Social Change in America: The Historical Handbook

2006

Social Change in America: The Historical Handbook

2006

Edited by Patricia C. Becker

BERNAN PRESS

Lanham, MD

© 2006 Bernan Press, an imprint of Bernan Associates, a division of The Kraus Organization Limited.

No part of this publication may be reproduced, stored in a retrieval system, or transmitted, in any form or by any means, electronic, mechanical, photocopying, recording, or otherwise, without the prior written permission of the copyright holder. Bernan Press does not claim copyright in U.S. government information.

ISBN: 1-59888-012-8

Cover photos: www.comstock.com; www.punchstock.com

Composed and printed by Automated Graphic Systems, Inc., White Plains, MD, on acid-free paper that meets the American National Standards Institute Z39-48 standard.

2007 2006   4 3 2 1

BERNAN PRESS
4611-F Assembly Drive
Lanham, MD 20706
800-274-4447
email: info@bernan.com
www.bernanpress.com

Contents

Chapter 3: Social Conditions

Chapter 4: Labor Force and Job Characteristics

Chapter 5: Housing

Chapter 6: Income, Wealth, and Poverty

Chapter 7: Education

Chapter 8: Crime and Criminal Justice

Chapter 9: Health

Chapter 10: Leisure, Volunteerism, and Religiosity

Chapter 11: Voting

Chapter 12: Government

Appendix

Figures and Tables

Chapter 3: Social Conditions

Chapter 4: Labor Force and Job Characteristics

Chapter 5: Housing

Chapter 6: Income, Wealth, and Poverty

Chapter 7: Education

Chapter 8: Crime and Criminal Justice

Chapter 9: Health

Chapter 10: Leisure, Volunteerism, and Religiosity

Chapter 11: Voting

Chapter 12: Government

Appendix Tables

About the Editors

Patricia C. Becker is a demographer with over 40 years of experience using federal statistics. A veteran census data user, she has served on several Census Bureau advisory committees. She is an active member of the Council of Professional Associations on Federal Statistics (COPAFS), and participates in most of the group's meetings. She is president of APB Associates, a Michigan-based consulting firm, executive director of the Southeast Michigan Census Council, and uses federal statistics in her everyday work. She has written many papers and offered presentations at professional meetings dealing with a wide variety of issues regarding the census and other federal statistical agencies. Ms. Becker is a founding member of the Association of Public Data Users (APDU), and she is currently the organization's Administrator. She received an A.B. in political science from the University of Michigan and an M.S. in sociology from the University of Wisconsin.

Mark Siegal is a research editor with Bernan Press. He is associate editor of several Bernan Press titles, including *Business Statistics of the United States, Vital Statistics of the United States,* and *Datapedia of the United States.* He received a B.S. in communication (with distinction in research) from Cornell University and a certificate in epidemiology from Tufts University.

Acknowledgments

Social Change in America is truly a cooperative effort and could not have been completed without the assistance of various individuals.

First, thanks to Mark Siegal of Bernan Press. Mark assisted with data research, as well as with designing the tables and charts.

Second, thanks to the editorial and production departments of Bernan Press, who under the direction of Tamera Wells-Lee did the copyediting, layout, and graphics preparation. Shana Hertz edited the manuscript. Rebecca Zayas prepared the layout and graphics. Shana and Rebecca capably handled all editorial and production aspects of this edition.

Thanks also to data analysts Katherine DeBrandt and Mary Meghan Ryan for additional data research and support.

Finally, thanks to our friends and colleagues at the federal statistical agencies, who willingly and enthusiastically answered my questions about the data published on their Web sites and provided information about the availability of unpublished data and analyses.

The publication of *Social Change in America* would not have been possible without the dedication and assistance of the above-listed individuals.

Patricia C. Becker

The Internet: The Latest Harbinger of Social Change

INTRODUCTION

As noted in the first edition of *Social Change in America*, the Internet is revolutionizing our society. This article has been expanded to include recent issues, such as increasing concerns about privacy and spam email, as well as the growing popularity of Web sites known as blogs.

RECENT HISTORY OF SOCIAL CHANGE

Social change is incremental. Sometimes it happens slowly, with decades passing before people are truly aware of the difference. Sometimes it happens quickly, turning American society "upside down" before anyone is aware of the change.

For the past half-century or so, it has been possible to characterize each decade by the major forces that shaped its politics and culture. The following is a summary of each decade's changes.

The 1950s: This was the decade of the baby boom (which peaked in 1957, as discussed in Chapter 1), suburban expansion, tract housing, fathers going to work, and mothers staying home with the children. Another important change that occurred in the 1950s was the introduction of television, which drastically changed the way information was communicated into American homes.

The 1960s: This decade saw real attitudinal and behavioral changes in the way racial minorities were treated. At the beginning of the decade, the South was still largely segregated, with communities seeking ways around the implementation of the landmark *Brown v. Board of Education* decision, which mandated integrated schools. In the North, government and private employers were struggling to provide equal opportunity in the workplace. By 1970, the majority of Americans had accepted the concept of equal opportunity, even if their attitudes did not change along with their behavior. Schools across the nation were becoming integrated; in the South, this was as a result of the *Brown* decision, while in the North, this occurred as courts increasingly found ways to integrate school systems segregated because of limited housing choices.

At the same time, America began its serious exploration of space. Following the creation of the National Aeronautics and Space Administration (NASA) in 1958, the first space flights took place in the early 1960s, culminating in the Apollo missions and the moon landing in 1969. The technology developed in these programs led to commercial applications in satellite transmissions, bringing the rest of the world closer to Americans through television and other communication options.

The 1970s: This was the decade in which women entered the workforce in droves. The baby boom was over. Women graduating from high school and college expected to work, with some women (due to either desire or economic necessity) remaining in the labor force even after marrying and having children. By 1980, workplaces were rapidly becoming integrated by gender and race, although "glass ceilings" at high levels still posed barriers to both women and minorities.

The 1980s: The arrival of the networked mainframe computer had a strong impact on this decade. Although the social changes of the 1960s and 1970s were still being absorbed, commerce was dramatically altered by the innovation of real-time access to central computers and, therefore, to central decision-making. For example, instead of only two airfare categories (coach and first class), there were suddenly dozens to consider, with availability in any specific category being managed centrally through information placed on networked terminals. Travel agents and airlines reservations agents (reachable only by telephone) never knew exactly what fares they would see on their screens, and could therefore only offer their customers what they saw at any given time. Similar changes in retail outlets, with cash registers interlinked and networked to central computers, permitted one-day sales and other such events.

The 1980s also brought bad news in the form of acquired immunodeficiency syndrome, or AIDS. According to the Centers for Disease Control and Prevention (CDC), the virus has existed in the United States, Haiti, and Africa since at least 1977–1978. In 1979, rare types of pneumonia, cancer, and other illnesses were being reported by doctors in Los Angeles and New York. The common link was that these conditions were not usually found in persons with healthy immune systems. In 1982, the CDC officially named the condition AIDS (acquired immunodeficiency syndrome). In 1984, the virus responsible for weakening the immune system was identified as HIV (human immunodeficiency virus). AIDS brought about important changes in adult sexual behavior.

The 1990s: This was decade of the personal computer and the real beginning of the Internet. The networked machines described above were not personal computers (PCs), but simply terminals connected by telephone lines to the central or home computer. They had no memory and little internal computing power of their own. When the system went down, so did they. PCs, on the other hand, were miniature, free-standing, fully-powered computers. They could be programmed and they had memory, or storage, for past activities.

A very early PC from about 1987 might have had 10 or 20 megabytes of hard drive memory. (A megabyte is slightly more than 1 million bytes, and a byte is roughly equivalent to a single letter or number.) Since this memory capacity was very limited, early PCs had little power. In the commercial world, they were first acquired by accountants, who used the VisiCalc program as well as Lotus spreadsheet software. Somewhat later, secretaries began to use PCs for word processing. Meanwhile, mainframe computers continued to be accessed using dumb terminals, so named because they had no capacity other than to connect to the central machine. The programmers and analysts who managed the mainframe capacity looked down on PCs.

Throughout the 1990s, PC speeds and hard drive (memory and storage) capacities increased exponentially. By the end of the decade, it was routine to have 20 gigabytes on board a PC, with a gigabyte being the equivalent of 1,024 megabytes, or almost 1.1 billion bytes.

The 2000s: This decade is more than half over as this book goes to press. It is clear that the Internet has become an integral factor in the lives of most Americans. Web sites and email addresses appear frequently in other media, such as newspapers and magazine articles, with the assumption that readers will be able to use this information. The oldest members of the baby boom have turned 60, and many sectors of society are getting ready for the changes that will come as this generation retires. Some fixed features of our economic lives are undergoing radical change, as defined-benefit pension systems and employer-paid health insurance benefits are rapidly disappearing. The overall economy continues its inexorable shift from the manufacturing sector to the service sector, and the future will depend on employment in knowledge-based industries. This, in turn, means that increasing levels of education will be required for success.

WHAT IS THE INTERNET?

The Internet is a system that allows computers to connect, communicate, and talk to each other. Thus, in order to have the Internet, we must have computers. We must also have a means of communication, through hardware devices called modems, and a protocol (or language) called TCP/IP, which stands for "transmission control protocol and Internet protocol." The Internet is not a single-computer network, such as one might find in a business or university. It is a "vast, globe-spanning network of networks (which communicate with one another based on these protocols). No single person, group, or organization runs the Internet. Instead, it is the purest form of electronic democracy."[1]

The number of interconnected networks is uncounted and grows continually. Even by accessing the Internet using a non-networked PC, the computer becomes an extension of that network. One of the most important things to understand about the Internet is that there is no central management, central control, or central source of funding. There are, however, cooperative organizations that exist to assist in developing standards and pro-

---

[1] Gralla, Preston. 1999. *How the Internet Works.* (Indianapolis: Que Publishing.) This book is the source for much of the information presented in this section.

vide education. One of these is the Internet Society, whose Internet Activities Board (IAB) handles many of the backbone issues that end users never see, but that are critical to making the system work. The World Wide Web Consortium (known as W3C), develops standards for the World Wide Web. Private companies, including InterNIC and others, are Internet registrars who assume responsibility for registering and keeping track of Internet domains (the Universal Resource Locators, or URLs, that identify each individual Web site) and Internet addresses composed of a series of numbers that users rarely see.

Information travels across the Internet in complex ways. The user begins at an individual PC or as part of a local area network (LAN) with a modem/router. The modem/router connects to a service—the Internet Service Provider or ISP—by dialing a telephone number, or through another type of device, such as a cable modem or a Digital Subscriber Line (DSL) modem. A large organization may have an even faster connection, such as a T1 or T3 telephone line. From there, the data are broken down into "packets" that the system can handle before being sent to routers, which do most of the work to direct Internet traffic. The data packets go from one router to another before arriving at a regional network, which serves a geographic area. The regional networks are connected by high-speed lines. When the data packets reach the regional network of their destination address, the process reverses itself until the data arrive at the intended address.

Electronic mail, or email, is older than the Internet. Back in the early 1980s, large mainframe computers were connected in ways that were predecessors to the Internet. Users on these mainframe systems had access to email, through the terminals described above.[2] However, it was not until the mid-1990s that the system evolved to allow attachments could be sent along with email. By that time, standard email software programs such as Internet Explorer and Eudora were available; before that, email software was "home-grown" and circulated in university and corporate settings. Attachments have made it possible to transmit information electronically that could formerly only be sent by postal mail or a facsimile (fax) machine. Computer files and documents can be shared and jointly edited in a way that was previously impossible.

Another critical innovation was the development of portable document file software, or PDF software, which is distributed for free by Adobe Systems. This software made it possible to distribute any document through the Internet. Even if the document was not originally created on a computer, it could be scanned (using scanning hardware) into a computer file, published as a PDF, and distributed.

One of the most powerful features of the Internet is its search function and hyperlinking capability. The power of modern computers makes it possible to conduct electronic searches, based on keywords, in seconds. Finding one document, the user may then discover hyperlinks that reveal an entirely different, yet related, document. Hyperlinks connect Web pages in clever, useful ways.

How has the Internet Changed American Lives?

The impact of the Internet is immeasurable and expansive, with significant technological advancements in its function being introduced every year.

Example 1: The Internet has revolutionized shopping. Prior to the 1980s, most non-store shopping was done using mail-order catalogues. However, by 1980, the cost of wide-ranging telephone lines had greatly decreased, leading to the availability and affordability of toll-free 800 numbers (which now include 888, 877, and 866 numbers). Thus, a consumer could call the company and place an order from a catalogue, which provided faster service and turnaround than was possible through mail. With the advent of the Internet, companies began to create Web sites, or virtual stores. Some of these are online versions of "brick-and-mortar" stores, some once marketed their wares via mail-order catalogues, while still others are a creation of the Internet itself. Amazon.com is the most well-known example of the latter phenomenon. The growth of Internet shopping has had a strong impact on traditional stores, which have had to adapt themselves to the new environment.

---

2 The author first gained access to email in 1982, using an account at Wayne State University in Detroit. At that point, most of her correspondents also had university email addresses. In those pre-Internet days, universities were connected through a system called "Bitnet," which later became the ".edu" domain on the Internet. Government agency staff did not have email accounts until several years later.

Almost all large retail establishments now have Web sites. Goods that used to only be sold in brick-and-mortar stores can now be purchased in cyberspace. These companies send email to current and potential customers, enticing them to shop at their Web site. This has resulted in a boon for package carriers (such as the U.S. Post Office, Federal Express, United Parcel Service, and the like), and a loss for on-the-ground stores. Many one- or two-establishment retail stores that offered clothing, office supplies, and household items have gone out of business, unable to compete with either the large chain suppliers on the Internet or the big box-type stores on the ground.

Example 2: The Internet has revolutionized travel purchases. As recently as 1980, people purchased airfare or rail tickets via telephone, in person, or through travel agents. As discussed above, there were only two categories of airfares: first class and coach. Travel agents were paid commissions by travel vendors, making their services generally free to the customer. Hotel and motel reservations were made in a similar fashion. Before there were toll-free numbers, the long distance call required to make a reservation was another reason to use a travel agent.

In the 1980s, networked computer systems such as Sabre (which ran off of mainframe computers) became the method used by travel agents to make reservations. They were forced to acquire the necessary hardware and to subscribe to the system. As the use of toll-free numbers became more prevalent, airlines began to reduce the commissions paid to the travel agencies, preferring to have travelers deal directly with their own reservations systems. As the World Wide Web grew in the 1990s, both airlines and hotel chains developed their own Web sites to enable travelers to make their reservations online. Commission payments to travel agents were reduced to zero, forcing many of them out of business or to charge customers for their services. By the late 1990s, Web sites such as Travelocity.com had grown into prominence, providing consumers with the opportunity to search across vendors for the best prices on airfares and hotels.

Example 3: The Internet has increased access to federal statistics. Prior to 1970, printed publications were the only way to access federal statistics. Beginning with the 1970 census, some data files began to be released on magnetic tape, which were accessible through mainframe computers. Federal agencies often charged large user fees to create these special tabulations, leading to the development of user consortia to share the data. The 1980 census was delivered in all of the traditional print formats, on magnetic tape, and on microfiche (a microfilm of report pages that could be read and printed from a special microfiche reader). Other federal agencies followed suit with subsequent publications.

By 1990, the need for data that could be accessed by a PC was evident, leading to the first publication of federal data in CD-ROM format. Unfortunately, adequate software to access the data on the CDs did not accompany the files, which one again left users to form consortia to develop the access mechanisms. At this point, the private sector had also seen the advantage of delivering data on CDs, and several vendors created special packages to make this data easier to access.

In the 1990s, the advent of the World Wide Web instigated radical changes in the delivery of public information. Every federal statistical agency developed a Web site. The federal government created a Web site called FedStats, self-defined as "the new window on the full range of official statistical information available to the public from the Federal Government. Use the Internet's powerful linking and searching capabilities to track economic and population trends, education, health care costs, aviation safety, foreign trade, energy use, farm production, and more. Access official statistics collected and published by more than 100 federal agencies without having to know in advance which agency produces them."[3]

The Internet, the Web, and PDF software have combined to shift the burden of created printed documents from the federal agencies to the users. Documentation, or metadata, is posted on federal Web sites in PDF format. The data are often accessible only through the same mechanism. The path of least resistance for federal agencies has been to create an "original" of a printed document using the same software and techniques as used in earlier decades, but then to post the resulting document on the Web instead of creating and distributing the

---

[3] FedStats. <http://www.fedstats.gov>. (Accessed Mar. 16, 2006.)

book itself. Thus, the user has to print the documentation or the data report instead of obtaining a bound print-ed copy from the U.S. Government Printing Office.

Example 4: The Internet has become an encyclopedia. Before the Internet, information was distributed in printed form. Users either purchased printed documents or used a library. As every student knows, research for school assignments is now conducted primarily on the Internet rather than out of books. Printed encyclopedias have been converted to electronic documents. There are even collaborative encyclopedias, such as Wikipedia (found at <http://www.wikipedia.org>), which allow any Internet user to write or edit articles. These collaborative social forces have created a free resource that rivals expert-authored encyclopedias. As of 2006, Wikipedia has over one million articles in English alone.

Example 5: The Internet has spawned new tools for communication, such as blogs. Weblogs, or blogs, are Web sites with a format similar to diaries. Blogs focus on timely content, easily created new pages, links to other blogs or Web sites, and individual posts designed for direct linking and easy discussion. Topics range from personal diaries to political soapboxes, including nearly any subject imaginable. Blogs are to the Internet what affordable laser printers were to desktop publishing. Any Internet user can set up a blog for free or at mini-mal expense, using services such as Blogger, LiveJournal, and MySpace, or by installing software on his or her own Web site.

Blogs have become increasingly popular in recent years. The earliest blogs began in the mid-1990s, and by the end of the decade, they numbered in the thousands. By 2003, there were approximately one million blogs. As of early 2006, there are at least 30 million blogs, and perhaps several times that number.[4]

The line between blogging and journalism can be blurry. Bloggers break some news stories before the main-stream media, and stories that are popular among blogs can also affect coverage in the media. In a turning-point example, bloggers played a key role in 2002, when Senator Trent Lott made comments supportive of racial segregation, which led to his stepping down as Senate Majority Leader.[5] Additionally, many newspapers and professional journalists now feature their own blogs.

DOWNSIDES OF THE INTERNET

While the impact of the Internet is mostly positive, there are some drawbacks:

Spam. As the number of email addresses has increased, the number of spam emails has grown exponentially. Spam is email that is not intended directly for the recipient, and consists of material the recipient usually does not want. Examples include advertising—especially for items related to sexual performance, pornography, appeals for money from phony charities, and phishing. Phishing involves an email that appears to have been sent from a legitimate financial institution, but is in fact designed to get the recipient to respond with private financial information. This information can then be used in criminal activity, such as applications for credit cards in the recipient's name. Internet service providers (ISPs) have developed increasingly sophisticated software to identify spam and segregate it from users' regular email inboxes. Nonetheless, the problem requires continuous vigilance on the part of the user.

Privacy. A downside of the technological advances of recent decades is an increasing concern with privacy. Information stored in electronic form is much more easily shared than paper documents. Reports of stolen credit card numbers and financial information abound. A special concern is medical records, as this private information, improperly shared, could lead to insurance denials and other negative consequences for the individual. In response, many Web sites sell items that guarantee privacy of credit card numbers and other financial information.

4 Sifry, Dave. *State of the Blogosphere, February 2006 Part 1: On Blogosphere Growth.* (Feb. 2006.) <http://www.sifry.com/alerts/archives/000419.html>. (Accessed Mar. 22, 2006.)

5 Rosen, Jay. *PressThink: The Legend of Trent Lott and the Weblogs.* (Mar. 2004.) <http://journalism.nyu.edu/pubzone/weblogs/pressthink/2004/03/15/lott_case.html>. (Accessed Mar. 22, 2006.)

Every Internet and email user must decide his or her own level of concern and the proper balance between the convenience of the Internet and concerns about privacy. Those who feel technologically competent have, for the most part, adapted to this new way of doing business. Those who feel intimidated or who have major concerns about privacy have continued to do business the old way, shopping in stores or by telephone, and using U.S. mail for communication. As time goes on, the number of people who do not use the Internet will decline.

CONCLUSION

This book and its predecessors[6] could not have been created without the Internet. Almost every piece of numeric information included in the text has been retrieved from a Web site. References to these sites are provided in footnotes and at the end of chapters, ensuring that readers will be able to access updated information, both now and in future years. The quality and accessibility of these Web sites is continually improving, as are those of many federal agencies. Web designers, with feedback from users, are improving their understanding of how information is accessed and how to make that access more user-friendly. Mechanisms for making the Internet available to the visually impaired have been developed and are continually being improved.

It's a great new world.

---

[6] Also published by Bernan Press: *A Statistical Portrait of the United States: Social Conditions and Trends, First Edition* (1998) and *Second Edition* (2002); and *Social Change in America: A Historic Handbook, First Edition* (2004).

As noted in the previous section, the Internet has created new tools for communicating and doing business. While many people in American society use electronic communication tools daily, the United States Congress has been slow to embrace modern technology, in general.

The following article, written by Richard S. Dunham of *Business Week*, provides an overview of how and why Congress has been slow to implement technology into its daily operations.

Modern Technology Meets Congressional Traditions

Back in 1914, Rep. Allan Walsh of New Jersey had a revolutionary idea. Walsh, an electrical engineer by training, suggested that the House allow its members to vote electronically. His plan was referred to the House Rules Committee and buried for 56 years. The House entered the 20th century in 1970, when it authorized a newfangled computerized voting system. Across the Capitol, however, the Senate still clings to its 18th-century sensibilities. And those hallowed traditions do not include modern technology. Nearly six years into the 21st century, there is no computerized voting and no senator is permitted to bring an electronic device onto the Senate floor.

With technology transforming American society and revolutionizing the way citizens receive news and information, Congress is decidedly schizophrenic about embracing the changes. Yes, some senators and representatives have whiz-bang Web sites. THOMAS, the congressional electronic information system named for Thomas Jefferson, provides the public with direct, free access to legislation and floor debate. Capitol Hill committee Web sites are treasure troves of data, testimony, reports, and useful Internet links. Many congressional campaigns use the latest information technology to identify voters and communicate with supporters. Electronic town hall meetings with constituents have become a fixture in the House. Trendy members have joined the latest info-fad with their own podcasts, and a few lawmakers even write their own blogs. But when it comes to embracing technology in the Capitol building, Congress remains decidedly old school.

Which brings us to Sen. Mike Enzi. The Wyoming Republican was an accountant, shoe store owner, and computer programmer before he won a Senate seat in 1996. A former Eagle Scout dubbed "Cyber Senator" because of his proud techno-geek status, Enzi saw no reason why he should not be allowed to carry his laptop computer onto the Senate floor so that he could study the issues at hand or communicate with his staff during lengthy debates. After all, 35 states provide computers in their chambers for lawmakers. "There is a lot of potential for using a computer to keep in touch with my staff while I am on the floor of the Senate," Enzi declared four months into his first term. "I can access volumes of information while I follow debates." To Enzi and a lot of tech aficionados, using the latest technology is important to understand the subjects about which they need to write laws. "It's only proper," Enzi reasoned, "that those charged with making sensible laws regarding the Internet, information access, computer use, and other areas actually use computers and know what they're about."

But Enzi ran head-first into the Senate rules, which state that any mechanical devices that "distract, interrupt, or inconvenience" members are strictly verboten. Enzi's laptop would violate both Senate decorum and traditions. "It appears that this request is a little ahead of its time," then-Sen. Wendell Ford, D-Ky., said during 1997 Senate Rules Committee hearings on the laptop issue. Nine years later, neither the Senate nor the House is yet ready to welcome laptops.

This resistance to technology applies even when security and safety might be at stake. After September 11, every member of Congress was issued a BlackBerry for instant communication in the event of an emergency. Lawmakers received training in the hot new technology, which has revolutionized instantaneous communication. But if a member is seen using one inside the chamber, he or she could face charges of violating the rules.

The Senate's Luddite inclinations extend to other areas. Although House candidates and presidential contenders routinely file their campaign contribution reports electronically, Senators and their opponents do not have to file that way. As a result, "it is almost impossible to get timely disclosure" from Senate campaigns, says Carol Darr, director of The George Washington University Institute for Politics, Democracy & the Internet. "It's not just technophobia. It's quite deliberate."

The reasoning: John Adams did not use a laptop or a BlackBerry, so neither should Mike Enzi. Quill pens, inkwells, and starched wigs are permitted, but a cell phone, a pager, or, heaven forbid, a laptop could get a lawmaker in big trouble. "It's the same reason we have spittoons and snuff boxes in the chamber," says Senate Historian Donald A. Ritchie. "You don't read the newspaper at your desk, you don't use your phone, and you don't eat your lunch." Or tap on your laptop. "The key word is decorum," explains Ritchie. "There's a veneration of the way the chamber has always operated."

While the Senate floor remains sacrosanct, Congress has slowly adopted modern technologies. In 1945, the Joint Committee on the Organization of Congress proposed to install equipment "for presentation of motion-picture or other visual displays for use in large-scale public hearings." Two years later, the House permitted television coverage of its opening session for two hours, "with pictures seen only in Washington, Philadelphia, and New York." Into the 1950s, committees decided whether to allow the new mass medium of television to cover their hearings. The House's electronic voting system, which was authorized in 1970, went online with a quorum call on January 23, 1973.

The House led the way to live television coverage of floor activities. On March 2, 1977, Speaker Thomas P. "Tip" O'Neill authorized a 90-day test of a closed-circuit system sent only to House offices. With the pilot program a success, the House voted 342-44 to go live on cable TV. The first lawmaker to stand before the microphone on March 19, 1979 was then-Rep. Albert Gore Jr. of Tennessee. "Television will change this institution," Gore predicted, "but the good will far outweigh the bad." The Senate followed in 1986.

But laptops are still unwelcome on the chamber floors. While there are a handful of computers near the Senate floor (hidden in the well and cloakroom), there is no groundswell for public displays of technology. Yes, senators can flaunt their laptops at committee hearings but not at their desks on the floor. "BlackBerries have dramatically increased our communication abilities, but laptops have more data storage, allow the user to type faster, and information is easier to read," Enzi says. "The more information you are able to access on the floor, the more time you can spend listening to the debate."

That's not to say that most members of Congress are gadget-averse. True, some still view 3x5 cards as modern information technology. But many have embraced PDAs and PCs. "These have become indispensable items ... especially when their time is double- and triple-booked," says Patrick Ross, a senior fellow at the Progress & Freedom Foundation. Indeed, Ross says that some lawmakers have been sighted "discreetly checking their BlackBerries" during debate.

One day that kind of guilty pleasure might be legal in the Senate chamber. But don't hold your breath. "When the Senate gets around to allowing laptops," laughs Senate Historian Ritchie, "laptops will be obsolete."

—Richard S. Dunham is senior White House correspondent and national political reporter for *Business Week*. He also has written for the *Dallas Times Herald*, the *Philadelphia Inquirer* and the *Cleveland Plain Dealer,* and he has contributed to two books (*The Founding City* [Chilton Books, 1976], and *The Handbook of Campaign Spending* [Congressional Quarterly Press, 1992]). He also writes the "Letter from America" column for the Finnish newspaper *Aamulehti*.

Beyond the political beat, Mr. Dunham is the 2005 president of the National Press Club. He also is former chairman of The Reporters Committee for Freedom of the Press. From 1992 to 1999, Mr. Dunham served on the Executive Committee of Periodical Correspondents, which oversees the press galleries on Capitol Hill for more than 2,000 newsmagazine and newsletter correspondents. As Executive Committee chairman from 1995 to 1997, he helped to coordinate press logistics for the national conventions and presidential inauguration.

He appears regularly on ABC World News This Morning and ABC Radio, and has offered political analysis for CNN, CNBC, MSNBC, the Fox News Channel, C-SPAN, the BBC, National Public Radio, and more than a dozen radio stations and networks.

A graduate of Central High School in Philadelphia, Mr. Dunham holds B.A. and M.A. degrees in history from the University of Pennsylvania. He resides in Arlington, Virginia, with his wife, Pam Tobey, a graphic artist at the *Washington Post*.

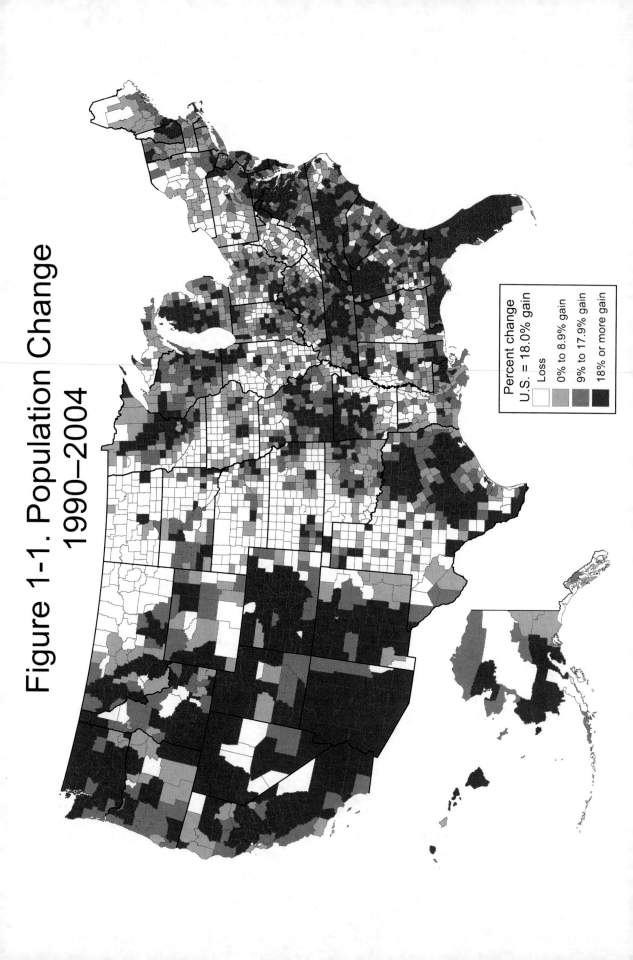

Figure 1-1. Population Change
1990–2004

Percent change
U.S. = 18.0% gain

Loss
0% to 8.9% gain
9% to 17.9% gain
18% or more gain

Chapter 1
Population

This chapter presents basic population information through current and historical perspectives, both for the United States alone and for the United States in the context of the rest of the world. These population indicators include the total population, the basic determinants of population growth (births, deaths, and migration), and the distribution of the population by age, race, and a variety of geographical categories.

WHAT IS THE TOTAL POPULATION OF THE UNITED STATES?

The official count of the U.S. population on the 2000 census was 281,421,906. By the end of January 2006, the population had increased to 298 million. At this rate, the 2010 population is projected to be about 309 million.

Internationally, the United States houses about 4.6 percent of the world's population, which was estimated to be nearly 6.5 billion at the end of 2005. This makes the United States the world's third most populous country, trailing China (1.31 billion) and India (1.08 billion). Most of the world's population (about 80 percent) lives in "developing" or "less developed" countries, according to the United Nations' scheme of development status. The "more developed" countries include the United States, most of Europe, and

countries such as Japan, Australia, and Canada; together, they account for about 20 percent of the world's population.

The United States' share of the world population is anticipated to decline only slightly between 2000 and 2025, when the U.S. population is projected to approach 350 million. However, the share of the world's population living in developed countries is projected to decline to about 15 percent in 2025. These figures assume that the characterization of the development status of countries will not change over the next 25 years. In reality, some countries that are currently characterized as "developing" will become "developed" by that time. (See Table 1-1.)

The U.S. growth rate in the 1990s—about 1 percent per year—was only slightly higher than the annual growth rate in the 1980s. This annual growth rate statistic approached 1.7 percent during the baby boom era of the 1950s, which represented the highest rate of population increase for the United States since early in the 20th century. The baby boom era birth rate in the United States was comparable to those of the world's developing countries in the 1990s. However, the worldwide growth rate has dropped in recent years to about 1.3 percent per year. Growth rates in all regions of the world, in both developed and less developed countries,

Table 1-1. United States and World Population, Selected Years, 2000–2050

(Numbers in thousands, percent.)

Year	World population	United States		Developed countries, excluding the United States		Less developed countries	
		Total population	Percent of world population	Total population	Percent of world population	Total population	Percent of world population
2000	6 081 528	282 339	4.6	911 117	15.0	4 888 072	80.4
2005	6 451 059	295 734	4.6	913 818	14.2	5 241 507	81.3
2010	6 825 750	309 163	4.5	914 916	13.4	5 601 672	82.1
2025	7 897 989	349 666	4.4	897 521	11.4	6 650 802	84.2
2050	9 224 376	420 081	4.6	815 385	8.8	7 988 910	86.6

Source: U.S. Census Bureau. International Data Base (IDB). <http://www.census.gov/ipc/www/idbnew.html>. (Accessed Mar. 1, 2006.)

Table 1-2. Average Annual Rates of Growth for the United States and for the World, 1950–2010

(Rate.)

Period	World	Less developed countries	More developed countries	United States
1950–1960	1.7	2.0	1.2	1.7
1960–1970	2.0	2.4	1.0	1.3
1970–1980	1.8	2.2	0.7	1.0
1980–1990	1.7	2.0	0.6	0.9
1990–2000	1.4	1.7	0.4	1.2
2000–2010	1.1	1.3	0.3	0.9

Source: U.S. Census Bureau. 2004. *Global Population Profile: 2002* (Report WP/02). (Washington, DC: U.S. Government Printing Office.)
U.S. Census Bureau. International Data Base (IDB). <http://www.census.gov/ipc/www/idbnew.html>. (Accessed Mar. 1, 2006.)

appear to have peaked. Average annual growth rates peaked in the 1950s for developed countries and in the 1960s for less developed countries; these have been declining for both groups ever since.

POPULATION BY STATE

The Census Bureau divides the United States into four geographical regions. The South and West regions combined are projected to account for most of U.S. population growth (88 percent) between now and 2030. The South is projected to remain the most populous region in the United States, while the West is projected to replace the Midwest as the second most populous region by the year 2010. California, the largest state, accounted for about 12 percent of the nation's population in 2000. Texas became the nation's second most populous state during the 1990s, while New York dropped to third. (As recently as the mid-1960s, New York had the largest state population.) According to current projections, Florida will replace New York as the third largest state within the next 10 years. (See Table 1-3.) At the other end of the size spectrum, Vermont, North Dakota, South Dakota, Wyoming, and Alaska are all projected to remain with total populations of less than 1 million in 2030.

As shown in Table 1-4, Nevada is currently the fastest-growing state in the nation, having experienced a population increase of more than 20 percent between 2000 and 2005. Other fast-growing states include Florida, Georgia, Arizona, Utah, and Idaho, all with double-digit increases over the past five years. In contrast, North Dakota is estimated to have lost population since the 2000 census, and several states (New York, Pennsylvania, Ohio, Michigan, Massachusetts, Louisiana, and West Virginia) have shown very small increases. (The populations of Louisiana and Mississippi were severely affected by Hurricane Katrina; accurate current estimates—as of early 2006—were not available.)

PEOPLE LIVING IN CITIES AND METROPOLITAN AREAS

About 83 percent of the U.S. population now lives within a metropolitan area. The general concept of a metropolitan area is that of an urban core of at least 50,000 persons, combined with adjacent communities that have a high rate of commuting to jobs within the core county or counties. Metropolitan areas comprise one or more entire counties, except in New England, where cities and towns are the basic geographic units.

Table 1-3. Population Estimates and Projections of Largest and Smallest States, 2000 and 2030

(Numbers in thousands.)

Largest 10 states

State and rank	2000	State and rank	2030
1. California	33 872	1. California	46 445
2. Texas	20 852	2. Texas	33 318
3. New York	18 976	3. Florida	28 686
4. Florida	15 982	4. New York	19 477
5. Illinois	12 419	5. Illinois	13 433
6. Pennsylvania	12 281	6. Pennsylvania	12 768
7. Ohio	11 353	7. North Carolina	12 228
8. Michigan	9 938	8. Georgia	12 018
9. New Jersey	8 414	9. Ohio	11 551
10. Georgia	8 186	10. Arizona	10 712

Smallest 10 states

State and rank	2000	State and rank	2030
1. Wyoming	494	1. Wyoming	523
2. Vermont	609	2. North Dakota	607
3. Alaska	627	3. Vermont	712
4. North Dakota	642	4. South Dakota	800
5. South Dakota	755	5. Alaska	868
6. Delaware	784	6. Delaware	1 013
7. Montana	902	7. Montana	1 045
8. Rhode Island	1 048	8. Rhode Island	1 153
9. Hawaii	1 212	9. Maine	1 411
10. New Hampshire	1 236	10. Hawaii	1 466

Source: U.S. Census Bureau. Population Division. Population Projections Branch.

Table 1-4. States Ranked by Population, 2005

(Number, percent.)

State and rank	Population estimates		Change, 2000–2005	
	July 1, 2005	April 1, 2000	Number	Percent
United States	296 410 404	281 424 602	14 985 802	5.3
1. California	36 132 147	33 871 653	2 260 494	6.7
2. Texas	22 859 968	20 851 792	2 008 176	9.6
3. New York	19 254 630	18 976 821	277 809	1.5
4. Florida	17 789 864	15 982 824	1 807 040	11.3
5. Illinois	12 763 371	12 419 647	343 724	2.8
6. Pennsylvania	12 429 616	12 281 054	148 562	1.2
7. Ohio	11 464 042	11 353 145	110 897	1.0
8. Michigan	10 120 860	9 938 480	182 380	1.8
9. Georgia	9 072 576	8 186 816	885 760	10.8
10. New Jersey	8 717 925	8 414 347	303 578	3.6
11. North Carolina	8 683 242	8 046 491	636 751	7.9
12. Virginia	7 567 465	7 079 030	488 435	6.9
13. Massachusetts	6 398 743	6 349 105	49 638	0.8
14. Washington	6 287 759	5 894 140	393 619	6.7
15. Indiana	6 271 973	6 080 517	191 456	3.1
16. Tennessee	5 962 959	5 689 262	273 697	4.8
17. Arizona	5 939 292	5 130 632	808 660	15.8
18. Missouri	5 800 310	5 596 683	203 627	3.6
19. Maryland	5 600 388	5 296 506	303 882	5.7
20. Wisconsin	5 536 201	5 363 715	172 486	3.2
21. Minnesota	5 132 799	4 919 492	213 307	4.3
22. Colorado	4 665 177	4 302 015	363 162	8.4
23. Alabama	4 557 808	4 447 351	110 457	2.5
24. Louisiana	4 523 628	4 468 958	54 670	1.2
25. South Carolina	4 255 083	4 011 816	243 267	6.1
26. Kentucky	4 173 405	4 042 285	131 120	3.2
27. Oregon	3 641 056	3 421 436	219 620	6.4
28. Oklahoma	3 547 884	3 450 652	97 232	2.8
29. Connecticut	3 510 297	3 405 602	104 695	3.1
30. Iowa	2 966 334	2 926 382	39 952	1.4
31. Mississippi	2 921 088	2 844 656	76 432	2.7
32. Arkansas	2 779 154	2 673 398	105 756	4.0
33. Kansas	2 744 687	2 688 824	55 863	2.1
34. Utah	2 469 585	2 233 198	236 387	10.6
35. Nevada	2 414 807	1 998 257	416 550	20.8
36. New Mexico	1 928 384	1 819 046	109 338	6.0
37. West Virginia	1 816 856	1 808 350	8 506	0.5
38. Nebraska	1 758 787	1 711 265	47 522	2.8
39. Idaho	1 429 096	1 293 956	135 140	10.4
40. Maine	1 321 505	1 274 923	46 582	3.7
41. New Hampshire	1 309 940	1 235 786	74 154	6.0
42. Hawaii	1 275 194	1 211 537	63 657	5.3
43. Rhode Island	1 076 189	1 048 319	27 870	2.7
44. Montana	935 670	902 195	33 475	3.7
45. Delaware	843 524	783 600	59 924	7.6
46. South Dakota	775 933	754 840	21 093	2.8
47. Alaska	663 661	626 931	36 730	5.9
48. North Dakota	636 677	642 204	-5 527	-0.9
49. Vermont	623 050	608 827	14 223	2.3
50. District of Columbia	550 521	572 059	-21 538	-3.8
51. Wyoming	509 294	493 782	15 512	3.1

Source: U.S. Census Bureau. Population Division.

The Office of Management and Budget (OMB) defines metropolitan areas for the purposes of collecting, tabulating, and publishing federal data.[1] In 1970, only about two-thirds of the U.S. population were classified as living in a metropolitan area. Part of this increase in metropolitan population (from 67 percent in 1970 to 83 percent in 2000) is attributable to changes in the definition of metropolitan areas. As the suburbs expand, more counties become included in the definitions of the metropolitan areas. The outward growth of suburbs, often called "urban sprawl," is caused by several factors, including population growth in the metropolitan area overall, the loss of population in central cities and inner suburbs, and the larger size of new average homes and lots. There are now 361 Metropolitan Statistical Areas, known as MSAs, in the United States, with another 8 in Puerto Rico.

After the 2000 census, a new type of area was defined: the Micropolitan Statistical Area. These areas are based around an urban core of between 10,000 and 50,000 persons, are also composed of whole counties (except in New England), and may include adjacent counties that are closely linked to the central county. About 10 percent of the U.S. population in 2004 lived in the country's 577 defined micropolitan areas.

The metropolitan and micropolitan areas are labeled "core-based statistical areas," and include 93 percent of the U.S. population. This leaves only 7 percent of the nation's population in counties that are not included in such an area; these counties are labeled as being "outside core-based statistical areas."

FARM, RURAL, AND NONMETROPOLITAN POPULATION

At the turn of the twentieth century, nearly two out of every five Americans (40 percent) lived on a farm. Today, persons living on farms represent fewer than 2 percent of the U.S. population. Part of this shift reflects changes in the agriculture industry itself. Fewer than half of the persons living on farms are employed in farming occupations today, and only about a third of people doing farm work live on farms. Most of this shift in residence, though, has occurred as Americans migrated from rural to urban settings.

The concept of "urban" is based on population density, usually defined in terms of 1,000 persons per square mile. The official definitions of "urban" and "rural" were changed at the time of the 2000 census.

Sophisticated geographic software can now calculate population density at the city block level. These blocks were aggregated to "densely settled territory" and defined as urbanized areas if they totaled at least 50,000 persons, and as urban clusters if they totaled between 10,000 and 50,000 persons. The population residing in urbanized areas or urban clusters is identified as urban, while the remaining population is identified as rural.[2]

In 2000, using these new definitions, 68 percent of Americans lived in urbanized areas, 11 percent resided in urban clusters, and 21 percent lived in rural areas. Of the population living in urbanized areas, 22 percent lived in the areas containing 5 million or more people, including New York, Chicago, Los Angeles, and Philadelphia.[3]

The shift away from agriculture and the tendency toward urbanization is occurring around the world, but there are still vast differences by country: in China, for example, about 70 percent of the population currently lives in rural areas; the vast majority of these people are involved with agriculture.

Table 1-5. Urban and Rural Population, 2000

(Number, percent.)

Area	Number	Percent distribution
Urban	222 360 539	79.0
Urbanized area	192 323 824	68.3
Urban cluster	30 036 715	10.7
Rural	59 061 367	21.0

Source: U.S. Census Bureau. Census 2000. Summary File 1. Table P2.

U.S. REGIONAL GROWTH AND MIGRATION

Between 2003 and 2004, 39 million people, or about 14 percent of the total U.S. population, moved from one address to another. Over half moved a short distance, taking up residence within the same county. Another quarter moved from one county to another in the same state; in many cases this involves a move within the same metropolitan area. The remaining quarter moved from a different state or from another country.[4] Renters are more likely to move than homeowners. As shown in Figure 1-2, the South is gaining residents at the expense of the other three regions in the nation. However, these data refer only to domestic migration; those who moved from and to other countries are not included.

---

[1] For more information about metropolitan areas, see <http://www.census.gov/population/www/estimates/aboutmetro.html>. For a complete list of areas, defined as of December 2005, see <http://www.whitehouse.gov/omb/bulletins/b0601.html>.

[2] The official definitions of urban and rural territory are located at <http://www.census.gov/population/censusdata/urdef.txt>.

[3] See Chapter 3 for further discussion of rural America.

[4] U.S. Census Bureau. *Geographical Mobility: 2002 to 2003* (Report P20-549). (Aug. 2004.) <http://www.census.gov/population/www/socdemo/migrate.html>. (Accessed Apr. 10, 2006.) This report issued the updated detailed tables for 2004.

Figure 1-2. In-migrants and Out-migrants Within the United States, by Region, 2003–2004

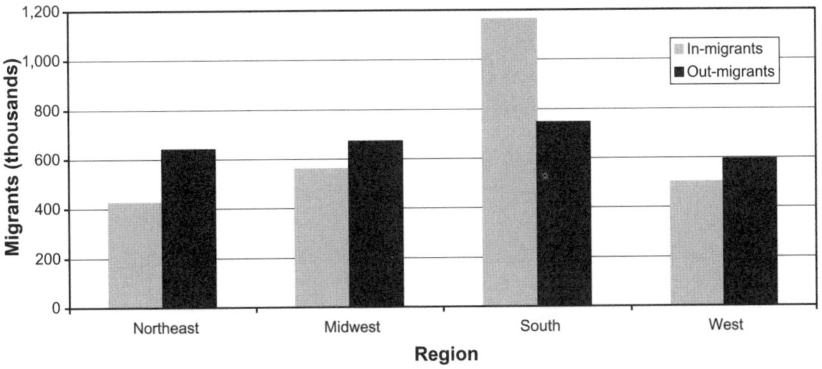

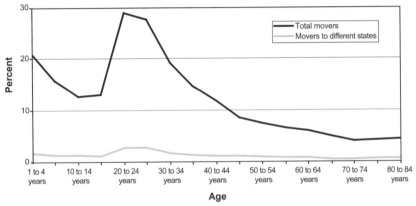

Source: U.S. Census Bureau. Current Population Survey.

Figure 1-3. Percent of Population that Moved, by Age, 2003–2004

Source: U.S. Census Bureau. Current Population Survey.

Figure 1-3 shows the tendency to move by age. Generally, young adults—especially those in their twenties—are more likely to move over the course of a year than people in any other age group. This figure is also higher for young children, because they move with their young parents. The likelihood of moving decreases substantially as people age. However, older persons who move are relatively likely to move to a different state, reflecting a pattern of migrating at retirement age to a different place, and then perhaps moving back to where their grown children reside as they become even older and more dependent.

One way to examine the likelihood of moving over a lifetime is to look at the proportion of persons living in a state who were born in that state. Americans have a cosmopolitan view of the United States, but there are several states in which over three-fourths of the population had been born in the state. Pennsylvania heads this list, with 78 percent of its population in 2000 having been born in the state. Most states with low proportions of population born there

were concentrated in the West. However, one Southern state, Florida (with only 30.5 percent of its population born in that state), ranked lowest for two reasons: its large retirement-age population from other states and its large numbers of immigrants (principally from Cuba).

AGE AND DEPENDENCY

As is the case worldwide, the population of the United States is slowly aging. At the turn of the twentieth century, only about 4 percent of the U.S. population was 65 years old and over. This percentage increased to 12.4 percent in 2000, and will likely reach 20 percent by the year 2030. The median age (the age that divides the population in half, with one half younger and one half older) in the United States increased from about 22.9 years in 1900 to 35.3 years in 2000, and is expected to be about 38.5 years by 2030.

The dependency ratio is the number of children and elderly persons per 100 persons 18 to 64 years of age.[5] This ratio was at its highest point during the early 1960s, due to the baby boom. There were about 82 dependents per 100 persons age 18 to 64 years at that time. Since the early 1960s, the dependency ratio has been declining (dropping to 62 per 100 persons in 2000), and is forecasted to continue declining until about the year 2010. At that point, it will begin to rise because of the increasing age of the population, as well as the (projected) increasing number of births. In 2050, the dependency ratio is projected to be about where it was in 1970, but the mix of dependents will be considerably different. In 1960, almost 4 out of every 5 dependents were children, and the remainder were elderly. By the year 2050, only about 53 percent of dependents will be children, with the remaining 47 percent being elderly.

HOW DO THE STATES DIFFER IN THE AGES OF THEIR POPULATIONS?

There is considerable variation by state in the age distribution of the population. Nationally, 26 percent of the population is under 18 years old, while 12 percent is 65 years old and over. The national median age, the point at which half the population is older and half is younger, is 35.3 years. Florida

Table 1-6. Ratio of Dependents to Persons Age 18 to 64 Years in the United States, Selected Years, 1900–2050

(Ratio.)

Year	Total dependents	Under 18 years	65 years and over
1900	79.9	72.6	7.3
1910	73.2	65.7	7.5
1920	72.0	64.0	8.0
1930	67.7	58.6	9.1
1940	59.7	48.8	10.9
1950	64.5	51.1	13.4
1960	82.2	65.3	16.9
1970	78.7	61.1	17.6
1980	64.9	46.2	18.7
1990	62.0	41.7	20.3
2000	61.5	41.4	20.1
2010	59.0	38.3	20.7
2020	67.2	40.0	27.2
2030	76.1	41.5	34.6
2040	78.0	41.6	36.4
2050	79.0	42.0	37.0

Source: U.S. Census Bureau. Population Division. Population Projections Branch.

age 65 years and over. The median age figure is a blend of the two extremes. Utah's median age is low because it has so many children, while Florida's is high because it has so many elderly persons. Texas's and Alaska's patterns are similar to Utah's, but not as extreme.

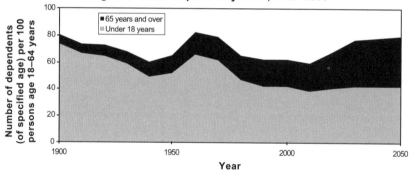

Figure 1-4. U.S. Dependency Ratio, 1900–2050

Source: U.S. Census Bureau. Population Division. Population Projections Branch.

used to have the highest median age, and it still has the highest proportion of population age 65 years and over. (See Table 1-7.) By 2004, the influx of young persons (mostly immigrants) into Florida dropped the state into fifth place for median age, surpassed by several small states with low growth rates and significant outmigration of younger population. (See Table 1-7.)

In contrast, the median age in Utah is only 28 years; this state leads the nation in proportion of population under 18 years old, and ranks second to last (ahead of Alaska) for proportion of population

BIRTHS AND FERTILITY

The number of children born in the United States peaked at about 4.3 million in 1960, dropped to 3.1 million in 1975, rose again to 4.2 million in 1990, and is currently around 4 million per year. This variation describes the cycle known as the "Baby Boom-Bust-Boomlet." The baby boom is described by demographers as the years between 1946 and 1964, the year in which the fertility rate dropped below 100 per 1,000 women of childbearing age (15 to 44 years old).

---

[5] The "dependency ratio" concept is based on the idea that persons in the "nondependent" age groups (18 to 64 years old) provide some or all of the economic support for the "dependent" age groups. This notion is not absolute, for there are many working people in the "dependent" group, and many non-working persons in the "nondependent" group. Many teenagers work, and many persons retire at younger or older ages than the traditional age of 65 years.

Table 1-7. States with the Largest and Smallest Proportion of Their Population Under 18 Years and 65 Years and Over, and Median Age, 2004

States with largest proportion

State and rank	Percent under 18 years	State and rank	Percent 65 years and over
1. Utah 2. Alaska 3. Texas 4. Arizona 5. California	31.0 28.7 27.9 26.9 26.7	1. Florida 2. West Virginia 2. Pennsylvania 4. North Dakota 4. Iowa	16.8 15.3 15.3 14.7 14.7

States with smallest proportion

State and rank	Percent under 18 years	State and rank	Percent 65 years and over
1. West Virginia 2. Maine 3. Vermont 4. North Dakota 5. Montana	21.2 21.4 21.7 21.9 22.5	1. Alaska 2. Utah 3. Georgia 4. Colorado 5. Texas	6.4 8.7 9.6 9.8 9.9

Median age

State and rank	Highest median age	State and rank	Lowest median age
1. Maine 2. Vermont 3. West Virginia 4. Montana 5. Florida	40.7 40.4 40.3 39.6 39.3	1. Utah 2. Texas 3. Alaska 4. Georgia 5. Arizona	28.0 32.9 33.4 34.0 34.1

Source: U.S. Census Bureau. American Community Survey 2004.

The boom was followed by a baby bust in the 1970s, when both the total number of births and the various birth rates dropped sharply. During this time, the number of women of childbearing age was lower (due to an earlier baby bust during the depression years of the 1930s and the World War II years). In addition, women were having fewer children and having them at a later point in life than in the past. Large numbers of women entered the labor force in the 1970s, and there were also significant increases in the use of contraceptives. Figure 1-5 shows these patterns.

By the 1980s, the early baby boomers had reached childbearing age. At this point, the number of births increased sharply, although the fertility rate increased only slightly. This "boomlet" was the product of having a large pool of available mothers who were, on average, having fewer children than their mothers did. In the 1990s, as the baby boomer women aged out of their childbearing years, the number of births and the birth and fertility rates began to drop. At the end of this period, and continuing into the current decade, rates rose slightly. The likely cause of this is increased immigration, which

Figure 1-5. Number of Births and Fertility Rate in the United States, 1940–2003

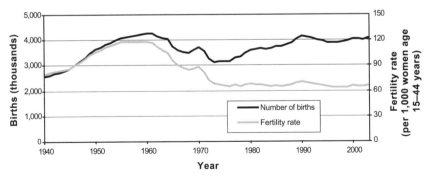

Source: National Center for Health Statistics. *National Vital Statistics Reports.*

consists primarily of people of childbearing age. However, the crude birth rate remains low, as the total population continues to increase.

Looking at birth figures another way, the Total Fertility Rate (TFR) was 2.042 in 2003, down from 2.056 in 2000. The TFR is the total number of children women will bear, on average, during their lifetimes. It is important to note that the TFR of the 2000s is, generally, at its lowest point in U.S. history, falling below the replacement rate of 2.1. (See Table 1-8.) This means that without immigration or a change in child-bearing patterns, the U.S. population would decrease over time. The figure of 2.042 is higher, however, than that of other industrialized countries such as those in western Europe.

NONMARITAL BIRTHS, TEEN BIRTHS

The birth rate for teenage mothers has dropped consistently over time, from a high of 68 per 1,000 girls age 15–19 years in 1970 to 42 in 2003. (See Figure 1-6.) However, the proportion of children born to unmarried mothers has increased steadily over this period of time. It was under 5 percent until 1958. Since then, this rate has increased steadily, reaching 35.7 percent, over one-third of all births, in 2004. Several societal changes explain this phenomenon, including the postponement of marriage and the increasing acceptance of single mothers who give birth to and raise their children.

Table 1-8. Selected Fertility Indicators for the United States, Selected Years, 1940–2003

(Number, rate.)

Year	Number of births (thousands)	Crude birth rate (per 1,000 population)	Fertility rate (per 1,000 women age 15–44 years)	Total fertility rate (implied lifetime births)
1940	2 559	19.4	79.9	2.301
1945	2 858	20.4	85.9	2.491
1950	3 632	24.1	106.2	3.091
1955	4 097	25.0	118.3	3.580
1960	4 258	23.7	118.0	3.449
1965	3 760	19.4	96.3	2.622
1970	3 731	18.4	87.9	2.480
1975	3 144	14.6	66.0	1.774
1980	3 612	15.9	68.4	1.840
1985	3 761	15.8	66.3	1.844
1990	4 158	16.7	70.9	2.081
1995	3 900	14.6	64.6	1.978
2000	4 059	14.4	65.9	2.056
2001	4 026	14.1	65.3	2.034
2002	4 022	13.9	64.8	2.013
2003	4 090	14.1	66.1	2.042

Source: Centers for Disease Control and Prevention. National Center for Health Statistics. *National Vital Statistics Reports* 54(2).

Figure 1-6. Birth Rates, by Age of Mother, 1970–2003

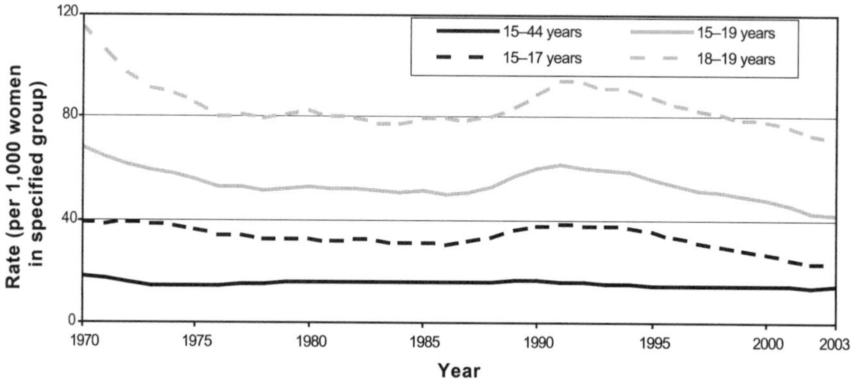

Source: Centers for Disease Control and Prevention. National Center for Health Statistics. *National Vital Statistics Reports.*

MORTALITY AND LIFE EXPECTANCY: THE CHANCES OF DYING

Life expectancy[6] for children born in the United States in 2003 was 77.6 years. Life expectancy is over 80 years for women and about 75 years for men. For both sexes, life expectancy has increased by more than a dozen years since the end of World War II. (See Figure 1-7.)

Another way to look at life expectancy is to project, for persons of a given age, the number of years left to live. This takes into account the fact that, for every age, some people of that birth year have already died. The focus can then be turned to those

Congress. Thus, Congress made no earlier attempt to enumerate Indians on reservations or in Indian territories. In 1890, there were only about 248,000 American Indians enumerated on the census, a proportion of less than 1 percent of the population in the continental United States. This racial group also composed less than 1 percent of the country's inhabitants, as enumerated on the 2000 census.

Although Blacks have remained the largest racial minority group in the United States, the proportion of the U.S. population that was of African origin actually declined between 1790 and the turn of the twentieth century. From 1920 to 1950, Blacks represented less than 10 percent of the U.S. population, through their representation has since increased

Figure 1-7. Life Expectancy, 1929–2003

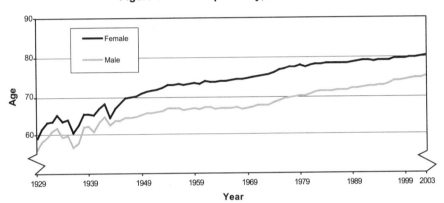

Source: Centers for Disease Control and Prevention. National Center for Health Statistics. *National Vital Statistics Reports.*

who are still living. For example, a person born in 1948 had an original life expectancy of 67 years. This same person, alive in 2003, and now 55 years old could expect to live for 26.5 more years, bringing his or her current life expectancy to 81. Insurance companies rely on this measure of life expectancy in setting rates.

RACIAL AND ETHNIC COMPOSITION

By the time of the birth of the United States as a nation, the predominant race among its approximately 4 million residents had already changed from American Indian to White. European settlers and their descendants composed about 80 percent of the U.S. population, as enumerated in the first U.S. Census in 1790, with Black slaves from Africa making up the bulk of the remainder. American Indians were not included in the census figures until the 1890 census, because the Constitution of the United States specifically excluded "Indians not taxed" from the apportionment of representatives in

slightly. The 2000 census reported the Black alone population at about 35 million, which made up about 12.3 percent of the total U.S. population.

The official federal government definition of race and ethnicity is embodied in Statistical Directive 15, issued by the Office of the Chief Statistician in the Office of Management and Budget (OMB). As originally promulgated in 1977, Directive 15 called for self-identification of persons into one of five racial groups: White; Black; American Indian; Asian and Pacific Islander; and "Other." A separate question elicited ethnic identification as Hispanic or Latino, and persons identifying as such could be of any race.

During the 1990s, a substantial research project and public hearing process was conducted to determine how, if at all, Directive 15 should be modified. Some wanted a "mixed race" category. Hawaiians wanted to be separate from Asians. Arabs wanted a category of their own. In the end, Directive 15 was

---

[6] Life expectancy is the average number of years that a group of infants born in a given year are expected to live, if they were to experience the age-specific death rates prevailing during the year of their birth.

modified in two important ways. First, a sixth racial category, Native Hawaiian and Other Pacific Islander, was added. This group is now tabulated and reported separately from the aggregation of Asian groups. Second, respondents were permitted to choose "one or more races," a process generally known as "multiple-checkoff." Nationally, about 1.4 percent of the population chose this option in the 2000 census. Finally, the separate question for Spanish/Hispanic/Latino ethnic designation was maintained.

This led to tabulations on race and Hispanic origin in 2000 that were not completely compatible with those published in 1990 or earlier. Blacks reporting only one race now make up 12.2 percent of the population. (See Table 1-9.) If all of the people who reported that they were Black and one or more other races are added in, the proportion rises to about 13 percent.

Despite the rising numbers and percentage of Black population in the nation, the Hispanic population has grown to be even larger. As tabulated in the census, Hispanics may be of any race. As shown in Table 1-9, the Hispanic or Latino population in 2004 totaled over 40.4 million, more than the Black or African American population—even when those who were both Black and another race are included. The reason for this change is that Hispanics are still immigrating into the United States. Most immigrants are young and likely to have more children

than non-immigrants. The Black population is growing at a much smaller rate.

Another group with a significant increase is the Asian population. Again, the primary reason is immigration and the fertility characteristics of the immigrant families. These trends are expected to continue over the next several decades, with Whites continuing to drop as a proportion of the total population. Current projections for 2050 show that non-Hispanic Whites will account for just about half of the total U.S. population, Blacks will make up about 15 percent of residents, Asians 8 percent of residents, and Hispanics (of any race), about 24 percent of the population.[7]

Table 1-9. Race and Ethnicity, 2004

(Number, percent.)

Race/ethnicity	Number	Percent
One race	280 285 784	98.1
White	216 036 244	75.6
Black or African American	34 772 381	12.2
American Indian and Alaska Native	2 151 322	0.8
Asian	12 097 281	4.2
Native Hawaiian and Other Pacific Islander	403 832	0.1
Some other race	14 824 724	5.2
Two or more races	5 405 717	1.9
Hispanic or Latino [1]	40 459 196	14.2

Source: U.S. Census Bureau. Population Division. American Community Survey 2004.

[1]May be of any race.

[7] U.S. Census Bureau. *U.S. Interim Projections by Age, Sex, Race, and Hispanic Origin.* (Mar. 2004.) <http://www.census.gov/ipc/www/ usinterimproj>. (Accessed Feb. 16, 2006.)

FOR FUTHER INFORMATION SEE:

Forstall, Richard, and James Fitzsimmons. 1993. *Metropolitan Growth and Expansion in the 1980s.* (Technical Working Paper No. 6). <http://www.census.gov/population/www/documentation/twps0006/twps0006.html>. (Accessed Feb. 16, 2006.)

McFalls, Joseph A., Jr. 1991. Population: A lively introduction. *Population Bulletin* 46(2).

U.S. Department of Health and Human Services. Centers for Disease Control and Prevention. National Center for Health Statistics. *Monthly Vital Statistics Reports* (various). <http://www.cdc.gov/nchs/products/pubs/pubd/mvsr/mvsr.htm>. (Accessed Feb. 16, 2006.)

WEB SITES:

National Center for Health Statistics. <http://www.cdc.gov/nchs>. (Accessed Feb. 16, 2006.)

Population Reference Bureau. <http://www.prb.org>. (Accessed Feb. 16, 2006.)

Urban Institute. <http://www.urban.org>. (Accessed Feb. 16, 2006.)

U.S. Census Bureau. <http://www.census.gov>. (Accessed Feb. 16, 2006.)

U.S. Census Bureau. International Database. <http://www.census.gov/ipc/www/idbnew.html>. (Accessed Feb. 16, 2006.)

U.S. Department of Agriculture. Economic Research Service. <http://www.ers.usda.gov>. (Accessed Feb. 16, 2006.)

Chapter 2
Households and Families

MARITAL STATUS

AGE AT MARRIAGE

Age at marriage, demographically speaking, makes a difference beyond the timing of the ceremony itself. It influences household formation, consumer purchases, and the number and timing of births. It can also influence such life events as educational attainment, career goals, and the likelihood of divorce, as well as the eventual total population of a nation.

Age at first marriage has been increasing in the United States since the mid-1960s, and is now at the highest level ever recorded. In 2004, the median age at first marriage was 27.4 years for men and 25.8 years for women. During the baby boom era of the 1950s, median age at first marriage was about 5 years younger for both men and women. To some degree, the baby boom era was the exception; at the turn of the twentieth century, the median age at first marriage was about 26 years for men and 22 years for women.

The delay in age of marriage can also be seen in the percentage of young adults who have never married. In 2004, 44 percent of men and 32 percent of women age 25 to 34 years had never been married. Both figures have been increasing steadily for the past several decades.

WILL PEOPLE MARRY AT ALL?

Despite the tendency to delay marriage, almost all of the young adults living in the United States will eventually marry. In 2004, only about 7 percent of people age 45 to 64 years had never married; the comparable figure for those 65 years old and over is 4 percent.[1]

There were about 4.7 million cohabiting couple households in the United States in 2004, defined as opposite sex unmarried partner households. The majority of these couples were made up of people who had never been married (58 percent); another third had been previously married but were divorced. (See Table 2-2.) The majority of these households had no children under 18 years old.

Table 2-1. Marital Status of People 15 Years and Over, 2004

(Numbers in thousands, percent distribution.)

Sex and age	Total (thousands)	Percent distribution			
		Married, spouse present or absent	Separated or divorced	Widowed	Never married
Both Sexes					
15 years and over	227 343	53.4	11.6	6.1	29.0
15 to 24 years	40 598	9.0	1.4	0.1	89.5
25 to 34 years	39 140	53.0	8.6	0.4	38.0
35 to 44 years	43 555	66.5	15.8	0.9	16.8
45 to 64 years	69 412	69.8	17.8	3.7	8.6
65 years and over	34 639	56.2	9.1	30.8	3.9
Male					
15 years and over	110 048	55.2	9.8	2.4	32.6
15 to 24 years	20 569	6.4	1.0	0.0	92.6
25 to 34 years	19 553	48.8	6.9	0.1	44.1
35 to 44 years	21 520	65.7	13.5	0.4	20.4
45 to 64 years	33 615	73.7	15.2	1.5	9.6
65 years and over	14 793	74.0	8.2	13.7	4.1
Female					
15 years and over	117 295	51.7	13.3	9.5	25.6
15 to 24 years	20 028	11.7	1.9	0.1	86.3
25 to 34 years	19 587	57.2	10.3	0.6	31.9
35 to 44 years	22 036	67.4	18.0	1.3	13.3
45 to 64 years	35 798	66.2	20.3	5.8	7.7
65 years and over	19 847	43.0	9.8	43.5	3.7

Source: U.S. Census Bureau. Current Population Survey.

---

[1] These statistics come from surveys conducted by the U.S. Census Bureau and published at <http://www.census.gov>.

Two out of five of the members of these households were under the age of 30. Thus, it appears that cohabitation is often an alternative to marriage, especially for young people with no children. The probability of premarital cohabitation leading to marriage is higher among White women (see Figure 2-2); it is also higher among couples with higher incomes, and among partners who have a religious affiliation.[2]

WILL MARRIAGES LAST?

About one-third of first marriages, among marriages that took place in 1965 or later, ended in divorce by their 15th anniversaries. Of those who divorced, the median duration of marriage was about 8 years. This has proved to be the time with the highest risk of divorce. Couples that remain married for longer than 8 years have an increasingly good chance of remaining married. The probability of marriage dis-

Table 2-2. Opposite Sex Unmarried Partner Households, 2004

(Numbers in thousands, percent.)

Characteristic	Percent, except as noted
Total Number of Unmarried Couples (Thousands)	4 677
Never married	58.0
Divorced	32.1
No children under 18 years	58.2
With children under 18 years	41.8
Under 30 years of age	38.7

Source: U.S. Census Bureau. Current Population Survey.

ruption is higher for partners who married as teenagers, partners who have less than a high school education, and partners with a low family income. People who did not grow up in an intact, two-parent household also have a higher chance of divorcing.[3]

Figure 2-1. Marital Status of People 15 Years and Over, 2004

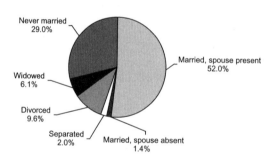

Source: U.S. Census Bureau. Current Population Survey.

Figure 2-2. Probability that Cohabitation Transitions to Marriage, 1995

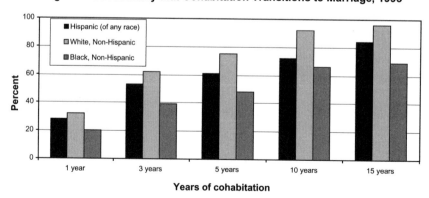

Source: Centers for Disease Control and Prevention. National Center for Health Statistics. 2002. *Vital Health Statistics* 23(22).

[2] Centers for Disease Control and Prevention. National Center for Health Statistics. 2002. Cohabitation, marriage, divorce, and remarriage in the United States. *Vital and Health Statistics* 23(22). <http://www.cdc.gov/nchs/data/series/sr_23/sr23_022.pdf>. (Accessed Feb. 16, 2006.)

[3] U.S. Census Bureau. *Number, Timing, and Duration of Marriages and Divorces: 2001* (Report P70-97). (Feb. 2005.) <http://www.census.gov/prod/2005pubs/p70-97.pdf>. (Accessed Feb. 16, 2006.)

"NON-TRADITIONAL" HOUSEHOLDS

As a result of the tendency to delay marriage (or to avoid it entirely, as described in the previous section) and the increased divorce rates, the last few decades have seen a proliferation of one-person households and nonfamily households. In 1960, at the height of an era that has come to epitomize the positive attributes of marriage and the two-parent family household, married-couple families accounted for 75 percent of all households and represented 87 percent of all families. Nonfamily households made up 15 percent of households. By 2004, married-couple families represented only 50 percent of all households, while one-third of all households were nonfamily households.[4] Families maintained by women (without a spouse) increased from about 10 percent to 19 percent of all families during this same period; those sustained by a man with no spouse present have also increased. In 2004, they represent 7 percent of all families. (See Table 2-3.)

The likelihood of children experiencing life in a single-parent family at some time during their childhood has increased considerably in the past several decades. In 2004, 31 percent of children under 18 years old were not living in a two-parent family; in 1970, about 12 percent of children lived with only one parent. Life in a single-parent family is even more likely for Black children: in 2004, fully two-thirds of them lived with only one parent or with neither parent.

Table 2-3. Household Type, 2004

(Numbers in thousands, percent.)

Type	Number (thousands)	Percent
Total	109 902	100.0
Family households	73 886	67.2
Married-couple family	55 224	50.2
Other family	18 662	17.0
Male householder, no wife present	4 811	4.4
Female householder, no husband present	13 851	12.6
Nonfamily households	36 016	32.8
Householder living alone	29 572	26.9
Householder not living alone	6 444	5.9

Source: U.S. Census Bureau. American Community Survey 2004.

A subset of nonfamily households is composed of unmarried couples, defined as persons of the opposite sex sharing living quarters. Since there are no questions directly related to the level of intimacy between such persons in most surveys, it is generally assumed that such persons are in fact "a couple." This assumption can be erroneous, as non-couple households, such as one in which an elderly widow rents a room to a male college student, can be included in this category. As discussed previously, the number of unmarried couples increased from about 500,000 in 1970 to about 4.7 million in 2004. Unmarried couples now represent about 8 percent of all couples (married and unmarried) in the United States, up from only about 1 percent 30 years ago. Children under 18 years old are living in just over one-third of these households.

Nonfamily households accounted for 43 percent of the growth in the total number of households during

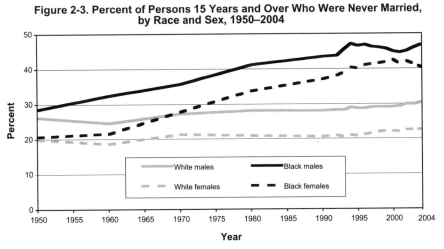

Figure 2-3. Percent of Persons 15 Years and Over Who Were Never Married, by Race and Sex, 1950–2004

Source: U.S. Census Bureau. Current Population Survey.

---

[4] The definitions of "household," "family," and "nonfamily household" used in this chapter are those used in U.S. Census Bureau publications. These data about households and families come from the census and the American Community Survey. A household is defined as all persons who occupy a housing unit; the term is essentially synonymous with "occupied housing unit." (Chapter 7 provides more information about housing.) A family is defined as a group of two or more persons who are related and live together in the same household. A nonfamily household is one consisting of only one person, or of two or more persons who are all unrelated to each other.

Figure 2-4. Percent Distribution of Households, 1940–2004

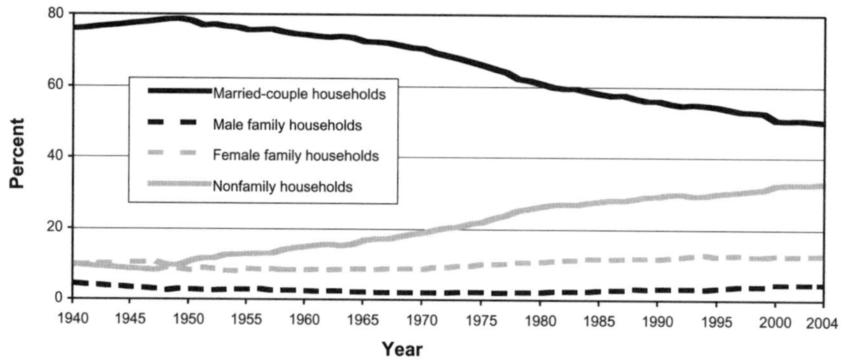

Source: U.S. Census Bureau. Current Population Survey. American Community Survey (data from 2000–2004).

the 1990s. Most of these households consist of persons living alone (about 83 percent). Men living alone tend to be younger than women living alone. (In 1995, the median age was about 44 years for men, and about 66 years for women.) The largest subgroup of women living alone was widows, with 30 percent over 75 years old.

Both household and family sizes have shrunk since 1970. There are many reasons for the decrease. One of the most important is increasing life expectancy, which means that both couples and single people are living a larger proportion of their total life span in households without children. Another important factor is the fact that women are having fewer children. (See discussion of fertility in Chapter 1.) Divorce, and the accompanying increase in one-parent households, is another contributing factor. Overall, the average household size declined from 3.33 to 2.60 between 1960 and 2004. In 2004, almost two-thirds of America's households, and over half of the family households, had no children under 18 years of age living in them.

Living with Grandma and Grandpa

In 2004, there were almost 5.7 million grandparents in the United States living with their grandchildren. In about half of these households, the grandparents were responsible for the grandchildren; the implication is that the children have no responsible parent in the household. Overall, 4.8 million children were living in such a situation. Responsible grandparents were 62 percent female. Over half were in the labor force (either working or unemployed), and about 1 in 5 was living below the poverty level.

Households that include a grandparent, a parent, a child, and perhaps a grandchild account for almost 4 percent of all households. In the majority of these households (2.5 million), the oldest generation is the householder, i.e., the person responsible for the household. This includes situations in which young mothers and their children live in their own mothers' households. Another 1.4 million multi-generational households are more traditional: they include a householder, his/her parent, and one or more children of the householder. In a fraction of these cases, the household consists of four generations: the (grand)parent, parent/householder, child and grandchild.[5] These households are relatively uncommon in the Plains states of Iowa, Minnesota, Montana, Nebraska, North Dakota, South Dakota, and Wisconsin. These states, as well as Wyoming, all show less than 2 percent of their households as multi-generational. This is also true in Maine and Vermont. On the other hand, the figure for Hawaii is 8.2 percent. Other states that are at least 1 percentage point above the national figure are Mississippi, Louisiana, and New Jersey.

How Are the Children Doing?

A Census Bureau study[6] describes child well-being in terms of five indicators: daily interactions, participation in extracurricular activities, academic achievement, educational expectations, and parents' feelings toward the child. A child's daily interaction was measured by activities such as eating meals with parents, being praised by a parent, and being talked to or played with just for fun. These types of interactions are more common for younger children (under 6 years old) than for their older siblings.

---

[5] U.S. Census Bureau. Table PHC-T-17: *Multigenerational Households for the United States, States, and for Puerto Rico.* Census 2000. (Sept. 2001.) <http://www.census.gov/population/www/cen2000/phc-t17.html>. (Accessed Feb. 16, 2006.) This item was tabulated for the first time in the 2000 census.

[6] U.S. Census Bureau. *A Child's Day: 2000 (Selected Indicators of Child Well-Being)* (Report P70-89). (Aug. 2003.) <http://www.census.gov/prod/2003pubs/p70-89.pdf>. (Accessed Feb. 16, 2006.) Data in this report came from the SIPP (Survey of Income and Program Participation), a large, national representative sample.

Figure 2-5. Percent Distribution of Children, by Household Type, 2004

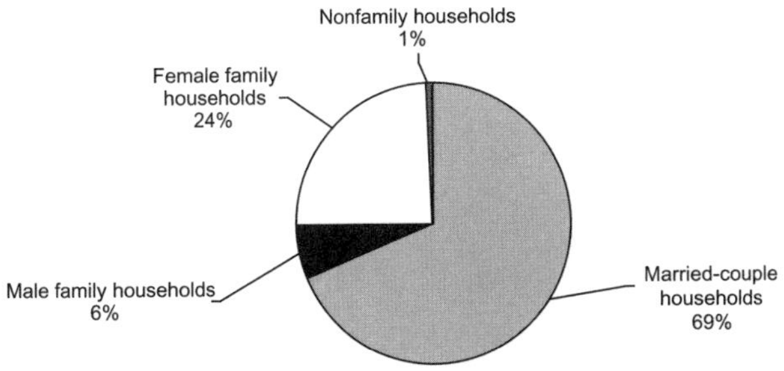

Nonfamily households
1%

Female family
households
24%

Male family households
6%

Married-couple
households
69%

Source: U.S. Census Bureau. American Community Survey 2004.

Only about one-third of children participate in extracurricular activities, be they sports, clubs, or lessons outside of school. Participation rates are higher when the child's parents are married, and are lower for children whose parents have lower educational attainment levels or incomes below or near the poverty line. Academic achievement was analyzed for children age 12 to 17 years. About 72 percent were at or beyond their appropriate grade level, and 22 percent had participated in classes for the gifted.

Educational expectations are reasonable, with 86 percent of parents wanting their children to graduate from college and 79 percent expecting them to do so. About half of all parents appear to have some negative feelings toward their children, considering them as harder to care for than most, doing things that are bothersome, taking up too much time, or causing angry feelings in the parents.

CHILD CARE ARRANGEMENTS

There are no widespread government-run child care centers in the United States. Yet the increased incidence of mothers of young children participating in the labor force, which has risen over the past several decades, has meant an increased need for child care arrangements, especially for families with preschoolers. In 2002, 11.6 million children, representing 63 percent of all children under 5 years old, required care during the time their mothers were at work, job training, or school. Of these children, about 7.4 million were cared for by relatives, mostly by fathers or grandparents. About 6.4 million were in some type of non-relative care, including organized facilities such as day care centers and nursery schools, and other people's homes.

Many preschool children experience more than one type of care. Almost 7 million have no regular arrangement.[7] All of these numbers are lower than the corresponding numbers from 5 years earlier, reflecting the declining number of births described in Chapter 1.

In the winter of 2002, there were 26.1 million children of grade-school age (age 5 to 14 years) with a working (employed) mother. Two-thirds of all children in this age group who lived with their mothers have mothers who worked. This represents an increase of nearly 3 million children over the 1997 figure. Child care arrangements for these children include the same options as for preschoolers, as well as enrichment activities such as organized sports, music lessons, and self-care; children in the latter group are often called "latchkey" children. Looking at all children age 5 to 14 years, about 16 percent participated in enrichment activities that served as childcare arrangements for their parents. These types of activity were slightly more frequent for older children (9 to 14 years old), for children who live in nonpoor families, and children whose mothers work at least part-time. Sports were the most frequent type of enrichment activity, followed by lessons, clubs (including scouting), and before/after-school programs.

About 6 million children were in self-care. As expected, the frequency of self-care is much higher for children 12–14 years old (40 percent of all children of this age) than for those 5–11 years old (15 percent of children in this age group). Most of the time, self-care is only one of the arrangements parents use for their children. The average number of hours a child was in self-care each week was about 5 hours for younger children and 7 hours for older

[7] U.S. Census Bureau. *Who's Minding the Kids? Child Care Arrangements: Winter 2002* (Report P70-101). (Oct. 2005.) <http://www.census.gov/prod/2005pubs/p70-101.pdf>. (Accessed Feb. 16, 2006.) The data in this report were derived from questions asked in the Survey of Income and Program Participation (SIPP).

**Figure 2-6. Child Care Arrangements for Preschool Children
Living with Employed Mothers, 2002**

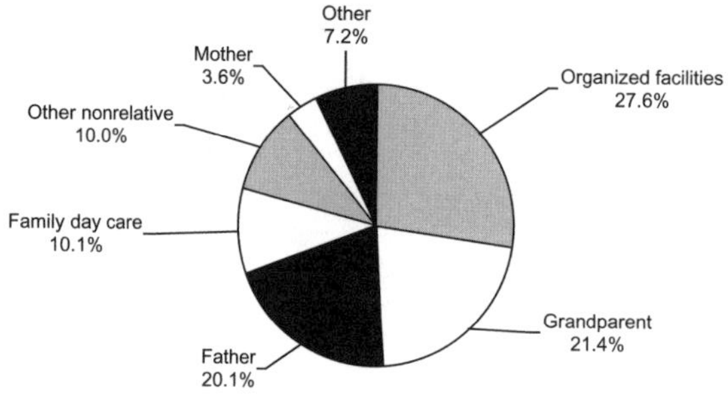

Other 7.2%
Mother 3.6%
Organized facilities 27.6%
Other nonrelative 10.0%
Family day care 10.1%
Grandparent 21.4%
Father 20.1%

Source: U.S. Census Bureau. Population Division. Fertility & Family Statistics Branch.
Who's Minding the Kids? Child Care Arrangements: Winter 2002 (P70-101).

children. A report by the Census Bureau in 1997 report noted that "among older children, self-care can be an important part of the natural process of independence, allowing children structured opportunities for successful transitions to adulthood."[8]

HOW MUCH DOES CHILD CARE COST?

The cost of child care is an important consideration in working parents' budgets, especially if the family's total income is low. In 2002, the average cost of child care for preschoolers with employed mothers was $122 per week and consumed almost 10 percent of the family's income. When mothers are not employed, the cost is $53 per week. For children age 5–14 years, the average cost per week is lower (about $60), primarily because the children usually are in school for most of the hours when child care is needed.

All told, full-time employed mothers spent about $95 per week on child care in 2002, with the cost averaging $75 per week for those with one child and about $114 per week for those with two or more children. Costs were highest in suburban areas and lowest outside of metropolitan areas, and generally rose with the income of the family.

Government assistance in paying for child care has increased, with the percentage of children covered nearly doubling from 2.4 percent to 4.1 percent. In all, the parents of about 1.4 million children received assistance. This is still a very small piece of the overall child care funding picture, even though welfare reform requires most parents to be at work or in school. Children whose families participate in TANF[9] or Medicaid are more likely to be covered than those whose families do not receive such assistance.

---

[8] U.S. Census Bureau. *Who's Minding the Kids? Child Care Arrangements: Spring 1997* (Report P70-86). (July 2002.) <http://www.census.gov/prod/2002pubs/p70-86.pdf>. (Accessed Feb. 16, 2006.) This report is the predecessor to the P70-101 report cited above.

[9] TANF is an acronym for Temporary Assistance to Needy Families, the name of the program under which welfare grants are made.

FOR FURTHER INFORMATION SEE:

Bianchi, Suzanne, and Daphne Spain. 1986. *American Women in Transition*. New York: Russell Sage Foundation.

Bianchi, Suzanne. 1990. America's children: Mixed prospects. *Population Bulletin* 45: 1-43.

U.S. Census Bureau. Families and living arrangements (formerly "Households and Families"). *Current Population Reports* (Series P-20). <http://www.census.gov/population/www/socdemo/hh-fam.html>. (Accessed Feb. 16, 2006.)

U.S. Census Bureau. Marital status and living arrangements. *Current Population Reports* (Series P-20). <http://www.census.gov/population/www/socdemo/ms-la.html>. (Accessed Feb. 16, 2006.)

WEB SITES:

National Center for Health Statistics. <http://www.cdc.gov/nchs>. (Accessed Feb. 16, 2006.)

U.S. Census Bureau. <http://www.census.gov>. (Accessed Feb. 16, 2006.)

U.S. Census Bureau. American FactFinder. <http://factfinder.census.gov>. (Accessed Feb. 16, 2006.)

Chapter 3
Social Conditions

AGING

The United States is an aging society. The number of elderly people continues to grow, both in absolute terms and as a proportion of the total population. This means that more societal resources must be devoted to serving this population.

In 2004, there were about 36.3 million people age 65 years and over in the United States, composing 12.4 percent of the total population. In contrast, there were only 3 million persons in this age group in 1900, constituting only 4 percent of the population. As shown in Figure 3-1, the proportion of elderly persons is projected to rise sharply over the next 40 years, especially after 2011, when the baby boomer generation begins to turn 65.

Why this sharp increase in the number and proportion of the elderly? Most importantly, advances in medical treatments are keeping people alive and in good health to a much more advanced age than even 50 years ago. This factor has already made a significant impact in many different ways. First, the health care system must increasingly serve the elderly, who constitute almost half of all hospital admissions. Second, increasing age has meant that more and more households are increasingly composed of one or two persons who have no children, as healthy senior citizens remain in their homes, rather moving into institutional care or their children's resi-

dences. Third, the booming elderly population has placed a significant strain on Social Security, which has already increased the standard retirement age for persons born in 1938 or later. Medicare funding is currently facing a similar problem. Finally, because retired people are living so much longer, they face an increasing challenge of managing to have sufficient income to continue to live in the style to which they are accustomed.

The Federal Interagency Forum on Aging-Related Statistics, a collaboration between several federal statistics agencies, has established a set of indicators to measure the status of older Americans—age 65 years and over—across time. The following sections report on many of these indicators.[1]

CHARACTERISTICS OF THE ELDERLY

Because the White non-Hispanic population has a longer life expectancy than minority groups, the proportion of the elderly population that is White non-Hispanic was 82 percent in 2004, much higher than this group's representation among the total population. Projections for 2050, however, show that pattern changing. The White non-Hispanic proportion is projected to drop to 61 percent, and the proportions of elderly population in other race groups and in the Hispanic origin ethnic group are projected to increase. (See Table 3-1.)

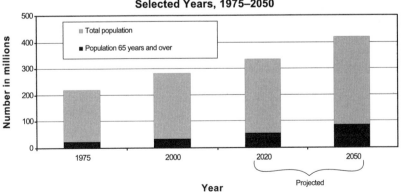

Figure 3-1. Total Population and Proportion 65 Years and Over, Selected Years, 1975–2050

Source: U.S. Census Bureau. *U.S. Interim Projections by Age, Sex, Race, and Hispanic Origin, 2004.*

---

[1] Federal Interagency Forum on Aging-Related Statistics. *Older Americans 2004: Key Indicators of Well-Being.* (Nov. 2004.) <http://www.agingstats.gov/chartbook2004/OA_2004.pdf>. (Accessed Feb. 17, 2006.)

As expected, the data show that elderly persons are more likely to be living alone and to be widowed. The "young old," people 65 to 74 years old, are more likely to be married; this proportion drops with age as the incidence of widowhood increases. Elderly men have a higher likelihood of being married, regardless of age, than do women. This happens because women are much more likely to be widowed than are men, and perhaps because men are more likely to remarry if their wives die. There are also far more women in these age groups than there are men. Overall, about three-quarters of men age 65 years or over are married, compared to less than half of the women. (See Table 3-2.)

The pattern varies somewhat by race and ethnicity. As shown in Table 3-3, elderly Asians are far more likely than other groups to have relatives (other than a spouse) living with them. Hispanics are also

more likely to be living with relatives. Elderly White non-Hispanics, especially women, are the most likely to be living alone.

Table 3-1. Projected Distribution of the Population 65 Years and Over, by Race and Hispanic Origin, 2004 and 2050

(Percent distribution.)

Race/ethnicity	2004 estimates	2050 projections
Total	100.0	100.0
White, non-Hispanic alone	81.9	61.3
Black alone	8.4	12.0
Asian alone	2.9	7.8
All other races alone or in combination	1.2	2.7
Hispanic (of any race)	6.0	17.5

Source: U.S. Census Bureau. Population Estimates and Projections.

Table 3-2. Marital Status of the Population 65 Years and Over, 2004

(Percent distribution, except as noted.)

Marital status	65 years and over	65 to 74 years	75 to 84 years	85 years and over
Total (Number in Thousands)	34 205	18 164	12 416	3 626
Total	100.0	100.0	100.0	100.0
Married, spouse present	54.3	63.7	48.7	26.4
Married, spouse absent	2.9	3.2	2.7	2.3
Widowed	30.5	18.2	38.7	63.8
Divorced	8.4	11.0	6.0	3.6
Never married	3.9	4.0	3.9	3.9
Men (Number in Thousands)	14 547	8 284	5 057	1 206
Men	100.0	100.0	100.0	100.0
Married, spouse present	71.8	75.5	70.0	53.9
Married, spouse absent	3.5	3.5	3.4	3.8
Widowed	13.4	7.5	17.7	36.0
Divorced	7.6	9.6	5.4	3.1
Never married	3.8	3.9	3.6	3.2
Women (Number in Thousands)	19 658	9 880	7 358	2 420
Women	100.0	100.0	100.0	100.0
Married, spouse present	41.3	53.8	34.1	12.6
Married, spouse absent	2.4	2.8	2.2	1.5
Widowed	43.1	27.2	53.2	77.7
Divorced	9.0	12.2	6.5	3.9
Never married	4.0	4.0	4.1	4.2

Source: U.S. Census Bureau. American Community Survey 2004.

Table 3-3. Living Arrangements of the Population 65 Years and Over, 2003

(Percent.)

Race/ethnicity	With spouse	With other relatives	With non-relatives	Alone
Men				
Total	73.0	5.0	3.0	19.0
White, non-Hispanic alone	75.0	3.5	2.7	18.7
Black alone	60.3	5.7	4.4	29.5
Asian alone	59.7	30.6	0.5	8.1
Hispanic (of any race)	68.3	15.0	4.7	12.0
Women				
Total	50.0	9.0	2.0	40.0
White, non-Hispanic alone	49.6	6.8	1.7	41.8
Black alone	45.6	13.2	2.1	39.1
Asian alone	42.8	35.6	2.2	19.4
Hispanic (of any race)	50.9	24.8	2.2	21.8

Source: Federal Interagency Forum on Aging-Related Statistics (Forum). Older Americans 2004: Key Indicators of Well-Being.

Table 3-4. Educational Attainment of the Population 65 Years and Over, Selected Years, 1950–2004

(Percent.)

Educational attainment level	1950	1960	1970	1980	1990	2000	2004
High school diploma or higher	17.0	19.1	27.1	38.8	53.2	65.5	71.6
Bachelor's degree or higher	3.4	3.7	5.5	8.3	10.7	15.4	17.9

Source: U.S. Census Bureau. Decennial Census 1950–2000 and American Community Survey 2004.
Note: Data for 2004 refer to the civilian noninstitutional population. Data for other years refer to the resident population.

Education levels among persons 65 years old and over have increased over time, much as education levels have increased across all age groups. In 2004, nearly three-quarters of this population had graduated from high school, with 18 percent having earned a four-year college degree. (See Table 3-4.)

ECONOMIC CIRCUMSTANCES

The economic condition of the nation's elderly has improved over time. In 1959, 35 percent of the population age 65 years and over lived below the poverty level. This rate declined sharply between 1965 and 1975. It continued to decrease at a slower rate, reaching 9 percent in 2004. However, the older the person, the more likely that he or she was living below the poverty level. Persons living alone show higher poverty rates as well.

In 2004, the median household income for persons 65 years old and over was $27,800. About 25 percent of the elderly had annual incomes below $15,000. At the other end of the scale, another 25 percent had incomes of $50,000 or more. The major predictors of higher income are being married and being among the "young old" (under 75 years old). These two factors are, of course, interrelated, as the young old are more likely to be married. They are also more likely to have earned income over the course of the year.

Almost all elderly households receive Social Security benefits. These provide the majority of total income for more than half of its beneficiaries, and is the only source of income for 18 percent of them. A recent change permits persons of full retirement age (65 years old and over) to receive Social Security benefits, regardless of their level of earned income. Figure 3-2 shows that Social Security is the single largest source of income for the elderly, followed by earnings, pensions, and asset income. Social Security provides 82 percent of aggregate income for the poorest group of elderly, but only 19 percent for the highest quintile of earners. These affluent households have significant income from assets, earnings, and pensions. The bottom line: the data clearly show that the elderly who are best off in their senior years are those who are able to keep working, at least part-time, who have pensions, and who have accumulated savings and investments from their younger years to provide income at this point in their lives.

HEALTH

As discussed in Chapter 1, life expectancy is continually increasing. In other words, Americans are living longer than ever before. The longer a person lives, the greater his or her life expectancy for the future. Thus, people who survive to age 65 can expect to live another 18 years, while those who are now 85 can expect another 6 or 7 years of life.

Figure 3-2. Shares of Aggregate Income, by Source, 2003

Source: Federal Interagency Forum on Aging-Related Statistics (Forum).
Older Americans 2004: Key Indicators of Well-Being.

Figure 3-3. Percent of Persons 65 Years and Over Reporting Good to Excellent Health, by Race and Hispanic Origin, 2000–2002

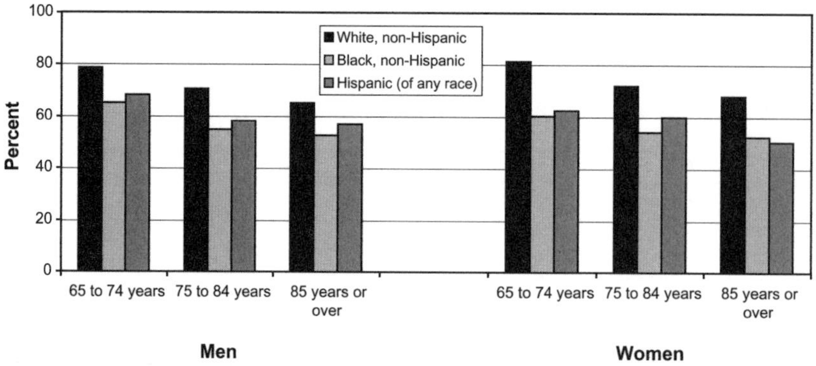

Source: Federal Interagency Forum on Aging-Related Statistics (Forum). *Older Americans 2004: Key Indicators of Well-Being.*

What are the causes of death for the elderly? Heart disease leads the list, followed by cancer and stroke. Diabetes, chronic obstructive pulmonary disease (such as emphysema), and pneumonia/influenza cause death less often. These rates may increase in the future as medical science finds new ways to treat the morbid effects of heart disease and cancer. In fact, the death rates for diabetes and chronic obstructive pulmonary disease have generally risen since 1980.

Chronic diseases exist over a long period of time and are rarely cured. Thus, they become a significant health and financial burden to the elderly, their families, and the nation's health system. Some of these are conditions that often lead to death (cancer, stroke, heart disease, and diabetes). Non-fatal conditions include arthritis and hypertension (high blood pressure); about half the elderly suffer from one, the other, or both. Another condition affecting elderly persons in large numbers is memory impairment, including Alzheimer's disease. The problem shows up in low numbers among the "young old," but affects more than one-third of persons 85 years old or over. It is somewhat more common in men than in women. Depressive symptoms also occur in 10 to 22 percent of the elderly, with the condition being more common among the "old old," persons 85 years old or over. Depressed people are also more likely to have physical illness, and to use the nation's health resources at a higher rate.

Overall, elderly persons rate their own health quite highly. These ratings differ significantly by race and Hispanic origin. However, as expected, younger elderly people rated their health more highly than

the population 85 years old and over. (See Figure 3-3.) Even so, more than half of the group that rate their health the lowest on average—Black men 85 years old and over—report having good to excellent health.

As we would expect, older Americans are more likely to suffer from disabilities than younger people. About 20 percent of this group reported a chronic disability in 1999, a smaller percentage than in 1984. However, there was a growth of 600,000 in the number of disabled persons, which increased from 6.2 to 6.8 million. In 1999, 21 percent of women age 65 years and over were unable to perform at least 1 of 6 "activities of daily living," including dressing, bathing, getting in or out of bed, getting around inside, using the toilet, or eating. Another 3 percent had limitations only in more difficult activities, labeled "instrumental activities of daily living," which include such actions as light housework, grocery shopping, and managing money. The figures for men are smaller, but as group, they are younger than the women. All of these percentages have declined over time.[2]

However, on the 2000 census, 42 percent of persons 65 years and over reported that they were "disabled," meaning that they had one or more conditions that had limited their activities for six months or more. This figure was 32 percent for those between 65 and 74 years old, and 54 percent for those 75 years old and over. This indicates that many people have chronic conditions, which are disabling but do not interfere with activities of daily living.

---

[2] Federal Interagency Forum on Aging-Related Statistics. *Older Americans 2004: Key Indicators of Well-Being.* (Nov. 2004.) <http://www.agingstats.gov/chartbook2004/OA_2004.pdf>. (Accessed Feb. 17, 2006.) These data come from a survey of Medicare recipients conducted by the National Center for Health Statistics.

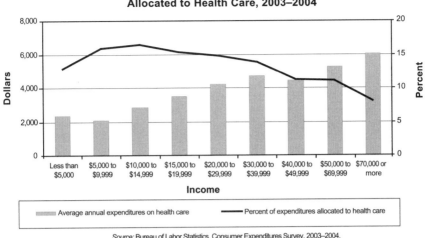

Figure 3-4. Health Care Expenditures and Percent of Total Expenditures Allocated to Health Care, 2003–2004

Source: Bureau of Labor Statistics. Consumer Expenditures Survey, 2003–2004.

Social activities and active lifestyles benefit older Americans and tend to improve their health status and life expectancy. Information on how people spend their time comes from the American Time Use Study. Researchers found that people age 60 and over spent about 30 percent of their time, or nearly half of their waking hours, in leisure activities; passive activities, such as watching television, were most common. Another 23 percent of the time was spent in productive activity, such as housework, paid work, volunteering, and shopping. The older the person, the more time spent sleeping and in leisure, with an accompanying reduction in the time spent in productive activity.[3]

Health care issues are, clearly, very important for senior citizens, and more of a concern for them than for younger people. Medical expenditures have generally risen in recent years, and rates tend go up with age. Middle income households (those with incomes between $5,000 and $30,000 a year) spend the greatest percentage of their incomes on health care. The lowest income households likely receive assistance from Medicaid. However, the amount of money spent on health care generally increases with income. (See Figure 3-4.) The new federal Medicare drug coverage plan, implemented in January 2006, may eventually alleviate some of the concerns over seniors' health costs, but this program has had significant problems in the early going. The Urban Institute estimates that, under current policies, the proportion of elderly families' income going to health care will increase from 17 percent to about 33 percent over the next several decades.[4]

Lack of access to health care is, fortunately, a rare problem. In 2000, 3 percent of elderly households reported that they had difficulty obtaining care, while another 5 percent said that they delayed obtaining care due to its cost. Table 3-5 shows the high frequency of service usage by the elderly population. The increases over a 10-year period are likely due to the increasing number of the "old old," persons 85 years of age and over. However, the average length of a hospital stay has decreased over the same period.

About 1 in 5 persons 85 years old and over resided in a nursing home in 2000. Men are less likely than women to be nursing home residents at any age, because they are more likely to have spouses at home to serve as caregivers. Older widowed women, without caregivers available, move into nursing homes more frequently.

IMPACT ON GOVERNMENT SPENDING

The aging of the population has necessitated a change in government spending priorities. Children and persons 60 years old and over consume the majority of net payments from government. Examples of these payment programs include Medicare,

---

[3] Alley, Dawn, and Dory Sabata. *Keeping Up with Time: A National Perspective of Time Use Among Older Adults.* <http://www.atususers.umd.edu/papers/atusconference/posters/>. (Accessed Mar. 16, 2006.)

[4] The Urban Institute. *Recent Research Findings on Retirement and Aging from the Urban Institute.* (Mar. 2005.) <http://www.urban.org/publications/900787.html>. (Accessed Feb. 17, 2006.)

Table 3-5. Rates of Health Care Service Usage by Medicare Beneficiaries, 1992–2001

(Rate per 1,000 population 65 years or over, days.)

Type of service	1992	1993	1994	1995	1996	1997	1998	1999	2000	2001
Hospitalization	306	300	331	336	341	351	354	365	361	364
Home health visits	3 822	4 648	6 352	7 608	8 376	8 227	5 058	3 708	2 913	2 295
Skilled nursing facility admissions	28	33	43	50	59	67	69	67	67	69
Physician visits and consultations	11 359	11 600	12 045	12 372	12 478	. . .	13 061	. . .	13 346	13 685
Average length of hospital stay (days)	8.4	8.0	7.5	7.0	6.6	6.3	6.1	6.0	6.0	5.9

Source: Federal Interagency Forum on Aging-Related Statistics (Forum). *Older Americans 2004: Key Indicators of Well-Being.*
Note: These data refer to Medicare beneficiaries in fee-for-service only, excluding those in Health Maintenance Organizations (HMOs).

. . . = Not available.

education, Social Security, and Medicaid. This demographic problem is the root of the current debate over Social Security, because the ratio between the number of wage earners paying into the system and the number of retirees collecting income from the system is changing rapidly. Current projections estimate that the Social Security trust fund will be exhausted sometime between 2038 and 2050. It is even more difficult to project future costs for Medicare than for Social Security, because of the uncertainty over health care expenses. Medicaid costs, which are the largest source of payments for long-term care of disabled and older people, are also projected to rise.

Overall, the Congressional Budget Office (CBO) projected in 2005 that Social Security would account for 6.3 percent of gross domestic product (GDP) by 2040, in contrast with its current level of 4.3 percent. If health care costs continue to increase at a pace similar to that of the 1990s and early 2000s, overall federal outlays for Medicare and Medicaid could climb from about 4 percent of GDP to more than 20 percent of GDP in 2050.[5] This would, inevitably, lead to increased taxes, whether in the form of income taxes or payroll taxes. One projection suggests that the payroll tax for Social Security would have to rise from its current 12.4 percent to over 21 percent in 2070, just to keep the trust funds in balance.[6]

SOCIAL SERVICES

Social services for the elderly will become increasingly important over time. The purpose of these services is to facilitate continued independent residence within the community, in order to prevent, or at least delay, the need for institutional care. As the number of elderly people increases, so do the needs for these services. At present, the supply is far short of the demand. For example, for several years Michigan had a "Medicaid waiver" program in place, in which funding was provided to the Area Agencies on Aging. These agencies could then provide services which would help people to avoid nursing homes. During the recent economic downturn, this program was eliminated, despite it costing more in Medicaid funds to keep an elderly person in a nursing home than to provide these services. The problem is especially acute for divorced and never-married older women, who are much more likely to be living below the poverty threshold than those who have been married and could benefit from retirement resources accumulated through their husbands' earnings.

CHILDREN

Children, defined as persons under 18 years of age, are the nation's future. They are also the country's collective responsibility, as they are generally unable to manage all of the necessary activities of life by themselves. The opportunities and challenges faced by children are determined primarily by the life status of their parents. It is difficult for low-income families to rise out of poverty. The Annie E. Casey foundation states, "Kids from poor families too often lack the opportunities and assets that will enable them to become successful adults. Compared to their more affluent peers, kids from low-income families are more likely to suffer from preventable illnesses, fail in school, become teenaged parents, and become involved with the justice system. As a result, these young people frequently reach adulthood without the necessary tools, experiences, and connections to succeed."[7]

---

[5] Holtz-Eakin, Douglas. *Implications of Demographic Change for the Budget and the Economy.* Congressional Budget Office, Testimony before the House Committee on Ways and Means, 109th Cong., 1st sess., May 19, 2005.

[6] Population Reference Bureau. 2002. Government spending in an older America. *Reports on America* 3(1).

[7] The Annie E. Casey Foundation. *2005 Kids Count Data Book.* <http://www.aecf.org/kidscount/sld/databook.jsp>. (Accessed Feb. 17, 2006.) This book is updated annually and is also available in hard copy form.

CHARACTERISTICS

The Census Bureau estimated that there were about 73.3 million children in the United States in 2004, an increase of slightly more than 1 percent from 2000. The growth rate was highest for children age 14 to 17 years, as the "baby boomlet" of the 1980s makes up a much larger cohort than the "baby bust" generation before it. By the mid-1990s, the baby boomlet was over. The number of children age 5–13 years was actually smaller in 2004 than in 2000. Children under 18 years of age compose one-quarter of the total population.

The poverty rate for children in 2004 was 18 percent, 5 percentage points higher than the rate for all persons. Among families with children, the rate was 16 percent, but rose to 38 percent for families headed by a female householder with no spouse present. The poverty rates for families with children under 5 years old were even higher, at 17 percent for all families and 46 percent for those headed by a female householder with no spouse present. (See Table 3-6.) These rates are all somewhat lower than the corresponding figures for 1990, but are generally higher than those in 2000. Both welfare reform in the late 1990s and the state of the economy—which was stronger in the late 1990s and weaker in the early 2000s—contribute to these patterns.

INDICATORS OF CHILDREN'S WELL-BEING

The Annie E. Casey Foundation and the Population Reference Bureau have developed a set of national indicators to evaluate the overall status of children's well-being. Many of these indicators have shown improvement over the past 30 years, although some have not. (See Table 3-7.) The percentage of babies weighing less than 5.5 pounds at birth, the standard definition of "low-birthweight babies," is slightly higher in 2004 than it was in 1975, despite a drop to about 6.8 percent in the mid-1980s. The increase is attributed to a greater frequency of multiple births, which have been caused by the increase in older mothers (35+ years) and the greater use of fertility drugs. However, the infant mortality rate has dropped by more than half since 1975. Nonetheless, it remains higher than that of most other industrialized nations. In the United States, about two-thirds of infant deaths occur in the first month after birth and most are due to health problems of the infant or complications from the pregnancy, such as preterm delivery and birth defects.[8] The child death rate has also decreased significantly over time, as have teenage death rates and teenage birth rates, both of which have leveled off at their lowest recorded measures.

Other measures have not shown much improvement over the past several decades. The incidence of low-weight babies has increased. The rates of high school dropouts and "idle" teens—those who have not been working or attending school—have dropped somewhat. The percentage of children in poverty has remained about the same over this period. However, this percentage was much higher (about 22 percent) in the early 1990s, and has also been in decline for several years. The percentage of families with children, headed by a single parent, has risen consistently since 1975. In 2004, 38 percent of these families had incomes below the poverty level.

Table 3-6. Poverty Rates for Children and Their Families, 1990, 2000, and 2004

(Percent.)

Characteristic	1990	2000	2004
All Children [1]	17.9	16.1	18.1
0–4 years	21.2	15.4	16.9
5–17 years	17.0	17.8	21.0
All Families with Children	14.9	13.6	15.5
With children under 5 years	18.3	17.0	16.7
All Families with Female Householder, No Husband Present, and with Children	42.3	34.3	37.6
With children under 5 years	57.4	46.4	46.2

Source: U.S. Census Bureau. 1990 and 2000 Census Reports and 2004 American Community Survey.

[1] Poverty rates are calculated only for children related to the householder. Children living in group quarters are not included in this table. Some foster children are also excluded.

---

[8] Federal Interagency Forum on Child and Family Statistics. *America's Children: Key Indicators of Well-Being 2005.* (July 2005). <http://www.childstats.gov/americaschildren/index.asp>. (Accessed Feb. 17, 2006.)

These indicators can be combined into a composite rank, enabling comparisons between states. (See Figure 3-5.) The leading state, in terms of children's well-being as measured by this set of indicators, is New Hampshire, followed by Vermont and Minnesota. At the other end of the scale, Mississippi ranks 50th of the 50 states, with its neighbors Alabama and Louisiana right above it.[9]

Table 3-7. National Indicators of Children's Well-Being, 1975 and 2002/2003

(Rate per 100,000, except where noted; percent.)

Characteristic	1975	2002/2003
Percent low-birthweight babies	7.4	7.8
Infant mortality rate (age under 1 year)	16.1	7.0
Child death rates (age 1 to 14 years)	44	21
Teen death rates (age 15 to 19 years)	100	68
Teen birth rate (per 1,000 females age 15 to 19 years)	56	43
Percent of teens who are high school dropouts (age 16 to 19 years)	12	8
Percent of teens who are not attending school and not working (age 16 to 19 years)	12	9
Percent of children living in families where no parent has full-time, year-round employment	33	33
Percent of children in poverty	17	18
Percent of families with children headed by a single parent	17	30

Source: Annie E. Casey Foundation. *2005 Kids Count Data Book.*

Another set of key indicators is published by the Federal Interagency Forum on Child and Family Statistics. These indicators include information on hunger, health indicators, behavior, and the social environment. In the early 2000s, children living in homes with incomes below the poverty level were three times more likely to experience food insecurity (concern over having enough to eat) and hunger than children in more affluent homes. On the behavior front, cigarette use among adolescents has declined, as have the violent crime victimization and offending rates. However, only a little over half of preschoolers are read to by a family member on a daily basis.

RURAL AMERICA

Rural America comprises over 2,000 counties, contains 75 percent of the nation's land, and is home to 17 percent of the U.S. population, or 49 million people. These numbers represent a decrease of 253 counties and 7.3 million people from the 1990 census.

How do we define "rural"? A general definition, used by the Economic Research Service (ERS) of the U.S. Department of Agriculture, has classified

Figure 3-5. National Composite Rank of Condition of Children, 2002/2003

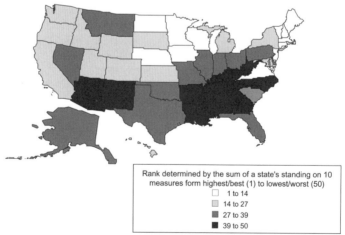

Rank determined by the sum of a state's standing on 10 measures form highest/best (1) to lowest/worst (50)
- ☐ 1 to 14
- ▨ 14 to 27
- ▨ 27 to 39
- ■ 39 to 50

Source: Annie E. Casey Foundation. *2005 Kids Count Data Book.*

---

[9] These statistics were compiled before Hurricane Katrina hit Louisiana and Mississippi in 2005.

counties as rural if they are not part of a Metropolitan Statistical Area. Micropolitan Statistical Areas and their counties are included in the rural definition.[10] While most counties within a Metropolitan Statistical Area are urban in character, some rural-like counties are included in these areas if a significant number of residents commute to the urban area for work. As used by the Census Bureau, the official definition of "urban" includes all territory in urbanized areas or "urban clusters," a new term for small built-up communities usually centered around a city or village. All territory outside the definition of "urban" is considered "rural."

POPULATION AND MIGRATION

At the time of the first census in 1790, the nation was about 95 percent rural. This figure declined slowly but steadily until 1970, when it reached 26 percent. The number also declined slowly over the next three decades, reaching 21 percent in 2000. What was behind these trends? First, the nation's economy was transformed from an agriculture-based economy to a manufacturing-based economy throughout the nineteenth and early twentieth centuries. Many people moved from rural to urban areas in order to find jobs. In addition, most immigrants, especially in the early twentieth century, headed for city residence, because that was where it was easiest to find work.

Why did this trend slow down, and even stabilize, in the late twentieth century? One reason is that the number of jobs in rural areas increased as the economy decentralized. Companies thought that they could find cheaper labor in rural areas, and a population with perhaps less inclination to unionize. As the primary mode of transportation switched from railroads to trucks, coupled with construction of the interstate highway system (beginning in 1957), it became ever easier to transport finished products from areas that were formerly considered remote. As the number of jobs in these areas increased, so did the population. Rural areas actually gained nearly 6 million new residents between 1970 and 1980, and another 1.2 million in the 1980s. Rural in-migration had not been as high since the 1880–1910 period, when many immigrants headed directly to rural areas to be farmers.

Another factor driving rural growth in the latter part of the twentieth century was the decrease in Black out-migration. In the mid-twentieth century, Blacks followed Whites to the metropolitan areas of the Northeast and Midwest. After 1965, Black migration shifted to metropolitan areas in the South, but was offset by the migration of Blacks into, or returning to, rural areas. This pattern was driven by job growth and, to some extent, by changing racial attitudes in the South. Family ties also played a role.[11] However, the rate of decline accelerated between 1990 and 2000, partly because major waves of new in-migration into urban areas. The rural population dropped by 2.6 million during this decade.

The rate of growth of the non-metropolitan population slowed down after 1995, reaching its lowest point during the 2000–2001 period. This was part of an overall drop in non-metropolitan mobility rates, reflecting both changing economic conditions and the aging of the population. Non-metropolitan population levels are boosted by in-migration from foreign countries, but not enough to offset the domestic migration loss. Geographically, the only region of the country to counter this trend is the Midwest, partly because of outward expansion of metropolitan areas into non-metropolitan counties. Some

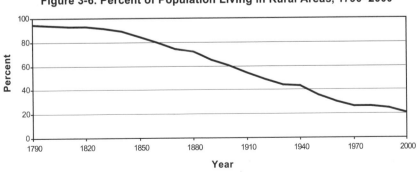

Figure 3-6. Percent of Population Living in Rural Areas, 1790–2000

Source: U.S. Census Bureau. Population Division.

---

[10] See Chapter 1 for more extensive discussion of Metropolitan and Micropolitan Statistical Areas.

[11] Fugitt, Glenn V., John A. Fulton, and Calvin L. Beale. 2001. *The Shifting Patterns of Black Migration From and Into the Nonmetropolitan South, 1965–95* (Rural Development Research Report No. 93). <http://www.ers.usda.gov/Publications/rdrr93/>. (Accessed Feb. 21, 2006.)

Figure 3-7. Net Migration for Blacks in the South, Selected Years, 1965–2000

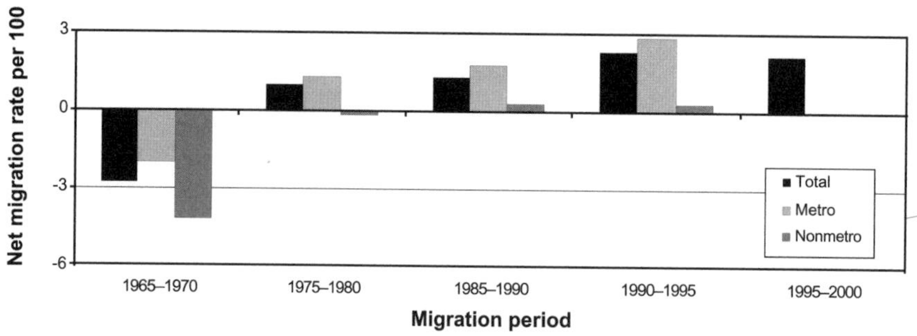

Source: Fuguitt, Glenn, John Fulton, and Calvin Beale. 2001. *The Shifting Pattern of Black Migration from and into the Nonmetropolitan South, 1965–95.* (U.S. Department of Agriculture, Economic Research Service, Rural Development Research Report No. 93.) U.S. Census Bureau. 2003. *Migration by Race and Hispanic Origin: 1995 to 2000.* (Census 2000 Special Report CENSR-13.)

areas, such as the northern Great Lakes area and parts of the West, are considered "high-amenity" locations and are attractive to urban migrants, including retirees. College graduates are especially likely to move out of the non-metropolitan areas and into cities and suburbs.[12]

HOUSING

Access to adequate and appropriate housing is important for all people. Rural housing is often thought to be less adequate than the housing in suburbs, just as central-city housing is perceived to be less adequate. For many years, the federal government has had programs in place to promote homeownership. While this is important, it does not address the problem of inadequate housing—whether owner or renter occupied.

The American Housing Survey (discussed in greater detail in the Chapter 5) provides data on the physical condition of housing in rural areas, as well as on the costs and the attitudes of the residents toward their housing and neighborhoods. Most rural residents lived in owner-occupied single family homes or in mobile homes. Townhouses, other attached housing units, and apartments are much more common in metropolitan areas. Rural homes are both smaller and less costly, on average, than urban homes.

An analysis of the 1997 American Housing Survey data shows that, in rural areas, housing is a bigger problem for the proportion of the population that is "wage-dependent," that is, the households whose

income depends on wages or salaried earnings. Typically, this excludes households whose prime work is farming. Low-income, wage-dependent householders are generally young, with young children, and find it hard to locate affordable housing which is in reasonably good condition. About 10 percent of owners and 15 percent of renters lived in physically inadequate housing, and about 13 percent of renters live in crowded conditions. Over 30 percent of these households lived in mobile homes in 1997, a housing category that combines less adequate and more highly cramped facilities with lower housing costs.[13]

Homeownership rates in nonmetropolitan areas are rising rapidly. They have been growing for nearly a decade, and continue to break records. At the start of 2004, about 75 percent of nonmetropolitan householders owned their own homes. There are variations by geography, with homeownership being most common in the upper Midwest (from Michigan to North Dakota) and least common in the West and along the lower Mississippi River. The rates are also higher for older persons.

Low-income households may benefit from federal, state, and local programs designed to make homeownership more affordable. One such program is the Department of Agriculture's single-family direct home loan program, which has been in operation for over 50 years in rural America. This has been the major federal program to provide low-income rural families with low-interest home mortgages over the last three decades.[14]

---

[12] John Cromartie. 2002. Nonmetro migration continues downward trend. *Rural America* 17(4): 70-73.

[13] Mikesell, James, and George Wallace. 2000. Unique housing challenges face rural America and its low-income workers. *Rural Conditions and Trends* 11(2): 75-79.

[14] James Mikesell. 2004. Rural homeownership rising. *Amber Waves*, 2004. <http://www.ers.usda.gov/Amberwaves/April04/Findings/RuralHomeownership.htm>. (Accessed Feb. 21, 2006.)

CHARACTERISTICS OF FARMS AND FARM OWNERS

Once every five years, the Census of Agriculture provides an analysis of the state of the nation's farms. Much of the data collected refer to crop and other farm production. A farm is defined as any place from which $1,000 or more of agricultural products (crops and livestock) are sold or normally would be sold during the census year. As of 2002, there were about 2.1 million farms in the United States. Almost half of these are classified as "residential/lifestyle" farms, where the operator(s) of the farm also report a non-farm occupation, with the farm bringing in less than $250,000 per year. (See Table 3-8.) Family farms, in which farming was the household's principal occupation, make up another 31 percent of all farms; the majority of these have sales of less than $100,000 annually.

Limited resource farms (5 percent of total farms) have household incomes under $20,000, farm assets of less than $150,000, and sales of under $100,000. These farms are located primarily in the eastern half of the nation, with a concentration in Appalachia and in the South. Overall, operators of these farms have less education than those in any other farm category; almost half have not completed high school and only 11 percent have attended college. Almost half are 65 years old or over. They compose a significant portion of the rural poor.[15]

THE ECONOMICS OF AGRICULTURE

More than half of all U.S. farm households lose money; many of them survive on off-farm income. However, in general, farmers are not a low-income group. Their median household income in 2001 was $45,100, about $3,000 higher than the median for all U.S. households. Farms in the "retirement" and "residential/lifestyle" typology groups generally show losses from farming operations, but these operators have significant off-farm income, either earned or coming from retirement income sources, such as pensions and investments.

A working farm is unlikely to show a profit until it achieves sales of at least $100,000 annually—the "high-sales" level. It takes sales of $500,000 or more before the net cash income from farming could exceed the income from off-farm sources. These data imply that small farmers take off-farm jobs out of necessity, and that the farm cannot produce enough income to sustain the household.[16] Large and very large farms make up only 7 percent of the total, but produce 58 percent of agricultural products. Nonfamily farms—those run by businesses as businesses—account for another 14 percent.

Table 3-8. Selected Characteristics of Farms, by Farm Typology Group, 2001

Farm type	Number	Percent of all farms	Average acres
TOTAL	2 149 683	100.0	446
Small Family Farms (Under $250,000 Sales Per Year)			
Limited resource (very poor)	96 127	4.5	100
Retirement (operator is retired)	247 230	11.5	156
Residential/lifestyle (owner has another occupation)	943 192	43.9	154
Farming occupation, under $100,000 sales per year	494 490	23.0	395
Farming occupation, $100,000–$249,000 sales per year	165 472	7.7	1 042
Large family farms ($250,000–$500,000 Sales Per Year)	85 098	4.0	1 948
Very large family farms (Over $500,000 Sales Per Year)	62 635	2.9	2 202
Non-family farms	55 440	2.6	1 698

Source: U.S. Department of Agriculture. Economic Research Service. *Structural and Financial Characteristics of U.S. Farms* (Agriculture Information Bulletin #797). (March 2005.) <http://www.ers.usda.gov/publications/aib797/aib797.pdf>. (Accessed Mar. 6, 2006.)

[15] Hoppe, Robert A., James Johnson, et al. *Structural and Financial Characteristics of Family Farms: 2001 Family Farm Report* (Report AIB-768). (May 2001.) <http://www.ers.usda.gov/publications/aib768>. (Accessed Feb. 21, 2006.) Updated data are not available because the Agricultural Research Management Survey (ARMS), the source of the data, was reduced in size.

[16] Banker, David E., and James M. MacDonald, eds. *Structural and Financial Characteristics of U.S. Farms: 2004 Family Farm Report* (Agriculture Information Bulletin No. 797). (Mar. 2005.) <http://www.ers.usda.gov/publications/AIB797>. (Accessed Feb. 21, 2006.)

IMMIGRATION AND IMMIGRANTS

LEGAL IMMIGRATION

The number of births minus the number of deaths (called the "natural increase" by demographers) and net migration are the determinants of growth for a country. One or both of these components can be the driving force of population change, depending on the country and the point in time of interest. In the United States, net immigration is projected to be a predominant factor in our future population growth. At levels presumed by the Census Bureau's middle projection series (which assume net immigration at current levels), immigrants who come to the United States between 1994 and 2050 and their offspring will be responsible for 60 percent of our total population growth during that period.

Another term for immigrants is "legal permanent residents." These are the people who hold coveted "green cards," which state that they legally reside in the United States. This status confers several privileges that are unavailable to non-citizens who do not hold green cards: those with green cards may permanently live and work anywhere in the country, own property, attend public schools and universities, and join some branches of the armed forces. People who apply to become American citizens are typically legal permanent residents.[17]

Recent concern about immigration to the United States has been fueled by the number of immigrants, and the perceived and actual influence that immigration exerts on the lives of non-immigrants. Historically, immigrants have borne the brunt of public scorn when economic conditions worsen. However, economic conditions were generally good during the 1990s, yet immigration remained a hotly contested issue in the media and at various levels of government. Part of the reason for this discussion is the differential effect of recent immigration on the resident population. Much of the negative impact is on minorities, according to some research, because the jobs recent immigrants are taking are concentrated at the bottom of the occupational ladder, where minorities are disproportionately represented.[18]

While the level of immigration is high by recent standards, the proportion of foreign-born persons in the population is not at record levels for the United States. In 2004, about 12 percent of the population was born abroad, more than double the percentage of foreign-born persons in 1970 (about 5 percent), but less than the figure at the turn of the century (about 15 percent).

The number of immigrants admitted to the United States varied considerably throughout the last part of the twentieth century, increasing from about 600,000 in the mid-1980s to almost two million in 1991. After that, the numbers began to decrease, dropping to 647,000 in 1999. One major statistical reason for the increase was the Immigration Reform and Control Act (IRCA) of 1986, which permitted immigration of former illegal aliens.[19] In 1995, a change in the law permitted such persons to apply directly for naturalization, thus removing them from the count of immigrants. Almost 2.7 immigrants were recorded under IRCA provisions between 1989 and 1994; about 75 percent of those removed "immigrated" in 1989 and 1990. Another reason for the decline was the Immigration Act of 1990, which placed a "flexible" cap on immigration at 700,000 during the 1992–1994 period, and 675,000 thereafter. After 2000, the numbers again began to rise.

In fiscal year 2004, about 946,000 immigrants were admitted to the United States. Of these, only 362,000 (38 percent) were actually new arrivals. The remaining 584,000 were already residing in the U.S. when their status was adjusted. As shown in Table 3-9, the largest single category is "immediate relatives of U.S. citizens," making up almost half the total. In the majority of these cases, the spouse is the U.S. citizen. The next major categories are family-sponsored immigrants (22.7 percent) and employment-based immigrants (16.4 percent). These two groups are "preference" immigrants, primarily made up of the spouses, children,

---

[17] Rytina, Nancy F. *U.S. Legal Permanent Residents: 2004*. (June 2005.) <http://uscis.gov/graphics/shared/statistics/publications/FlowReportLegalPermResidents2004.pdf>. (Accessed Feb. 21, 2006.)

[18] See George J. Borjas, "The New Economics of Immigration," *Atlantic Monthly*, November 1996.

[19] IRCA is an acronym for Immigration Reform and Control Act of 1986. This legislation legalized the immigration of approximately 3 million persons (roughly 1 percent of the U.S. population) who had entered the United States illegally or as temporary visitors after January 1, 1982. The size of the illegal population likely peaked in the mid-1980s, prior to the IRCA legalization program, declined for a few years, and now appears to be increasing again. One indication is the number of apprehensions of aliens (arrests of aliens who are in violation of immigration law). The number of apprehensions, which had peaked in the 1980s prior to IRCA and which then declined sharply after IRCA, began to increase again in the 1990s. Apprehensions totaled about 1.3 million in 1993; the country of origin was Mexico for 96 percent of apprehensions. The law also created sanctions against employers for hiring illegal aliens not authorized to work in the United States. For further discussion, see Michael Fix and Jeffrey S. Passel, *Immigration and Immigrants* (Washington, DC: The Urban Institute, 1994) and Immigration and Naturalization Service, *1994 Statistical Yearbook,* as well as the yearbook for various other years.

or siblings of U.S. citizens and people eligible for immigration because they have desirable occupations or education. Refugees and asylees are another important immigrant group.

Beginning in the early 1990s, Congress mandated a new "diversity" program, which guaranteed about 55,000 visas to countries that had been "adversely affected" by the 1965 Immigration Act; another 5 percent of immigrants in 2004 were admitted to the United States under this provision. These immigrants were balanced by an estimated 220,000 persons who left the United States, known as the "emigrants."[20] Most immigrants are young, with 40 percent between the ages of 25 and 39 years. The youngest are children adopted by American parents; they accounted for most of the children under 5 years old among the immigrant group.

Table 3-9. Immigrants Admitted, by Type, 2004

(Percent, except as noted.)

Type	Percent, except as noted
Total, All Immigrants (Number)	946 142
Family-sponsored immigrants	22.7
Employment-based immigrants	16.4
Immediate relatives of U.S. citizens	42.9
Refugees and asylees	7.5
Other immigrants	10.5

Source: U.S. Department of Homeland Security. Office of Immigration Statistics. *2004 Yearbook of Immigration Statistics.*

During the twentieth century, there was a dramatic shift in the countries of origin of immigrants, with fewer arriving from Europe and more originating in Central America and Asia. As was the case throughout the 1990s, Mexico remained the source country for the largest group of immigrants (even excluding IRCA legalizations, which were also predominantly for Mexicans), representing about 18 percent of all immigrants in 2004. The other top five sending countries included the Philippines, Vietnam, China, and India. The largest sending area in Europe encompassed the republics of the former Soviet Union. (See Figure 3-8.)

Immigrants tend to cluster in a relatively small number of states, with two-thirds of the 2004 group concentrated in six states: California (home to 27 percent of immigrants in 2004), New York (11 percent), Texas (10 percent), Florida (8 percent), New Jersey (5 percent), and Illinois (5 percent).

It is important to note that a large number of persons legally enter the United States each year, but are not immediately enumerated as "immigrants" in official statistics, despite the fact that many end up staying in the United States permanently. Some "classes" of persons can "adjust" to permanent status (and are thus counted as immigrants) after being in the United States for one year (e.g., people granted asylum or refugee status). Such persons are counted as "immigrants" only after they take this adjustment step, even though they may have been in the United States for several years. A major category of non-immigrant entry is the H-1B visas, permitting employers to bring in workers (or to keep workers already in the country) to meet employment needs that cannot be met by American citizens. Most of these jobs are technical in nature and require at least a bachelor's degree. The number of immigrants in the category has declined in recent years, but still amounted to near 400,000 in 2004. However, the largest number of foreigners entering the country each year (more than 30 million) are non-immigrants admitted as temporary visitors, with most coming to the United States on vacation or for pleasure.

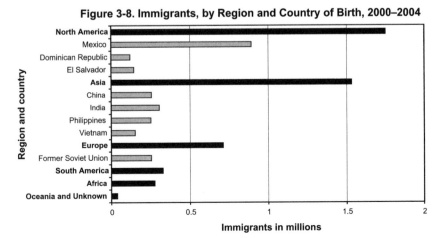

Figure 3-8. Immigrants, by Region and Country of Birth, 2000–2004

Immigrants in millions

Source: U.S. Department of Homeland Security. Office of Immigration Statistics. *2004 Yearbook of Immigration Statistics.*

[20] Martin, Philip, and Elizabeth Midgley. 2003. Immigration: Shaping and reshaping America. *Population Bulletin* 58(2): 3–44.

ILLEGAL IMMIGRATION

The term "illegal immigrants" conjures up notions of undocumented persons (i.e., without visa or other permit to enter the United States) sneaking across the Rio Grande River at night, carrying their belongings in a sack over their heads. In fact, the majority of illegal immigrants enter the United States legally and simply overstay their visit when their visas expire. Immigrants most often enter the United States as students, visitors, or temporary workers: in 2004, over 30 million persons were admitted to the United States on a temporary basis. Such persons represent about 60 percent of undocumented immigrants.

The Census Bureau has estimated a net international migration of 6.3 million between April 1, 2000 (the official date of the 2000 census) and July 1, 2005. The Pew Hispanic Center estimates that the number of undocumented residents had reached 10.3 million in March 2004, and was nearly 11 million in March 2005. Over half of this population is Mexican. In fact, most of the Mexicans now coming to the United States are undocumented. The net annual increase of illegal immigrants over the past decade has been around half a million people. More people than that actually arrived without authorization, but some of them later leave the United States.

In addition to the high immigration states described above, North Carolina and Arizona have emerged as centers for this population. The undocumented group is a large share (at least 40 percent) of the total foreign-born population in a large band of states, stretching from New Mexico in the west to Georgia in the east. In contrast, less than 20 percent of the foreign-born population of New York is undocumented.[21]

EMIGRATION

Not all immigrants stay in the United States. In fact, at some times in our history (e.g., during the Great Depression era of the 1930s), more persons left the United States to live in another country than entered the United States. However, measuring emigration is difficult because no official records exist—when a person decides to move out of the country, he or she doesn't have to tell the government.

There are two categories of emigrants: native-born Americans choosing to live elsewhere, and foreign-born persons (legal or undocumented) who return to their native countries. Native-born emigration is the smaller category. The best available estimates put the number of emigrants at about 17,000 persons annually during the 1990s.[22] Some of this population will eventually return, an event which is also not recorded for U.S. citizens. The number of foreign-born emigrants is much larger, perhaps around 200,000 per year.[23] A significant segment of this group is Mexican, as large numbers of people in this group move quite freely across the border in both directions.

NATURALIZATION

Between 1907 and 2001, almost 24 million American citizens achieved citizen status through the naturalization system. Surprisingly, the greatest numbers did not come in the early part of the twentieth century, when hundreds of thousands of European immigrants immigrated to the United States (before federal law curtailed immigration in 1924). The greatest number of naturalizations in a decade occurred between 1991 and 2000, when 7.4 million people became citizens.

In 2004, a year with 537,151 naturalizations, over 40 percent of new citizens came originally from Asia; the highest number of new citizens came from India, followed by Vietnam, China, and the Philippines. However, the single largest sending country was Mexico, representing 13 percent of all naturalizations. The new citizens' leading state of residence was California (26 percent of naturalizations in 2004), followed by New York, Florida, Texas, New Jersey, and Illinois. Not surprisingly, this pattern is similar to that reported earlier for new immigrants.

---

[21] Jeffrey S. Passel. *Estimates of the Size and Characteristics of the Undocumented Population.* (Mar. 2005.) <http://pewhispanic.org/reports/report.php?ReportID=44>. (Accessed Feb. 21, 2006.)
Gibbs, James C., et al. *Evaluating Components of International Migration: Native Emigrants* (Population Division Working Paper No. 63). (Jan. 2003.) <http://www.census.gov/population/www/documentation/twps0063.html>. (Accessed Feb. 21, 2006.)

[22] Mulder, Tammany J., Betsy Guzmán, and Angela Brittingham. *Evaluating Components of International Migration: Foreign-Born Emigrants* (Population Division Working Paper No. 62). (Apr. 2002.) <http://www.census.gov/population/www/documentation/twps0062.html>. (Accessed Feb. 21, 2006.)

[23] Office of Immigration Statistics (OIS), Management Directorate, Department of Homeland Security (DHS) publishes the *Yearbook of Immigration Statistics* each year (formerly entitled *Statistical Yearbook of the Immigration and Naturalization Service*). It may be accessed at <http://uscis.gov/graphics/shared/statistics/yearbook/index.htm>. Note that this office was relocated to the Department of Homeland Security; it was formerly located in the Immigration and Naturalization Service of the Department of Justice. OIS also publishes a series of "Flow Reports," which provide readers with summary information.

FOREIGN-BORN

The net result of the events described above was that 12 percent of the 2004 U.S. population was born abroad. Of these 34.3 million people, about 18 percent entered the country after 2000, and another 33 percent arrived during the 1990s. About 42 percent of these new residents were naturalized citizens, while 58 percent were not (including almost all of the people who immigrated after 1999). About half of the foreign-born population came from Latin America; 3 in 5 of this group are Mexican in origin. Another 27 percent came from Asia, and 14 percent arrived from Europe. The remainder immigrated from Africa, Oceania, or other parts of North America (primarily Canada).

LANGUAGE SPOKEN IN HOME AND ANCESTRY

Among the total population age 5 years and over in 2004, 19 percent speak a language other than English in the home. Note that this figure is higher than the percentage of foreign-born population, because children who are born in the United States to immigrants are likely to speak their parents' native tongue(s). However, more than half of the 50 million people who speak a language other than English in their homes also speak English "very well." This leaves 22 million, or about 8 percent of the population, unable to speak English very well. Some of these people live in households where someone speaks English well, others are linguistically isolated. The leading language spoken, as expected, is Spanish, accounting for over half of the people who spoke a different language at home. Other Indo-European languages (including Russian) and Asian languages account for most of the remainder.

The ancestry question on the census is designed to determine the respondent's national origin, regardless of how long the person and his or her ancestors have been in the United States. The leading countries of origin are the traditional European sending countries of the nineteenth and early twentieth century: Germany, England, and Ireland. Seven percent of respondents indicated an ancestry of "United States" or "American"; many African Americans respond this way. Russia is the largest Eastern European designation, accounting for about 2.6 million respondents. About 1.2 million responses indicated one or more of the predominantly Muslim Middle Eastern, or "Arab," countries as the country of origin.

FOR FURTHER INFORMATION SEE:

Annie E. Casey Foundation. 2005. *2005 Kids Count Data Book.* (Baltimore, MD: Annie E. Casey Foundation.)

———. 2005. *2005 Kids Count Pocket Guide.* (Baltimore, MD: Annie E. Casey Foundation.)

———. 2002. *Children At Risk: State Trends 1990-2000, A First Look at Census 2000 Supplementary Survey Data.* (A PRB/KIDS COUNT Special Report.) (Baltimore, MD: Annie E. Casey Foundation.)

Dacquel, Laarni T., and Donald C. Dahmann. 1993. *Residents of Farms and Rural Areas: 1991* (Current Population Reports, Series P-20, no. 472). (Washington, DC: U.S. Department of Agriculture, Economic Research Service, and U.S. Census Bureau.)

Federal Interagency Forum on Aging-Related Statistics. *Older Americans 2004: Key Indicators of Well-Being.* <http://www.agingstats.gov/chartbook2004/default.htm>. (Accessed Feb. 21, 2006.) Also contact: Kristen Robinson, Ph.D., Staff Director. 6525 Belcrest Road, Room 790. Hyattsville, MD 20782.

He, Wan, Manisha Sengupta, Victoria A. Velkoff, and Kimberly A. DeBarros. 2005. *65+ in the United States: 2005* (Washington, DC: U.S. Bureau of the Census, Report P23-209.)

Fix, Michael, and Jeffrey S. Passel. 1994. *Immigration and Immigrants.* (Washington, DC: The Urban Institute.)

———. *U.S. Immigration at the Beginning of the 21st Century.* (Testimony prepared for the House Subcommittee on Immigration and Claims, House Committee on the Judiciary.) 107th Cong., 1st sess., August 2, 2001.

Martin, Philip, and Elizabeth Midgley. 2003. Immigration: Shaping and reshaping America. *Population Bulletin* 58(2): 3-44.

Social Security Administration. Office of Policy. Office of Research, Evaluation, and Statistics. *Fast Facts and Figures About Social Security.* (Aug. 2000.) <http://www.ssa.gov/policy/docs/chartbooks/fast_facts/2000>. (Accessed Feb. 21, 2006.)

———. *Income of the Population 55 and Older.* (Mar. 2005). <http://www.ssa.gov/policy/docs/statcomps/income_pop55>. (Accessed Feb. 21, 2006.)

U.S. Department of Homeland Security. Office of Immigration Statistics. Management Directorate. *2004 Yearbook of Immigration Statistics.* (Jan. 2006.) <http://uscis.gov/graphics/shared/statistics/yearbook/Yearbook2004.pdf>. (Accessed Feb. 21, 2006.)

Zedlewski, Sheila R., Roberta O. Barnes, et al. 1990. *The Needs of the Elderly in the 21st Century.* (Washington, DC: Urban Institute Press.)

WEB SITES:

Federal Interagency Forum on Aging Related Statistics. <http://www.agingstats.gov>. (Accessed Feb. 21, 2006.)

Federal Interagency Forum on Child and Family Statistics. <http://www.childstats.gov>. (Accessed Feb. 21, 2006.)

National Agricultural Statistics Service. <http://www.nass.usda.gov>. (Accessed Feb. 21, 2006.)

Population Reference Bureau. <http://www.prb.org>. (Accessed Feb. 21, 2006.)

Social Security Administration. Office of Policy. <http://www.ssa.gov/policy>. (Accessed Feb. 21, 2006.)

U.S. Census Bureau. <http://www.census.gov>. (Accessed Feb. 21, 2006.)

U.S. Census Bureau. American FactFinder. <http://factfinder.census.gov>. (Accessed Feb. 21, 2006.)

U.S. Department of Agriculture. Economic Research Service. <http://www.ers.usda.gov>. (Accessed Feb. 21, 2006.)

U.S. Department of Homeland Security. Office of Immigration Statistics. <http://uscis.gov/graphics/shared/statistics/index.htm>. (Accessed Feb. 21, 2006.)

Chapter 4
Labor Force and Job Characteristics

INTRODUCTION

Statistics concerning people working and looking for work are critical indicators of the nation's economic standing and the socioeconomic conditions of its population. Employment is essential for providing the means through which most persons satisfy the material requirements of their families and themselves, as well as their own psychic needs.

The first statistic in this category is the labor force, defined as the number of people who are employed plus the number who are looking for work. The second statistic, the unemployment rate, is defined as the percentage of the labor force that is not employed and is looking for work. The lower the unemployment rate, the healthier the economy.

LABOR FORCE GROWTH

The United States' labor force has expanded at a remarkable pace in recent decades. In 2005, about 149 million Americans were in the labor force, 63 million more than in 1970. This impressive expansion was due to by two important factors: the growth of the working-age population (16 years old and over), and the sustained increase of women's participation in the labor force. While men have had a slightly reduced rate of participation in the labor force in recent decades, due to their tendency to retire earlier than in the past and their lengthening life spans, women have continued to increase their presence in the job market. (See Figure 4-1 and Table 4-1.)

The increase in the population of working age is explained by all of the factors affecting population growth: the baby boom following World War II, lengthening life span, and immigration. People are also more likely to remain in the labor force (even for part-time work) after the "normal" retirement age of 65, partly to supplement retirement incomes and partly because better health permits more activity. The number of people age 65 and over who are part of the civilian labor force increased from 2.8 million in 1985 to 4.9 million in 2004, and will continue to increase as the large baby boom generation ages into this category. Even among people 75 years and over, about 900,000, or 6 percent of this age group, is still in the labor force.

Table 4-1. Population and Labor Force Growth, Selected Years, 1950–2005

(Number in thousands, percent.)

Year	Civilian noninstitutional population [1]	Civilian labor force	Labor force participation rate
Both Sexes			
1950	104 995	62 208	59.2
1960	117 245	69 628	59.4
1970	137 085	82 771	60.4
1980	167 745	106 940	63.8
1990	189 164	125 840	66.5
2000	212 577	142 583	67.1
2005	226 082	149 320	66.0
Men			
1950	50 725	43 819	86.4
1960	55 662	46 388	83.3
1970	64 304	51 228	79.7
1980	79 398	61 453	77.4
1990	90 377	69 011	76.4
2000	101 964	76 280	74.8
2005	109 151	80 033	73.3
Women			
1950	54 270	18 389	33.9
1960	61 582	23 240	37.7
1970	72 782	31 543	43.3
1980	88 348	45 487	51.5
1990	98 787	56 829	57.5
2000	110 613	66 303	59.9
2005	116 931	69 288	59.3

Source: U.S. Bureau of Labor Statistics.

[1]16 years old and over.

Figure 4-1. Labor Force Participation Rate, 1950–2005

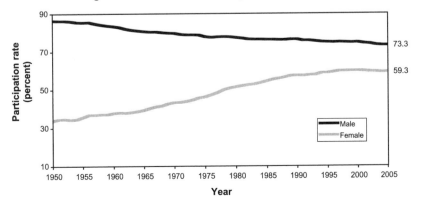

Source: U.S. Bureau of Labor Statistics.

The proportion of the female population age 16 years and over that was either working or actively looking for work increased from 39 percent in 1965 to 59 percent in 2005. This sharp rise in women's work activity, combined with the increase in the female population, has more than doubled the number of American women in the labor force over the last third of the century, increasing it from 26.2 million in 1965 to 69.3 million in 2005.

Of course, owing to the rapid growth of the population, the number of men in the labor force also increased over this period, from 48.2 million in 1965 to 80 million in 2005. This increase occurred despite the slow downdrift in the rate of labor force participation among men.

The sustained and very strong rise in the rate of labor force participation among women over the past 40 years has more than offset the slight decline among men, resulting in an increase in the rate of labor force participation among all persons. This rate grew from 61 percent in 1965 to 66 percent in 2005. All of these figures were slightly higher in the late 1990s, but declined between 2000 and 2005, due to a weaker economy. When jobs are hard to find, a larger proportion of people stop looking for them.

WHY PEOPLE AREN'T WORKING

Most of the 76.8 million people who aren't working or looking for work do not want a job. This group includes retirees, older women who were never in the labor force, people staying home to raise children, and students. Only 22.7 million people in this group are 25 to 54 years old, the prime working-age years. Almost three-quarters of those who are not in the labor force are women.

However, there are about 5 million people in 2006 who wanted a job but did not have one and were not actively seeking work. Of these, 1.5 million are available to work. One-quarter of them are discouraged workers, believing that no work is available, that they lack the necessary skills or training, or that they are the wrong age. Others cite family responsibilities, being in school or training, being in ill health, having a disability, or some other reason for not looking for work, even though they would accept a job if one were offered.

MOTHERS IN THE LABOR FORCE

One factor contributing to the increasing labor force participation rate for women is their attachment to jobs. Unlike in the past, women are marrying at later ages, and, on average, are postponing having chil-

dren. In addition, the mothers of young children no longer tend to leave the job market. As shown in Table 4-2, about 56 percent of all children under 6 years old had a mother who was either employed or looking for work in 2004. The figure for families maintained by women, with no spouse present, was even higher, coming in at nearly 70 percent.

Table 4-2. Number of Children Under 6 Years Old, by Type of Family and Labor Force Status of Mother, 2004

(Number in thousands, percent distribution.)

Characteristic	Number (thousands)	Percent distribution
All children under 6 years	22 864	100
Mother in labor force	12 781	56
Children in married-couple families	16 400	100
Mother in labor force	9 168	56
Children in families maintained by women	5 117	100
Mother in labor force	3 480	68
Children in families maintained by men	1 346	100

Source: U.S. Census Bureau. American Community Survey 2004.

As shown in Table 4-3, there have been some significant changes in these patterns over the past few years. Between 1993 and 2004, the proportion of married-couple families where only the husband worked remained about the same, while the proportion of married couples where both husband and wife worked decreased. The difference lies in a significant increase in the number of married-couple families in which there is no earner, or there are earners other than the husband or wife. This reflects the increasing number of elderly households that are beyond working age, which either have no income or have only the income generated by younger people in the household, such as their children. The pattern for families maintained by men, with no spouse present, is similar, but there is little change in the pattern for families maintained by women, with no spouse present. The latter is likely a reflection of welfare reform, which has caused the increase in elderly families to be balanced out by an increase in the number of younger households in which women are working.

The fact that women have developed stronger attachment to their jobs, with many also attaining relatively high-paying positions, may contribute to the slight but persistent decline in the labor force participation among working-age men. For men age 35 to 44 years, for example, the labor force participation rate has declined from 81 percent in 1965 to 74 percent in 2004. While the slow downward drift in the labor force participation among these men may be largely attributable to other factors (such as an

Table 4-3. Families by Presence and Relationship of Employed Members and Family Type, 1993 and 2004

(Number in thousands, percent distribution.)

Characteristic	1993		2004	
	Number (thousands)	Percent distribution	Number (thousands)	Percent distribution
Married-Couple Families	53 248	100.0	57 188	100.0
No earners	7 281	13.7	9 420	16.5
Husband, not wife	10 832	20.3	11 712	20.5
Wife, not husband	3 184	6.0	3 843	6.7
Husband and wife	31 266	58.7	28 991	50.7
Other earners only	685	1.3	3 222	5.6
Families Maintained by Women [1]	11 087	100.0	13 614	100.0
No earners	2 607	23.5	3 255	23.9
Householder is earner	7 080	63.9	8 722	64.1
Other earners only	1 399	12.6	1 636	12.0
Families Maintained by Men [1]	2 859	100.0	5 071	100.0
No earners	312	10.9	772	15.2
Householder is earner	2 227	77.9	3 617	71.3
Other earners only	319	11.2	682	13.5

Source: U.S. Bureau of Labor Statistics.
Note: Detail may not sum to totals due to rounding.

[1]No spouse present.

easing of the rules to allow those with some disability to cease working), some men have assumed the role of homemakers, while their wives have assumed the role of the primary family earner. Married-couple families in which only the wife is an earner make up about 7 percent of all such families.

TRENDS IN UNEMPLOYMENT

Throughout the 1990s, with the American economy continuing to expand vigorously, the ranks of the unemployed—persons without a job who were actively looking for work—continued to shrink. The proportion of the labor force that was unemployed had dropped to only 4.0 percent in 2000. By contrast, the unemployment rate had been much higher during most of the preceding quarter of a century, having approached a peak of 10 percent in the early 1980s.

The official government definitions of "employed" and "unemployed" tend to measure the low range of an unemployment rate. A person age 16 years or over is considered employed if he or she did any work at all for pay or profit during the week for which the data are collected. This includes part-time and occasional work such as lawn care, snow shoveling, and babysitting. People are also considered employed when they are on vacation, out of work because of illness, on leave, involved in a labor strike, or prevented from working because of bad weather. To be counted as unemployed, a person age 16 years or over must not have a job, must not have actively looked for work during the past four weeks, and must be available for work or be on layoff from a job to which he or she expects to be called back. People who only search for employment through want ads are considered out of the labor force rather than unemployed.[1]

Of course, unemployment is a highly cyclical phenomenon, rising sharply when economic growth slackens and dropping quickly once the economy recovers its productive rhythm. This largely explains the fluctuations in the unemployment rate shown in Figure 4-2. In 2001, a new recession emerged. The unemployment rate rose all that year, reaching 5.7 percent in November. The annual average rate for 2002 was 5.8, a full percentage point higher than the rate in 2001. The picture improved after 2003, with the unemployment rate falling to 5.1 percent for 2005. (See Figure 4-2.)

Some population groups are much more likely to encounter unemployment than others. Teenagers, who may be looking for their first regular jobs, or who may only be looking for temporary jobs while studying and preparing for a career, have by far the

---

[1] Bureau of Labor Statistics. Frequently Asked Questions: Basic Concepts of Employment and Unemployment. (Oct. 2001.) <http://www.bls.gov/cps/cps_faq.htm>. (Accessed Feb. 17, 2006.)
   See also: Bureau of Labor Statistics. How the Government Measures Unemployment. (Oct. 2001.) <http://www.bls.gov/cps/cps_htgm.htm>. (Accessed Feb. 17, 2006.) Note that the Current Population Survey (CPS) provides monthly estimates for all states, the District of Columbia, and the New York and Los Angeles metropolitan areas. The survey provides annual average estimates for some large cities and metropolitan areas; these data are published in the "Geographic Profile of Employment and Unemployment." All other local unemployment estimates are derived from the Local Area Unemployment Statistics (LAUS) program.

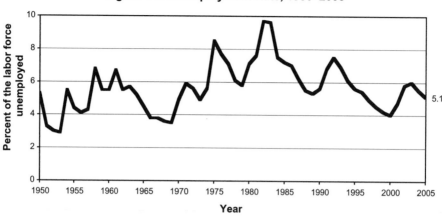

Figure 4-2. Unemployment Rate, 1950–2005

Source: U.S. Bureau of Labor Statistics.

highest rate of unemployment among the major population groups. In 2005, the unemployment rate for teenagers (16 to 19 years old) averaged 16.6 percent. For adults, unemployment was also a problem. As shown in Table 4-4, the joblessness rate for workers age 20 years and over averaged 4.4 percent for men and 4.6 percent for women.

Table 4-4. Unemployment Rate, 2005

(Annual average rate.)

Characteristic	Unemployment rate
Total, all workers	5.1
Men, 20 years and over	4.4
Women, 20 years and over	4.6
Teenagers (both sexes), 16–19 years	16.6

Source: U.S. Bureau of Labor Statistics.

The fact that the unemployment rates for adult men and women have recently been nearly equal is another reflection of the progress made by women in becoming a large and relatively permanent proportion of the nation's labor force. Only a few decades ago, women were more likely to be perceived as a "secondary" source of workers. Indeed, in past years, women were much more likely to leave and reenter the labor force many times, in response to changes in labor demand or in their family circumstances. Because women historically went back and forth between being in the labor force and leaving, they generally had a higher unemployment rate than men. For example, in 1970, when unemployment averaged only 3.5 percent for men 20 years old and over, the average rate for women in the same age group was 4.8 percent.

EMPLOYMENT STATUS OF BLACKS AND HISPANICS

Although the general labor market indicators for the United States performed particularly well in the 1990s, there are some groups of workers that continued to lag far behind the national averages. This was particularly the case for Black workers and, to a lesser extent, for workers of Hispanic origin. The historic unemployment rates for these two groups, as well as for Whites, are shown in Table 4-5. The substantial differential between the unemployment rates of White workers and those of Blacks and Hispanics has changed little over the past several decades. The percentage of Black workers trying to find job has consistently run 2 to 2.5 times the comparable rate for White workers. Persons of Hispanic origin, a group that has been growing rapidly in the United States, have generally experienced lower unemployment rates than Blacks, but much higher rates than those for Whites.

Table 4-5. Unemployment Rates, Selected Years, 1970–2005

(Annual average rate.)

Year	Total, all races	White	Black	Hispanic [1]
1970	4.9	4.5	. . .	. . .
1980	7.1	6.3	14.3	10.1
1990	5.6	4.8	11.4	8.2
2000	4.0	3.5	7.6	5.7
2005	5.1	4.4	10.0	6.0

Source: U.S. Bureau of Labor Statistics.

[1] May be of any race.
. . . = Not available.

EXTENT OF WORK DURING THE YEAR

The statistics examined thus far relate to the employment and unemployment rates during a given year. However, these numbers, while very important, do not fully reflect the dynamics of labor force activity. Since many people only work or look for work for part of the year, the total number of Americans with some labor force activity during a given year is usually much greater than is shown in the averages for that year. For example, students may work or look for work only in the summer. Some people operate seasonal businesses. Some only work during busy retail seasons, such as December.

Table 4-6. Extent of Labor Force Activity, 2003 and 2004

(Number in thousands, percent.)

Characteristic	2003	2004
Extent of Labor Force Activity		
Civilian noninstitutional population, 16 years and over	222 509	225 236
Total who worked or looked for work	153 448	154 785
Percent of the population	69.0	68.7
Total who worked during the year [1]	150 689	152 235
Percent of the population	67.7	67.6
Total with unemployment	16 444	15 063
Percent with unemployment	10.7	9.7
Percent Distribution by Extent of Employment		
Total who worked during the year [1]	100.0	100.0
Full-time [2]	79.8	79.9
All year	66.3	66.8
Part of year [3]	13.7	13.1
Part-time [4]	20.2	20.1
All year	10.2	10.2
Part of year [3]	9.9	9.9

Source: U.S. Bureau of Labor Statistics.

[1] Time worked includes paid vacation and sick leave.
[2] Usually worked 35 hours or more per week.
[3] Worked less than 50 weeks.
[4] Usually worked 1 to 34 hours per week.

In 2004, the average number of employed persons was 139 million, but the total number of people with at least some employment during the year was over 154 million. While the average number of persons looking for work during the year was 8.1 million, and the year's average unemployment rate was 5.5 percent, the total number of persons encountering some unemployment during the course of the year was 16.4 million, equaling 10.7 percent of all those with some labor force activity during the year. (See Table 4-6.) These significant differences show the impact of the labor market on individuals.

Of all the persons with a job during 2004, about 67 percent worked on a full-time basis for the entire year. Another 13 percent also worked mostly on a full-time basis, but for only part of the year. The remainder, about 20 percent, worked mostly on a part-time basis for periods that varied from a few weeks to the entire year. As shown in Table 4-6, the numbers for 2003 and 2004 are almost the same.

PERSONS WITH MORE THAN ONE JOB

Many American workers hold more than one job. In fact, about 7.5 million managed to hold two or more jobs simultaneously during 2005. These "multiple jobholders" accounted for 5.3 percent of the average number of employed persons for the year.

The reasons that workers cite for holding more than one job vary considerably. Financial necessity is one major reason. Others include a variety of non-financial motivators, such as getting experience in a new field or building up a "side business."

OCCUPATION, INDUSTRY, AND EDUCATION OF WORKERS

One of the most important changes in the American economy is the gradual shift from goods-producing jobs (manufacturing) to service-providing jobs. Over time, manufacturing has become much more efficient and "productive," meaning that it takes fewer workers to create the same amount of goods to sell. At the same time, the "service sector" of the economy has grown tremendously. All of the jobs that support the technology Americans use every day are service jobs. The health care industry—including doctors, hospitals, clinics, laboratories—has also grown tremendously.

These changes have, in turn, led to a re-ordering of the occupational landscape, with a rapid increase in white-collar and services occupations and a relative decline in traditional blue-collar occupations. Most notable has been the increase in managerial and professional occupations. At the same time, there has been a steady erosion in the proportion of workers holding lower-skill jobs.

Table 4-7 shows the distribution of workers among the various occupation and industry groups into which the economy is classified.[2] In the occupation section, the management, professional, sales, and office categories constitute the traditional white-collar jobs. Service occupations are sometimes classi-

[2] Both occupational and industry classifications have been changed in recent years. Table 4-7 reflects the current classifications, using the Standard Occupation Classification (SOC) and the North American Industry Classification System (NAICS). These changes make historical comparisons difficult and beyond the scope of this book. For more information, see: U.S. Census Bureau. Industry and Occupation FAQs, 2000. <http://www.census.gov/hhes/www/ioindex/faqs.html#top>. (Accessed Feb. 17, 2006.)

fied as pink-collar jobs, while the final five groups make up the blue-collar segment of the economy. The managerial and professional categories constituted about 35 percent of all jobs in 2005, as compared to 16 percent in 1989. These are the jobs that generally require at least some college, and many of these jobs are located in the "service sector." Service sector jobs make up 16 percent of the total, sales and office jobs account for 25 percent of the total, and traditional blue-collar jobs make up the remaining 24 percent of the total.

Looking at industry, the manufacturing sector declined from 16 percent of all jobs in 1989 to 11 percent of all jobs in 2005. This represents the continuation of a long trend; the comparable rates were 23 percent in 1980 and 26 percent in 1970. Service sector jobs now account for more than half the total. The 1990s revision of the industry code, from the old Standard Industrial Classification (SIC) to the new North American Industrial Classification System (NAICS), reflected this trend by providing considerably more detail on the service sector side. For example, the NAICS industry sector titled "Information" did not exist in the SIC.

Table 4-7. Employment by Occupation and Industry, 2005

(Number in thousands, percent.)

Group type	Number in thousands	Percent distribution
Total Employed	141 728	100.0
Occupation Group		
Management, business, and financial operations occupations	20 451	14.4
Professional and related occupations	28 796	20.3
Protective service occupations	2 892	2.0
Service occupations, except protective	20 239	14.3
Sales and related occupations	16 435	11.6
Office and administrative support occupations	19 529	13.8
Farming, fishing, and forestry occupations	976	0.7
Construction and extraction occupations	9 145	6.5
Installation, maintenance, and repair occupations	5 225	3.7
Production occupations	9 377	6.6
Transportation and material moving occupations	8 662	6.1
Industry Group		
Agriculture, forestry, fishing, and hunting	2 197	1.6
Mining	624	0.4
Construction	11 197	7.9
Durable goods manufacturing	10 333	7.3
Nondurable goods manufacturing	5 919	4.2
Wholesale trade	4 579	3.2
Retail trade	16 825	11.9
Transportation and utilities	7 360	5.2
Information	3 402	2.4
Financial activities	10 203	7.2
Professional and business services	14 294	10.1
Education and health services	29 174	20.6
Leisure and hospitality	12 071	8.5
Other services	7 020	5.0
Public administration	6 530	4.6

Source: U.S. Bureau of Labor Statistics.

Table 4-8. Education and Occupation, 2004

(Percent distribution.)

Occupation	Total	Not a high school graduate	High school graduate only	Some college	College graduate or more
Total	100.0	10.3	30.1	29.4	30.3
Management, business, and financial occupations	100.0	2.3	18.3	26.8	52.7
Professional and related occupations	100.0	1.0	9.1	23.6	66.3
Service occupations	100.0	19.8	38.1	31.7	10.4
Sales and related occupations	100.0	7.7	30.4	34.1	27.7
Office and administrative occupations	100.0	4.9	37.7	41.2	16.1
Farming, forestry, and fishing occupations	100.0	44.0	33.0	17.9	5.2
Construction and extraction occupations	100.0	26.5	45.3	22.3	5.9
Installation, maintenance, and repair occupations	100.0	13.2	43.6	35.5	7.7
Production occupations	100.0	21.4	47.2	24.2	7.2
Transportation and material moving occupations	100.0	20.2	48.2	24.1	7.5

Source: U.S. Census Bureau. Current Population Survey 2004.

Table 4-8 shows the relationship between education and occupation. More than half of the people holding professional specialty jobs reported having completed four years of college. Many have even higher levels of educational attainment, including physicians, dentists, attorneys, and judges. Another 29 percent have at least some college. The people in this category who lack college educations are usually small business owners. In contrast, people without a high school diploma are a significant proportion of only of the service and blue-collar occupation groups, but are a minority in these sectors as well. Completion of high school and, increasingly, college is becoming essential for jobs at all skill levels.

YEARS WITH CURRENT EMPLOYER

The average number of years that the typical worker spends with the same employer has changed little over the past two decades. For all workers 25 years of age and over—men and women combined—the median number of years with the current employer was 4.9 in 2004, almost the same as reported in previous job tenure surveys in 1983 and 1991. However, the stability of these "average" numbers masks important changes in tenure for some groups of workers, namely a general increase for women and a rather sharp and troubling decline for middle-aged and pre-retirement men. (See Table 4-9.)

When the job tenure numbers are broken down by sex, they clearly show that women are staying in their jobs for longer periods of time, while men have experienced a strong decline in the average number of years spent with the same employer. For men in the older age groups, this may be a reflection of the voluntary trend toward earlier retirement or a switch to part-time and/or less burdensome work. The same cannot be said for the men in the middle age groups, who have also experienced large declines in job tenure. For these men, there has been an obvious decline in job security, probably as the result of the "downsizing" of many American firms. This trend has forced many of them to restart their careers with new employers.

Due to these developments, the traditional gap in average job tenure between men and women has shrunk significantly. In 1983, the median length of job tenure for a worker age 25 years and over was 5.9 years for men, but only 4.2 years for women. The January 2004 job tenure survey yielded a median length of tenure of 5.1 years for men and 4.7 years for women. Naturally, the job tenure numbers tend to increase with age. However, they dipped again for persons 65 years old and over, as many of these workers are in post-retirement jobs of relatively short duration.

Table 4-9. Median Years with Current Employer, Selected Years, 1983–2004

(Years.)

Sex and age	January 1983	January 1987	January 1991	February 1996	February 1998	February 2000	January 2002	January 2004
Total								
25 years and over	5.0	5.0	4.8	5.0	4.7	4.7	4.7	4.9
25 to 34 years	3.0	2.9	2.9	2.8	2.7	2.6	2.7	2.9
35 to 44 years	5.2	5.5	5.4	5.3	5.0	4.8	4.6	4.9
45 to 54 years	9.5	8.8	8.9	8.3	8.1	8.2	7.6	7.7
55 to 64 years	12.2	11.6	11.1	10.2	10.1	10.0	9.9	9.6
65 years and over	9.6	9.5	8.1	8.4	7.8	9.4	8.6	9.0
Men								
25 years and over	5.9	5.7	5.4	5.3	4.9	4.9	4.9	5.1
25 to 34 years	3.2	3.1	3.1	3.0	2.8	2.7	2.8	3.0
35 to 44 years	7.3	7.0	6.5	6.1	5.5	5.3	5.0	5.2
45 to 54 years	12.8	11.8	11.2	10.1	9.4	9.5	9.1	9.6
55 to 64 years	15.3	14.5	13.4	10.5	11.2	10.2	10.2	9.8
65 years and over	8.3	8.3	7.0	8.3	7.1	9.0	8.1	8.2
Women								
25 years and over	4.2	4.3	4.3	4.7	4.4	4.4	4.4	4.7
25 to 34 years	2.8	2.6	2.7	2.7	2.5	2.5	2.5	2.8
35 to 44 years	4.1	4.4	4.5	4.8	4.5	4.3	4.2	4.5
45 to 54 years	6.3	6.8	6.7	7.0	7.2	7.3	6.5	6.4
55 to 64 years	9.8	9.7	9.9	10.0	9.6	9.9	9.6	9.2
65 years and over	10.1	9.9	9.5	8.4	8.7	9.7	9.5	9.6

Source: U.S. Bureau of Labor Statistics.

HOW AMERICANS TRAVEL TO THEIR JOBS

Most American workers drive alone to and from their jobs, and their tendency to do so has been increasing. Nearly three-quarters of workers used this mode of transportation in 1990, representing a considerable increase from 1980; the rates for 2000 and 2004 are only slightly higher than that in 1990. (See Table 4-10.) In contrast, the proportion of workers riding with others or using public transportation has continued to shrink, despite public and private efforts to reverse this trend (through subsidizing fares, instituting special traffic lanes, and prioritizing parking for carpools). Only 10 percent of American workers carpooled in 2004, down from 20 percent in 1980. There was also a further decline—to less than 5 percent—in the proportion of workers using public transportation. The small proportion of workers who walked to their jobs has consistently declined since 1980, while the proportion using other modes of transportation (such as bicycles, motorcycles, etc.) also shrank between 1980 and 2004. However, the number of employees who "worked at home" has grown over the past 20 years.

Average commuting time has changed little since 1980. Census data show that the 2004 average (mean) travel time was about 24.7 minutes, compared with 21.7 minutes in 1980. However, as Table 4-11 shows, there was a wide variation in reported travel time: about 4 percent of the workers (excluding those working at home) reported that it took them less than 5 minutes to reach their jobs. At the other extreme, about 8 percent of respondents had to travel more than 1 hour to reach their jobs.

UNION REPRESENTATION

American workers are less likely to belong to a union now than in the past. While the extent of union membership differed significantly across the industrial spectrum, the proportion of all wage and salary workers[3] belonging to unions or employee associations similar to labor unions declined from nearly 25 percent in the late 1970s to only 12.5 percent in 2004. (See Table 4-12.) This proportional decline is related both to the rapid increase in employment in service-providing industries, where participation in the union movement has traditionally been very low, and to the decline or relative stagnation in employment in goods-producing industries, where union membership has historically been more prevalent.

Table 4-10. Means of Transportation to Work, Selected Years, 1980–2004

(Percent.)

Means of travel to work	1980	1990	2000	2004
Total	100.0	100.0	100.0	100.0
Car, truck, or van	84.1	86.5	87.9	87.8
Drove alone	64.4	73.2	75.7	77.7
Carpooled	19.7	13.4	12.2	10.1
Public transportation (including taxicab)	6.4	5.3	4.7	4.7
Walked	5.6	3.9	2.9	2.4
Other means	1.6	1.3	0.7	1.3
Worked at home	2.3	3.0	3.3	3.8

Source: U.S. Census Bureau. Census reports and American Community Survey 2004.

Table 4-11. Travel Time to Work, Selected Years, 1990–2004

(Percent, except as noted.)

Travel time to work (minutes)	1990	2000	2004
Total, Working Away from Home	100.0	100.0	100.0
Less than 5 minutes	3.9	3.4	3.7
5–9 minutes	12.5	11.0	11.2
10–14 minutes	16.1	15.0	14.6
15–19 minutes	17.0	15.8	15.5
20–24 minutes	14.5	14.5	14.6
25–34 minutes	18.3	19.0	19.1
35–44 minutes	5.2	5.9	6.2
45–59 minutes	6.4	7.4	7.5
60–89 minutes	4.5	5.2	5.4
90 minutes or more	1.6	2.8	2.2
Median (minutes)	20.2	21.7	21.7

Source: U.S. Census Bureau. Census reports and American Community Survey 2004.

Table 4-12. Union or Association Members, Selected Years, 1977–2004

(Number in thousands, percent.)

Year	Total wage and salary employment (thousands)	Wage and salary employees who were union or employee association members (thousands)	Union or association members as a percent of wage and salary employment
1977	81 334	19 335	23.8
1980	87 480	20 095	23.0
1985	94 521	16 996	18.0
1990	109 905	16 740	16.1
1995	110 038	16 360	14.9
2001	122 482	16 837	13.4
2002	122 009	16 108	13.2
2003	122 358	15 776	12.9
2004	123 554	15 472	12.5

Source: U.S. Census Bureau. Current Population Survey.
Note: Data for 1985 may not be directly comparable with the data for 1977 and 1980 because of some survey changes. Furthermore, data beginning with 1995 may also not be strictly comparable with data for prior years.

---

[3] A "wage" worker is one who is usually paid by the hour, such as a factory and service employee. A "salary" worker is usually paid a set annual or monthly amount. These categories exclude workers who are self-employed or who work in a family-owned business.

The actual number of workers belonging to unions remained fairly stable, in absolute terms, during the 1990s, after declining rapidly in the 1980s. The number of workers in unions has grown since 2000. However, because total wage and salary employment has continued to increase rapidly, the proportion of workers belonging to unions has continued to shrink as a percentage of the total. The increase also reflects some modest success in organizing unions within the service sector.

OCCUPATIONAL-RELATED INJURIES, ILLNESSES, AND FATALITIES

Although an increasing share of the American work force has moved into white-collar occupations, where the risk of injuries and work-related illnesses has traditionally been very low, millions of Americans still occupy jobs where such risk is relatively high. Although relatively rare, fatalities stemming from work-related injuries continue to be a problem in certain fields of work.

Concern about the safety and health of American workers has increased significantly in recent decades, and employers in the United States are now responsible for reporting any injuries or job-related illnesses among their employees. According to these reports, there were 4.3 million nonfatal injuries and work-related illnesses among American workers in 2004 that required either recuperation away from work or restriction of duties. This statistic translates to a rate of 4.8 injuries/illnesses per 100 workers. Of these, about 1.3 million involved days away from work.

The major occupational groups with the highest relative risks of injury and/or illnesses are those in the traditional blue-collar worker categories. These workers are more than twice as likely as the overall workforce to sustain an injury or illness resulting in lost work days. Over half of the injuries in 2004 were suffered by workers age 25 to 44 years. The relative risk of work-related injuries or illnesses was higher for men than for women, particularly in the younger age groups (16 to 34 years old). In the older age groups, the risk was only slightly higher for men than for women.

Table 4-13. Nonfatal Occupational Injuries and Illnesses Involving Days Away from Work, 2004

(Number of cases.)

Industry	Number
Total Cases, All Industries	1 259 320
Total goods-producing	408 400
Natural resources and mining	29 100
Construction	153 200
Manufacturing	226 090
Total service-providing	850 930
Trade, transportation, and utilities	387 650
Information	21 150
Financial activities	34 930
Professional and business services	90 500
Education and health services	189 980
Leisure and hospitality	95 380
Other services	31 350
Total Cases, All Occupations	1 259 320
Management occupations	23 080
Business and financial operations occupations	6 330
Computer and mathematical occupations	2 800
Architecture and engineering occupations	6 960
Life, physical, and social science occupations	3 130
Community and social services occupations	9 540
Legal occupations	700
Education, training, and library occupations	6 460
Arts, design, entertainment, sports, and media occupations	7 190
Healthcare practitioners and technical occupations	48 890
Healthcare support occupations	73 070
Protective service occupations	10 920
Food preparation and serving-related occupations	75 670
Building and grounds cleaning and maintenance occupations	73 740
Personal care and service occupations	24 180
Sales and related occupations	82 000
Office and administrative support occupations	89 540
Farming, fishing, and forestry occupations	17 510
Construction and extraction occupations	144 050
Installation, maintenance, and repair occupations	107 940
Production occupations	186 600
Transportation and material moving occupations	257 210

Source: U.S. Bureau of Labor Statistics.

Figure 4-3. Fatal Occupational Injuries, by Major Event or Exposure, 2004

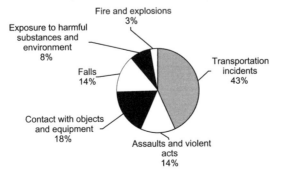

Source: U.S. Bureau of Labor Statistics.

There were 5,700 fatal work injuries during 2004, averaging about 16 for each day of the year. Transportation incidents accounted for 43 percent of the total, but were responsible for most of the deaths in transportation and material moving occupations, including those of truck drivers. Violent acts and assaults accounted for 14 percent of all fatalities. Farmers and other agricultural workers were especially at risk of dying from being struck by an object, while falls occurred disproportionately in the construction trades. Homicide was largely a white-collar phenomenon, and also had a higher incidence rate among taxi drivers and chauffeurs.

THE RETIREMENT YEARS

Americans are spending increasing numbers of years in retirement. This is because their life span has increased considerably over the past century, while, at the same time, there has been an increased tendency to retire from their jobs at ever earlier ages. (Changes in Social Security law, designed to counteract this trend, began to take effect in 2003.) The result of these two crosscurrents has been a large increase in the number of years that the average worker expects to spend in retirement. For this reason, the eventual availability of retirement benefits—and the amount of those benefits—has become an issue of extreme importance to American workers.

Social Security benefits, under a government-sponsored program, have been available to most retired workers since 1940. The coverage of this program has been significantly expanded over the years, becoming almost universal in scope. However, for many retirees, the benefits available under this program have not been sufficient to maintain desired living standards. To relieve this problem, additional retirement benefits provided through employer-specific or union-sponsored pension plans have become increasingly popular, and the coverage provided by these benefits expanded significantly throughout the last part of the twentieth century. Recently, these benefits, which are known as "defined-benefit" plans, are often being phased out, replaced either by no plan at all, or by a "defined-contribution" benefit, such as the popular 401(k) plans.

A defined-benefit plan obligates the employer (or union) to pay retirees an annuity at retirement age, with the amount based on a formula specified in the plan. Defined-contribution plans generally specify the amount of the employer contributions, as well as what the employees may contribute. These plans do not specify the actual benefits to be paid upon retirement, which will depend on the amount of funds available at the time. The amount of funds available hinges largely upon the success with which the funds are invested.

In defined-contribution plans, the employers contribute a set amount (or percentage of wages/salaries), often matching the worker's contribution. Workers may make additional contributions up to a limit set by federal law. In these plans, workers are responsible for determining how the plan's funds are invested. In 2005, workers are twice as likely to be participating in defined-contribution plans as to be participating in defined-benefit plans.

For government workers, whether federal, state, or local, employer-sponsored pension plans have long been prevalent. By 1999, 92 percent of full-time government workers had this type of coverage. In the private sector, however, the proportion of workers covered by employer-specific or union-sponsored pension plans has been much lower. This proportion averaged about 50 percent from the 1970s to the early 1990s, but increased to 60 percent in 2005 among all workers, and to 69 percent among full-time workers. (See Table 4-14.) Pension access is much more prevalent for workers covered by union contracts than for those without such protection, for those in white-collar and blue-collar occupations, and for those who are paid higher wages.[4]

However, working for an employer with a pension plan does not imply that all workers are covered. Some may opt out, while other workers may be too new to qualify for coverage, or else fail to meet other criteria for coverage. Private sector coverage rates (the proportion of workers actually participating in their employers' plans) were about 50 percent in 2005, rising to 60 percent for full-time workers, but dropping to only 19 percent for part-time workers. As employers have shifted jobs from full-time status to part-time, overall coverage rates are dropping as well.

---

[4] U.S. Bureau of Labor Statistics. *National Compensation Survey: Employee Benefits in Private Industry in the United States, March 2005* (Summary 05-01). (Aug. 2005). <http://www.bls.gov/ncs/ebs/sp/ebsm0003.pdf>. (Accessed Feb. 17, 2006.) Comparable updated information on government employee benefits is not available.

CURRENT EMPLOYEE BENEFITS

Full-time employees have come to expect a range of benefits, especially from larger employers. Table 4-15 shows the pattern for a variety of commonly-offered items. Some benefits, such as paid holidays, paid vacations, medical insurance, and life insurance used to be nearly universal. Over the years, there has been attrition in the number of full-time employees receiving these "standard" benefits.

Furthermore, in the case of medical insurance, employees have increasingly been required to share the cost; about two-thirds of all private companies required cost-sharing for medical insurance in 2005. The contribution amount varies by type of coverage and employer, but is often more than $100 per month for individual plans and more than $400 per month for family plans. These costs have been rising for several years and are expected to continue to do so.

Table 4-14. Employees with Access to and Participating in Pension Plans, 2005

(Percent.)

Characteristic	Percent of workers with access			Percent of workers participating		
	All retirement plans	Defined benefit	Defined contribution	All retirement plans	Defined benefit	Defined contribution
All Workers	60	22	53	50	21	42
Worker Characteristics						
White-collar occupations	70	25	64	61	24	53
Blue-collar occupations	60	26	50	51	26	38
Service occupations	32	7	28	22	7	18
Full-time	69	25	62	60	25	50
Part-time	27	10	23	19	9	14
Union	88	73	49	85	72	43
Nonunion	56	16	54	46	15	41
Average wage less than $15 per hour	46	12	41	35	11	29
Average wage $15 per hour or higher	78	35	69	71	34	59
Establishment Characteristics						
Goods-producing	71	33	61	64	32	50
Service-providing	56	19	51	47	18	39
1 to 99 workers	44	10	40	37	9	32
100 workers or more	78	37	69	67	36	53
Geographic Areas						
Metropolitan areas	60	23	54	52	22	42
Nonmetropolitan areas	55	15	50	44	15	38

Source: U.S. Bureau of Labor Statistics. *National Compensation Survey: Employee Benefits in Private Industry in the United States.* (March 2005.) <http://www.bls.gov/ncs/ebs/sp/ebsm0003.pdf>. (Accessed Mar. 6, 2006.)

Figure 4-4. Percent of Employees Participating in Selected Benefit, 2005

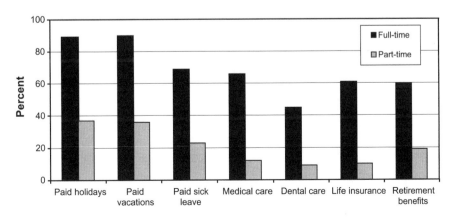

Source: U.S. Bureau of Labor Statistics.

Table 4-15. Employees with Access to Employee-Provided Benefit Programs, 2005

(Percent.)

Characteristic	Medical care	Dental care	Vision care	Outpatient prescription drug coverage	Paid holidays	Paid sick leave	Paid vacations	Life insurance
All Workers	70	46	29	64	77	58	77	52
Worker Characteristics								
White-collar occupations	77	54	33	69	85	74	83	59
Blue-collar occupations	77	47	30	71	81	46	80	55
Service occupations	44	25	19	41	49	36	59	28
Full-time	85	56	35	78	89	69	90	64
Part-time	22	14	9	20	37	23	36	12
Union	92	73	57	87	87	61	86	65
Nonunion	68	43	26	61	75	58	77	50
Average wage less than $15 per hour	58	34	21	53	68	47	70	40
Average wage $15 per hour or higher	87	62	40	80	88	75	88	67
Establishment Characteristics								
Goods-producing	85	56	36	80	85	49	86	63
Service-providing	66	43	27	59	74	61	75	48
1 to 99 workers	59	31	19	52	68	49	70	37
100 workers or more	84	65	41	79	87	70	87	70
Geographic Areas								
Metropolitan areas	71	48	30	65	77	60	78	52
Nonmetropolitan areas	66	39	24	60	74	50	76	51

Source: U.S. Bureau of Labor Statistics. *National Compensation Survey: Employee Benefits in Private Industry in the United States.* (March 2005.)
<http://www.bls.gov/ncs/ebs/sp/ebsm0003.pdf>. (Accessed Mar. 6, 2006.)

FOR FURTHER INFORMATION SEE:

Data on the labor force are produced by two federal agencies, the Bureau of Labor Statistics (BLS) and the Census Bureau. Decennial census data are generally published, or made available electronically, by the Census Bureau. Labor force data from the Current Population Survey (CPS) are more often published by BLS. Data from the American Community Survey are made available electronically by the Census Bureau. Information on commuting is drawn from the decennial census. Some data on pensions are produced by the Pension and Welfare Benefits Administration, another Department of Labor agency.

Jacobs, Eva E., ed. 2001. *Handbook of U.S. Labor Statistics,* 5th ed. (Lanham, MD: Bernan Press.)

Spain, Daphne, and Suzanne M. Bianchi. 1986. *Balancing Act: Motherhood, Marriage, and Employment Among American Women.* (New York: Russell Sage.)

WEB SITES:

U.S. Bureau of Labor Statistics. <http://www.bls.gov>. (Accessed Feb. 17, 2006.)

U.S. Bureau of Transportation Statistics. <http://www.bts.gov>. (Accessed Feb. 17, 2006.)

U.S. Census Bureau. <http://www.census.gov>. (Accessed Feb. 16, 2006.)

U.S. Census Bureau. American FactFinder. <http://factfinder.census.gov>. (Accessed Feb. 16, 2006.)

U.S. Department of Labor. Employee Benefits Security Administration. <http://www.dol.gov/ebsa>. (Accessed Feb. 17, 2006.)

Chapter 5
Housing

INTRODUCTION

Perhaps the earliest example of housing as a social indicator can be found in the work of social reformer Jacob Riis, whose graphic descriptions (in 1890) of slum conditions in the United States led to the passage of legislation to alleviate tenement ills. Since that time, there has been a considerable amount of study and legislation concerning all aspects of housing. For the great majority of householders, slum conditions are unknown today. An American family's home is likely to be the largest expenditure of their lifetime. Housing is the largest component of family budgets; for most Americans, homeownership is the best vehicle for accumulating wealth. In 2003, the nation's housing inventory included almost 121 million homes, apartments, and mobile homes, more than double the number of units from just 40 years earlier. Like population, the greatest housing increase is occurring in the Sun Belt region of the South and West. (See Table 5-1.) This area of the country continues to increase its share of housing at the expense of the Northeast and Midwest. These areas are growing as well, but at a slower rate.

The nation's 121 million housing units included 105.8 million occupied units and about 11.3 million vacant units, of which about 5.8 million were part of the active housing market. The remaining units were held off the market for various reasons. Some were for seasonal, recreational, or other occasional use, while others housed migrant farm workers. Still others were not marketable because of their condition or because their owners chose not to place them on the market. (See Table 5-2.)

Americans like single-family homes. In 2004, about 81 percent of homeowners lived in single-family detached units; another 6 percent lived in row housing (single-family attached); and 7 percent resided in mobile homes. One-quarter of renters lived in single-family detached houses. (See Table 5-3.) There are substantial size differences in single-family owner and renter units. The typical single detached owner home is about 1,800 square feet, while the typical renter unit is about 1,300 square feet. The typical owner-occupied unit has a lot size of about a third of an acre, while rental units have, on average, a lot size closer to a quarter of an acre.

Table 5-1. Regional Distribution of Housing Units, 1990 and 2003

(Numbers in thousands, percent distribution.)

Region	1990		2003		Percent change, 1990 to 2003
	Housing units	Percent distribution	Housing units	Percent distribution	
United States, total ...	102 764	100.0	120 777	100.0	17.5
Northeast	20 811	20.3	22 602	18.7	8.6
Midwest	24 993	24.3	27 893	23.1	11.6
South	36 065	35.1	44 659	37.0	23.8
West	20 895	20.3	25 623	21.2	22.6

Source: U.S. Census Bureau. Housing Characteristics: 2000 and American Housing Survey 2003.

Table 5-2. Distribution of Housing Units, by Occupancy/Vacancy Status, 2003

(Numbers in thousands, percent distribution.)

Unit type	Number (in thousands)	Percent distribution
All Housing Units	120 777	100.0
Occupied	105 842	87.6
Vacant	11 369	9.4
All Occupied Units	105 842	100.0
Owner-occupied	72 238	68.3
Renter-occupied	33 604	31.7
All Vacant Units	11 369	100.0
In the market	5 813	51.1
For rent	3 597	31.6
For sale	1 284	11.3
Rented or sold, not occupied	932	8.2
Not in the market	5 556	48.9
For seasonal, recreational, or occasional use	2 647	23.3
Other vacant (boarded, not offered, etc.) ...	2 909	25.6

Source: U.S. Census Bureau. American Housing Survey 2003.

Table 5-3. Housing Structure Type, by Tenure, 2004

(Percent.)

Type	Owners	Renters
Total Housing Units	100.0	100.0
1, detached	81.3	24.9
1, attached	5.7	5.8
2	1.5	8.8
3 or 4	0.9	11.8
5 to 9	0.8	12.9
10 to 19	0.6	11.7
20 to 49	0.7	8.4
50 or more	1.1	10.9
Mobile home	7.3	4.7

Source: U.S. Census Bureau. American Community Survey 2004.

HOMEOWNERSHIP

Since early in the 20th century, public policy at various levels of government has encouraged both the construction and ownership of single-family homes. Homeownership has often been cited as a major part of the American Dream. However, that dream has not been realized by all Americans, as significant gaps still exist among household groups.

Measurement of homeownership in the United States began in the last decade of the 19th century, when just under half of all households were occupied by their owners. As vast numbers of immigrants moved into mostly rented quarters in American cities, homeownership rates slipped slightly downward, reaching a low point of 46 percent in 1920. The boom economy of the 1920s reversed that trend, but the disastrous effects of the Great Depression in the 1930s were particularly felt by the housing market. The 1940 census classified only 44 percent of households as owner-occupied. (See Figure 5-1.)

The decades after World War II brought unprecedented growth to the homeownership rate. Between 1940 and 1950, the United States went from a nation of renters to one of homeowners. The 1950 census categorized 55 percent of households as owner-occupied; this proportion increased to 62 percent on the 1960 census. The two following decades showed slight gains, rising 1 percentage point to 63 percent in 1970 and another percentage point to 64 percent in 1980. These apparently modest increases in the homeownership rate represented a net addition of 19 million new homeowners. A small decline in the homeownership rate was recorded on the 1990 census. However, the pattern reversed itself again and increased for younger

households in the 2000 census. By 2004, the rate had risen to a record high of 67 percent.

There are differences in homeownership rates by age of householder and by race and Hispanic origin. (See Table 5-4.) The rate rises with age. Non-Hispanic Whites are more likely to be homeowners than members of minority groups. These patterns have not changed a great deal over the past 25 years.

INDICATORS OF HOUSING QUALITY

When Franklin Roosevelt stated in his second inaugural address in 1936, "I see one-third of a nation ill-housed, ill-clad, ill-nourished,"[1] little was known about the characteristics of housing in the United States. Congress responded by authorizing housing questions for the 1940 census. That first comprehensive look at housing quality focused almost exclusively on physical aspects. Standard housing required complete plumbing that was not in need of major repair (later termed "not dilapidated"). Thus, "substandard" housing became a term used to refer to housing that lacked complete plumbing or was in poor condition. However, interviewer ratings of structural conditions (sound, deteriorating, dilapidated) were dropped after the 1970 census, when enumeration by the Census Bureau began to be done by mail.

The use of complete plumbing continues. Figure 5-2 shows the dramatic drop in the incidence of lacking complete plumbing as a housing problem over the past 60 years. It is now effectively a non-issue.

The American Housing Survey (formerly the Annual Housing Survey), which is conducted through personal interviews, provides an opportunity for the

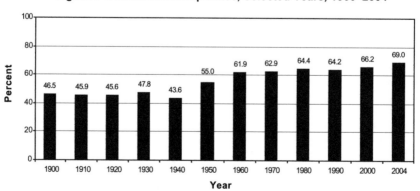

Figure 5-1. Homeownership Rates, Selected Years, 1900–2004

Source: U.S. Census Bureau. Housing Vacancy Survey 2004.

[1] U.S. Congressional Budget Office. 1989. *Inaugural Addresses of the Presidents of the United States from George Washington 1789 to George Bush 1989, Bicentennial Edition.* (Washington, DC: U.S. Government Printing Office), p. 277.

Table 5-4. Homeownership Rates, by Age and Race of Householder, 1980–2004

(Percent.)

Characteristic	1980	1990	2000	2004
Total	64.4	64.2	66.2	67.1
Age				
15 to 24 years	22.1	17.1	17.9	17.7
25 to 34 years	51.6	45.3	45.6	47.0
35 to 44 years	71.2	66.2	66.2	67.1
45 to 64 years	77.3	77.3	76.9	77.2
65 years and over	70.1	75.2	78.1	79.2
Race/ethnicity				
White	67.8	68.2	71.3	72.8
Black	44.4	43.4	46.3	49.1
American Indian, Alaska Native	53.4	53.8	55.5	55.6
Asian and Pacific Islander	52.5	52.2	53.2	59.8
Other race	36.9	36.1	40.5	58.6
Hispanic (of any race)	43.4	42.4	45.7	48.1

Source: U.S. Census Bureau. 1980, 1990, and 2000 Censuses. American Community Survey 2004.

enumerator to observe the characteristics of the house and the neighborhood in which it is located. The results from the 2003 survey are shown in Table 5-5 and Figure 5-3. While housing structural deficiencies are relatively uncommon, with most types occurring in less than 5 percent of all housing, neighborhood problems, such as streets needing repairs, trash accumulation, and crime, occur much more often.

AGE OF HOUSING

In 1940, the median age of housing units in the United States was about 25 years, indicating that one-half of all units had been built before 1915. The median age dropped to 23 years for both 1970 and 1980, after several decades of high rates of residential construction. However, in recent years, the median age has gradually moved upward, reaching over 30 years in 2003. Generally speaking, owner-occupied housing units are newer, by five years, than renter-occupied units. Housing units occupied by elderly householders tend to be older (with a median of 39 years), primarily because many elderly persons have lived in the same house for decades. Elderly householders are also less likely to purchase a newly built owner-occupied unit. Elderly renters, on the other hand, live in somewhat newer structures (with a median age of 34 years), most likely because many apartment units designated for the elderly were built in the 1980s and 1990s.

CROWDING

Crowding, usually defined as having more than one person per room in a housing unit, has been used as a housing quality measure since at least 1940. The 1940 census found that more than one-fifth of all households were crowded. Smaller household sizes and larger homes reduced the crowding rate

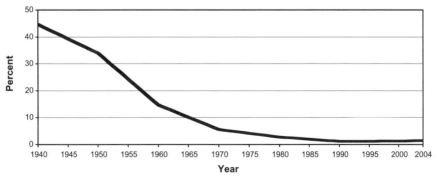

Figure 5-2. Percent of Housing Units Lacking Complete Plumbing, Selected Years, 1940–2004

Source: U.S. Census Bureau. Decennial Census Reports. American Community Survey 2004.

Table 5-5. Enumerator-Reported Housing and Neighborhood Quality Issues, 2003

(Percent.)

Characteristic	Total	Owner	Renter
Signs of rodents in the past three months	7.1	6.2	9.0
Holes in floors	1.6	0.6	1.7
Open holes or cracks in the interior	6.4	3.7	7.6
Broken plaster or peeling paint	3.0	1.5	3.7
Rooms without electric outlets	1.9	1.2	1.9
Streets need repairs	41.0	33.9	40.0
Accumulation of trash, litter, or junk	10.2	6.3	14.2
Commercial or industrial neighborhood	28.1	15.9	43.1
Industrial/factory neighborhood	3.8	2.3	5.8
Missing roofing material	4.5	2.8	4.8
Missing bricks, siding, or outside wall material	3.7	2.1	4.0
Broken windows	4.7	2.9	5.1
Foundation crumbling or has open crack or hole	3.2	2.2	3.4

Source: U.S. Census Bureau. American Housing Survey 2003.

to 3.1 percent by 2004. Renters were more likely to be living in crowded conditions than owners (6.0 percent for renters; 1.7 percent for owners).

RECENT QUALITY TRENDS

The American Housing Survey became operational in 1973. It contains a number of housing quality indicators that were designed, in part, to replace the items on substandard living that were not to be collected after the 1970 census. These items include questions about plumbing, heating, water and sewer systems, service breakdowns, and upkeep and maintenance. When tabulated in different com-

Table 5-6. Indicators of Housing Quality, 2003

(Percent.)

Characteristic	Total	Owner	Renter
Overall Opinion of Neighborhood			
Worst	2.4	1.5	4.6
Middle	28.1	23.8	37.3
Best	69.5	74.7	58.2
Median score (scale of 1 to 10)	7.8	7.6	8.1
Overall Opinion of Own Building			
Worst	1.7	0.8	3.5
Middle	26.4	20.4	39.4
Best	71.9	78.8	57.1
Median score (scale of 1 to 10)	7.7	7.5	8.2
Presence of Selected Amenities			
Porch, deck, balcony, or patio	82.8	91.4	70.1
Fireplace	31.5	43.7	11.5
Separate dining room	45.6	57.2	27.9
Garage or carport	58.7	75.7	31.5

Source: U.S. Census Bureau. American Housing Survey 2003.

binations, they can label a housing unit as "inadequate," "with physical problems," "needing rehabilitation," or "substandard."

American Housing Survey interviewers observe certain conditions of neighborhoods The leading problem, cited for four in ten housing units, is streets in need of repair. It is followed by problems, such as street noise and traffic, that come with living in a commercial or industrial neighborhood. Owner/renter status is not a significant factor in the recitation of individual problems, but overall there are more problems in renters' neighborhoods than in owners' neighborhoods. The likely correlation is that neighborhoods occupied primarily by renters are often older and less affluent. (See Table 5-5.)

What do the American families themselves think of their homes and neighborhoods? When asked to rate their homes and neighborhoods on a scale of 1 to 10, with 1 being the worst and 10 the best, most respondents seemed satisfied with their housing conditions. In Table 5-6, "worst" is a rating of 1, 2, or 3, and "best" is a rating of 8, 9, or 10. Owners rated both their homes and their neighborhoods more highly than did renters. It is important to note, however, that these ratings are subjective, and that people become accustomed to the characters of the homes and neighborhoods in which they live. Research in Detroit in the 1970s indicated that respondents would rate their homes and neighborhoods at a level far higher than would an independent observer. Table 5-6 also reports on indicators of quality in the respondent's housing. A fair number of housing units have one or more of the housing amenities listed, with porches or balconies being the most common.

Figure 5-3. Percent of Households with Breakdowns in the Last 3 Months, 2003

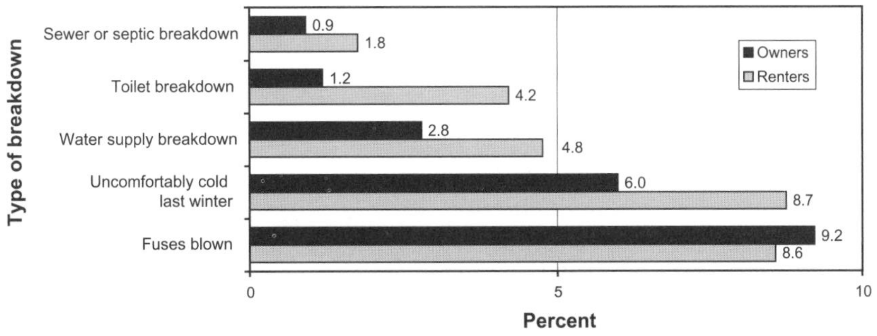

Source: U.S. Census Bureau. American Housing Survey 2003.

The American Housing Survey includes information about the frequency of breakdowns or the failures of systems within the housing unit. Overall, about 1 in 15 households experienced some kind of system failure over a year's time. Figure 5-3 indicates that the most frequent system problems were with blown fuses, with owners reporting the problem more often than renters. Renters were especially subjected to heating failures, resulting in their being uncomfortably cold.

HOUSEHOLD CHARACTERISTICS AND AMENITIES

The definitions of requirements and amenities for housing units have changed significantly over the past half-century. Questions about the availability of some household items (for example, electricity, lighting, and radios) have been dropped from the decennial census and other surveys, because they are virtually universally available in the United States. In 1940, about 44 percent of households reported having a mechanical refrigerator. By 1995, more than 99 percent had this appliance, and there was no discernible difference among owners, renters, or various categories of household groups. Color televisions have become similarly universal.

Most single-family homes now have washers and dryers, while only one in five multi-family units have these appliances. The presence of dishwashers, on the other hand, is more closely tied to the age of the structure. Dishwashers are found in only 30 percent of homes built before 1950, but in 77 percent of homes built since 1990. Other features, such as basements, are correlated with geographical location. Basements are common in the Northeast and Midwest, but are quite rare in the South and West. The South and West have a higher proportion of mobile homes than the other areas of the country.

HEATING EQUIPMENT

The presence and type of heating equipment in homes has long been viewed as being directly related to the health and safety of the occupants. In 1940, about 42 percent of occupied housing units did not have central heating; by 2004, this figure had been reduced to 7 percent. (See Figure 5-4.) Currently, about 11 million households do not have central heating. Some of these homes, of course, are located in parts of the country where central heating is not really necessary, such Hawaii and South Florida. In fact, about 600,000 housing units in these areas have no heating equipment at all. However, other housing units in this group are located in the mid-South, where it often gets cold enough to require central heating. In this region, some lower-value units occupied by poorer households do not have this amenity. In many housing units lacking central heating, unvented room heaters are used at substantial risk to the dwelling's occupants.[2]

Table 5-7. Type of Household Heating Fuel, 1940–2004

(Percent.)

Heating fuel	1940	1960	1980	2004
All households	100	100	100	100
Utility gas	11	43	53	51
LP gas	0	5	6	6
Electricity	0	2	18	32
Fuel oil, kerosene	10	32	18	8
Coal	55	12	1	0
Wood	23	4	3	2
Other, none	1	2	1	1

Source: U.S. Census Bureau. 1940, 1960, and 1980 Census of Housing reports. American Community Survey 2004.

2 U.S. Census Bureau. American Housing Survey 2003 (Report H150/03). (Sept. 2004.) <http://www.census.gov/prod/2004pubs/ H150-03.pdf>. (Accessed Mar. 7, 2006.)

HOUSEHOLD ENERGY USE AND EXPENDITURES

Over the past 60 years, there have been enormous changes in the way that families in the United States heat their homes. In 1940, more than three out of four households used solid fuels, such as coal and wood. By 2004, coal had virtually disappeared, and the use of wood was down to 2 percent. The use of piped utility gas (or "natural" gas), which increased substantially after World War II due to the extension of gas pipelines to suburban areas, was used by 51 percent of all households. (See Figure 5-4.)

in the Northeast. As mentioned above, electric heating is most common in the South, but is also used by one-third of all households in the West. Of course, the southern portions of the West region (including Southern California, Arizona, and New Mexico) resemble the South in terms of their heating needs. The cost of heating is higher in the Northeast, where the cost per million Btu of energy is $8.64, than in the Midwest ($6.68 per million Btu). This apparently occurs because natural gas is a less costly heating fuel than fuel oil. Energy costs per million Btu are even higher in the South, with its high use of electricity, but the overall costs in this region are the lowest in the country.

Figure 5-4. Distribution of Household Heating Fuel, by Type, 1940 and 2004

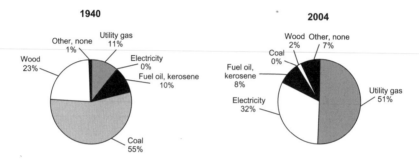

Source: U.S. Census Bureau. 1940 Census of Housing and American Community Survey 2004.

The development of more efficient reverse-cycle heating and cooling equipment, together with the high population and housing growth in warmer areas of the country where this equipment is most effective, has resulted in a rapid increase in the number of households using electricity as the main source of house-heating fuel. In 2003, there were more than 30 million homes using electricity; nearly two-thirds of these were located in the South.

According to the Residential Energy Consumption Survey, conducted by the Energy Information Administration, the average U.S. household spent $1,493 on energy in 2001. About two-thirds of this cost was for electricity (to provide lighting and run appliances), while space heating accounted for 10 percent. The remainder of the costs were for water heating and air conditioning.

Table 5-8 shows the differences in the types of space heating fuel used in different parts of the country, along with the varying costs of energy. Natural gas is used most heavily in the Midwest, while fuel oil remains an important heating source

HOUSING COSTS AND AFFORDABILITY

In recent years, the issue of affordability has begun to overshadow physical condition in discussions of housing quality. In this context, "affordability" generally concerns the relationship of gross rent or homeowner cost to household income. The traditional conclusion of household budget experts in the United States was that households that spent more than 25 percent of income on housing were spending excessively; this could also be indicative of housing or affordability problems. The proportion of population falling under this somewhat arbitrary standard has edged upward to the current level of 30 percent. Most federal and local housing assistance programs require participants to contribute 30 percent of their income toward rent. (Prior to 1981, the requirement was 25 percent of income.) Income-eligible households that spend more than 50 percent of their income on rent are considered to have "worst-case needs," and consequently receive top priority for federal aid.

Data in earlier sections have suggested that the quality of the nation's housing stock has substan-

Figure 5-5. Median Ratio of Value of Owner-Occupied Units to Current Income, 2003

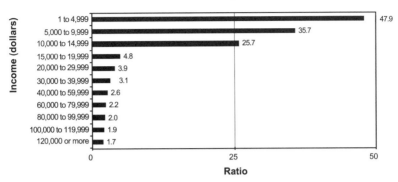

Source: U.S. Census Bureau. American Housing Survey 2003.

Figure 5-6. Median Monthly Housing Costs as Percent of Current Income, 2003

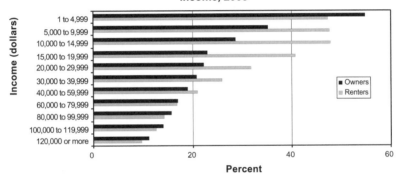

Source: U.S. Census Bureau. American Housing Survey 2003.

tially improved. However, despite the good economy of the 1990s, almost half of all households were paying more than 30 percent of their income for housing, while almost one-fourth were paying more than 50 percent. Part of the problem may be due to households overextending themselves by contracting for more housing costs than they can afford.

Discussions of housing costs and the relation to income are couched in slightly different terms for owners than for renters. A distinction must be made between mortgaged and non-mortgaged homes, because their cost structure is different. For owners, the largest single component of their housing cost is principal and interest for mortgaged units. Moreover, there is the presumption of a greater range of housing choices for homeowners because of their substantially higher incomes. The median household income in 2003 for renters was $24,300, while the median income level for owners was more than double, at $51,100.

As shown in Figure 5-5, lower-income households must purchase homes at prices nearly five times their income, which in turn may produce mortgage payments (including taxes) that greatly exceed the 30 percent of income deemed reasonable to spend on housing. High-income families, who have median housing values at only one to two times their income, do not have this problem. However, it should be noted that some subsidies may be available for the very low income families, which may make their housing costs more affordable. The lower the household income, the greater the proportion that must be spent on housing, even with the availability of subsidies. Figure 5-6 shows the same trend with a different statistic—median monthly housing costs. Generally, renters have higher housing costs than owners. Note that housing costs are very high for lower-income households. These costs decrease steadily as income increases.

Table 5-8. Energy-Relevant Characteristics of Households, by Census Region and Structure Type, 2001

(Numbers in millions, percent.)

Characteristic	Total	Census region				Type of housing unit		
		Northeast	Midwest	South	West	Single-family	Multi-family	Mobile homes
Number of households (millions)	107.0	20.3	24.5	38.9	23.3	73.7	26.5	6.8
Percent owner-occupied	67.9	64.0	71.4	72.2	60.5	85.8	14.7	83.8
Number of Households With Space Heating, Major Fuels Used (Millions)								
Electricity	43.8	4.8	6.2	23.1	9.7	27.5	12.6	3.7
Natural gas	60.5	10.6	19.1	16.6	14.2	45.6	12.7	2.2
Fuel oil	8.5	6.4	0.9	0.9	0.2	6.3	1.9	0.2
Kerosene	2.7	0.7	0.5	0.9	0.2	2.0	. . .	0.6
LP gas	6.6	0.6	2.0	1.4	1.0	5.3	. . .	1.2
Structure Type (Percent)								
Single-family	68.9	59.3	74.7	73.5	63.5	NA	NA	NA
Multifamily	24.8	37.5	20.4	18.1	29.3	NA	NA	NA
Mobile homes	6.4	3.2	5.0	10.0	7.2	NA	NA	NA
Homes With: (Percent)								
Basement	36.6	61.5	61.0	20.3	16.4	48.0	NA	NA
Garage or carport	54.6	44.6	64.7	51.5	57.6	76.6	NA	28.4
Clothes washer	78.6	72.6	80.8	84.0	72.7	94.9	31.7	84.5
Clothes dryer	73.7	65.5	78.5	77.7	68.8	90.1	27.2	76.1
Personal computer	56.1	54.1	57.5	53.1	61.5	63.0	84.1	40.0

Source: U.S. Department of Energy. Energy Information Administration. *A Look at Residential Energy Consumption in 2001.*

. . . = Not available.
NA = Not applicable.

Affordability can also be measured by taking home prices, incomes, interest rates, and other factors into account. For example, the National Association of Realtors calculates a composite Housing Affordability Index. (See Table 5-9.) When the index measures 100, a family earning the median household income has the amount needed to purchase a home priced exactly at the median. In the spring of 2004, the index was 132.6, indicating that such a household had more than enough to purchase a median-priced home. The primary reason for the recent improvement in the Housing Affordability Index is the historically low mortgage rates that have been available in the early years of this decade. As interest rates rise, housing may become less affordable.

The Census Bureau also issues estimates of affordability by including factors such as assets, cash on hand, debt, price, and interest rates. However, the last year for which data are available is 1995, when about 56 percent of all families could afford a modestly-priced house. Only 10 percent of renter families could afford the same home. A modestly-priced house is one that is priced at the 25th percentile of all owner-occupied homes in the geographic area. The ability to purchase a modestly priced house differs significantly by race and ethnicity, and by

whether a family currently owns or rents. Owner families are far more likely to be able to afford to relocate than renter families, and more White renter families can afford to purchase a home than minority renter families.[3]

More recent data for housing costs and affordability are shown in Figure 5-7. The ratio between income and housing value has risen over the years, even as both incomes and home values have increased. In 1970, the median value of housing was slightly less than double (1.95) the median household income. This figure rose to 2.67 in 1970 and remained relatively stable until 2000. However, the skyrocketing housing market of the early 2000s caused this ratio to increase to 3.41 by 2004. This indicates that housing has become increasingly less affordable.

HOME PURCHASE LENDING TRENDS

About 30 years ago, Congress passed a law known as the Home Mortgage Disclosure Act (HMDA). Its purpose is to monitor the home-related lending activities of financial institutions. The corresponding data can tell us whether or not individual banks and financial institutions engage in discriminatory lending, or "red-lining." HMDA was originally applicable

[3] U.S. Census Bureau. *Who Could Afford to Buy a House in 1995?* (Current Housing Reports, Series H121/99-1). (Aug. 1999.) <http://www.census.gov/prod/99pubs/h121-991.pdf>. (Accessed Mar. 7, 2006.)

Table 5-9. Composite Housing Affordability Index, Selected Years, 1991–2004

(Dollars, rate, index.)

Year	Median price existing single-family home (dollars)	Mortgage rate	Median family income (dollars)	Qualifying income (dollars)	Composite affordability index
1991	100 300	9.3	35 939	31 825	112.9
2000	139 000	8.0	50 732	39 264	129.2
2002	158 100	6.6	51 680	38 592	133.9
2003	170 000	5.7	52 682	38 064	138.4
2004	184 100	5.7	54 527	41 136	132.6

Source: National Association of Realtors.

only to banks; however, the law has been expanded several times to include other financial institutions, such as credit unions and mortgage companies, and to cover applications for home improvement loans as well as primary mortgages. The Federal Financial Institutions Examination Council (FFIEC) was formed several years later for the purpose of aggregating and reporting the information recorded under HMDA by the financial institutions, with each reporting to its own oversight agency.

Overall, in 2003, the nearly 8,000 lenders covered by HMDA reported a total of 31 million loans and applications. Table 5-10 shows the results of these loan applications by income and race and ethnicity of the applicant. As expected, all approval rates increased with income. However, the approval rates for Black applicants were consistently lower than the rates for any other group, regardless of income. American Indians and Hispanics had the next lowest rates of approval. Asians, on the other hand, had very high approval rates. These numbers show that the problem of discriminatory lending may be

still present. The FFIEC data set permits analysis of the data at the census tract level and for individual lending institutions.

NON-TRADITIONAL HOUSING

Not every U.S. resident lives in a household or a housing unit. In 2000, about 7.8 million people, or almost 3 percent of the U.S. population, lived in a group quarters facility. Group quarters are places in which unrelated people live and eat together. Because they are not housing units, the decennial census collects no housing data for them, and they are not included in the American Housing Survey.[4] Group quarters are classified into two main categories: institutional and non-institutional. Generally speaking, institutionalized people are not free to come and go at will, whereas persons living in non-institutionalized group quarters have the same freedom as people living in housing units.

Table 5-11 shows the overall distribution of the

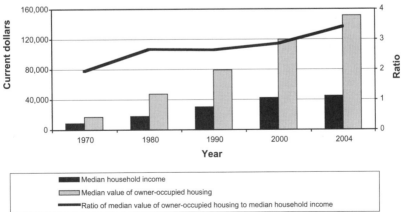

Figure 5-7. Median Household Income and Median Value of Owner-Occupied Housing, Selected Years, 1970–2004

- Median household income
- Median value of owner-occupied housing
- Ratio of median value of owner-occupied housing to median household income

Source: U.S. Census Bureau. Current Population Survey. Census of Housing. American Community Survey 2004.

[4] Group quarters were also not included in the American Community Survey (ACS) from 2000 through 2005. ACS data for 2006, scheduled to be released in the summer of 2007, will be the first to include a sample of this population.

group quarters by type of place. The largest single category is college dormitories, which housed over 2 million residents in 2000; this included everyone living in housing managed by a college or university. The other large specific categories are correctional institutions (housing almost 2 million people) and nursing homes (housing 1.7 million people). Figure 5-8 shows the distribution by sex. Children under 18 years old accounted for a small proportion (about 4 percent) of the total group quarters population; most of them were categorized as living in facilities classified in the "other" categories, which included children's group homes and shelters for teenage runaways. Among adults age 18 to 64 years old, college dormitories and correctional institutions accounted for most of the group quarters population. Almost all of the adults in correctional institutions were men, while college dormitories were almost evenly split between the sexes. Military quarters accounted for a small proportion of the group quarters population in this age group,

The 2000 census employed a variety of enumeration techniques intended to reach as many of the homeless as possible. On a single night, March 27, 2000, enumeration was conducted in facilities including emergency shelters, shelters with temporary lodging for children, shelters for abused women and their children, transitional shelters, and hotels/motels used to provide shelter for people without conventional housing. The next day, March 28, Census enumerators counted people at soup kitchens and mobile food vans. Finally, on March 29, people in targeted non-sheltered outdoor locations were enumerated.

Nationally, the total number of persons enumerated in emergency and transitional shelters in 2000 was 170,706. The Census Bureau is careful to note that this tabulation "is not representative of, and should not be construed to be, the total population without conventional housing, nor is it representative of the entire population that could be defined as living in

Table 5-10. Home Loan Applications Approved, 2003

(Percent.)

Characteristic	Approved	Denied	Withdrawn	File closed	Total
Race/ethnicity					
American Indian, Alaska Native	63.7	24.0	9.5	2.7	100.0
Asian and Pacific Islander	78.0	11.4	8.2	2.4	100.0
Black	63.6	24.3	8.9	3.2	100.0
Hispanic (of any race)	70.2	18.4	8.5	2.8	100.0
White	79.8	11.6	6.8	1.8	100.0
Other	71.2	15.3	10.1	3.3	100.0
Joint (White/minority)	76.9	11.8	9.4	1.9	100.0
Income (Percentage of MSA Median) [1]					
Less than 50	64.0	25.5	8.1	2.4	100.0
50 to 79	74.5	15.7	7.3	2.4	100.0
80 to 99	77.8	12.5	7.4	2.3	100.0
100 to 119	79.3	11.1	7.5	2.1	100.0
120 or more	80.9	9.3	7.8	2.0	100.0

Source: Federal Financial Institutions Examination Council (FFIEC). Nationwide Summary Statistics for 2003 HMDA Data, Fact Sheet, July 2004.

[1]Metropolitan statistical median is median family income of the metropolitan statistical area in which the property to the loan is located.

and were also primarily made up of men. Among the elderly, over three-quarters of the group quarters population lived in nursing homes, with most of the remainder residing in a variety of non-institutionalized housing situations.

EMERGENCY AND TRANSITIONAL SHELTER POPULATION

The population group that falls under this category, often called "the homeless," is composed of the proportion of population that does not live in conventional housing (either housing units or group quarters). It is essentially impossible to enumerate everyone in this population group, as they have no addresses at which they can be definitively located.

emergency and transitional shelters."[5] However, while the total number may be too low, the demographic characteristics of the enumerated population should be considered representative of the population that does not live in conventional housing.

Blacks and Hispanics are over-represented in the emergency and transitional shelter population, as compared to their share of the total population in 2000. About one-quarter of the homeless population is made up of children. In two states, New York and California, children accounted for more than one-third of the homeless population.

Shelters are primarily located in cities. Thus, states with a larger urban population (as well as a larger

[5] U.S. Census Bureau. *Emergency and Transitional Shelter Population: 2000* (Census Special Reports, Report CENSR/01-2). (Oct. 2001.) <http://www.census.gov/prod/2001pubs/censr01-2.pdf>. (Accessed Mar. 7, 2006.)

Table 5-11. Group Quarters Population, 2000

(Number, percent.)

Characteristic	Population	Percent distribution
Total group quarters	7 778 633	
Under 18 Years	322 911	100.0
Institutionalized population	158 118	49.0
Correctional institutions	21 130	6.5
Nursing homes	48	0.0
Other institutions	136 940	42.4
Non-institutionalized population	164 793	51.0
College dormitories (includes college quarters off campus)	10 528	3.3
Military quarters	2 260	0.7
Other non-institutional group quarters	152 005	47.1
18 to 64 Years	5 462 101	100.0
Institutionalized population	2 259 845	41.4
Correctional institutions	1 939 007	35.5
Nursing homes	162 652	3.0
Other institutions	158 186	2.9
Non-institutionalized population	3 202 256	58.6
College dormitories (includes college quarters off campus)	2 053 495	37.6
Military quarters	352 889	6.5
Other non-institutional group quarters	795 872	14.6
65 Years and Over	1 993 621	100.0
Institutionalized population	1 641 076	82.3
Correctional institutions	15 882	0.8
Nursing homes	1 557 800	78.1
Other institutions	67 394	3.4
Non-institutionalized population	352 545	17.7
College dormitories (includes college quarters off campus)	105	0.0
Military quarters	6	0.0
Other non-institutional group quarters	352 434	17.7

Source: U.S. Census Bureau. Table P38. Census 2000 Summary File 1.

total population) are likely to have more of them. Almost one in five homeless people enumerated nationwide (19 percent) was found living in New York City. Other cities with large homeless populations included Los Angeles, Chicago, Boston, Cleveland, Philadelphia, and Seattle.

The National Coalition for the Homeless (NCH) says that there is no easy way to determine the number of homeless and that the question of enumeration itself is misleading. "In most cases, homelessness is a temporary circumstance—not a permanent condition. A more appropriate measure of the magnitude of homelessness is therefore the number of people who experience homelessness over time, not the number of single quarter 'homeless people.'"[6]

There is a difference between a "point-in-time" count of the homeless, such as that conducted for the 2000 census, and an estimate of the number of people who are homeless over a given period of time (such as three months during a given year). The latter count is referred to as a "period prevalence count." Many people are periodically homeless; they lose housing, find it, and then lose it again. For example, a man may live for with his sig-

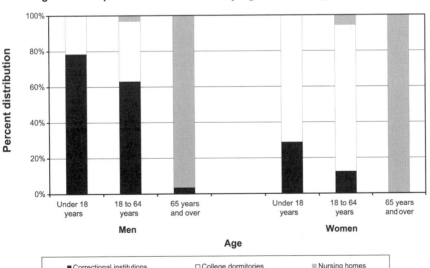

Figure 5-8. Population in Institutions, by Age, Sex, and Type of Institution, 2000

■ Correctional institutions   □ College dormitories   ▨ Nursing homes

Source: U.S. Census Bureau. Table QT-P12. Census 2000 Summary File 1.

6 National Coalition for the Homeless. *How Many People Experience Homelessness?* (NCH Fact Sheet #2). (June 2005.) <http://www.nationalhomeless.org/publications/facts/How_Many.pdf>/ (Accessed Mar. 7, 2006.)

Figure 5-9. Population in Institutions, by Sex and Type of Institution, 2000

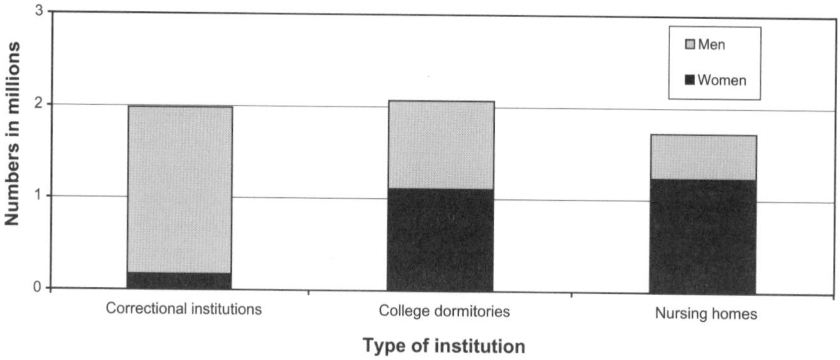

Source: U.S. Census Bureau. Table QT-P12. Census 2000 Summary File 1.

nificant other for a period of time, then be homeless. His mother then takes him in, but later tells him to leave, and so on. According to NCH, point-in-time counts overestimate the proportion of people who are chronically homeless, especially those who are mentally ill and/or substance abusers. These people may have a much harder time finding permanent housing. In addition, any attempt to count the homeless will inadvertently overlook those who cannot be found or identified.

Several studies identified by NCH all give much higher counts of homeless persons than the 170,000 reported on the 2000 census. They also assert that homelessness is increasing, primarily because the number of shelter beds is growing. However, NCH also emphasizes that the focus should be on ending homelessness, rather than on knowing the precise number of homeless persons in the country.

Table 5-12. Characteristics of the Population in Emergency or Transitional Shelters, 2000

(Numbers in thousands, percent.)

Characteristic	Total	Percent distribution
United States	170 706	100.0
Race/ethnicity		
White alone	69 637	40.8
Black alone	69 046	40.4
American Indian, Alaska Native alone	4 092	2.4
Asian alone	3 922	2.3
Native Hawaiian and other Pacific Islander alone	489	0.3
Some other race alone	15 842	9.3
Two or more races	7 678	4.5
Hispanic (of any race)	34 013	19.9
White alone, not Hispanic	57 173	33.5
State		
New York	31 856	18.7
California	27 701	16.2
Texas	7 608	4.5
Florida	6 766	4.0
Illinois	6 378	3.7
Massachusetts	5 405	3.2
New Jersey	5 500	3.2
Pennsylvania	5 463	3.2
Washington	5 387	3.2
Ohio	5 224	3.1
All other states	63 418	37.1
Age		
Under 18 years	43 887	25.7
18 years and over	126 819	74.3

Source: Smith, Annetta C., and Denise I. Smith. 2001. *Emergency and Transitional Shelter Population: 2000* (Census Special Reports, Series CENSR/01-2). (Washington, DC: U.S. Government Printing Office.)

FOR FURTHER INFORMATION SEE:

The primary sources of housing data are the decennial census, the annual American Community Survey, and the American Housing Survey. All of these data sets and their reports are available at <http://www.census.gov> and/or through American FactFinder at <http://factfinder.census.gov>.

WEB SITES:

National Association of Realtors. <http://www.realtor.org>. (Accessed Mar. 7, 2006.)

National Coalition for the Homeless. <http://www.nationalhomeless.org>. (Accessed Mar. 7, 2006.)

U.S. Department of Energy. Energy Information Administration. <http://www.eia.doe.gov>. (Accessed Mar. 7, 2006.)

U.S. Department of Housing and Urban Development. <http://www.hud.gov> and <http://www.huduser.org>. (Accessed Mar. 7, 2006.)

Chapter 6
Income, Wealth, and Poverty

INCOME

UNDERSTANDING INCOME STATISTICS

The term "income" has multiple meanings. It refers to the different ways of measuring the money available to households, families, and individuals. The income of individual persons who are working is better labeled as "earnings." Earnings (or earned income) are only one of several sources of income potentially available to households and families. Other means of income include self-employment income, Social Security payments, welfare, private pensions, income from investments, and child support payments.

In census terms, a household is defined as all of the people living in an occupied housing unit. A family is defined more narrowly, consisting of two or more related people who live in the same household. Thus, a one-person household (someone living alone) is not a family; neither is a household entirely made up of unrelated individuals. A household can include two or more families, and can be made up of any combination of one or more families and one or more unrelated individuals.

HOUSEHOLD INCOME

As measured by the Census Bureau, the national median household income was $44,389 in 2004. This means that half of all households had incomes that were higher than this figure, and half had incomes that were lower. In real terms (adjusted for inflation), this actually represents a small decline from 2003.

Which types of households had higher median incomes, and which types had lower median incomes? Demographic groups with higher median income levels (over $60,000 in 2004) included married-couple households, households headed by an Asian or Pacific Islander householder, households headed by a 45- to 64-year-old householder, and households headed by a college graduate. Demographic groups with lower median income levels (below $35,000 in 2004) included non-family households (primarily one-person households), family households headed by women, Black households, households headed by very young (under 25 years old) or elderly (65 years old or over) householders, and households headed by a householder with less than a high school diploma. Income levels have been rising across the board, but gains have been especially strong for households headed by a highly educated householder.

Comparing the 2004 data with tabulations for 1993, the median income level increased for every group. Median income in real dollars was at a low point in 1993, following the difficult economic period of 1990–1991. The overall increase was about 10 percent, rising from $40,200 in 1993 to $44,400 in 2004. These gains were especially large for Black households and for households headed by a foreign-born person.

Figure 6-1 shows the historic income pattern by race and ethnicity. The slope of increase rose sharply in the 1990s, at a much faster pace than in previous decades, before dropping after 2000. This statistic helps explain why the 1990s were such a prosperous decade, and how the economic downturn that began in 2001 has since affected income.

Figure 6-1. Median Household Income, by Race and Hispanic Origin, 1972–2004

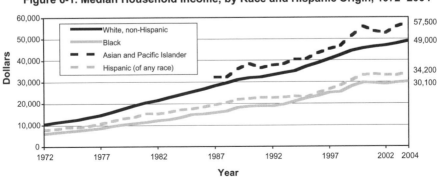

Source: U.S. Census Bureau. Current Population Survey.

However, it must be noted that the income differences by race and ethnic group remain constant, even as the slope increases or decreases. As a group, Black households still have the lowest income in the United States, with income levels only two-thirds of those claimed by White households. Asian and Pacific Islander households have the highest income. However, this is partly due to the higher average number of wage earners in their households. When per capita income is calculated (by dividing the household income by the number of people in the household), White, and especially non-Hispanic White, households had the highest income levels.

INCOME INEQUALITY

Another trend was evident during the 1970–2000 period: increasing "income inequality." This tendency was not restricted to the United States. Income inequality also increased in the Organization for Economic Cooperation and Development (OECD) countries during this period.

What does this often-used term mean, and why is it important to persons in the United States? American society is firmly rooted in the belief in equality of opportunity. However, this does not mean that Americans believe that income should be equal regardless of skill, effort, and education (nor that certain segments of society—such as Blacks and women—should be excluded from that belief). At the same time, residents of the United States seem to believe that lifestyle differences between the poorest and richest Americans should be diminishing, not increasing, over time.

Similarly, Americans tend to believe that extremes of poverty, if not wealth, are somehow foreign to U.S. culture, despite the persistent appearance of both. For example, few Americans would argue against the chief executive officer (CEO) of a large company earning more than an assembly-line worker in one of the company plants. But what is the appropriate ratio of their incomes? Should the CEO make 10 times the income of the assembly-line worker, or 50 or 100 times as much? Should that gap be increasing or diminishing, and under what conditions? A recent article indicated that the CEOs of many large corporations, including Lockheed Martin, Black and Decker, Fannie Mae, CSX, Gannett, and Mobil earn annual salary, bonus, and stock options ranging from $4 million to $24 million. Exec-utive salaries of that magnitude range between 80 and 800 times the average income of U.S. workers in 1995. While some feel such income differences are obscene, there is no sign of change to come.

The Census Bureau uses two measures to estimate income inequality. One is called the Gini index, also known as the index of income concentration. The Gini index would be 0.0 if all households had equal shares of income. If one household had all of the

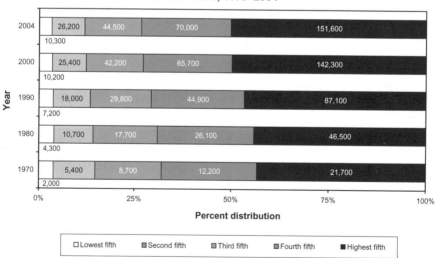

Figure 6-2. Percent Share of Household Income and Mean Income, by Each Fifth, Selected Years, 1970–2004

Source: U.S. Census Bureau. Current Population Survey.

income, and the rest had none, the index would be 1.0. Thus, the lower the index figure, the more equal the distribution of income among households. In 2004, the Gini Index was 0.466, a significant increase over the 1995 figure of 0.450.

Another way of measuring income inequality is to examine the differences between income levels at the top and at the bottom. This involves ranking households by income·and dividing the ranked list into quintiles, with one-fifth (or 20 percent) of households in each. As Figure 6-2 shows, the proportion of income going to the top quintile has gradually increased over time, while the proportion going to the bottom two quintiles has gradually decreased. This signifies increasing income inequality. The lowest quintile has seen only a 22 percent increase in real income over the recent 34-year period (1970–2004), while the increase in income for the highest quintile was 65 percent. The second and third quintiles had even smaller increases than the lowest quintile (15 percent and 21 percent, respectively). As is often said, "the rich get richer and the poor get poorer."

There are a number of factors behind this trend. One of the most important is the increasing number of dual-earner households, with both husband and wife in the labor force. This trend has sharply increased the number of high income households. People subsisting only on government benefits (welfare and/or Social Security) have seen some increase in real income over the past 30 years. The minimum wage has increased, but not enough to pull the working poor up into what many call the middle class. The decrease in unionized manufac-

turing jobs and the increase in hourly, part-time service-sector jobs has had a severe impact on the earnings of workers with lesser amounts of education. The proportion of retired households has increased, and these households generally have lower income than households with earners.

In fact, the lowest income quintile is characterized by persons living alone (56 percent of households in the quintile), householders age 65 years and over (38 percent), and households with no earner (56 percent). In contrast, almost all of the households in the highest quintile are married-couple families (86 percent), households with earner(s) in the prime earning years of 35 to 54 years old (60 percent), and households with two or more earners (43 percent). (See Table 6-1.)

NON-CASH INCOME

The discussion above focused on money income alone. In recent years, the Census Bureau has conducted research on the effect of defining income in other ways. The most important non-money-income factors are government transfers. Income taxes and Social Security payroll taxes reduce income, while the Earned Income Tax Credit (EIC), employer-paid health insurance, and government subsidies increase income. The Census Bureau has created 15 different measures of income, each of which take one or more of these factors into account.

The impact of using these definitions, whether alone or in combination, is measured by the changes in percentage differences between the offi-

Table 6-1. Percent Distribution of Households, by Selected Characteristics Within Income Quintile, 2004

(Percent distribution.)

Characteristic	Total	Lowest fifth	Highest fifth
Race/ethnicity			
White, non-Hispanic	100.0	17.4	22.7
Black	100.0	32.4	9.3
Hispanic (of any race)	100.0	24.8	11.0
Family type			
Married-couple families	100.0	7.4	31.5
Male householder, no wife present	100.0	14.3	15.3
Female householder, no husband present	100.0	30.6	6.9
Male householder living alone	100.0	33.6	7.2
Female householder living alone	100.0	48.4	3.0
Age			
15–24 years	100.0	33.2	5.7
25–34 years	100.0	15.5	15.7
35–44 years	100.0	12.3	26.3
45–54 years	100.0	12.8	30.3
55–64 years	100.0	17.2	24.3
65 years and over	100.0	37.1	7.7
Earners			
No earners	100.0	56.4	2.3
One earner	100.0	18.9	11.1
Two earners or more	100.0	2.7	36.7

Source: U.S. Census Bureau. Current Population Survey.

cial median income figure and the revised figure. For most types of households, these changes do not make a significant difference in the measurement of income, but do make a difference in their relative income as compared to other types of households. For example, using the official measure of income, elderly households have less than half the median income of married-couple family households. When disposable income is calculated, elderly households improve to 60 percent: $33,500 for elderly households and $55,600 for married-couple households in 2004.[1]

TRENDS BY EDUCATIONAL LEVEL

Educational attainment appears to be playing an increasingly important role in determining income. (See Table 6-2.) Some education level categories dropped between 1991 and 2004, which indicates that income levels for these groups were not keeping up with inflation. However, the median income differences between less educated households and more educated households remained relatively constant. In all four years shown, householders with professional degrees (such as medical, dental, and law degrees) had about five times more income than households in which the householder had less than a 9th grade education.

However, it should be noted that the number of households with poorly educated householders

decreased during this 10-year period, dropping from 9.3 million to 6.8 million for those with less than 9th grade education, and from 10.3 million to 9.4 million for those with some high school but no diploma. At the same time, the total number of households increased by about 10 percent. The losses in households at the low end of the education scale were more than balanced out by gains at the top end. Households in which the householder had a bachelor's degree or more increased from 20.8 million to 28.5 million during the same period.

CHANGES IN INCOME OVER LIFETIME

The income level in the United States is not static. Thus, discussions about the poor or the rich in the 1970s, as compared to the 2000s, does not mean that those groups contain same individuals at both time periods. There is considerable evidence of large annual, as well as lifetime, shifts in income level. Life cycle events such as leaving the parental home, graduating from college, getting one's first job, marriage, divorce, disability, and retirement (not necessarily in that order) can have profound impact on income. Typically, income level peaks between the ages of 45 to 54 years old, and then begins to taper off (on average) as people begin to retire. However, patterns vary. Women maintaining families due to divorce or the death of a spouse, for example, have reduced income, compared to their previous status in a married-couple household.

Table 6-2. Trends in Household Median Income, by Educational Attainment of Householder, Selected Years, 1991–2004

(2004 dollars.)

Educational attainment level	1991	1995	2001	2004
Median income, householders 25 years and older	41 971	43 370	46 517	45 996
Educational Attainment				
Less than 9th grade	17 882	18 516	19 336	19 541
9th to 12th grade, no diploma	23 716	22 523	24 811	22 476
High school graduate or GED	38 529	38 620	38 475	37 378
Some college, no degree	47 541	45 734	48 884	47 390
Associate degree	53 695	51 842	54 595	54 004
Bachelor's degree	65 874	65 060	71 672	68 626
Master's degree	74 622	79 957	84 197	80 282
Professional degree	105 427	100 944	106 711	100 000
Doctorate degree	95 103	98 476	99 034	100 000

Source: U.S. Census Bureau. Current Population Survey.
Note: Medians calculated from grouped data ending with the category $100,000 and over.

---

[1] For an explanation of the different types of income calculation, see: U.S. Census Bureau. The Effects of Government Taxes and Transfers on Income and Poverty: 2004. (Feb. 2006.) <http://www.census.gov/hhes/www/poverty/effect2004/effectofgovtandt2004.html>. (Accessed Feb. 27, 2006.)

Figure 6-3. Median Net Worth of Families, by Race and Hispanic Origin, 1995 and 2004

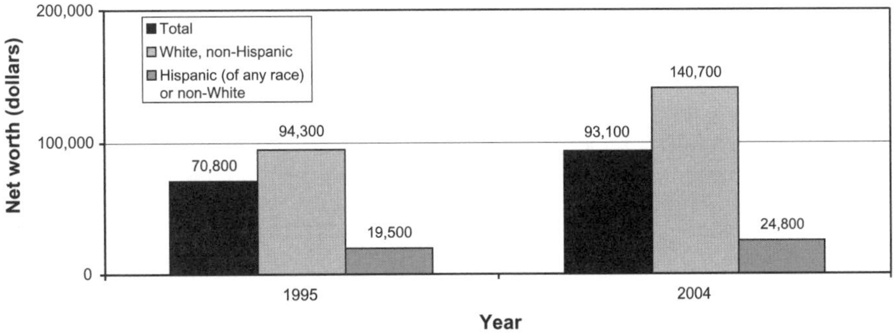

Source: The Federal Reserve Board. 2004 Survey of Consumer Finances. *Federal Reserve Bulletin.*

WEALTH

NET WORTH

Income is not the only influence on the economic well-being of an individual. Wealth is another factor. One often-used gauge of wealth is "net worth," which is defined as the market value of assets (such as equity in one's home, stocks, savings, and checking account balances) minus liabilities (such as mortgages and debt on credit cards). The median net worth for all U.S. households in 2004 was $93,100. Unlike previous studies, this calculation of net worth includes 401(k) savings.

Households in the lowest income quintile had a median net worth of about $7,400, while those in the highest income quintile had a median net worth of $185,000. For non-Hispanic White households, median net worth in 2004 ($140,700) was about six times the median net worth of minority households ($24,800). (See Figure 6-3.)

Since the passage of time offers increased opportunities for accumulating wealth, it is not surprising that net worth increases with age of the householder, until the householder reaches retirement age. The median net worth of households headed by a person under 35 years old was only $14,200 in 2004, but increased to $248,700 for householders

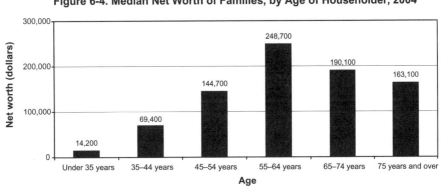

Figure 6-4. Median Net Worth of Families, by Age of Householder, 2004

Source: The Federal Reserve Board. 2004 Survey of Consumer Finances. *Federal Reserve Bulletin.*

in the 55- to 64-year-old age group, before declining for older households. (See Figure 6-4.) As is the case with income, the net worth of married-couple households is typically greater than the net worth of households maintained by a man or woman without a spouse present. Regardless of the age of householder, households maintained by a married couple typically have double the net worth of other household types. Households headed by a woman under 35 years old had the lowest median net worth. Education is also strongly associated with wealth: the median net worth of households headed by a college graduate was about triple that of households in which the householder had only a high school education.

TYPES OF ASSETS

The nation's homeowners, who represent about 67 percent of households in the United States, had a median net worth of $184,000 in 2004, compared to only about $4,000 net worth for households that rent. Among homeowners, home equity (its net value) was a substantial of their total net worth. Median value of the primary residence was about $160,000.

In the 1990s, families began to hold less of their financial assets in regular savings or checking accounts, while putting more into tax-deferred retirement accounts, publicly traded stocks, and mutual funds. (See Table 6-3.) By 2000, about half of all families' financial assets (excluding home

equity) were in such investments. Ownership of vehicles (including cars, trucks, motorcycles, mobile homes, boats, and airplanes) was one of the most commonly held non-financial assets, with 83 percent of households having one or more vehicle with a median value of $10,000. There has been a slight decrease in the tendency of families to own such assets, and an increased tendency for households to lease, rather than buy, their automobiles. This was particularly prevalent among higher-income households.

SAVING

In 2004, slightly over half (56 percent) of families were savers. This represents a decline of 3 percentage points from the 2001 figure; this drop generally reflects the poor economy of the early part of this decade, demonstrated by a 6.2 percent decline in median wages. The percentage of savers increases with income, education, and net worth. Non-Hispanic White families are more likely to be savers than families in other racial and ethnic groups. The age of the head of the household makes surprisingly little difference in the percentage of savers, except that the elderly persons (75 years old and over) are less likely to save.

The leading reasons for saving are (1) retirement and (2) liquidity, i.e. to have money in the bank in case of emergency. Education is a distant third, while saving for purchases has become increasingly less common.

Table 6-3. Distribution of Net Worth, by Asset Type, Selected Years, 1993–2000

(Percent distribution.)

Type of asset	1993 (1995 dollars)	1995 (1995 dollars)	1998 (2000 dollars)	2000 (2000 dollars)
All Assets	100.0	100.0	100.0	100.0
Interest-earning assets at financial institutions	11.4	9.6	8.1	8.9
Other interest-earning assets	4.0	4.5	2.7	1.7
Regular checking accounts	0.5	0.6	0.4	0.3
Stocks and mutual fund shares	8.3	8.4	18.8	15.6
Own home	44.4	44.4	33.7	32.3
Rental property	6.7	6.2	4.5	3.7
Other real estate	4.6	4.3	3.2	3.6
Vehicles	6.4	8.3	4.4	3.7
Business or profession	6.4	5.6	7.3	7.7
U.S. savings bonds	0.8	0.8	0.6	0.5
IRA or Keogh accounts	6.7	8.3	7.0	8.6
401(k) and thrift savings plans	. . .	. . .	8.6	9.7
Other financial investments	3.0	2.8	2.6	1.6
Unsecured liabilities	. . .	-3.6	-3.4	-3.0

Source: U.S. Census Bureau. *Net Worth and Asset Ownership of Households: 1998 and 2000* and *Household Net Worth and Asset Ownership: 1995.*
Note: Because net worth is assets less liabilities, unsecured liabilities are subtracted from the distribution of net worth and are shown as negative.

. . . = Not available.

Table 6-4. Families Holding Debt, by Type of Debt and Median Amount of Debt, 2004

(Percent, dollars.)

Type of debt	Percent with specified debt	Median amount (dollars)
Mortgage and home equity loans	47.9	95 000
Other residential property	4.0	87 000
Installment loans	46.0	11 500
Other lines of credit	1.6	3 000
Credit card balances	46.2	2 200
Other debt	7.6	4 000
Any debt	76.4	55 300

Source: The Federal Reserve Board. 2004 Survey of Consumer Finances. *Federal Reserve Bulletin.*

DEBT

In the average household in 2000, debt represented about 12 percent of its assets. This fraction (known as the "leverage ratio") did not change much during the 1990s. The median debt for all households, including mortgage debt and home equity loans, credit card debt, and installment purchases was about $55,000 in 2004. (See Table 6-4 and Figure 6-5.) The median credit card debt (the outstanding balance after paying the most recent bill) was about $2,200 in 2004, up from $1,100 in 1992. The proportion of households with credit card debt increased from about 40 percent in 1989 to 48 percent in 1995. This proportion dropped to 44 percent in 1998, but rose to 47 percent in 2004. It is important to note that, while current data are not available, the burden of debt has likely increased since 1998 (and especially since 2001, as the economy has worsened).

POVERTY

DEFINING POVERTY

The official measurement of poverty in America began in the mid-1960s, during the presidency of Lyndon Johnson. It was the advent of his administration's "War on Poverty" that introduced a variety of anti-poverty programs into the country. Prior to the mid-1960s, no official government gauge existed to measure the extent and distribution of poverty in the United States. An often-used measure of poverty during the early 1960s was the number of families with annual incomes below $3,000 combined with the number of unrelated persons with annual income below $1,500. Such a fixed gauge did not take into account differences in family size (and in varying living expenses) or the changes over time in the amount of income required to sustain a family.

In the early 1960s, Mollie Orshansky, an economist at the Social Security Administration (SSA), devised a gauge that did factor in differences in size and composition of families. She also devised a mechanism for adjusting the poverty "thresholds" for inflation. Within a few years, the Orshansky, or SSA, poverty definition was being used as a budget and planning tool by federal agencies and as the basis for eligibility for certain programs. In 1969, the SSA definition of poverty was adopted by the Budget Bureau[2] for use in the official statistical series for the U.S. government that was to be published by the U.S. Census Bureau. The poverty definition provides a sliding scale of income thresholds by family size, age of householder, and number of related

Figure 6-5. Percent Distribution of Debt for Families, by Type of Debt, 2004

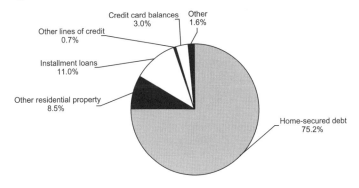

Source: The Federal Reserve Board. 2004 Survey of Consumer Finances. *Federal Reserve Bulletin.*

---

2 Budget Bureau. 1969. Circular No. A-46. Transmittal Memorandum No. 9, August 29, 1969. The Budget Bureau is the predecessor of the present-day Office of Management and Budget.

Table 6-5. Poverty Thresholds for Families, 2004

(Dollars.)

Size of family unit	Weighted average poverty threshold
One person	
Under 65 years	9 827
65 years and over	9 060
Two persons	
Householder under 65 years	12 649
Householder 65 years and over	11 418
Three persons	14 776
Four persons	19 484
Five persons	23 497
Six persons	27 025
Seven persons	31 096
Eight persons	34 778
Nine persons or more	41 836

Source: U.S. Census Bureau. Current Population Survey.

children under 18 years of age. (See Table 6-5.)

The original basis for these income thresholds was a minimally adequate food budget devised by the Department of Agriculture and the ratio of food to total spending for a typical family in 1969 (which was about a third). Thus, minimum food requirements for various family compositions were multiplied by a factor of three to come up with the original poverty thresholds. Families or individuals with income below their appropriate threshold were classified as poor; those with income above their poverty threshold were classified as not poor.

In 2004, the poverty threshold for a family of four was $19,484; and other thresholds varied from a low of $9,060 for a person 65 years old or over living alone to $41,836 for a family with nine or more members. Poverty thresholds are updated every year to reflect changes in cost of living, as measured by the Consumer Price Index (CPI-U). Thus, the poverty threshold for a family of four was $2,973 in 1959, $8,414 in 1980, $10,989 in 1985, $13,359 in 1990, $15,569 in 1995, and $17,603 in 2000. (See Figure 6-6.)

Over the years, the SSA definition of poverty has been criticized by those who perceive it as too stringent, as well as by those who think it is too lenient. The definition has been the subject of several major studies that have examined the perceived to be technical deficiencies, although most criticisms have existed since the definition was first proposed. Some of these criticisms were anticipated by Orshansky in her original research.[3] The latest study, conducted by the National Research Council in 1995, suggested important new changes to the concept and measurement of poverty.[4]

To date, there has not been a convergence between the technical/programmatic need for a change in the definition of poverty and the political climate necessary for such a change to occur. (No president wants an increase in poverty—a likely

Figure 6-6. Average Poverty Threshold for a Four-Person Family and Consumer Price Index (CPI-U), 1959–2004

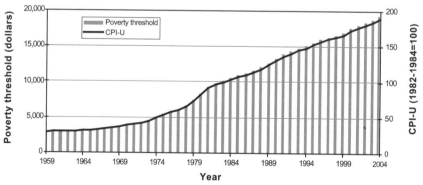

Source: U.S. Census Bureau. Current Population Survey.

---

[3] Orshansky, Mollie. 1965. Counting the poor: Another look at the poverty profile. *Social Security Bulletin* 28(1). Also see: Orshansky, Mollie. 1965. Who's who among the poor: A demographic view of poverty. *Social Security Bulletin* 28(7).

[4] Citro, Constance F., and Robert T. Michael, eds. 1995. *Measuring Poverty: A New Approach.* (Washington, DC: National Academy Press.) Earlier work in this area includes: Department of Health, Education, and Welfare. 1976. *The Measure of Poverty.* (Washington, DC: U.S. Government Printing Office.) Also see: U.S. Census Bureau. 1985. *Proceedings of a Conference on the Measurement of Noncash Benefits* (December 12–14 1985). (Washington, DC: U.S. Department of Commerce.)

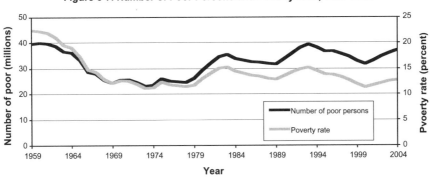

Figure 6-7. Number of Poor Persons and Poverty Rate, 1959–2004

Source: U.S. Census Bureau. Current Population Survey.

product of a change in definition—on his or her "watch," regardless of whether or not it was statistically induced.) For example, the poverty threshold for a family of four cited above was essentially the same as that already used for all families ($3,000) at the time of its adoption as the official measure. However, an analysis of the experimental measure of poverty currently being developed at the Census Bureau is discussed below.

TRENDS IN THE NUMBER OF POOR

Using the official definition of poverty, the number of poor people decreased dramatically in the 1960s and the early 1970s, dropping from a high of nearly 40 million persons in 1960 to a low of 23 million by 1973. (See Figure 6-7.) The proportion of the U.S. population living in households with poverty-level income also fell, declining from a high of 22 percent in 1960 to half that figure by 1973. The early 1970s marked a turning point in income growth in the United States. This was the point at which income, adjusted for inflation, began to stagnate. While there was some fluctuation (with business cycles) in the number and proportion of poor persons between the mid-1970s and the early 1990s, neither the number of poor nor the poverty rate has ever returned to the low levels of the early 1970s.

The cycle began to improve in 1994, and continued in this manner through 2000. The official 2000 poverty rate of 11.3 percent was almost as low as it was in 1972–1973. The number of poor showed a somewhat different picture, because the total population is constantly growing. However, this figure also declined, in spite of the population increase. The poverty rate began to increase after this low

point in 2000, climbing to 12.7 percent in 2004. Why poverty in America has not been eradicated, despite significant government programs and investment, is the subject of considerable debate. Conservatives tend to assert that government intervention has perpetuated poverty and created a dependent class. Liberals tend to put the blame on insufficient government assistance, along with environmental influences and economic conditions that perpetuate poverty. Data can be brought forth to support either position. A frequently lost detail in these arguments is that, among individual people and families, there is considerable movement up and down the income ladder; the poor in 1995 are not the same people (or even the children of the people) who were poor in 1965. About one out of four persons who were poor in a given year were not poor the next, according to longitudinal data for the mid-1980s and early 1990s. Welfare reform, enacted into law in 1996, made some difference, but the fate of former welfare recipients is often subject to the overall economic situation.

WHO IS POOR?

Demographic groups with higher than average proportions of population in poverty include children, Blacks, Hispanics, women living alone, non-citizens, people living in central cities, and families headed by a woman with no husband present. Population groups with lower than average proportions include non-Hispanics Whites, people 35 to 59 years old, native-born people, suburban residents, and married-couple families. The improvements over the late 1990s were primarily among some of the worst-off groups, including Blacks, Hispanics, younger people (under 25 years old), and female-headed families.

Figure 6-8. Poverty Rate for Persons Under 18 Years and Persons 65 Years and Over, 1959–2004

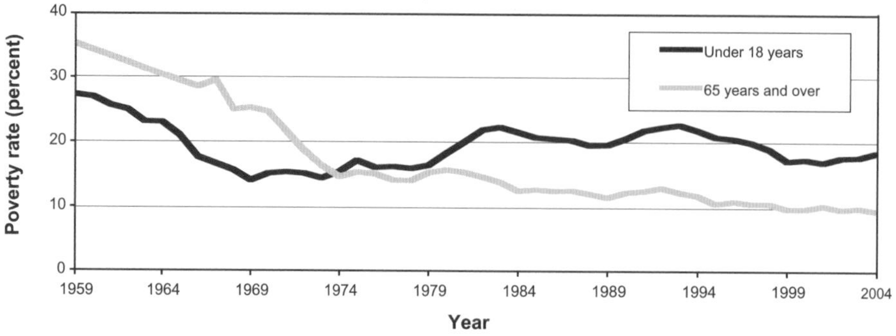

Source: U.S. Census Bureau. Current Population Survey; Census 2000; American Community Survey (data for 2001–2004).

One of the groups that has experienced significant long-term reductions in poverty since 1959 is the elderly. Persons 65 years old and over had a poverty rate of over 35 percent in 1959, which was higher than any other age group. However, by 2004, the poverty rate for the elderly had declined to less than a third of its 1959 level (10.1 percent), and has been lower than the rate for all ages combined since the early 1980s. Much of this reduction has been attributed to the automatic inflation adjustment of Social Security benefits, which began in the early 1970s, as well as to the increasing proportion of the aged eligible for such benefits. However, a larger than average proportion of elderly persons have incomes just above the poverty level, and are thus at risk of falling below the subsistence level if faced with unavoidable and unusually large expenses.

Children, on the other hand, experienced little reduction in poverty between 1959 (when government figures became available) and 2001. The 18.4 percent poverty rate for children under 18 years old in 2004 was higher than in the mid-1970s. (See Figure 6-8.) This rate was lower than of the rate for the elderly until the early 1970s, but is currently almost twice that of older age groups. More than one out of six American children under 6 years old lived in a poor household in 2004. Because of their relatively high poverty rate, children under 18 years of age represented 25 percent of all poor persons in 2004.

Among racial groups, Blacks have seen their official poverty level decline considerably in the past 30 years. Over half (55 percent) of Blacks were poor in 1959, when poverty statistics were first tabulated. The poverty rate for this group declined to 22 percent in 2000, its lowest figure ever, but was back up to 35 percent in 2004. Progress has been made, despite the presence of several countervailing trends that tend to increase poverty in this group— particularly the incidence of single-parent families. Much of the Social Security Administration's original concern with measuring poverty pertained to women left alone to sustain their children without benefit of a spouse; such families historically had higher poverty rates than married-couple families. Originally, this concern was fostered by widowhood, but children growing up in single-parent families are now likely to have parents who are divorced or who have had children outside of marriage.

For families headed by single women, the 2004 poverty rate was about the same for Hispanics (37.0 percent) as for Blacks, whereas the poverty rate for White families in this group was 22 percent. (See Figure 6-9.) Married-couple households have much lower poverty rates, at about than 5 percent overall and 8 percent for Blacks. Hispanic married-couple families had a poverty rate more than three times that of non-Hispanic White families (14 percent versus 5 percent), and almost twice that of Black families. Even though the poverty rate for

Figure 6-9. Poverty Status in the Past 12 Months for Families, by Type and Race and Hispanic Origin of Householder, 2004

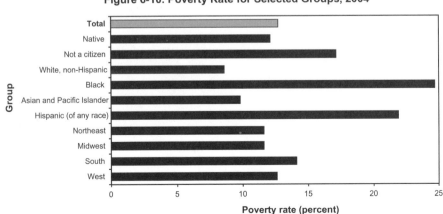

Source: U.S. Census Bureau. American Community Survey 2004.

Hispanic families was higher than that for Blacks within each family type, the overall poverty rate for families with an Hispanic householder was about the same as that for Black families. This was due to the vastly different family composition of these two groups: only one-fourth of Hispanic families are maintained by women without husbands, and fewer than half of poor Hispanic families are headed by women alone.

Unrelated individuals (people who live alone or with people who are not related to them, such as a roommate, boarder, etc.) have increased both in absolute terms and as a proportion of all poor per-

sons. More than one of five of these unrelated persons was poor in 2004, which was less than half of their poverty rate in the early 1960s (when a larger proportion of this group was made up of elderly persons living alone). However, the number of unrelated poor individuals increased from about 5 million in 1959 to 11 million in 2004; this group also represented about 30 percent of the poor, over twice their level of representation in 1959.

Other characteristics (other than membership in a minority group or living in a single-parent family) are also associated with higher than average poverty rates. (See Figure 6-10.) Foreign-born non-citizens

Figure 6-10. Poverty Rate for Selected Groups, 2004

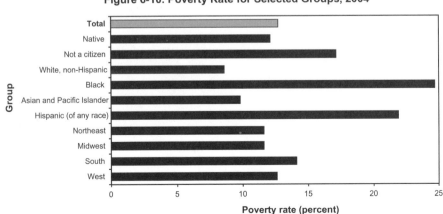

Source: U.S. Census Bureau. Current Population Survey.

have higher rates of poverty than persons born in the United States (17 percent versus 12 percent); persons living in large central cities have poverty rates that are twice as high those of persons living in suburban areas, while those living in rural areas have a rate that falls between the city and suburban rates; work effort is highly correlated with poverty status, as only 8 percent of persons in a family with a worker were poor, compared with 29 percent in families with no workers.

DEPTH OF POVERTY

Classifying people as either "in poverty" or "not in poverty" is a fairly simple, dichotomous way of analyzing economic position. The Census Bureau has developed two "depth of poverty" measures that more fully reflect the distribution of economic well-being.

The first measure is the ratio of income to poverty. This is a measure of the degree of poverty, both among those below the poverty threshold and those who are just above it. In 2004, 44 percent of the nation's poor were very poor, with incomes of less than 50 percent of their poverty threshold. As might be expected, the population groups most represented in this measure included the young (under 25 years old), minorities (Blacks and Hispanics), children, and unrelated individuals. The latter, of course, are limited to one person contributing to their income. Another group of people, about 12.4 million, were living just above the poverty level in 2004, with incomes of up to 1.25 percent of their poverty thresholds.

The second measure of depth of poverty is called the income deficit. This is the difference in dollars between the family's income and its threshold, which averaged $7,800 in 2004. The deficit tends to be higher for families and lower for unrelated individuals (in part because the poverty threshold for single persons living alone is so low). On a per capita basis, the deficit is higher for unrelated individuals than for people living in families.

THE GEOGRAPHY OF POVERTY

Poverty is not evenly spread throughout the country. By state, Mississippi had the highest poverty rate in 2004, followed by Kentucky, Alabama, and Louisiana. In contrast, 14 states had poverty rates below 10 percent, with the lowest levels found in New Hampshire, Minnesota, Vermont, and New Jersey. Within cities, poor people tended to live in their own neighborhoods; the poverty rate in cities was more than twice that of suburbs. Rural areas often have concentrations of people living below the poverty level. This isolation of poor people from the more affluent segments of the population is increasing, influenced by the flight of middle-class Blacks to the suburbs, housing discrimination against disadvantaged groups such as immigrants, and a growing mismatch between where low-income workers live and where their jobs are located.[5]

EXPERIMENTAL POVERTY MEASURES

The Census Bureau has, to date, developed several experimental poverty measures. The work is based on two important components: (1) How does one measure a family's (or person's) needs?; and (2) What resources should be counted as income for meeting those needs? A 1995 report by the National Research Council Panel is the basis for this project, with research being conducted to refine some of the measurement methods and to examine how various adaptations of the panel's recommendations would affect the number of poor and the poverty rate.

The research, with 2004 data, focuses on four definitions of resources: money income, market income, post-social insurance income, and disposable income. This produced a wide variation in poverty rates, ranging from 10.4 percent using the disposable income method to 19.4 percent using market income.[6]

[5] Lichter, Daniel T., and Martha L. Crowley. 2002. Poverty in America: Beyond welfare reform. *Population Bulletin* 47(2).

[6] For more information, see: U.S. Census Bureau. *The Effects of Government Taxes and Transfers on Income and Poverty: 2004.* (Feb. 2006.) <http://www.census.gov/hhes/www/poverty/effect2004/effectofgovtandt2004.html>. (Accessed Feb. 28, 2006)

FOR FURTHER INFORMATION SEE:

Bucks, Brian K., Arthur B. Kennickell, and Kevin B. Moore. Recent changes in U.S. family finances: Evidence from the 2001 and 2004 Survey of Consumer Finances (*Federal Reserve Bulletin*, Feb. 2004). <http://www.federalreserve.gov/pubs/bulletin/2006/financesurvey.pdf>. (Accessed Mar. 17, 2006.)

Burt, Martha, and Barbara Cohen. 1989. *America's Homeless: Numbers, Characteristics, and Programs That Serve Them*. (Washington, DC: Urban Institute Press.)

Citro, Constance F., and Robert T. Michael, eds. 1995. *Measuring Poverty: A New Approach*. (Washington, DC: National Academy Press.)

DeNavas-Walt, Carmen, Bernadette D. Proctor, and Cheryl Hill Lee. *Income, Poverty, and Health Insurance Coverage in the United States: 2004* (Current Population Report P60-229). (Aug. 2005.) <http://www.census.gov/prod/2005pubs/p60-229.pdf>. (Accessed Mar. 17, 2006.)

The Federal Reserve Board. 2006. 2004 Survey of Consumer Finances. *Federal Reserve Bulletin*.

Jones, Jr., Arthur E., and Daniel Weinberg. *The Changing Shape of the Nation's Income Distribution: 1947–1998* (Current Population Report P60-204). (June 2000.) <http://www.census.gov/prod/2000pubs/p60-204.pdf>. (Accessed Mar. 17, 2006.)

Link, Bruce, et al. 1994. Lifetime and five-year prevalence of homelessness in the United States. *American Journal of Public Health* 84(12): 1907-1912.

Lichter, Daniel T., and Martha L. Crowley. 2002. *Poverty in America: Beyond Welfare Reform*. (Washington, DC: Population Reference Bureau.)

Orzechowski, Shawna, and Peter Sepielli. *Household Net Worth and Asset Ownership: 1998 and 2000* (Current Population Report P70-88). (May 2003.) <http://www.census.gov/prod/2003pubs/p70-88.pdf>. (Accessed Mar. 17, 2006.)

WEB SITES:

Federal Reserve System. <http://www.federalreserve.gov>. (Accessed Mar. 17, 2006.) This site provided the Bucks report cited above.

U.S. Census Bureau. <http://www.census.gov>. (Accessed Mar. 17, 2006.) The Income Data and Poverty Data sections were used for this chapter, supplementing the Income and Poverty reports cited above.

Chapter 7
Education

SCHOOL ENROLLMENT

In October 2004, a total of more than 75 million people (more than one out of every four persons in the United States) were currently enrolled in school. While most were students in elementary school, high school, or college, there were 8.7 million children enrolled in nursery school or kindergarten. The college student figures, about 17.3 million overall, include 2.8 million people over the age of 34—the end of the traditional school enrollment age range. Groups at the enrollment age extremes have seen the largest proportional increases in school attendance over the past several decades.[1]

The proportion of children age 3 and 4 years who are enrolled in nursery school has increased continuously over the past several decades, rising to include about 54 percent of all children of this age. Children of higher-income families are more likely to be enrolled, most likely because of the cost involved in paying for private education. College-graduate mothers and mothers in the labor force are also significantly more likely to enroll their young children in nursery school. The availability of full-day programs means that, for some children, the school serves as a day-care facility as well.

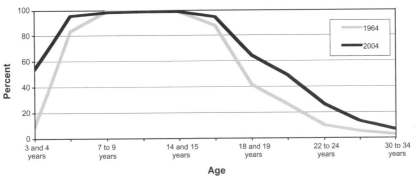

Figure 7-1. School Enrollment Rates, by Age, 1964 and 2004

Source: U.S. Census Bureau. Current Population Survey.

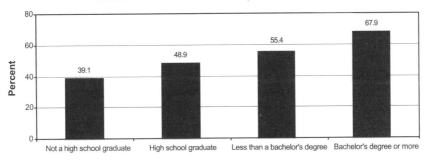

Figure 7-2. Nursery School Enrollment of Children 3 and 4 Years Old, by Mother's Level of Education, October 2004

Source: U.S. Census Bureau. Current Population Survey.

---

[1] Shin, Hyon B. 2005. *School Enrollment in the United States—Social and Economic Characteristics of Students: October 2003* (Current Population Report P20-554). <http://www.census.gov/prod/2005pubs/p20-554.pdf>. (Accessed Jan. 30, 2006.) The data reported here do not include students enrolled in vocational or technical training programs unless it leads to a diploma or a degree. Although the cited report presents 2003 data, 2004 data are available at <http://www.census.gov> and are used in this chapter.

Pre-primary enrollment is still linked to income, despite government efforts—such as Head Start and other state and locally administered pre-primary programs—to make this education available to any student (or student's parent) who desires it. Government programs are typically restricted to families with low incomes. For example, about 60 percent of 3- and 4-year-olds in families with incomes over $40,000 were enrolled in nursery school in 2004, compared with about 47 percent of children in families with incomes under $20,000. Children whose mothers have less than a high school education are less likely to be enrolled than those whose mothers have at least a bachelor's degree. However, there is some evidence that these gaps are becoming narrower.

Kindergarten, elementary, and high school enrollment patterns are closely linked with the total population in these age groups. In the late 1990s, the "baby boomlet" of the 1980s brought school enrollments back to the level of the baby boom years; in both 1970 and 1999, there were 49 million children enrolled in elementary and high school.

The number was expected to decrease by 2004; instead, it stayed at 49 million. Two factors are responsible. First, high school enrollment has increased, as students remain in school longer. Second, the high immigration levels of the 1990s contribute to these high enrollment figures. In 2004, almost one student in five had a foreign-born parent, including 6 percent who were themselves foreign born. These patterns, which emerged in the mid-1990s, had many school districts scrambling to provide sufficient enrollment capacity, after years of dealing with a surplus of classroom space.

About 90 percent of elementary and high school students attend public schools. Children living outside of metropolitan areas are slightly less likely to attend private school. At the nursery school level, about half the children enrolled are in a public school environment and half in a private school environment, with children living in suburbs more likely to attend a private school. For kindergarten, the figure rises to 86 percent enrolled in public schools.

In 2004, the National Center for Education Statistics revised the way in which it considers post-secondary education. Instead of separating colleges from vocational training, it now classifies areas of study as either academic or career, and further subdivides career majors into sub-baccalaureate (non-four-year degree) and baccalaureate levels.[2] About 14.8 million students were enrolled in the various categories of post-secondary education in the 1999–2000 academic year.

Of the 6.9 million students enrolled in four-year programs in 1999–2000, only one-third were enrolled in an academic area of study (defined as an area of study that is comprehensive, theoretical, and not oriented to a specific occupation). The remainder had career-oriented majors, of which the most common was business/marketing. Of those enrolled in two-year programs, 20 percent were enrolled in academic areas; most of these students were likely planning to continue on to four-year degrees. The most common career majors for students in two-year programs were business/marketing, computer science, and health care. Often, students in this group are of working age, between 25 and 64 years old, and have at least a high school diploma. One-third report that they have completed a bachelor's degree. Another data set, covering persons 18 to 44 years of age, shows that while participation in credentialed programs (leading to a college degree, diploma, or certificate) decreases by age, participation in other types of adult learning activities remains high—at about 50 percent—for all age groups.[3]

HIGH SCHOOL DROPOUTS

At the other end of the enrollment spectrum, high school dropout rates have tended to decline over the past 25 years, reaching an annual figure of about 3.8 percent of 10th through 12th graders in 2003. For Whites, the rate has not changed much; there is a drop from somewhat higher levels in the 1970s. For Blacks, the dropout rate is now half its 1970 rate, but remains higher than that of Whites (5.2 percent for Blacks, 4.2 percent for Whites in 2004). The annual dropout rate for Hispanics (8.0 percent) is higher than that for either Blacks or Whites. The dropout rate for Asians and Pacific Islanders, reported for the first time in 1999, was less than 1 percent in 2004.

[2] U.S. Department of Education. National Center for Education Statistics. 2004. *Undergraduate Enrollments in Academic, Career, and Vocational Education* (Issue Brief NCES 2004-108). <http://nces.ed.gov/pubs2004/2004018.pdf>. (Accessed Jan. 30, 2006.)
  For a summary of trends in time, see also: U.S. Department of Education. National Center for Education Statistics. 2005. *Trends in Undergraduate Education* (Issue Brief NCES 2005-012). <http://nces.ed.gov/pubs2005/2005012.pdf>. (Accessed Jan. 30, 2006.)
[3] U.S. Department of Education. National Center for Education Statistics. 2001. *The Condition of Education, 2001.* <http://nces.ed.gov/pubs2001/2001072.pdf>. (Accessed Jan. 30, 2006.)

Figure 7-3. Annual High School Dropout Rate, by Race and Hispanic Origin, 1970–2004

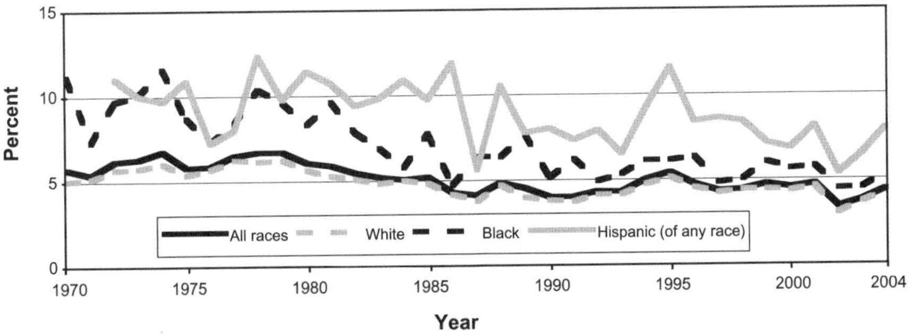

Year

Source: U.S. Census Bureau. Current Population Survey.
Note: Beginning in 2003, respondents could choose more than one race. The data from 2003 forward represent those respondents who chose only one race category.

Annual dropout rates do not show the cumulative effect that dropping out of school may have on the population. In 2000, 10 percent of 18- to 24-year-olds were not high school graduates and were not attending school. This figure was 26 percent for young persons living in households with a family income of under $20,000. In contrast, the rate was only 4 percent for children of families with incomes of $50,000 or more.

COLLEGE ENROLLMENT AND COMPOSITION OF STUDENT BODY

About 17.4 million people were enrolled in college in 2004. Of that group, 10.6 million were in the prime college age group of 18- to 24-years-old. Nearly half the population age 18 to 21 years was enrolled in college, and about a quarter of the 22- to 24-year-old age group was enrolled as well.

In 2000, over half (56 percent) of the 18- to 24-year-olds in the nation were either currently or formerly enrolled in college. This represents a very substantial increase over the 31 percent figure from 25 years earlier. The number of 18- and 19-year-olds enrolled in college in 2000 was only somewhat higher than

the comparable figure in 1975—about 3.5 million. However, total college enrollment has increased from 10.9 to 15.3 million during that period.

Older students make up the difference. The number of college students age 35 years and over has increased from 1.2 million to 2.5 million, and these older students now represent 16 percent of all enrollment. Reasons for this change include the drastic changes in the work force since 1975—including more women in the labor force, the large increase in the number of persons age 35 to 55 years, and the availability of community college programs.

Both Blacks and Hispanics represented larger proportions of the total college population in 2000 than they did in the early 1970s. Blacks had increased from about 8 percent to about 14 percent of all college students, and Hispanics had increased from about 3 percent to about 9 percent of all persons enrolled in college. Hispanics were still somewhat underrepresented in college, as compared to their proportions among the total population (about 13 percent), while Blacks had achieved parity between the two figures.

Figure 7-4. Selected Characteristics of College Students, 1974 and 2004

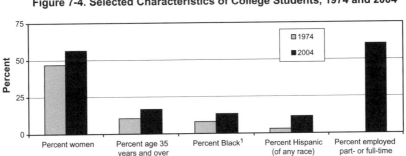

Student characteristic

Source: U.S. Census Bureau. Current Population Survey.
Note: Employment data for college students in 1974 are not available.
[1] The 2004 data are for respondents who identified themselves as Black alone.

Women, who represented about one-third of all college students in 1950, became the majority of all college students in the United States during the late 1970s. By 2000, they represented about 56 percent of total college enrollment.

GAUGING PROGRESS IN SCHOOL

One gauge of how well students are doing in school is the proportion of students enrolled below their modal grade. Modal grade is the year of school in which the largest proportion of students of a given age is enrolled. For example, the modal grade for 11-year-olds is the sixth grade. In 2004, 31 percent of students were enrolled below their modal grade by the time they were 15 to 17 years old. When these students were between 6 and 8 years old (in 1995), only 18 percent of the cohort was enrolled below its modal grade. Since 1971, the proportion of students enrolled below their modal grade has been increasing for each age group.[4] Currently, about 1 student in 10 is held back sometime between kindergarten and high school.

The National Assessment of Educational Progress (NAEP) provides comparisons of progress on standardized tests over time. These scores serve as additional gauges of progress in school and of how well our educational system is preparing students for an increasingly technical world of work. The average mathematics proficiency scores achieved by 17-year-old students between 1977 and 1999 indicated an increase in proficiency; however, a significant drop is shown in the 2004 statistics. Reading proficiency scores remained stable between 1977 and 1999, but also showed a slight drop in 2004.

The Scholastic Assessment Test (SAT) is used as an admission criterion for college and is taken by students who are contemplating college attendance. It is usually taken during the senior year of high school. The proportion of high school graduates who take the SAT has risen as the availability of college education has increased. The proportion of minorities who take the SAT has also increased. Even though the average scores of minorities (with the exception of the math scores of Asian-American students) were lower than those of Whites, the average mathematics and verbal scores in 2000 for all test-takers, regardless of race, were as high as they have been since the early 1970s (although not as high as they were in 1972). Average SAT scores have increased considerably for minority test-takers, while average scores for Whites have fallen a few percentage points in the past 20 years. Little change was evident in the 2000–2004 period.[5]

COMPUTER USAGE

Computer literacy is likely to influence the employment opportunities available to today's students and is likely to restrict the opportunities of those without computer skills. The proportion of households with a computer increased from about 8 percent in 1984 to 62 percent in 2003; over half of all home computers (55 percent) also have Internet access.

Over 75 percent of students age 3 to 17 years live in homes with computer access. The likelihood of having a computer increases both with the age of the student and with the family's income. Home computer access was nearly universal (94 percent) for children living in families with incomes of $75,000 or more in 2003. Younger children are

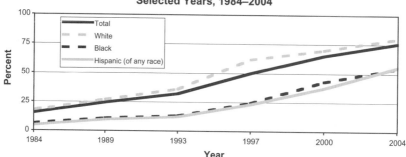

Figure 7-5. Percent of 3- to 17-Year-Olds with Computer Access at Home, Selected Years, 1984–2004

Source: U.S. Census Bureau. Current Population Survey.
Note: 2004 data are for race alone.

[4] U.S. Census Bureau. *School Enrollment.* <http://www.census.gov/population/www/socdemo/school.html>. (Accessed Jan. 30, 2006.) Note that many factors may be involved in students being one year behind the modal grade. They may have started school late (this happens more often for boys), or the state law may require students born after September 1 to enroll the following year.

[5] U.S. Department of Education. National Center for Education Statistics. 2005. *Digest of Education Statistics: 2004.* <http://nces.ed.gov/programs/digest/d04/>. (Accessed Jan. 30, 2006.)

most likely to use the computer to play games, while those age 10 years and over use it for school assignments and for email.[6]

EDUCATIONAL ATTAINMENT AND OUTCOMES

CHANGE AND CONTINUED VARIATION

It was not until the mid-1960s that at least half of the adult population of the United States had completed four or more years of high school. The increase in the average educational attainment of the U.S. population has continued to improve over the past several decades. Overall, 85 percent of the population 25 years of age and over was composed of high school graduates in 2004, and almost 28 percent were college graduates. (See Figure 7-6.)

The proportion of Black adults 18 years old and over who have completed at least high school is almost the same as that of Whites (80 percent to 85 percent), although the proportion completing college is still considerably lower than the proportion of White college graduates (16 percent for Blacks, 26 percent for Whites). Adults of Hispanic origin trail both their White and Black peers, with only 59 percent having graduated from high school and 10 percent having graduated from college in 2004. On the other hand, Asians and Pacific Islanders have much higher completion rates: 87 percent of this population 18 years old and over had completed high school in 2004, and 46 percent had completed college. All of these figures are somewhat higher if we look only at young adults between 25 and 34 years of age.

There is considerable variation among states, partly due to these racial and ethnic differences and to the varied racial composition of each state. Three states—Arkansas, Louisiana, and Texas—had high school graduation rates of less than 80 percent in 2004. In several states with relatively small minority populations—Utah, Nebraska, New Hampshire, Alaska, Minnesota, Wyoming, Vermont, and Montana—more than 90 percent of the adult population has graduated from high school or possesses an equivalent diploma.

In 2004, over one-half of the U.S. population age 25 years and over had attended college for at least one course, and more than one out of four adults had a bachelor's degree or more. A bachelor's degree typically takes four years of full-time study beyond the high school level, although there are some variations (in both directions) in the time needed for completion. Here again, there are considerable differences by state, with four states and the District of Columbia having more than 35 percent of their populations holding a bachelor's degree or more, while in West Virginia and Arkansas, less than 20 percent of residents have achieved this level of education. (See Figure 7-7.)

The economic returns from additional schooling are considerable. In 2003, persons 18 years old and over who had completed high school but no college had average earnings of about $27,900, while those with a bachelor's degree could expect earnings of about $51,200. Individuals with a doctorate had average earnings of $88,500. In addition, the average number of months with work activity tends to increase with educational attainment, indicating a lower likelihood of periodic unemployment.[7] Table 7-1 shows the distribution of educational levels in a variety of occupation groups.

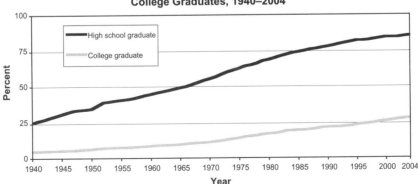

Figure 7-6. Percent of People 25 Years and Over Who Are High School and College Graduates, 1940–2004

Source: U.S. Census Bureau. Current Population Survey.

---

[6] Day, Jennifer Cheeseman, Alex Janus, and Jessica Davis. 2005. *Computer and Internet Use in the United States: 2003.* <http://www.census.gov/prod/2005pubs/p23-208.pdf>. (Accessed Jan. 30, 2006.)

[7] Newberger, Eric C., and Andrea Curry. 2000. *Educational Attainment in the United States: March 1999* (Current Population Report P20-528). <http://www.census.gov/prod/2000pubs/p20-528.pdf>. Also see its March 2004 update in tabular form at <http://www.census.gov/population/www/socdemo/educ-attn.html>. (Accessed Jan. 30, 2006.)

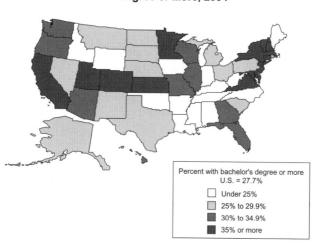

Figure 7-7. Percent of People 25 Years and Over with a Bachelor's Degree or More, 2004

Percent with bachelor's degree or more
U.S. = 27.7%

☐ Under 25%
25% to 29.9%
30% to 34.9%
35% or more

Source: U.S. Census Bureau. Current Population Survey.

ADULT LITERACY

One measure of educational outcomes is adult literacy. The 2003 National Assessment of Adult Literacy (NAAL) found little change in adults' ability to read and understand sentences, as compared to the previous study in 1992. However, quantitative literacy, or the ability to do tasks that involve computation, did improve significantly over that period. The NAAL defines literacy as "using printed and written information to function in society, to achieve one's goals, and to develop one's knowledge and potential."

The study measured literacy in three categories and categorized the scores in four levels for each. Prose literacy involves reading materials arranged in sentences and paragraphs, such as newspaper articles. Document literacy involves items such as bills, maps, bus schedules, and prescription labels. Quantitative activities require simple calculations such as filling out tax forms or balancing bank statements. The four levels are Proficient, Intermediate, Basic, and Below Basic, as well as a category for those who are non-literate in English.

Thirty million adults (age 16 and over), or about 13 percent of the population, have Below Basic prose literacy levels. Of these 30 million, 7 million exhibit a skill level so low that they may be defined as "non-literate." In addition, another 4 million people are non-literate in English, although they may have literacy in another language. Document literacy levels are equally poor, while quantitative literacy levels are even worse, with 22 percent of the population at the Below Basic level.

Table 7-1. Education and Occupation for Population 25 to 64 Years of Age, 2004

(Percent distribution.)

Occupation	Not a high school graduate	High school graduate only	Some college	Bachelor's degree	Master's degree or more
Total	7.1	29.4	30.3	21.9	11.2
Management, business, and financial occupations	1.8	19.1	29.4	34.8	14.9
Professional and related occupations	0.8	10.1	24.9	35.5	28.7
Service occupations	18.9	43.3	28.3	8.1	1.5
Sales and related occupations	7.4	35.9	31.7	21.0	4.0
Office and administrative occupations	3.4	40.1	40.6	13.7	2.3
Farming, forestry, and fishing occupations	39.2	42.5	16.7	1.7	0.0
Construction and extraction occupations	11.8	40.9	35.5	11.3	1.1
Installation, maintenance, and repair occupations	6.3	41.3	30.6	18.4	3.9
Production occupations	26.9	45.8	20.7	5.6	0.9
Transportation and material moving occupations	20.6	48.4	23.9	6.5	0.7

Source: U.S. Census Bureau. Current Population Survey.

What are the characteristics of these citizens with Below Basic prose literacy? They include more than half (55 percent) of the population that has not graduated from high school, 44 percent of those who never spoke English before starting school, and 39 percent of all Hispanics. Being elderly (65 years old or over), having disabilities, and being African American are also characteristics associated with a high risk of poor literacy skills. The consequences of low literacy include lower income and a higher risk of unemployment.[8]

TEACHERS: QUANTITY AND QUALITY

An estimated 3.3 million teachers were engaged in elementary and secondary classroom instruction in 2002; 3.0 million teach in public schools. The number of teachers increased by 20 percent during the 1990s, a growth rate slightly higher than the increase in the number of students. Consequently, the student/teacher ratio declined slightly, from 16.8 to 15.9 students per teacher in public schools in 2002. This figure represents a substantial improvement over the 27.4 ratio of students per teacher in 1955.

Virtually all public school teachers have bachelor's degrees, and 45 percent hold a master's degree.

This figure varies little by characteristics of the teachers or schools, except that older teachers are more likely to have earned the advanced degree. A large majority of teachers have participated in professional development activities, most often involving curriculum or performance standards, integration of educational technology into the curriculum, in-depth study of their subject area, or new teaching methods. The majority feel well-prepared to meet the demands of their teaching assignments.[9]

TEACHER SALARIES

Teacher salaries are one gauge of the public's willingness (or ability) to invest in education. Like the salaries of other professions, teacher salaries declined (in real terms) during the 1970s, and only returned to their 1972 levels in 1987. In 2003, the average salary for all public school teachers was $45,800. There is little difference between salary levels for elementary and secondary teachers, although salaries tend to increase with higher educational attainment levels and with seniority. Projections for teacher salaries in the coming decade show little change, with expected increases of only 2 percent (holding inflation constant).[10]

Figure 7-8. Current Expenditures Per Student for Public Elementary and Secondary Schools, 2002–2003

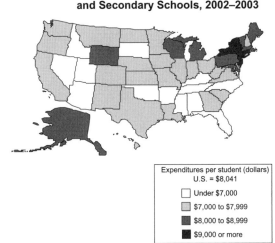

Expenditures per student (dollars)
U.S. = $8,041

☐ Under $7,000
▨ $7,000 to $7,999
▩ $8,000 to $8,999
■ $9,000 or more

Source: U.S. Department of Education. National Center for Education Statistics. Common Core of Data, 2002–2003.

[8] U.S. Department of Education. National Center for Education Statistics. 2005. *The 2003 National Assessment of Adult Literacy*. <http://nces.ed.gov/pubs2003/2003495rev.pdf>. (Accessed Feb. 9, 2006.)

[9] U.S. Department of Education. National Center for Education Statistics. 2001. *Teacher Preparation and Professional Development: 2000*. <http://nces.ed.gov/pubs2001/2001088.pdf>. (Accessed Jan. 30, 2006.)

[10] U.S. Department of Education. National Center for Education Statistics. 2005. Table 77—Estimated average annual salary of teachers in public elementary and secondary schools: Selected years, 1959–60 to 2002–03. *Digest of Education Statistics: 2004*. <http://nces.ed.gov/programs/digest/d04/tables/dt04_077.asp (Accessed Jan. 30, 2006.)

EXPENDITURES ON EDUCATION

Annual expenditures per student are another measure of the proportion of public investment devoted to each student's education. Actual current expenditures per elementary and secondary student increased from $600 to $9,000 between 1965 and 2002. Adjusted for inflation, this amount represents an increase of about 165 percent. However, most of this growth took place early in the period; the inflation-adjusted increase between 1990 and 2002 was only 23 percent.

There are wide variations in per student expenditures by state (see Figure 7-8). In 2002–2003, New Jersey led the nation with $12,600 annual current expenditures per student, followed by New York at $12,000. At the other end of the scale, Utah's figure is only $4,800, followed by Mississippi at $5,800. Nationally, about 62 percent of expenditures go directly to instruction, with 34 percent spent on support services and 4 percent on other non-instruction activity. These proportions change little with varying levels of overall expenditures.

FOR FURTHER INFORMATION SEE:

Day, Jennifer Cheeseman, and Kristine Witkowski. 1999. *Financing the Future: Postsecondary Students, Costs, and Financial Aid: 1993–94* (Current Population Report P70-60). <http://www.sipp.census.gov/sipp/p70s/p70-60.pdf>. (Accessed Jan. 30, 2006.)

Shin, Hyon B. 2005. *School Enrollment in the United States—Social and Economic Characteristics of Students: October 2003* (Current Population Report P20-554). <http://www.census.gov/prod/2005pubs/p20-554.pdf>. Updated tables are available at <http://www.census.gov/population/www/socdemo/school.html>. (Accessed Jan. 30, 2006.)

Stoops, Nicole. 2004. *Educational Attainment in the United States: 2003.* <http://www.census.gov/prod/2004pubs/p20-550.pdf>. Updated tables with 2004 data are available at <http://www.census.gov/population/www/socdemo/educ-attn.html>. (Accessed Jan. 30, 2006.)

U.S. Department of Education. National Center for Education Statistics. 2005. *Digest of Education Statistics: 2004.* <http://nces.ed.gov/programs/digest/d04/>. (Accessed Jan. 30, 2006.)

U.S. Department of Education. National Center for Education Statistics. 2001. *The Condition of Education, 2001.* <http://nces.ed.gov/pubs2001/2001072.pdf>. (Accessed Jan. 30, 2006.)

U.S. Department of Education. National Center for Education Statistics. 2004. *Undergraduate Enrollments in Academic, Career, and Vocational Education* (Issue Brief NCES 2004-108). <http://nces.ed.gov/pubs2004/2004018.pdf>. (Accessed Jan. 30, 2006.)

For a summary of trends over time, see: U.S. Department of Education. National Center for Education Statistics. 2005. *Trends in Undergraduate Education* (Issue Brief NCES 2005-012). <http://nces.ed.gov/pubs2005/2005012.pdf>. (Accessed Jan. 30, 2006.)

WEB SITES:

U.S. Census Bureau. <http://www.census.gov>.

U.S. Department of Education. National Center for Education Statistics. <http://nces.ed.gov>.

Chapter 8
Crime and Criminal Justice

INTRODUCTION

Knowing about "crime" is difficult. There are serious questions concerning the understanding, definition, and measurement of this issue. In 1967, the President's Commission on Law Enforcement and Administration of Justice made the following observation: "A skid-row drunk lying in a gutter is a crime. So is the killing of an unfaithful wife. A Cosa Nostra conspiracy to bribe public officials is crime. So is a strong-arm robbery by a 15-year-old boy ... These crimes can no more be linked together for purposes of analysis than can measles and schizophrenia, or lung cancer and a broken ankle ... Thinking of 'crime' as a whole is futile."[1] The irony in the above statement further illustrates the difficulty in analyzing crime: since that statement was written, many jurisdictions have decriminalized public drunkenness, making the commission's first example no longer relevant.

Crime has more than just a temporal dimension. It also has a spatial dimension. For example, throughout the early decades of the twentieth century, the use of marijuana, cocaine, and opium and its derivatives became illegal in the United States. However, in some countries, the use of these substances is not illegal, while in other countries, drug use is more severely punished than it is in the United States.

The measurement problem is equally vexing, as crimes such as embezzlement and drug possession cannot be identified until the perpetrator is caught. Some others cannot ever be adequately categorized. For example, if a retail establishment discovers less inventory than expected while conducting a routine check, there is no way to know whether this the result of shoplifting, employee theft, a simple error, or some other circumstance.

Laying these problems aside, this chapter will address how people understand and perceive crime, the resulting criminal justice process, and the outcomes of that process.

THE GREAT PARADOX

Since 1990, the United States has experienced both a sharply declining crime rate and an exploding prison population. After reaching a high of almost 5,900 in 1991, the crime index declined to 4,160 in 2001, with a further decline shown in preliminary data for 2002. The crime index, which represents the number of crimes per 100,000 population, experienced a decline of almost 30 percent over the 10-year period. In 2004, the crime index was discontinued.[2] However, the decrease in violent crime continued into the first half of 2005, with a decline of half of one percent from 2004; property crimes decreased by 2.8 percent during the same period.

In contrast, the number of prisoners in federal and state prisons increased from 0.8 million in 1990 to almost 1.5 million in 2000, an increase of about 88 percent. However, the annual growth rate of the incarcerated population had slowed to 1.9 percent by 2004, down from an average annual rate of 3.5 percent in 1995. Expenditures for criminal justice activities also increased significantly, reaching $57 billion in 2001.

The explanation for this paradox lies in the country's demographics. Baby boomers, the largest cohort of population, were born between 1946 and 1964. In 2006, they are between 42 and 60 years old. Following the baby boom, the birth rate dropped sharply; children born in the late 1960s and 1970s (also known as Generation X) comprise a much smaller cohort, in terms of population size, than the baby boomers. As shown later in this chapter, most crimes are committed by people between the ages of 18 and 34 years. There are now significantly fewer people in this age range, and thus fewer people to commit crimes. Meanwhile, the nation has been developing at a rapid clip. This demographic pattern has led to the sharp drop in the number of crimes.

---

[1] President's Commission on Law Enforcement and the Administration of Justice. 1967. *The Challenge of Crime in a Free Society*. (Washington, DC: U.S. Government Printing Office.)

[2] An item in "Frequently Asked Questions" section of the FBI Web site states, "In June, 2004, the CJIS Advisory Policy Board (APB) approved discontinuing the use of the Crime Index in the UCR Program and its publications. The CJIS APB recommended that the FBI publish a violent crime total and a property crime total until a more viable index is developed. In recent years, the Crime Index has not been a true indicator of the degree of criminality of a locality. The Crime Index was calculated by adding the totals of seven Part I crimes. (The Modified Crime Index included arson.) Currently, larceny-thefts account for almost 60 percent of the total crimes reported. Consequently, the volume of larcenies overshadows more serious but less frequently committed crimes." See <http://www.fbi.gov/ucr/ucrquest.htm>. (Accessed Feb. 28, 2006.)

At the same time, convicted criminals from the large baby boomer population occupy today's prisons and jails, and there are many of them. These criminals account for the high numbers in the corrections population. In 2004, over 7 million people were in the purview of the corrections system (either in jail, in prison, or on parole). This amounted to 2.4 percent, or 1 in 42, of all U.S. residents. However, the incarceration rate—the number of people coming into the corrections system—finally leveled off in 2002, after dramatic increases throughout the 1980s and 1990s.[3]

Public concern about crime has increased dramatically, despite the falling crime rate. In a series of surveys conducted by the Gallup Organization, people were asked what they considered to be the most important problem facing the country. The "crime; violence" category was quite low from 1988 until 1991. It began to rise in 1992, and peaked at 52 percent in 1994. It then began to drop, returning to its low level (1 percent) by March 2002. However, it is important to note that respondents were asked to name the "most important problem facing this country today." Thus, the rate at which crime was mentioned was partly dependent on the importance of other problems to respondents. For example, "the economy" ranked high in the early 1990s, but dropped to a much lower level during the prosperous latter half of the decade before rising again in 2002 (due to the recession in 2001). Economic issues were cited by 14 percent of respondents in late 2005. The Iraq War, which was not an issue before 2002, was listed by 22 percent of respondents in 2005.[4]

CRIME AND VICTIMS

In *Webster's New Universal Unabridged Dictionary*, crime is defined as "an action or an instance of negligence … that is legally prohibited." There are many kinds of crime, including commercial crime, industrial crime, other white-collar crime, and common crime. While commercial crime may pose a heavy cost to society, such as from the savings and loan scandals of the 1980s or from the various industrial crimes involving pollution, commercial and industrial crimes are not subject to simple measurement, nor do they come to mind when most people think of crime. In the United States, most people think of crime as those offenses regularly reported by the FBI in its Uniform Crime Reports (UCR).

The UCR divides crimes into two major categories: violent crimes (or crimes against persons) and property crimes. Violent crimes include murder and nonnegligent manslaughter, forcible rape, robbery, and aggravated assault. Property crimes include burglary, larceny-theft, motor vehicle theft, and arson. For the purposes of this chapter, property crimes will be referred to as serious crimes. The UCR develops its data by collecting information taken from crimes reported to law enforcement agencies and provided to the FBI by almost every police agency in the country.

The National Crime Victimization Survey (NCVS), conducted by the Bureau of Justice Statistics, is a survey of a national sample of households in which information about crime victimization was obtained for each household member 12 years of age and

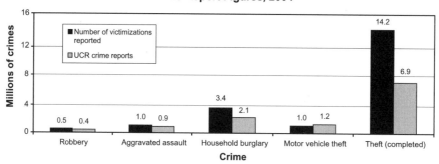

Figure 8-1. Comparison of National Crime Victimization Survey Estimates and Uniform Crime Report Figures, 2004

Source: Bureau of Justice Statistics. *Criminal Victimization in the United States, 2004.*
For UCR: Federal Bureau of Investigation. *Crime in the United States, 2004.*

[3] U.S. Department of Justice. Bureau of Justice Statistics. <http://www.ojp.usdoj.gov/bjs/correct.htm>. (Accessed Mar. 16, 2006.)

[4] Gallup Organization. *The Gallup Report* (several reports between 1988 and 2002). 2005 data were obtained from <http://poll.gallup.com/content/default.aspx?ci=14338>. (Accessed Feb. 28, 2006.)

over. Crimes such as household burglary, motor vehicle theft, and theft for which no victim was present are called property crimes by NCVS, while crimes occurring in the presence of the victim are called personal crimes.

Although neither the UCR nor the NCVS provides a perfect measurement of crime in the United States, they complement each other's findings. As stated by the U.S. Department of Justice, "The UCR Program's primary objective is to provide a reliable set of criminal justice statistics for law enforcement administration, operation, and management, as well as to indicate fluctuations in the level of crime in America. The NCVS was established to obtain and provide previously unavailable information about victims, offenders, and crime (including crime not reported to the police)."[5]

While the two programs employ different methodologies, they measure a similar subset of serious crimes. For example, because the UCR receives reports from almost all police agencies, it can provide good information on the geographic distribution of crime. The NCVS, which is based on a national sample, does not collect data for small geographic areas. However, it does provide better information

on the true incidence of crime, since many crimes are not reported to the police. Every effort is made to define criminal events in the same way for both of these surveys. The major differences are that the NCVS does not include murder and nonnegligent manslaughter, since there is no living victim to interview, and that the NCVS includes simple assault in its count of violent crimes, while the UCR does not.

Figure 8-1 shows the number of crimes reported by the FBI via the UCR, as compared to those reported by the Bureau of Justice Statistics via the NCVS.[6] There are a number of hypotheses explaining the differences, but one stands out: when the victim feels that the police are powerless, or that it is not worth the effort to report the crime, the crime will not be reported. This is probably why reports of theft, for example, differ so greatly between the two sources. If the victim feels that there is a chance for recovery by the police, or the item is covered by insurance that would require a police report for the insurance claim to go through (such as the theft of a motor vehicle), the crime is much more likely to be reported. According to 2004 NCVS data, 50 percent all of violent crimes and 39 percent of all property crimes were reported to police, with the highest reporting figures for aggravated assault with an

Figure 8-2. Violent Crime Rates, 2004

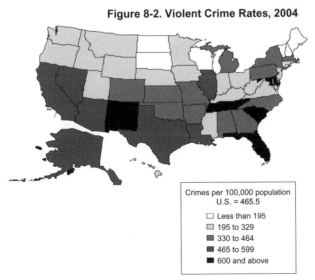

Crimes per 100,000 population
U.S. = 465.5

☐ Less than 195
◻ 195 to 329
▨ 330 to 464
▩ 465 to 599
■ 600 and above

Source: Federal Bureau of Investigation. *Crime in the United States, 2004.*

---

[5] U.S. Department of Justice. Federal Bureau of Investigation. *Frequently Asked Questions about Uniform Crime Reports.* <http://www.fbi.gov/ucr/ucrquest.htm>. (Accessed Mar. 16, 2006.)

[6] It is important to note that, while the great majority of places are covered, the UCRs do not include data for every place in the nation. Missing data are estimated for national and regional summaries. They are often omitted in state and lower-level data presentation.

Table 8-1. Estimated Rate of Personal Victimization, 2004

(Rate per 1,000 persons age 12 years and over, except where noted.)

Characteristic	All personal crimes	Violent crimes						Personal theft	Property crimes (per 1,000 households)		
		Total	Rape/sexual assault	Robbery	Assault				Household burglary	Motor vehicle theft	Theft
					Total	Aggravated	Simple				
ALL PERSONS	22.5	21.4	0.9	2.1	18.5	4.3	14.2	161.1	29.6	8.8	122.8
Sex											
Male	. . .	25.0	0.1	2.9	22.1	5.8	16.3	1.0	. . .	. . .	. . .
Female	. . .	18.1	1.6	1.3	15.1	2.8	12.3	0.9	. . .	. . .	. . .
Age											
12–15 years	. . .	49.7	2.2	3.8	43.6	6.2	37.5	2.1	. . .	. . .	. . .
16–19 years	. . .	45.9	2.5	4.8	38.6	11.3	27.2	3.3	. . .	. . .	. . .
20–24 years	. . .	43.0	2.5	3.1	37.4	9.4	28.0	0.7	. . .	. . .	. . .
25–34 years	. . .	23.7	0.7	2.4	20.6	4.8	15.8	0.6	. . .	. . .	. . .
35–49 years	. . .	17.9	0.5	2.1	15.2	3.9	11.4	0.7	. . .	. . .	. . .
50–64 years	. . .	11.0	0.3	1.1	9.6	1.9	7.8	0.5	. . .	. . .	. . .
65 years and over	. . .	2.1	0.1	0.3	1.8	0.5	1.3	0.8	. . .	. . .	. . .
Race											
White	. . .	21.0	0.8	1.8	18.4	4.0	14.4	0.8	. . .	. . .	. . .
Black	. . .	26.0	1.7	3.7	20.7	6.7	13.9	1.5	. . .	. . .	. . .
Other	. . .	12.7	0.0	2.6	10.1	1.8	8.3	1.0	. . .	. . .	. . .
Ethnicity											
Hispanic	. . .	18.2	0.6	2.8	14.9	3.2	11.7	0.7	. . .	. . .	. . .
Non-Hispanic	. . .	21.9	0.9	2.0	19.1	4.4	14.6	1.0	. . .	. . .	. . .
Household Income											
Less than $7,500	. . .	38.4	2.4	29.5	29.5	7.3	22.3	3.1	59.3	4.9	132.8
$7,500–$14,999	. . .	39.0	0.4	4.4	34.2	7.8	26.5	1.1	38.5	9.7	133.3
$15,000–$24,999	. . .	24.4	1.6	2.1	20.7	5.6	15.0	0.7	40.1	8.7	119.0
$25,000–$34,999	. . .	22.1	0.6	2.1	19.4	5.0	14.3	0.6	27.6	11.1	130.6
$35,000–$49,999	. . .	21.6	0.9	1.4	19.4	4.3	15.1	1.4	33.4	9.3	133.6
$50,000–$74,999	. . .	22.1	0.6	1.3	20.3	4.9	15.4	0.8	21.8	9.0	136.2
$75,000 or more	. . .	17.0	0.6	1.3	15.1	2.5	12.6	1.1	23.9	7.4	145.1

Source: Bureau of Justice Statistics. *Criminal Victimization in United States, 2004.*

. . . = Not available.

injury, robbery with an injury, and motor vehicle theft. The lowest reporting levels were for theft with a small monetary value and sexual assaults (including rape). These figures represent an improvement over the 1993 levels.[7]

VICTIMIZATION

A major purpose of the NCVS is to identify and characterize victims of crime. For example, the most likely victim of violent crime, or a crime in which the victim and the offender are in contact at the time of the criminal event, is male, 16 to 19 years old, Black, and with a household income of under $15,000. (See Table 8-1.) Higher-income households are more likely to fall victim to property crime, but lower-income households are still more likely to be victims of burglary, the most invasive of the property crimes. The reason that very low income households (under $7,500) have a lower rate of motor vehicle theft is that these households are less likely to own cars.

CRIME DISTRIBUTION

Crime is not distributed evenly around the country. For example, Figure 8-2 shows that states such as California have violent crime rates well above the average for the country as a whole. A few states, such as South Carolina and Maryland, have inexplicably high crime rates. There is no geographic pattern.

ARRESTS

Table 8-2 shows the number of arrests in the United States in 2004 for a variety of offenses, as well as the incidence rate of arrests compared to the total population. In addition to showing the types of offenses reflected in the Uniform Crime Reports, this table shows all of the other offenses for which arrests were made, except for traffic offenses. ("Driving under the influence" is not considered a simple traffic offense and is therefore included on the list of offenses.) The total of drug abuse violations is included here; these offenses make up the single largest category of arrests. The figure for drug abuse violations includes arrests for both drug possession and drug trafficking.

Crime is largely a young person's prerogative. Figure 8-3 shows arrest rate per 100,000 population for selected age groups. It is clear that teenagers are the most likely to be commit crimes and to be arrested. Half or more of all arrests for arson and vandalism involve persons under 21 years old.

---

[7] U.S. Department of Justice. Bureau of Justice Statistics. 2005. *Criminal Victimization in the United States, 2004* (NCJ210674). <http://www.ojp.usdoj.gov/bjs/pub/pdf/cv04.pdf>. (Accessed Mar. 16, 2006.)

Figure 8-3. Proportion of Arrests, by Age and Offense, 2004

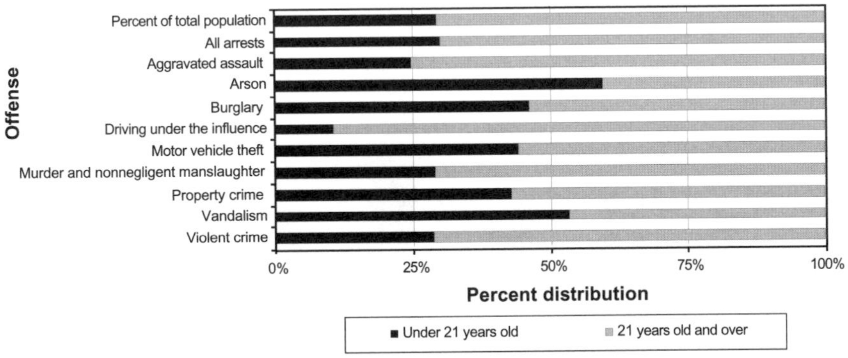

Source: Federal Bureau of Investigation. *Crime in the United States, 2004.*

DOES CRIME PAY?

The likelihood that an arrest will be made in a crime varies by the type of offense. Figure 8-4 shows the clearance rates for index crimes in 2004. "To clear" roughly equals "to solve," and indicates that the case was turned over to the courts for prosecution. This category also includes situations in which the offender cannot be prosecuted because of death, the victim's refusal to cooperate, or another reason. These data demonstrate that many crimes in the United States remain unsolved. In 2004, the national clearance rate for crime index crimes was 46 percent.

Overall, clearance rates for violent crimes are higher than those for property crimes. Although the clearance rate for murder is higher than any other crime, over one-third of murders still go unsolved. Robbery and the property crimes—burglary, larceny, and motor vehicle theft—show extremely low clearance rates. As stated by the FBI, "violent crimes often undergo a more vigorous investigative effort than crimes against property. Additionally, victims and/or witnesses often identify the perpetrators."[8]

CONVICTIONS AND SENTENCES

The criminal justice system in the United States divides the responsibility for judicial processing and corrections between state and local jurisdictions and the federal government. Many offenses are under federal jurisdiction, such as serious crimes that take place on federal property, or those related to national issues, such as violations of antitrust or customs laws. Other crimes have been turned into

Table 8-2. Number of Arrests and Arrest Rate, by Type of Offense, 2004

(Number, rate of arrests per 100,000 inhabitants.)

Offense charged	Number	Rate
Total [1]	10 044 735	4 777.2
Murder and nonnegligent manslaughter	9 998	4.8
Forcible rape	18 693	8.9
Robbery	79 336	37.7
Aggravated assault	316 636	150.6
Burglary	211 548	100.6
Larceny-theft	866 217	412.0
Motor vehicle theft	105 746	50.3
Arson	11 121	5.3
Violent crime [2]	424 663	202.0
Property crime [3]	1 194 632	568.2
Other assaults	923 089	439.0
Forgery and counterfeiting	86 122	41.0
Fraud	199 974	95.1
Embezzlement	12 616	6.0
Stolen property	93 344	44.4
Vandalism	199 058	94.7
Weapons	127 546	60.7
Prostitution and commercialized vice	64 786	30.8
Sex offenses (except forcible rape and prostitution)	65 311	31.1
Drug abuse violations	1 251 059	595.0
Gambling	7 746	3.7
Offenses against the family and children ...	88 738	42.2
Driving under the influence	1 014 064	482.3
Liquor laws	439 648	209.1
Drunkenness	399 077	189.8
Disorderly conduct	494 217	235.0
Vagrancy	25 667	12.2
All other offenses (except traffic)	2 747 535	1 306.7
Suspicion	2 521	1.2
Curfew and loitering law violations	99 746	47.4
Runaways	86 097	40.9

Source: U.S. Department of Justice. Federal Bureau of Investigation. *Crime in the United States, 2004.*

[1]Does not include suspicion.
[2]Violent crimes are offenses of murder and nonnegligent manslaughter, forcible rape, robbery, and aggravated assault.
[3]Property crimes are offenses of burglary, larceny-theft, motor vehicle theft, and arson.

[8] U.S. Department of Justice. Federal Bureau of Investigation. *Crime in the United States, 2001* (p. 220). <http://www.fbi.gov/ucr/01cius.htm>. (Accessed Mar. 16, 2006.)

Figure 8-4. Offenses Cleared by Arrest, 2004

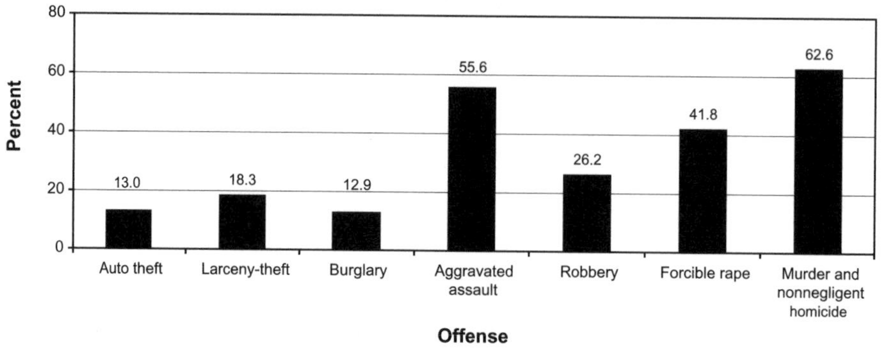

Auto theft 13.0 · Larceny-theft 18.3 · Burglary 12.9 · Aggravated assault 55.6 · Robbery 26.2 · Forcible rape 41.8 · Murder and nonnegligent homicide 62.6

Source: Federal Bureau of Investigation. *Crime in the United States, 2004.*

federal crimes through legislation; the drug laws are representative of this process. Both state governments and the federal government have an interest in many of the same offenses. In general, when the state and federal interests are the same, the federal government has the jurisdictional option in individual cases.

As shown in Figure 8-5, sentences imposed in U.S. district courts vary by the nature of the offense. As expected, the longest sentences are imposed for kidnapping, murder, robbery, and assault, which average about five years. Property offense sentences are much shorter, averaging about two years. Drug offenses (even for simple possession) receive much longer sentences. Racketeering and extortion are also subject to severe penalties. The length of imposed sentences has shortened somewhat in recent years, perhaps in response to the overcrowding in prisons. Many convicted criminals

also serve a much shorter sentence than the one originally imposed by the court.

Although a significant number of crimes involve the federal system, crime is still primarily a state problem. Almost all felony convictions take place in state courts. Sentencing patterns differ considerably between state and federal courts. Overall, an offender is more likely to be sentenced to prison in the federal system (72 percent in federal court versus 68 percent in state court). Average prison sentences imposed by the federal court are also longer than those imposed by state courts for most offenses. For violent offenses, the state figure is higher (60 months compared to 36 months). The fact that almost all murder cases are tried in state courts accounts for the higher average. For drug trafficking, the average federal sentence is 57 months, versus 24 months in state courts. (See Figure 8-5.)

Figure 8-5. Median Months of Incarceration Imposed by U.S. District Courts and State Courts, 2002

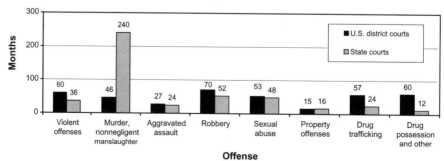

Source: Bureau of Justice Statistics. *Compendium of Federal Justice Statistics, 2002; Felony Sentences in State Courts, 2002.*

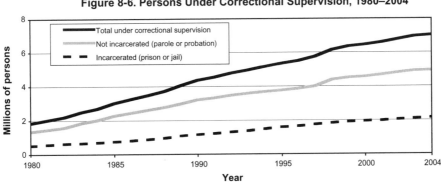

Figure 8-6. Persons Under Correctional Supervision, 1980–2004

Source: Bureau of Justice Statistics. Correctional Surveys.

Most of the offenders convicted in state courts in 2002 (83 percent) were male. For violent offenses, the percentage increased to 89 percent. The overall racial division was 60 percent White and 37 percent Black. Among offenders convicted of violent crimes, 39 percent were Black, although rapists were more likely to be White. Over two-thirds of convictions were of persons between 21 and 39 years of age.[9]

CORRECTIONS

The corrections system in the United States consists principally of prisons, jails, probation, and parole. Generally, prisons are institutions designed to house convicted felons; they are usually managed by the federal or state governments. Jails are usually locally run (by cities and counties), and are designed to house criminals with sentences of a year or less, persons being held while awaiting trial, and others in temporary or short-term incarceration situations. In recent years, jails have also been used to house overflow from the overcrowded prison system.

Parole is the process by which prison inmates are released before their full sentences are completed. The inmate remains under the supervision of the correctional system, usually until his or her original sentence is completed. Probation, either supervised or unsupervised, is generally a sentence given in lieu of either prison or jail. However, there are occasions (usually at a judge's discretion) in

which the offender is given a combination of incarceration and probation.

The number of adults in the custody of state or federal prisons or local jails increased sharply between 1980 and 2000, before rising more slowly through 2004. (See Figure 8-6.) Another measure is the incarceration rate (the number of persons incarcerated per 100,000 population); this figure has increased by 250 percent since 1980. A similar increase occurred in the non-incarcerated population, or those on probation or parole. Tougher crime-fighting policies and longer sentences have exacerbated this growth. The growth in the prison population and the commensurate growth in the number of prisons has constituted a new growth industry. Since 1990, the number of jails and prisons has increased significantly, with cities and towns competing for new facilities with their eyes on the number of jobs that would be generated.

The increase in the prison population has had a profound impact on many neighborhoods, especially in the inner cities. Figure 8-7 shows the incarceration rate per 100,000 by race, ethnicity, and sex. In 2004, Black males were more than 8 times as likely to be incarcerated as White non-Hispanic males; the rate for Hispanic men was about triple that for White men. Incarceration rates for women were much lower, but maintained the same general ratios.

9 U.S. Department of Justice. Bureau of Justice Statistics. 2004. *Felony Sentences in State Courts, 2002* (NCJ report 203916). <http://www.ojp.usdoj.gov/bjs/pub/pdf/fssc02.pdf>. (Accessed Mar. 15, 2006.)

In 2001, the rising prison population trend began to change. "It appears that the state prison population has reached some stability," said Allen Beck, a statistician with the Bureau of Justice Statistics.[10] The growth rate for 2001 was 1.6 percent, the lowest in three decades. The growth rate has continued to be low in the years since. With lower crime rates, steady rates of parole violation, and the movement of the baby bust (or Generation X) cohort through the prime years of criminal activity, the incarcerated prison population could actually decrease in the near future.

EXPENDITURES

Expenditures in all parts of the criminal justice system and at all levels of government have been rising steadily. In 2003, $185.5 billion was expended for criminal justice activities, more than quadruple the amount spent in 1982 (not adjusted for inflation). Corrections accounted for the biggest share of the increase, due to the burgeoning prison population and number of facilities described above. In 2003, the United States spent $646 per capita to maintain the criminal justice system. Of this, $289 went to police protection, $237 to corrections, and the balance to other legal and judicial functions. Local governments had the primary responsibility and expenditure of funds for police protection, while state governments were responsible for most of the corrections funding. Judicial and legal functions were about evenly divided between state and local

governments, with the federal government spending a smaller amount.[11]

SENTENCING POLICIES

During the 1990s, Congress and many state governments passed mandatory sentencing and "truth in sentencing" laws that, in effect, increased the amount of time convicted offenders would remain incarcerated, thus decreasing the number of cells available at any given time. The public also tends to support the use of mandatory sentences. In a 2004 survey of police chiefs about drug offenses, conducted by the Police Foundation, only 6 percent thought the mandatory sentencing strategy was "very effective," while another 16 percent thought that it was "fairly effective." (See Table 8-3.)

It appears that there is a conflict between various American value systems. On one hand, there is the desire to suppress crime and punish criminals. On the other, there is the desire to be fair to first offenders and others who appear to want to work within the system. Although various professionals do not feel that strategies such as mandatory sentences are effective, the public seems to clamor for something to be done. The political establishment appears to be listening, as more and more of these types of laws are being enacted at both the state and federal level. Only time will tell if this conflict worsens or resolves itself.

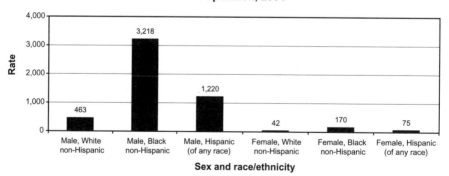

Figure 8-7. Sentenced Prisoners Under State or Federal Jurisdiction Per 100,000 Population, 2004

Source: Bureau of Justice Statistics. *Prisoners in 2004.*

---

[10] Quoted in the *Detroit Free Press*, April 11, 2002.

[11] U.S. Department of Justice. Bureau of Justice Statistics. *Justice Expenditure and Employment Extracts, 2003.* <http://www.ojp.usdoj.gov/bjs/pub/sheets/cjee03.zip>. (Accessed Mar. 15, 2006.)

Figure 8-8. Percent Change in Criminal Justice Expenditures Activity, 1982–2001

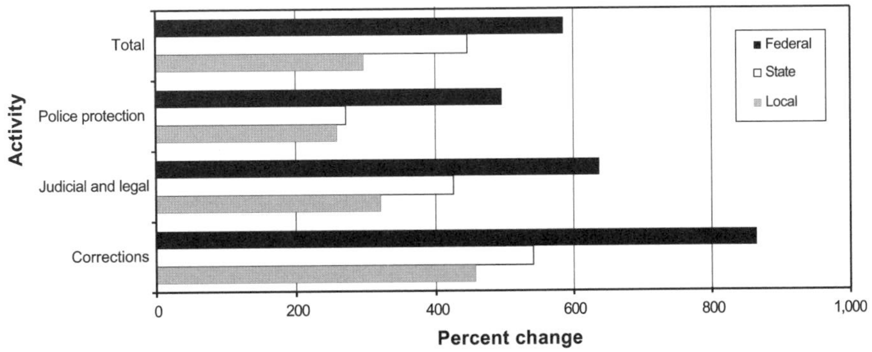

Source: Bureau of Justice Statistics. *Justice Expenditures and Employment in the United States, 2001.*

A review of current sentencing guidelines suggests that the record is mixed. As the new decade and century have begun, several new issues have arisen, including the core principles on which guidelines have been based and their compatibility with a new concept called "restorative justice."[12] This idea promotes reparation rather than retribution, with the community deciding the appropriate punishment for the crime. Of course, it would only apply to less serious crimes and non-repeat offenders. Restorative justice is sharply different from previous practices, emphasizing a subjective understanding of the crime and the circumstances surrounding it. Disproportionate sentences for what is objectively the same crime are acceptable. In the current sentencing guidelines atmosphere, the approach is top down rather than bottom up. It appears that a hybrid approach needs to be developed.

Another issue which has received a great deal of attention is the combination of mandatory minimum sentences and truth in sentencing (TIS). The latter refers to attempts to reduce the disparity between the sentences imposed by courts and the actual time that the offenders serve in prison. The 1994 Violent Crime Control and Law Enforcement Act included a provision that provided grants to states, enabling them to increase their prison capacity if they imposed TIS requirements on violent offenders, who would then be required to serve at least 85 percent of their sentences in prisons. A recent examination of the effects of this legislation concluded that these laws had little effect, as states were already moving in the direction of longer prison terms.[13] TIS guidelines conflict with the concept of restorative justice, and compromise is thus required between these two concepts.

Table 8-3. Survey of U.S. Police Chiefs' Attitudes Toward the Effectiveness of Mandatory Minimum Sentences for Drug Possession, by Size of Community, 2004

Question: "From your perspective, how effective have mandatory minimum sentences for drug possession been in reducing drug trafficking in your community—very effective, fairly effective, somewhat effective, or not really the answer to the problem in your community?"

(Percent.)

Responses	All police chiefs	Large cities	Medium communities	Small towns
Very effective	6	5	7	6
Fairly effective	16	23	18	12
Only somewhat effective	38	30	43	39
Not really the answer	29	37	26	27
Don't have a mandatory minimum sentencing [1]	8	3	5	11
Not sure	3	2	1	5

Source: Police Foundation. 2004. *Drugs and Crime Across America: Police Chiefs Speak Out.* (Washington, DC: Police Foundation and Drug Strategies.)

[1] Response volunteered.

---

[12] Lubitz, Robin L., and Thomas W. Ross. *Sentencing & Corrections: Issues for the 21st Century* (Papers from the Executive Sessions on Sentencing and Corrections, No. 10). (June 2001.) <http://www.ncjrs.gov/pdffiles1/nij/186480.pdf>. (Accessed Mar. 16, 2006.)

[13] Rosich, Katherine J., and Kamala Mallik Kane. 2005. Truth in sentencing and state sentencing practices. *NIJ Journal* 252 (July 2005).

FOR FURTHER INFORMATION SEE:

U.S. Department of Justice. Bureau of Justice Statistics. *Criminal Victimization in the United States.*
<http://www.ojp.usdoj.gov/bjs/abstract/cv04.htm>. (Accessed Mar. 16, 2006.)

U.S. Department of Justice. Bureau of Justice Statistics. *Sourcebook of Criminal Justice Statistics.*
<http://www.albany.edu/sourcebook>. (Accessed Mar. 16, 2006.)

U.S. Department of Justice. Federal Bureau of Investigation. *Uniform Crime Reports.*
<http://www.fbi.gov/ucr/ucr.htm#cius>. (Accessed Mar. 16, 2006.)

WEB SITES:

U.S. Department of Justice. Bureau of Justice Statistics. <http://www.ojp.usdoj.gov/bjs/>. (Accessed Mar. 16, 2006.)
BJS publishes a series of bulletins that cover a wide variety of topics in criminal justice. These include annual
updates of the types of data presented in this chapter.

U.S. Department of Justice. Federal Bureau of Investigation. <http://www.fbi.gov>. (Accessed Mar. 16, 2006.)

U.S. Department of Justice. Federal Bureau of Prisons. <http://www.bop.gov>. (Accessed Mar. 16, 2006.)

University of Michigan. Inter-University Consortium for Political and Social Research (ICPSR).
<http://www.icpsr.umich.edu/index.html>. (Accessed Mar. 16, 2006.)

Chapter 9
Health

HEALTHY PEOPLE

Is the U.S. population more or less healthy today than it was a few decades ago? The population is living longer, with the average life expectancy having increased to nearly 78 years in 2003—an increase of 5 years since 1970. (See Chapter 1 for more information.) Yet, there are health concerns today that were virtually nonexistent 30 years ago, such as HIV/AIDS, SARS, West Nile virus, and avian influenza. There is also a current emphasis on risk factors that were only peripheral concerns a few decades ago, such as fat intake, obesity, and smoking.

The U.S. Department of Health and Human Services (HHS) has developed an initiative entitled Healthy People 2010, with the goals of "increasing the span of healthy life for all Americans, decreasing health disparities among Americans, and achieving access to preventive services for all Americans." This initiative has defined the term "health-related quality of life," which reflects a "personal sense of physical and mental health, and the ability to react to factors in the physical and social environments." This leads to the definition of "years of healthy life," reflecting the "time spent in less than optimal health because of chronic or acute limitations." In these terms, healthy life expectancy has not risen nearly as quickly as overall life expectancy, meaning that more time at the end of life is spent in less than optimal health conditions.

MORTALITY

When changes in age composition are taken into account (to determine the age-adjusted death rate), death rates for the United States are shown to have continued to decline over the past 25 years for the population as a whole. The crude death rate in 2003—831 deaths per 100,000 population—is considerably below the 1970 rate of 945 deaths per 100,000 population. The infant mortality rate in the United States, 6.9 per 1,000 live births in 2003, was one of the lowest in the world.

Cause of death varies considerably by age. Since about three out of four deaths in the United States each year occur for persons over 65 years old, their causes of death predominate when the causes are not disaggregated by age. This makes the major causes of death diseases of the heart, at 29 percent of deaths; malignant neoplasms (various forms of cancer), at 23 percent of deaths; cerebrovascular diseases (stroke), at 7 percent of deaths; chronic lower respiratory diseases (such as emphysema), at 5 percent of deaths; and accidents, at 4 percent of deaths. However, accidents are the leading cause of death for persons under 45 years old. (See Figure 9-1.) Some causes of death are among the top 10 causes for each age group, including accidents, cancer, diseases of the heart, and cerebrovascular diseases. Other diseases, such as diabetes, HIV, or congenital anomalies, are significant causes of death for specific age groups.

Figure 9-1. Leading Causes of Death, by Age, 2003

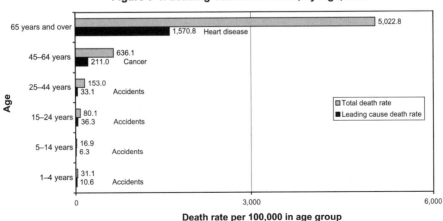

Source: Centers for Disease Control and Prevention. National Center for Health Statistics. *National Vital Statistics Report* 53(15).

For any given age group, the top five causes of death account for the vast majority of deaths, with the 10th most common cause typically causing only about 1 percent of deaths in a group in a given year. Among children under 15 years old, accidents remain the leading cause, accounting for about one-third of deaths in this age group. Motor vehicle accidents predominate for 5- to 14-year-old children, while other types of accidents are more common among younger children. Homicide and suicide are the fourth and fifth most common causes of death for children age 5 to 14 years. For young adults age 15 to 24 years, motor vehicle accidents are the number one cause of death, followed by homicide and suicide.

Among persons age 25–44 years, accidents are the leading cause of death, followed by cancer, heart disease, suicide, homicide, and HIV. In the next oldest group, age 45–64 years, the death rate from accidents remains about the same, but drops to third place overall, as the incidence of heart diseases and cancer increase with advancing age. Heart disease and cancer are also the top two causes of death for the elderly (65 years old and over).[1]

DIFFERENCES BETWEEN STATES

As shown in Figure 9-2, there is considerable variation in death rates, even when these rates are age adjusted, among the states. In 2003, 10 states had death rates above 925 per 100,000 population; all were located in the South, with the exceptions of Nevada, West Virginia, and Oklahoma. Four states showed rates below 750 per 100,000 population: Connecticut, Hawaii, Minnesota, and New Hampshire. The southern states generally have larger concentrations of lower-income Black populations; death rates are higher among this group.

HIV/AIDS

The HIV/AIDS epidemic in the United States is measured beginning in 1981. Through 2004, a total of about 949,000 cases had been diagnosed and reported throughout the country. Of these, 55 percent had died. The epidemic hit its peak in terms of cases diagnosed in 1992–1993 (about 79,000 per year), and two years later in terms of deaths (about 50,000 per year). By 2001, the number of new cases dropped to 39,000, and the number of deaths dropped to about 17,000. A slight increase in reported cases occurred between 2001 and 2004, but the number of deaths dropped significantly. (See Figure 9-3.)

Most of the cases occurring among children under 13 were caused by infection from the mother around the time of birth-perinatal HIV transmission. In 1994, treatment with the drug zidovudine (ZDV) was found to reduce perinatal HIV transmission, leading to a significant decline in the number of AIDS cases among children. In 2004, only 48 new pediatric cases were diagnosed.

Figure 9-2. Age-Adjusted Death Rates, 2002

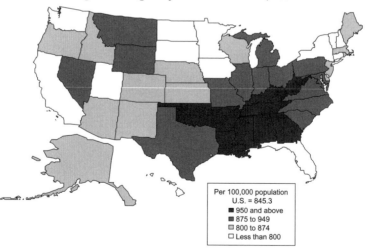

Per 100,000 population
U.S. = 845.3
■ 950 and above
■ 875 to 949
▨ 800 to 874
☐ Less than 800

Source: Centers for Disease Control and Prevention. National Center for Health Statistics.
National Vital Statistics Report 53(15).

---

[1] Hoyert, Donna L., Hsiang-Ching Kung, and Betty L. Smith. Deaths: Preliminary data for 2003. National Vital Statistics Report 53(15). (Feb. 28, 2005.) <http://www.cdc.gov/nchs/data/nvsr/nvsr53/nvsr53_15.pdf>. (Accessed Mar. 6, 2006.) The figures reported are the preliminary data for 2003.

Figure 9-3. AIDS Diagnoses and Deaths for Persons 13 Years of Age and Over, 1981–2004

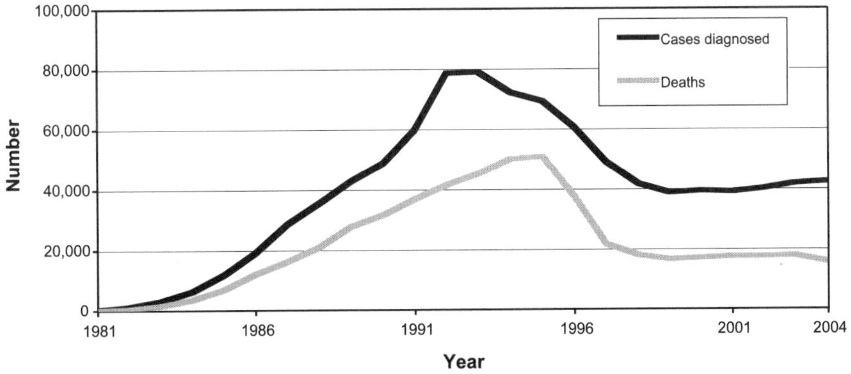

Source: Centers for Disease Control and Prevention. HIV/AIDS Surveillance Reports.

Table 9-1. Reported AIDS Cases, by Exposure Category, Race, and Sex, 2004

(Number, percent distribution.)

Characteristic	Total AIDS cases		Male		Female	
	Number	Percent distribution	Number	Percent distribution	Number	Percent distribution
Total, age 13 years and over	44 615	100.0	32 756	100.0	11 859	100.0
Exposure category						
Men who have sex with men	15 607	35.0	15 607	47.6	NA	NA
Injecting drug use	6 919	15.5	4 564	13.9	2 355	19.9
Men who have sex with men and inject drugs	1 696	3.8	1 696	5.2	NA	NA
Heterosexual contact	8 651	19.4	3 373	10.3	5 278	44.5
Other/risk not reported	11 742	26.3	7 516	22.9	4 226	36.0
Race/ethnicity						
White, non-Hispanic	13 129	29.4	11 157	34.1	1 972	16.6
Black, non-Hispanic	21 419	48.0	13 833	42.2	7 586	64.0
Hispanic (of any race)	9 174	20.6	7 090	21.6	2 084	17.6
Asian and Pacific Islander	494	1.1	395	1.2	99	0.8
American Indian, Alaska Native	210	0.5	148	0.5	62	0.5

Source: Centers for Disease Control and Prevention. HIV/AIDS Surveillance Report, 2004.
Note: Total includes 133 males and 56 females of unknown race or multiple races.

NA = Not applicable.

By 2001, there were an estimated half a million people currently living with HIV or AIDS, with approximately 31,000 new HIV infections occurring that year. About 40 percent of the people with HIV develop full-blown AIDS. About 75 percent are men. The proximate cause of the infection in about half of these male cases is homosexual sex. Women are more likely to become exposed to the virus through drug use or heterosexual sex. However, the actual proximate cause of the infection is often not identified. Blacks, both males and females, have a much higher incidence of AIDS cases than do Whites; the rate for Hispanics is in between these two. In over half of the Hispanic AIDS cases in 2001, the patient was born outside the United States.[2]

ENVIRONMENTAL FACTORS

Changes in the quality of the environment and the effects of pollution on health and death rates have been of particular concern over the past 35 years. Concern about illnesses caused by the condition of the environment takes on an extraordinarily broad focus—from sick-building syndrome (in which building occupants experience acute health problems that appear to be linked to the time spent in that particular structure) to lead exposure (a problem in Idaho, where lead that was left in the pilings of long-closed mines sifted into school yards) to the public water systems that carry unsafe levels of bacteria. Some environmental diseases occur naturally (e.g., mosquito-borne malaria), while some are the result of human activities (e.g., asbestos poisoning).

[2] Centers for Disease Control and Prevention. HIV/AIDS Surveillance Report (Year-end edition) 13(2). (Sept. 2002.) <http://www.cdc.gov/hiv/stats/hasr1302.htm>. (Accessed Mar. 6, 2006.) This includes data reported through December 2001.

The fraction of all deaths attributable to environmental causes has decreased dramatically in the United States throughout the last century. Environmental causes were responsible for 40 percent of all deaths at the turn of the 20th century, but caused only 5 percent of deaths in 1970. There is little evidence that this proportion has changed significantly since 1970.

HEALTHY PEOPLE AND STEPS TO A HEALTHIERUS

The U. S. Department of Health and Human Services's Healthy People 2010 program is an update of the earlier Healthy People 2000 program. The effort specifies a set of "Leading Health Indicators," which reflect the major health concerns in the nation at the beginning of the 21st century. They were selected "on the basis of their ability to motivate action, the availability of data to measure progress, and their importance as public health issues."[3] The leading health indicators are physical activity, overweight and obesity, tobacco use, substance abuse, responsible sexual behavior, mental health, injury and violence, environmental quality, immunization, and access to health care.

An accompanying initiative is Steps to a HealthierUS, which was established in 2003 to promote the creation of health promotion programs, community initiatives, and health care and insurance systems that put prevention first; and state and federal policies that "invest in the promise of prevention" and cooperation among policy makers, local health

agencies, and the public to invest in disease prevention rather than focusing on treating diseases after they arise. The initiative focuses on five disease categories: diabetes, obesity, asthma, heart disease and stroke, and cancer. It also focuses on three lifestyle choices which have significant impacts on health: poor nutrition and physical inactivity, tobacco use, and youth risk-taking.[4]

CHRONIC DISEASES

According to the National Center for Chronic Disease and Health Promotion, an agency of the Centers for Disease Control, "chronic diseases such as heart disease, cancer, and diabetes are leading causes of disability and death in the United States." These diseases cause about 1.7 million deaths annually, or 7 out of every 10 deaths in the nation. Chronic diseases cause major limitations in daily living for about 25 million people, and account for more than 70 percent of the $1 trillion spent on health care each year. They are also among the most preventable of diseases. The leading chronic disease killers include heart disease, cancer, stroke, chronic obstructive pulmonary disease (such as emphysema), and diabetes.

The major risk factors for chronic disease include cigarette smoking; lack of physical activity; poor nutrition; overweight and obesity; high blood pressure (hypertension); high blood cholesterol; a lack of usage of screening tests such as mammography, sigmoidoscopy/colonoscopy, and the fetal occult blood test; and a lack of health insurance.[5] The category of chronic diseases also includes conditions

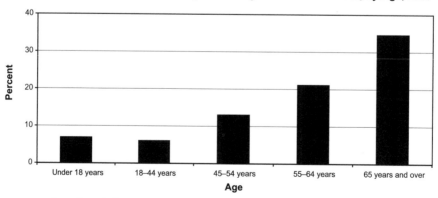

Figure 9-4. Limitation of Activity Caused by Chronic Conditions, by Age, 2003

Source: Centers for Disease Control and Prevention. National Center for Health Statistics. *Health, United States, 2005.*

[3] U.S. Department of Health and Human Services. What are the leading health indicators? *Healthy People 2010.* <http://www.healthypeople.gov/LHI/lhiwhat.htm>. (Accessed Mar. 6, 2006.)

[4] U.S. Department of Health and Human Services. *Steps to a HealthierUS.* (Jan. 2005). <http://www.healthierus.gov/steps/steps_brochure.html>. (Accessed Mar. 6, 2006.)

[5] Centers for Disease Control and Prevention. *The Burden of Chronic Disease and Their Factors.* (Feb. 2004.) <http://www.cdc.gov/nccdphp/burdenbook2004/> (Accessed Mar. 6, 2006.)

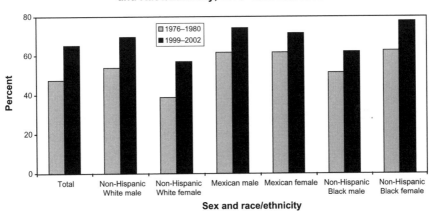

Figure 9-5. Percent of Population 20–74 Years That Is Overweight, by Sex and Race/Ethnicity, 1976–1980 and 1999–2002

Source: Centers for Disease Control and Prevention. National Center for Health Statistics. *Health, United States, 2005.*

that are disabling but not life-threatening. These include arthritis, loss of hearing, poor eyesight, and orthopedic problems. Figure 9-4 shows the impact of these conditions, by age, on the ability to be active. As expected, these problems are most significant for the elderly population.

PHYSICAL ACTIVITY

Emphasis on regular physical activity has increased strongly over the past several decades. It is considered important for maintaining a healthy body, enhancing psychological well-being, and preventing premature death. Participation in leisure-time physical activity is considerably below the recommended level; in 2002, 25 percent of adults reported that they engaged in no exercise, recreational, or physical activity. Almost half of all high school students were not enrolled in a physical education class in 2001; the target goal for physical activity in this age group was 85 percent. Several population categories have low rates of physical activity. These include women, people with lower income and lower education levels, African Americans, Hispanics, and adults in the northeastern and southern states.

OVERWEIGHT AND OBESITY

Being overweight is one of the most prevalent and serious health conditions in the United States. If being overweight had no side effect other than to make clothing purchases more difficult, it would be

of little more than aesthetic concern. But being overweight is associated with a host of other ailments, including high cholesterol, which can lead to high blood pressure, heart disease, and other chronic conditions. As shown in Figure 9-5, the proportion of the adult population (age 20 to 74 years) that is overweight increased from 47 percent in the 1976–1980 period to 65 percent in the 1999–2002 period. Men are slightly more likely to be overweight than women, although Black women (78 percent) are more frequently overweight than Black men (62 percent). The Healthy People 2010 target is for no more than 11 percent of children and adolescents, and 23 percent of adults age 20 years and over, to be overweight or obese.

Despite the increased proportion of population that is overweight, the percentage of population with high serum cholesterol has actually declined over the past 40 years, dropping from about 33 percent to 17 percent during the 1999–2002 period. For men, the proportion of population with high cholesterol has declined from about 31 percent to 17 percent; for women, the rate has dropped from 37 percent to 17 percent. Similarly, the percentage of the population that suffers from hypertension has also declined, falling from about 38 percent of adults (20 years old and over) in the early 1960s to 26 percent in the 1999–2002 period. For both men and women, this decline has occurred since 1980. The proportion of population suffering from this condition actually increased between 1960 and 1980. These figures include people whose blood pressure is only normal due to anti-hypertensive medication.

What is behind the paradox of this increase in overweight but decrease in cholesterol levels and hypertension? One partial explanation is that a large fraction of adults stopped smoking over this same period. Former smokers have long complained of gaining weight when they quit smoking. A 1995 study appears to confirm this.[6] Former smokers who quit over the past 10 years were considerably more likely to have become overweight than their peers who had never smoked. About one-fourth of the increase in the rate of overweight for men and about one-sixth of the increase in the rate of overweight for women can be attributed to quitting smoking.

SUBSTANCE ABUSE: DRUGS, ALCOHOL, AND TOBACCO

Being overweight and lack of exercise are not the only factors contributing to serious health problems in the United States. Substance abuse—including cigarettes, alcohol, and illegal substances—also persists. Alcohol use is the most pervasive, with a fairly constant proportion of the population reporting having used it at some time during the past month. In 2003, 50 percent of the population reported using alcohol in the past month, down from 63 percent in 1979. Alcohol usage has declined considerably

Table 9-2. Alcohol Use, Selected Years, 1979–2003

(Percent using in past month.)

Characteristic	1979	1985	1990	1995	1999	2003
12 years and over	63	60	53	52	52	50
12–17 years	50	71	33	21	19	18
18–25 years	75	70	63	61	60	61
26–34 years	72	71	64	63	62	60
35 years and over	60	58	50	53	53	51

Source: Centers for Disease Control and Prevention. National Center for Health Statistics. *Health, United States, 2005.*

However, this theory regarding smoking cessation does not explain the large increase in the occurrence of overweight children and adolescents. In the past 35 years, the percentage of 6- to 17-year-old children who are overweight has quadrupled, with much of this increase occurring (as it has in adults) since the late 1970s. About 11 percent of these children are classified as "seriously overweight." Obese children are likely to become obese adults and suffer the health consequences of being overweight. They are also more likely to attempt dangerous weight-reducing activities: about 5 percent of youth in a 1995 survey responded that they had taken laxatives or vomited to lose or maintain weight during the previous month.[7]

Decreased participation in physical activity with increasing age is part of the problem for children as well as adults. Regular participation in vigorous physical activity was reported by about 63 percent of youngsters in grades 9 through 12, while another 25 percent participated in moderate physical activity. There were variations within this age group, with older students less likely to engage in physical activity than younger students.

among teenagers. In 1979, 50 percent of 12- to 17-year-old teenagers reporting having had a drink in the past month; the comparable figure for 2003 was 18 percent. Similar drops were evident among older persons, although they were less dramatic. Drinking levels remain quite high among young adults 18 to 34 years of age (see Table 9-2), and certain historical patterns persist. For persons 18 to 25 years old, alcohol use remains more prevalent in men than in women (65 percent versus 55 percent), and more prevalent in Whites than in Blacks (63 percent versus 47 percent) or Hispanics (50 percent).

In 2003, about 32 percent of Americans age 18 years and over indicated that they had at least three drinks per week—a level of drinking considered to be "moderate" or "heavier." Therefore, 68 percent were "light" drinkers or abstainers, drinking less than three drinks per week or none at all. About 15 percent of the population could be characterized as "binge drinkers," or drinkers who had had 5 or more drinks on 12 or more days over the past year.[8] While the possible consequences of alcohol abuse—both health and societal—are widely

---

[6] Legal, Katerina M., et al. 1995. The influence of smoking cessation on the prevalence of overweight in the United States. *New England Journal of Medicine* 333(1995): 1165-70.

[7] Centers for Disease Control and Prevention. National Center for Health Statistics. *Youth Risk Behavior Surveillance—United States, 1999.* (June 2000.) <http://www.cdc.gov/mmwr/preview/mmwrhtml/ss4905a1.htm>. (Accessed Mar. 6, 2006.)

8 Centers for Disease Control and Prevention. National Center for Health Statistics. *Health, United States, 2005.* <http://www.cdc.gov/nchs/data/hus/hus05.pdf>. (Accessed Mar. 6, 2006.)

known, groups such as Mothers Against Drunk Driving (MADD) have only somewhat recently brought issues about drinking, such as the consequences of driving while intoxicated, to the attention of the public.

After alcohol, the most pervasive drug is tobacco, and specifically cigarettes. Smoking reached a high of about 4,300 cigarettes a year (about 12 per day) per person age 18 years and over in 1963. This level remained quite high until about 20 years ago. Significant annual declines brought the figure down to about 2,000 cigarettes per year in 2002. The percentage of adults who were current smokers declined from 42 percent in 1965 to 37 percent in 1974, and then to 21 percent in 2003. This decline is observed among all age groups, among both men and women, and among both Whites and Blacks. Still, almost one out of four Americans smoked cigarettes in 2001. As shown in Table 9-3, not smoking cigarettes is highly correlated with educational attainment levels among adults. However, there has been a significant decline in smoking at all educational levels. The Healthy People 2010 target is to cut the 1999 level in half, down to 12 percent of all adults.

Perhaps one of the biggest societal changes that has occurred since 1980 has been the shift in public attitudes and behavior toward smoking. The U.S. Surgeon General's report of 1964 was the first significant government argument against smoking; it linked casual smoking to lung cancer as well as other ailments. Yet, prior to 1980, it was common to smoke cigarettes, pipes, and cigars in most workplaces and in public accommodations, such as restaurants and airplanes. After 1980, amid mounting evidence of the detrimental health effects of smoking, the effects of secondhand smoke in the workplace, and the legal right and obligation of employers to protect their workers, smoking in the workplace began to be severely limited. It was first restricted by employers to particular locations, before being banned entirely from the interior of buildings.

As of 2005, 9 states (California, Connecticut, Delaware, Maine, Massachusetts, New York, Rhode Island, Vermont, and Washington) have banned smoking in most public places, earning them A ratings from the American Lung Association. Another 11 states received a B or C grade, while the remaining 30 were recorded as failing. Other activities measured by state included the cigarette tax level, the amount of funding devoted to smoking prevention, and how youth access issues were dealt with.[9]

Table 9-3. Age-Adjusted Prevalence of Current Cigarette Smoking by Persons 25 Years and Over, 1974 and 2003

(Percent.)

Sex, race, and year	Total	No high school diploma or GED	High school diploma or GED	Some college, no bachelor's degree	Bachelor's degree or higher
All Persons					
1974	36.9	43.7	36.2	35.9	27.2
2003	21.1	29.7	27.8	21.1	10.2
All Males					
1974	42.9	52.3	42.4	41.8	28.3
2003	23.3	34.4	29.9	22.7	11.2
White Males					
1974	41.9	51.5	42.0	41.6	27.8
2003	23.2	33.6	29.6	23.3	11.2
Black Males					
1974	53.4	58.1	*50.7	*45.3	*41.4
2003	26.3	37.4	33.4	19.5	*10.3
All Females					
1974	32.0	36.6	32.2	30.1	25.9
2003	19.1	24.9	25.8	19.7	9.3
White Females					
1974	31.7	36.8	31.9	30.4	25.5
2003	19.6	25.0	26.8	20.6	9.4
Black Females					
1974	35.6	36.1	40.9	32.3	*36.3
2003	18.9	26.9	23.3	17.0	11.4

Source: Centers for Disease Control and Prevention. National Center for Health Statistics. *Health, United States, 2005.*
Note: Totals for each category include unknown education. GED stands for general education development test.

* = Estimates are considered unreliable.

9 American Lung Association. <http://www.lungusa.org>. (Accessed Mar. 6, 2006.)

While alcohol abuse remains the primary substance abuse problem (as measured by admissions for treatment), illicit drug use has also been a serious concern for several decades. Drug use is rising, with admissions increasing by 53 percent between 1993 and 2003. Heroin was the cause of the most admissions, followed by cocaine and marijuana/hashish. Other substance abuse included stimulants, sedatives and tranquilizers, hallucinogens, PCP, and inhalants. Over the 1993–2003 period, the proportion of admissions for cocaine abuse declined, while those for heroin increased. This may have been due to the increased availability of "high purity heroin," which can be inhaled instead of being injected.[10]

Substance abuse among teenagers has long been of special concern. As shown in Table 9-4, this remains a serious issue, but there has been improvement over the past 20 years in all the reported categories (except for cigarettes). However, recent data show that half of high school seniors drink alcoholic beverages, with 3 in 10 engaging in binge drinking. Marijuana use remains high as well.

CONTRACEPTIVE USE, ABORTION, AND SEXUALLY TRANSMITTED DISEASES

CONTRACEPTIVE USE

The federal government was first involved in family planning services in the 1960s, as part of the "War on Poverty" declared by President Lyndon Johnson in 1964. The first funding was earmarked to provide family planning services for women receiving public assistance. In 1970, Title X of the Public Health Service Act created a comprehensive federal program to provide family planning services (but prohibited abortion as a family planning method); these services were available to anyone in need. Additional public support for family planning has come from Medicaid, the social services block grant, and state contributions.

As described by the Alan Guttmacher Institute, family planning services have been plagued by political controversy since their inception. Conservatives

Table 9-4. Use of Selected Substances by High School Seniors and Eighth Graders, Selected Years, 1980–2004

(Percent using substance in past month, except where noted.)

Substance and grade in school	1980	1990	2000	2004
Cigarettes				
High school seniors	30.5	29.4	31.4	25.0
All eighth graders	. . .	. . .	14.6	9.2
Marijuana				
High school seniors	33.7	14.0	21.6	19.9
All eighth graders	. . .	. . .	9.1	6.4
Cocaine				
High school seniors	5.2	1.9	2.1	2.3
All eighth graders	. . .	. . .	1.2	0.9
Inhalants				
High school seniors	1.4	2.7	2.2	1.5
All eighth graders	. . .	. . .	4.5	4.5
MDMA (Ecstasy)				
High school seniors	. . .	. . .	3.6	1.2
All eighth graders	. . .	. . .	1.4	0.8
Alcohol				
High school seniors	72.0	57.1	50.0	48.0
All eighth graders	. . .	. . .	22.4	18.6
Binge Drinking [1]				
High school seniors	41.2	32.2	30.0	29.2
All eighth graders	. . .	. . .	14.1	11.4

Source: Centers for Disease Control and Prevention. National Center for Health Statistics. *Health, United States, 2005.*

[1]Five or more alcoholic drinks in a row at least once in the prior two-week period.
. . . = Not available.

---

[10] Substance Abuse and Mental Health Services Administration (SAMHSA). Data from the TEDS and DASIS reporting system. <http://www.drugabusestatistics.samhsa.gov>. (Accessed Mar. 6, 2006.) The TEDS data set also provides many state-level tabulations.

have claimed that the availability of confidential contraceptive services encourages sexual activity among teenagers and that family planning clinics promote abortion. Supporters point to the success of the family planning services network, whose annual average of 6.5 million clients represents one-quarter of the women receiving these types of services. The network services go primarily to poor or low-income women, the majority of whom are White, and to women under 30 years old. In addition to advice on contraceptive methods, the clinics provide Pap smears, pelvic examinations, testing and treatment for gynecological infections, and testing for HIV and other sexually transmitted diseases (STDs). This work has been carried out in an atmosphere of severely reduced funding; when adjusted for inflation, the funding level in 2000 was 60 percent lower than the level from 20 years earlier.[11]

As indicated in a previous chapter (Chapter 2—Households and Families), average family size in the United States has declined considerably over the past several decades, with the unplanned pregnancy rate dropping as well. A major contributor to the decrease in the number of children born to American women has been the increased use of and improvements in contraceptives. However, half of all pregnancies are still unintended, and half of all unintended pregnancies end in abortion. These unintended pregnancies occur most often among young women (and account for over 75 percent of pregnancies in women under 20 years old), unmarried women, and women living below the poverty level. A 1994 study showed that almost half of all women of childbearing age have had at least one unintended pregnancy, with the figure rising as high as 60 percent among women in their thirties.[12]

Almost all sexually active women in the 15- to 44-year-old age group who are not pregnant and do not wish to become so report using some method of contraception. The most commonly used method is an oral contraceptive, also known as the "Pill." This method is reported as being used by 3 out of 10 women who use some birth control method. The second most common reversible method is the male condom. A small number of women use the recently developed injection, which provides protection for several weeks or months. (See Figure 9-6.) Another 27 percent of women are sterilized.

ABORTION TRENDS

Abortion was legalized in the United States by the Supreme Court in the 1972 *Roe v. Wade* decision. In recent years, the actual number of induced abortions has tended to decrease. The ratio of abortions to live births has also tended to decline, after initial increases in the late 1970s. Between 1975 (when such data were first collected) and 1979, the number of abortions performed increased from about 1 million to 1.5 million, and the ratio of abortions to live births increased from 331 to 420 per 1,000 live births. From 1979 to 1993, the actual number of abortions remained relatively stable, despite a large increase in the number of women of childbearing age (from 52 to 59 million women) during this period. The number of abortions peaked at 1.6 million in 1990, before declining to about 1.3 million in 2000; this level was maintained into 2002.

Figure 9-6. Percent Distribution by Method of Birth Control Used, 2002

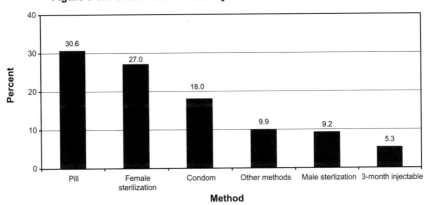

Source: Centers for Disease Control and Prevention. National Center for Health Statistics. *2002 National Survey of Family Growth.*

11 The Alan Guttmacher Institute. *Fulfilling the Promise: Public Policy and U.S. Family Planning Clinics.* (Jan. 2000.) <http://www.guttmacher.org/pubs/fulfill.pdf>. (Accessed Mar. 6, 2006.)
12 Henshaw, Stanley K. 1998. Unintended pregnancy in the United States. *Family Planning Perspectives* 30(1): 24-29 & 46.

However, a better way of measuring is to look at the abortion rate. Two methods of calculating the rate are available: abortions per 1,000 women of childbearing age and abortions per 1,000 live births. By either measure, the rates have dropped steadily from their peak in 1981. Figure 9-7 shows this trend over time.

SEXUALLY TRANSMITTED DISEASES

Sexually transmitted diseases (STDs) have increased as a public health problem in the United States during the past three decades. Despite the fact that the number of cases per 100,000 population for syphilis and gonorrhea declined throughout the 1990s, the incidence rate of chlamydia was on the rise. Five STDs are among the 10 most frequently treated infections, including chlamydia, gonorrhea, HIV/AIDS, syphilis, and hepatitis B. Women are more likely than men to become infected with an STD.

The most commonly reported STD (and, for that matter, any type of infection) in the United States is chlamydia trachomatis. While this condition is usually asymptomatic, it often leads to pelvic inflammatory disease (PID), a major cause of infertility, ectopic pregnancy, and chronic pelvic pain in women. A chlamydial infection can also facilitate the transmission of HIV, and can be passed from mother to child during delivery. The rate of chlamydia has been increasing steadily since it was first reported in 1984, partly because diagnostic tests and reporting have improved. The number of reported cases reached nearly 1 million in 2004. Chlamydia affects many more women than men,

and the rate for women has been increasing at a faster pace. It primarily infects young people between the ages of 15 and 29.

Rates for other STDs, such as gonorrhea and syphilis, have been decreasing over time. These diseases are almost non-existent in northern New England and in the northern Rocky Mountain region. The syphilis rate has dropped so much—almost 90 percent in the 1990s alone—that the Centers for Disease Control and Prevention (CDC), a unit of the Department of Health and Human Services, has developed the National Plan to Eliminate Syphilis from the United States. However, the rate of syphilis has increased every year since 2001, primarily among men, who experienced an 11 percent increase in the 2003–2004 period alone. Geographically, the highest rates of syphilis are found in the Deep South. Several other STDs are tracked by the public health system, but their incidence rates are quite low. Genital herpes falls in this category.[13] Rates for gonorrhea are at their lowest reported levels ever, but still exceed the Healthy People 2010 goal.

Teenagers and young adults are at higher risk of acquiring STDs than older adults, as they are more likely to have multiple sexual partners and are more likely to engage in sex without appropriate protection. In addition, they are less likely to seek treatment for STDs because of confidentiality concerns, transportation, and inability to pay. Recent estimates suggest that while 15- to 24-year-olds represent 25 percent of the ever sexually active population, this group acquires nearly half of all new STDs.[14]

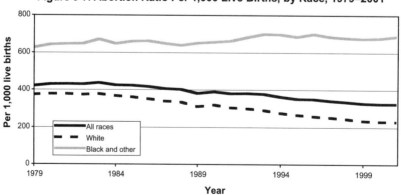

Figure 9-7. Abortion Ratio Per 1,000 Live Births, by Race, 1979–2001

Source: U.S. Census Bureau. *Statistical Abstract of the United States, 2006.*

[13] Centers for Disease Control and Prevention. Division of STD Prevention. *Sexually Transmitted Disease Surveillance 2004.* <http://www.cdc.gov/std/stats>. (Accessed Mar. 6, 2006.)

[14] Centers for Disease Control and Prevention. <http://www.cdc.gov/std/stats/adol.htm>. (Accessed Mar. 3, 2006.)

Between 1970 and 1990, there was a steady rise in the proportion of teenage women who indicated they had ever had sexual intercourse. Compared to older adults, sexually active adolescents (10- to 19-year-olds) and young adults (20- to 24-year-olds) are at higher risk for acquiring STDs, due to a combination of behavioral, biological, and cultural reasons. One problem for this age group is the lack of access to quality STD prevention services, due to a lack of insurance or other ability to pay, lack of transportation, discomfort with facilities and services designed for adults, and concerns about confidentiality.

Another problem among adolescents is the common practice of oral sex. While non-coital sex avoids the risk of pregnancy and some of the emotional problems associated with intercourse, it still carries a significant risk of transmitting STDs. Research has shown that teenagers are likely to engage in oral sex before they begin to have intercourse.[15]

DISABILITY

DEFINING AND GAUGING DISABILITY

The term "disability" has many connotations; it can be defined very broadly or very narrowly. The proportion of the population with a disability varies considerably, depending on the definition. A relatively narrow definition says that employed or formerly employed persons are considered to be disabled if they are "unable to engage in substantial gainful activity." This definition is used by the U.S. government in the Social Security Disability program. A considerably broader definition is used in the Americans with Disabilities Act of 1990 (ADA), which defines disability as a "physical or mental impairment that substantially limits one or more of the major life activities."

Early surveys relating to disability focused on the presence of a physical, mental, or other health condition that limited the kind or amount of work a person could perform. In recent surveys used to determine the extent of disability, the ADA definition is typically operationalized by asking questions relating to: (a) "limitations in functional activities," such as seeing, hearing, using stairs, lifting, and carry-

ing; (b) "activities of daily living" (ADLs), such as washing, eating, and dressing; and (c) "instrumental activities of daily living" (IADLs), such as difficulty going outside the home or keeping track of money or bills. ADA assessment also includes questions relating to ability to work and, for children, limitations in their ability to complete school work and engage in other usual activities.

On the 2000 census, respondents were asked about several categories of disability: sensory, physical, mental, and self-care. In addition, adults age 16 years and over were asked about disabilities related to going outside the home, and persons of working age (age 16–64 years) were asked about disabilities that prevented them from holding a job. People could report that they were disabled in none, one, or more than one of these categories.

The likelihood of having some type of disability increases with age. In 2000, about 6 percent of children between 5 and 15 years of age had a disability, compared with 14 percent of adults 21 to 64 years old and 54 percent of persons 75 years old and over. Disability is correlated with advancing age; persons 65 years old and over accounted for 28 percent of all persons who reported a disability. Among children, boys tended to have higher disability rates than girls, while for adults, the rates by sex were similar. Among older adults, women tended to have slightly higher disability rates, primarily because there were more women than men in the very oldest age groups. (See Figure 9-8.)

TYPES OF DISABILITY AND EFFECTS ON LIVELIHOOD

The first type of disability is sensory. This category includes eyesight and hearing disorders. One in seven older Americans (14 percent) reports blindness, deafness, or a severe hearing or vision impairment. Physical disability refers to "a condition that substantially limits one or more basic physical activities such as walking, climbing stairs, reaching, lifting, or carrying."[16] This is the most common disability, reported by 29 percent of senior citizens and about 6 percent of working-age adults. Mental disability is defined as a problem with learning, remembering, or concentrating. It is the most common disability among children age 5 to 15 years,

---

15 Remez, Lisa. 2000. Oral sex among adolescents: Is it sex or is it abstinence? *Family Planning Perspectives* 32(6).

16 U.S. Census Bureau. Question 16b. <http://www.census.gov/dmd/www/pdf/d02p.pdf>. (Accessed Mar. 6, 2006.) The questionnaire itself is the best reference for each of the six individual disability categories discussed here.

Figure 9-8. Percent of Persons with Disabilities, by Age Group, 2004

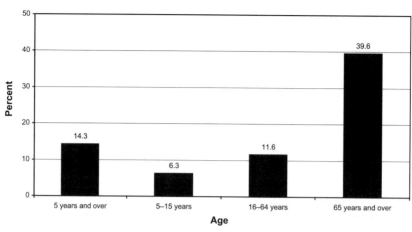

Source: U.S. Census Bureau. American Community Survey 2004.

affecting 5 percent of the total population in that age group. About 11 percent of seniors are affected by this problem.

Self-care disabilities refer to problems bathing, dressing, or getting around inside the home. It is a relatively uncommon problem, experienced by only 1 percent of children and adults and 10 percent of seniors. Going outside the home was asked in reference to shopping or visiting a doctor's office. Six percent of adults reported this category of disability; the figure for senior citizens rose to 25 percent. Finally, working-age adults were asked if they had a disability which caused difficult in working at a job or business; 12 percent responded "yes." There is some evidence, however, that people who have trouble finding work may report a disability, such as "back trouble," to explain their lack of looking; this rate is likely to rise when the economy falters.

HEALTH INSURANCE COVERAGE

WHO IS NOT COVERED

Unlike some countries, the United States does not have a national health insurance program that covers everyone, regardless of age or income. Thus, for many people in the United States, the greatest impediment to a healthy life is the lack of adequate health insurance. Lack of coverage can delay or prevent treatment for a specific ailment, as well as impede access to information or preventive services.

In 2004, about 16 percent of the U.S. population (45.8 million people) had no health insurance at any

time during the year. In addition, other people were covered by health insurance for only part of the year. This is often the result of short-term unemployment, a change in employment, or a policy lapse due to unpaid insurance premiums. The number of uninsured people for 2004 was higher than that for 2003. Due to the worsening economy (and consequently, the loss of employer-sponsored health insurance) and continuing high immigration, the number of uninsured Americans has been rising for several years.

Men were somewhat more likely than women to be uninsured in 2004, perhaps because they were less likely to be on public assistance and, consequently, covered by Medicaid. Young adults (age 18 to 34 years) were more likely to lack insurance than other age groups. Hispanics were considerably more likely than Blacks or non-Hispanic Whites to lack insurance, with a non-coverage rate of 33 percent. Migrant farm workers were usually not covered by health insurance. Immigrant non-citizens were more than three times as likely as native-born Americans to lack insurance. (See Figure 9-10.)

SOURCES OF COVERAGE

There are three main government health insurance programs: one to provide coverage for persons age 65 years and over, regardless of income level (Medicare); one to provide coverage for low-income Americans (Medicaid); and a one to provide care for the military and veterans. Together, these programs provide health insurance coverage to slightly more than one-fourth of the U.S. population, with

Medicare covering 14 percent, Medicaid covering about 13 percent, and military health insurance covering about 4 percent. Some people may have coverage from more than one of these sources.

The great majority of the insured, representing some 245 million people (or 84 percent of the total population), have some form of private health insurance. Since there are gaps in the insurance coverage of government-sponsored programs, some persons who have government coverage also have private health insurance. Almost all private health insurance is obtained through employment. Persons with unstable employment or with part-time work were considerably more likely than full-time workers to be uninsured. Such persons may not be immediately eligible for a government program like Medicaid because their income was too high (or had recently been too high), but may not feel as though they can continue to afford private insurance coverage.[17]

In the United States, the amount of coverage varies considerably between health plans. Some plans only cover catastrophic illnesses and may have large co-payment amounts that must be paid by the insured individual, while other plans cover everything from prescriptions to long-term hospital care. In addition, while a plan may "cover" virtually all health conditions, health insurance plans have caps that limit the amount the healthcare provider will be paid for a particular service. This may be considerably less than the actual charge. In some cases, the insured individual is responsible for any amount above the charge allowed by the insurance company; in other instances, the healthcare provider will accept the insurance company's allowed charges as full payment.

People without health insurance have a difficult time receiving needed treatment. In 2001, only 21 percent of this population visited a doctor or dentist, and only 10 percent obtained routine check-ups. Even for those who did visit a doctor or dentist, one-quarter did not receive service. Persons who reported being in fair or poor health status were more likely to visit doctors and to receive services when they asked for them.[18]

Figure 9-9. Percent of Persons Without Health Insurance for the Entire Year, Average 2003–2004

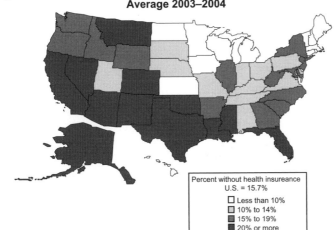

Percent without health insureance
U.S. = 15.7%

☐ Less than 10%
☐ 10% to 14%
■ 15% to 19%
■ 20% or more

Source: U.S. Census Bureau. Current Population Survey.

---

17 U.S. Census Bureau. *Income, Poverty, and Health Insurance Coverage: 2004* (Current Population Report P60-229). (Aug. 2005.) <http://www.census.gov/prod/2005pubs/p60-229.pdf>. (Accessed Mar. 6, 2006.) Additional information on the relationship between employment and health insurance is included in Chapter 4.

18 U.S. Census Bureau. *Health Status, Health Insurance, and Health Services Utilization: 2001* (Current Population Report P70-106). (Feb. 2006.) <http://www.census.gov/prod/2006pubs/p70-106.pdf>. (Accessed Mar. 6, 2006.)

Figure 9-10. Percent of Persons Without Health Insurance, 2004

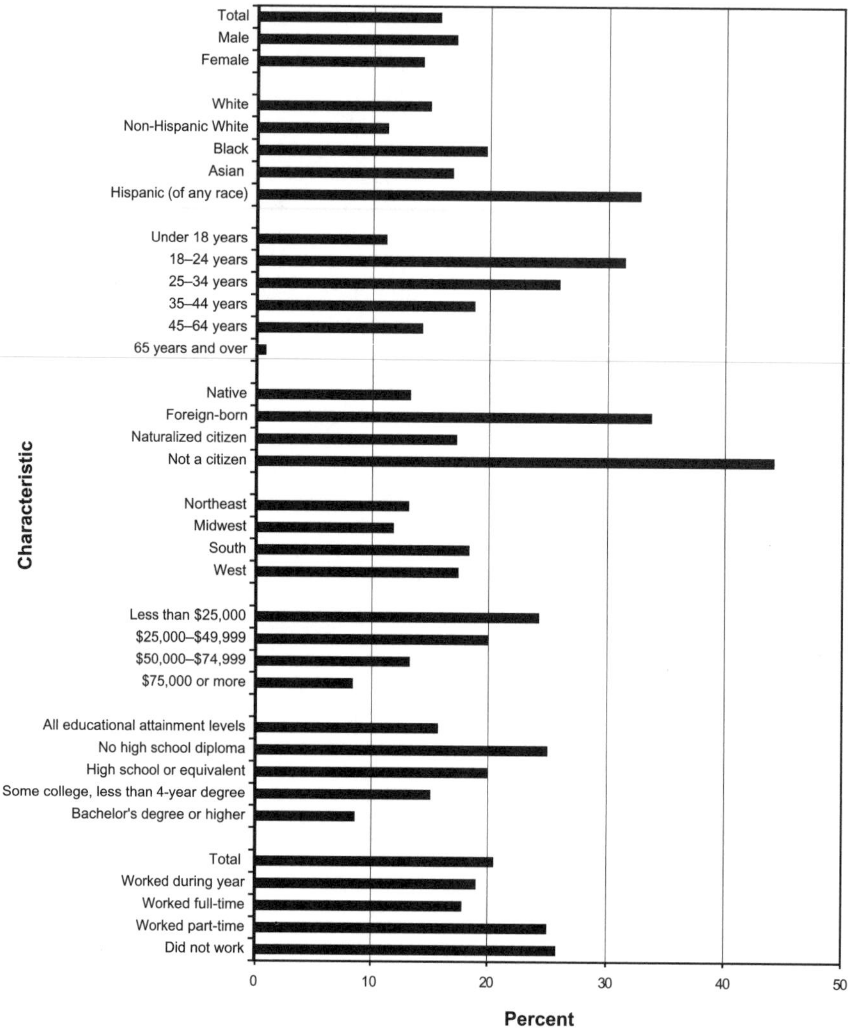

Source: U.S. Census Bureau. Current Population Survey.

FOR FURTHER INFORMATION:

Centers for Disease Control and Prevention. *HIV/AIDS Surveillance Report, 2000* (Year-end edition, vol. 12 no. 2). (Sept. 2001.) <http://www.cdc.gov/hiv/stats/hasr1202.htm>. (Accessed Mar. 6, 2006.)

Centers for Disease Control and Prevention. *The Burden of Chronic Diseases and Their Risk Factors.* (Feb. 2004.) <http://www.cdc.gov/nccdphp/burdenbook2004/>. (Accessed Mar. 6, 2006.)

Centers for Disease Control and Prevention. National Center for Health Statistics. *Health, United States, 2005.* <http://www.cdc.gov/nchs/data/hus/hus05.pdf>. (Accessed Mar. 6, 2006.)

Donovan, Patricia. 1997. Confronting a hidden epidemic: The Institute of Medicine's report on sexually transmitted diseases. *Family Planning Perspectives* 29(2).

WEB SITES:

Alan Guttmacher Institute. <http://www.guttmacher.org>. (Accessed Mar. 6, 2006.)

Centers for Disease Control and Prevention. <http://www.cdc.gov>. (Accessed Mar. 6, 2006.)

Centers for Disease Control and Prevention. National Center for Health Statistics. <http://www.cdc.gov/nchs>. (Accessed Mar. 6, 2006.)

National Clearinghouse for Alcohol and Drug Information. <http://www.health.org>. (Accessed Mar. 6, 2006.)

Substance Abuse and Mental Health Services Administration. <http://www.samhsa.gov>. (Accessed Mar. 6, 2006.)

U.S. Census Bureau (for health insurance data and data on disabilities). <http://www.census.gov>. (Accessed Mar. 6, 2006.)

Chapter 10
Leisure, Volunteerism, and Religiosity

TRENDS IN LEISURE TIME

What do Americans do with their non-working, or (in the case of children) non-school hours? While most non-work time is spent on commuting and the everyday tasks of daily living, Americans have, on average, about 40 hours a week to spend on leisure activities. Such activities can take a variety of forms, from watching television to participating in an athletic pursuit, to volunteer work, or to singing in a church choir.

According to data from time-use studies, Americans used to spend a large portion of their free time in civic activities, such as working for a political party, attending religious services or participating in activities at their church or synagogue, and in membership in such organizations as parent-teacher associations and labor unions. Membership in civic groups has declined over the past two decades, as has the amount of time spent socializing, visiting, and attending church, according to data from the General Social Survey and the Gallup Poll. However, time spent watching television has increased considerably. Americans, on average, spend between 2 and 3 hours a day watching television, or approximately 40 percent of their free time. One author feels these two trends—declining civic association and increased television watching—are causally related.[1]

There is a large gap between Americans' perception of how much time they have for leisure and the actual amount of time they have, according to a recent study. The perception is considerably short of reality.[2] Time-diary data indicate that both men and women were spending less time on average at paid work in 1995 than they did in 1965, and that free time had increased for both, whether or not they were employed. However, according to a 2004 survey, women still spend more time than men on family care, and somewhat less time at paid work.[3]

Table 10-1 shows the impact that working and having children in the home makes on the availability of time for leisure and sports activities. People who are employed have much less time for any type of leisure activity than do those who are not working, and those without children have more time than those with children. The age of the children does not make a significant difference. However, both groups spend more time at leisure activities on weekends and holidays than on weekdays.

TYPES OF LEISURE ACTIVITIES

Not only does the amount of leisure time vary throughout the life cycle, but the favorite free time activities of Americans vary by age.[4] For example, the most popular sports activity among Americans age 65 years and over is exercise walking, in which about 46 percent participated. For children between 7 and 11 years old, bicycle riding and swimming were the most popular sports activities, with about half of children participating in one or both. Teenagers, age 12 to 17, are also into bike riding and swimming, but the percentage of participants is smaller. For young adults (18 to 24 years old), exer-

Table 10-1. Daily Time Spent on Leisure and Sports Activities, 2004

(Hours.)

Characteristic	Weekdays		Weekends/holidays	
	Men	Women	Men	Women
Employed				
With children under 6 years old	3.3	2.8	5.8	4.0
With children under 18 years old	3.3	3.0	5.9	4.5
Without children	4.0	3.7	6.6	5.5
Not Employed				
With children under 6 years old	6.1	4.3	5.7	5.2
With children under 18 years old	6.6	4.5	6.6	5.8
Without children	8.3	6.7	8.7	7.1

Source: U.S. Bureau of Labor Statistics. American Time Use Survey 2004.

---

[1] Putnam, Robert D. 1966. The strange disappearance of civic America. *The American Prospect* 7(24).

[2] Robinson, John P., and Geoffrey Godbey. 1997. *Time for Life: The Surprising Ways Americans Use Their Time.* (University Park, PA: Pennsylvania State University Press.)

[3] Bureau of Labor Statistics. American Time Use Survey. <http://www.bls.gov/tus>. (Accessed Mar. 8, 2006.)

[4] U.S. Census Bureau. 2006. Table 1238. *Statistical Abstract of the United States, 2006.* (Washington, DC: U.S. Census Bureau.)

cise walking, exercising with equipment such as stationary bicycles or steppers, and swimming head the list, along with sports such as billiards and bowling. Similar numbers of men and women enjoyed activities such as cross-country skiing and volleyball. Participants in other sports were predominantly of one sex or the other: men were predominant in the "ball" games (football, baseball, and basketball), as well as golf and hunting, while aerobics was primarily an activity for women. Looking at income, persons with higher incomes are more likely to be involved in swimming, bicycle riding, or golf; these are all sports that usually require an expenditure of personal funds in order to participate.

For all types of leisure activities, the one enjoyed by more people than any other is eating out, followed by reading books and entertaining friends or relatives at home. These activities were enjoyed by nearly half the U.S. population at least once during a 12-month period, with most engaging in them at least two or three times a month.[5] The other activities high on the list were also quite passive: barbecuing, playing cards, and going to the beach.

One specific category of leisure activities is the arts. This category consists of participating in or attending music, dance, or theater performances; and visiting museums, historic parks, and arts/craft fairs. Of these types of activities, arts/craft fairs were the most popular, with a 33 percent participation rate in 2002.[6] Historic parks and art museums were next on the list. Generally, adults of all ages participate equally in these types of activities, except that persons 75 years old and over show lower rates. However, education makes a big difference. For all types of arts activities, participation increases significantly as the level of educational attainment rises.

Looking at spectator attendance at sporting events, baseball remains the top attractor, with about one person in eight (12 percent) saying they attended one or more games in the course of a year. Next is high school sports, with an attendance rate of 9 percent, followed by college football at 7 percent. These data show clearly that sports events, both professional and school-based, are attractive to only a small minority of the population.[7]

Physical activity has become increasingly important, as people have become aware of its correlation with good health. However, in 2003, only about one-quarter of all adults reported engaging in regu-

Table 10-2. Leisure-Time Physical Activity Among Adults 18 Years of Age and Over, 2003

(Percent.)

Characteristic	Inactive [1]	Some leisure-time activity [2]	Regular leisure-time activity [3]
Total, age-adjusted	37.6	29.5	32.8
18–24 years	29.6	28.2	42.3
25–44 years	34.0	31.0	34.9
45–64 years	38.2	30.5	31.3
65–74 years	45.8	25.8	28.4
75 years and over	57.5	24.8	17.7
Male	35.4	29.2	35.4
Female	39.5	29.9	30.6
White, non-Hispanic	33.4	30.9	35.8
Black, non-Hispanic	48.5	26.0	25.5
Hispanic or Latino (of any race)	51.9	23.6	24.4
No high school diploma or GED ...	61.2	20.6	18.1
High school diploma or GED	45.5	27.5	27.0
Some college or more	28.1	33.8	38.2
Poor	55.1	22.0	22.9
Near poor	50.5	24.8	24.7
Nonpoor	31.4	32.0	36.7
Northeast	34.4	29.2	36.4
Midwest	34.7	32.2	33.1
South	42.6	27.7	29.7
West	34.9	29.9	35.2

Source: Centers for Disease Control and Prevention. National Center for Health Statistics. *Health, United States, 2005.*

[1]Reported no sessions of light/moderate or vigorous leisure-time activity of at least 10 minutes duration.
[2]Reported at least one session of light/moderate or vigorous physical activity of at least 10 minutes duration, but did not meet the definition for regular leisure-time activity.
[3]Reported three or more sessions per week of vigorous activity lasting at least 20 minutes or five or more sessions per week of light/moderate activity lasting at least 30 minutes in duration.

lar physical activity. (See Table 10-2.) Women were slightly less likely to participate than men. Regular participation declined, as expected, with age. However, engaging in such activity was highly correlated with educational attainment.

What else do people do with their time? Some other activities—which some people might think would more appropriately be classified as work—are nevertheless reported as leisure activities by large portions of the U.S. population. For example, 42 percent of adults 18 years old and over indicated home improvement and repair as a leisure activity in 2002. Charity work remains important, engaged in by nearly a third of the adult population. Over half indicate participation in exercise programs, 30 percent play sports (while 35 percent attend sports events, many of which are not organized), and 47

[5] U.S. Census Bureau. 2006. Table 1230. *Statistical Abstract of the United States, 2006.* (Washington, DC: U.S. Census Bureau.)
[6] U.S. Census Bureau. 2006. Table 1226. *Statistical Abstract of the United States, 2006.* (Washington, DC: U.S. Census Bureau.)
[7] U.S. Census Bureau. 2006. Table 1229. *Statistical Abstract of the United States, 2006.* (Washington, DC: U.S. Census Bureau.)

Figure 10-1. Percent of High School Seniors Participating in Extracurricular Activities, 2001

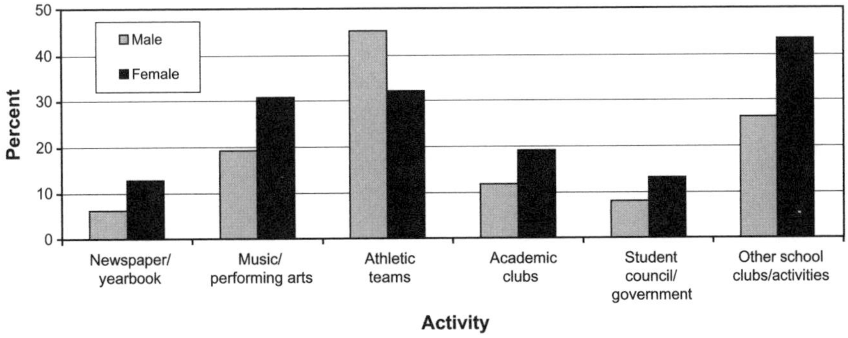

Source: University of Michigan. Institute for Social Research. *Monitoring the Future.*

percent spend time gardening. Three in five say that they attend movies. As with activities in the arts, participation in these activities increases with education and with income; clearly, it costs money to engage in most leisure activities. Again, there are few differences by age except for the 75 years old and over age group. However, as we would expect, playing sports does decrease with age, as does engagement in spectator activities such as movies, sporting events, and amusement parks. In fact, attending movies—possibly the most common "date" event—is reported by 83 percent of persons 18 to 24 years old.[8]

Students who participated in extracurricular activities were found to have higher school attendance, better performance on standardized math and reading tests, and more aspirations to higher education than non-participants. There is some evidence to suggest that the sense of attachment to school fostered by participation in extracurricular activities decreases the likelihood of school failure and dropping out.[9]

In reference to organized physical activity at the high school level, slightly more than half of all students were enrolled in physical education classes in 2003. As expected, boys were more likely to be enrolled than girls, and participation levels decreased as the students moved through from 9th to 12th grade. However, 58 percent were involved with a school sports team (64 percent of boys; 51 percent of girls), and the dropoff with age was consid-

erably smaller in this category. These data may reflect the fact that, in many schools, physical education is not a mandatory requirement after the 9th or 10th grade. The most popular high school sports program for boys is football, followed by basketball, track and field, and baseball. The highest rates of participation for girls are found in basketball, track and field, volleyball, and softball.[10]

EXPENDITURES ON LEISURE

Expenditures per American consumer unit (usually a household) on entertainment and reading almost doubled, from $1,311 in 1985 to $2,187 in 2003. The latter figure made up about 5 percent of average household total expenditures. This includes expenditures on fees and admissions, television and sound equipment, play and sports equipment, and reading; television and sound equipment consumed about a third of the total. Examining the data another way, total recreation expenditures rose from $295 billion in 1990 to 661 billion in 2003, and increased from 7.6 to 8.5 percent of all personal consumption expenditures.[11] The largest dollar category at both points in time was spending on video and audio products, computer equipment, and musical instruments. Computer equipment spending (including peripherals such as printers and software) almost quintupled, increasing from $9 billion in 1990 to $46 billion in 2003.

These figures on consumer spending for leisure do not include spending on travel (or lodging), and

---

[8] U.S. Census Bureau. 2006. Table 1227. *Statistical Abstract of the United States, 2006.* (Washington, DC: U.S. Census Bureau.)

[9] U.S. Department of Education. National Center for Education Statistics. *Extracurricular Participation and Student Engagement* (Report 95-741). (June 1995.) <http://nces.ed.gov/pubs95/95741.pdf>. (Accessed Mar. 8, 2006.)

[10] U.S. Census Bureau. 2006. Tables 1236 and 1237. *Statistical Abstract of the United States, 2006.* (Washington, DC: U.S. Census Bureau.)

[11] U.S. Census Bureau. 2006. Tables 1222 and 1223. *Statistical Abstract of the United States, 2006.* (Washington, DC: U.S. Census Bureau.)

thus underestimate actual expenditures on leisure. Leisure travel increased from 863 million "person trips" in 1998 to 944 million in 2004. The average length of pleasure trips appears to have remained relatively stable at about 4 nights per trip. About three-quarters of these trips are by auto or truck, while one-fifth are by air. Slightly less than half involve a stay in a hotel, motel, or bed and breakfast inn.[12]

VOLUNTEERISM AND GIVING

HOW MANY VOLUNTEERS?

Some people feel guilty about spending time in leisure activities because of the historic emphasis in American society on success in the world of work. Since the image of having a strong work ethic is so highly prized in the United States, taking part in (or having time to take part in) leisure activity is equated with sloth by some people. "The ancient Athenian ideal of leisure, the absence of the necessity of being occupied, is not only rarely realized but most Americans regard contemplation as simply a waste of time—being busy has become a primary indicator of importance."[13]

Rather than spending it on themselves, some people spend their free time on others through voluntary activities, with some taking part through formal organizations and others through informal assistance (such as providing child care for a neighbor

or relative). Such activities can take a wide range of forms, from volunteering to fight fires with the local fire station to assisting teachers at the local elementary school. Volunteerism can foster a sense of helping others by doing something worthwhile with one's leisure time.

In 2005, 65.4 million people age 16 years and over, or about 29 percent of the population, volunteered with a formal organization. Women volunteered at a somewhat higher rate than men, as did people with higher educational attainment levels and people with part-time jobs. By age, the 35- to 44-year-old age group has the highest volunteering rate, followed by those 45 to 54 years old. The median number of annual volunteer hours is 50. The only demographic group with a significantly higher median is the 65 years old and over age group, which spent about twice as many hours per year in these activities.[14]

The types of activities in which people volunteer are shown in Figure 10-2. Religious activities lead the list, followed by educational/youth service and social/community service. These figures refer to the main organization for which the survey respondent volunteers; about 30 percent of volunteers perform services for more than one organization. Figure 10-3 shows the types of activities volunteers perform. Fundraising heads the list, followed by various activities involving food, tutoring/teaching, and general activities, including providing transportation.

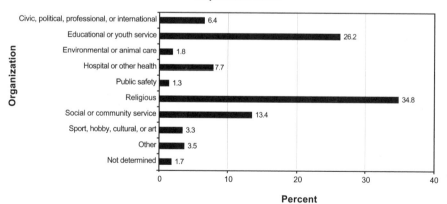

Figure 10-2. Percent Distribution of Volunteers, by Type of Organization, September 2005

Source: U.S. Bureau of Labor Statistics. *Volunteering in the United States, 2005.*

---

[12] U.S. Census Bureau. 2002. Table 1237. *Statistical Abstract of the United States, 2002.* (Washington, DC: U.S. Census Bureau.) Data obtained from the Travel Industry Association of America.

[13] Godbey, Geoffrey. "The Problem of Free Time—It's Not What You Think." Academy of Leisure Sciences. <http://www.academyofleisuresciences.org/alswp8.html>. (Accessed Mar. 17, 2006.)

[14] Bureau of Labor Statistics. *Volunteering in the United States, 2005* (USDL 05-2278). (Dec. 9, 2005.) <http://www.bls.gov/news.release/volun.nr0.htm>. (Accessed Mar. 8, 2006.) Data refer to the year between September 2004 and September 2005.

Figure 10-3. Percent Distribution of Volunteers, by Type of Activity, September 2005

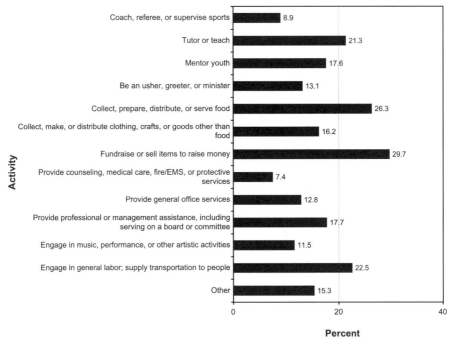

Source: U.S. Bureau of Labor Statistics. *Volunteering in the United States, 2005.*

Most volunteers become involved in one of three ways. About 40 percent approached the organization themselves. Another 43 percent were asked, either by someone in the organization (or school), or by a relative, friend, or co-worker. People who had volunteered in the past but not in the past year were asked why. Almost half cited lack of time as the main reason, while another group had health or physical problems that kept them from doing this work.

GOVERNMENT INVOLVEMENT IN VOLUNTEERISM

Government encouragement of volunteer efforts expanded in the 1990s, amid continued discussion about whether or not charitable organizations have sufficient resources to pick up social services when government support for such services is diminished. In the 1960s, the federal government initiated two volunteer programs—one with an international focus (the Peace Corps) and one with a domestic

orientation (AmeriCorps). About 182,000 Peace Corps volunteers have served in 138 countries since 1961, typically spending 2 years in a country requesting assistance. They have provided a wide variety of assistance, from water, sanitation, and health programs to teaching English and helping to launch small businesses. In 2005, there were about 8,000 Peace Corps volunteers serving in over 70 countries throughout the world.

AmeriCorps enlists about 50,000 Americans each year to provide intensive service to meet community needs in a variety of areas, including education, the environment, public safety, and homeland security. They generally work with nonprofit organizations such as Habitat for Humanity, the American Red Cross, and Teach for America. Open to citizens and lawful permanent residents 17 years old and over, these volunteers serve as full- or part-time workers over a 10- to 12-month period. The program provides an education award, which can be used for further schooling or to pay back qualified student loans; some volunteers also receive a modest annual living allowance.

Another AmeriCorps program is the National Civilian Community Corps (NCCC), which was modeled after the Depression-era Civilian Conservation Corps (CCC). The CCC put thousands of people to work in the United States during the Great Depression in the 1930s. NCCC service is restricted to 18- to 24-year-olds, who work in teams and focus on environmental improvements, although some programs are also involved in public safety, education, and disaster relief. There were about 1,200 NCCC members in 2005.

AmeriCorps is a component of the Corporation for National Service, which also includes Senior Corps and Learn and Serve. The National Senior Service Corps helps persons 55 years old and over find volunteer activities, with three programs that receive federal funds: the Grandparents Program (which provides support to children with special needs), the Senior Companions Program (which helps frail elderly persons live independently), and the Retired and Senior Volunteers Program (which provides a wide range of community services). Learn and Serve is a program for students. Service-learning, as it is often called, is a method in which students learn and develop through active participation in thoughtfully organized service that meets the needs of communities. It is coordinated between an elementary school, secondary school, institution of higher education, or community service program and the community being served. The program helps foster civic responsibility. It is integrated into the academic curriculum of participating schools, or satisfies the education components of the community service program in which the participating students are enrolled. Service-learning also provides structured time for students or participants to reflect on the service experience.[15]

School districts in the United States are attempting to increase community service participation of students, with some requiring a minimum number of hours of community service to graduate from high school. Others attempt to encourage participation without requiring students to do so. A recent survey revealed that 52 percent of students in grades 6 through 12 were involved in community service in

Table 10-3. Percent of Students in Grades 6–12 Participating in Community Service, 1999

(Percent.)

Characteristic	Percent
TOTAL	52
Grade Level	
6–8	48
9–10	50
11–12	61
Sex	
Male	47
Female	57
Race/Ethnicity	
White	56
Black	48
Hispanic (of any race)	38
Other	54
Language Spoken Most Frequently at Home by Student	
English	53
Other	35
Parents' Education	
Less than high school	37
High school diploma or equivalent	46
Some college, including vocational/technical	50
Bachelor's degree	62
Professional/graduate degree	64
School Type	
Public	50
Private	
Religious	71
Nonsectarian	68
Enrollment	
Less than 300	56
300–599	48
600–999	52
1,000 or more	54
School Practice	
Requires and arranges service	60
Requires service only	35
Arranges service only	54
Neither requires nor arranges service	29

Source: U.S. Department of Education. 2000. National Center for Education Statistics. *Youth Service-Learning and Community Service Among 6th- Through 12th-Grade Students in the United States: 1996 and 1999* (NCES 2000–028).

1999. Over half of these students also participated in service-based learning. Teenage volunteerism often occurs because the school arranges the program in which the students participate. This type of activity is more likely to occur in private (religious or non-sectarian) schools than in public schools, and more often involves children whose parents have a college degree or more.[16] (See Table 10-3.)

---

[15] For more information, see <http://www.learnandserve.org/about/service_learning.html> and <http://www.seniorcorps.org>.

[16] U.S. Department of Education. National Center for Education Statistics. *The Condition of Education* (a discussion on learner outcomes). <http://nces.ed.gov/programs/coe>. (Accessed Mar. 8, 2006.)

Figure 10-4. Percent of Men and Women Volunteering, by Educational Attainment, September 2005

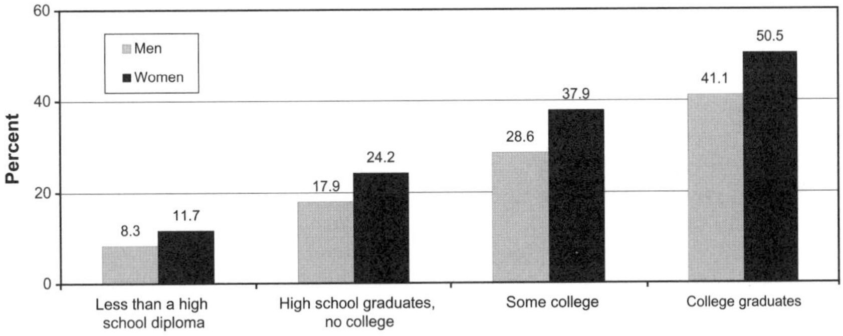

Source: U.S. Bureau of Labor Statistics. *Volunteering in the United States, 2005.*

GIVING

Charitable giving complements volunteerism. It represents the gift of money as opposed to time. Many people, of course, do both. Most households (89 percent) in the United States reported contributing to charity in 2001; their average annual contribution was $1,620, or 3.2 percent of their total income. Giving was even higher among households that included people who also volunteered, with an average contribution of nearly $2,300. Overall, 42 percent of households both volunteer and give, 46 percent report contributing only, 2 percent volunteer only, and 10 percent do neither. Factors that influence giving include being asked for gifts, having been involved with giving and volunteering as youths, opinions of the household's economic outlook, and participation in religious services.[17]

Religious organizations are both the most likely to receive charitable gifts and to have the highest average contribution. Other types of organizations that receive gifts from at least 20 percent of all households include education, health, human services (including United Way), and youth development programs.

As in many other areas of American life, the Internet is becoming important for both volunteering and giving. According to VolunteerMatch, a non-profit service that lists volunteer opportunities from almost 20,000 organizations in 27 different categories nationwide, the events of September 11, 2001, prompted a significant increase in people seeking such opportunities on the Internet. Referrals, which match a volunteer with an opportunity, have risen as well.[18] The Independent Sector notes that the both volunteering and charitable giving via the Internet are increasing, with about 1 in 8 households with Internet access using this route.

Charitable giving is also linked to the giver's level of confidence in the charity seeking the gift. A 1999 survey showed that youth development and recreational services and human service organizations ranked highest in givers' esteem; more than two-thirds of respondents reported that they had high confidence in these types of organizations. Educational organizations also rank high, along with religious institutions. Organizations at the other end of the scale included political parties, lobbying organizations, Congress, and the federal government in general. Confidence and giving levels were also linked to well-known events. For example, overall public confidence in religious organizations waned in the light of the several well-publicized scandals that occurred during the late 1980s. Finally, donors were more likely to have confidence in local charities than in national organizations.[19]

Giving is also inevitably tied to the state of the economy. When asked about their giving levels during "tough times," respondents to an Independent Sector survey stated that they would reduce their giving by amounts ranging from $130, or 23 percent, for the poorest households, to at least $1,300, or 33 percent, for the wealthiest households. The greatest decline is projected for households earning

---

17 Independent Sector. *Giving and Volunteering in the United States: 2001.* (Washington, DC: Independent Sector, <http://www.independentsector.org>.) Also see: U.S. Census Bureau. 2002. Tables 552 and 553. *Statistical Abstract of the United States, 2002.* (Washington, DC: U.S. Census Bureau.)

18 *The Detroit News,* article of April 1, 2002.

19 Independent Sector. *Taking the Pulse of Americans' Attitudes Toward Charities.* <http://www.independentsector.org/programs/research/factfind3.pdf>. (Accessed Mar. 8, 2006.)

between $25,000 and $50,000 per year, with an expected decline of 45 percent (from $1,300 to $710).[20]

RELIGIOSITY

RELIGIOUS IDENTIFICATION

The most important trend in religious identification in recent years is the significant growth in the proportion of the population not reporting their religion as Christianity or Judaism. In 2002, 1 in 8 Americans identified with another specific religion, such as Greek Orthodoxy, Mormonism, Buddhism, or Hinduism. This is one effect of the substantial Asian immigration to the United States over the past two decades. Still, over half the population identifies itself as Protestant, with another one-quarter identifying as Catholic. The proportion reporting no religion has also increased in recent decades.[21] Among Protestants, Baptists are the leading denomination, with about one-third of the total, followed by Methodists. About half of all Christians describe themselves as "born-again" or "evangelical," according to a recent Gallup poll.

The Gallup Organization reports on a composite Index of Leading Religious Indicators, which includes measures such as belief in God, having a religious preference, being a member of a church or synagogue, attending church or synagogue weekly, and respondents' views of the role of religion in their lives. In the 1950s, the index score peaked at 746 (of a possible 1,000). It declined slowly over

the years, with a low point of 650 in 1988, but increased during the 1990s and was measured at 671 in 2001. Its top components are belief in God (95 percent) and stating a religious preference (92 percent). The lowest component is church attendance in the past week (41 percent). About 58 percent indicate that religion is very important in their lives.

The proportion of people who neither belong to a church or synagogue, nor attend services unrelated to major holidays or life events has been growing over time; it increased from 41 percent in 1978 to 47 percent in 2001. The Gallup Organization labels people in this category the "unchurched." Many of these people, however, have been or will be "churched" at some point in their lives. Affiliation with religious institutions tends to be highest among families with children, and lowest among young people and people who are single.

Among people who do belong to congregations, about one-quarter are actively engaged with the institution: they tend to be more spiritually committed and to devote more time and money to these organizations than members who are not engaged. About half the members are minimally engaged, and one in five is actively disengaged, with most of these members rarely attending services.

A higher proportion of the elderly attend church regularly, as compared to other age groups (39 percent of those over age 65, compared with 26 percent of young adults). Women tend to attend religious services more regularly than men, with about one-third

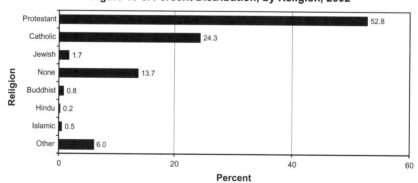

Figure 10-5. Percent Distribution, by Religion, 2002

Religion	Percent
Protestant	52.8
Catholic	24.3
Jewish	1.7
None	13.7
Buddhist	0.8
Hindu	0.2
Islamic	0.5
Other	6.0

Source: The Association of Religion Data Archives. General Social Survey, 2002.

[20] Independent Sector. 2003. *Giving in Tough Times.* (Washington, DC: Independent Sector. http://www.independentsector.org/programs/research/toughtimes.html>.)
[21] The Gallup Organization. *The Gallup Poll Monthly.* (Princeton: The Gallup Poll. <http://www.gallup.com>.)

of women and one-quarter of men in the United States reporting weekly attendance. Blacks report weekly attendance more frequently than do Whites (40 percent versus 29 percent). Weekly attendance is considerably more likely among residents living in the South (38 percent) and the Northeast (34 percent) than among residents of the Midwest (26 percent) or West, where only 19 percent report weekly church attendance. There is not much difference in attendance by educational attainment level (27 percent with a college degree and 33 percent with no college degree), but there is significant difference by political affiliation. Republicans are considerably more likely to be weekly churchgoers (44 percent) than either Democrats or Independents (25 percent and 22 percent, respectively).

RELIGION AND POLITICS

The U.S. Constitution states that Congress cannot make any laws specifying the establishment of a state religion and that Americans are free to worship as they see fit. While politics may not shape religion in America, religious affiliation does influence political values. The general tendency is that the more devout a person is, the more politically conservative he or she is. This not only affects viewpoints on matters such as abortion, homosexuality, and family, but also perceptions of national security and environmental issues. While the fundamentalist classification cuts across denominations, Baptists make up the largest share of "born-again" or evangelical Christians.

Views on the amount of influence religion has on American life are subject to real time events. Polls showed that in the wake of the September 11, 2001, attacks, the proportion of Americans believing religious participation was on the rise increased substantially. By March 2002, however, the proportion was back to where it had been before September 11. About half of Americans believe that the United States has special protection from God; this view is held by 71 percent of evangelical White Christians, but only by 40 percent of mainline Protestants and Catholics. Almost all White evangelicals believe that America's strength is based on religious faith; in contrast, only 20 percent of people identifying themselves as secular hold this view.[22]

A July 2003 study by the Pew Center shows that 62 percent of Americans think that President Bush "strikes the right balance" in his frequent mentions of his religious faith, and 58 percent believe the president's reliance on religion in policy-making is reasonable. However, many Americans "express a general discomfort when exposed to actual religious statements by various politicians." However, 58 percent say that religion does not affect their voting decisions.[23]

[22] The Pew Research Center for the People and the Press. *Americans Struggle with Religion's Role at Home and Abroad.* (Mar. 2002.) <http://pewforum.org/publications/reports/poll2002.pdf>. (Accessed Mar. 8, 2006.)

[23] Pew Research Center for the People and the Press. *Religion and Politics: Contention and Consensus.* (July 2003.) <http://pewforum.org/publications/surveys/religion-politics.pdf>. (Accessed Mar. 8, 2006.)

FOR FURTHER INFORMATION SEE:

The Gallup Organization. *The Gallup Poll Monthly*. (Princeton: The Gallup Poll. <http://www.gallup.com>.)

WEB SITES:

Corporation for National and Community Service. <http://www.cns.gov>. (Accessed Mar. 8, 2006.)

Independent Sector. <http://www.independentsector.org>. (Accessed Mar. 8, 2006.)

Peace Corps. <http://www.peacecorps.gov>. (Accessed Mar. 8, 2006.)

Pew Research Center for People and the Press. <http://www.people-press.org>. (Accessed Mar. 8, 2006.)

U.S. Census Bureau. *Statistical Abstract of the United States*. <http://www.census.gov/statab/www>. (Accessed Mar. 8, 2006.)

Chapter 11
Voting

ELIGIBILITY TO VOTE

Until 1920, the right to vote to elect the president, Congress, and local officials was restricted to a minority of the adult population in the United States. Women did not have the right to vote. Indeed, prior to 1900, the voting franchise was generally limited to White males. Early in the nation's history, some states (especially those in New England) required religious tests, and others required ownership of property in order to be eligible to vote. Since eligibility was determined by each state, the removal of these requirements was uneven, although they had largely disappeared by the time of the Civil War. In the aftermath of that war, Congress enacted constitutional amendments to elevate the status of former slaves to full citizenship. These amendments included the right to vote—this was the 15th Amendment to the U.S. Constitution, enacted in 1870. The greatest expansion of the electorate was the inclusion of females, which began in 1869 when Wyoming Territory gave women the vote. By the time the 19th Amendment was added to the Constitution in 1920, 15 states had granted women full suffrage. That amendment extended eligibility to all American women, regardless of residence.

After the Civil War, Black citizens' attempts to register and vote were often frustrated, especially in the South, by devices such as poll taxes and literacy tests. The latter was especially susceptible to manipulation by unsympathetic electoral officials. Efforts to overturn discrimination against the Black citizens who tried to exercise their right to vote culminated in the 24th Amendment to the U.S. Constitution in 1964. That amendment prohibited the payment of poll taxes as a requirement for voting in federal elections. The Voting Rights Act of 1965 and subsequent amendments abolished literacy tests as a prerequisite for voting and reduced the residency requirement for voting in presidential elections to 30 days.

In 1971, the 26th Amendment lowered the voting age for all persons from 21 to 18 years. Currently, all persons who are 18 years of age or over, who are citizens of the United States, who meet local residence requirements, and who are not convicted felons or mentally incompetent are eligible to vote in federal elections.

REGISTRATION

In most jurisdictions in the United States, a registration process is required before becoming eligible to vote. In most cases, the voter must register at least 30 days prior to the election.[1] Once registered, a person stays on the election rolls as long as he or she lives at the same address and meets the state requirement for frequency of voting (usually at least once every four years). Some states have permanent registration, regardless of voter turnout. Barriers to registration have been substantially removed since World War II. Through a combination of constitutional amendments, acts of Congress, and Supreme Court decisions, registration has been greatly simplified. For example, residence requirements were once as much as 2 years in some states; the maximum residence requirement for federal elections is now 30 days.

The National Voter Registration Act (NVRA) of 1993 and the Help America Vote Act (HAVA), which amended the NRVA in 2002, are the most recent attempts to expand the core of registered voters. These acts require a biennial report to Congress on patterns of voter registration; the latest, issued in June 2005, is the sixth in the series and the first to be produced by the Election Assistance Commission (EAC).[2] Voter registration increased in the 2004 election to over the 2000 level, but did not keep pace with the rate of growth in the voting age population. The EAC estimated that the share of the voting age population that was actually registered dropped slightly, from 78.9 percent in 2000 to 78.5 percent in 2004.

The NVRA implemented the "motor-voter" program, through which a citizen may choose to have his or her voter registration automatically updated when the address on his or her driver's license or state identification card is changed. The act also required states to accept registrations by mail, and encouraged the establishment of voter registration programs in public agencies which serve the poor.

In its 2005 report, the EAC made strong recommendations concerning the electronic transmission of information between motor vehicle offices and other voter registration agencies, such as county and local clerks.

---

[1] North Dakota does not have a registration requirement. Wisconsin, Minnesota, Maine, New Hampshire, Idaho, and Wyoming permit election day registration.

[2] Election Assistance Commission. June 2005. *The Impact of the National Voter Registration Act on the Administration of Elections for Federal Office, 2003–2004.* <http://www.eac.gov/election_resources/NVRA-2004-Survey.pdf>. (Accessed Jan. 11, 2006.)

Turnout in National Elections

Having a higher proportion of eligible voters participate in national elections is considered by some as
a measure of the health of the body politic, but this
is an oversimplification. "More is better" is not necessarily indicative of a healthy democratic society.
Nazi Germany routinely proclaimed voter turnouts
approaching unanimity in the various referenda they
conducted. Some countries attempt to guarantee
high turnouts by making voting compulsory, fining
nonvoters who do not provide a valid excuse.
However, there is no evidence that these devices
promote more beneficial results. On the other hand,
an unusually low turnout in a national election
would indicate a level of apathy that would be considered unhealthy in a democratic society.

Since the vote was extended to a majority of the
population, the highest turnout in an election in the
United States occurred in the presidential election
of 1960, when 63 percent of eligible voters participated. (See Figure 11-1.) This contrasts with a 49
percent turnout in 1996, a post-World-War-II low. In
presidential election years, there is an approximately 5 percentage point drop-off in votes for members
of the House of Representatives; this is made up of
people who cast votes for a presidential candidate
but do not do so for congressional or other races on
the ballot. Presidential elections occur every 4 years
(the most recent one in 2004), while elections for
Congress and some state and local offices occur
every two years. Elections in non-presidential years
exhibit substantially lower voting participation levels,

with declines of 13 to 17 percentage points. This
discrepancy results from lower voter interest in
these elections due to the absence of the contest
for president, plus situations in which incumbents
are unopposed or where long-time incumbents are
perceived to be invulnerable.[3]

Voting participation differs substantially among the
50 states. For example, in 2004, Minnesota
achieved the highest turnout at 76 percent, and
Hawaii was lowest with 48 percent. Oregon's high
turnout (71 percent) may be related to its practice of
conducting elections entirely by mail.[4] States with
voter turnout below the national average were disproportionately located in the South. (See Figure
11-2 and Table 11-1.)

Table 11-1. Voter Turnout, November 2004

(Percent of voting-age population that voted in 2004
election.)

State	Percent
United States	60.7
States with Highest Turnout	
Minnesota	76.1
Wisconsin	74.1
Maine	73.7
Oregon	71.4
New Hampshire	70.4
States with Lowest Turnout	
Hawaii	47.9
Texas	52.0
Arkansas	52.1
South Carolina	52.4
Georgia	53.9

Source: U.S. Election Assistance Commission.

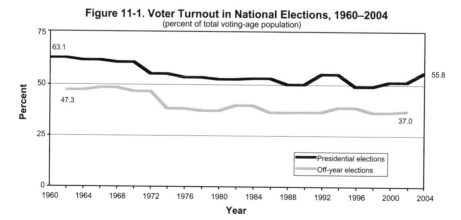

Figure 11-1. Voter Turnout in National Elections, 1960–2004
(percent of total voting-age population)

Source: U.S. Election Assistance Commission.

---

[3] Survey data, such as the data discussed here which come from the Census Bureau's Current Population Survey, tend to overestimate
voting participation relative to administrative tallies of votes cast. The reason for this is that many people who do not vote will report on
a survey that they did vote in a particular election. For further discussion, see: U.S. Census Bureau. 2002. Voting and registration in
the election of November 2000. *Current Population Report P20-542.*

[4] For an explanation of the Oregon voting process, see: <http://www.oregonvotes.org/elec101.htm>. (Accessed Jan. 6, 2006.)

Figure 11-2. Voter Turnout, 2004

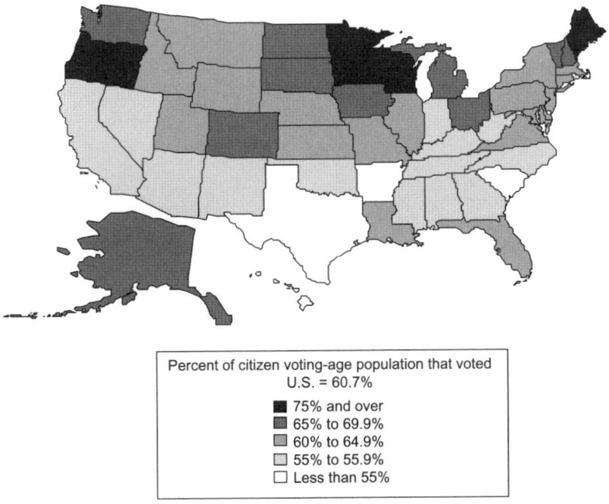

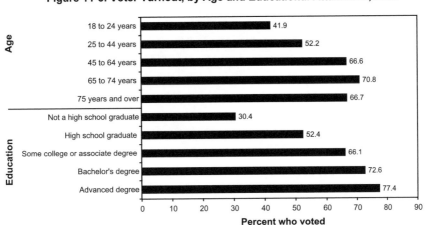

Percent of citizen voting-age population that voted
U.S. = 60.7%

■ 75% and over
■ 65% to 69.9%
■ 60% to 64.9%
□ 55% to 55.9%
□ Less than 55%

Source: U.S. Election Assistance Commission.

Numerous studies have demonstrated that participation in elections varies by population group. Turnout increases with age, with the youngest of the potentially eligible voters (those under age 25) having the lowest turnout. In 2004, persons 65 to 74 years old voted at nearly twice the rate of persons 18 to 24 years old. (See Figure 11-3.) Educational level and income are also strong predictors of turnout. Those with college degrees or more and those with high incomes vote at levels up to 40 percentage points higher than persons at the opposite ends of these scales.

Members of minority groups have traditionally exhibited lower electoral participation, although the gap between Blacks and Whites has narrowed since the 1960s as formal and informal barriers to registration and voting have been removed. (See Figure 11-4.) These data, calculated using the citizen voting age population as a base, show Hispanics behind Blacks in voter turnout, but by a much smaller margin than if the figures were calculated using the total voting age population.

Figure 11-3. Voter Turnout, by Age and Educational Attainment, 2004

Age

- 18 to 24 years — 41.9
- 25 to 44 years — 52.2
- 45 to 64 years — 66.6
- 65 to 74 years — 70.8
- 75 years and over — 66.7

Education

- Not a high school graduate — 30.4
- High school graduate — 52.4
- Some college or associate degree — 66.1
- Bachelor's degree — 72.6
- Advanced degree — 77.4

Percent who voted (0, 10, 20, 30, 40, 50, 60, 70, 80, 90)

Source: U.S. Census Bureau.

Figure 11-4. Voter Turnout in Presidential Elections, 1980–2004
(percent of citizen voting-age population)

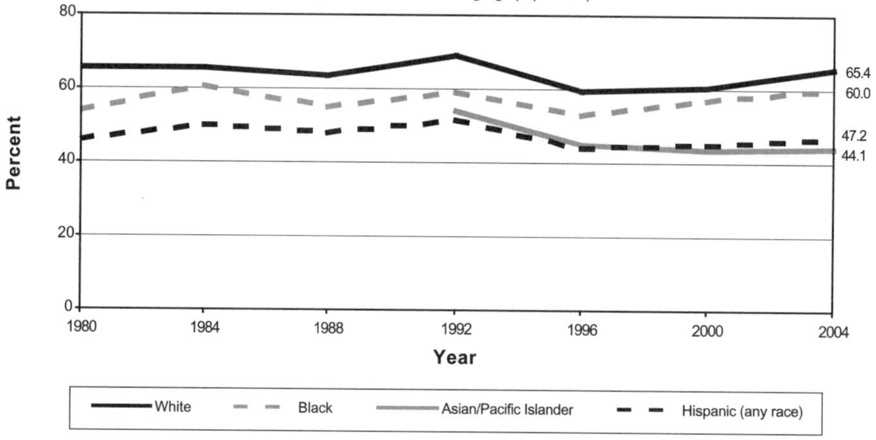

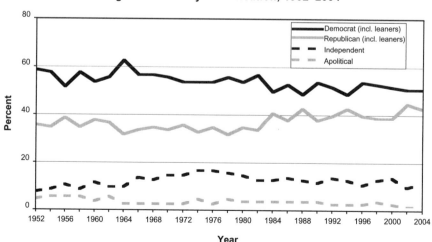

Source: U.S. Census Bureau.

PARTY IDENTIFICATION

Identification with the two major political parties in the United States (Democratic and Republican) has remained relatively constant over the past 50 years, with variations closely tied to the party holding the White House. (See Figure 11-5.) The proportion reporting themselves "independent" or "apolitical" grew over the years, from 1952 (9 percent) to 2000 (12 percent). However, this rate had dropped back to 10 percent by 2004. The drop is compensated by an increase in Republican identification, likely due to the national mood after the terrorist attacks of September 11, 2001.

About one-third of voters currently identify themselves weakly with one party or the other, while 31 percent are strong partisans. Among both Republicans and Democrats, the proportion saying they are an "Independent [party]" has grown at the expense of stronger identification with either party. Democrats still lead Republicans in overall identification patterns, but the margin has been shrinking over time.[5]

Looking at party identification by selected demographic and economic characteristics (see Table 11-2), there is remarkably little change over time in the proportions of various group populations who identi-

Figure 11-5. Party Identification, 1952–2004

Source: American National Election Studies. *The ANES Guide to Public Opinion and Electoral Behavior, 2004.*

[5] See tables available from: Center for Political Studies. Institute for Social Research. University of Michigan. <http://www.umich.edu/~nes>. (Accessed Jan. 6, 2006.) This organization originated the concept of "leaning" toward a particular party identification.

Table 11-2. Percent of Voters Identifying as Republican or Democrat, Selected Years, 1952–2004

(Percent.)

Characteristic	1952	1964	1976	1988	2000	2004
Total Republican	34	30	33	41	37	41
Males	33	30	33	45	41	44
Females	35	30	33	38	34	37
Whites	36	33	37	48	42	49
Blacks	17	8	6	12	7	7
Not a high school graduate	28	20	24	26	30	20
College graduate or more	53	46	48	52	48	45
Very low income	29	24	26	30	22	29
Very high income	59	48	68	77	54	51
Professionals	42	43	42	48	44	38
Blue collar workers	27	21	24	33	31	38
Union households	28	17	22	33	28	30
Non-union households	36	34	36	43	38	43
Total Democrat	57	61	52	47	50	49
Males	58	61	50	43	46	45
Females	56	61	52	50	53	53
Whites	56	59	47	39	44	42
Blacks	63	82	85	80	83	81
Not a high school graduate	59	70	62	56	58	55
College graduate or more	44	48	40	42	44	51
Very low income	57	65	60	55	62	54
Very high income	28	44	23	19	36	46
Professionals	51	49	44	43	46	56
Blue collar workers	66	70	58	51	55	49
Union households	66	77	62	55	61	59
Non-union households	54	56	49	45	48	48

Source: American National Election Studies. *The ANES Guide to Public Opinion and Electoral Behavior, 2004.* <http://www.umich.edu/~nes/nesguide/nesguide.htm>. (Accessed Feb. 2, 2006.)

fy themselves as Republicans. In 2004, men were more likely than women to fall in this category. College graduates, high-income persons, and professionals have always had higher rates of Republican identification than their opposites: non-high school graduates, low-income persons, and blue-collar workers. However, more blue-collar workers and more union members have identified themselves as Republicans in recent years than in the past; the party experienced a major gain in 2004, in which formerly independent voters became identified with Republicans. Again, the impact of the presidential winner is apparent, as it was in 1964, when Barry Goldwater was heavily defeated by Lyndon Johnson. For most of the groups shown, Republican identification was at its low point that year.

HOW ELECTIONS ARE CONDUCTED

After the 2000 presidential election was decided by the Supreme Court, amid many complaints about voting procedures in Florida and other states, a movement took shape to help make these procedures clearer and more uniform across the country. The impact of the Help America Vote Act of 2002 (HAVA) on registration procedures is discussed above. Information about the actual conduct of elections is available from the 2004 Election Day Survey.[6]

One important change has been in the kind of voting methods employed during elections. Historically, smaller jurisdictions used paper ballots, while larger jurisdictions used either voting machines or punch card systems. By 2004, less than 2 percent of all ballots were cast on paper. Optical scan systems were in place for 39 percent of voters, and electronic systems were used by 23 percent. The Election Assistance Commission (EAC) has distributed several billion dollars to states for the purpose of upgrading voting equipment and establishing statewide voter registration databases. The EAC is also responsible for developing guidelines to help states spend these funds and establish a new process for certifying voting equipment.

In 2005, the Government Accountability Office (GAO) released a report on the security and reliability of electronic voting machines. The report stated, "While electronic voting systems hold promise for a more accurate and efficient election process, numerous entities have raised concerns about their security and reliability, citing instances of weak security controls, system design flaws, inadequate system version control, inadequate security testing, incorrect system configuration, poor security management, and vague or incomplete voting system standards," among other issues. One major problem is that the software that operates these electronic systems is proprietary and cannot be verified by independent observers. There is also no paper

[6] United States Election Assistance Commission. 2005. *2004 Election Day Survey.* <http://www.eac.gov/election_survey_2004/intro.htm>. (Accessed Jan. 6, 2006.)

audit trail or record of the votes that were actually cast, making recounts impossible. As of early 2006, many jurisdictions had implemented these new voting systems, even though appropriate safeguards were not yet in place.

Another important trend has been voting by methods other than the traditional one of showing up at the polls on election day. Rules for using absentee ballots vary by state, with some states strongly encouraging this method of voting. Some states offer an early voting option, where voters cast ballots before election day. A provision of HAVA allows for "provisional votes" when there is a question about the voter's eligibility. About 1.9 million provisional ballots were cast in 2004, with 1.2 million of them ultimately being counted. This system was used most prominently in California, especially by persons of Hispanic origin; 73 percent of the 668,000 provisional ballots cast there were counted.

PAYING FOR POLITICAL CAMPAIGNS

U.S. political campaigns have become increasingly expensive over the years, even with inflation taken into account. (See Figure 11-6.) In the 2003–2004 election cycle (January 1, 2003, through December 31, 2004), a total of almost $1.5 billion was raised and over $1.4 billion spent by the federal committees of the two major parties. These figures are nearly double the figure raised and spent over the comparable period for the 2000 presidential election. Candidate campaigns raised and spent about $674 million, while political parties, other individuals, and groups spent $192 million independently advocating for one side or the other. Over the four-year period for the 2004 presidential election, the two main presidential candidates and their supporters spent about $2.2 billion, including about $207 million in public funds for the 2004 presidential election.

Direct fundraising by the two presidential candidates after the nominating conventions was prohibited by the Bipartisan Campaign Reform Act of 2002 (BRCA), often referred to as the McCain-Feingold Act. This law prohibits the national political parties from raising or spending nonfederal funds—otherwise known as "soft money"—on federal elections. It requires party committees to fund federal election activities with only federal funds (i.e. "hard money") or with money raised under specific limitations and reporting requirements. It also limits fundraising activities. Most specifically, BRCA limits the amounts that corporations, labor unions, and wealthy individuals can contribute to federal candidates and to the national parties.

Passage of this law gave impetus to the so-called "527" organizations, which are permitted to raise money freely and spend it on political activity, as long as they are not endorsing specific candidates and are independent of the political parties. "527" refers to the section of the Internal Revenue Code which exempts political organizations from federal income tax. Prominent examples in 2004 included Swift Boat Veterans for Truth and MoveOn.org. According to the Center for Responsive Politics, 527 organizations raised and spent about $600 million in the 2003–2004 campaign cycle.

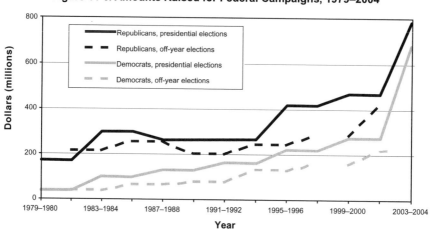

Figure 11-6. Amounts Raised for Federal Campaigns, 1979–2004

Source: Federal Election Commission.

Individual candidates for the U.S. Senate and House of Representatives raised more than $1.2 billion in total for the 2004 election, an increase of 25 percent over 2002. (See Figure 11-7.) Senate fundraising took an unexplained dip in 2002, but went right back up in 2004.

Political Action Committees (PACs) continue to represent a significant portion of political funds raised. PAC contributions to all federal candidates for the 2003–2004 election cycle were $310 million, up 10 percent from 2001–2002. Democratic House and Senate candidates received $134 million of these funds, Republicans received $174 million, while candidates from other parties received about $2.5 million. Incumbents are the primary beneficiaries of PAC money; they received 79 percent of the funds in 2003–2004.[7]

Paying for political campaigns out of public funds was first proposed by President Theodore Roosevelt in his 1907 State of the Union address. However, legislation to finance presidential election campaigns with tax dollars was not enacted until 1971, with the first funds dispersed for the 1976 election. The funds are authorized through an option offered to each taxpayer on their income tax returns. Originally $1, the voluntary checkoff amount is now $3. The checkoff neither increases the amount of taxes owed nor decreases any refund due.

Funding is available to any presidential candidate seeking nomination by a political party. The candi-

date must show broad-based public support, defined as raising at least $5,000 in at least 20 states through contributions of $250 or less per person. Candidates must also agree to limit primary election campaign spending to $10 million,[8] limit spending in individual states according to an established formula, and limit spending from personal funds to $50,000.[9] In the general election, Republican and Democratic nominees are eligible for a public grant of $20 million, but must agree to limit their spending to this amount plus (if desired) $50,000 in personal funds. There are also provisions for minor party candidates to receive such funding, based on the party's performance in the preceding presidential election. In addition, each major party may receive $4 million to finance its nominating convention. If violations of the law are identified during an audit, the candidates and convention committees must repay the public funds to the U.S. Treasury.

During the primary campaigns for the 2004 presidential election, Democratic candidates received a total of $28 million in matching funds. The largest amounts went to Sen. John Edwards ($6.7 million), Gen. Wesley Clark ($7.6 million), and Sen. Joseph Lieberman ($4.3 million). Republican George W. Bush, the incumbent, declined matching funds; he had no primary opposition. In the general election, each major party nominee received $74.6 million and raised an additional $21 million for legal and accounting costs. Private fundraising for campaign activities in the general election is not permitted.

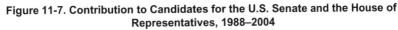

Figure 11-7. Contribution to Candidates for the U.S. Senate and the House of Representatives, 1988–2004

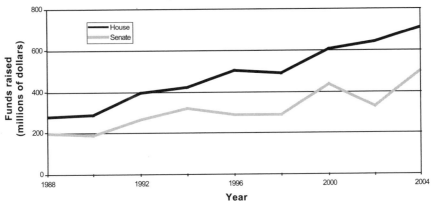

Source: Federal Election Commission.

---

[7] Federal Election Commission. 2005. *PAC Activity Increases for 2004 Elections.* (Apr. 13, 2005.) <http://www.fec.gov/press/press2005/20050412pac/PACFinal2004.html>. (Accessed Feb. 2, 2006.)

[8] All figures cited here are subject to cost of living adjustments (COLA), and thus are higher for recent and future elections.

[9] Federal Election Commission. *Public Funding of Presidential Elections.* <http://www.fec.gov/pages/brochures/pubfund.shtml>. (Accessed Feb. 2, 2006.)

FOR FURTHER INFORMATION SEE:

Office of the Federal Register. National Archives and Records Administration. 2004. *The United States Government Manual, 2004–2005*. <http://www.gpoaccess.gov/gmanual/browse-gm-04.html>. (Accessed Jan. 6, 2006.)

U.S. Census Bureau. 2005. *Statistical Abstract of the United States, 2004–2005*. (Washington, DC: U.S. Census Bureau.)

U.S. Census Bureau. 2004. Voting and registration in the election of November 2002. *Current Population Reports P20-552*. <http://www.census.gov/prod/2004pubs/p20-552.pdf>. (Accessed Jan. 6, 2006.).

United States Election Assistance Commission. 2005. *The Impact of the National Voter Registration Act of 1993 on the Administration of Elections for Federal Office, 2003–2004*. <http://www.eac.gov/docs/NVRA-2004-Survey.pdf>. (Accessed Jan. 6, 2006.)

WEB SITES:

Center for Responsive Politics. <http://www.opensecrets.org>.

Election Assistance Commission. <http://www.eac.gov>.

Federal Election Commission. <http://www.fec.gov>.

National Election Studies at the University of Michigan. <http://www.umich.edu/~nes>.

U.S. Census Bureau. <http://www.census.gov>.

VoteTrust USA. <http://www.votetrustusa.org>.

Chapter 12

Government

INTRODUCTION

This chapter brings some perspective, context, and background to discussions about government and government spending in the United States. Looking at American government through the prism of these statistics, this chapter will address such questions as:

- Compared to other countries, is government a large or small part of the U.S. economy?

- How many governments are there in the United States?

- Just how big is the government sector compared to the private sector?

- What are the overall sources of government revenues? Do the sources differ much for federal, state and local governments? Do they differ much from area to area?

- On what does government spend its money? How much does government spending vary for different areas?

- Has the emphasis of government activity changed much over the past several decades?

GOVERNMENT AND THE ECONOMY: AN INTERNATIONAL COMPARISON

Classic conservative-liberal discussions in the United States have often been framed around the issues of whether the government is too big, too intrusive, too much of a drag on the economy, or whether it needs to play more of a role in certain societal concerns, such as caring for neglected people, labor/management issues, and education funding. Compared with other countries, just how big is our government—federal, state, and local—relative to the economy?[1]

One measure of the size of a country's government relative to the size of its economy is a comparison of taxes relative to gross domestic product (GDP).[2] This is a fair measure because taxes are, by far, the single largest source of governmental revenue. Relative to other industrialized countries, the United States was ranked 27th out of 30 OECD[3] countries in 2004, a position that has varied little since 1980. (See Figure 12-1 and Appendix Table A12-1.) To some, this low rank is positive because they see taxes as a drag on the economy—the higher the ranking, the less money for business investment. Others also see this in positive terms, but with an entirely different slant—the United States has a

Figure 12-1. Tax Revenue as a Percent of Gross Domestic Product, 2004

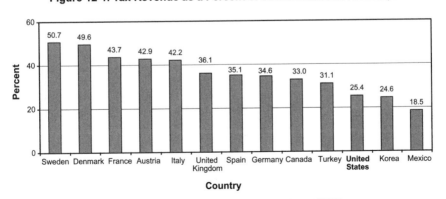

Source: Organisation for Economic Co-operation and Development (OECD).

---

[1] It is important to be cautious in comparing government activity among different countries. First, the definition of government can vary considerably. Some countries are highly socialistic, where almost everything is government; others are free-market where government is minimal. Second, it is very difficult to determine the defining line between national and sub-national government activity.

[2] Gross domestic product (GDP) is quantitative economic measure of a country's economy. In this instance, taxes become the measure of the size of government. Although the resulting comparison requires some caution in interpretation, it is a reasonable measure of the impact of government on an economy.

[3] OECD is the "Organisation for Economic Co-operation and Development," headquartered in Paris. OECD members include Canada, Mexico, the United States, Australia, Japan, Korea, New Zealand, and 23 European nations. See <http://www.oecd.org> for more information.

much greater taxing capacity than it is using. This "extra" capacity might be available to help reduce social problems, maintain or extend infrastructure, or make important government investments in the future for activities such as education. However interpreted, the fact remains that, compared with these other industrialized countries, the United States is a "low tax" nation.

GOVERNMENT AND THE ECONOMY: A STATE COMPARISON

Just as we can observe the varying economic role of government within nations, we can examine the same thing within our own states. Each state can be visualized as an individual entity with the economic attributes of a separate nation, and its economic growth can be gauged by the measures similar to those used for a nation's GDP. This measure is known as gross state product (GSP). Some states (California, for example) have such large economies that they would be among the top 10 in the world if they were countries.

GSP, a statistic produced by the Bureau of Economic Analysis, is the state equivalent of the national-level GDP. The role of government in a state's economy can be measured by looking at the percentage of GSP that can be attributed to government. The range for 2003, excluding the District of Columbia, ran from 8.4 percent in Delaware to 22.7 percent in Hawaii. (See Table 12-1.) There are some geographical patterns among the 2003 rankings. For example, three of the six New England states are among the bottom five, while the high rankings of Alaska and Hawaii show their dependency on federal government activities.

Government has composed a decreasing share of most states' economies since 1977, the year when GSP was first measured. At the national level, the percentage of GSP represented by government dropped from 13.5 percent in 1977 to 12.1 percent in 2003. The picture for the future largely depends on the degree to which states continue programs formerly conducted at the federal level. Welfare is a prime example of this type of program.

THE STRUCTURE OF GOVERNMENT

Just as government has a different economic impact in each state, the structure of government takes on a very different cast in different parts of the country. Although people sometimes perceive that government has a certain uniformity, in reality it is a series of 50 variations at the state level.

Table 12-1. Government as a Percent of Gross State Product, 2003

(Percent.)

State	Percent
Highest States	
Hawaii	22.7
New Mexico	19.9
Alaska	19.8
Mississippi	17.4
Virginia	17.2
Lowest States	
Delaware	8.4
Massachusetts	8.7
Connecticut	8.9
New Hampshire	9.2
Pennsylvania	9.7

Source: Bureau of Economic Analysis.

The role of counties varies widely. In about half the states, county governments share responsibilities with sub-county governments and special districts. In New England, counties are very weak; in fact, county governments do not exist at all in Connecticut and Rhode Island. In those two states, the primary local governments are cities and towns.

However, in about 20 states, there are no county subdivisions; counties carry out most of the governmental functions (other than school districts) in territory which is not incorporated. Maryland and Virginia have no sub-county governments at all; when a city incorporates, it is no longer part of its old county. Instead, it becomes a county-equivalent.

Even the federal government—ostensibly the same wherever one travels—has different looks in various parts of the country. For example, the federal government owns a considerable portion of the land in some states and very little in others. Of all the land area in the United States, more than one-quarter—a rather surprising 29.6 percent—belongs to the federal government. This percentage was 33.9 percent in 1960. It fell between the mid-1970s and mid-1980s, reaching the current level in the late 1980s. Although it might seem that the federally-owned portion of land would be highest in the District of Columbia (26.3 percent), all the states in the Western region, except Hawaii, exceed that figure—some by a considerable amount. In six of those Western and Pacific area states, more than half of the land is federally owned, led by Nevada at 91 percent. (See Figure 12-2.)

Within other regions, there is considerable variation in how much land belongs to the federal government. The nine Northeast states range from 0.5 percent (Connecticut) to 14.4 percent (New Hampshire). The 12 Midwest states range from 1.2 percent in Kansas to 10.0 percent in Michigan. The

Figure 12-2. Percent of Federally Owned Land, 2003

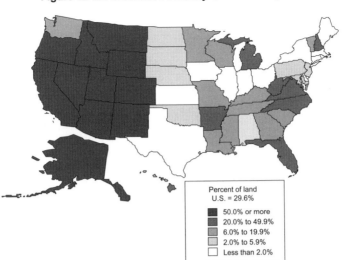

Percent of land
U.S. = 29.6%

- ■ 50.0% or more
- ■ 20.0% to 49.9%
- ▨ 6.0% to 19.9%
- ░ 2.0% to 5.9%
- □ Less than 2.0%

Source: U.S. Census Bureau. Table 347. *Statistical Abstract of the United States, 2004–2005.*

percentage of land ownership and the type of land owned (national forests, military bases, grazing lands, national parks, and the like) give the federal government a very different presence among the states. These differences might influence feelings about taxes, specific laws, or media treatment that likely translate into different social, political, and economic views of the federal government by the citizens. Whether these thoughts are extended to governments as a whole is unknown. Yet the public does have opinions about which levels of government they like and the various facets of government that please or displease them.

VARIATIONS IN THE STRUCTURE OF STATE AND LOCAL GOVERNMENTS

The immediacy and importance of local government today make it difficult to remember that local governments are not mentioned in the U.S. Constitution. The Tenth Amendment divides all powers between just two governmental levels, a central federal government and state-level government. Each state constitution sets the rules for dividing power between the state governments and their subordinate governments. Local governments are, to quote John F. Dillon, a renowned Iowa judge and local government legal commentator, "creatures of the state."[4] Using their legal authority, states have developed a tapestry of state and local government structures that are showcases for our federal system as laboratories of government. The richness and diversity of the state and local governing institutions are the result of the different mixes of geography, history, and economic factors.

The first thing one notices about governments is just how many of them there are—about 87,600 in 2002. The largest number was in Illinois (6,904) and the fewest, excluding the District of Columbia, in Hawaii (20). The number of governments correlates roughly with population—that is, more people, more governments—with Illinois, Pennsylvania (5,032), Texas (4,785), and California (4,410) in the top four spots. Ohio (3,637) and New York (3,421) came in sixth and eighth, and Michigan (2,805) was in twelfth position. However, Kansas, Nebraska, and North Dakota—all with fairly low population rankings— appear among the top dozen states in terms of numbers of governments. (See Table 12-2.)

The governing systems that exist today have both historical roots and modern origins. For example, townships in Midwestern states have a direct link to the Federal Northwest Territory Ordinance of 1787, which mandated their creation.[5] The growth in special district governments in California since 1977 is attributed by some to the passage of Proposition 13 in 1978.

---

4 Dillon, John F. 1911. *Commentaries on the Law of Municipal Corporations*. (Boston: Little, Brown and Co.)

5 The Federal General Revenue Sharing Program was a direct distribution of federal funds to state and local governments. It began in the early 1970s and continued for about 15 years. This may have been a factor in the maintenance of very small general purpose governments, such as townships. However, townships in the Midwest have been around for two centuries, and show little inclination to dissolve. On the contrary, at least in Michigan, township government has grown larger and stronger. As population size increases, these communities tend to retain the township form of government rather than incorporate as cities.

Table 12-2. Rank of States, by Number of Internal Governments and Population, 2002

(Number, rank.)

State	Governments		Population		Difference in government/ population rank
	Number	Rank	Number (thousands)	Rank	
Illinois	6 904	1	12 601	5	4
Pennsylvania	5 032	2	12 335	6	4
Texas	4 785	3	21 780	2	1
California	4 410	4	35 116	1	3
Kansas	3 888	5	2 716	32	27
Ohio	3 637	6	11 421	7	1
Minnesota	3 483	7	5 020	21	14
Missouri	3 423	8	5 673	17	9
New York	3 421	9	19 158	3	6
Indiana	3 086	10	6 159	14	4
Wisconsin	3 049	11	5 441	20	9
Michigan	2 805	12	10 050	8	4
Nebraska	2 792	13	1 729	38	25
North Dakota	2 736	14	634	48	34
Iowa	1 976	15	2 937	30	15

Source: U.S. Census Bureau. 2002 Census of Governments. *Government Organization, 2002.* <http://www.census.gov/prod/2003pubs/gc021x1.pdf>. (Accessed Feb. 23, 2006.)

The sheer number of governments is only one measure of the differences that exist in governing styles among the states. Each individual state decides the division of duties, detailing which services are provided and how they are financed. From public welfare to public elementary and secondary education, highways, and sewerage treatment, there are significant differences in approaches.

Some state governments take on certain functions themselves, based on financial, administrative, political, geographic, or historical criteria. In Hawaii, for example, all public elementary and secondary education is a state activity. Though all states fund a significant portion of elementary and secondary education, the administration in other states is generally carried out by local governments—either by general purpose governments (common on the East Coast) or special school districts. Streets and highways in Virginia are largely a state government activity; in most other states, the responsibility is more evenly divided. In Maryland, elementary and secondary school construction is a state activity, but the operation of schools is a local government responsibility.

The states have developed two categories of subordinate governments, general purpose and special purpose, to provide local services. General purpose governments usually perform a variety of services for their citizens, such as public safety and health, various types of public works, social services, and the like. Usually, the general purpose governments carry designations such as counties, municipalities,

villages, and towns or townships.[6] Townships and other sub-county unincorporated governments exist in only 20 states, and have active governments in only 12 of these states. In the six New England states, most government functions are carried out through towns. In the Middle Atlantic states of New York, New Jersey, and Pennsylvania, and in the upper Midwest states of Michigan, Minnesota, and Wisconsin, towns or townships are active governments that provide a range of the same types of services provided by cities. In the other eight states, township governments have few or no governmental functions, with the appropriate services being provided by the counties instead.

Special purpose governments are created to provide either a single service or a very limited number of services to a population or an area. The most common special purpose government is a school district. The 2002 Census of Governments enumerated about 13,500 of these districts throughout the United States. There is a wide variety of other types of special districts. Some are large and well known, such as the Port Authority of New York and New Jersey. By and large, however, special districts are neither a well-known nor well-understood facet of local government.

While the numbers of some types of governments have changed considerably over the past few decades, some have changed little. (See Table 12-3.) Among general purpose governments, only the count of municipalities shows significant change, having experienced an increase of 16 percent from

---

[6] There is wide variety in the naming conventions for local governments. The Midwestern township is called a "town" in Wisconsin. County-equivalent governments are called "parishes" in Louisiana and "boroughs" in Alaska. In New Jersey, however, boroughs are municipal corporations. For an excellent description of these patterns, state by state, see *A Guide to State and Local Census Geography*, a joint venture of the U.S. Census Bureau and the Association of Public Data Users, 1990 CPH-I-18, June 1993.

Table 12-3. Local Governments, by Type of Government, Selected Years, 1952–2002

(Number.)

Year	Total	County	Municipal	Township	Special district	School district
1952	102 392	3 052	16 807	17 202	12 340	67 355
1962	91 237	3 043	17 997	17 144	18 323	34 678
1972	78 269	3 044	18 517	16 991	23 885	15 781
1982	81 831	3 041	19 076	16 734	28 078	14 851
1987	83 237	3 042	19 200	16 691	29 532	14 721
1992	84 955	3 043	19 279	16 656	31 555	14 422
1997	87 453	3 043	19 372	16 629	34 683	13 726
2002	87 525	3 034	19 429	16 504	35 052	13 506

Source: U.S. Census Bureau. 2002 Census of Governments. *Government Organization, 2002.* <http://www.census.gov/prod/2003pubs/gc021x1.pdf>. (Accessed Feb. 23, 2006.)

1952 to 2002. The reason for growth here is partly due to the fact that municipalities are designed to serve populations; as populations grow, the number of municipalities generally does as well.[7] In contrast, counties and townships, which have a geographic base, do not change much over time.

The special purpose governments—special districts and school districts—are quite different than the general purpose governments. The count of school districts decreased by 80 percent between 1951 and 2002. This largely reflects the consolidation of relatively small schools with multi-grade classrooms into larger school districts in order to provide a more balanced and cost-effective educational system, as well as the means for high school education within each district. In some states, primarily in the Midwest, the results of this process were quite dramatic. Nebraska, for example, went from 6,392 districts in 1951 to 575 in 2002.

Special districts show the opposite trend from school districts, up 184 percent from 1952 to 2004. The states that used special districts the most frequently in 1952, Illinois and California, remain the primary users of this form of government today. Other states with more than 1,000 special districts include Colorado, Indiana, Kansas, Missouri, Nebraska, New York, Pennsylvania, Texas, and Washington. On the other hand, many states have less than 300 such districts. The reasons for the differences are rooted in individual state politics (such as Proposition 13 in California), economies, and histories. New York, by way of contrast, limits the activity of this type of government to fire districts (which account for about 90 percent of the New York special district total), health districts, and a few miscellaneous activities. Nevertheless, special districts are where government structure shows the most dynamic adaptability.

COMPARING PUBLIC AND PRIVATE SECTORS OF THE ECONOMY

Talk of "big" government in the United States is often directed at the size and influence of the federal government. The place of state and local governments in these discussions seems to be absent or minimized. However, there is another way to look at the relative size of these governments that provides a good perspective on the size of government below the federal level.

The "Fortune 500" is a popular and widely used listing of the biggest and most important corporations in the United States. Ranking U.S. state governments against this list, based on their general revenues, demonstrates their size relative to the largest businesses in the United States. (See Table 12-4.) That California ranks fourth, New York sixth, and Texas tenth might not be surprising. However, the smallest state government in terms of general revenue, South Dakota, falls below the smallest of the Fortune 500 companies. Further, these are just the state governments. If local governments were included, five California county governments (Los Angeles, Orange, San Bernardino, Santa Clara, and San Diego), two city governments (Los Angeles and San Francisco), one school district (Los Angeles Unified), and one special district (Los Angeles County Transportation Commission) would each rank higher than South Dakota.

This comparison of government with the private sector holds true in many different areas. In the obscure but financially important field of retirement and pension systems, for example, the very largest system in terms of assets is a state retirement system—the California Public Employee Retirement System—with assets about 57 percent greater than those of the General Motors Corporation. State and local government public employee retirement sys-

---

[7] Municipalities also grow in size, if not in number, through annexation. The procedures that permit existing municipalities to annex adjacent areas vary for each state. The level of difficulty in annexation procedures likely has an effect on the development of new municipalities. In addition, there is often a difference in statutory taxing authority between townships and cities. A desire to keep taxes low is a factor in discouraging township incorporation into cities.

Table 12-4. Rank of State Governments in Combined Ranking with Fortune 500 Corporations, 2003

(Rank; corporations based on revenue; state governments based on general revenue.)

State	Combined rank of states with Fortune 500 corporations
California	4
New York	6
Texas	10
Florida	19
Michigan	22
Ohio	22
Pennsylvania	23
New Jersey	25
Illinois	26
Massachusetts	53
North Carolina	54
Georgia	54
Washington	54
Virginia	56
Minnesota	71
Wisconsin	72
Indiana	72
Missouri	85
Maryland	86
Tennessee	93
South Carolina	97
Louisiana	97
Oregon	98
Alabama	100
Kentucky	104
Connecticut	105
Arizona	109
Oklahoma	137
Colorado	145
Mississippi	147
Iowa	153
Arkansas	166
Utah	172
Kansas	187
New Mexico	197
West Virginia	202
Nevada	247
Nebraska	270
Alaska	274
Hawaii	277
Maine	277
Rhode Island	315
Idaho	330
New Hampshire	344
Delaware	349
Montana	380
Vermont	463
Wyoming	484
North Dakota	487
South Dakota	(¹)

Source: U.S. Census Bureau. *Fortune Magazine.*

¹General revenue is exceeded by sales of all Fortune 500 corporations.

tems occupy 9 of the top 10 and 32 of the top 50 spots in this ranking of pension/retirement systems.[8]

A regional ranking of almost any financial activity, such as revenues, expenditures, indebtedness, assets, employment, or payroll—no matter the location—would yield similar results. State and major local governments would rank as, or among, the leaders in most categories. State and local governments are significant "businesses" and economic forces, no matter how they are measured. As said by one of the authors of the State Governments/Fortune 500 ranking: "This ranking dramatizes that the governors are the chief executive officers of some of the largest human enterprises in the country. If you want to get a good sense of the significance of a governor's managerial responsibilities, just look at corporations that are similar in size to his or her state."[9]

Even though the responsibilities might be similar, there is a significant disparity in the financial compensation of public and private chief executive officers (CEOs). While the compensation of private sector executives of Fortune 500 companies extends into the hundreds of thousands or millions of dollars, the highest governor's salary is $179,000 (New York) and the lowest is $70,000 (Maine). In 19 states, the governor's salary is less than $100,000.[10] It is also relevant to point out that the annual salary of the most important and powerful chief executive in the world, the president of the United States, is $400,000.

THE MONEY THAT FUNDS GOVERNMENT

Taxes are the largest and most visible source of government funding. There are also four other important sources: fees or charges for specific services, "contributions" for social insurance and other retirement programs, intergovernmental revenue, and miscellaneous items such as fines, interest earnings, sales of property, and lottery revenue.

The mix among these components varies considerably depending on the level of government. (See Figure 12-3.) Most of the federal government's income comes from income taxes (individual and corporate) and from the social insurance taxes that support Social Security and Medicare. Looking at the states, sales taxes are a very important source of revenue; aggregated nationwide, they are almost equal to income taxes on individuals and corporations. The states also have a great variety of revenue sources, including gasoline taxes, license fees, taxes on insurance premiums, and so forth. As with the federal government, states collect retirement system contributions for their own employees (often including teachers). Both local and state governments receive a significant propor-

[8] Pensions and Investments Online. The Top 200 Pension Funds/Sponsors. <http://www.pionline.com/page.cms?pageId=277>. (Accessed Feb. 24, 2006)

[9] Press release, "Duke Study Ranks Governments in Comparison with the Fortune 500." (January 1993).

[10] The Council of State Governments. 2004. Table 4.3 (The governors: Compensation). *Book of the States 2004.* (Lexington, KY: Council of State Governments.) Salary figures accurate as of December 2003.

Figure 12-3. Revenue by Major Source, 2002–2003 and 2004

Federal Government, 2004

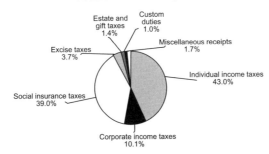

State Government, 2002–2003   Local Government, 2002–2003

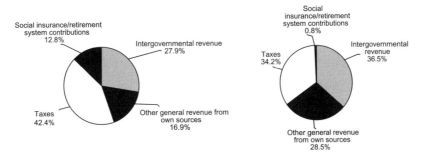

Source: Congressional Budget Office. *The Budget and Economic Outlook: Fiscal Years 2006–2015.*
U.S. Census Bureau. Governments Division.

tion of their revenue from the federal government. Local governments depend on property and income taxes, but also rely heavily on intergovernmental revenue and other forms of general revenue.

Federal revenues have increased rapidly over the past several decades. As shown in Figure 12-4, the federal budget level was at just about $100 billion in 1962. It passed $200 billion in the early 1970s, $500 billion around 1980, and $1,000 billion (or $1 trillion) in 1990. During almost all of this period, expenditures exceeded revenue, thus adding to the federal debt. This trend was reversed in 1998, but headed back toward the negative in 2002.

School systems are supported by local property taxes, the state government, and the federal gov-

ernment. The proportions vary by state. (See Table 12-5.) In Hawaii, public education is essentially state-funded; the schools are an arm of the state government. Michigan revised its tax structure for education in 1994, making individual school districts less dependent on local property taxes and more dependent on state sources for revenue.

TAXES

The contribution of taxes to overall government revenue was demonstrated earlier. But what types of taxes? Without delving into the arguments of progressivity or its effect on economic development, it is useful to look at the variations that exist in the American tax system.

Table 12-5. Percent of Elementary-Secondary Education Revenue Funded by Federal, State, and Local Government Sources, 2002–2003

(Percent, rank.)

State	Total	Federal sources	Local sources	State sources	Rank by state funded
United States, Average	100.0	8.4	42.7	49.0	
Hawaii	100.0	8.2	1.7	90.1	1
Arkansas	100.0	11.8	14.1	74.2	2
Minnesota	100.0	5.6	20.7	73.7	3
New Mexico	100.0	14.6	12.8	72.6	4
Vermont	100.0	7.1	23.5	69.3	5
Delaware	100.0	7.6	26.6	65.8	6
Michigan	100.0	7.6	29.2	63.2	7
Washington	100.0	8.2	29.3	62.4	8
West Virginia	100.0	10.7	28.4	60.9	9
North Carolina	100.0	9.0	30.8	60.3	10
Nevada	100.0	6.9	33.1	59.9	11
Kentucky	100.0	10.3	30.0	59.6	12
Idaho	100.0	9.6	31.4	59.0	13
Kansas	100.0	7.7	33.4	59.0	14
California	100.0	10.0	32.0	58.0	15
Alabama	100.0	10.9	31.9	57.1	16
Indiana	100.0	7.3	35.6	57.1	17
Alaska	100.0	18.2	24.8	57.0	18
Utah	100.0	9.1	34.9	55.9	19
Wisconsin	100.0	6.0	39.2	54.8	20
Mississippi	100.0	14.8	31.3	53.9	21
Oklahoma	100.0	12.7	35.9	51.4	22
Oregon	100.0	8.9	39.8	51.3	23
Wyoming	100.0	8.8	40.3	50.9	24
New Hampshire	100.0	5.2	45.8	49.0	25
Georgia	100.0	7.8	43.8	48.5	26
South Carolina	100.0	9.4	42.2	48.4	27
Louisiana	100.0	13.5	38.3	48.2	28
Iowa	100.0	7.2	46.0	46.8	29
Montana	100.0	14.4	39.4	46.2	30
New York	100.0	6.8	46.9	46.2	31
Missouri	100.0	7.4	47.2	45.4	32
Arizona	100.0	11.4	43.7	44.9	33
Florida	100.0	10.0	45.5	44.5	34
Tennessee	100.0	10.2	45.4	44.4	35
Ohio	100.0	6.2	49.7	44.1	36
Colorado	100.0	6.4	50.2	43.4	37
New Jersey	100.0	4.2	53.3	42.5	38
Maine	100.0	7.9	50.0	42.1	39
Rhode Island	100.0	6.3	52.2	41.5	40
Massachusetts	100.0	6.2	52.4	41.4	41
Virginia	100.0	6.8	53.7	39.6	42
Texas	100.0	9.6	51.3	39.1	43
Maryland	100.0	6.6	55.3	38.2	44
Pennsylvania	100.0	7.5	55.8	36.7	45
North Dakota	100.0	15.0	48.5	36.5	46
Connecticut	100.0	5.1	58.6	36.3	47
Illinois	100.0	8.5	55.9	35.6	48
Nebraska	100.0	8.9	56.6	34.5	49
South Dakota	100.0	15.4	50.4	34.1	50
District of Columbia	100.0	13.7	86.3	0.0	51

Source: U.S. Census Bureau. *Public Elementary-Secondary Education Finances: 2002–2003.*

When social insurance premiums are excluded, income taxes—personal and corporate—account for seven out of every eight federal tax dollars. Individual income taxes alone provide nearly three-fourths of federal tax revenue. This is why discussions about reforming the federal government tax system start and end with individual income taxes. Other specific taxes, such as the estate tax and the gift tax, account for very small proportions of federal revenue, although they often take on a much bigger role in the political context.

State and local governments have an entirely different tax mix than the federal government. For local governments, the property tax is, without question, the dominant levy, although it is less preeminent

Figure 12-4. Federal Goverment Revenues and Outlays, 1962–2004

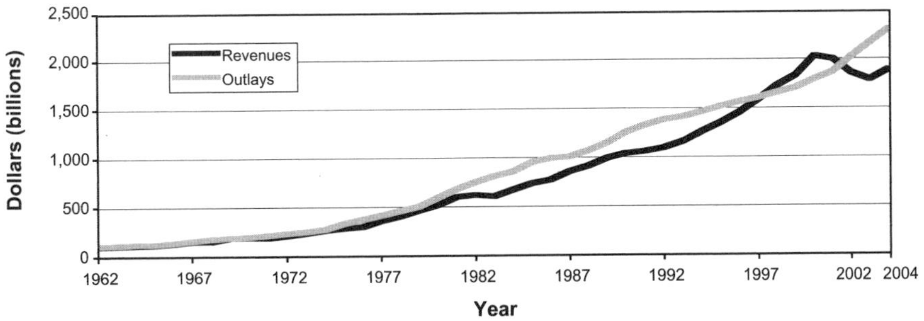

Source: Congressional Budget Office. The Budget and Economic Outlook: Fiscal Years 2006–2015.

than it once was. From 1950 through 1970, property taxes composed about 85 percent of all local government taxes. From 1970 through 1980, the percentage drifted down to about 76 percent of the total; this proportion has not changed much since then. Though property tax restriction movements of the late 1970s, such as those in California and Massachusetts, provided additional impetus, the trend toward less reliance on property taxes had already been firmly established earlier in that decade. (See Table 12-6.)

Three interrelated movements, beginning in the 1970s, contributed to the reduced role of property taxes. The property tax restriction movement was mentioned above. The second was property tax relief programs, some of which replaced property taxes with intergovernmental revenue from the states. The third was the diversification of local revenues, as state legislatures allowed local governments to impose other taxes, including both income and sales taxes. The states, though they allowed local governments more use of other taxes, still kept a tight rein. In many instances, those same

taxes were primary state tax producers, such as general sales taxes.

State governments rely on two pillars for taxes, general sales taxes and individual income taxes. These accounted for 34 percent and 38 percent, respectively, of all state government taxes in fiscal year 2003. States supplement the two taxes with a variety of other levies, such as specific sales taxes (motor fuel, alcohol, tobacco, and utilities, for example), license taxes, death and gift taxes, and severance taxes (on removal of natural resources). These state government totals provide some good general comparisons to current trends in federal and local government taxes.

What the national totals hide, however, is some of the differences found among the state tax systems. Table 12-7 provides examples of the wide variations in state tax systems. Alaska, which has built its tax system largely around its oil and gas reserves, levies neither an individual income nor a general sales tax. Delaware is the U.S. home of many large corporations, which are drawn there by business-

Table 12-6. Percent Distribution of Local Taxes, Selected Years, 1950–2003

(Percent.)

Tax	1950	1960	1970	1980	1990	2000	2003
Total Taxes	100.0	100.0	100.0	100.0	100.0	100.0	100.0
Property tax	88.2	87.4	84.9	75.9	74.5	71.6	73.4
Nonproperty tax	11.8	12.6	15.1	24.1	25.5	28.4	26.6
General sales tax	. . .	4.8	5.0	9.4	10.7	12.2	11.4
Motor fuels tax	. . .	0.2	0.1	0.1	0.3	0.3	0.3
Individual income tax	0.8	1.4	4.2	5.8	4.8	5.1	4.5
Other taxes	11.0	6.2	5.8	8.7	9.7	10.8	10.4

Source: U.S. Census Bureau.

. . . = Not available.

friendly corporation laws. It has taken advantage of this significant corporate presence by levying corporate license taxes; the corporate license tax has given it sufficient leeway so that, while Delaware does impose an individual income tax, it does not have a general sales tax. Pennsylvania has what most economists would say is a balanced tax system, with a fairly even reliance on its two major sources. Texas does not impose an individual income tax. Until recently, Texas obtained a significant percentage of its total from severance taxes, but has made a successful effort to move away from those taxes, as they had become an unreliable source of revenue source. Washington emphasizes the use of the general sales tax, with no income tax. Right next door in Oregon, just the reverse is true.

How Onerous Is the Tax Burden Relative to Personal Income?

While states obviously choose different paths for obtaining tax revenues, the question arises as to whether there are measures of what the states do collect, compared to what they have the capacity to collect. This is especially important in arguments about equity. In other words, measured against their ability to raise revenue, what efforts are states making in supplying services to citizens? Are "poor" states putting relatively less, the same, or more

Table 12-7. Top Three Tax Sources for Selected States, 2004

(Percent.)

State and tax source	Percent
Alaska	
1. Severance	50.2
2. Corporate net income	26.4
3. Insurance premiums	3.9
Delaware	
1. Individual income	32.9
2. Corporate license	23.9
3. Occupation and business, n.e.c.	9.3
Pennsylvania	
1. General sales	30.7
2. Individual income	28.9
3. Motor fuel sales	7.0
Texas	
1. General sales	50.3
2. Motor fuel sales	9.5
3. Severance	6.2
Washington	
1. General sales	60.6
2. Property taxes	11.0
3. Motor fuel sales	6.7

Source: U.S. Census Bureau.

n.e.c. = Not elsewhere classified.

resources toward supplying services than "rich" states?[11]

One method for calculating this impact is simply to examine the amount of taxation per resident of the state (per capita). Table 12-8 presents a ranking of the states for the taxes per capita in 2004. The overall distribution of the states is remarkable. The tax burden in Hawaii, at $3,048, is 51 percent higher than the national average of $2,025 and 123 percent higher than Texas. There is no particular geographic or size of state pattern to the distribution.

Where Does the Money Go?

Table 12-9 shows us the distribution of money, by major categories, at the federal level. As discussed above, the total amount of federal expenditures has risen dramatically, more than quadrupling between 1980 and 2004. Up through 2000, spending on national defense rose at a much lower rate, dropping from 22 percent of the overall budget to 16 percent. However, defense spending increased dramatically with the onset of the Iraq War and was back up to nearly 20 percent of the total budget in 2004.

Spending on human resources programs quadrupled, growing from 53 percent of the budget to 64 percent. This category includes Medicare and Social Security disbursements, which are entitlements; these budget lines now account for about half the total expenditures in the human resources category. However, the "income security" category includes retirement and disability payments and unemployment compensation for federal government workers. Together, these allocations total about half of the income security section of the budget. Food and nutrition assistance, including the Food Stamp program, equals 15 percent of the budget. Another very large component of federal expenditures is interest on the national debt. This figure dropped after 1995, when serious efforts to balance the budget were put into place by Congress, but may increase again in the near future.

Figure 12-4 shows the overall pattern of federal revenues and expenditures over the past 40 years. Expenditures exceeded revenues, thus increasing the national debt, between 1971 and 1997. Between 1998 and 2000, the efforts to balance the federal budget resulted in an excess of revenues.

---

[11] The U.S. Advisory Commission on Intergovernmental Relations (ACIR) made an effort to focus attention on this issue, starting in the early 1980s. The earlier ACIR work on this subject extends back to the 1960s. Starting in 1982, the commission issued a series of reports entitled "Measuring State Fiscal Capacity," in which it developed alternatives to the tax/personal income measure. A report issued in 1986, "Measuring State Fiscal Capacity: Alternative Methods and Their Uses" (Report M-150, September 1986) provides a good discussion of six potential fiscal capacity measures: per capita personal income, gross state product, total taxable resources, export-adjusted income, the representative tax system, and the representative revenue system. The ACIR ended its work in 1996. For more information, see: <http://www.library.unt.edu/gpo/ACIR/Default.html>. (Accessed Feb. 24, 2006.)

Table 12-8. States Ranked by Per Capita Taxes, 2004

(Dollars.)

State and rank	Taxes per capita	Percent difference from U.S. average
United States	2 025	NA
1. Hawaii	3 048	50.5
2. Wyoming	2 968	46.6
3. Connecticut	2 937	45.0
4. Minnesota	2 889	42.7
5. Delaware	2 862	41.3
6. Vermont	2 845	40.5
7. Massachusetts	2 602	28.5
8. New Jersey	2 412	19.1
9. California	2 388	17.9
10. New York	2 384	17.7
11. Michigan	2 379	17.5
12. Wisconsin	2 275	12.3
13. Washington	2 240	10.6
14. Rhode Island	2 228	10.1
15. Maryland	2 216	9.4
16. Maine	2 200	8.6
17. New Mexico	2 103	3.9
18. Nebraska	2 083	2.9
19. West Virginia	2 066	2.0
20. Pennsylvania	2 043	0.9
21. Kentucky	2 041	0.8
22. Nevada	2 030	0.2
23. Arkansas	2 027	0.1
24. Illinois	2 005	-1.0
25. Alaska	1 967	-2.9
26. Ohio	1 961	-3.1
27. North Carolina	1 941	-4.2
28. North Dakota	1 938	-4.3
29. Kansas	1 931	-4.6
30. Indiana	1 917	-5.3
31. Virginia	1 908	-5.8
32. Idaho	1 901	-6.1
33. Oklahoma	1 824	-9.9
34. Louisiana	1 777	-12.2
35. Florida	1 769	-12.7
36. Mississippi	1 765	-12.8
37. Montana	1 754	-13.4
37. Utah	1 754	-13.4
39. Iowa	1 738	-14.2
40. Oregon	1 698	-16.2
41. Arizona	1 672	-17.4
42. Georgia	1 650	-18.5
43. South Carolina	1 621	-20.0
44. Tennessee	1 616	-20.2
45. Missouri	1 585	-21.7
46. Alabama	1 549	-23.5
47. New Hampshire	1 543	-23.8
48. Colorado	1 533	-24.3
49. South Dakota	1 378	-31.9
50. Texas	1 367	-32.5

Source: U.S. Census Bureau.

NA = Not applicable.

However, in 2001, the pattern reversed itself once more. Expenditures on the Iraq War and natural disasters, such as Hurricane Katrina, coupled with significant tax cuts, have created this problem in recent years.

Table 12-10 focuses on expenditures by state and local governments. The first and greatest expenditure at this level is education, including both the operation of the elementary and secondary school systems and support for the public institutions of higher education in the states. Three of every ten state/local dollars go to education. The second greatest expenditure is for public welfare, which consumes about 14 percent of state/local budgets. Capital outlay is another significant budget item. The remaining expenditure categories cover a wide range of functions, including transportation needs (primarily road construction), hospitals, government administration, and disbursement of insurance trust income, such as unemployment compensation.

Figure 12-5 provides details on the distribution of different types of taxes at the state level. Nationally and across all states, individual income taxes account for about one-third of state taxes. General sales taxes account for another one-third. The remaining taxes come from a variety of sources.

An issue of significant concern around the country is the proportion of federal government expenditures that come back to each state. These data are reported annually in the Census Bureau's Consolidated Federal Funds Report. The state that receives the most funds, in total dollars, is California, followed closely by Virginia. The state that receives the most money per capita is Alaska (see Figure 12-6), with more than $12,000 per person per year. Virginia's high rank is a result of the Pentagon's location in the northern part of the state. As a result, the state receives credit for Department of Defense spending there and receives, by far, the highest per capita expenditures for defense.

Figure 12-5. Percent Distribution of State Taxes, 2004

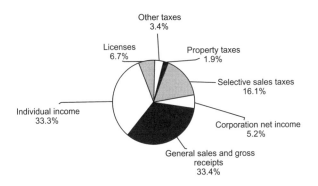

Source: U.S. Census Bureau. Government Division.

Table 12-9. Federal Budget Outlays—Defense, Human and Physical Resources, and Net Interest Payments, Selected Years, 1970–2005

(Percents, except as noted; for fiscal year ending in year shown; minus sign (-) indicates offsets.)

Outlays	1970	1975	1980	1985	1990	1995	2000	2004	2005 estimate
Federal Outlays, Total (Dollars in Billions)	195.6	332.3	590.9	946.4	1 253.1	1 515.8	1 789.1	2 292.2	2 479.4
National defense	41.8	26.0	22.7	26.7	23.9	17.9	16.5	19.9	18.8
Human resources	38.5	52.1	53.0	49.9	49.4	60.9	62.3	64.8	64.0
Education, training, employment, and social services	4.4	4.8	5.4	3.0	3.0	3.4	3.0	3.8	3.9
Health	3.0	3.9	3.9	3.5	4.6	7.6	8.6	10.5	10.4
Medicare	3.2	3.9	5.4	7.0	7.8	10.5	11.0	11.8	11.9
Income security	8.0	15.1	14.6	13.6	11.9	14.8	14.2	14.5	14.2
Social Security	15.5	19.5	20.1	19.9	19.8	22.2	22.9	21.6	21.0
Veterans' benefits and services	4.4	5.0	3.6	2.8	2.3	2.5	2.6	2.6	2.7
Physical resources	8.0	10.7	11.2	6.0	10.1	3.9	4.7	5.1	5.3
Energy	0.5	0.9	1.7	0.6	0.3	0.3	0.0	0.0	0.1
Natural resources and environment	1.6	2.2	2.3	1.4	1.4	1.4	1.4	1.3	1.2
Commerce and housing credit	1.1	3.0	1.6	0.5	5.4	-1.2	0.2	0.2	0.4
Transportation	3.6	3.3	3.6	2.7	2.4	2.6	2.6	2.8	2.8
Community and regional development	1.2	1.3	1.9	0.8	0.7	0.7	0.6	0.7	0.8
Net interest	7.3	7.0	8.9	13.7	14.7	15.3	12.5	7.0	7.2
International affairs	2.2	2.1	2.2	1.7	1.1	1.1	1.0	1.2	1.3
Agriculture	2.6	0.9	1.5	2.7	0.9	0.6	2.0	0.7	1.2
Administration of justice	0.5	0.9	0.8	0.7	0.8	1.1	1.6	2.0	1.6
General government	1.2	3.1	2.2	1.2	0.8	0.9	0.7	1.0	0.8
Undistributed offsetting receipts	-4.4	-4.1	-3.4	-3.5	-2.9	-2.9	-2.4	-2.6	-2.6

Source: U.S. Office of Management and Budget. *Budget of the United States Government: Fiscal Year 2006.*

At the low end of the scale, expenditures are less than $6,000 per capita in 11 states. Nevada is the lowest, followed by Wisconsin and Minnesota, while Michigan ranks seventh from the bottom. Clearly, the upper Midwest loses out on this scale of measurement.

PUBLIC EMPLOYMENT

In 2004, the federal government employed about 2.4 million people, while another 15.8 million worked for state and local governments. (See Table 12-11.) At the federal level, the single largest "employer" used to be the Postal Service, followed by the Department of Defense. With the advent of the Iraq War, the Department of Defense is now first, although the Postal Service payroll is higher. Health and hospitals also have large numbers of employees, as does natural resources, which includes all the National Park Service rangers. At

Table 12-10. State and Local Expenditures, by Function, 2002–2003

(Dollars in millions, percent.)

Expenditure	Amount	Percent
Total Expenditures	2 159.8	100.0
Capital outlay	228.7	10.6
Education	621.3	28.8
Libraries	8.9	0.4
Social services and income maintenance		
Public welfare	306.5	14.2
Hospitals	93.2	4.3
Health	61.7	2.9
Transportation	142.3	6.6
Public safety	162.3	7.5
Natural resources, parks, and recreation	54.6	2.5
Housing and community develoment	35.3	1.6
Sewers and solid waste management	51.7	2.4
Government administration	98.7	4.6
Interest on general debt	77.3	3.6
Utility expenditure	144.6	6.7
Insurance trust expenditure	193.3	8.9
Other	108.3	5.0

Source: U.S. Census Bureau. *Government Finances, 2002–2003.*

Table 12-11. Federal and State and Local Government Employment and Payroll, 2004

(Ranked by leading number of employees; number, dollars in millions.)

Function	Full-time employees	Annual payroll (millions of dollars)
Total Federal Government	2 445 287	151 237
1. National defense and international relations	663 708	30 895
2. Postal service	611 238	40 111
3. Natural resources	182 108	11 205
4. Police	150 711	9 764
5. Hospitals	143 131	8 184
Total State and Local Governments	15 788 784	658 353
1. Elementary and secondary education—instructional	4 487 240	198 567
2. Elementary and secondary education—other	1 986 185	54 062
3. Higher education—other	1 219 254	44 426
4. Hospitals	912 496	37 631
5. Correction	701 905	28 320

Source: U.S. Census Bureau. Governments Division.

Figure 12-6. Federal Government Expenditure Per Capita Amounts by State for Defense Department and All Other Agencies, Fiscal Year 2003

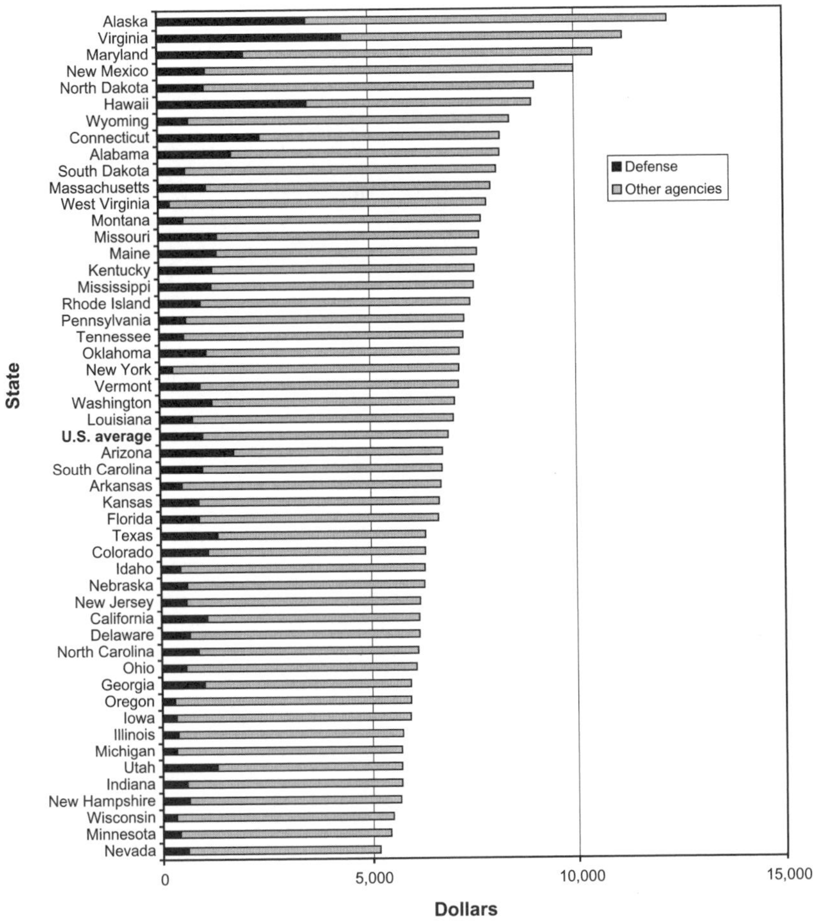

Source: U.S. Census Bureau. *Consolidated Federal Funds Report for Fiscal Year 2003.*

the state/local level, and paralleling the expenditures data reviewed earlier, education is by far the largest employment category. Corrections, or the operation of jails and management of prisoners, is also significant. Hospitals have higher employment relative to other measures because they utilize workers around the clock.

Table 12-12 shows some characteristics of federal workers and how they have changed over the past several years. The average age and average length of service is rising; i.e., the federal workforce is aging. It is important to note that the proportion of workers with a bachelor's degree or more has increased somewhat over this period of time. Minority employment has increased slightly. The number of employees with veterans' preferences has decreased, as veterans are passing out of the labor force.

Table 12-12. Federal Employment Trends, Selected Years, 1990–2003

(Percent, except where noted.)

Characteristic	1990	1995	1996	1997	1998	1999	2000	2001	2002	2003
Average age (years) of full-time employees	42.3	44.3	44.8	45.2	45.6	45.9	46.3	46.5	46.5	46.7
Average length of service (years)	13.4	15.5	15.9	16.3	16.6	16.9	17.1	17.1	16.8	16.8
Retirement Eligible										
Civil Service Retirement System	8	10	11	12	13	15	17	19	23	27
Federal Employees Retirement System	3	5	6	7	8	10	11	10	11	12
Bachelor's degree or higher	35	39	39	40	40	40	41	41	41	41
Gender										
Men	57	56	56	56	56	55	55	55	55	55
Women	43	44	44	44	44	45	45	45	45	45
Race and National Origin										
Total minorities	27.4	28.9	29.1	29.4	29.7	30.0	30.4	30.6	30.8	31.1
Black	16.7	16.8	16.7	16.7	16.7	17.0	17.1	17.1	17.0	17.0
Hispanic (of any race)	5.4	5.9	6.1	6.2	6.4	6.5	6.6	6.7	6.9	7.1
Asian/Pacific Islander	3.5	4.2	4.3	4.4	4.5	4.5	4.5	4.6	4.7	4.8
American Indian/Alaska native	1.8	2.0	2.0	2.1	2.1	2.2	2.2	2.2	2.2	2.1
Disabled	7	7	7	7	7	7	7	7	7	7
Veterans' preference	30	26	26	25	25	25	24	24	23	22
Vietnam Era veterans	17	17	17	15	14	14	14	13	13	13
Retired military	4.9	4.2	4.3	4.2	3.9	3.9	3.9	4.2	4.4	4.6

Source: U.S. Office of Personnel Management. Office of Workforce Information. The Fact Book, Federal Civilian Workforce: 2004 Edition. <http://www.opm.gov/feddata/factbook/2004/factbook.pdf>. (Accessed Feb. 23, 2006.)

FOR FURTHER INFORMATION SEE:

Council of State Governments. 2001. *Book of the States* (Volume 33). (Lexington, KY: Council of State Governments.)

Harvard University. 1996. John F. Kennedy School of Government. *The Federal Budget and the States 1995.* (Cambridge, MA: Taubman Center, Harvard University.)

National Association of the State Budget Officers. (Spring 2001–Spring 2005). Fiscal Survey of the States. <http://www.nasbo.org/publications.php>. (Accessed Dec. 19, 2005.)

National Association of the State Budget Officers. (2000–2003). State Expenditure Report. <http://www.nasbo.org/publications.php>. (Accessed Dec. 19, 2005.)

National Conference of State Legislatures. State Budget and Tax Actions. <http://www.ncsl.org/programs/fiscal/index.htm>. (Accessed Dec. 19, 2005.)

U.S. Advisory Commission on Intergovernmental Relations. *Significant Features of Fiscal Federalism.* <http://www.library.unt.edu/gpo/acir/BrowseTitles.htm#sfff>. (Accessed Dec. 19, 2005.)

U.S. Census Bureau. 2001. *Statistical Abstract of the United States, 2001* (121st Edition). (Washington, DC: U.S. Census Bureau.)

WEB SITES:

Congressional Budget Office. <http://www.cbo.gov>. (Accessed Dec. 19, 2005.)

Council of State Governments. <http://www.csg.org>. (Accessed Dec. 19, 2005.)

Governing Magazine. <http://www.governing.com>. (Accessed Dec. 19, 2005.)

National Conference of State Legislatures. <http://www.ncsl.org>. (Accessed Dec. 19, 2005.)

U.S. Census Bureau. <http://www.census.gov>. (Accessed Dec. 19, 2005.)

U.S. Department of Commerce. Bureau of Economic Analysis. <http://www.bea.gov>. (Accessed Dec. 19, 2005.)

Appendix

Detailed Tables
Population

Table A1-1. Resident Population Projections of the United States: Middle, Low, High, and Zero International Migration Series, 2001–2100

(Numbers in thousands; consistent with the 1990 census, as enumerated.)

Year	Middle series	Low series	High series	Zero international migration growth
2001	277 803	276 879	278 869	275 279
2002	280 306	278 801	282 087	276 709
2003	282 798	280 624	285 422	278 112
2004	285 266	282 352	288 841	279 493
2005	287 716	284 000	292 339	280 859
2006	290 153	285 581	295 911	282 219
2007	292 583	287 106	299 557	283 579
2008	295 009	288 583	303 274	284 945
2009	297 436	290 018	307 060	286 322
2010	299 862	291 413	310 910	287 710
2011	302 300	292 778	314 846	289 108
2012	304 764	294 120	318 893	290 514
2013	307 250	295 436	323 044	291 924
2014	309 753	296 723	327 293	293 334
2015	312 268	297 977	331 636	294 741
2016	314 793	299 197	336 069	296 144
2017	317 325	300 379	340 589	297 539
2018	319 860	301 521	345 192	298 921
2019	322 395	302 617	349 877	300 288
2020	324 927	303 664	354 642	301 636
2021	327 468	304 667	359 515	302 958
2022	330 028	305 628	364 524	304 251
2023	332 607	306 545	369 671	305 511
2024	335 202	307 412	374 960	306 735
2025	337 815	308 229	380 397	307 923
2026	340 441	308 999	385 971	309 070
2027	343 078	309 727	391 672	310 172
2028	345 727	310 413	397 507	311 230
2029	348 391	311 056	403 483	312 246
2030	351 070	311 656	409 604	313 219
2031	353 749	312 204	415 839	314 153
2032	356 411	312 692	422 154	315 049
2033	359 059	313 124	428 554	315 910
2034	361 695	313 499	435 041	316 737
2035	364 319	313 819	441 618	317 534
2036	366 934	314 086	448 287	318 304
2037	369 544	314 303	455 053	319 049
2038	372 148	314 472	461 917	319 773
2039	374 750	314 594	468 882	320 478
2040	377 350	314 673	475 949	321 167
2041	379 951	314 710	483 122	321 843
2042	382 555	314 707	490 401	322 506
2043	385 163	314 667	497 790	323 160
2044	387 776	314 591	505 290	323 807
2045	390 398	314 484	512 904	324 449
2046	393 029	314 346	520 633	325 087
2047	395 671	314 181	528 480	325 723
2048	398 326	313 990	536 447	326 359
2049	400 998	313 778	544 539	326 998
2050	403 687	313 546	552 757	327 641
2051	406 396	313 296	561 106	328 291
2052	409 127	313 030	569 589	328 949
2053	411 884	312 752	578 211	329 617
2054	414 667	312 461	586 975	330 297
2055	417 478	312 160	595 885	330 991
2056	420 318	311 850	604 943	331 700
2057	423 191	311 532	614 157	332 427
2058	426 097	311 206	623 527	333 172
2059	429 037	310 873	633 058	333 937
2060	432 011	310 533	642 752	334 724

Source: U.S. Census Bureau. Population Projections Program. Population Division.

Table A1-1. Resident Population Projections of the United States: Middle, Low, High, and Zero International Migration Series, 2001–2100—*Continued*

(Numbers in thousands; consistent with the 1990 census, as enumerated.)

Year	Middle series	Low series	High series	Zero international migration growth
2061	435 021	310 187	652 615	335 533
2062	438 067	309 833	662 648	336 365
2063	441 149	309 471	672 853	337 220
2064	444 265	309 098	683 233	338 098
2065	447 416	308 716	693 790	338 999
2066	450 600	308 321	704 524	339 922
2067	453 815	307 913	715 438	340 866
2068	457 061	307 488	726 530	341 830
2069	460 337	307 048	737 804	342 814
2070	463 639	306 589	749 257	343 815
2071	466 968	306 109	760 892	344 833
2072	470 319	305 608	772 707	345 865
2073	473 694	305 086	784 704	346 909
2074	477 090	304 540	796 883	347 966
2075	480 504	303 970	809 243	349 032
2076	483 937	303 375	821 785	350 107
2077	487 387	302 756	834 510	351 189
2078	490 853	302 111	847 420	352 278
2079	494 334	301 442	860 514	353 372
2080	497 830	300 747	873 794	354 471
2081	501 341	300 029	887 263	355 574
2082	504 866	299 286	900 922	356 681
2083	508 406	298 521	914 773	357 792
2084	511 959	297 732	928 818	358 907
2085	515 529	296 923	943 062	360 026
2086	519 113	296 093	957 506	361 149
2087	522 712	295 244	972 153	362 277
2088	526 327	294 375	987 006	363 409
2089	529 958	293 488	1 002 069	364 546
2090	533 605	292 584	1 017 344	365 689
2091	537 269	291 664	1 032 834	366 838
2092	540 948	290 727	1 048 542	367 992
2093	544 645	289 775	1 064 472	369 153
2094	548 357	288 808	1 080 626	370 319
2095	552 086	287 826	1 097 007	371 492
2096	555 830	286 830	1 113 615	372 672
2097	559 590	285 820	1 130 457	373 857
2098	563 365	284 796	1 147 532	375 048
2099	567 153	283 758	1 164 842	376 243
2100	570 954	282 706	1 182 390	377 444

Source: U.S. Census Bureau. Population Projections Program. Population Division.

Table A1-2. Resident Population Projections of the United States, by Age, 2000–2050

(Numbers in thousands; consistent with the 2000 census, as enumerated.)

Year	Total	Under 18 years	18 to 64 years	65 years and over
2000	282 125	72 373	174 690	35 061
2001	284 797	72 633	176 855	35 309
2002	287 449	72 915	178 982	35 552
2003	290 116	73 153	181 084	35 878
2004	292 801	73 383	183 167	36 251
2005	295 507	73 639	185 172	36 696
2006	298 217	73 852	187 169	37 196
2007	300 913	74 015	189 049	37 850
2008	303 598	74 082	190 825	38 690
2009	306 272	74 203	192 588	39 482
2010	308 936	74 432	194 260	40 244
2011	311 601	74 760	195 720	41 121
2012	314 281	75 205	196 525	42 551
2013	316 971	75 726	197 272	43 973
2014	319 668	76 323	198 005	45 340
2015	322 366	77 018	198 557	46 791
2016	325 063	77 753	199 107	48 202
2017	327 756	78 482	199 580	49 694
2018	330 444	79 179	200 009	51 256
2019	333 127	79 730	200 515	52 882
2020	335 805	80 300	200 873	54 632
2021	338 490	80 869	201 278	56 342
2022	341 195	81 436	201 650	58 109
2023	343 921	81 997	202 015	59 909
2024	346 669	82 551	202 450	61 668
2025	349 439	83 098	202 817	63 524
2026	352 229	83 634	203 336	65 258
2027	355 035	84 157	203 972	66 906
2028	357 862	84 672	204 702	68 488
2029	360 711	85 186	205 499	70 026
2030	363 584	85 707	206 424	71 453
2031	366 466	86 238	207 635	72 593
2032	369 336	86 778	208 972	73 586
2033	372 196	87 333	210 335	74 528
2034	375 046	87 905	211 630	75 512
2035	377 886	88 495	212 749	76 641
2036	380 716	89 103	213 958	77 655
2037	383 537	89 727	215 378	78 432
2038	386 348	90 366	216 960	79 022
2039	389 151	91 018	218 621	79 512
2040	391 946	91 682	220 214	80 050
2041	394 734	92 357	221 864	80 513
2042	397 519	93 040	223 477	81 002
2043	400 301	93 727	225 023	81 550
2044	403 081	94 420	226 480	82 182
2045	405 862	95 117	227 786	82 959
2046	408 646	95 814	229 065	83 767
2047	411 435	96 508	230 406	84 521
2048	414 230	97 195	231 778	85 257
2049	417 035	97 876	233 199	85 960
2050	419 854	98 549	234 599	86 706

Source: U.S. Census Bureau. Population Projections Program. Population Division.

Table A1-3. Resident Population of the United States: Estimates, by Age and Sex, 2005 and 2015

(Numbers in thousands; consistent with the 2000 census, as enumerated.)

Age	2005			2015		
	Total	Male	Female	Total	Male	Female
Population, All Ages	295 507	145 113	150 394	322 366	158 489	163 877
Under 5 years	20 495	10 471	10 024	22 358	11 423	10 935
5 to 9 years	19 467	9 954	9 512	21 623	11 044	10 579
10 to 14 years	20 838	10 670	10 167	20 984	10 718	10 265
15 to 19 years	21 172	10 862	10 310	20 243	10 366	9 877
20 to 24 years	20 823	10 657	10 166	21 810	11 137	10 673
25 to 29 years	19 753	10 016	9 737	22 195	11 269	10 926
30 to 34 years	19 847	9 987	9 860	21 858	11 075	10 783
35 to 39 years	20 869	10 449	10 420	20 543	10 337	10 206
40 to 44 years	22 735	11 282	11 452	20 250	10 108	10 142
45 to 49 years	22 453	11 076	11 377	20 926	10 387	10 539
50 to 54 years	19 983	9 771	10 212	22 376	10 992	11 383
55 to 59 years	17 359	8 415	8 944	21 649	10 532	11 117
60 to 64 years	13 017	6 203	6 814	18 761	8 985	9 776
65 to 69 years	10 123	4 712	5 412	15 621	7 336	8 285
70 to 74 years	8 500	3 804	4 697	10 987	4 988	5 998
75 to 79 years	7 376	3 094	4 282	7 761	3 351	4 409
80 to 84 years	5 576	2 117	3 459	5 600	2 226	3 374
85 to 89 years	3 206	1 072	2 135	3 857	1 363	2 494
90 to 94 years	1 431	397	1 034	2 069	629	1 440
95 to 99 years	412	91	321	723	185	537
100 years and over	71	12	58	173	35	138

Source: U.S. Census Bureau. Population Estimates Program. Population Division.

Table A1-4. World Population, by Region and Development Category, Selected Years, 1950–2050

(Midyear population in millions, figures may not add to totals due to rounding.)

Region	1950	1960	1970	1980	1990	2000	2010	2025	2050
World	2 555	3 040	3 708	4 455	5 275	6 079	6 812	7 834	9 079
Less developed countries	1 749	2 129	2 705	3 374	4 132	4 887	5 588	6 582	7 836
More developed countries	807	910	1 003	1 081	1 143	1 192	1 224	1 252	1 243
Africa	227	283	361	473	627	803	977	1 247	1 786
Sub-Saharan Africa	183	227	291	382	508	657	804	1 036	1 532
North Africa	44	56	71	91	119	147	174	211	255
Near East	44	58	75	101	135	171	212	280	396
Asia	1 368	1 628	2 038	2 494	2 978	3 435	3 838	4 375	4 832
Latin American and the Caribbean	166	218	286	362	443	524	596	690	782
Europe and the New Independent States	572	639	702	750	788	802	810	814	776
Western Europe	304	326	352	367	377	390	398	398	373
Eastern Europe	88	99	108	117	122	121	120	117	104
New Independent States	180	214	242	266	289	291	292	300	300
North America	166	199	227	252	278	314	344	388	462
Oceania	12	16	19	23	27	31	35	40	45
Excluding China:									
World	1 982	2 374	2 868	3 446	4 109	4 786	5 436	6 350	7 627
Less developed countries	1 176	1 464	1 866	2 366	2 967	3 595	4 213	5 100	6 386
Asia	795	962	1 198	1 486	1 813	2 143	2 463	2 892	3 383
Less developed countries	711	868	1 094	1 369	1 689	2 016	2 336	2 772	3 283

Source: U.S. Census Bureau. 2004. *Global Population Profile: 2002* (Report WP/02). (Washington, DC: U.S. Government Printing Office.)
Note: Reference to China encompasses China, Hong Kong SAR, and Taiwan.

Table A1-5. Population, Vital Events, and Rates, by Region and Development Category, 2002

(Population and events in thousands, figures may not add to totals due to rounding.)

Region	Midyear population	Births	Deaths	Natural increase	Birth per 1,000 population	Deaths per 1,000 population	Rate of natural increase (percent)
World	6 228 394	128 578	54 997	73 581	21	9	1.2
Less developed countries	5 029 539	115 120	42 794	72 326	23	9	1.4
More developed countries	1 198 856	13 458	12 203	1 255	11	10	0.1
Africa	838 720	30 133	12 097	18 036	36	14	2.2
Sub-Saharan Africa	686 522	26 538	11 285	15 253	39	16	2.2
North Africa	152 199	3 595	813	2 783	24	5	1.8
Near East	178 574	4 905	1 071	3 833	28	6	2.1
Asia	3 517 862	68 104	26 671	41 434	19	8	1.2
Latin America and the Caribbean	538 680	11 282	3 256	8 026	21	6	1.5
Europe and the New Independent States	803 255	9 186	8 974	212	11	11	Z
Western Europe	392 237	4 096	3 843	254	10	10	0.1
Eastern Europe	120 864	1 296	1 314	-18	11	11	Z
New Independent States	290 154	3 794	3 818	-24	13	13	Z
North America	319 705	4 432	2 701	1 731	14	8	0.5
Oceania	31 598	536	227	309	17	7	1.0
Excluding China:							
World	4 918 062	111 397	46 250	65 147	23	9	1.3
Less developed countries	3 720 158	97 966	34 053	63 912	26	9	1.7
Asia	2 208 482	50 950	17 929	33 020	23	8	1.5
Less developed countries	2 081 416	49 725	16 867	32 858	24	8	1.6

Source: U.S. Census Bureau. 2004. *Global Population Profile: 2002* (Report WP/02). (Washington, DC: U.S. Government Printing Office.)
Note: Reference to China encompasses China, Hong Kong SAR, and Taiwan.

Z = Between -0.05 percent and +0.05 percent.

Households and Families

Table A2-1. Marital Status of People 15 Years and Over, 1970 and 2004

(Numbers in thousands, percent.)

Sex and age	March 2004							Percent never married	March 1970 Percent never married [1]
	Number								
	Total	Married, spouse present	Married, spouse absent	Separated	Divorced	Widowed	Never married		
Both Sexes									
Total, 15 years and over ..	227 343	118 128	3 212	4 540	21 809	13 794	65 860	29.0	24.9
15 to 19 years	20 296	195	28	85	72	12	19 904	98.1	93.9
20 to 24 years	20 302	3 251	184	198	223	14	16 431	80.9	44.5
25 to 29 years	18 996	8 125	306	386	879	50	9 250	48.7	14.7
30 to 34 years	20 144	11 998	329	554	1 552	87	5 623	27.9	7.8
35 to 44 years	43 555	28 270	710	1 286	5 581	380	7 328	16.8	5.9
45 to 54 years	41 047	27 601	706	1 102	6 416	836	4 386	10.7	6.1
55 to 64 years	28 365	19 731	432	566	4 293	1 750	1 593	5.6	7.2
65 years and over	34 639	18 958	516	363	2 794	10 663	1 346	3.9	7.6
Male									
Total, 15 years and over ..	110 048	59 064	1 660	1 811	8 980	2 648	35 885	32.6	28.1
15 to 19 years	10 327	53	11	33	32	5	10 192	98.7	97.4
20 to 24 years	10 242	1 182	73	53	81	2	8 850	86.4	54.7
25 to 29 years	9 535	3 515	169	128	320	8	5 395	56.6	19.1
30 to 34 years	10 018	5 685	181	219	690	20	3 223	32.2	9.4
35 to 44 years	21 520	13 716	422	493	2 416	84	4 388	20.4	6.7
45 to 54 years	20 072	13 895	367	453	2 715	203	2 437	12.1	7.5
55 to 64 years	13 543	10 308	198	250	1 697	293	797	5.9	7.8
65 years and over	14 792	10 708	239	180	1 030	2 031	603	4.1	7.5
Female									
Total, 15 years and over ..	117 295	59 064	1 552	2 729	12 829	11 146	29 975	25.6	22.1
15 to 19 years	9 969	142	18	51	39	7	9 711	97.4	90.3
20 to 24 years	10 059	2 069	111	146	142	11	7 581	75.4	35.8
25 to 29 years	9 460	4 609	137	258	559	42	3 855	40.8	10.5
30 to 34 years	10 127	6 313	149	335	863	67	2 400	23.7	6.2
35 to 44 years	22 036	14 554	288	793	3 165	297	2 940	13.3	5.2
45 to 54 years	20 975	13 705	338	648	3 701	633	1 949	9.3	4.9
55 to 64 years	14 823	9 423	234	316	2 596	1 458	796	5.4	6.8
65 years and over	19 847	8 249	277	183	1 763	8 632	742	3.7	7.7

Source: U.S. Census Bureau. Current Population Survey.

[1]The 1970 percentages include 14-year-olds, and thus are for 14 years and over and 14–19 years.

Table A2-2. Marital Status of the Population 15 Years and Over, by Sex and Race, Selected Years, 1950–2004

(Numbers in thousands.)

Year	Total	Married, spouse present	Unmarried			
			Total	Never married	Widowed	Divorced
MALE						
All Races						
1950 [1]	54 601	36 866	17 735	14 400	2 264	1 071
1960 [1]	60 273	41 781	18 492	15 274	2 112	1 106
1970	70 559	47 109	23 450	19 832	2 051	1 567
1980	81 947	51 813	30 134	24 227	1 977	3 930
1990	91 955	55 833	36 121	27 505	2 333	6 283
1993	94 854	56 833	38 021	28 775	2 468	6 778
1994	96 768	57 068	39 700	30 228	2 222	7 250
1995	97 704	57 570	39 953	30 286	2 284	7 383
1996	98 593	57 656	40 937	30 691	2 478	7 768
1997	100 159	57 923	42 236	31 315	2 690	8 231
1998	101 123	58 633	42 491	31 591	2 569	8 331
1999	102 048	59 039	43 010	31 912	2 542	8 556
2000	103 114	59 684	43 429	32 253	2 604	8 572
2001	105 584	61 209	44 375	33 077	2 540	8 758
2002	106 819	61 268	45 551	34 229	2 636	8 686
2003	108 696	62 142	46 554	34 881	2 697	8 976
2004	110 048	62 535	47 513	35 885	2 648	8 980
White						
1950 [1]	49 302	33 451	15 850	12 892	1 986	972
1960 [1]	54 130	38 042	16 088	13 286	1 816	986
1970	62 868	42 732	20 135	17 080	1 722	1 333
1980	71 887	46 721	25 167	20 174	1 642	3 351
1990	78 908	49 542	29 367	22 078	1 930	5 359
1993	80 755	50 305	30 451	22 738	1 954	5 759
1994	82 026	50 226	31 800	23 704	1 878	6 218
1995	82 566	50 658	31 909	23 667	1 921	6 321
1996	83 463	50 882	32 581	23 894	2 128	6 559
1997	84 540	50 860	33 680	24 471	2 264	6 945
1998	85 219	51 299	33 920	24 775	2 106	7 038
1999	85 750	51 645	34 105	24 827	2 084	7 194
2000	86 443	51 888	34 555	25 113	2 196	7 246
2001	88 215	52 903	35 312	25 814	2 117	7 381
2002	89 233	52 924	36 309	26 686	2 218	7 405
2003	89 998	53 382	36 616	26 772	2 257	7 587
2004	90 814	53 517	37 298	27 551	2 231	7 516
Black						
1950 [1]	5 299	3 415	1 885	1 508	278	99
1960 [1]	6 143	3 739	2 404	1 988	296	120
1970	6 936	3 949	2 987	2 468	307	212
1980	8 292	4 053	4 239	3 410	308	521
1990	9 948	4 489	5 459	4 319	338	802
1993	10 442	4 431	6 012	4 750	426	836
1994	10 639	4 486	6 153	5 007	295	851
1995	10 825	4 632	6 193	5 031	310	852
1996	10 922	4 515	6 407	5 115	277	1 015
1997	11 113	4 623	6 491	5 137	340	1 014
1998	11 283	4 675	6 608	5 191	382	1 035
1999	11 483	4 709	6 775	5 250	391	1 134
2000	11 687	5 005	6 682	5 246	328	1 108
2001	11 527	4 978	6 549	5 139	333	1 077
2002	11 695	5 142	6 553	5 266	319	968
2003	11 791	5 022	6 769	5 417	323	1 029
2004	11 987	4 974	7 012	5 605	312	1 095

Source: U.S. Census Bureau. Current Population Survey.

[1] 1950 and 1960 data are for the population 14 years old and over. For these years, Black data are for the non-White population.

Table A2-2. Marital Status of the Population 15 Years and Over, by Sex and Race, Selected Years, 1950–2004—*Continued*

(Numbers in thousands.)

Year	Total	Married, spouse present	Unmarried			
			Total	Never married	Widowed	Divorced
FEMALE						
All Races						
1950 [1]	57 102	37 577	19 525	11 418	6 734	1 373
1960 [1]	64 607	42 583	22 024	12 252	8 064	1 708
1970	77 766	48 148	29 618	17 167	9 734	2 717
1980	89 914	52 965	36 950	20 226	10 758	5 966
1990	99 838	56 797	43 040	22 718	11 477	8 845
1993	102 400	57 768	44 631	23 534	11 214	9 883
1994	104 032	58 185	45 847	24 645	11 073	10 129
1995	105 028	58 984	46 045	24 693	11 082	10 270
1996	106 031	58 905	47 127	25 528	11 078	10 521
1997	107 076	58 829	48 247	26 073	11 058	11 116
1998	108 168	59 333	48 835	26 713	11 029	11 093
1999	109 628	60 001	49 626	27 520	10 944	11 162
2000	110 660	60 527	50 133	27 763	11 061	11 309
2001	113 451	61 889	51 562	28 056	11 526	11 980
2002	114 639	62 102	52 537	28 861	11 408	12 268
2003	116 361	62 892	53 469	29 499	11 297	12 673
2004	117 295	63 345	53 950	29 975	11 146	12 829
White						
1950 [1]	51 404	34 042	17 362	10 241	5 902	1 219
1960 [1]	57 860	38 545	19 315	10 796	7 099	1 420
1970	68 888	43 286	25 602	14 703	8 559	2 340
1980	77 882	47 277	30 604	16 318	9 296	4 990
1990	84 508	49 986	34 522	17 438	9 800	7 284
1993	86 045	50 668	35 377	17 660	9 512	8 205
1994	86 765	50 766	36 000	18 235	9 424	8 341
1995	87 484	51 390	36 094	18 250	9 399	8 445
1996	88 134	51 388	33 745	18 691	9 392	8 662
1997	88 756	50 987	37 769	19 139	9 404	9 226
1998	89 489	51 410	38 079	19 614	9 351	9 115
1999	90 463	51 979	38 485	20 105	9 245	9 135
2000	91 138	52 317	38 821	20 184	9 336	9 301
2001	92 989	52 911	40 078	20 539	9 723	9 816
2002	93 764	53 118	40 646	21 052	9 593	10 001
2003	94 363	53 434	40 929	21 276	9 405	10 248
2004	94 928	53 722	41 207	21 594	9 275	10 338
Black						
1950 [1]	5 698	3 534	2 164	1 178	832	154
1960 [1]	6 747	4 038	2 709	1 456	965	288
1970	8 108	4 384	3 723	2 248	1 120	355
1980	10 108	4 508	5 600	3 401	1 319	880
1990	11 966	4 813	7 152	4 416	1 392	1 344
1993	12 495	4 820	7 676	4 867	1 401	1 408
1994	12 872	4 863	8 009	5 190	1 322	1 497
1995	13 097	4 942	8 155	5 250	1 380	1 525
1996	13 292	4 947	8 345	5 451	1 330	1 564
1997	13 514	5 058	8 457	5 584	1 307	1 566
1998	13 715	4 983	8 732	5 689	1 370	1 673
1999	13 964	5 054	8 909	5 840	1 395	1 674
2000	14 167	5 123	9 045	6 008	1 367	1 670
2001	14 236	5 257	8 979	5 868	1 376	1 735
2002	14 442	5 262	9 180	6 068	1 354	1 758
2003	14 458	5 265	9 193	5 966	1 374	1 853
2004	14 678	5 216	9 462	6 210	1 357	1 895

Source: U.S. Census Bureau. Current Population Survey.

[1] 1950 and 1960 data are for the population 14 years old and over. For these years, Black data are for the non-White population.

Table A2-3. Marriages and Divorces, Selected Years, 1950–2003

(Numbers in thousands, rate per 1,000 population.)

Year	Marriages[1]						Divorces and annulments		
	Number (thousands)	Rate per 1,000 population					Number	Rate per 1,000 population	
		Total	Men, 15 years and over	Women, 15 years and over	Unmarried women			Total	Married women, 15 years and over
					15 years and over	15–44 years			
1950	1 667	11.1	...	...	...	...	385	2.6	...
1955	1 531	9.3	...	...	...	...	377	2.3	...
1960	1 523	8.5	...	...	...	...	393	2.2	...
1965	1 800	9.3	...	...	...	...	479	2.5	...
1970	2 159	10.6	31.1	28.4	76.5	140.2	708	3.5	14.9
1971	2 190	10.6	...	...	...	...	773	3.7	...
1972	2 282	10.9	...	...	...	...	845	4.0	...
1973	2 284	10.8	...	...	...	...	915	4.3	...
1974	2 230	10.5	...	...	...	...	977	4.6	...
1975	2 153	10.0	27.9	25.6	66.9	118.5	1 036	4.8	20.3
1976	2 155	9.9	...	...	...	...	1 083	5.0	...
1977	2 178	9.9	...	...	...	...	1 091	5.0	...
1978	2 282	10.3	...	...	...	...	1 130	5.1	...
1979	2 331	10.4	...	...	...	...	1 181	5.3	...
1980	2 390	10.6	28.5	26.1	61.4	102.6	1 189	5.2	22.6
1981	2 422	10.6	...	...	...	...	1 213	5.3	...
1982	2 456	10.6	...	...	...	...	1 170	5.1	...
1983	2 446	10.5	...	...	...	...	1 158	5.0	...
1984	2 477	10.5	28.0	25.8	59.5	99.0	1 169	5.0	21.5
1985	2 413	10.1	27.0	24.9	57.0	94.9	1 190	5.0	21.7
1986	2 407	10.0	26.6	24.5	56.2	93.9	1 178	4.9	21.2
1987	2 403	9.9	26.3	24.3	55.7	92.4	1 166	4.8	20.8
1988	2 396	9.8	26.0	24.0	54.6	91.0	1 167	4.8	20.7
1989	2 403	9.7	25.8	23.9	54.2	91.2	1 157	4.7	20.4
1990	2 443	9.8	26.0	24.1	54.5	91.3	1 182	4.7	20.9
1991	2 371	9.4	...	...	54.2	86.8	1 187	4.7	20.9
1992	2 362	9.3	...	...	53.3	88.2	1 215	4.8	21.2
1993	2 334	9.0	...	...	52.3	86.8	1 187	4.6	20.5
1994	2 362	9.1	...	...	51.5	84.0	1 191	4.6	20.5
1995	2 336	8.9	...	...	50.8	83.0	1 169	4.4	19.8
1996	2 344	8.8	...	...	49.7	81.5	1 150	4.3	19.5
1997	2 384	8.9	...	...	...	...	1 163	4.3	...
1998	2 244	8.4	...	...	...	...	1 135	4.2	...
1999	2 358	8.6	...	...	...	...	...	4.1	...
2000	2 329	8.3	...	...	...	...	...	4.1	...
2001	2 345	8.2	...	...	...	...	...	4.0	...
2002	2 254	7.8	...	...	...	...	...	4.0	...
2003	2 187	7.5	...	...	...	...	...	3.8	...

Source: U.S. Census Bureau. *Statistical Abstract of the United States: 2006.*

[1]Beginning in 1980, includes nonlicensed marriages registered in California.
. . . = Not available.

Table A2-4. Marriages and Divorces, by State, Selected Years, 1990–2004

(Numbers in thousands, rate per 1,000 population. [1])

State	Marriages [2]						Divorces [3]					
	Number			Rate			Number			Rate		
	1990	2000	2004	1990	2000	2004	1990	2000	2004	1990	2000	2004
United States	2 443.0	2 329.0	2 178.4	9.8	8.3	7.4	1 182.0	. . .	. . .	4.7	4.2	3.7
Alabama	43.3	45.0	40.6	10.6	10.3	9.0	25.3	23.5	21.5	6.1	5.4	4.7
Alaska	5.7	5.6	5.4	10.2	8.9	8.3	2.9	2.7	3.1	5.5	4.4	4.8
Arizona	37.0	38.7	37.9	10.0	7.9	6.6	25.1	21.6	24.4	6.9	4.4	4.2
Arkansas	35.7	41.1	35.7	15.3	16.0	13.0	16.8	17.9	17.4	6.9	6.9	6.3
California [4]	236.7	196.9	172.3	7.9	5.9	4.8	128.0	. . .	. . .	4.3	. . .	. . .
Colorado	31.5	35.6	34.5	9.8	8.6	7.5	18.4	. . .	20.2	5.5	. . .	4.4
Connecticut	27.8	19.4	16.5	7.9	5.9	4.7	10.3	6.5	10.3	3.2	2.0	2.9
Delaware	5.6	5.1	5.1	8.4	6.7	6.1	3.0	3.2	3.1	4.4	4.2	3.7
District of Columbia	4.7	2.8	2.9	8.2	5.4	5.3	2.7	1.5	0.9	4.5	3.0	1.7
Florida	142.3	141.9	156.4	10.9	9.3	9.0	81.7	81.9	82.7	6.3	5.3	4.8
Georgia	64.4	56.0	64.5	10.3	7.1	7.3	35.7	30.7	. . .	5.5	3.9	. . .
Hawaii	18.1	25.0	28.4	16.4	21.2	22.5	5.2	4.6	. . .	4.6	3.9	. . .
Idaho	15.0	14.0	15.2	13.9	11.0	10.9	6.6	6.9	7.1	6.5	5.4	5.1
Illinois	97.1	85.5	77.8	8.8	7.0	6.1	44.3	39.1	33.1	3.8	3.2	2.6
Indiana	54.3	34.5	48.4	9.6	5.8	7.8	. . .	. . .	. . .	. . .	. . .	. . .
Iowa	24.8	20.3	20.5	9.0	7.0	6.9	11.1	9.4	8.3	3.9	3.3	2.8
Kansas	23.4	22.2	19.1	9.2	8.3	7.0	12.6	10.6	9.1	5.0	4.0	3.3
Kentucky	51.3	39.7	36.8	13.5	10.0	8.9	21.8	21.6	20.5	5.8	5.4	4.9
Louisiana	41.2	40.5	30.2	9.6	9.3	6.7	. . .	. . .	. . .	. . .	. . .	. . .
Maine	11.8	10.5	10.9	9.7	8.3	8.3	5.3	5.8	4.7	4.3	4.6	3.6
Maryland	46.1	40.0	37.7	9.7	7.7	6.8	16.1	17.0	17.1	3.4	3.3	3.1
Massachusetts	47.8	37.0	41.2	7.9	6.0	6.4	16.8	18.6	14.1	2.8	3.0	2.2
Michigan	76.1	66.4	62.6	8.2	6.7	6.2	40.2	39.4	35.0	4.3	4.0	3.5
Minnesota	33.7	33.4	30.1	7.7	6.9	5.9	15.4	14.8	14.2	3.5	3.1	2.8
Mississippi	24.3	19.7	17.8	9.4	7.1	6.1	14.4	14.4	13.1	5.5	5.2	4.5
Missouri	49.3	43.7	36.5	9.6	7.9	6.3	26.4	26.5	21.9	5.1	4.8	3.8
Montana	7.0	6.6	6.8	8.6	7.4	7.4	4.1	2.1	3.5	5.1	2.4	3.8
Nebraska	12.5	13.0	12.9	8.0	7.8	7.4	6.5	6.4	6.4	4.0	3.8	3.6
Nevada	123.4	144.3	145.8	99.0	76.7	62.4	13.3	18.1	14.8	11.4	9.6	6.4
New Hampshire	10.6	11.6	9.8	9.5	9.5	7.6	5.3	7.1	5.0	4.7	5.8	3.9
New Jersey	58.0	50.4	50.1	7.6	6.1	5.8	23.6	25.6	26.0	3.0	3.1	3.0
New Mexico	13.2	14.5	14.1	8.8	8.3	7.4	7.7	9.2	8.8	4.9	5.3	4.6
New York	169.3	162.0	124.4	8.6	8.9	6.5	57.9	62.8	57.8	3.2	3.4	3.0
North Carolina	52.1	65.6	65.9	7.8	8.5	7.7	34.0	36.9	37.7	5.1	4.8	4.4
North Dakota	4.8	4.6	4.1	7.5	7.3	6.5	2.3	2.0	1.8	3.6	3.2	2.8
Ohio	95.8	88.5	75.9	9.0	7.9	6.6	51.0	49.3	42.4	4.7	4.4	3.7
Oklahoma	33.2	15.6	22.8	10.6	4.6	6.5	24.9	12.4	. . .	7.7	3.7	. . .
Oregon	25.2	26.0	29.0	8.9	7.8	8.1	15.9	16.7	14.8	5.5	5.0	4.1
Pennsylvania	86.8	73.2	65.1	7.1	6.1	5.3	40.1	37.9	30.7	3.3	3.2	2.5
Rhode Island	8.1	8.0	8.2	8.1	8.0	7.6	3.8	3.1	3.3	3.7	3.1	3.0
South Carolina	55.8	42.7	34.5	15.9	10.9	8.2	16.1	14.4	13.4	4.5	3.7	3.2
South Dakota	7.7	7.1	6.5	11.1	9.6	8.4	2.6	2.7	2.5	3.7	3.6	3.2
Tennessee	66.6	88.2	67.5	13.9	15.9	11.4	32.3	33.8	29.8	6.5	6.1	5.0
Texas	182.8	196.4	176.3	10.5	9.6	7.8	94.0	85.2	81.9	5.5	4.2	3.6
Utah	19.0	24.1	13.2	11.2	11.1	5.5	8.8	9.7	9.3	5.1	4.5	3.9
Vermont	6.1	6.1	6.0	10.9	10.2	9.6	2.6	5.1	2.4	4.5	8.6	3.9
Virginia	71.3	62.4	62.5	11.4	9.0	8.4	27.3	30.2	30.1	4.4	4.3	4.0
Washington	48.6	40.9	40.1	9.5	7.0	6.5	28.8	27.2	25.2	5.9	4.7	4.1
West Virginia	13.2	15.7	13.2	7.2	8.7	7.3	9.7	9.3	8.6	5.3	5.2	4.7
Wisconsin	41.2	36.1	34.1	7.9	6.8	6.2	17.8	17.6	17.0	3.6	3.3	3.1
Wyoming	4.8	4.9	4.8	10.7	10.3	9.4	3.1	2.8	2.7	6.6	5.9	5.3

Source: U.S. Census Bureau. *Statistical Abstract of the United States: 2006.*

[1] Based on total population residing in area; population enumerated as of April 1 for 1980; estimated as of July 1 for all other years.
[2] Data are counts of marriages performed, except as noted.
[3] Includes annulments.
[4] Marriage data include nonlicensed marriages registered.
. . . = Not available.

Table A2-5. Households, by Type, Selected Years, 1940–2004

(Number.)

Year	Total households	Family households				Nonfamily households		
		Total	Married-couple	Other family		Total	Male householder	Female householder
				Male householder	Female householder			
1940 [1]	34 949	31 491	26 571	1 510	3 410	3 458	1 599	1 859
1947	39 107	34 964	30 612	1 129	3 223	4 143	1 388	2 755
1948	40 532	36 629	31 900	1 020	3 709	3 903	1 198	2 705
1949	42 182	38 080	33 257	1 197	3 626	4 102	1 308	2 794
1950	43 554	38 838	34 075	1 169	3 594	4 716	1 668	3 048
1951	44 673	39 502	34 391	1 154	3 957	5 171	1 732	3 439
1952	45 538	40 235	35 164	1 119	3 952	5 303	1 757	3 546
1953	46 385	40 540	35 577	1 206	3 757	5 845	1 902	3 943
1954	46 962	40 998	35 926	1 315	3 757	5 964	1 925	4 039
1955	47 874	41 732	36 251	1 328	4 153	6 142	2 059	4 083
1956	48 902	42 593	37 047	1 408	4 138	6 309	2 058	4 250
1957	49 673	43 262	37 718	1 241	4 304	6 411	2 038	4 374
1958	50 474	43 426	37 911	1 278	4 237	7 047	2 329	4 718
1959	51 435	43 971	38 410	1 285	4 276	7 464	2 449	5 015
1960	52 799	44 905	39 254	1 228	4 422	7 895	2 716	5 179
1961	53 557	45 383	39 620	1 199	4 564	8 174	2 779	5 395
1962	54 764	46 262	40 404	1 268	4 590	8 502	2 932	5 570
1963	55 270	46 872	40 888	1 295	4 689	8 398	2 838	5 560
1964	56 149	47 381	41 341	1 204	4 836	8 768	2 965	5 803
1965	57 436	47 838	41 689	1 167	4 982	9 598	3 277	6 321
1966	58 406	48 399	42 263	1 163	4 973	10 007	3 299	6 708
1967	59 236	49 086	42 743	1 190	5 153	10 150	3 419	6 731
1968	60 813	50 012	43 507	1 195	5 310	10 801	3 658	7 143
1969	62 214	50 729	44 086	1 221	5 422	11 485	3 890	7 595
1970	63 401	51 456	44 728	1 228	5 500	11 945	4 063	7 882
1971	64 778	52 102	44 928	1 254	5 920	12 676	4 403	8 273
1972	66 676	53 163	45 724	1 331	6 108	13 513	4 839	8 674
1973	68 251	54 264	46 297	1 432	6 535	13 986	5 129	8 858
1974	69 859	54 917	46 787	1 421	6 709	14 942	5 654	9 288
1975	71 120	55 563	46 951	1 485	7 127	15 557	5 912	9 645
1976	72 867	56 056	47 297	1 424	7 335	16 811	6 548	10 263
1977	74 142	56 472	47 471	1 461	7 540	17 669	6 971	10 698
1978	76 030	56 958	47 357	1 564	8 037	19 071	7 811	11 261
1979	77 330	57 498	47 662	1 616	8 220	19 831	8 064	11 767
1980	79 108	58 426	48 180	1 706	8 540	20 682	8 594	12 088
1980 [2]	80 776	59 550	49 112	1 733	8 705	21 226	8 807	12 419
1981	82 368	60 309	49 294	1 933	9 082	22 059	9 279	12 780
1982	83 527	61 019	49 630	1 986	9 403	22 508	9 457	13 051
1983	83 918	61 393	49 908	2 016	9 469	22 525	9 514	13 011
1984	85 407	61 997	50 090	2 030	9 878	23 410	9 752	13 658
1984 [3]	85 290	62 015	50 081	2 038	9 896	23 276	9 689	13 587
1985	86 789	62 706	50 350	2 228	10 129	24 082	10 114	13 968
1986	88 458	63 558	50 933	2 414	10 211	24 900	10 648	14 252
1987	89 479	64 491	51 537	2 510	10 445	24 988	10 652	14 336
1988	91 066	65 133	51 809	2 715	10 608	25 933	11 310	14 624
1988 [4]	91 124	65 204	51 675	2 834	10 696	25 919	11 282	14 637
1989	92 830	65 837	52 100	2 847	10 890	26 994	11 874	15 120
1990	93 347	66 090	52 317	2 884	10 890	27 257	11 606	15 651
1991	94 312	66 322	52 147	2 907	11 268	27 990	12 150	15 840
1992	95 669	67 173	52 457	3 025	11 692	28 496	12 428	16 068
1993	96 391	68 144	53 171	3 026	11 947	28 247	12 254	15 993
1993 [5]	96 426	68 216	53 090	3 065	12 061	28 210	12 297	15 914
1994	97 107	68 490	53 171	2 913	12 406	28 617	12 462	16 155
1995	98 990	69 305	53 858	3 226	12 220	29 686	13 190	16 496
1996	99 627	69 594	53 567	3 513	12 514	30 033	13 348	16 685
1997	101 018	70 241	53 604	3 847	12 790	30 777	13 707	17 070
1998	102 528	70 880	54 317	3 911	12 652	31 648	14 133	17 516
1999	103 874	71 535	54 770	3 976	12 789	32 339	14 368	17 971
2000	104 705	72 025	55 311	4 028	12 687	32 680	14 641	18 039
2001	108 209	73 767	56 592	4 275	12 900	34 442	15 345	19 097
2002	109 297	74 329	56 747	4 438	13 143	34 969	15 579	19 390
2003	111 278	75 596	57 320	4 656	13 620	35 682	16 020	19 662
2004	112 000	76 217	57 719	4 716	13 781	35 783	16 136	19 647

Source: U.S. Census Bureau. Current Population Survey.

[1]Based on 1940 census.
[2]Revised using population controls based on the 1980 census.
[3]Incorporates Hispanic-origin population controls.
[4]Data based on 1988 revised processing.
[5]Revised using population controls based on the 1990 census.

Table A2-6. Unmarried-Couple Households, by Presence of Children, Selected Years, 1960–2004

(Numbers in thousands.)

Year	Partners of opposite sex sharing living quarters			Total unmarried partners		
	Total	Without children under 15 years	With children under 15 years	Total	Without children under 15 years	With children under 15 years
1960 Census	439	242	197	. . .	. . .	. . .
1970 Census	523	327	196	. . .	. . .	. . .
1977	957	754	204	. . .	. . .	. . .
1978	1 137	865	272	. . .	. . .	. . .
1979	1 346	985	360	. . .	. . .	. . .
1980	1 589	1 159	431	. . .	. . .	. . .
1981	1 808	1 305	502	. . .	. . .	. . .
1982	1 863	1 387	475	. . .	. . .	. . .
1983	1 891	1 366	525	. . .	. . .	. . .
1984	1 988	1 373	614	. . .	. . .	. . .
1985	1 983	1 380	603	. . .	. . .	. . .
1986	2 220	1 558	662	. . .	. . .	. . .
1987	2 334	1 614	720	. . .	. . .	. . .
1988	2 588	1 786	802	. . .	. . .	. . .
1989	2 764	1 906	858	. . .	. . .	. . .
1990	2 856	1 966	891	. . .	. . .	. . .
1991	3 039	2 077	962	. . .	. . .	. . .
1992	3 308	2 187	1 121	. . .	. . .	. . .
1993	3 510	2 274	1 236	. . .	. . .	. . .
1994	3 661	2 391	1 270	. . .	. . .	. . .
1995	3 668	2 349	1 319	. . .	. . .	. . .
1996	3 958	2 516	1 442	2 858	1 623	1 236
1997	4 130	2 660	1 470	3 087	1 787	1 300
1998	4 236	2 716	1 520	3 139	1 844	1 295
1999	4 486	2 981	1 505	3 380	2 048	1 331
2000	4 736	3 061	1 675	3 822	2 259	1 563
2001	4 893	3 178	1 716	4 101	2 435	1 665
2002	4 898	3 245	1 654	4 193	2 475	1 718
2003	5 054	3 337	1 717	4 622	2 745	1 877
2004	5 080	3 292	1 788	4 677	2 724	1 953

Source: U.S. Census Bureau. Current Population Survey.

. . . = Not available.

Table A2-7. Average Population Per Household and Family, Selected Years, 1940–2004

(Average population, except as noted.)

Year	Households Total (thousands)	Population per household All ages	Under 18 years	18 years and over	Family households Total (thousands)	Population per family All ages	Under 18 years	18 years and over
1940	34 949	3.67	1.14	2.53	32 166	3.76	1.24	2.52
1947	39 107	3.56	. . .	. . .	35 794	3.67	. . .	. . .
1948	40 532	3.49	1.10	2.48	37 237	3.64	1.19	2.44
1949	42 182	3.42	1.09	2.33	38 624	3.58	1.19	2.39
1950	43 554	3.37	1.06	2.31	39 303	3.54	1.17	2.37
1951	44 673	3.34	1.10	2.23	39 929	3.54	1.23	2.31
1952	45 538	3.32	1.12	2.20	40 578	3.54	1.25	2.29
1953	46 385	3.28	1.09	2.19	40 832	3.53	1.24	2.29
1954	46 962	3.34	1.13	2.20	41 202	3.59	1.30	2.29
1955	47 874	3.33	1.14	2.19	41 951	3.59	1.30	2.29
1956	48 902	3.32	1.15	2.17	42 889	3.58	1.31	2.27
1957	49 673	3.33	1.17	2.16	43 497	3.60	1.34	2.27
1958	50 474	3.34	1.19	2.15	43 696	3.64	1.37	2.27
1959	51 435	3.34	1.20	2.14	44 232	3.65	1.39	2.26
1960	52 799	3.33	1.21	2.12	45 111	3.67	1.41	2.26
1961	53 557	3.34	1.22	2.13	45 539	3.70	1.42	2.27
1962	54 764	3.31	1.21	2.10	46 418	3.67	1.42	2.25
1963	55 270	3.33	1.22	2.10	47 059	3.68	1.43	2.25
1964	56 149	3.33	1.23	2.10	47 540	3.70	1.44	2.25
1965	57 436	3.29	1.21	2.09	47 956	3.70	1.44	2.26
1966	58 406	3.27	1.19	2.08	48 509	3.69	1.42	2.27
1967	59 236	3.26	1.17	2.08	49 214	3.67	1.41	2.27
1968	60 813	3.20	1.14	2.06	50 111	3.63	1.38	2.25
1969	62 214	3.16	1.11	2.05	50 823	3.60	1.36	2.24
1970	63 401	3.14	1.09	2.05	51 586	3.58	1.34	2.25
1971	64 778	3.11	1.07	2.04	52 227	3.57	1.32	2.25
1972	66 676	3.06	1.03	2.03	53 296	3.53	1.29	2.25
1973	68 251	3.01	1.00	2.02	54 373	3.48	1.25	2.23
1974	69 859	2.97	0.96	2.00	55 053	3.44	1.21	2.23
1975	71 120	2.94	0.93	2.01	55 712	3.42	1.18	2.23
1976	72 867	2.89	0.89	2.00	56 245	3.39	1.15	2.23
1977	74 142	2.86	0.87	1.99	56 710	3.37	1.13	2.24
1978	76 030	2.81	0.83	1.98	57 215	3.33	1.10	2.23
1979	77 330	2.78	0.81	1.97	57 804	3.31	1.08	2.23
1980	80 776	2.76	0.79	1.97	59 550	3.29	1.05	2.23
1981	82 368	2.73	0.76	1.96	60 309	3.27	1.03	2.23
1982	83 527	2.72	0.75	1.97	61 019	3.25	1.01	2.24
1983	83 918	2.73	0.74	1.99	61 393	3.26	1.00	2.26
1984	85 407	2.71	0.73	1.98	61 997	3.24	0.99	2.25
1985	86 789	2.69	0.72	1.97	62 706	3.23	0.98	2.24
1986	88 458	2.67	0.71	1.96	63 558	3.21	0.98	2.23
1987	89 479	2.66	0.71	1.96	64 491	3.19	0.96	2.22
1988	91 066	2.64	0.70	1.94	65 133	3.17	0.96	2.21
1989	92 830	2.62	0.69	1.93	65 837	3.16	0.96	2.21
1990	93 347	2.63	0.69	1.94	66 090	3.17	0.96	2.21
1991	94 312	2.63	0.69	1.94	66 322	3.18	0.96	2.22
1992	95 669	2.62	0.69	1.93	67 173	3.17	0.97	2.20
1993	96 391	2.63	0.70	1.94	68 144	3.16	0.96	2.20
1993 [1]	96 426	2.66	0.71	1.95	68 216	3.19	0.99	2.20
1994	97 107	2.67	0.72	1.95	68 490	3.20	0.99	2.21
1995	98 990	2.65	0.71	1.93	69 305	3.19	0.99	2.20
1996	99 627	2.65	0.71	1.94	69 594	3.20	1.00	2.20
1997	101 018	2.64	0.71	1.93	70 241	3.19	0.99	2.20
1998	102 528	2.62	0.70	1.92	70 880	3.18	0.99	2.19
1999	103 874	2.61	0.69	1.92	71 535	3.18	0.98	2.19
2000	104 705	2.62	0.69	1.93	72 025	3.17	0.98	2.19
2001	108 209	2.58	0.67	1.91	73 767	3.14	0.96	2.18
2002	109 297	2.58	0.66	1.92	74 329	3.15	0.96	2.19
2003	111 278	2.57	0.66	1.91	75 596	3.13	0.95	2.18
2004	112 000	2.57	0.66	1.92	76 217	3.13	0.95	2.19

Source: U.S. Census Bureau. Current Population Survey.

[1] Revised using population controls based on the 1990 census.
. . . = Not available.

Table A2-8. Living Arrangements of Children Under 18 Years Old, Selected Years, 1960–2004

(Numbers in thousands, percent distribution.)

Year	Total children under 18 years (thousands)	Percent distribution					
		Living with two parents	Living with one parent			Living with other relatives	Living with non-relatives only
			Total	Mother only	Father only		
1960 Census	63 727	87.7	9.1	8.0	1.1	2.5	0.7
1968	70 326	85.4	11.8	10.7	1.1	2.4	0.4
1969	70 317	85.1	12.1	11.0	1.1	2.3	0.5
1970 [1]	69 162	85.2	11.9	10.8	1.1	2.2	0.7
1971	70 255	83.4	13.5	12.4	1.1	2.4	0.7
1972	68 811	83.1	14.0	12.8	1.2	2.3	0.6
1973	67 950	82.1	14.9	13.6	1.2	2.4	0.6
1974	67 047	81.4	15.6	14.4	1.3	2.3	0.7
1975	66 087	80.3	17.0	15.5	1.5	2.1	0.5
1976	65 129	80.0	17.1	15.8	1.2	2.3	0.6
1977	64 062	79.2	17.7	16.3	1.4	2.5	0.6
1978	63 206	77.7	18.5	17.0	1.6	3.1	0.7
1979	62 389	77.4	18.5	16.9	1.6	3.4	0.7
1980 [1]	63 427	76.7	19.7	18.0	1.7	3.1	0.6
1981	62 918	76.4	20.1	18.1	1.9	3.0	0.6
1982 [2]	62 407	75.0	22.0	20.0	1.9	2.5	0.6
1983 [2]	62 281	74.9	22.5	20.5	2.0	2.2	0.5
1984	62 139	74.9	22.6	20.4	2.2	2.0	0.5
1985	62 475	73.9	23.4	20.9	2.5	2.1	0.6
1986	62 763	73.9	23.5	21.0	2.5	2.1	0.4
1987	62 932	73.1	23.9	21.3	2.6	2.4	0.6
1988	63 179	72.7	24.3	21.4	2.9	2.4	0.6
1989	63 637	73.1	24.3	21.5	2.8	2.1	0.4
1990	64 137	72.5	24.7	21.6	3.1	2.2	0.5
1991	65 093	71.7	25.5	22.4	3.1	2.2	0.6
1992	65 965	70.7	26.6	23.3	3.3	2.0	0.6
1993	66 893	70.5	26.7	23.3	3.4	2.2	0.6
1994	69 508	69.2	26.7	23.5	3.2	3.1	1.0
1995	70 254	68.7	27.0	23.5	3.5	3.3	1.0
1996	70 908	68.0	27.9	24.0	3.9	3.0	1.1
1997	70 983	68.2	27.9	23.6	4.3	2.8	1.1
1998	71 377	68.1	27.7	23.3	4.4	3.0	1.2
1999	71 703	68.0	27.8	23.4	4.3	3.0	1.3
2000	72 012	69.1	26.7	22.4	4.2	3.0	1.2
2001	72 006	69.1	26.7	22.4	4.4	3.0	1.1
2002	72 321	68.7	27.3	22.8	4.6	2.9	1.1
2003	73 001	68.4	27.5	23.0	4.6	3.0	1.1
2004	73 205	67.8	28.0	23.3	4.6	3.2	1.1

Source: U.S. Census Bureau. Current Population Survey.

[1] Revised using population controls based on the 1990 census.
[2] Introduction of improved data collection and processing procedures that helped identify parent-child subfamilies.

Detailed Tables
Social
Conditions

Table A3-1. Population, Urban and Rural, Selected Years, 1790–2000

(Number, percent.)

Year	United States Total population	United States Change Population	United States Change Percent	Urban Number of places 2,500 or more	Urban Population	Urban Change Population	Urban Change Percent	Rural Population	Rural Change Population	Rural Change Percent	Percent of total population Urban	Percent of total population Rural
Previous Urban Definition												
1790	3 929 214	. . .	. . .	. . .	201 655	. . .	. . .	3 727 559	. . .	. . .	5.1	94.9
1800	5 308 483	1 379 269	35.1	33	322 371	120 716	59.9	4 986 112	1 258 553	33.8	6.1	93.9
1810	7 239 881	1 931 398	36.4	46	525 459	203 088	63.0	6 714 422	1 728 310	34.7	7.3	92.7
1820	9 638 453	2 398 572	33.1	61	693 255	167 796	31.9	8 945 198	2 230 776	33.2	7.2	92.8
1830	12 860 702	3 222 249	33.4	90	1 127 247	433 992	62.6	11 733 455	2 788 257	31.2	8.8	91.2
1840	17 063 353	4 202 651	32.7	131	1 845 055	717 808	63.7	15 218 298	3 484 843	29.7	10.8	89.2
1850	23 191 876	6 128 523	35.9	237	3 574 496	1 729 441	93.7	19 617 380	4 399 082	28.9	15.4	84.6
1860	31 443 321	8 251 445	35.6	392	6 216 518	2 642 022	73.9	25 226 803	5 609 423	28.6	19.8	80.2
1870	38 558 371	7 115 050	22.6	663	9 902 361	3 685 843	59.3	28 656 010	3 429 207	13.6	25.7	74.3
1880	50 189 209	11 630 838	30.2	940	14 129 735	4 227 374	42.7	36 059 474	7 403 464	25.8	28.2	71.8
1890	62 979 766	12 790 557	25.5	1 351	22 106 265	7 976 530	56.5	40 873 501	4 814 027	13.4	35.1	64.9
1900	76 212 168	13 232 402	21.0	1 743	30 214 832	8 108 567	36.7	45 997 336	5 123 835	12.5	39.6	60.4
1910	92 228 496	16 016 328	21.0	2 269	42 064 001	11 849 169	39.2	50 164 495	4 176 159	9.1	45.6	54.4
1920	106 021 537	13 793 041	15.0	2 728	54 253 282	12 189 281	29.0	51 768 255	1 603 760	3.2	51.2	48.8
1930	123 202 624	17 181 087	16.2	3 183	69 160 599	14 907 317	27.5	54 042 025	2 273 770	4.4	56.1	43.9
1940	132 164 569	8 961 945	7.3	3 485	74 705 338	5 544 739	8.0	57 459 231	3 417 206	6.3	56.5	43.5
1950	151 325 798	19 161 229	14.5	4 077	90 128 194	15 422 856	20.6	61 197 604	3 738 373	6.5	59.6	40.4
1960	179 323 175	27 997 377	18.5	5 023	113 063 593	22 935 399	25.4	66 259 582	5 061 978	8.3	63.1	36.9
Current Urban Definition												
1950	151 325 798	19 161 229	14.5	4 307	96 846 817	. . .	. . .	54 478 981	. . .	. . .	64.0	36.0
1960	179 323 175	27 997 377	18.5	5 445	125 268 750	28 421 933	29.3	54 045 425	-424 556	-0.8	69.9	30.1
1970	203 302 031	23 978 856	13.4	6 433	149 646 617	24 377 867	19.5	53 565 309	-489 116	-0.9	73.6	26.3
1980	226 542 199	23 240 168	11.4	7 749	167 050 992	17 404 375	11.6	59 494 813	5 929 504	11.1	73.7	26.3
1990	248 709 873	22 167 674	9.8	8 510	187 053 487	20 002 495	12.0	61 656 386	2 161 573	3.6	75.2	24.8
2000	281 421 906	32 712 033	13.2	. . .	222 360 539	35 307 052	18.9	59 061 367	-2 595 019	-4.2	79.0	21.0

Source: U.S. Census Bureau. Historical Decennial Census data.

. . . = Not available.

Table A3-2. Profile of General Demographic Characteristics, 2004

(Number, percent.)

Characteristic	Number	Percent of total population
TOTAL POPULATION	285 691 501	100.0
SEX		
Male	139 782 818	48.9
Female	145 908 683	51.1
AGE		
Under 5 years	20 008 152	7.0
5 to 9 years	19 659 110	6.9
10 to 14 years	21 084 611	7.4
15 to 19 years	19 077 645	6.7
20 to 24 years	19 327 806	6.8
25 to 34 years	38 692 519	13.5
35 to 44 years	43 571 574	15.2
45 to 54 years	41 219 069	14.4
55 to 59 years	16 227 169	5.7
60 to 64 years	12 618 545	4.4
65 to 74 years	18 163 750	6.4
75 to 84 years	12 415 691	4.4
85 years and over	3 625 860	1.3
Median age (years)	36.2	NA
18 years and over	212 767 197	74.5
21 years and over	202 103 066	70.7
62 years and over	41 217 820	14.4
65 years and over	34 205 301	12.0
18 years and over	212 767 197	74.5
Male	102 545 454	35.9
Female	110 221 743	38.6
65 years and over	34 205 301	12.0
Male	14 546 816	5.1
Female	19 658 485	6.9
RACE		
One race	280 285 784	98.1
Two or more races	5 405 717	1.9
Total population	285 691 501	100.0
One race	280 285 784	98.1
White	216 036 244	75.6
Black or African American	34 772 381	12.2
American Indian and Alaska Native	2 151 322	0.8
Cherokee tribal grouping	331 491	0.1
Chippewa tribal grouping	92 041	*
Navajo tribal grouping	230 401	0.1
Sioux tribal grouping	67 666	*
Asian	12 097 281	4.2
Asian Indian	2 245 239	0.8
Chinese, except Taiwanese	2 829 627	1.0
Filipino	2 148 227	0.8
Japanese	832 039	0.3
Korean	1 251 092	0.4
Vietnamese	1 267 510	0.4
Other Asian	1 523 547	0.5
Native Hawaiian and Other Pacific Islander	403 832	0.1
Native Hawaiian	154 666	*
Guamanian or Chamorro	68 336	*
Samoan	60 520	*
Other Pacific Islander	120 310	*
Some other race	14 824 724	5.2
Two or more races	5 405 717	1.9
White and Black or African American	1 141 232	0.4
White and American Indian and Alaska Native	1 370 675	0.5
White and Asian	881 813	0.3
Black or African American and American Indian and Alaska Native	204 832	0.1

Source: U.S. Census Bureau. American Community Survey 2004.

NA = Not applicable.
* = Less than 0.05 percent.

Table A3-2. Profile of General Demographic Characteristics, 2004—*Continued*

(Number, percent.)

Characteristic	Number	Percent of total population
Race Alone or in Combination with One or More Other Races:		
Total population	285 691 501	100.0
White	220 707 536	77.2
Black or African American	36 597 015	12.8
American Indian and Alaska Native	4 006 160	1.4
Asian	13 466 479	4.7
Native Hawaiian and Other Pacific Islander	743 314	0.3
Some other race	15 983 697	5.6
HISPANIC ORIGIN AND RACE		
Total population	285 691 501	100.0
Hispanic or Latino (of any race)	40 459 196	14.2
Mexican	25 894 763	9.1
Puerto Rican	3 874 322	1.4
Cuban	1 437 828	0.5
Other Hispanic or Latino	9 252 283	3.2
Not Hispanic or Latino	245 232 305	85.8
White alone	192 362 875	67.3
Black or African American alone	34 142 554	12.0
American Indian or Alaska Native alone	1 852 775	0.6
Asian alone	11 955 401	4.2
Native Hawaiian and Other Pacific Islander alone	364 656	0.1
Some other race alone	601 187	0.2
Two or more races:	3 952 857	1.4
Two races including some other race	185 083	0.1
Two races excluding some other race, and three or more races	3 767 774	1.3
RELATIONSHIP		
Household population	285 691 501	100.0
Householder	113 448 071	39.7
Spouse	57 012 791	20.0
Child	85 030 196	29.8
Other relatives	16 419 200	5.8
Nonrelatives	13 781 243	4.8
Unmarried partner	6 035 051	2.1
HOUSEHOLDS BY TYPE		
Total households	109 902 090	38.5
Family households (families)	73 885 953	25.9
With own children under 18 years	34 976 246	12.2
Married-couple families	55 223 574	19.3
With own children under 18 years	24 319 914	8.5
Female householder, no husband present	13 850 917	4.8
With own children under 18 years	8 308 267	2.9
Nonfamily households	36 016 137	12.6
Householder living alone	29 572 372	10.4
65 years and over	9 948 787	3.5
Households with one or more people under 18 years	38 657 986	13.5
Households with one or more people 65 years and over	25 156 235	8.8
Average household size	2.60	NA
Average family size	3.18	NA

Source: U.S. Census Bureau. American Community Survey 2004.

NA = Not applicable.

Table A3-3. Profile of Selected Social Characteristics, 2004

(Number, percent.)

Characteristic	Number	Percent of total population
SCHOOL ENROLLMENT		
Population 3 Years and Over Enrolled in School	75 475 565	100.0
Nursery school, preschool	4 673 868	6.2
Kindergarten	4 018 983	5.3
Elementary school (grades 1-8)	32 500 451	43.1
High school grade (grades 9-12)	16 626 365	22.0
College or graduate school	17 655 898	23.4
EDUCATIONAL ATTAINMENT		
Population 25 Years and Over	186 534 177	100.0
Less than 9th grade	11 698 807	6.3
9th to 12th grade, no diploma	18 277 242	9.8
High school graduate (including equivalency)	55 055 121	29.5
Some college, no degree	37 875 025	20.3
Associate degree	13 216 578	7.1
Bachelor's degree	32 030 270	17.2
Graduate or professional degree	18 381 134	9.8
Percent high school graduate or higher	84	NA
Percent bachelor's degree or higher	27	NA
MARITAL STATUS		
Males 15 Years and Over	108 732 377	100.0
Never married	33 290 195	30.6
Now married, except separated	61 315 221	56.4
Separated	1 852 825	1.7
Widowed	2 626 726	2.4
Divorced	9 647 410	8.9
Females 15 Years and Over	116 207 251	100.0
Never married	29 204 857	25.1
Now married, except separated	59 727 165	51.4
Separated	2 962 912	2.6
Widowed	11 030 558	9.5
Divorced	13 281 759	11.4
FERTILITY		
Number of Women 15 to 50 Years Old Who Had a Birth in the Past 12 Months	4 088 512	100.0
Unmarried women (widowed, divorced, and never married)	1 170 797	28.6
Per 1,000 unmarried women	34	NA
Per 1,000 women 15 to 50 years old	55	NA
Per 1,000 women 15 to 19 years old	30	NA
Per 1,000 women 20 to 34 years old	105	NA
Per 1,000 women 35 to 50 years old	22	NA
GRANDPARENTS		
Number of Grandparents Living With Own Grandchildren Under 18 Years in Households	5 675 375	100.0
Responsible for grandchildren	2 374 694	41.8
Less than 1 year	531 984	9.4
1 or 2 years	536 072	9.4
3 or 4 years	383 420	6.8
5 or more years	923 218	16.3
Characteristics of Grandparents Responsible for Own Grandchildren Under 18 Years		
Who are female	63	NA
Who are married	72	NA
Who are in labor force	59	NA
Who are in poverty	20	NA
VETERAN STATUS		
Civilian population 18 years and over	212 052 116	100.0
Civilian veterans	23 756 268	11.2

Source: U.S. Census Bureau. American Community Survey 2004.

NA = Not applicable.

Table A3-3. Profile of Selected Social Characteristics, 2004—*Continued*

(Number, percent.)

Characteristic	Number	Percent of total population
DISABILITY STATUS		
Population 5 years and over	264 965 834	100.0
With a disability	37 858 580	14.3
Population 5 to 15 years	44 889 036	100.0
With a disability	2 824 147	6.3
Population 16 to 64 years	185 871 497	100.0
With a disability	21 495 471	11.6
Population 65 years and over	34 205 301	100.0
With a disability	13 538 962	39.6
RESIDENCE 1 YEAR AGO		
Population 1 Year and Over	281 761 953	100.0
Same house	237 517 689	84.3
Different house in the U.S.	42 548 139	15.1
Same county	27 417 194	9.7
Different county	15 130 945	5.4
Same state	8 518 584	3.0
Different state	6 612 361	2.4
Abroad	1 696 125	0.6
PLACE OF BIRTH		
Total population	285 691 501	100.0
Native	251 411 745	88.0
Born in United States	247 866 360	86.8
State of residence	169 678 117	59.4
Different state	78 188 243	27.4
Born in Puerto Rico, U.S. Island areas, or born abroad to American parent(s)	3 545 385	1.2
Foreign-born	34 279 756	12.0
U.S. CITIZENSHIP STATUS		
Foreign-Born Population	34 279 756	12.0
Naturalization U.S. citizen	14 399 448	5.0
Not a U.S. citizen	19 880 308	7.0
YEAR OF U.S. ENTRY		
Population Born Outside the United States	37 825 141	100.0
Native	3 545 385	9.4
Foreign-born	34 279 756	90.6
Native	3 545 385	9.4
Entered U.S. 2000 or later	394 826	1.0
Entered U.S. before 2000	3 150 559	8.3
Foreign-born	34 279 756	90.6
Entered U.S. 2000 or later	6 281 567	16.6
Entered U.S. before 2000	27 998 189	74.0
WORLD REGION OF BIRTH OF FOREIGN-BORN		
Foreign-Born Population (Excluding Population Born at Sea)	34 279 584	100.0
Europe	4 890 431	14.3
Asia	9 254 705	27.0
Africa	1 147 378	3.4
Oceania	189 596	0.6
Latin America	17 973 287	52.4
Northern America	824 187	2.4
LANGUAGE SPOKEN AT HOME		
Population 5 Years and Over	265 683 349	100.0
English only	216 050 424	81.3
Language other than English	49 632 925	18.7
Speak English less than very well	22 305 496	8.4
Spanish	30 521 800	11.5
Speak English less than very well	14 636 751	5.5
Other Indo-European languages	9 633 742	3.6
Speak English less than very well	3 316 723	1.2
Asian and Pacific Islander languages	7 614 353	2.9
Speak English less than very well	3 807 072	1.4
Other languages	1 863 030	0.7
Speak English less than very well	544 950	0.2

Source: U.S. Census Bureau. American Community Survey 2004.

Table A3-3. Profile of Selected Social Characteristics, 2004—*Continued*

(Number, percent.)

Characteristic	Number	Percent of total population
ANCESTRY (TOTAL REPORTED)		
Total Population	285 691 501	100.0
American	20 061 233	7.0
Arab	1 304 485	0.5
Czech	1 462 413	0.5
Danish	1 477 096	0.5
Dutch	5 087 191	1.8
English	28 410 295	9.9
French (except Basque)	9 496 451	3.3
French Canadian	2 233 999	0.8
German	48 202 654	16.9
Greek	1 309 766	0.5
Hungarian	1 527 156	0.5
Irish	34 487 790	12.1
Italian	16 817 286	5.9
Lithuanian	719 280	0.2
Norwegian	4 585 209	1.6
Polish	9 385 233	3.3
Portuguese	1 335 171	0.5
Russian	3 016 988	1.1
Scotch-Irish	5 323 888	1.9
Scottish	5 752 571	2.0
Slovak	809 066	0.3
Subsaharan African	2 072 057	0.7
Swedish	4 325 823	1.5
Swiss	1 033 014	0.4
Ukrainian	893 502	0.3
Welsh	1 913 101	0.7
West Indian (excluding Hispanic origin groups)	2 163 912	0.8

Source: U.S. Census Bureau. American Community Survey 2004.

Table A3-4. Profile of Selected Economic Characteristics, 2004

(Number, percent.)

Characteristic	Number	Percent
EMPLOYMENT STATUS		
Population 16 Years and Over	220 794 313	100.0
In labor force	145 437 824	65.9
Civilian labor force	144 720 309	65.6
Employed	134 259 460	60.8
Unemployed	10 460 849	4.7
Armed Forces	717 515	0.3
Not in labor force	75 356 489	34.1
Civilian Labor Force	144 720 309	65.6
Unemployed	7	NA
Females 16 Years and Over	114 171 503	100.0
In labor force	67 261 759	30.5
Civilian labor force	67 160 975	30.4
Employed	62 226 143	28.2
Own Children Under 6 Years	22 863 721	10.4
All parents in family in labor force	13 596 151	6.2
Own Children 6 to 17 Years	45 787 059	20.7
All parents in family in labor force	31 224 826.0	14.1
Population 16 to 19 Years	14 932 330	6.8
Not enrolled in school and not a high school graduate	1 137 746	0.5
Unemployed or not in the labor force	688 000	0.3
COMMUTING TO WORK		
Workers 16 years and over	130 831 187	100.0
Car, truck, or van—drove alone	101 635 318	77.7
Car, truck, or van—carpooled	13 183 471	10.1
Public transportation (excluding taxicab)	5 978 055	4.6
Walked	3 115 757	2.4
Other means	1 895 142	1.4
Worked at home	5 023 444	3.8
Mean travel time to work (minutes)	25	NA
EMPLOYED CIVILIAN POPULATION 16 YEARS AND OVER	134 259 460	100.0
OCCUPATION		
Management, professional, and related occupations	45 845 041	34.2
Service occupations	21 749 672	16.2
Sales and office occupations	35 117 275	26.2
Farming, fishing, and forestry occupations	902 224	0.7
Construction, extraction, maintenance and repair occupations	13 109 418	9.8
Production, transportation, and material moving occupations	17 535 830	13.1
INDUSTRY		
Agriculture, forestry, fishing and hunting, and mining	2 414 847	1.8
Construction	10 006 794	7.4
Manufacturing	16 226 119	12.1
Wholesale trade	5 049 763	3.8
Retail trade	15 744 773	11.7
Transportation and warehousing, and utilities	6 718 486	5.0
Information	3 427 421	2.6
Finance and insurance, and real estate and rental and leasing	9 571 229	7.1
Professional, scientific, and management, and administrative and waste management services	13 035 328	9.7
Educational services, and health care, and social assistance	27 400 004	20.4
Arts, entertainment, and recreation, and accommodation, and food services	11 472 519	8.6
Other services, except public administration	6 531 271	4.9
Public administration	6 660 906	5.0
CLASS OF WORKER		
Private wage and salary workers	104 253 095	77.6
Government workers	19 974 153	14.9
Self-employed workers in own not incorporated business	9 652 071	7.2
Unpaid family workers	380 141	0.3

Source: U.S. Census Bureau. American Community Survey 2004.

NA = Not applicable.

Table A3-4. Profile of Selected Economic Characteristics, 2004—*Continued*

(Number, percent.)

Characteristic	Number	Percent
INCOME AND BENEFITS (IN 2004 INFLATION-ADJUSTED DOLLARS)		
Total households	109 902 090	100.0
Less than $10,000	9 748 420	8.9
$10,000 to $14,999	6 912 624	6.3
$15,000 to $24,999	13 556 809	12.3
$25,000 to $34,999	13 156 447	12.0
$35,000 to $49,999	17 027 247	15.5
$50,000 to $74,999	20 896 809	19.0
$75,000 to $99,999	12 161 904	11.1
$100,000 to $149,999	10 353 574	9.4
$150,000 to $199,999	3 135 578	2.8
$200,000 or more	2 952 678	2.7
Median household income (dollars)	44 684	NA
Mean household income (dollars)	60 070	NA
With earnings	87 998 999	80.1
Mean earnings (dollars)	61 341	NA
With Social Security	29 155 647	26.5
Mean Social Security income (dollars)	13 046	NA
With retirement income	18 891 187	17.2
Mean retirement income (dollars)	17 798	NA
With Supplemental Security Income	4 177 140	3.8
Mean Supplemental Security Income (dollars)	6 907	NA
With cash public assistance income	2 675 483	2.4
Mean cash public assistance income (dollars)	3 116	NA
With Food Stamp benefits in the past 12 months	7 939 033	7.2
Family Households	73 885 953	100.0
Less than $10,000	4 053 670	5.5
$10,000 to $14,999	2 963 242	4.0
$15,000 to $24,999	7 454 780	10.1
$25,000 to $34,999	8 106 752	11.0
$35,000 to $49,999	11 518 072	15.6
$50,000 to $74,999	15 726 964	21.3
$75,000 to $99,999	9 966 992	13.5
$100,000 to $149,999	8 829 466	12.0
$150,000 to $199,999	2 708 993	3.7
$200,000 or more	2 557 022	3.5
Median family income (dollars)	53 692	NA
Mean family income (dollars)	69 593	NA
Per capita income (dollars)	24 020	NA
Nonfamily Households	36 016 137	48.8
Median nonfamily income (dollars)	27 226	NA
Mean nonfamily income (dollars)	38 165	NA
Median earnings:	26 691	NA
Male full-time, year-round workers (dollars)	41 194	NA
Female full-time, year-round workers (dollars)	31 374	NA
PERCENTAGE OF FAMILIES AND PEOPLE WHOSE INCOME IN THE PAST 12 MONTHS IS BELOW THE POVERTY LEVEL		
All Families	10	NA
With related children under 18 years	16	NA
With related children under 5 years only	17	NA
Married-couple families	5.00	NA
With related children under 18 years	6.90	NA
With related children under 5 years only	6	NA
Families with female householder, no husband present	29	NA
With related children under 18 years	38	NA
With related children under 5 years only	46	NA
All People	13	NA
Under 18 years	18	NA
Related children under 18 years	18	NA
Related children under 5 years	21	NA
Related children 5 to 17 years	17	NA
18 years and over	11	NA
18 to 64 years	12	NA
65 years and over	9	NA
People in families	12	NA
Unrelated individuals 15 years and over	22	NA

Source: U.S. Census Bureau. American Community Survey 2004.

NA = Not applicable.

Table A3-5. Profile of Selected Housing Characteristics, 2004

(Number, percent.)

Characteristic	Number	Percent
HOUSING OCCUPANCY		
Total Housing Units	122 671 734	100.0
Occupied housing units	109 902 090	89.6
Vacant housing units	12 769 644	10.4
Homeowner vacancy rate	2	NA
Rental vacancy rate	8	NA
UNITS IN STRUCTURE		
1-unit, detached	75 057 202	61.2
1-unit, attached	6 891 601	5.6
2 units	5 042 360	4.1
3 or 4 units	5 739 277	4.7
5 to 9 units	6 088 586	5.0
10 to 19 units	5 521 813	4.5
20 or more units	9 526 484	7.8
Mobile home	8 717 845	7.1
Boat, RV, van, etc.	86 566	0.1
YEAR STRUCTURE BUILT		
2000 or later	7 535 088	6.1
1995 to 1999	10 115 631	8.2
1990 to 1994	8 892 303	7.2
1980 to 1989	18 406 439	15.0
1970 to 1979	21 462 868	17.5
1960 to 1969	15 137 038	12.3
1950 to 1959	14 826 857	12.1
1940 to 1949	7 959 497	6.5
1939 or earlier	18 336 013	15.0
ROOMS		
1 room	1 189 672	1.0
2 rooms	3 908 800	3.2
3 rooms	11 467 134	9.4
4 rooms	21 803 418	17.8
5 rooms	26 719 750	21.8
6 rooms	23 140 319	18.9
7 rooms	15 116 712	12.3
8 rooms	9 666 527	7.9
9 rooms or more	9 659 402	7.9
Median (rooms)	5	NA
BEDROOMS		
No bedroom	1 550 579	1.3
1 bedroom	14 744 165	12.0
2 bedrooms	34 786 589	28.4
3 bedrooms	48 833 466	39.8
4 bedrooms	18 338 502	15.0
5 bedrooms or more	4 418 433	3.6
OCCUPIED HOUSING UNITS	109 902 090	100.0
HOUSING TENURE		
Owner-occupied	73 754 173	67.1
Renter-occupied	36 147 917	32.9
Average household size of owner-occupied unit	3	NA
Average household size of renter-occupied unit	2	NA
YEAR HOUSEHOLDER MOVED INTO UNIT		
2000 or later	47 762 934	43.5
1995 to 1999	20 805 196	18.9
1990 to 1994	12 057 348	11.0
1980 to 1989	13 158 677	12.0
1970 to 1979	8 431 663	7.7
1969 or earlier	7 686 272	7.0

Source: U.S. Census Bureau. American Community Survey 2004.

NA = Not applicable.

Table A3-5. Profile of Selected Housing Characteristics, 2004—*Continued*

(Number, percent.)

Characteristic	Number	Percent
VEHICLES AVAILABLE		
No vehicles available	9 626 376	8.8
1 vehicle available	36 506 960	33.2
2 vehicles available	42 350 190	38.5
3 or more vehicles available	21 418 564	19.5
HOUSE HEATING FUEL		
Utility gas	55 763 928	50.7
Bottled, tank, or LP gas	6 839 664	6.2
Electricity	34 815 624	31.7
Fuel oil, kerosene, etc.	9 184 460	8.4
Coal or coke	158 318	0.1
Wood	1 791 422	1.6
Solar energy	36 264	*
Other fuel	428 954	0.4
No fuel used	883 456	0.8
SELECTED CHARACTERISTICS		
Lacking complete plumbing facilities	461 894	0.4
Lacking complete kitchen facilities	571 708	0.5
No telephone service available	4 764 467	4.3
OCCUPANTS PER ROOM		
1.00 or less	106 511 410	96.9
1.01 to 1.50	2 567 069	2.3
1.51 or more	823 611	0.8
OWNER-OCCUPIED UNITS	73 754 173	100.0
VALUE		
Less than $50,000	7 454 042	10.1
$50,000 to $99,999	15 100 516	20.5
$100,000 to $149,999	13 993 069	19.0
$150,000 to $199,999	10 451 920	14.2
$200,000 to $299,999	10 781 732	14.6
$300,000 to $499,999	9 956 999	13.5
$500,000 to $999,999	4 981 509	6.8
$1,000,000 or more	1 034 386	1.4
Median (dollars)	151 366	NA
MORTGAGE STATUS AND SELECTED MONTHLY OWNER COSTS		
Housing units with a mortgage	49 782 384	67.5
Less than $300	265 760	0.4
$300 to $499	1 999 050	2.7
$500 to $699	4 879 431	6.6
$700 to $999	10 665 631	14.5
$1,000 to $1,499	15 012 317	20.4
$1,500 to $1,999	8 284 385	11.2
$2,000 or more	8 675 810	11.8
Median (dollars)	1 212	NA
Housing units without a mortgage	23 971 789	32.5
Less than $100	473 006	0.6
$100 to $199	3 185 126	4.3
$200 to $299	5 832 993	7.9
$300 to $399	5 220 046	7.1
$400 or more	9 260 618	12.6
Median (dollars)	345	NA

Source: U.S. Census Bureau. American Community Survey 2004.

NA = Not applicable.
* = Less than 0.05 percent.

Table A3-5. Profile of Selected Housing Characteristics, 2004—*Continued*

(Number, percent.)

Characteristic	Number	Percent
SELECTED MONTHLY OWNER COSTS AS A PERCENTAGE OF HOUSEHOLD INCOME		
Housing unit with a mortgage	49 782 384	67.5
Less than 20.0 percent	18 837 782	25.5
20.0 to 24.9 percent	8 398 483	11.4
25.0 to 29.9 percent	6 228 983	8.4
30.0 to 34.9 percent	4 164 847	5.6
35.0 percent or more	11 946 686	16.2
Not computed	205 603	0.3
Housing unit without a mortgage	23 971 789	32.5
Less than 10.0 percent	9 796 061	13.3
10.0 to 14.9 percent	4 764 390	6.5
15.0 to 19.9 percent	2 851 272	3.9
20.0 to 24.9 percent	1 761 205	2.4
25.0 to 29.9 percent	1 143 743	1.6
30.0 to 34.9 percent	802 593	1.1
35.0 percent or more	2 620 238	3.6
Not computed	232 287	0.3
RENTER-OCCUPIED UNITS	36 147 917	100.0
GROSS RENT		
Less than $200	1 331 724	3.7
$200 to $299	1 400 313	3.9
$300 to $499	5 578 208	15.4
$500 to $749	11 112 318	30.7
$750 to $999	7 692 958	21.3
$1,000 to $1,499	4 975 776	13.8
$1,500 or more	1 873 549	5.2
No cash rent	2 183 071	6.0
Median (dollars)	694	NA
GROSS RENT AS A PERCENTAGE OF HOUSEHOLD INCOME		
Less than 15.0 percent	4 673 416	12.9
15.0 to 19.9 percent	4 372 792	12.1
20.0 to 24.9 percent	4 374 549	12.1
25.0 to 29.9 percent	3 950 411	10.9
30.0 to 34.9 percent	2 948 416	8.2
35.0 percent or more	12 978 991	35.9
Not computed	2 849 342	7.9

Source: U.S. Census Bureau. American Community Survey 2004.

NA = Not applicable.

Labor Force and Job Characteristics

Table A4-1. Employment Status of the Civilian Noninstitutional Population, 1947–2004

(Thousands of persons, percent.)

Year	Civilian noninsti-tutional population	Civilian labor force		Employed				Unemployed		Not in labor force
		Total	Participation rate	Total	Percent of population	Agriculture	Nonagri-cultural industries	Number	Unemploy-ment rate	
1947	101 827	59 350	58.3	57 038	56.0	7 890	49 148	2 311	3.9	42 477
1948	103 068	60 621	58.8	58 343	56.6	7 629	50 714	2 276	3.8	42 447
1949	103 994	61 286	58.9	57 651	55.4	7 658	49 993	3 637	5.9	42 708
1950	104 995	62 208	59.2	58 918	56.1	7 160	51 758	3 288	5.3	42 787
1951	104 621	62 017	59.2	59 961	57.3	6 726	53 235	2 055	3.3	42 604
1952	105 231	62 138	59.0	60 250	57.3	6 500	53 749	1 883	3.0	43 093
1953 [1]	107 056	63 015	58.9	61 179	57.1	6 260	54 919	1 834	2.9	44 041
1954	108 321	63 643	58.8	60 109	55.5	6 205	53 904	3 532	5.5	44 678
1955	109 683	65 023	59.3	62 170	56.7	6 450	55 722	2 852	4.4	44 660
1956	110 954	66 552	60.0	63 799	57.5	6 283	57 514	2 750	4.1	44 402
1957	112 265	66 929	59.6	64 071	57.1	5 947	58 123	2 859	4.3	45 336
1958	113 727	67 639	59.5	63 036	55.4	5 586	57 450	4 602	6.8	46 088
1959	115 329	68 369	59.3	64 630	56.0	5 565	59 065	3 740	5.5	46 960
1960 [1]	117 245	69 628	59.4	65 778	56.1	5 458	60 318	3 852	5.5	47 617
1961	118 771	70 459	59.3	65 746	55.4	5 200	60 546	4 714	6.7	48 312
1962 [1]	120 153	70 614	58.8	66 702	55.5	4 944	61 759	3 911	5.5	49 539
1963	122 416	71 833	58.7	67 762	55.4	4 687	63 076	4 070	5.7	50 583
1964	124 485	73 091	58.7	69 305	55.7	4 523	64 782	3 786	5.2	51 394
1965	126 513	74 455	58.9	71 088	56.2	4 361	66 726	3 366	4.5	52 058
1966	128 058	75 770	59.2	72 895	56.9	3 979	68 915	2 875	3.8	52 288
1967	129 874	77 347	59.6	74 372	57.3	3 844	70 527	2 975	3.8	52 527
1968	132 028	78 737	59.6	75 920	57.5	3 817	72 103	2 817	3.6	53 291
1969	134 335	80 734	60.1	77 902	58.0	3 606	74 296	2 832	3.5	53 602
1970	137 085	82 771	60.4	78 678	57.4	3 463	75 215	4 093	4.9	54 315
1971	140 216	84 382	60.2	79 367	56.6	3 394	75 972	5 016	5.9	55 834
1972 [1]	144 126	87 034	60.4	82 153	57.0	3 484	78 669	4 882	5.6	57 091
1973 [1]	147 096	89 429	60.8	85 064	57.8	3 470	81 594	4 365	4.9	57 667
1974	150 120	91 949	61.3	86 794	57.8	3 515	83 279	5 156	5.6	58 171
1975	153 153	93 775	61.2	85 846	56.1	3 408	82 438	7 929	8.5	59 377
1976	156 150	96 158	61.6	88 752	56.8	3 331	85 421	7 406	7.7	59 991
1977	159 033	99 009	62.3	92 017	57.9	3 283	88 734	6 991	7.1	60 025
1978 [1]	161 910	102 251	63.2	96 048	59.3	3 387	92 661	6 202	6.1	59 659
1979	164 863	104 962	63.7	98 824	59.9	3 347	95 477	6 137	5.8	59 900
1980	167 745	106 940	63.8	99 303	59.2	3 364	95 938	7 637	7.1	60 806
1981	170 130	108 670	63.9	100 397	59.0	3 368	97 030	8 273	7.6	61 460
1982	172 271	110 204	64.0	99 526	57.8	3 401	96 125	10 678	9.7	62 067
1983	174 215	111 550	64.0	100 834	57.9	3 383	97 450	10 717	9.6	62 665
1984	176 383	113 544	64.4	105 005	59.5	3 321	101 685	8 539	7.5	62 839
1985	178 206	115 461	64.8	107 150	60.1	3 179	103 971	8 312	7.2	62 744
1986 [1]	180 587	117 834	65.3	109 597	60.7	3 163	106 434	8 237	7.0	62 752
1987	182 753	119 865	65.6	112 440	61.5	3 208	109 232	7 425	6.2	62 888
1988	184 613	121 669	65.9	114 968	62.3	3 169	111 800	6 701	5.5	62 944
1989	186 393	123 869	66.5	117 342	63.0	3 199	114 142	6 528	5.3	62 523
1990 [1]	189 164	125 840	66.5	118 793	62.8	3 223	115 570	7 047	5.6	63 324
1991	190 925	126 346	66.2	117 718	61.7	3 269	114 449	8 628	6.8	64 578
1992	192 805	128 105	66.4	118 492	61.5	3 247	115 245	9 613	7.5	64 700
1993	194 838	129 200	66.3	120 259	61.7	3 115	117 144	8 940	6.9	65 638
1994 [1]	196 814	131 056	66.6	123 060	62.5	3 409	119 651	7 996	6.1	65 758
1995	198 584	132 304	66.6	124 900	62.9	3 440	121 460	7 404	5.6	66 280
1996	200 591	133 943	66.8	126 708	63.2	3 443	123 264	7 236	5.4	66 647
1997 [1]	203 133	136 297	67.1	129 558	63.8	3 399	126 159	6 739	4.9	66 837
1998 [1]	205 220	137 673	67.1	131 463	64.1	3 378	128 085	6 210	4.5	67 547
1999 [1]	207 753	139 368	67.1	133 488	64.3	3 281	130 207	5 880	4.2	68 385
2000 [1]	212 577	142 583	67.1	136 891	64.4	2 464	134 427	5 692	4.0	69 994
2001	215 092	143 734	66.8	136 933	63.7	2 299	134 635	6 801	4.7	71 359
2002	217 570	144 863	66.6	136 485	62.7	2 311	134 174	8 378	5.8	72 707
2003 [1]	221 168	146 510	66.2	137 736	62.3	2 275	135 461	8 774	6.0	74 658
2004 [1]	223 357	147 401	66.0	139 252	62.3	2 232	137 020	8 149	5.5	75 956

Source: U.S. Bureau of Labor Statistics.

[1]Not strictly comparable with data for prior years.

Table A4-2. Civilian Labor Force Participation Rates, 1980–2005

(Percent.)

Year	16 years and over	16–19 years	20 years and over						
			Total	20–24 years	25–34 years	35–44 years	45–54 years	55–64 years	65 years and over
Both Sexes									
1980	63.8	56.7	64.5	77.2	79.9	80.0	74.9	55.7	12.5
1981	63.9	55.4	64.8	77.3	80.5	80.7	75.7	55.0	12.2
1982	64.0	54.1	65.0	77.2	81.0	81.2	75.9	55.1	11.9
1983	64.0	53.5	65.0	77.2	81.3	81.6	76.0	54.5	11.7
1984	64.4	53.9	65.3	77.6	81.8	82.4	76.5	54.2	11.1
1985	64.8	54.5	65.7	78.2	82.5	83.1	77.3	54.2	10.8
1986	65.3	54.7	66.2	78.9	82.9	83.7	78.0	54.0	10.9
1987	65.6	54.7	66.5	79.0	83.3	84.3	78.5	54.4	11.1
1988	65.9	55.3	66.8	78.7	83.3	84.6	79.6	54.6	11.5
1989	66.5	55.9	67.3	78.7	83.8	85.1	80.5	55.5	11.8
1990	66.5	53.7	67.6	77.8	83.6	85.2	80.7	55.9	11.8
1991	66.2	51.6	67.3	76.7	83.2	85.2	81.0	55.5	11.5
1992	66.4	51.3	67.6	77.1	83.7	85.1	81.5	56.2	11.5
1993	66.3	51.5	67.5	77.0	83.3	84.9	81.6	56.4	11.2
1994	66.6	52.7	67.7	77.0	83.2	84.8	81.7	56.8	12.4
1995	66.6	53.5	67.7	76.6	83.8	84.6	81.4	57.2	12.1
1996	66.8	52.3	67.9	76.8	84.1	84.8	82.1	57.9	12.1
1997	67.1	51.6	68.4	77.6	84.4	85.1	82.6	58.9	12.2
1998	67.1	52.8	68.3	77.5	84.6	84.7	82.5	59.3	11.9
1999	67.1	52.0	68.3	77.5	84.6	84.9	82.6	59.3	12.3
2000	67.1	52.0	68.3	77.8	84.6	84.8	82.5	59.2	12.9
2001	66.8	49.6	68.2	77.1	84.0	84.6	82.3	60.4	13.0
2002	66.6	47.4	68.1	76.4	83.7	84.1	82.1	61.9	13.2
2003	66.2	44.5	67.9	75.4	82.9	83.9	82.1	62.4	14.0
2004	66.0	43.9	67.7	75.0	82.7	83.6	81.8	62.3	14.4
2005	66.0	43.7	67.8	74.6	82.8	83.8	81.7	62.9	15.1
Men									
1980	77.4	60.5	79.4	85.9	95.2	95.5	91.2	72.1	19.0
1981	77.0	59.0	79.0	85.5	94.9	95.4	91.4	70.6	18.3
1982	76.6	56.7	78.7	84.9	94.7	95.3	91.2	70.2	17.8
1983	76.4	56.2	78.5	84.8	94.2	95.2	91.2	69.4	17.4
1984	76.4	56.0	78.3	85.0	94.3	95.4	91.2	68.5	16.3
1985	76.3	56.8	78.1	85.0	94.7	95.0	91.0	67.9	15.8
1986	76.3	56.4	78.1	85.8	94.6	94.8	91.0	67.3	16.0
1987	76.2	56.1	78.0	85.2	94.6	94.6	90.7	67.6	16.3
1988	76.2	56.9	77.9	85.0	94.3	94.5	90.9	67.0	16.5
1989	76.4	57.9	78.1	85.3	94.4	94.5	91.1	67.2	16.6
1990	76.4	55.7	78.2	84.4	94.1	94.3	90.7	67.8	16.3
1991	75.8	53.2	77.7	83.5	93.6	94.1	90.5	67.0	15.7
1992	75.8	53.4	77.7	83.3	93.8	93.7	90.7	67.0	16.1
1993	75.4	53.2	77.3	83.2	93.4	93.4	90.1	66.5	15.6
1994	75.1	54.1	76.8	83.1	92.6	92.8	89.1	65.5	16.9
1995	75.0	54.8	76.7	83.1	93.0	92.3	88.8	66.0	16.8
1996	74.9	53.2	76.8	82.5	93.2	92.4	89.1	67.0	16.9
1997	75.0	52.3	77.0	82.5	93.0	92.6	89.5	67.6	17.1
1998	74.9	53.3	76.8	82.0	93.2	92.6	89.2	68.1	16.5
1999	74.7	52.9	76.7	81.9	93.3	92.8	88.8	67.9	16.9
2000	74.8	52.8	76.7	82.6	93.4	92.7	88.6	67.3	17.7
2001	74.4	50.2	76.5	81.6	92.7	92.5	88.5	68.3	17.7
2002	74.1	47.5	76.3	80.7	92.4	92.1	88.5	69.2	17.9
2003	73.5	44.3	75.9	80.0	91.8	92.1	87.7	68.7	18.6
2004	73.3	43.9	75.8	79.6	91.9	91.9	87.5	68.7	19.0
2005	73.3	43.2	75.8	79.1	91.7	92.1	87.7	69.3	19.8

Source: U.S. Bureau of Labor Statistics.

Table A4-2. Civilian Labor Force Participation Rates, 1980–2005—*Continued*

(Percent.)

Year	16 years and over	16–19 years	20 years and over						
			Total	20–24 years	25–34 years	35–44 years	45–54 years	55–64 years	65 years and over
Women									
1980	51.5	52.9	51.3	68.9	65.5	65.5	59.9	41.3	8.1
1981	52.1	51.9	52.1	69.6	66.7	66.8	61.1	41.4	8.0
1982	52.6	51.4	52.7	69.8	68.0	68.0	61.6	41.8	7.9
1983	52.9	50.8	53.1	69.9	69.0	68.7	61.9	41.5	7.8
1984	53.6	51.8	53.7	70.4	69.8	70.2	62.9	41.7	7.5
1985	54.5	52.1	54.7	71.8	70.9	71.8	64.4	42.0	7.3
1986	55.3	53.0	55.5	72.4	71.6	73.1	65.9	42.3	7.4
1987	56.0	53.3	56.2	73.0	72.4	74.5	67.1	42.7	7.4
1988	56.6	53.6	56.8	72.7	72.7	75.2	69.0	43.5	7.9
1989	57.4	53.9	57.7	72.4	73.5	76.0	70.5	45.0	8.4
1990	57.5	51.6	58.0	71.3	73.5	76.4	71.2	45.2	8.6
1991	57.4	50.0	57.9	70.1	73.1	76.5	71.9	45.2	8.5
1992	57.8	49.1	58.5	70.9	73.9	76.7	72.6	46.5	8.3
1993	57.9	49.7	58.5	70.9	73.4	76.6	73.5	47.2	8.1
1994	58.8	51.3	59.3	71.0	74.0	77.1	74.6	48.9	9.2
1995	58.9	52.2	59.4	70.3	74.9	77.2	74.4	49.2	8.8
1996	59.3	51.3	59.9	71.3	75.2	77.5	75.4	49.6	8.6
1997	59.8	51.0	60.5	72.7	76.0	77.7	76.0	50.9	8.6
1998	59.8	52.3	60.4	73.0	76.3	77.1	76.2	51.2	8.6
1999	60.0	51.0	60.7	73.2	76.4	77.2	76.7	51.5	8.9
2000	59.9	51.2	60.6	73.1	76.1	77.2	76.8	51.9	9.4
2001	59.8	49.0	60.6	72.7	75.5	77.1	76.4	53.2	9.6
2002	59.6	47.3	60.5	72.1	75.1	76.4	76.0	55.2	9.8
2003	59.5	44.8	60.6	70.8	74.1	76.0	76.8	56.6	10.6
2004	59.2	43.8	60.3	70.5	73.6	75.6	76.5	56.3	11.1
2005	59.3	44.2	60.4	70.1	73.9	75.8	76.0	57.0	11.5

Source: U.S. Bureau of Labor Statistics.

Detailed Tables
Housing

Table A5-1. Housing Financial Characteristics, by State, 2004

(Dollars, percent.)

State	Owner-occupied housing units				Renter-occupied housing units	
	Percent owner-occupied	Median housing value	With a mortgage		Median monthly housing costs	Percent spending 30 percent or more of household income on rent and utilities
			Median monthly housing costs	Percent spending 30 percent or more of household income on selected monthly owner costs		
United States	67.1	151 366	1 212	32.4	694	44.1
Alabama	71.9	94 671	872	26.0	519	39.6
Alaska	65.5	179 304	1 421	26.1	808	36.3
Arizona	68.7	145 741	1 130	33.4	691	47.3
Arkansas	65.5	79 006	773	22.7	517	40.6
California	58.6	391 102	1 733	44.1	914	49.9
Colorado	68.6	211 740	1 355	36.3	724	47.0
Connecticut	69.7	236 559	1 603	31.2	811	43.2
Delaware	72.9	171 589	1 191	25.4	743	37.5
District of Columbia	43.6	334 702	1 612	33.5	799	43.5
Florida	70.5	149 291	1 143	37.9	766	50.5
Georgia	67.7	136 912	1 126	31.1	677	43.9
Hawaii	58.9	364 840	1 648	37.3	871	42.9
Idaho	72.4	120 825	953	28.2	566	45.1
Illinois	69.2	167 711	1 370	33.8	698	42.5
Indiana	71.8	110 020	963	24.4	589	37.8
Iowa	73.8	95 901	942	21.5	533	37.9
Kansas	69.5	102 458	1 013	24.1	567	38.1
Kentucky	70.1	98 438	888	25.6	503	39.5
Louisiana	66.2	95 910	902	27.3	540	42.3
Maine	72.9	143 182	1 020	27.5	582	40.8
Maryland	69.5	216 529	1 406	27.9	837	40.7
Massachusetts	64.6	331 200	1 645	35.2	852	42.9
Michigan	74.7	145 177	1 137	29.3	628	43.4
Minnesota	75.3	181 135	1 260	29.2	673	41.7
Mississippi	69.6	79 023	843	30.7	529	42.0
Missouri	70.8	117 033	954	24.4	567	39.1
Montana	68.5	119 319	974	33.0	520	40.2
Nebraska	68.4	106 656	1 051	24.1	547	37.6
Nevada	61.2	202 937	1 274	38.6	787	43.7
New Hampshire	72.6	216 639	1 472	33.3	810	42.5
New Jersey	68.1	291 294	1 847	38.4	877	44.8
New Mexico	69.3	110 788	935	31.2	546	39.7
New York	55.6	220 981	1 525	37.3	796	47.4
North Carolina	69.0	117 771	1 028	29.7	610	40.9
North Dakota	68.1	84 354	902	21.6	466	32.1
Ohio	69.8	122 384	1 090	27.6	587	41.7
Oklahoma	68.2	85 060	871	25.0	525	39.9
Oregon	63.0	181 544	1 217	35.0	681	47.6
Pennsylvania	72.8	116 520	1 114	28.8	611	41.8
Rhode Island	61.8	240 150	1 469	35.9	740	45.0
South Carolina	69.7	113 910	987	28.8	610	40.3
South Dakota	69.1	95 523	952	26.5	493	34.6
Tennessee	70.0	110 198	954	29.1	564	40.2
Texas	65.1	99 858	1 166	29.9	648	42.0
Utah	69.7	157 275	1 164	33.1	662	42.9
Vermont	73.3	154 318	1 174	32.2	674	38.5
Virginia	69.2	179 191	1 323	29.0	757	41.6
Washington	64.1	204 719	1 389	35.1	727	47.5
West Virginia	74.0	81 826	769	24.7	461	36.7
Wisconsin	69.9	137 727	1 155	29.8	609	40.9
Wyoming	69.9	119 654	954	24.1	534	31.3

Source: U.S. Census Bureau. American Community Survey 2004.

Table A5-2. Housing Unit Characteristics, 2003

(Numbers in thousands, rate.)

Characteristic	Total housing units	Seasonal	Year-round			
				Occupied		
			Total	Total	Owner	Renter
TOTAL	120 777	3 566	117 211	105 842	72 238	33 604
Units in Structure						
1, detached	74 916	2 034	72 882	67 753	59 642	8 111
1, attached	7 227	205	7 023	6 272	3 679	2 593
2 to 4	9 965	102	9 863	8 474	1 426	7 048
5 to 9	6 012	73	5 938	5 135	501	4 634
10 to 19	5 433	77	5 355	4 468	485	3 983
20 to 49	3 964	116	3 848	3 294	389	2 905
50 or more	4 289	129	4 160	3 592	601	2 991
Mobile home or trailer	8 971	829	8 142	6 854	5 514	1 340
Cooperatives and Condominiums						
Cooperatives	693	59	634	558	378	180
Condominiums	6 080	492	5 589	4 722	3 416	1 305
Year Structure Built						
2000 to 2004	6 237	201	6 036	5 228	4 239	989
1995 to 1999	8 851	226	8 624	7 922	6 315	1 607
1990 to 1994	7 155	227	6 928	6 344	5 117	1 226
1985 to 1989	8 865	238	8 627	7 936	5 374	2 562
1980 to 1984	7 584	218	7 365	6 641	4 298	2 343
1975 to 1979	12 314	387	11 927	10 876	7 308	3 568
1970 to 1974	11 188	449	10 739	9 598	6 051	3 547
1960 to 1969	15 482	480	15 002	13 781	9 187	4 594
1950 to 1959	13 433	400	13 033	11 933	8 696	3 237
1940 to 1949	8 152	237	7 915	7 098	4 643	2 456
1930 to 1939	6 362	182	6 180	5 432	3 192	2 239
1920 to 1929	5 479	70	5 410	4 750	2 799	1 951
1919 or earlier	9 672	249	9 423	8 304	5 018	3 285
Median	1 970	1 971	1 970	1 970	1 972	1 967
Suitability for Year-Round Use						
Built and heated for year-round use ...	119 603	2 392	117 211	105 842	72 238	33 604
Not suitable	1 055	1 055	NA	NA	NA	NA
Not reported	120	120	NA	NA	NA	NA
Time Sharing						
Vacant, including URE	14 935	3 566	11 369	NA	NA	NA
Ownership time shared	71	24	47	NA	NA	NA
Not time shared	14 864	3 542	11 322	NA	NA	NA
Duration of Vacancy						
Vacant units	13 494	3 036	10 458	NA	NA	NA
Less than 1 month vacant	2 258	449	1 808	NA	NA	NA
1 month up to 2 months	1 148	149	1 000	NA	NA	NA
2 months up to 6 months	2 490	499	1 991	NA	NA	NA
6 months up to 1 year	1 173	294	879	NA	NA	NA
1 year up to 2 years	815	93	722	NA	NA	NA
2 years or more	2 442	516	1 926	NA	NA	NA
Never occupied	598	277	322	NA	NA	NA
Don't know	2 570	759	1 810	NA	NA	NA
Last Used as a Permanent Residence						
Vacant seasonal	3 566	3 566	NA	NA	NA	NA
Less than 1 month since occupied as permanent home	92	92	NA	NA	NA	NA
1 month up to 2 months	46	46	NA	NA	NA	NA
2 months up to 6 months	95	95	NA	NA	NA	NA
6 months up to 1 year	92	92	NA	NA	NA	NA
1 year up to 2 years	82	82	NA	NA	NA	NA
2 years or more	819	819	NA	NA	NA	NA
Never occupied as permanent home ...	1 680	1 680	NA	NA	NA	NA
Don't know	658	658	NA	NA	NA	NA
Not reported	2	2	NA	NA	NA	NA
Metropolitan/Nonmetropolitan Areas						
Inside metropolitan statistical areas ...	94 488	1 388	93 100	85 064	56 425	28 639
In central cities	35 217	231	34 986	31 300	16 701	14 599
Suburbs	59 271	1 157	58 114	53 765	39 724	14 041
Outside metropolitan statistical areas ...	26 289	2 178	24 111	20 778	15 813	4 965

Source: U.S. Census Bureau. American Housing Survey 2003.

NA = Not applicable.

Table A5-2. Housing Unit Characteristics, 2003—*Continued*

(Numbers in thousands, rate.)

Characteristic	Year-round—*Continued* Vacant Total	For rent	Rental vacancy rate	For sale only	Rented or sold	Occasional use/URE	Other vacant	New construction, 4 years	Mobile homes
TOTAL	11 369	3 597	9.6	1 284	932	2 647	2 909	6 758	8 971
Units in Structure									
1, detached	5 129	675	7.6	882	505	1 455	1 612	4 256	NA
1, attached	750	252	8.8	82	65	173	178	566	NA
2 to 4	1 390	710	9.1	52	89	193	346	213	NA
5 to 9	803	526	10.1	33	56	104	84	187	NA
10 to 19	887	588	12.7	14	59	124	103	303	NA
20 to 49	554	378	11.4	26	34	73	43	270	NA
50 or more	568	261	7.9	38	62	140	66	190	NA
Mobile home or trailer	1 288	208	13.3	156	63	384	477	773	8 971
Cooperatives and Condominiums									
Cooperatives	75	13	6.8	14	8	31	10	8	86
Condominiums	867	135	9.2	144	85	392	110	513	9
Year Structure Built									
2000 to 2004	808	232	18.5	196	120	169	92	6 237	709
1995 to 1999	703	203	11.1	114	67	201	119	521	1 693
1990 to 1994	585	190	13.2	55	52	190	97	NA	1 084
1985 to 1989	691	255	9.0	69	57	193	118	NA	879
1980 to 1984	725	263	10.0	61	60	184	157	NA	985
1975 to 1979	1 051	363	9.2	120	87	243	239	NA	1 245
1970 to 1974	1 141	404	10.1	99	85	262	290	NA	1 366
1960 to 1969	1 221	398	7.9	130	69	297	327	NA	790
1950 to 1959	1 101	313	8.7	127	106	247	307	NA	127
1940 to 1949	816	252	9.2	85	52	179	248	NA	32
1930 to 1939	748	192	7.8	72	70	164	250	NA	60
1920 to 1929	660	182	8.5	62	39	125	251	NA	NA
1919 or earlier	1 119	349	9.5	94	67	194	415	NA	NA
Median	1 970	1 971	NA	1 973	1 973	1 972	1 959	2 000	1 984
Suitability for Year-Round Use									
Built and heated for year-round use	11 369	3 597	9.6	1 284	932	2 647	2 909	6 734	8 718
Not suitable	NA	NA	NA	NA	NA	NA	NA	25	217
Not reported	NA	NA	NA	NA	NA	NA	NA	NA	36
Time Sharing									
Vacant, including URE	11 369	3 597	90.5	1 284	932	2 647	2 909	1 068	2 117
Ownership time shared	47	17	100.0	6	3	8	13	4	7
Not time shared	11 322	3 580	90.4	1 278	929	2 639	2 896	1 063	2 110
Duration of Vacancy									
Vacant units	10 458	3 597	90.7	1 284	932	1 737	2 909	1 001	1 949
Less than 1 month vacant	1 808	960	91.3	158	211	282	197	187	249
1 month up to 2 months	1 000	564	87.5	81	123	76	156	92	86
2 months up to 6 months	1 991	885	89.1	254	230	245	377	136	388
6 months up to 1 year	879	261	95.5	167	67	137	247	79	156
1 year up to 2 years	722	128	92.0	134	52	103	305	25	144
2 years or more	1 926	243	90.2	155	83	345	1 099	33	444
Never occupied	322	45	93.1	99	48	64	65	255	104
Don't know	1 810	511	93.4	234	117	485	463	194	377
Last Used as a Permanent Residence									
Vacant seasonal	NA	NA	NA	NA	NA	NA	NA	222	829
Less than 1 month since occupied as permanent home	NA	NA	NA	NA	NA	NA	NA	13	25
1 month up to 2 months	NA	NA	NA	NA	NA	NA	NA	3	11
2 months up to 6 months	NA	NA	NA	NA	NA	NA	NA	5	18
6 months up to 1 year	NA	NA	NA	NA	NA	NA	NA	3	19
1 year up to 2 years	NA	NA	NA	NA	NA	NA	NA	NA	24
2 years or more	NA	NA	NA	NA	NA	NA	NA	NA	212
Never occupied as permanent home	NA	NA	NA	NA	NA	NA	NA	152	389
Don't know	NA	NA	NA	NA	NA	NA	NA	45	132
Not reported	NA	NA	NA	NA	NA	NA	NA	NA	NA
Metropolitan/Nonmetropolitan Areas									
Inside metropolitan statistical areas	8 036	2 916	9.2	939	697	1 617	1 866	5 365	4 804
In central cities	3 686	1 583	9.7	333	335	568	868	1 250	632
Suburbs	4 350	1 333	8.6	606	362	1 050	998	4 116	4 172
Outside metropolitan statistical areas	3 333	680	11.9	345	235	1 030	1 043	1 393	4 167

Source: U.S. Census Bureau. American Housing Survey 2003.

NA = Not applicable.

Table A5-2. Housing Unit Characteristics, 2003—*Continued*

(Numbers in thousands, rate.)

Characteristic	Total housing units	Seasonal	Year-round			
				Occupied		
			Total	Total	Owner	Renter
Regions						
Northeast	22 602	725	21 877	20 133	12 964	7 169
Midwest	27 893	962	26 931	24 488	17 889	6 599
South	44 659	1 246	43 413	38 145	26 699	11 446
West	25 623	632	24 991	23 077	14 686	8 390
Place Size						
Less than 2,500 persons	5 941	332	5 610	4 977	3 795	1 182
2,500 to 9,999 persons	14 063	478	13 585	12 371	8 851	3 520
10,000 to 19,999 persons	10 093	94	9 999	9 126	6 240	2 885
20,000 to 49,999 persons	15 742	121	15 621	14 234	9 319	4 915
50,000 to 99,999 persons	11 185	59	11 126	10 211	6 228	3 983
100,000 to 249,999 persons	9 415	25	9 390	8 486	4 935	3 551
250,000 to 499,999 persons	6 649	27	6 622	5 932	3 225	2 706
500,000 to 999,999 persons	4 286	30	4 256	3 828	1 974	1 854
1,000,000 persons or more	7 963	57	7 905	7 129	2 984	4 144
Homes Currently for Sale or Rent						
Up for rent only	3 718	NA	3 718	89	89	NA
Up for rent or for sale	275	NA	275	49	49	NA
For sale only	2 676	NA	2 676	1 330	1 330	NA
Not on the market	75 451	NA	75 451	69 283	69 283	NA
Not reported	1 488	NA	1 488	1 488	1 488	NA
Reasons For Extra Unit Owned						
Extra units	6 151	3 503	2 647	NA	NA	NA
Previous usual residence	862	257	605	NA	NA	NA
Used for recreational purposes	3 398	2 364	1 034	NA	NA	NA
Investment purposes	841	432	408	NA	NA	NA
Unable to sell property	56	19	37	NA	NA	NA
Inherited property	349	206	143	NA	NA	NA
Other reasons	1 178	637	541	NA	NA	NA
Not reported	365	135	230	NA	NA	NA
Location of Extra Unit						
Within 150 miles of current residence	2 888	1 652	1 236	NA	NA	NA
150 miles or more from current residence	2 235	1 353	882	NA	NA	NA
Not reported	1 028	499	529	NA	NA	NA
Nights Owner Spent At Extra Unit						
0–2 nights	1 363	695	668	NA	NA	NA
3–7 nights	222	140	82	NA	NA	NA
8 nights or more	3 253	1 926	1 328	NA	NA	NA
Not reported	1 312	742	570	NA	NA	NA
Nights Owner Rented Extra Unit						
0–2 nights	4 294	2 574	1 720	NA	NA	NA
3–7 nights	17	9	8	NA	NA	NA
8 nights or more	737	332	405	NA	NA	NA
Not reported	1 102	588	515	NA	NA	NA

Source: U.S. Census Bureau. American Housing Survey 2003.

NA = Not applicable.

Table A5-2. Housing Unit Characteristics, 2003—*Continued*

(Numbers in thousands, rate.)

Characteristic	Year-round—*Continued*							New construc-tion, 4 years	Mobile homes
	Vacant								
	Total	For rent	Rental vacancy rate	For sale only	Rented or sold	Occasional use/URE	Other vacant		
Regions									
Northeast	1 744	518	6.7	182	142	444	459	604	671
Midwest	2 443	840	11.1	318	225	462	597	1 385	1 560
South	5 268	1 571	11.9	559	350	1 329	1 459	3 190	5 128
West	1 914	668	7.3	225	215	412	395	1 579	1 613
Place Size									
Less than 2,500 persons	633	148	NA	72	43	159	210	225	570
2,500 to 9,999 persons	1 215	374	NA	144	119	278	299	530	833
10,000 to 19,999 persons	874	328	NA	114	83	157	191	395	346
20,000 to 49,999 persons	1 387	611	NA	149	124	216	287	700	275
50,000 to 99,999 persons	915	328	NA	84	90	184	229	436	193
100,000 to 249,999 persons	904	397	NA	93	81	107	227	359	148
250,000 to 499,999 persons	691	348	11.3	72	53	89	128	243	92
500,000 to 999,999 persons	428	211	10.1	41	41	51	84	155	43
1,000,000 persons or more	777	302	6.7	67	78	151	179	150	18
Homes Currently for Sale or Rent									
Up for rent only	3 629	3 372	100.0	NA	NA	257	NA	240	129
Up for rent or for sale	226	225	100.0	NA	NA	1	NA	19	91
For sale only	1 346	NA	NA	1 284	NA	62	NA	319	282
Not on the market	6 168	NA	NA	NA	932	2 327	2 909	4 867	6 232
Not reported	NA	NA	NA	NA	NA	NA	NA	74	68
Reasons For Extra Unit Owned									
Extra units	2 647	NA	NA	NA	NA	2 647	NA	391	1 191
Previous usual residence	605	NA	NA	NA	NA	605	NA	38	120
Used for recreational purposes	1 034	NA	NA	NA	NA	1 034	NA	229	804
Investment purposes	408	NA	NA	NA	NA	408	NA	47	49
Unable to sell property	37	NA	NA	NA	NA	37	NA	5	11
Inherited property	143	NA	NA	NA	NA	143	NA	NA	28
Other reasons	541	NA	NA	NA	NA	541	NA	108	222
Not reported	230	NA	NA	NA	NA	230	NA	10	40
Location of Extra Unit									
Within 150 miles of current residence	1 236	NA	NA	NA	NA	1 236	NA	133	535
150 miles or more from current residence	882	NA	NA	NA	NA	882	NA	175	462
Not reported	529	NA	NA	NA	NA	529	NA	82	194
Nights Owner Spent At Extra Unit									
0–2 nights	668	NA	NA	NA	NA	668	NA	31	236
3–7 nights	82	NA	NA	NA	NA	82	NA	11	22
8 nights or more	1 328	NA	NA	NA	NA	1 328	NA	249	714
Not reported	570	NA	NA	NA	NA	570	NA	101	219
Nights Owner Rented Extra Unit									
0–2 nights	1 720	NA	NA	NA	NA	1 720	NA	290	954
3–7 nights	8	NA	NA	NA	NA	8	NA	3	NA
8 nights or more	405	NA	NA	NA	NA	405	NA	17	44
Not reported	515	NA	NA	NA	NA	515	NA	82	193

Source: U.S. Census Bureau. American Housing Survey 2003.

NA = Not applicable.

Detailed Tables
Income, Wealth, and Poverty

Table A6-1. Income Limits for Each Fifth and Top 5 Percent of Households, 1967–2004

(Households as of March of the following year. Income in current and 2004 CPI-U-RS adjusted dollars. [1])

Year	Number (thousands)	Upper limits of each fifth (dollars)				Lower limit of top 5 percent (dollars)
		Lowest	Second	Third	Fourth	
Current Dollars						
1967 [2]	60 813	3 000	5 850	8 303	11 840	19 000
1968	62 214	3 323	6 300	9 030	12 688	19 850
1969	63 401	3 575	6 860	9 921	13 900	21 800
1970	64 778	3 688	7 065	10 276	14 661	23 175
1971 [3]	66 676	3 800	7 244	10 660	15 200	24 138
1972 [4]	68 251	4 050	7 800	11 528	16 500	26 555
1973	69 859	4 397	8 455	12 510	18 012	28 950
1974 [5,6]	71 163	4 860	9 015	13 321	19 333	30 600
1975 [6]	72 867	5 000	9 384	14 180	20 360	32 129
1976 [7]	74 142	5 405	10 070	15 340	22 070	35 000
1977	76 030	5 734	10 800	16 462	24 000	38 000
1978	77 330	6 318	11 946	18 075	26 288	42 055
1979 [8]	80 776	7 000	13 000	20 001	29 000	46 860
1980	82 368	7 478	14 024	21 500	31 480	50 661
1981	83 527	8 024	15 000	23 200	34 300	55 200
1982	83 918	8 400	15 976	24 410	36 400	60 086
1983 [9]	85 290	8 949	16 640	25 539	38 596	63 500
1984	86 789	9 500	17 780	27 393	41 380	68 500
1985 [10]	88 458	9 941	18 704	28 975	43 578	72 004
1986	89 479	10 247	19 600	30 419	45 982	77 106
1987 [11]	91 124	10 800	20 500	32 000	48 363	80 928
1988	92 830	11 382	21 500	33 506	50 593	85 640
1989	93 347	12 096	23 000	35 350	53 710	91 750
1990	94 312	12 500	23 662	36 200	55 205	94 748
1991	95 669	12 591	24 000	37 070	56 759	96 400
1992 [12]	96 426	12 600	24 140	37 900	58 007	99 020
1993 [13]	97 107	12 967	24 679	38 793	60 300	104 639
1994 [14]	98 990	13 426	25 200	40 100	62 841	109 821
1995 [15]	99 627	14 400	26 914	42 002	65 124	113 000
1996	101 018	14 768	27 760	44 006	68 015	119 540
1997	102 528	15 400	29 200	46 000	71 500	126 550
1998	103 874	16 116	30 408	48 337	75 000	132 199
1999	106 434	17 136	31 920	50 384	79 232	142 000
2000 [16]	108 209	17 920	33 000	52 174	81 766	145 220
2001	109 297	17 970	33 314	53 000	83 500	150 499
2002	111 278	17 916	33 377	53 162	84 016	150 002
2003	112 000	17 984	34 000	54 453	86 867	154 120
2004	113 146	18 500	34 738	55 325	88 029	157 185

Source: U.S. Census Bureau. Housing and Household Economic Statistics Division. Income Surveys Branch. March Current Population Survey.

[1]The CPI-U-RS is a price index of inflation that incorporates most of the improvements in methodology made to the current CPI-U since 1978 into a single, uniform series. See *Money Income in the United States: 1999* or the appendix of *Money Income in the United States: 1998* for more information. Before 1977, the CPI-U-RS is extrapolated.
[2]Data reflect implementation of a new March CPS processing system.
[3]Data reflect introduction of 1970 census-based sample design and population controls.
[4]Data reflect full implementation of 1970 census-based sample design.
[5]Data reflect implementation of a new March CPS processing system. Questionnaire expanded to ask income questions.
[6]Some of these estimates were derived using Pareto interpolation and may differ from published data, which were derived using linear interpolation.
[7]First-year medians were derived using both Pareto and linear interpolation. Before this year, all medians were derived using linear interpolation.
[8]Data reflect implementation of 1980 census population controls. Questionnaire expanded to show 27 possible values from 5 possible sources of income.
[9]Data reflect implementation of Hispanic population weighting controls and introduction of 1980 census-based sample design.
[10]Recording of amounts for earnings from longest job were increased to $199,999. Data reflect full implementation of 1980 census-based sample design.
[11]Data reflect implementation of a new March CPS processing system.
[12]Data reflect implementation of 1990 census population controls.
[13]Data collection method changed from paper and pencil to computer-assisted interviewing. In addition, the March 1994 income supplement was revised to allow for the coding of different income amounts on selected questionnaire items. Child support and alimony limits decreased to $49,999. Limits increased in the following categories: earnings to $999,999; Social Security to $49,999; Supplemental Security Income and public assistance income to $24,999; and veterans' benefits to $99,999.
[14]Data reflect introduction of 1990 census-based sample design.
[15]Data reflect full implementation of the 1990 census-based sample design and metropolitan definitions, 7,000-household sample reduction, and revised race edits.
[16]Based on November 2001 weighting correction.

Table A6-1. Income Limits for Each Fifth and Top 5 Percent of Households, 1967–2004
—Continued

(Households as of March of the following year. Income in current and 2004 CPI-U-RS adjusted dollars. [1])

Year	Number (thousands)	Upper limits of each fifth (dollars)				Lower limit of top 5 percent (dollars)
		Lowest	Second	Third	Fourth	
2004 Dollars						
1967 [2]	60 813	14 378	28 037	39 794	56 745	91 061
1968	62 214	15 313	29 031	41 611	58 467	91 470
1969	63 401	15 786	30 292	43 808	61 379	96 263
1970	64 778	15 537	29 764	43 291	61 765	97 633
1971 [3]	66 676	15 328	29 220	43 000	61 313	97 366
1972 [4]	68 251	15 849	30 523	45 112	64 568	103 916
1973	69 859	16 193	31 137	46 071	66 333	106 615
1974 [5, 6]	71 163	16 285	30 207	44 636	64 781	102 534
1975 [6]	72 867	15 472	29 039	43 880	63 004	99 423
1976 [7]	74 142	15 818	29 471	44 894	64 590	102 431
1977	76 030	15 774	29 711	45 287	66 024	104 538
1978	77 330	16 664	31 509	47 674	69 337	110 924
1979 [8]	80 776	16 877	31 344	48 223	69 920	112 981
1980	82 368	16 237	30 450	46 682	68 352	109 999
1981	83 527	15 926	29 773	46 048	68 080	109 564
1982	83 918	15 741	29 939	45 744	68 213	112 600
1983 [9]	85 290	16 101	29 939	45 950	69 443	114 250
1984	86 789	16 437	30 763	47 395	71 595	118 518
1985 [10]	88 458	16 645	31 318	48 515	72 966	120 562
1986	89 479	16 850	32 229	50 020	75 611	126 789
1987 [11]	91 124	17 174	32 599	50 886	76 906	128 690
1988	92 830	17 463	32 987	51 408	77 625	131 397
1989	93 347	17 795	33 836	52 004	79 014	134 976
1990	94 312	17 518	33 161	50 732	77 366	132 782
1991	95 669	17 029	32 460	50 137	76 767	130 382
1992 [12]	96 426	16 625	31 851	50 006	76 536	130 649
1993 [13]	97 107	16 693	31 770	49 939	77 625	134 704
1994 [14]	98 990	16 927	31 771	50 557	79 228	138 459
1995 [15]	99 627	17 725	33 128	51 699	80 159	139 089
1996	101 018	17 702	33 276	52 750	81 529	143 292
1997	102 528	18 074	34 270	53 987	83 915	148 523
1998	103 874	18 652	35 192	55 942	86 801	152 999
1999	106 434	19 424	36 181	57 110	89 809	160 957
2000 [16]	108 209	19 656	36 197	57 229	89 688	159 290
2001	109 297	19 176	35 550	56 557	89 103	160 598
2002	111 278	18 819	35 059	55 841	88 250	157 562
2003	112 000	18 467	34 914	55 916	89 202	158 262
2004	113 146	18 500	34 738	55 325	88 029	157 185

Source: U.S. Census Bureau. Housing and Household Economic Statistics Division. Income Surveys Branch. March Current Population Survey.

[1]The CPI-U-RS is a price index of inflation that incorporates most of the improvements in methodology made to the current CPI-U since 1978 into a single, uniform series. See *Money Income in the United States: 1999* or the appendix of *Money Income in the United States: 1998* for more information. Before 1977, the CPI-U-RS is extrapolated.
[2]Data reflect implementation of a new March CPS processing system.
[3]Data reflect introduction of 1970 census-based sample design and population controls.
[4]Data reflect full implementation of 1970 census-based sample design.
[5]Data reflect implementation of a new March CPS processing system. Questionnaire expanded to ask income questions.
[6]Some of these estimates were derived using Pareto interpolation and may differ from published data, which were derived using linear interpolation.
[7]First-year medians were derived using both Pareto and linear interpolation. Before this year, all medians were derived using linear interpolation.
[8]Data reflect implementation of 1980 census population controls. Questionnaire expanded to show 27 possible values from 5 possible sources of income.
[9]Data reflect implementation of Hispanic population weighting controls and introduction of 1980 census-based sample design.
[10]Recording of amounts for earnings from longest job were increased to $199,999. Data reflect full implementation of 1980 census-based sample design.
[11]Data reflect implementation of a new March CPS processing system.
[12]Data reflect implementation of 1990 census population controls.
[13]Data collection method changed from paper and pencil to computer-assisted interviewing. In addition, the March 1994 income supplement was revised to allow for the coding of different income amounts on selected questionnaire items. Child support and alimony limits decreased to $49,999. Limits increased in the following categories: earnings to $999,999; Social Security to $49,999; Supplemental Security Income and public assistance income to $24,999; and veterans' benefits to $99,999.
[14]Data reflect introduction of 1990 census-based sample design.
[15]Data reflect full implementation of the 1990 census-based sample design and metropolitan definitions, 7,000-household sample reduction, and revised race edits.
[16]Based on November 2001 weighting correction.

Table A6-2. Share of Aggregate Income Received by Each Fifth and Top 5 Percent of Households, 1967–2004

(Households as of March of the following year.)

Year	Number (thousands)	Upper limits of each fifth (dollars)					Lower limit of top 5 percent (dollars)
		Lowest	Second	Third	Fourth	Highest fifth	
All Races							
1967 [1]	60 813	4.0	10.8	17.3	24.2	43.6	17.2
1968	62 214	4.2	11.1	17.6	24.5	42.6	16.3
1969	63 401	4.1	10.9	17.5	24.5	43.0	16.6
1970	64 778	4.1	10.8	17.4	24.5	43.3	16.6
1971 [2]	66 676	4.1	10.6	17.3	24.5	43.5	16.7
1972 [3]	68 251	4.1	10.4	17.0	24.5	43.9	17.0
1973	69 859	4.2	10.4	17.0	24.5	43.9	16.9
1974 [4,5]	71 163	4.3	10.6	17.0	24.6	43.5	16.5
1975 [5]	72 867	4.3	10.4	17.0	24.7	43.6	16.5
1976 [6]	74 142	4.3	10.3	17.0	24.7	43.7	16.6
1977	76 030	4.2	10.2	16.9	24.7	44.0	16.8
1978	77 330	4.2	10.2	16.8	24.7	44.1	16.8
1979 [7]	80 776	4.1	10.2	16.8	24.6	44.2	16.9
1980	82 368	4.2	10.2	16.8	24.7	44.1	16.5
1981	83 527	4.1	10.1	16.7	24.8	44.3	16.5
1982	83 918	4.0	10.0	16.5	24.5	45.0	17.0
1983 [8]	85 407	4.0	9.9	16.4	24.6	45.1	17.0
1984	86 789	4.0	9.9	16.3	24.6	45.2	17.1
1985 [9]	88 458	3.9	9.8	16.2	24.4	45.6	17.6
1986	89 479	3.8	9.7	16.2	24.3	46.1	18.0
1987 [10]	91 124	3.8	9.6	16.1	24.3	46.2	18.2
1988	92 830	3.8	9.6	16.0	24.2	46.3	18.3
1989	93 347	3.8	9.5	15.8	24.0	46.8	18.9
1990	94 312	3.8	9.6	15.9	24.0	46.6	18.5
1991	95 669	3.8	9.6	15.9	24.2	46.5	18.1
1992 [11]	96 426	3.8	9.4	15.8	24.2	46.9	18.6
1993 [12]	97 107	3.6	9.0	15.1	23.5	48.9	21.0
1994 [13]	98 990	3.6	8.9	15.0	23.4	49.1	21.2
1995 [14]	99 627	3.7	9.1	15.2	23.3	48.7	21.0
1996	101 018	3.6	9.0	15.1	23.3	49.0	21.4
1997	102 528	3.6	8.9	15.0	23.2	49.4	21.7
1998	103 874	3.6	9.0	15.0	23.2	49.2	21.4
1999	106 434	3.6	8.9	14.9	23.2	49.4	21.5
2000 [15]	108 209	3.6	8.9	14.8	23.0	49.8	22.1
2001	109 297	3.5	8.7	14.6	23.0	50.1	22.4
2002	111 278	3.5	8.8	14.8	23.3	49.7	21.7
2003	112 000	3.4	8.7	14.8	23.4	49.8	21.4
2004	113 146	3.4	8.7	14.7	23.2	50.1	21.8

Source: U.S. Census Bureau. Housing and Household Economic Statistics Division. Income Surveys Branch. March Current Population Survey.

[1] Data reflect implementation of a new March CPS processing system.
[2] Data reflect introduction of 1970 census-based sample design and population controls.
[3] Data reflect full implementation of 1970 census-based sample design.
[4] Data reflect implementation of a new March CPS processing system. Questionnaire expanded to ask income questions.
[5] Some of these estimates were derived using Pareto interpolation and may differ from published data, which were derived using linear interpolation.
[6] First-year medians were derived using both Pareto and linear interpolation. Before this year, all medians were derived using linear interpolation.
[7] Data reflect implementation of 1980 census population controls. Questionnaire expanded to show 27 possible values from 5 possible sources of income.
[8] Data reflect implementation of Hispanic population weighting controls and introduction of 1980 census-based sample design.
[9] Recording of amounts for earnings from longest job were increased to $199,999. Data reflect full implementation of 1980 census-based sample design.
[10] Data reflect implementation of a new March CPS processing system.
[11] Data reflect implementation of 1990 census population controls.
[12] Data collection method changed from paper and pencil to computer-assisted interviewing. In addition, the March 1994 income supplement was revised to allow for the coding of different income amounts on selected questionnaire items. Child support and alimony limits decreased to $49,999. Limits increased in the following categories: earnings to $999,999; Social Security to $49,999; Supplemental Security Income and public assistance income to $24,999; and veterans' benefits to $99,999.
[13] Data reflect introduction of 1990 census-based sample design.
[14] Data reflect full implementation of the 1990 census-based sample design and metropolitan definitions, 7,000-household sample reduction, and revised race edits.
[15] Based on November 2001 weighting correction.

Table A6-3. Households, by Median and Mean Income, 1967–2004

(Households as of March of the following year. Income in current and 2004 CPI-U-RS adjusted dollars. [1])

Year	Number (thousands)	Median income		Mean income	
		Current dollars	2004 dollars	Current dollars	2004 dollars
All Races					
1967 [2]	60 813	7 143	34 234	7 989	38 289
1968	62 214	7 743	35 680	8 760	40 366
1969	63 401	8 389	37 044	9 544	42 144
1970	64 778	8 734	36 795	10 001	42 133
1971 [3]	66 676	9 028	36 416	10 383	41 882
1972 [4]	68 251	9 697	37 947	11 286	44 165
1973	69 859	10 512	38 713	12 157	44 771
1974 [5,6]	71 163	11 197	37 519	13 094	43 875
1975 [6]	72 867	11 800	36 515	13 779	42 639
1976 [7]	74 142	12 686	37 127	14 922	43 671
1977	76 030	13 572	37 337	16 100	44 291
1978	77 330	15 064	39 733	17 730	46 764
1979 [8]	80 776	16 461	39 688	19 554	47 146
1980	82 368	17 710	38 453	21 063	45 733
1981	83 527	19 074	37 859	22 787	45 229
1982	83 918	20 171	37 800	24 309	45 555
1983 [9]	85 407	20 885	37 577	25 401	45 702
1984	86 789	22 415	38 782	27 464	47 518
1985 [10]	88 458	23 618	39 545	29 066	48 667
1986	89 479	24 897	40 939	30 759	50 579
1987 [11]	91 124	26 061	41 442	32 410	51 538
1988	92 830	27 225	41 771	34 017	52 192
1989	93 347	28 906	42 524	36 520	53 725
1990	94 312	29 943	41 963	37 403	52 418
1991	95 669	30 126	40 746	37 922	51 290
1992 [12]	96 426	30 636	40 422	38 840	51 246
1993 [13]	97 107	31 241	40 217	41 428	53 331
1994 [14]	98 990	32 264	40 677	43 133	54 381
1995 [15]	99 627	34 076	41 943	44 938	55 313
1996	101 018	35 492	42 544	47 123	56 486
1997	102 528	37 005	43 430	49 692	58 320
1998	103 874	38 885	45 003	51 855	60 014
1999	106 434	40 696	46 129	54 737	62 044
2000 [16]	108 209	41 990	46 058	57 135	62 671
2001	109 297	42 228	45 062	58 208	62 114
2002	111 278	42 409	44 546	57 852	60 768
2003	112 000	43 318	44 482	59 067	60 654
2004	113 146	44 389	44 389	60 528	60 528

Source: U.S. Census Bureau. Housing and Household Economic Statistics Division. Income Surveys Branch. March Current Population Survey.

[1]The CPI-U-RS is a price index of inflation that incorporates most of the improvements in methodology made to the current CPI-U since 1978 into a single, uniform series. See *Money Income in the United States: 1999* or the appendix of *Money Income in the United States: 1998* for more information. Before 1977, the CPI-U-RS is extrapolated.
[2]Data reflect implementation of a new March CPS processing system.
[3]Data reflect introduction of 1970 census-based sample design and population controls.
[4]Data reflect full implementation of 1970 census-based sample design.
[5]Data reflect implementation of a new March CPS processing system. Questionnaire expanded to ask income questions.
[6]Some of these estimates were derived using Pareto interpolation and may differ from published data, which were derived using linear interpolation.
[7]First-year medians were derived using both Pareto and linear interpolation. Before this year, all medians were derived using linear interpolation.
[8]Data reflect implementation of 1980 census population controls. Questionnaire expanded to show 27 possible values from 5 possible sources of income.
[9]Data reflect implementation of Hispanic population weighting controls and introduction of 1980 census-based sample design.
[10]Recording of amounts for earnings from longest job were increased to $199,999. Data reflect full implementation of 1980 census-based sample design.
[11]Data reflect implementation of a new March CPS processing system.
[12]Data reflect implementation of 1990 census population controls.
[13]Data collection method changed from paper and pencil to computer-assisted interviewing. In addition, the March 1994 income supplement was revised to allow for the coding of different income amounts on selected questionnaire items. Child support and alimony limits decreased to $49,999. Limits increased in the following categories: earnings to $999,999; Social Security to $49,999; Supplemental Security Income and public assistance income to $24,999; and veterans' benefits to $99,999.
[14]Data reflect introduction of 1990 census-based sample design.
[15]Data reflect full implementation of the 1990 census-based sample design and metropolitan definitions, 7,000-household sample reduction, and revised race edits.
[16]Based on November 2001 weighting correction.

Detailed Tables
Education

Table A7-1. School Enrollment of the Population 3 to 34 Years of Age, by Level and Control of School, 1955–2004

(Numbers in thousands.)

Year	Total enrolled	Nursery school			Kindergarten			Elementary school		
		Total	Public	Private	Total	Public	Private	Total	Public	Private
All Races										
1955	37 426	. . .	. . .	. . .	1 628	1 365	263	25 458	22 078	3 379
1956	39 353	. . .	. . .	. . .	1 758	1 566	192	26 169	22 474	3 695
1957	41 166	. . .	. . .	. . .	1 824	1 471	353	27 248	23 076	4 172
1958	42 900	. . .	. . .	. . .	1 991	1 569	422	28 184	23 800	4 385
1959	44 370	. . .	. . .	. . .	2 032	1 678	354	29 382	24 680	4 702
1960	46 260	. . .	. . .	. . .	2 092	1 691	401	30 349	25 814	4 535
1961	47 708	. . .	. . .	. . .	2 299	1 926	373	30 718	26 221	4 497
1962	48 704	. . .	. . .	. . .	2 319	1 914	405	30 661	26 148	4 513
1963	50 356	. . .	. . .	. . .	2 340	1 936	404	31 245	26 502	4 742
1964	52 490	471	91	380	2 830	2 349	481	31 734	26 811	4 923
1965	54 701	520	127	393	3 057	2 439	618	32 474	27 596	4 878
1966	56 167	688	215	473	3 115	2 527	588	32 916	28 208	4 706
1967	57 656	713	230	484	3 312	2 678	635	33 440	28 877	4 562
1968	58 791	816	262	554	3 268	2 709	559	33 761	29 527	4 234
1969	59 913	860	245	615	3 276	2 682	594	33 788	29 825	3 964
1970	60 357	1 096	333	763	3 183	2 647	536	33 950	30 001	3 949
1971	61 106	1 066	317	749	3 263	2 689	574	33 507	29 829	3 678
1972	60 142	1 283	402	881	3 135	2 636	499	32 242	28 693	3 549
1973	59 392	1 324	400	924	3 074	2 582	493	31 469	28 201	3 268
1974	60 259	1 607	423	1 184	3 252	2 726	526	31 126	27 956	3 169
1975	60 969	1 748	574	1 174	3 393	2 851	542	30 446	27 166	3 279
1976	60 482	1 526	476	1 050	3 490	2 962	528	29 774	26 698	3 075
1977	60 013	1 618	562	1 056	3 191	2 665	526	29 234	25 983	3 251
1978	58 616	1 824	587	1 237	2 989	2 493	496	28 490	25 252	3 238
1979	57 854	1 869	636	1 233	3 025	2 593	432	27 865	24 756	3 109
1980	57 348	1 987	633	1 354	3 176	2 690	486	27 449	24 398	3 051
1981	58 390	2 058	663	1 396	3 161	2 616	545	27 795	24 758	3 037
1982	57 905	2 153	729	1 423	3 299	2 746	553	27 412	24 381	3 031
1983	57 745	2 350	809	1 541	3 361	2 706	656	27 198	24 203	2 994
1984	57 313	2 354	761	1 593	3 484	2 953	531	26 838	24 120	2 718
1985	58 014	2 491	854	1 637	3 815	3 221	594	26 866	23 803	3 063
1986	58 153	2 554	835	1 719	3 961	3 328	633	27 121	24 163	2 958
1987	58 691	2 587	848	1 739	4 018	3 423	595	27 524	24 760	2 765
1988	58 847	2 639	838	1 770	3 958	3 420	538	28 223	25 443	2 778
1989	59 236	2 877	971	1 906	3 868	3 293	575	28 637	25 897	2 740
1990	60 588	3 401	1 212	2 188	3 899	3 332	567	29 265	26 591	2 674
1991	61 276	2 933	1 094	1 839	4 152	3 531	621	29 591	26 632	2 958
1992	62 082	2 899	1 098	1 801	4 130	3 507	623	30 165	27 066	3 102
1993	62 730	3 018	1 230	1 788	4 180	3 499	681	30 604	27 688	2 914
1993 [1]	64 414	3 032	1 258	1 774	4 275	3 589	686	31 219	28 278	2 941
1994	69 272	4 259	1 940	2 319	3 863	3 278	585	31 512	28 131	3 381
1995	69 769	4 399	2 012	2 387	3 877	3 174	704	31 815	28 384	3 431
1996	70 297	4 212	1 868	2 344	4 034	3 353	681	31 515	28 153	3 362
1997	72 031	4 500	2 254	2 246	3 933	3 271	663	32 369	29 308	3 061
1998	72 109	4 577	2 265	2 313	3 828	3 128	700	32 573	29 124	3 449
1999	72 395	4 578	2 269	2 309	3 825	3 167	658	32 873	29 264	3 609
2000	72 214	4 401	2 217	2 184	3 832	3 173	659	32 898	29 378	3 520
2001	73 124	4 289	2 161	2 128	3 737	3 145	591	33 166	29 800	3 366
2002	74 046	4 471	2 246	2 225	3 571	2 976	594	33 132	29 658	3 474
2003	74 911	4 928	2 567	2 361	3 719	3 098	622	32 565	29 204	3 361
2004	75 461	4 739	2 487	2 252	3 992	3 417	575	32 556	29 166	3 389

Source: U.S. Census Bureau. Current Population Survey.

[1]Revised, controlled to 1990 census-based population estimates; previous 1993 data controlled to 1980 census-based population estimates. Prior to 1994, total enrolled does not include the population age 35 years and over.
. . . = Not available.

Table A7-1. School Enrollment of the Population 3 to 34 Years of Age, by Level and Control of School, 1955–2004—Continued

(Numbers in thousands.)

Year	High school			College			College full time
	Total	Public	Private	Total	Public	Private	
All Races							
1955	7 961	7 181	780	2 379	1 515	864	. . .
1956	8 543	7 668	875	2 883	1 824	1 059	. . .
1957	8 956	8 059	897	3 138	2 054	1 084	. . .
1958	9 482	8 485	998	3 242	2 088	1 155	. . .
1959	9 616	8 571	1 045	3 340	2 120	1 220	2 464
1960	10 249	9 215	1 033	3 570	2 307	1 262	2 681
1961	10 959	9 817	1 141	3 731	2 376	1 354	2 902
1962	11 516	10 431	1 085	4 208	2 820	1 388	3 237
1963	12 438	11 186	1 251	4 336	2 897	1 439	3 260
1964	12 812	11 403	1 410	4 643	3 025	1 618	3 556
1965	12 975	11 517	1 457	5 675	3 840	1 835	4 414
1966	13 364	11 985	1 377	6 085	4 178	1 908	4 847
1967	13 790	12 498	1 292	6 401	4 540	1 861	4 976
1968	14 145	12 793	1 352	6 801	4 948	1 854	5 357
1969	14 553	13 400	1 153	7 435	5 439	1 995	5 810
1970	14 715	13 545	1 170	7 413	5 699	1 714	5 763
1971	15 183	14 057	1 126	8 087	6 271	1 816	6 204
1972	15 169	14 015	1 155	8 313	6 337	1 976	6 314
1973	15 347	14 162	1 184	8 179	6 224	1 955	6 089
1974	15 447	14 275	1 172	8 827	6 905	1 922	6 351
1975	15 683	14 503	1 180	9 697	7 704	1 994	7 105
1976	15 742	14 541	1 201	9 950	7 739	2 211	7 176
1977	15 753	14 505	1 248	10 217	7 925	2 292	7 196
1978	15 475	14 231	1 244	9 838	7 427	2 410	6 979
1979	15 116	13 994	1 122	9 978	7 699	2 280	7 010
1980	14 556	. . .	. . .	10 180	. . .	. . .	7 147
1981	14 642	13 523	1 119	10 734	8 159	2 576	7 569
1982	14 123	13 004	1 118	10 919	8 354	2 565	7 736
1983	14 010	12 792	1 218	10 825	8 185	2 640	7 711
1984	13 777	12 721	1 057	10 859	8 467	2 392	7 822
1985	13 979	12 764	1 215	10 863	8 379	2 483	7 720
1986	13 912	12 746	1 166	10 605	8 153	2 452	7 507
1987	13 647	12 577	1 070	10 915	8 556	2 361	7 560
1988	13 093	12 095	998	10 937	8 663	2 278	7 771
1989	12 786	11 980	806	11 066	8 576	2 490	7 905
1990	12 719	11 818	903	11 306	8 889	2 417	8 154
1991	13 010	12 069	945	11 589	9 078	2 511	8 461
1992	13 219	12 268	952	11 671	9 282	2 386	8 503
1993	13 522	12 542	977	11 409	9 031	2 374	8 308
1993 [1]	13 989	12 985	1 004	11 901	9 440	2 461	8 706
1994	14 616	13 539	1 077	15 022	11 694	3 329	9 573
1995	14 963	13 750	1 213	14 715	11 372	3 343	9 544
1996	15 309	14 113	1 197	15 226	12 014	3 212	9 839
1997	15 793	14 634	1 159	15 436	12 091	3 345	10 236
1998	15 584	14 299	1 285	15 547	11 984	3 563	10 184
1999	15 916	14 638	1 278	15 203	11 659	3 544	10 112
2000	15 770	14 431	1 339	15 314	12 008	3 305	10 159
2001	16 059	14 830	1 230	15 873	12 421	3 452	10 404
2002	16 374	15 064	1 310	16 497	12 834	3 664	11 141
2003	17 062	15 785	1 276	16 638	13 109	3 529	11 490
2004	16 791	15 498	1 293	17 383	13 652	3 731	11 990

Source: U.S. Census Bureau. Current Population Survey.

[1]Revised, controlled to 1990 census-based population estimates; previous 1993 data controlled to 1980 census-based population estimates. Prior to 1994, total enrolled does not include the population age 35 years and over.
. . . = Not available.

Table A7-2. Percent of the Population 3 Years of Age and Over Enrolled in School, by Age, 1947–2004

(Percent.)

Year	Total, 3 to 34 years	Total, 3 years and over	3 and 4 years	5 and 6 years	7 to 9 years	10 to 13 years	14 and 15 years
All Races							
1947	42.3	. . .	. . .	58.0	98.4	98.6	91.6
1948	43.1	. . .	. . .	56.0	98.3	98.0	92.7
1949	43.9	. . .	. . .	59.3	98.5	98.7	93.5
1950	44.2	. . .	. . .	58.2	98.9	98.6	94.7
1951	45.4	. . .	. . .	54.5	99.0	99.2	94.8
1952	46.8	. . .	. . .	54.7	98.7	98.9	96.2
1953	48.8	. . .	. . .	55.7	99.4	99.4	96.5
1954	50.0	. . .	. . .	77.3	99.2	99.5	95.8
1955	50.8	. . .	. . .	78.1	99.2	99.2	95.9
1956	52.3	. . .	. . .	77.6	99.4	99.2	96.9
1957	53.6	. . .	. . .	78.6	99.5	99.5	97.1
1958	54.8	. . .	. . .	80.4	99.5	99.5	96.9
1959	55.5	. . .	. . .	80.0	99.4	99.4	97.5
1960	56.4	. . .	. . .	80.7	99.6	99.5	97.8
1961	56.8	. . .	. . .	81.7	99.4	99.3	97.6
1962	57.8	. . .	. . .	82.2	99.2	99.3	98.0
1963	58.5	. . .	. . .	82.7	99.4	99.3	98.4
1964	54.5	. . .	9.5	83.3	99.0	99.0	98.6
1965	55.5	. . .	10.6	84.4	99.3	99.4	98.9
1966	56.1	. . .	12.5	85.1	99.3	99.3	98.6
1967	56.6	. . .	14.2	87.4	99.4	99.1	98.2
1968	56.7	. . .	15.7	87.6	99.1	99.1	98.0
1969	57.0	. . .	16.1	88.4	99.3	99.1	98.1
1970	56.4	. . .	20.5	89.5	99.3	99.2	98.1
1971	56.2	. . .	21.2	91.6	99.1	99.2	98.6
1972	54.9	. . .	24.4	91.9	99.0	99.3	97.6
1973	53.5	. . .	24.2	92.5	99.1	99.2	97.5
1974	53.6	. . .	28.8	94.2	99.1	99.5	97.9
1975	53.7	. . .	31.5	94.7	99.3	99.3	98.2
1976	53.1	31.7	31.3	95.5	99.2	99.2	98.2
1977	52.5	. . .	32.0	95.8	99.5	99.4	98.5
1978	51.2	29.3	34.2	95.3	99.3	99.0	98.4
1979	50.3	28.7	35.1	95.8	99.2	99.1	98.1
1980	49.7	28.2	36.7	95.7	99.1	99.4	98.2
1981	48.9	27.9	36.0	94.0	99.2	99.3	98.0
1982	48.6	27.4	36.4	95.0	99.2	99.1	98.5
1983	48.4	27.1	37.6	95.4	98.9	99.4	98.3
1984	47.9	26.6	36.3	94.5	99.0	99.4	97.8
1985	48.3	26.8	38.9	96.1	99.1	99.3	98.1
1986	48.2	26.6	39.0	95.3	99.3	99.1	97.6
1987	48.6	26.6	38.3	95.1	99.6	99.5	98.6
1988	48.7	26.5	38.2	96.0	99.6	99.7	98.9
1989	49.1	26.4	39.1	95.2	99.2	99.4	98.8
1990	50.2	26.8	44.4	96.5	99.7	99.6	99.0
1991	50.7	26.9	40.5	95.4	99.6	99.7	98.8
1992	51.4	26.9	39.7	95.5	99.4	99.4	99.1
1993	51.8	26.9	40.4	95.4	99.5	99.5	98.9
1993 [1]	51.9	. . .	40.1	95.3	99.5	99.5	98.9
1994	53.3	27.9	47.3	96.7	99.3	99.4	98.8
1995	53.7	27.8	48.7	96.0	98.7	99.1	98.9
1996	54.1	27.8	48.3	94.0	97.2	98.1	98.0
1997	55.6	28.3	52.6	96.6	98.8	99.3	98.9
1998	55.8	27.9	52.1	95.6	98.8	99.0	98.4
1999	56.0	27.7	54.2	96.0	98.5	98.8	98.2
2000	55.9	27.5	52.1	95.6	98.1	98.3	98.7
2001	55.7	27.2	52.2	95.3	98.2	98.4	98.1
2002	56.1	27.3	54.5	95.2	98.0	98.5	98.4
2003	56.2	27.2	55.1	94.5	98.1	98.4	97.5
2004	56.2	27.2	54.0	95.4	98.1	98.6	98.5

Source: U.S. Census Bureau. Current Population Survey.

[1] Revised, controlled to 1990 census-based population estimates; previous 1993 data controlled to 1980 census-based population estimates.
. . . = Not available.

Table A7-2. Percent of the Population 3 Years of Age and Over Enrolled in School, by Age, 1947–2004—*Continued*

(Percent.)

Year	16 and 17 years	18 and 19 years	20 and 21 years	22 to 24 years	25 to 29 years	30 to 34 years	35 years and over
All Races							
1947	67.6	24.3	[2]10.2	. . .	3.0	1.0	. . .
1948	71.2	26.9	[2]9.7	. . .	2.6	0.9	. . .
1949	69.5	25.3	[2]9.2	. . .	3.8	1.1	. . .
1950	71.3	29.4	[2]9.0	. . .	3.0	. . .	. . .
1951	75.1	26.3	[2]8.3	. . .	2.5	. . .	. . .
1952	73.4	28.7	[2]9.5	. . .	2.6	1.1	. . .
1953	74.7	31.2	[2]11.1	. . .	2.9	1.7	. . .
1954	78.0	32.4	[2]11.2	. . .	4.1	1.5	. . .
1955	77.4	31.5	[2]11.1	. . .	4.2	1.6	. . .
1956	78.4	35.4	[2]12.8	. . .	5.1	1.9	. . .
1957	80.5	34.9	[2]14.0	. . .	5.5	1.8	. . .
1958	80.6	37.6	13.4	. . .	5.7	2.2	. . .
1959	82.9	36.8	18.8	8.6	5.1	2.2	. . .
1960	82.6	38.4	19.4	8.7	4.9	2.4	. . .
1961	83.6	38.0	21.5	8.4	4.4	2.0	. . .
1962	84.3	41.8	23.0	10.3	5.0	2.6	. . .
1963	87.1	40.9	25.0	11.4	4.9	2.5	. . .
1964	87.7	41.6	26.3	9.9	5.2	2.6	. . .
1965	87.4	46.3	27.6	13.2	6.1	3.2	. . .
1966	88.5	47.2	29.9	13.2	6.5	2.7	. . .
1967	88.8	47.6	33.3	13.6	6.6	4.0	. . .
1968	90.2	50.4	31.2	13.8	7.0	3.9	. . .
1969	89.7	50.2	34.1	15.4	7.9	4.8	. . .
1970	90.0	47.7	31.9	14.9	7.5	4.2	. . .
1971	90.2	49.2	32.2	15.4	8.0	4.9	. . .
1972	88.9	46.3	31.4	14.8	8.6	4.6	. . .
1973	88.3	42.9	30.1	14.5	8.5	4.5	. . .
1974	87.9	43.1	30.2	15.1	9.6	5.7	. . .
1975	89.0	46.9	31.2	16.2	10.1	6.6	. . .
1976	89.1	46.2	32.0	17.1	10.0	6.0	3.9
1977	88.9	46.2	31.8	16.5	10.8	6.9	. . .
1978	89.1	45.4	29.5	16.3	9.4	6.4	1.6
1979	89.2	45.0	30.2	15.8	9.6	6.4	1.7
1980	89.0	46.4	31.0	16.3	9.3	6.5	1.6
1981	90.6	49.0	31.6	16.5	9.0	6.9	1.7
1982	90.6	47.8	34.0	16.8	9.6	6.3	1.6
1983	91.7	50.4	32.5	16.6	9.6	6.4	1.7
1984	91.5	50.1	33.9	17.3	9.1	6.3	1.5
1985	91.7	51.6	35.3	16.9	9.2	6.1	1.7
1986	92.3	54.6	33.0	17.9	8.8	6.0	1.8
1987	91.7	55.6	38.7	17.5	9.0	5.9	1.8
1988	91.6	55.7	39.1	18.3	8.3	5.9	2.1
1989	92.7	56.0	38.5	19.9	9.3	5.7	2.0
1990	92.5	57.3	39.7	21.0	9.7	5.8	2.1
1991	93.3	59.6	42.0	22.2	10.2	6.2	2.2
1992	94.1	61.4	44.0	23.7	9.8	6.1	2.1
1993	94.0	61.6	42.7	23.6	10.2	5.9	2.2
1993 [1]	93.9	61.4	42.6	23.5	10.2	5.9	. . .
1994	94.4	60.2	44.9	24.1	10.8	6.7	2.3
1995	93.6	59.4	44.9	23.2	11.6	6.0	2.2
1996	92.8	61.5	44.4	24.8	11.9	6.1	2.3
1997	94.3	61.5	45.9	26.4	11.8	5.7	2.3
1998	93.9	62.2	44.8	24.9	11.9	6.6	2.1
1999	93.6	60.6	45.3	24.5	11.1	6.2	2.1
2000	92.8	61.2	44.1	24.6	11.4	6.7	1.9
2001	93.4	61.0	45.5	25.1	11.7	6.8	2.0
2002	94.3	63.3	47.8	25.6	12.1	6.6	2.1
2003	94.9	64.5	48.3	27.8	11.8	6.8	1.9
2004	94.5	64.4	48.9	26.3	13.0	6.6	2.0

Source: U.S. Census Bureau. Current Population Survey.

[1]Revised, controlled to 1990 census-based population estimates; previous 1993 data controlled to 1980 census-based population estimates.
[2]Data for population 20 to 24 years old.
. . . = Not available.

Table A7-3. Annual High School Dropout Rates, by Sex, 1967–2004

(Numbers in thousands, rate.)

Year	Total Students Total	Total Students Dropouts	Total Dropout rate	Male Students Total	Male Students Dropouts	Male Dropout rate	Female Students Total	Female Students Dropouts	Female Dropout rate
All Races									
Grades 10–12									
1967	9 350	486	5.2	4 605	237	5.1	4 745	249	5.2
1968	9 814	506	5.2	4 831	247	5.1	4 983	259	5.2
1969	10 212	551	5.4	5 069	273	5.4	5 142	278	5.4
1970	10 281	588	5.7	5 145	288	5.6	5 138	302	5.9
1971	10 451	562	5.4	5 193	297	5.7	5 258	266	5.1
1972	10 664	659	6.2	5 305	317	6.0	5 358	341	6.4
1973	10 851	683	6.3	5 407	370	6.8	5 444	313	5.7
1974	11 026	742	6.7	5 421	402	7.4	5 605	340	6.1
1975	11 033	639	5.8	5 485	296	5.4	5 548	343	6.2
1976	10 996	644	5.9	5 534	360	6.5	5 463	285	5.2
1977	11 300	734	6.5	5 657	392	6.9	5 643	342	6.1
1978	11 116	743	6.7	5 558	415	7.5	5 558	328	5.9
1979	11 136	744	6.7	5 479	369	6.7	5 658	377	6.7
1980	10 891	658	6.0	5 445	362	6.6	5 448	296	5.4
1981	10 868	639	5.9	5 379	322	6.0	5 487	316	5.8
1982	10 611	577	5.4	5 310	305	5.7	5 301	271	5.1
1983	10 331	535	5.2	5 130	294	5.7	5 200	241	4.6
1984	10 041	507	5.0	4 986	268	5.4	5 054	238	4.7
1985	9 704	504	5.2	4 831	259	5.4	4 874	245	5.0
1986	9 829	421	4.3	4 910	213	4.3	4 917	208	4.2
1987	9 802	403	4.1	4 921	215	4.4	4 879	187	3.8
1988	9 590	461	4.8	4 960	256	5.2	4 628	206	4.5
1989	8 974	404	4.5	4 519	203	4.5	4 453	199	4.5
1990	8 679	347	4.0	4 356	177	4.1	4 323	170	3.9
1991	8 612	348	4.0	4 380	167	3.8	4 231	180	4.3
1992	8 939	384	4.3	4 580	175	3.8	4 357	207	4.8
1993	9 021	382	4.2	4 570	199	4.4	4 452	183	4.1
1993 [1]	9 430	404	4.3	4 787	211	4.4	4 640	192	4.1
1994	9 922	497	5.0	5 048	249	4.9	4 873	247	5.1
1995	10 106	544	5.4	5 161	297	5.8	4 946	247	5.0
1996	10 249	485	4.7	5 175	240	4.6	5 072	244	4.8
1997	10 645	454	4.3	5 330	251	4.7	5 313	203	3.8
1998	10 791	479	4.4	5 486	237	4.3	5 305	243	4.6
1999	11 067	520	4.7	5 659	243	4.3	5 411	277	5.1
2000	10 773	488	4.5	5 417	280	5.2	5 356	208	3.9
2001	10 777	507	4.7	5 534	293	5.3	5 243	214	4.1
2002	10 989	367	3.3	5 504	193	3.5	5 484	174	3.2
2003	11 378	429	3.8	5 705	225	4.0	5 674	203	3.6
2004	11 166	486	4.4	5 624	266	4.7	5 542	220	4.0

Source: U.S. Census Bureau. Current Population Survey.

[1] Revised, controlled to 1990 census-based population estimates; previous 1993 data controlled to 1980 census-based population estimates.

Table A7-4. Average Reading Scale Scores as Gauged by the National Assessment of Educational Progress, Selected Years, 1971–2004

(Score.)

Year	Total	Race/ethnicity			Sex		Type of school	
		White	Black	Hispanic	Male	Female	Public	Private
9 Years of Age								
1971	208	214	170	. . .	201	214	. . .	. . .
1975	210	217	181	183	204	216	. . .	. . .
1980	215	221	189	190	210	220	214	227
1984	211	218	186	187	207	214	209	223
1988	212	218	189	194	207	216	210	223
1990	209	217	182	189	204	215	208	228
1992	211	218	185	192	206	215	209	225
1994	211	218	185	186	207	215	209	225
1996	212	220	191	195	207	218	210	227
1999	212	221	186	193	209	215	210	226
2004 modified [1]	216	. . .	. . .	. . .	212	219	214	. . .
2004 bridge [1]	219	226	200	205	216	221	217	. . .
13 Years of Age								
1971	255	261	222	. . .	250	261	. . .	. . .
1975	256	262	226	233	250	262	. . .	. . .
1980	258	264	233	237	254	263	257	271
1984	257	263	236	240	253	262	255	271
1988	257	261	243	240	252	263	256	268
1990	257	262	241	238	251	263	255	270
1992	260	266	238	239	254	265	257	276
1994	258	265	234	235	251	266	256	276
1996	258	266	234	238	251	264	256	273
1999	259	267	238	244	254	265	257	276
2004 modified [1]	257	. . .	. . .	. . .	252	262	255	. . .
2004 bridge [1]	259	266	244	242	254	264	257	. . .
17 Years of Age								
1971	285	291	239	. . .	279	291	. . .	. . .
1975	286	293	241	252	280	291	. . .	. . .
1980	285	293	243	261	282	289	284	298
1984	289	295	264	268	284	294	287	303
1988	290	295	274	271	286	294	289	300
1990	290	297	267	275	284	296	289	311
1992	290	297	261	271	284	296	288	310
1994	288	296	266	263	282	295	286	306
1996	288	295	266	265	281	295	287	294
1999	288	295	264	271	281	295	286	307
2004 modified [1]	283	. . .	. . .	. . .	276	289	281	. . .
2004 bridge [1]	285	293	264	264	278	292	283	. . .

Source: U.S. Department of Education. National Center for Education Statistics. *National Assessment of Educational Progress, The Nation's Report Card.* <http://nces.ed.gov/nationsreportcard>. (Accessed Feb. 17, 2006.)

Note: **Level 150**: Simple, discrete reading tasks; students at this level can follow brief written directions. They can also select words, phrases, or sentences to describe a simple picture and can interpret simple written clues to identify a common object. Performance at this level suggests the ability to carry out simple, discrete reading tasks.

Level 200: Partially developed skills and understanding; students at this level can locate and identify facts from simple informational paragraphs, stories, and news articles. In addition, they can combine ideas and make inferences based on short, uncomplicated passages. Performance at this level suggests the ability to understand specific or sequentially related information.

Level 250: Interrelate ideas and make generalizations; students at this level use intermediate skills and strategies to search for, locate, and organize the information they find in relatively lengthy passages and can recognize paraphrases of what they have read. They can also make inferences and reach generalizations about main ideas and the author's purpose from passages dealing with literature, science, and social studies. Performance at this level suggests the ability to search for specific information, interrelate ideas, and make generalizations.

Level 300: Understand complicated information; students at this level can understand complicated literary and informational passages, including material about topics they study at school. They can also analyze and integrate less familiar material about topics they study at school as well as provide reactions to and explanations of the text as a whole. Performance at this level suggests the ability to find, understand, summarize, and explain relatively complicated information.

Level 350: Learn from specialized reading materials; students at this level can extend and restructure the ideas presented in specialized and complex texts. They are also able to understand the links between ideas, even when those links are not explicitly stated, and to make appropriate generalizations. Performance at this level suggests the ability to synthesize and learn from specialized reading materials.

[1] For the 2004 administration of the long-term trend assessment in reading, several changes were made to the assessment design. When changes are made in a trend assessment, studies are required to ensure that the results can continue to be reported on the same trend line—that is, that they are validly comparable to earlier results. Analyses were needed to ensure that the 2004 results under the new design were comparable to the results from previous long-term trend assessments. Therefore, two assessments were conducted in 2004. One was a modified assessment that used the new design and the other was a "bridge" assessment that replicated the former design. The bridge assessment links the results of the modified assessment to the existing trend line so that comparisons of the results of the bridge and modified assessments could detect any shifts in results that may be due to changes in test design.

. . . = Not available.

Table A7-5. Average Mathematics Scale Scores as Gauged by the National Assessment of Educational Progress, Selected Years, 1973–2004

(Score.)

Year	Total	Race/ethnicity			Sex		Type of school	
		White	Black	Hispanic	Male	Female	Public	Private
9 Years of Age								
1973	219	225	190	202	218	220	. . .	. . .
1978	219	224	192	203	217	220	217	230
1982	219	224	195	204	217	221	217	232
1986	222	227	202	205	222	222	220	230
1990	230	235	208	214	229	230	229	238
1992	230	235	208	212	231	228	228	242
1994	231	237	212	210	232	230	229	245
1996	231	237	212	215	233	229	230	239
1999	232	239	211	213	233	231	231	242
2004 modified [1]	239	. . .	. . .	. . .	239	240	239	. . .
2004 bridge [1]	241	247	224	230	243	240	241	. . .
13 Years of Age								
1973	266	274	228	239	268	267	. . .	. . .
1978	264	272	230	238	264	265	263	279
1982	269	274	240	252	269	268	267	281
1986	269	274	249	254	270	268	269	276
1990	270	276	249	255	271	270	269	280
1992	273	279	250	259	274	272	272	283
1994	274	281	252	256	276	273	273	285
1996	274	281	252	256	276	272	273	286
1999	276	283	251	259	277	274	274	288
2004 modified [1]	279	. . .	. . .	. . .	279	278	278	. . .
2004 bridge [1]	281	288	262	265	283	279	280	. . .
17 Years of Age								
1973	304	310	270	277	309	301	. . .	. . .
1978	300	306	268	276	304	297	300	314
1982	298	304	272	277	301	296	297	311
1986	302	308	279	283	305	299	301	320
1990	305	309	289	284	306	303	304	318
1992	307	312	286	292	309	305	305	320
1994	306	312	286	291	309	304	304	319
1996	307	313	286	292	310	305	306	316
1999	308	315	283	293	310	307	307	321
2004 modified [1]	305	. . .	. . .	. . .	307	304	304	. . .
2004 bridge [1]	307	313	285	289	308	305	306	. . .

Source: U.S. Department of Education. National Center for Education Statistics. *National Assessment of Educational Progress, The Nation's Report Card.* <http://nces.ed.gov/nationsreportcard>. (Accessed Feb. 17, 2006.)

Note: **Level 150**: Simple arithmetic facts; students at this level know some basic addition and subtraction facts, and most can add two-digit numbers without regrouping. They recognize simple situations in which addition and subtraction apply. They are also developing rudimentary classification skills.

Level 200: Beginning skills and understandings; students at this level have considerable understanding of two-digit numbers. They can add two-digit numbers but are still developing an ability to regroup in subtraction. They know some basic multiplication and division facts, recognize relations among coins, can read information from charts and graphs, and use simple measurement instruments. They are developing some reasoning skills.

Level 250: Numerical operations and beginning problem solving; students at this level have an initial understanding of the four basic operations. They are able to apply whole number addition and subtraction skills to one-step word problems and money situations. In multiplication, they can find the product of a two-digit and a one-digit number. They can also compare information from graphs and charts and are developing an ability to analyze simple logical relations.

Level 300: Moderately complex procedures and reasoning; students at this level are developing an understanding of number systems. They can compute with decimals, simple fractions, and commonly encountered percents. They can identify geometric figures, measure lengths and angles, and calculate areas of rectangles. These students are also able to interpret simple inequalities, evaluate formulas, and solve simple linear equations. They can find averages, make decisions based on information drawn from graphs, and use logical reasoning to solve problems. They are developing the skills to operate with signed numbers, exponents, and square roots.

Level 350: Multistep problem solving and algebra; students at this level can apply a range of reasoning skills to solve multistep problems. They can solve routine problems involving fractions and percents, recognize properties of basic geometric figures, and work with exponents and square roots. They can solve a variety of two-step problems using variables, identify equivalent algebraic expressions, and solve linear equations and inequalities. They are developing an understanding of functions and coordinate systems.

[1]For the 2004 administration of the long-term trend assessment in mathematics, several changes were made to the assessment design. When changes are made in a trend assessment, studies are required to ensure that the results can continue to be reported on the same trend line—that is, that they are validly comparable to earlier results. Analyses were needed to ensure that the 2004 results under the new design were comparable to the results from previous long-term trend assessments. Therefore, two assessments were conducted in 2004. One was a modified assessment that used the new design and the other was a "bridge" assessment that replicated the former design. The bridge assessment links the results of the modified assessment to the existing trend line so that comparisons of the results of the bridge and modified assessments could detect any shifts in results that may be due to changes in test design.

. . . = Not available.

Table A7-6. Presence of a Computer and the Internet at Home for Children 3 to 17 Years of Age, October 2003

(Numbers in thousands, percent.)

Characteristic	Number of children 3–17 years old	Presence of computer at home				Presence of Internet access at home			
		Yes		No		Yes		No	
		Number	Percent	Number	Percent	Number	Percent	Number	Percent
TOTAL	61 897	46 746	75.5	15 151	24.5	40 923	66.1	20 974	33.9
Age									
3 to 5 years	12 204	8 565	70.2	3 638	29.8	7 512	61.6	4 692	38.4
6 to 9 years	15 793	11 584	73.3	4 209	26.7	9 981	63.2	5 812	36.8
10 to 14 years	21 147	16 496	78.0	4 651	22.0	14 407	68.1	6 740	31.9
15 to 17 years	12 753	10 101	79.2	2 652	20.8	9 023	70.8	3 730	29.2
Sex									
Male	31 778	23 886	75.2	7 892	24.8	20 900	65.8	10 878	34.2
Female	30 119	22 860	75.9	7 259	24.1	20 023	66.5	10 095	33.5
Race and Hispanic Origin									
White alone	47 410	37 732	79.6	9 679	20.4	33 583	70.8	13 828	29.2
Non-Hispanic White alone	37 164	32 140	86.5	5 024	13.5	29 321	78.9	7 843	21.1
Black alone	9 705	5 238	54.0	4 467	46.0	4 098	42.2	5 607	57.8
Asian alone	2 273	1 901	83.7	372	16.3	1 685	74.2	587	25.8
Hispanic (of any race)	11 167	6 129	54.9	5 037	45.1	4 672	41.8	6 495	58.2
White alone or in combination	49 023	39 021	79.6	10 002	20.4	34 681	70.7	14 342	29.3
Non-Hispanic White alone or in combination	37 164	32 140	86.5	5 024	13.5	29 321	78.9	7 843	21.1
Black alone or in combination	10 401	5 708	54.9	4 693	45.1	4 500	43.3	5 901	56.7
Asian alone or in combination	2 735	2 315	84.7	420	15.3	2 059	75.3	676	24.7
Region									
Northeast	11 009	8 928	81.1	2 081	18.9	8 154	74.1	2 855	25.9
Midwest	14 025	10 885	77.6	3 141	22.4	9 569	68.2	4 457	31.8
South	21 969	15 682	71.4	6 288	28.6	13 527	61.6	8 442	38.4
West	14 894	11 252	75.5	3 642	24.5	9 675	65.0	5 219	35.0
Household Type									
Total families	61 237	46 339	75.7	14 898	24.3	40 564	66.2	20 673	33.8
Married-couple family	43 602	35 897	82.3	7 705	17.7	32 400	74.3	11 202	25.7
Male householder	3 364	2 161	64.2	1 203	35.8	1 739	51.7	1 625	48.3
Female householder	14 271	8 281	58.0	5 990	42.0	6 425	45.0	7 846	55.0
Nonfamily households	660	407	61.6	253	38.4	360	54.5	301	45.5
Household Size									
1 to 3 people	13 876	9 660	69.6	4 216	30.4	8 249	59.5	5 627	40.5
4 to 5 people	36 755	28 881	78.6	7 874	21.4	25 938	70.6	10 817	29.4
More than 5 people	11 266	8 206	72.8	3 061	27.2	6 736	59.8	4 530	40.2
Family Income									
Total in families	61 237	46 339	75.7	14 898	24.3	40 564	66.2	20 673	33.8
Less than $5,000	1 506	545	36.2	961	63.8	335	22.2	1 171	77.8
$5,000–$9,999	2 415	1 065	44.1	1 350	55.9	667	27.6	1 748	72.4
$10,000–$14,999	3 135	1 413	45.1	1 722	54.9	956	30.5	2 180	69.5
$15,000–$19,999	2 422	1 192	49.2	1 229	50.8	845	34.9	1 577	65.1
$20,000–$29,999	6 581	3 957	60.1	2 624	39.9	3 109	47.2	3 472	52.8
$30,000–$39,999	6 597	4 862	73.7	1 736	26.3	4 009	60.8	2 589	39.2
$40,000–$49,999	4 759	3 911	82.2	848	17.8	3 434	72.1	1 325	27.9
$50,000–$59,999	4 883	4 191	85.8	692	14.2	3 834	78.5	1 049	21.5
$60,000–$74,999	5 444	4 907	90.1	537	9.9	4 657	85.5	787	14.5
$75,000–$99,999	6 293	5 891	93.6	403	6.4	5 686	90.4	607	9.6
$100,000–$149,999	4 881	4 743	97.2	138	2.8	4 613	94.5	268	5.5
$150,000 or more	2 917	2 832	97.1	85	2.9	2 781	95.4	135	4.6
Not reported	9 403	6 830	72.6	2 574	27.4	5 639	60.0	3 764	40.0
Education of Householder									
Less than high school graduate	9 746	4 539	46.6	5 207	53.4	3 129	32.1	6 617	67.9
High school graduate or GED	18 082	12 363	68.4	5 719	31.6	10 358	57.3	7 724	42.7
Some college or associate degree	17 465	14 311	81.9	3 154	18.1	12 613	72.2	4 852	27.8
Bachelor's degree	11 131	10 319	92.7	812	7.3	9 824	88.3	1 307	11.7
Advanced degree	5 474	5 214	95.3	259	4.7	4 999	91.3	474	8.7
Employment Status of Householder									
Employed	47 160	37 246	79.0	9 913	21.0	33 024	70.0	14 136	30.0
Unemployed	2 573	1 571	61.1	1 002	38.9	1 271	49.4	1 302	50.6
Not in labor force	12 164	7 929	65.2	4 236	34.8	6 629	54.5	5 535	45.5

Source: U.S. Census Bureau. *Computer and Internet Use in the United States: 2003* (Current Population Reports, P23-208).
<http://www.census.gov/prod/2005pubs/p23-208.pdf>. (Accessed Feb. 17, 2006.)

Table A7-6.   Presence of a Computer and the Internet at Home for Children 3 to 17 Years of Age, October 2003—*Continued*

(Numbers in thousands, percent.)

Characteristic	Number of children 3–17 years old	Presence of computer at home				Presence of Internet access at home			
		Yes		No		Yes		No	
		Number	Percent	Number	Percent	Number	Percent	Number	Percent
Occupation of Householder									
Never worked/not in labor force	11 797	7 639	64.7	4 159	35.3	6 402	54.3	5 395	45.7
Management, business, and financial	7 844	7 156	91.2	688	8.8	6 710	85.5	1 135	14.5
Professional	10 054	8 968	89.2	1 087	10.8	8 355	83.1	1 699	16.9
Service	7 438	4 723	63.5	2 715	36.5	3 835	51.6	3 603	48.4
Sales	5 381	4 364	81.1	1 016	18.9	3 990	74.2	1 391	25.8
Office and administrative support	5 921	4 523	76.4	1 398	23.6	3 887	65.6	2 034	34.4
Farming, fishing, and forestry	629	284	45.2	344	54.8	236	37.5	393	62.5
Construction and extraction	3 364	2 320	69.0	1 044	31.0	1 917	57.0	1 447	43.0
Installation, maintenance, and repair	2 202	1 815	82.4	386	17.6	1 613	73.3	589	26.7
Production	4 100	2 710	66.1	1 390	33.9	2 172	53.0	1 928	47.0
Transportation and material moving	3 167	2 243	70.8	924	29.2	1 807	57.1	1 360	42.9
Industry of Householder									
Never worked/not in labor force	11 797	7 639	64.7	4 159	35.3	6 402	54.3	5 395	45.7
Agriculture, forestry, fishing, and hunting	1 050	654	62.2	397	37.8	543	51.7	507	48.3
Mining	267	215	80.5	52	19.5	189	70.6	78	29.4
Construction	4 319	3 148	72.9	1 171	27.1	2 674	61.9	1 645	38.1
Manufacturing	7 301	5 669	77.6	1 632	22.4	4 800	65.7	2 501	34.3
Wholesale and retail trade	7 005	5 362	76.6	1 643	23.4	4 719	67.4	2 286	32.6
Transportation and utilities	2 829	2 229	78.8	599	21.2	2 044	72.3	785	27.7
Information	1 141	1 040	91.2	101	8.8	937	82.1	204	17.9
Financial activities	3 144	2 707	86.1	437	13.9	2 508	79.8	636	20.2
Professional and business services	4 998	4 032	80.7	966	19.3	3 719	74.4	1 278	25.6
Educational and health services	9 820	7 893	80.4	1 927	19.6	6 989	71.2	2 831	28.8
Leisure and hospitality	3 108	1 980	63.7	1 128	36.3	1 662	53.5	1 445	46.5
Other services	2 507	1 947	77.6	561	22.4	1 681	67.0	827	33.0
Public administration	2 612	2 231	85.4	380	14.6	2 056	78.7	555	21.3

Source: U.S. Census Bureau. *Computer and Internet Use in the United States: 2003* (Current Population Reports, P23-208). <http://www.census.gov/prod/2005pubs/p23-208.pdf>. (Accessed Feb. 17, 2006.)

Table A7-7. Years of School Completed by People 25 Years of Age and Over, by Sex, Selected Years, 1940–2004

(Numbers in thousands, median years.)

Year and sex	Total, 25 years and over	Years of school completed						Median
		Elementary		High school		College		
		0 to 4 years	5 to 7 years	1 to 3 years	4 years	1 to 3 years	4 years	
Both Sexes								
1940	74 776	10 105	34 413	11 182	10 552	4 075	3 407	8.6
1947	82 578	8 611	32 308	13 487	16 926	5 533	4 424	9.0
1950	87 484	9 491	31 617	14 817	17 625	6 246	5 272	9.3
1952	88 358	8 004	30 274	15 228	21 074	6 714	6 118	10.1
1957	95 630	8 561	29 316	16 951	24 832	6 985	7 172	10.6
1959	97 478	7 816	28 490	17 520	26 219	7 888	7 734	11.0
1960	99 465	8 303	31 218	19 140	24 440	8 747	7 617	10.6
1962	100 664	7 826	28 438	17 751	28 477	9 170	9 002	11.4
1964	102 421	7 295	27 551	18 419	30 728	9 085	9 345	11.7
1965	103 245	6 982	27 063	18 617	31 703	9 139	9 742	11.8
1966	103 876	6 705	26 478	18 859	32 391	9 235	10 212	12.0
1967	104 864	6 400	26 178	18 647	33 173	9 914	10 550	12.0
1968	106 469	6 248	25 467	18 724	34 603	10 254	11 171	12.1
1969	107 750	6 014	24 976	18 527	36 133	10 564	11 535	12.1
1970	109 310	5 747	24 519	18 682	37 134	11 164	12 062	12.2
1971	110 627	5 574	24 029	18 601	38 029	11 782	12 612	12.2
1972	111 133	5 124	22 503	18 855	39 171	12 117	13 364	12.2
1973	112 866	5 100	21 838	18 420	40 448	12 831	14 228	12.3
1974	115 005	5 106	21 200	18 274	41 460	13 665	15 300	12.3
1975	116 897	4 912	20 633	18 237	42 353	14 518	16 244	12.3
1976	118 848	4 601	19 912	18 204	43 157	15 477	17 496	12.4
1977	120 870	4 509	19 567	18 318	43 602	16 247	18 627	12.4
1978	123 019	4 445	19 309	18 175	44 381	17 379	19 332	12.4
1979	125 295	4 324	18 504	17 579	45 915	18 393	20 579	12.5
1980	130 409	4 390	18 426	18 086	47 934	19 379	22 193	12.5
1981	132 899	4 358	17 868	18 041	49 915	20 042	22 674	12.5
1982	135 526	4 119	17 232	18 006	51 426	20 692	24 050	12.6
1983	138 020	4 119	16 714	17 681	52 060	21 531	25 915	12.6
1984	140 794	3 884	16 258	17 433	54 073	22 281	26 862	12.6
1985	143 524	3 873	16 020	17 553	54 866	23 405	27 808	12.6
1986	146 606	3 894	15 672	17 484	56 338	24 729	28 489	12.6
1987	149 144	3 640	15 301	17 417	57 669	25 479	29 637	12.7
1988	151 635	3 714	14 550	17 847	58 940	25 799	30 787	12.7
1989	154 155	3 861	14 061	17 719	59 336	26 614	32 565	12.7
1990	156 538	3 833	13 758	17 461	60 119	28 075	33 291	12.7
1991	158 694	3 803	13 046	17 379	61 272	29 170	34 026	12.7
1992	160 827	3 449	11 989	17 672	57 860	35 520	34 337	. . .
1993	162 826	3 380	11 747	17 067	57 589	37 451	35 590	. . .
1994	164 512	3 156	11 359	16 925	56 515	40 014	36 544	. . .
1995	166 438	3 074	10 873	16 566	56 450	41 249	38 226	. . .
1996	168 323	3 027	10 595	17 102	56 559	41 372	39 668	. . .
1997	170 581	2 840	10 472	17 211	57 586	41 774	40 697	. . .
1998	172 211	2 834	9 948	16 776	58 174	42 506	41 973	. . .
1999	173 754	2 742	9 655	15 674	57 935	43 176	43 803	. . .
2000	175 230	2 742	9 438	15 674	58 086	44 445	44 845	. . .
2001	180 389	2 810	9 518	16 279	58 272	46 281	47 228	. . .
2002	182 142	2 902	9 668	16 378	58 456	46 042	48 696	. . .
2003	185 183	2 915	9 361	16 323	59 292	46 910	50 383	. . .
2004	186 876	2 858	8 888	15 999	59 811	47 571	51 749	. . .

Source: U.S. Census Bureau. 1947, and 1952 to 2002 March Current Population Survey; 2003 and 2004 Annual Social and Economic Supplement to the Current Population Survey (noninstitutionalized population, excluding members of the Armed Forces living in barracks); 1960 Census of Population, 1950 Census of Population, and 1940 Census of Population (resident population).

Note: Beginning in 2001, data are from the expanded CPS sample and were created using population controls based on Census 2000 data. A new question results in different categories than for years prior to 1992. Data shown as "high school, 4 years" is now collected by the category "high school graduate." Data shown as "college, 1 to 3 years" is now collected by "some college" and two "associate degree" categories. Data shown as "college, 4 years or more" is now collected by the categories, "bachelor"s degree," "master"s degree," "doctorate degree," and "professional degree." Due to the change in question format, median years of schooling cannot be derived. Total includes persons who did not report on years of school completed.

. . . = Not available.

Table A7-7. Years of School Completed by People 25 Years of Age and Over, by Sex, Selected Years, 1940–2004—*Continued*

(Numbers in thousands, median years.)

Year and sex	Total, 25 years and over	Years of school completed						Median
		Elementary		High school		College		
		0 to 4 years	5 to 7 years	1 to 3 years	4 years	1 to 3 years	4 years	
Male								
1940	37 463	5 550	17 639	5 333	4 507	1 824	2 021	8.6
1947	40 483	4 615	16 086	6 535	7 353	2 625	2 478	8.9
1950	42 627	5 074	15 852	6 974	7 511	2 888	3 008	9.0
1952	42 368	4 396	14 876	7 048	8 760	3 164	3 480	9.7
1957	46 208	4 610	14 634	8 003	10 230	3 347	4 359	10.3
1959	47 041	4 257	14 039	8 326	10 870	3 801	4 765	10.7
1960	47 997	4 522	15 562	8 988	10 175	4 127	4 626	10.3
1962	48 283	4 213	13 927	8 399	11 932	4 315	5 497	11.1
1964	48 975	3 959	13 467	8 537	12 902	4 394	5 714	11.5
1965	49 242	3 774	13 308	8 529	13 334	4 370	5 923	11.7
1966	49 410	3 614	12 992	8 611	13 672	4 342	6 180	11.8
1967	49 756	3 417	12 736	8 463	14 015	4 755	6 372	12.0
1968	50 510	3 261	12 407	8 564	14 613	4 945	6 721	12.1
1969	51 031	3 095	12 182	8 398	15 177	5 263	6 917	12.1
1970	51 784	3 031	11 925	8 355	15 571	5 580	7 321	12.2
1971	52 357	2 933	11 703	8 264	16 008	5 798	7 653	12.2
1972	52 351	2 634	10 854	8 413	16 424	5 972	8 055	12.3
1973	53 067	2 598	10 488	8 120	17 011	6 376	8 473	12.3
1974	54 167	2 637	10 186	7 966	17 488	6 756	9 135	12.4
1975	55 036	2 568	9 760	7 985	17 769	7 274	9 679	12.4
1976	55 902	2 371	9 463	7 923	18 048	7 699	10 397	12.5
1977	56 917	2 296	9 330	7 969	18 290	8 104	10 926	12.5
1978	57 922	2 230	9 195	7 821	18 620	8 657	11 398	12.5
1979	58 986	2 190	8 785	7 636	19 250	9 100	12 025	12.6
1980	61 389	2 212	8 627	8 046	20 080	9 593	12 832	12.6
1981	62 509	2 141	8 322	8 084	21 019	9 734	13 208	12.6
1982	63 764	2 074	7 987	7 960	21 749	10 020	13 974	12.6
1983	65 004	2 103	7 750	7 867	22 048	10 310	14 926	12.7
1984	66 350	1 945	7 688	7 837	22 990	10 678	15 211	12.7
1985	67 756	1 947	7 629	7 783	23 552	11 164	15 682	12.7
1986	69 503	1 978	7 446	7 872	24 260	11 856	16 091	12.7
1987	70 677	1 794	7 259	7 909	24 998	12 062	16 654	12.7
1988	71 911	1 852	6 849	8 247	25 638	12 057	17 268	12.7
1989	73 225	1 956	6 659	8 076	25 897	12 725	17 913	12.8
1990	74 421	2 004	6 557	8 000	26 426	13 271	18 164	12.8
1991	75 487	2 018	6 299	7 887	27 189	13 720	18 373	12.8
1992	76 579	1 737	5 726	8 085	25 774	16 631	18 627	. . .
1993	77 644	1 709	5 594	7 821	25 766	17 521	19 234	. . .
1994	78 539	1 669	5 427	7 789	25 404	18 544	19 705	. . .
1995	79 463	1 598	5 231	7 691	25 378	18 933	20 631	. . .
1996	80 339	1 537	5 067	7 930	25 649	19 301	20 854	. . .
1997	81 620	1 454	5 023	8 212	26 226	19 332	21 374	. . .
1998	82 376	1 431	4 727	8 017	26 575	19 792	21 832	. . .
1999	82 917	1 339	4 651	7 736	26 368	20 043	22 782	. . .
2000	83 611	1 341	4 577	7 298	26 651	20 493	23 252	. . .
2001	86 096	1 419	4 673	7 615	26 956	21 120	24 313	. . .
2002	86 996	1 457	4 743	7 894	26 947	21 127	24 828	. . .
2003	88 597	1 482	4 566	8 026	27 356	21 568	25 598	. . .
2004	89 558	1 496	4 308	7 766	27 889	21 763	26 336	. . .

Source: U.S. Census Bureau. 1947, and 1952 to 2002 March Current Population Survey; 2003 and 2004 Annual Social and Economic Supplement to the Current Population Survey (noninstitutionalized population, excluding members of the Armed Forces living in barracks); 1960 Census of Population, 1950 Census of Population, and 1940 Census of Population (resident population).

Note: Beginning in 2001, data are from the expanded CPS sample and were created using population controls based on Census 2000 data. A new question results in different categories than for years prior to 1992. Data shown as "high school, 4 years" is now collected by the category "high school graduate." Data shown as "college, 1 to 3 years" is now collected by "some college" and two "associate degree" categories. Data shown as "college, 4 years or more" is now collected by the categories, "bachelor's degree," "master's degree," "doctorate degree," and "professional degree." Due to the change in question format, median years of schooling cannot be derived. Total includes persons who did not report on years of school completed.

. . . = Not available.

Table A7-7. Years of School Completed by People 25 Years of Age and Over, by Sex, Selected Years, 1940–2004—*Continued*

(Numbers in thousands, median years.)

Year and sex	Total, 25 years and over	Years of school completed						Median
		Elementary		High school		College		
		0 to 4 years	5 to 7 years	1 to 3 years	4 years	1 to 3 years	4 years	
Female								
1940	37 313	4 554	16 773	5 849	6 044	2 251	1 386	8.7
1947	42 095	3 996	16 222	6 952	9 573	2 908	1 946	8.9
1950	44 857	4 417	15 824	7 843	10 114	3 358	2 264	9.6
1952	45 990	3 608	15 398	8 180	12 314	3 550	2 638	10.4
1957	49 422	3 951	14 682	8 948	14 602	3 638	2 813	10.9
1959	50 437	3 559	14 451	9 194	15 349	4 087	2 969	11.2
1960	51 468	3 781	15 656	10 151	14 267	4 620	2 991	10.9
1962	52 381	3 613	14 511	9 352	16 545	4 855	3 505	11.6
1964	53 447	3 333	14 086	9 881	17 825	4 686	3 629	11.8
1965	54 004	3 207	13 753	10 085	18 369	4 767	3 820	12.0
1966	54 467	3 090	13 488	10 246	18 719	4 892	4 032	12.0
1967	55 107	2 985	13 439	10 185	19 157	5 162	4 178	12.0
1968	55 959	2 987	13 060	10 160	19 991	5 309	4 450	12.1
1969	56 719	2 919	12 796	10 131	20 955	5 301	4 619	12.1
1970	57 527	2 716	12 595	10 327	21 563	5 584	4 743	12.1
1971	58 270	2 641	12 327	10 339	22 021	5 984	4 959	12.2
1972	58 782	2 490	11 649	10 442	22 746	6 145	5 309	12.2
1973	59 799	2 502	11 350	10 300	23 437	6 454	5 755	12.2
1974	60 838	2 469	11 015	10 308	23 972	6 910	6 165	12.3
1975	61 861	2 344	10 871	10 252	24 584	7 243	6 565	12.3
1976	62 946	2 230	10 449	10 281	25 109	7 779	7 098	12.3
1977	63 953	2 213	10 236	10 349	25 312	8 142	7 701	12.4
1978	65 097	2 214	10 114	10 353	25 761	8 721	7 934	12.4
1979	66 309	2 133	9 720	9 945	26 665	9 293	8 554	12.4
1980	69 020	2 178	9 800	10 040	27 854	9 786	9 362	12.4
1981	70 390	2 217	9 545	9 957	28 896	10 309	9 466	12.5
1982	71 762	2 045	9 245	10 046	29 677	10 673	10 076	12.5
1983	73 016	2 015	8 964	9 814	30 012	11 220	10 990	12.5
1984	74 444	1 939	8 571	9 596	31 083	11 603	11 651	12.6
1985	75 768	1 926	8 390	9 770	31 314	12 242	12 126	12.6
1986	77 102	1 916	8 226	9 612	32 078	12 874	12 399	12.6
1987	78 467	1 846	8 042	9 508	32 671	13 417	12 983	12.6
1988	79 724	1 862	7 700	9 599	33 303	13 741	13 519	12.6
1989	80 930	1 904	7 402	9 643	33 440	13 888	14 652	12.6
1990	82 116	1 829	7 200	9 462	33 693	14 806	15 126	12.7
1991	83 207	1 784	6 747	9 491	34 083	15 449	15 652	12.7
1992	84 248	1 712	6 263	9 587	32 086	18 889	15 709	...
1993	85 181	1 672	6 154	9 246	31 823	19 930	16 357	...
1994	85 973	1 487	5 932	9 135	31 111	21 470	16 838	...
1995	86 975	1 476	5 642	8 874	31 072	22 317	17 594	...
1996	87 984	1 491	5 528	9 171	30 911	22 071	18 813	...
1997	88 961	1 387	5 450	8 999	31 360	22 442	19 323	...
1998	89 835	1 403	5 220	8 758	31 599	22 714	20 142	...
1999	90 837	1 404	5 004	8 707	31 566	23 133	21 021	...
2000	91 620	1 400	4 861	8 378	31 435	23 953	21 594	...
2001	94 293	1 392	4 845	8 664	31 316	25 161	22 915	...
2002	95 146	1 445	4 926	8 484	31 509	24 915	23 868	...
2003	96 586	1 433	4 795	8 297	31 936	25 342	24 784	...
2004	97 319	1 363	4 580	8 233	31 921	25 808	25 413	...

Source: U.S. Census Bureau. 1947, and 1952 to 2002 March Current Population Survey; 2003 and 2004 Annual Social and Economic Supplement to the Current Population Survey (noninstitutionalized population, excluding members of the Armed Forces living in barracks); 1960 Census of Population, 1950 Census of Population, and 1940 Census of Population (resident population).

Note: Beginning in 2001, data are from the expanded CPS sample and were created using population controls based on Census 2000 data. A new question results in different categories than for years prior to 1992. Data shown as "high school, 4 years" is now collected by the category "high school graduate." Data shown as "college, 1 to 3 years" is now collected by "some college" and two "associate degree" categories. Data shown as "college, 4 years or more" is now collected by the categories, "bachelor's degree," "master's degree," "doctorate degree," and "professional degree." Due to the change in question format, median years of schooling cannot be derived. Total includes persons who did not report on years of school completed.

. . . = Not available.

Table A7-8. Percent of Population 25 Years and Over Who Have Completed High School or College, by Race, Hispanic Origin, and Sex, Selected Years, 1940–2004

(Percent.)

Year, age, and educational attainment level	All races			White			Black[1]		
	Total	Male	Female	Total	Male	Female	Total	Male	Female
25 YEARS AND OVER									
Completed 4 Years of High School or More									
1940	24.5	22.7	26.3	26.1	24.2	28.1	7.7	6.9	8.4
1947	33.1	31.4	34.7	35.0	33.2	36.7	13.6	12.7	14.5
1950	34.3	32.6	36.0	. . .	. . .	. . .	13.7	12.5	14.7
1952	38.8	36.9	40.5	. . .	. . .	. . .	15.0	14.0	15.7
1957	41.6	39.7	43.3	43.2	41.1	45.1	18.4	16.9	19.7
1959	43.7	42.2	45.2	46.1	44.5	47.7	20.7	19.6	21.6
1962	46.3	45.0	47.5	48.7	47.4	49.9	24.8	23.2	26.2
1964	48.0	47.0	48.9	50.3	49.3	51.2	25.7	23.7	27.4
1965	49.0	48.0	49.9	51.3	50.2	52.2	27.2	25.8	28.4
1966	49.9	49.0	50.8	52.2	51.3	53.0	27.8	25.8	29.5
1967	51.1	50.5	51.7	53.4	52.8	53.8	29.5	27.1	31.5
1968	52.6	52.0	53.2	54.9	54.3	55.5	30.1	28.9	31.0
1969	54.0	53.6	54.4	56.3	55.7	56.7	32.3	31.9	32.6
1970	55.2	55.0	55.4	57.4	57.2	57.6	33.7	32.4	34.8
1971	56.4	56.3	56.6	58.6	58.4	58.8	34.7	33.8	35.4
1972	58.2	58.2	58.2	60.4	60.3	60.5	36.6	35.7	37.2
1973	59.8	60.0	59.6	61.9	62.1	61.7	39.2	38.2	40.1
1974	61.2	61.6	60.9	63.3	63.6	63.0	40.8	39.9	41.5
1975	62.5	63.1	62.1	64.5	65.0	64.1	42.5	41.6	43.3
1976	64.1	64.7	63.5	66.1	66.7	65.5	43.8	42.3	45.0
1977	64.9	65.6	64.4	67.0	67.5	66.5	45.5	45.6	45.4
1978	65.9	66.8	65.2	67.9	68.6	67.2	47.6	47.9	47.3
1979	67.7	68.4	67.1	69.7	70.3	69.2	49.4	49.2	49.5
1980	68.6	69.2	68.1	70.5	71.0	70.1	51.2	51.1	51.3
1981	69.7	70.3	69.1	71.6	72.1	71.2	52.9	53.2	52.6
1982	71.0	71.7	70.3	72.8	73.4	72.3	54.9	55.7	54.3
1983	72.1	72.7	71.5	73.8	74.4	73.3	56.8	56.5	57.1
1984	73.3	73.7	73.0	75.0	75.4	74.6	58.5	57.1	59.7
1985	73.9	74.4	73.5	75.5	76.0	75.1	59.8	58.4	60.8
1986	74.7	75.1	74.4	76.2	76.5	75.9	62.3	61.5	63.0
1987	75.6	76.0	75.3	77.0	77.3	76.7	63.4	63.0	63.7
1988	76.2	76.4	76.0	77.7	77.7	77.6	63.5	63.7	63.4
1989	76.9	77.2	76.6	78.4	78.6	78.2	64.6	64.2	65.0
1990	77.6	77.7	77.5	79.1	79.1	79.0	66.2	65.8	66.5
1991	78.4	78.5	78.3	79.9	79.8	79.9	66.7	66.7	66.7
1992	79.4	79.7	79.2	80.9	81.1	80.7	67.7	67.0	68.2
1993	80.2	80.5	80.0	81.5	81.8	81.3	70.4	69.6	71.1
1994	80.9	81.0	80.7	82.0	82.1	81.9	72.9	71.7	73.8
1995	81.7	81.7	81.6	83.0	83.0	83.0	73.8	73.4	74.1
1996	81.7	81.9	81.6	82.8	82.7	82.8	74.3	74.3	74.2
1997	82.1	82.0	82.2	83.0	82.9	83.2	74.9	73.5	76.0
1998	82.8	82.8	82.9	83.7	83.6	83.8	76.0	75.2	76.7
1999	83.4	83.4	83.4	84.3	84.2	84.3	77.0	76.7	77.2
2000	84.1	84.2	84.0	84.9	84.8	85.0	78.5	78.7	78.3
2001	84.1	84.1	84.2	84.8	84.4	85.1	78.8	79.2	78.5
2002	84.1	83.8	84.4	84.8	84.3	85.2	78.7	78.5	78.9
2003	84.6	84.1	85.0	85.1	84.5	85.7	80.0	79.6	80.3
2004	85.2	84.8	85.4	85.8	85.3	86.3	80.6	80.4	80.8

Source: U.S. Census Bureau. 1947, and 1952 to 2002 March Current Population Survey; 2003 and 2004 Annual Social and Economic Supplement to the Current Population Survey (noninstitutionalized population, excluding members of the Armed Forces living in barracks); 1960 Census of Population, 1950 Census of Population, and 1940 Census of Population (resident population).

[1]Includes Black and other races from 1940 to 1962; from 1963 to 2003, data are for the Black population only.
. . . = Not available.

Table A7-8. Percent of Population 25 Years and Over Who Have Completed High School or College, by Race, Hispanic Origin, and Sex, Selected Years, 1940–2004
—Continued

(Percent.)

Year, age, and educational attainment level	Hispanic[2]			Non-Hispanic White			Non-Hispanic Black		
	Total	Male	Female	Total	Male	Female	Total	Male	Female
25 YEARS AND OVER									
Completed 4 Years of High School or More									
1940	...	...	...	...	...	...	...	...	...
1947	...	...	...	...	...	...	...	...	...
1950	...	...	...	...	...	...	...	...	...
1952	...	...	...	...	...	...	...	...	...
1957	...	...	...	...	...	...	...	...	...
1959	...	...	...	...	...	...	...	...	...
1962	...	...	...	...	...	...	...	...	...
1964	...	...	...	...	...	...	...	...	...
1965	...	...	...	...	...	...	...	...	...
1966	...	...	...	...	...	...	...	...	...
1967	...	...	...	...	...	...	...	...	...
1968	...	...	...	...	...	...	...	...	...
1969	...	...	...	...	...	...	...	...	...
1970	...	...	...	...	...	...	...	...	...
1971	...	...	...	...	...	...	...	...	...
1972	...	...	...	...	...	...	...	...	...
1973	...	...	...	...	...	...	...	...	...
1974	36.5	38.3	34.9	...	...	...	...	...	...
1975	37.9	39.5	36.7	...	...	...	...	...	...
1976	39.3	41.4	37.3	...	...	...	...	...	...
1977	39.6	42.3	37.2	...	...	...	...	...	...
1978	40.8	42.2	39.6	...	...	...	...	...	...
1979	42.0	42.3	41.7	...	...	...	...	...	...
1980	45.3	46.4	44.1	...	...	...	...	...	...
1981	44.5	45.5	43.6	...	...	...	...	...	...
1982	45.9	48.1	44.1	...	...	...	...	...	...
1983	46.2	48.6	44.2	...	...	...	...	...	...
1984	47.1	48.6	45.7	...	...	...	...	...	...
1985	47.9	48.5	47.4	...	...	...	...	...	...
1986	48.5	49.2	47.8	...	...	...	...	...	...
1987	50.9	51.8	50.0	...	...	...	...	...	...
1988	51.0	52.0	50.0	...	...	...	...	...	...
1989	50.9	51.0	50.7	...	...	...	...	...	...
1990	50.8	50.3	51.3	...	...	...	...	...	...
1991	51.3	51.4	51.2	...	...	...	...	...	...
1992	52.6	53.7	51.5	...	...	...	...	...	...
1993	53.1	52.9	53.2	84.1	84.5	83.8	70.4	69.6	71.1
1994	53.3	53.4	53.2	84.9	85.1	84.7	72.9	71.7	73.8
1995	53.4	52.9	53.8	85.9	86.0	85.8	73.8	73.4	74.1
1996	53.1	53.0	53.3	86.0	86.1	85.9	74.3	74.3	74.2
1997	54.7	54.9	54.6	86.3	86.3	86.3	74.9	73.5	76.0
1998	55.5	55.7	55.3	87.1	87.1	87.1	76.0	75.2	76.7
1999	56.1	56.0	56.3	87.7	87.7	87.7	77.4	77.2	77.5
2000	57.0	56.6	57.5	88.4	88.5	88.4	78.9	79.1	78.7
2001	56.8	55.5	58.0	88.6	88.6	88.6	79.1	79.5	78.8
2002	57.0	56.1	57.9	88.7	88.5	88.9	79.2	79.0	79.4
2003	57.0	56.3	57.8	89.4	89.0	89.7	80.3	79.9	80.7
2004	58.4	57.3	59.5	90.0	89.9	90.1	81.1	80.8	81.2

Source: U.S. Census Bureau. 1947, and 1952 to 2002 March Current Population Survey; 2003 and 2004 Annual Social and Economic Supplement to the Current Population Survey (noninstitutionalized population, excluding members of the Armed Forces living in barracks); 1960 Census of Population, 1950 Census of Population, and 1940 Census of Population (resident population).

[2]May be of any race.
... = Not available.

Table A7-8. Percent of Population 25 Years and Over Who Have Completed High School or College, by Race, Hispanic Origin, and Sex, Selected Years, 1940–2004
—Continued

(Percent.)

Year, age, and educational attainment level	All races			White			Black[1]		
	Total	Male	Female	Total	Male	Female	Total	Male	Female
25 YEARS AND OVER									
Completed 4 Years of College or More									
1940	4.6	5.5	3.8	4.9	5.9	4.0	1.3	1.4	1.2
1947	5.4	6.2	4.7	5.7	6.6	4.9	2.5	2.4	2.6
1950	6.2	7.3	5.2	. . .	. . .	. . .	2.3	2.1	2.4
1952	7.0	8.3	5.8	. . .	. . .	. . .	2.4	2.0	2.7
1957	7.6	9.6	5.8	8.0	10.1	6.0	2.9	2.7	3.0
1959	8.1	10.3	6.0	8.6	11.0	6.2	3.3	3.8	2.9
1962	8.9	11.4	6.7	9.5	12.2	7.0	4.0	3.9	4.0
1964	9.1	11.7	6.8	9.6	12.3	7.1	3.9	4.5	3.4
1965	9.4	12.0	7.1	9.9	12.7	7.3	4.7	4.9	4.5
1966	9.8	12.5	7.4	10.4	13.3	7.7	3.8	3.9	3.7
1967	10.1	12.8	7.6	10.6	13.6	7.9	4.0	3.4	4.4
1968	10.5	13.3	8.0	11.0	14.1	8.3	4.3	3.7	4.8
1969	10.7	13.6	8.1	11.2	14.3	8.5	4.6	4.8	4.5
1970	11.0	14.1	8.2	11.6	15.0	8.6	4.5	4.6	4.4
1971	11.4	14.6	8.5	12.0	15.5	8.9	4.5	4.7	4.3
1972	12.0	15.4	9.0	12.6	16.2	9.4	5.1	5.5	4.8
1973	12.6	16.0	9.6	13.1	16.8	9.9	6.0	5.9	6.0
1974	13.3	16.9	10.1	14.0	17.7	10.6	5.5	5.7	5.3
1975	13.9	17.6	10.6	14.5	18.4	11.0	6.4	6.7	6.2
1976	14.7	18.6	11.3	15.4	19.6	11.6	6.6	6.3	6.8
1977	15.4	19.2	12.0	16.1	20.2	12.4	7.2	7.0	7.4
1978	15.7	19.7	12.2	16.4	20.7	12.6	7.2	7.3	7.1
1979	16.4	20.4	12.9	17.2	21.4	13.3	7.9	8.3	7.5
1980	17.0	20.9	13.6	17.8	22.1	14.0	7.9	7.7	8.1
1981	17.1	21.1	13.4	17.8	22.2	13.8	8.2	8.2	8.2
1982	17.7	21.9	14.0	18.5	23.0	14.4	8.8	9.1	8.5
1983	18.8	23.0	15.1	19.5	24.0	15.4	9.5	10.0	9.2
1984	19.1	22.9	15.7	19.8	23.9	16.0	10.4	10.4	10.4
1985	19.4	23.1	16.0	20.0	24.0	16.3	11.1	11.2	11.0
1986	19.4	23.2	16.1	20.1	24.1	16.4	10.9	11.2	10.7
1987	19.9	23.6	16.5	20.5	24.5	16.9	10.7	11.0	10.4
1988	20.3	24.0	17.0	20.9	25.0	17.3	11.2	11.1	11.4
1989	21.1	24.5	18.1	21.8	25.4	18.5	11.8	11.7	11.9
1990	21.3	24.4	18.4	22.0	25.3	19.0	11.3	11.9	10.8
1991	21.4	24.3	18.8	22.2	25.4	19.3	11.5	11.4	11.6
1992	21.4	24.3	18.6	22.1	25.2	19.1	11.9	11.9	12.0
1993	21.9	24.8	19.2	22.6	25.7	19.7	12.2	11.9	12.4
1994	22.2	25.1	19.6	22.9	26.1	20.0	12.9	12.8	13.0
1995	23.0	26.0	20.2	24.0	27.2	21.0	13.2	13.6	12.9
1996	23.6	26.0	21.4	24.3	26.9	21.8	13.6	12.4	14.6
1997	23.9	26.2	21.7	24.6	27.0	22.3	13.3	12.5	13.9
1998	24.4	26.5	22.4	25.0	27.3	22.8	14.7	13.9	15.4
1999	25.2	27.5	23.1	25.9	28.5	23.5	15.4	14.2	16.4
2000	25.6	27.8	23.6	26.1	28.5	23.9	16.5	16.3	16.7
2001	26.2	28.2	24.3	26.6	28.7	24.6	15.7	15.3	16.1
2002	26.7	28.5	25.1	27.2	29.1	25.4	17.0	16.4	17.5
2003	27.2	28.9	25.7	27.6	29.4	25.9	17.3	16.7	17.8
2004	27.7	29.4	26.1	28.2	30.0	26.4	17.6	16.6	18.5

Source: U.S. Census Bureau. 1947, and 1952 to 2002 March Current Population Survey; 2003 and 2004 Annual Social and Economic Supplement to the Current Population Survey (noninstitutionalized population, excluding members of the Armed Forces living in barracks); 1960 Census of Population, 1950 Census of Population, and 1940 Census of Population (resident population).

[1] Includes Black and other races from 1940 to 1962; from 1963 to 2003, data are for the Black population only.
. . . = Not available.

Table A7-8. Percent of Population 25 Years and Over Who Have Completed High School or College, by Race, Hispanic Origin, and Sex, Selected Years, 1940–2004 —*Continued*

(Percent.)

Year, age, and educational attainment level	Hispanic[2]			Non-Hispanic White			Non-Hispanic Black		
	Total	Male	Female	Total	Male	Female	Total	Male	Female
25 YEARS AND OVER									
Completed 4 Years of College or More									
1940	...	...	...	...	...	...	...	...	...
1947	...	...	...	...	...	...	...	...	...
1950	...	...	...	...	...	...	...	...	...
1952	...	...	...	...	...	...	...	...	...
1957	...	...	...	...	...	...	...	...	...
1959	...	...	...	...	...	...	...	...	...
1962	...	...	...	...	...	...	...	...	...
1964	...	...	...	...	...	...	...	...	...
1965	...	...	...	...	...	...	...	...	...
1966	...	...	...	...	...	...	...	...	...
1967	...	...	...	...	...	...	...	...	...
1968	...	...	...	...	...	...	...	...	...
1969	...	...	...	...	...	...	...	...	...
1970	...	...	...	...	...	...	...	...	...
1971	...	...	...	...	...	...	...	...	...
1972	...	...	...	...	...	...	...	...	...
1973	...	...	...	...	...	...	...	...	...
1974	5.5	7.1	4.0	...	...	...	...	...	...
1975	6.3	8.3	4.6	...	...	...	...	...	...
1976	6.1	8.6	4.0	...	...	...	...	...	...
1977	6.2	8.1	4.4	...	...	...	...	...	...
1978	7.0	8.6	5.7	...	...	...	...	...	...
1979	6.7	8.2	5.3	...	...	...	...	...	...
1980	7.9	9.7	6.2	...	...	...	...	...	...
1981	7.7	9.7	5.9	...	...	...	...	...	...
1982	7.8	9.6	6.2	...	...	...	...	...	...
1983	7.9	9.2	6.8	...	...	...	...	...	...
1984	8.2	9.5	7.0	...	...	...	...	...	...
1985	8.5	9.7	7.3	...	...	...	...	...	...
1986	8.4	9.5	7.4	...	...	...	...	...	...
1987	8.6	9.7	7.5	...	...	...	...	...	...
1988	10.1	12.3	8.1	...	...	...	...	...	...
1989	9.9	11.0	8.8	...	...	...	...	...	...
1990	9.2	9.8	8.7	...	...	...	...	...	...
1991	9.7	10.0	9.4	...	...	...	...	...	...
1992	9.3	10.2	8.5	...	...	...	...	...	...
1993	9.0	9.5	8.5	23.8	27.2	20.7	12.2	11.9	12.4
1994	9.1	9.6	8.6	24.3	27.8	21.1	12.9	12.8	13.0
1995	9.3	10.1	8.4	25.4	28.9	22.1	13.2	13.6	12.9
1996	9.3	10.3	8.3	25.9	28.8	23.2	13.6	12.4	14.6
1997	10.3	10.6	10.1	26.2	29.0	23.7	13.3	12.5	13.9
1998	11.0	11.1	10.9	26.6	29.3	24.1	14.7	13.9	15.4
1999	10.9	10.7	11.0	27.7	30.6	25.0	15.5	14.3	16.5
2000	10.6	10.7	10.6	28.1	30.8	25.5	16.6	16.4	16.8
2001	11.1	10.8	11.4	28.7	31.3	26.3	15.7	15.3	16.0
2002	11.1	11.0	11.2	29.4	31.7	27.3	17.2	16.5	17.7
2003	11.4	11.2	11.6	30.0	32.3	27.9	17.4	16.8	18.0
2004	12.1	11.8	12.3	30.6	32.9	28.4	17.7	16.6	18.5

Source: U.S. Census Bureau. 1947, and 1952 to 2002 March Current Population Survey; 2003 and 2004 Annual Social and Economic Supplement to the Current Population Survey (noninstitutionalized population, excluding members of the Armed Forces living in barracks); 1960 Census of Population, 1950 Census of Population, and 1940 Census of Population (resident population).

[2]May be of any race.
... = Not available.

Table A7-8. Percent of Population 25 Years and Over Who Have Completed High School or College, by Race, Hispanic Origin, and Sex, Selected Years, 1940–2004 —*Continued*

(Percent.)

Year, age, and educational attainment level	All races			White			Black[1]		
	Total	Male	Female	Total	Male	Female	Total	Male	Female
25 TO 29 YEARS									
Completed 4 Years of High School or More									
1940	38.1	36.0	40.1	41.2	38.9	43.4	12.3	10.6	13.6
1947	51.4	49.4	53.3	54.9	52.9	56.8	22.3	19.6	24.7
1950	52.8	50.6	55.0	. . .	. . .	. . .	23.6	21.3	25.5
1952	57.1	55.3	58.7	. . .	. . .	. . .	28.1	27.9	28.3
1957	60.2	57.9	62.4	63.3	60.7	65.7	31.6	27.4	35.2
1959	63.9	63.9	64.0	67.2	66.9	67.4	39.5	40.6	38.6
1962	65.9	65.8	66.1	69.2	69.2	69.3	41.6	38.9	43.8
1964	69.2	68.8	69.5	72.1	71.8	72.4	45.0	41.6	47.9
1965	70.3	70.5	70.1	72.8	72.7	72.8	50.3	50.3	50.4
1966	71.0	70.9	71.2	73.8	73.2	74.4	47.9	48.9	47.0
1967	72.5	72.1	72.9	74.8	74.3	75.3	53.4	51.7	55.0
1968	73.2	73.7	72.7	75.3	75.5	75.0	55.8	58.1	53.6
1969	74.7	75.6	73.8	77.0	77.5	76.6	55.8	59.8	52.3
1970	75.4	76.6	74.2	77.8	79.2	76.4	56.2	54.5	57.9
1971	77.2	78.1	76.4	79.5	80.8	78.3	57.5	54.1	60.7
1972	79.8	80.5	79.2	81.5	82.3	80.8	64.1	61.8	66.2
1973	80.2	80.6	79.8	82.0	82.4	81.6	64.2	63.1	64.9
1974	81.9	83.1	80.8	83.4	84.1	82.7	68.2	71.1	66.0
1975	83.1	84.5	81.8	84.4	85.7	83.2	71.0	72.2	70.1
1976	84.7	86.0	83.5	85.9	87.3	84.6	73.8	72.5	74.9
1977	85.4	86.6	84.2	86.8	87.6	86.0	74.4	77.5	72.0
1978	85.3	86.0	84.6	86.3	86.8	85.8	77.3	78.5	76.3
1979	85.6	86.3	84.9	87.0	87.7	86.4	74.8	73.9	75.4
1980	85.4	85.4	85.5	86.9	86.8	87.0	76.6	74.8	78.1
1981	86.3	86.5	86.1	87.6	87.6	87.6	77.3	78.4	76.4
1982	86.2	86.3	86.1	86.9	87.0	86.8	80.9	80.5	81.3
1983	86.0	86.0	86.0	86.9	86.9	86.9	79.4	78.9	79.8
1984	85.9	85.6	86.3	86.9	86.8	87.0	78.9	75.9	81.5
1985	86.1	85.9	86.4	86.8	86.4	87.3	80.6	80.8	80.4
1986	86.1	85.9	86.4	86.5	85.6	87.4	83.4	86.5	80.6
1987	86.0	85.5	86.4	86.3	85.6	87.0	83.3	84.8	82.1
1988	85.7	84.4	87.0	86.5	84.8	88.2	80.7	80.6	80.7
1989	85.5	84.4	86.5	86.0	84.8	87.1	82.2	80.6	83.6
1990	85.7	84.4	87.0	86.3	84.6	88.1	81.7	81.5	81.8
1991	85.4	84.9	85.8	85.8	85.1	86.6	81.7	83.5	80.1
1992	86.3	86.1	86.5	87.0	86.5	87.6	80.9	82.5	79.5
1993	86.7	86.0	87.4	87.3	86.1	88.5	82.8	85.0	80.9
1994	86.1	84.5	87.6	86.5	84.7	88.3	84.1	82.9	85.0
1995	86.8	86.3	87.4	87.4	86.6	88.2	86.5	88.1	85.1
1996	87.3	86.5	88.1	87.5	86.3	88.8	85.6	87.2	84.2
1997	87.4	85.8	88.9	87.6	85.8	89.4	86.2	85.2	87.1
1998	88.1	86.6	89.6	88.1	86.3	90.0	87.6	87.6	87.6
1999	87.8	86.1	89.5	87.6	85.8	89.3	88.2	87.7	88.6
2000	88.1	86.7	89.4	88.3	86.6	90.0	85.9	86.6	85.3
2001	86.8	85.3	88.3	86.4	84.6	88.3	86.3	85.4	87.0
2002	86.4	84.7	88.1	85.9	84.1	87.7	86.6	85.0	88.0
2003	86.5	84.9	88.2	85.7	83.8	87.6	87.6	86.4	88.5
2004	86.6	85.2	88.0	85.9	83.7	88.1	87.9	90.1	86.1

Source: U.S. Census Bureau. 1947, and 1952 to 2002 March Current Population Survey; 2003 and 2004 Annual Social and Economic Supplement to the Current Population Survey (noninstitutionalized population, excluding members of the Armed Forces living in barracks); 1960 Census of Population, 1950 Census of Population, and 1940 Census of Population (resident population).

[1] Includes Black and other races from 1940 to 1962; from 1963 to 2003, data are for the Black population only.
. . . = Not available.

Table A7-8.   Percent of Population 25 Years and Over Who Have Completed High School or College, by Race, Hispanic Origin, and Sex, Selected Years, 1940–2004 —Continued

(Percent.)

Year, age, and educational attainment level	Hispanic[2]			Non-Hispanic White			Non-Hispanic Black		
	Total	Male	Female	Total	Male	Female	Total	Male	Female
25 TO 29 YEARS									
Completed 4 Years of High School or More									
1940	. . .	. . .	. . .	. . .	. . .	. . .	. . .	. . .	. . .
1947	. . .	. . .	. . .	. . .	. . .	. . .	. . .	. . .	. . .
1950	. . .	. . .	. . .	. . .	. . .	. . .	. . .	. . .	. . .
1952	. . .	. . .	. . .	. . .	. . .	. . .	. . .	. . .	. . .
1957	. . .	. . .	. . .	. . .	. . .	. . .	. . .	. . .	. . .
1959	. . .	. . .	. . .	. . .	. . .	. . .	. . .	. . .	. . .
1962	. . .	. . .	. . .	. . .	. . .	. . .	. . .	. . .	. . .
1964	. . .	. . .	. . .	. . .	. . .	. . .	. . .	. . .	. . .
1965	. . .	. . .	. . .	. . .	. . .	. . .	. . .	. . .	. . .
1966	. . .	. . .	. . .	. . .	. . .	. . .	. . .	. . .	. . .
1967	. . .	. . .	. . .	. . .	. . .	. . .	. . .	. . .	. . .
1968	. . .	. . .	. . .	. . .	. . .	. . .	. . .	. . .	. . .
1969	. . .	. . .	. . .	. . .	. . .	. . .	. . .	. . .	. . .
1970	. . .	. . .	. . .	. . .	. . .	. . .	. . .	. . .	. . .
1971	. . .	. . .	. . .	. . .	. . .	. . .	. . .	. . .	. . .
1972	. . .	. . .	. . .	. . .	. . .	. . .	. . .	. . .	. . .
1973	. . .	. . .	. . .	. . .	. . .	. . .	. . .	. . .	. . .
1974	52.5	55.1	49.9	. . .	. . .	. . .	. . .	. . .	. . .
1975	51.7	51.1	52.1	. . .	. . .	. . .	. . .	. . .	. . .
1976	58.1	57.6	58.4	. . .	. . .	. . .	. . .	. . .	. . .
1977	58.1	62.1	54.8	. . .	. . .	. . .	. . .	. . .	. . .
1978	56.6	58.5	54.7	. . .	. . .	. . .	. . .	. . .	. . .
1979	57.0	55.5	58.5	. . .	. . .	. . .	. . .	. . .	. . .
1980	58.6	58.3	58.8	. . .	. . .	. . .	. . .	. . .	. . .
1981	59.8	59.1	60.4	. . .	. . .	. . .	. . .	. . .	. . .
1982	60.9	60.7	61.2	. . .	. . .	. . .	. . .	. . .	. . .
1983	58.3	57.8	58.9	. . .	. . .	. . .	. . .	. . .	. . .
1984	58.6	56.8	60.2	. . .	. . .	. . .	. . .	. . .	. . .
1985	60.9	58.6	63.1	. . .	. . .	. . .	. . .	. . .	. . .
1986	59.1	58.2	60.0	. . .	. . .	. . .	. . .	. . .	. . .
1987	59.8	58.6	61.0	. . .	. . .	. . .	. . .	. . .	. . .
1988	62.0	59.4	65.0	. . .	. . .	. . .	. . .	. . .	. . .
1989	61.0	61.0	61.0	. . .	. . .	. . .	. . .	. . .	. . .
1990	58.2	56.6	59.9	. . .	. . .	. . .	. . .	. . .	. . .
1991	56.7	56.4	57.1	. . .	. . .	. . .	. . .	. . .	. . .
1992	60.9	61.1	60.6	. . .	. . .	. . .	. . .	. . .	. . .
1993	60.9	58.3	64.0	91.2	90.6	91.8	82.8	85.0	80.9
1994	60.3	58.0	63.0	91.1	90.0	92.3	84.1	82.9	85.0
1995	57.1	55.7	58.7	92.5	92.0	93.0	86.5	88.1	85.1
1996	61.1	59.7	62.9	92.6	92.0	93.1	85.6	87.2	84.2
1997	61.8	59.2	64.9	92.9	91.7	94.0	86.2	85.2	87.1
1998	62.8	59.9	66.3	93.6	92.5	94.6	87.6	87.6	87.6
1999	61.6	57.4	66.0	93.0	91.9	94.1	88.7	88.2	89.2
2000	62.8	59.2	66.4	94.0	92.9	95.2	86.8	87.6	86.2
2001	62.4	58.3	67.3	93.4	93.1	93.7	86.8	86.0	87.5
2002	62.4	60.2	65.0	93.0	92.1	93.8	87.6	85.8	88.9
2003	61.7	59.6	64.2	93.7	92.8	94.5	88.5	87.4	89.4
2004	62.4	60.1	65.2	93.3	92.1	94.5	88.7	91.3	86.6

Source: U.S. Census Bureau. 1947, and 1952 to 2002 March Current Population Survey; 2003 and 2004 Annual Social and Economic Supplement to the Current Population Survey (noninstitutionalized population, excluding members of the Armed Forces living in barracks); 1960 Census of Population, 1950 Census of Population, and 1940 Census of Population (resident population).

[2]May be of any race.
. . . = Not available.

Table A7-8. Percent of Population 25 Years and Over Who Have Completed High School or College, by Race, Hispanic Origin, and Sex, Selected Years, 1940–2004 —*Continued*

(Percent.)

Year, age, and educational attainment level	All races			White			Black[1]		
	Total	Male	Female	Total	Male	Female	Total	Male	Female
25 TO 29 YEARS									
Completed 4 Years of College or More									
1940	5.9	6.9	4.9	6.4	7.5	5.3	1.6	1.5	1.7
1947	5.6	5.8	5.4	5.9	6.2	5.7	2.8	2.6	2.9
1950	7.7	9.6	5.9	. . .	. . .	. . .	2.9	2.4	3.2
1952	10.1	13.8	6.7	. . .	. . .	. . .	4.6	3.2	5.8
1957	10.4	13.5	7.5	11.1	14.5	7.8	4.1	3.3	5.0
1959	11.1	14.8	7.6	11.9	15.9	8.1	4.6	5.6	3.7
1962	13.1	17.2	9.2	14.3	18.7	10.0	4.2	5.7	3.0
1964	12.8	16.6	9.2	13.6	17.5	9.9	5.5	7.5	3.9
1965	12.4	15.6	9.5	13.0	16.4	9.8	6.8	7.3	6.8
1966	14.0	16.8	11.3	14.7	17.9	11.8	5.9	5.4	6.4
1967	14.6	17.2	12.1	15.5	18.3	12.7	5.4	4.2	6.3
1968	14.7	18.0	11.6	15.6	19.1	12.3	5.3	5.3	5.3
1969	16.0	19.4	12.8	17.0	20.6	13.4	6.7	8.1	5.5
1970	16.4	20.0	12.9	17.3	21.3	13.3	7.3	6.7	8.0
1971	16.9	20.1	13.8	17.9	21.3	14.6	6.4	6.4	6.5
1972	19.0	22.0	16.0	19.9	23.1	16.7	8.3	7.1	9.4
1973	19.0	21.6	16.4	19.9	22.8	17.0	8.1	7.1	8.8
1974	20.7	23.9	17.6	22.0	25.3	18.8	7.9	8.8	7.2
1975	21.9	25.1	18.7	22.8	26.3	19.4	10.7	11.4	10.1
1976	23.7	27.5	20.1	24.6	28.7	20.6	13.0	12.0	13.6
1977	24.0	27.0	21.1	25.3	28.5	22.1	12.6	12.8	12.4
1978	23.3	26.0	20.6	24.5	27.6	21.4	11.8	10.7	12.6
1979	23.1	25.6	20.5	24.3	27.1	21.5	12.4	13.3	11.7
1980	22.5	24.0	21.0	23.7	25.5	22.0	11.6	10.5	12.5
1981	21.3	23.1	19.6	22.4	24.3	20.5	11.6	12.1	11.1
1982	21.7	23.3	20.2	22.7	24.5	20.9	12.6	11.8	13.2
1983	22.5	23.9	21.1	23.4	25.0	21.8	12.9	13.1	12.8
1984	21.9	23.2	20.7	23.1	24.3	21.9	11.6	12.9	10.5
1985	22.2	23.1	21.3	23.2	24.2	22.2	11.5	10.3	12.6
1986	22.4	22.9	21.9	23.5	24.1	22.9	11.8	10.1	13.3
1987	22.0	22.3	21.7	23.0	23.3	22.8	11.4	11.6	11.1
1988	22.5	23.2	21.9	23.5	24.0	22.9	12.2	12.6	11.9
1989	23.4	23.9	22.9	24.4	24.8	24.0	12.7	12.0	13.3
1990	23.2	23.7	22.8	24.2	24.2	24.3	13.4	15.1	11.9
1991	23.2	23.0	23.4	24.6	24.1	25.0	11.0	11.5	10.6
1992	23.6	23.2	24.0	25.0	24.2	25.7	11.3	12.0	10.6
1993	23.7	23.4	23.9	24.7	24.4	25.1	13.2	12.6	13.8
1994	23.3	22.5	24.0	24.2	23.6	24.8	13.7	11.7	15.4
1995	24.7	24.5	24.9	26.0	25.4	26.6	15.3	17.2	13.6
1996	27.1	26.1	28.2	28.1	27.2	29.1	14.6	12.4	16.4
1997	27.8	26.3	29.3	28.9	27.2	30.7	14.4	12.1	16.4
1998	27.3	25.6	29.0	28.4	26.5	30.4	15.8	14.2	17.0
1999	28.2	26.8	29.5	29.3	27.6	30.9	15.0	13.1	16.5
2000	29.1	27.9	30.1	29.6	27.8	31.3	17.5	18.1	17.0
2001	28.4	25.5	31.3	28.5	25.1	32.1	16.8	15.6	17.9
2002	29.3	26.9	31.8	29.7	26.5	33.1	17.5	17.4	17.7
2003	28.4	26.0	30.9	28.3	25.3	31.5	17.2	17.5	17.0
2004	28.7	26.1	31.4	28.9	25.8	32.1	16.9	13.4	19.7

Source: U.S. Census Bureau. 1947, and 1952 to 2002 March Current Population Survey; 2003 and 2004 Annual Social and Economic Supplement to the Current Population Survey (noninstitutionalized population, excluding members of the Armed Forces living in barracks); 1960 Census of Population, 1950 Census of Population, and 1940 Census of Population (resident population).

[1] Includes Black and other races from 1940 to 1962; from 1963 to 2003, data are for the Black population only.
. . . = Not available.

Table A7-8. Percent of Population 25 Years and Over Who Have Completed High School or College, by Race, Hispanic Origin, and Sex, Selected Years, 1940–2004 —Continued

(Percent.)

Year, age, and educational attainment level	Hispanic[2]			Non-Hispanic White			Non-Hispanic Black		
	Total	Male	Female	Total	Male	Female	Total	Male	Female
25 TO 29 YEARS									
Completed 4 Years of College or More									
1940	. . .	. . .	. . .	. . .	. . .	. . .	. . .	. . .	. . .
1947	. . .	. . .	. . .	. . .	. . .	. . .	. . .	. . .	. . .
1950	. . .	. . .	. . .	. . .	. . .	. . .	. . .	. . .	. . .
1952	. . .	. . .	. . .	. . .	. . .	. . .	. . .	. . .	. . .
1957	. . .	. . .	. . .	. . .	. . .	. . .	. . .	. . .	. . .
1959	. . .	. . .	. . .	. . .	. . .	. . .	. . .	. . .	. . .
1962	. . .	. . .	. . .	. . .	. . .	. . .	. . .	. . .	. . .
1964	. . .	. . .	. . .	. . .	. . .	. . .	. . .	. . .	. . .
1965	. . .	. . .	. . .	. . .	. . .	. . .	. . .	. . .	. . .
1966	. . .	. . .	. . .	. . .	. . .	. . .	. . .	. . .	. . .
1967	. . .	. . .	. . .	. . .	. . .	. . .	. . .	. . .	. . .
1968	. . .	. . .	. . .	. . .	. . .	. . .	. . .	. . .	. . .
1969	. . .	. . .	. . .	. . .	. . .	. . .	. . .	. . .	. . .
1970	. . .	. . .	. . .	. . .	. . .	. . .	. . .	. . .	. . .
1971	. . .	. . .	. . .	. . .	. . .	. . .	. . .	. . .	. . .
1972	. . .	. . .	. . .	. . .	. . .	. . .	. . .	. . .	. . .
1973	. . .	. . .	. . .	. . .	. . .	. . .	. . .	. . .	. . .
1974	5.7	7.2	4.6	. . .	. . .	. . .	. . .	. . .	. . .
1975	8.8	10.0	7.3	. . .	. . .	. . .	. . .	. . .	. . .
1976	7.4	10.3	4.8	. . .	. . .	. . .	. . .	. . .	. . .
1977	6.7	7.2	6.4	. . .	. . .	. . .	. . .	. . .	. . .
1978	9.6	9.6	9.7	. . .	. . .	. . .	. . .	. . .	. . .
1979	7.3	7.9	6.8	. . .	. . .	. . .	. . .	. . .	. . .
1980	7.7	8.4	6.9	. . .	. . .	. . .	. . .	. . .	. . .
1981	7.5	8.6	6.5	. . .	. . .	. . .	. . .	. . .	. . .
1982	9.7	10.7	8.7	. . .	. . .	. . .	. . .	. . .	. . .
1983	10.4	9.6	11.1	. . .	. . .	. . .	. . .	. . .	. . .
1984	10.6	9.6	11.6	. . .	. . .	. . .	. . .	. . .	. . .
1985	11.1	10.9	11.2	. . .	. . .	. . .	. . .	. . .	. . .
1986	9.0	8.9	9.1	. . .	. . .	. . .	. . .	. . .	. . .
1987	8.7	9.2	8.2	. . .	. . .	. . .	. . .	. . .	. . .
1988	11.4	12.1	10.6	. . .	. . .	. . .	. . .	. . .	. . .
1989	10.1	9.6	10.6	. . .	. . .	. . .	. . .	. . .	. . .
1990	8.1	7.3	9.1	. . .	. . .	. . .	. . .	. . .	. . .
1991	9.2	8.1	10.4	. . .	. . .	. . .	. . .	. . .	. . .
1992	9.5	8.8	10.3	. . .	. . .	. . .	. . .	. . .	. . .
1993	8.3	7.1	9.8	27.2	27.2	27.1	13.2	12.6	13.8
1994	8.0	6.6	9.8	27.1	26.8	27.4	13.7	11.7	15.4
1995	8.9	7.8	10.1	28.8	28.4	29.2	15.3	17.2	13.6
1996	10.0	10.2	9.8	31.6	30.9	32.3	14.6	12.4	16.4
1997	11.0	9.6	10.1	32.6	31.2	34.1	14.4	12.1	16.4
1998	10.4	9.5	11.3	32.3	30.5	34.2	15.8	14.2	17.0
1999	8.9	7.5	10.4	33.6	32.0	35.1	15.0	13.1	16.5
2000	9.7	8.3	11.0	34.0	32.3	35.8	17.8	18.4	17.4
2001	10.5	8.2	13.3	33.7	30.4	36.9	17.2	16.0	18.2
2002	8.9	8.3	9.7	35.9	32.6	39.2	18.0	17.9	18.1
2003	10.0	8.4	12.0	34.2	31.4	37.1	17.5	17.7	17.4
2004	10.9	9.6	12.4	34.5	31.4	37.5	17.1	13.6	20.0

Source: U.S. Census Bureau. 1947, and 1952 to 2002 March Current Population Survey; 2003 and 2004 Annual Social and Economic Supplement to the Current Population Survey (noninstitutionalized population, excluding members of the Armed Forces living in barracks); 1960 Census of Population, 1950 Census of Population, and 1940 Census of Population (resident population).

[2]May be of any race.
. . . = Not available.

Table A7-9. Mean Earnings of Workers 18 Years of Age and Over, by Educational Attainment, Race, Sex, and Hispanic Origin, 1975–2003

(Dollars, numbers in thousands.)

Sex and year	Total		Not a high school graduate		High school graduate		Some college/ associate degree		Bachelor's degree[1]		Advanced degree[1]	
	Mean earnings (dollars)	Number with earnings	Mean earnings (dollars)	Number with earnings	Mean earnings (dollars)	Number with earnings	Mean earnings (dollars)	Number with earnings	Mean earnings (dollars)	Number with earnings	Mean earnings (dollars)	Number with earnings
Both Sexes												
1975	8 552	97 881	6 198	24 916	7 843	39 827	8 388	16 917	12 332	9 764	16 725	6 457
1976	9 180	100 510	6 720	25 035	8 393	40 570	8 813	17 786	13 033	10 132	17 911	6 985
1977	9 887	103 119	7 066	24 854	9 013	41 696	9 607	18 905	14 207	10 357	19 077	7 309
1978	10 812	106 436	7 759	23 787	9 834	43 510	10 357	20 121	15 291	11 001	20 173	8 017
1979	11 795	110 826	8 420	23 783	10 624	45 497	11 377	21 174	16 514	11 751	21 874	8 621
1980	12 665	111 919	8 845	23 028	11 314	46 795	12 409	21 384	18 075	12 175	23 308	8 535
1981	13 624	113 301	9 357	22 296	12 109	47 332	13 176	21 759	19 006	12 579	25 281	9 336
1982	14 351	113 451	9 387	20 789	12 560	46 584	13 503	22 602	20 272	13 425	26 915	10 051
1983	15 137	115 095	9 853	20 020	13 044	47 560	14 245	23 208	21 532	13 929	28 333	10 377
1984	16 083	118 183	10 384	20 206	13 893	48 452	14 936	24 463	23 072	14 653	30 192	10 410
1985	17 181	120 651	10 726	19 692	14 457	49 674	16 349	25 402	24 877	15 373	32 909	10 510
1986	18 149	122 757	11 203	19 665	15 120	50 104	17 073	26 113	26 511	15 788	34 787	11 087
1987	19 016	124 874	11 824	19 748	15 939	50 815	18 054	26 404	26 919	16 497	35 968	11 411
1988	20 060	127 564	11 889	19 635	16 750	51 297	19 066	27 217	28 344	17 308	37 724	12 109
1989	21 414	129 094	12 242	19 137	17 594	51 846	20 255	28 078	30 736	17 767	41 019	12 265
1990	21 793	130 080	12 582	18 698	17 820	51 977	20 694	28 993	31 112	18 128	41 458	12 285
1991	22 332	130 371	12 613	17 553	18 261	46 508	20 551	35 732	31 323	20 475	46 039	10 103
1992	23 227	130 860	12 809	16 612	18 737	45 340	20 867	37 339	32 629	21 091	48 652	10 479
1993	24 674	133 119	12 820	16 575	19 422	44 779	21 539	39 429	35 121	21 815	55 789	10 521
1994	25 852	135 096	13 697	16 479	20 248	44 614	22 226	40 135	37 224	22 712	56 105	11 155
1995	26 792	136 221	14 013	16 990	21 431	44 546	23 862	40 142	36 980	23 285	56 667	11 258
1996	28 106	138 703	15 011	17 075	22 154	45 908	25 181	40 410	38 112	24 028	61 317	11 281
1997	29 514	140 367	16 124	16 962	22 895	45 976	26 235	40 802	40 478	25 035	63 229	11 591
1998	30 928	142 053	16 053	16 742	23 594	45 987	27 566	41 412	43 782	25 818	63 473	12 095
1999	32 356	144 640	16 121	16 737	24 572	46 082	28 403	42 860	45 678	26 215	67 697	12 749
2000[2]	34 514	147 966	17 738	17 425	25 692	45 977	29 939	43 874	49 595	27 488	71 194	13 200
2001	35 805	147 829	18 793	17 293	26 795	45 641	30 782	43 214	50 623	27 980	72 869	13 700
2002	36 308	148 492	18 826	16 931	27 280	45 407	31 046	43 776	51 194	28 257	72 824	14 119
2003[3]	37 046	148 660	18 734	16 282	27 915	45 064	31 498	44 048	51 206	28 672	74 602	14 592
Male												
1975	11 091	57 297	7 843	15 613	10 475	21 347	10 805	9 851	15 758	5 960	19 672	4 526
1976	11 923	58 419	8 522	15 634	11 189	21 499	11 376	10 282	16 714	6 135	21 202	4 868
1977	12 888	59 441	8 939	15 369	12 092	21 846	12 299	10 848	18 187	6 341	22 786	5 038
1978	14 154	60 586	9 894	14 550	13 188	22 650	13 382	11 352	19 861	6 611	24 274	5 422
1979	15 430	62 464	10 628	14 711	14 317	23 318	14 716	11 781	21 482	6 889	26 411	5 765
1980	16 382	62 825	11 042	14 273	15 002	24 023	15 871	11 663	23 340	7 132	27 846	5 733
1981	17 542	63 547	11 668	13 701	15 900	24 435	16 870	11 784	24 353	7 393	30 072	6 235
1982	18 244	63 489	11 513	12 868	16 160	24 059	17 108	12 103	25 758	7 865	32 109	6 594
1983	19 175	63 816	12 052	12 376	16 728	24 449	18 052	12 261	27 239	8 010	33 635	6 719
1984	20 452	65 005	12 775	12 325	18 016	24 827	18 863	12 818	29 203	8 387	35 804	6 648
1985	21 823	66 439	13 124	12 137	18 575	25 496	20 698	13 385	31 433	8 794	39 768	6 627
1986	23 057	67 189	13 703	12 208	19 453	25 562	21 784	13 502	33 376	8 908	41 836	7 009
1987	24 015	67 951	14 544	12 117	20 364	25 981	22 781	13 433	33 677	9 286	43 140	7 134
1988	25 344	69 006	14 551	11 993	21 481	26 080	23 827	14 019	35 906	9 466	45 677	7 449
1989	27 025	69 798	14 727	11 774	22 508	26 469	25 555	14 384	38 692	9 737	50 144	7 434
1990	27 164	70 218	14 991	11 412	22 378	26 753	26 120	14 844	38 901	9 807	49 768	7 402
1991	27 494	70 145	15 056	10 679	22 663	24 110	25 345	18 076	38 484	11 126	54 449	6 154
1992	28 448	70 409	14 934	10 335	22 978	23 610	25 660	18 768	40 039	11 353	58 324	6 344
1993	30 568	71 183	14 946	10 151	23 973	23 388	26 614	19 532	43 499	11 810	68 221	6 302
1994	32 087	72 246	16 633	9 981	25 038	23 418	27 636	19 859	46 278	12 324	67 032	6 663
1995	33 251	72 634	16 748	10 312	26 333	23 473	29 851	19 918	46 111	12 251	69 588	6 679
1996	34 705	73 955	17 826	10 583	27 642	23 966	31 426	20 208	46 702	12 562	74 406	6 636
1997	36 556	74 596	19 575	10 348	28 307	24 152	32 641	20 359	50 056	13 008	78 032	6 728
1998	38 134	75 213	19 155	10 085	28 742	24 155	34 179	20 545	55 057	13 486	77 217	6 942
1999	40 257	76 233	18 855	9 917	30 414	24 235	35 326	21 173	57 706	13 683	84 051	7 225
2000[2]	42 772	78 319	21 007	10 535	31 446	24 439	37 372	21 526	62 609	14 375	88 077	7 442
2001	43 648	78 342	21 508	10 572	32 363	24 239	37 429	21 390	63 354	14 507	90 130	7 631
2002	44 310	78 757	22 091	10 526	32 673	24 174	38 377	21 599	63 503	14 667	90 761	7 788
2003[3]	44 726	78 869	21 447	10 173	33 266	24 292	38 451	21 534	63 084	14 849	91 831	8 019

Source: U.S. Census Bureau. 1947, and 1952 to 2002 March Current Population Survey; 2003 and 2004 Annual Social and Economic Supplement to the Current Population Survey (noninstitutionalized population, excluding members of the Armed Forces living in barracks); 1960 Census of Population, 1950 Census of Population, and 1940 Census of Population (resident population).

[1] For data prior to 1991, some college/associate degree equals 1 to 3 years of college completed; a bachelor's degree equals 4 years of college completed; and an advanced degree equals 5 or more years of college completed.
[2] Beginning in 2000, earnings data are from the expanded CPS sample and were calculated using population controls based on the 2000 census.
[3] Starting in 2003, respondents could choose more than one race. The race data in this table from 2003 onward represent those respondents who indicated only one racial identity.

Table A7-9. Mean Earnings of Workers 18 Years of Age and Over, by Educational Attainment, Race, Sex, and Hispanic Origin, 1975–2003—*Continued*

(Dollars, numbers in thousands.)

Sex and year	Total		Not a high school graduate		High school graduate		Some college/ associate degree		Bachelor's degree[1]		Advanced degree[1]	
	Mean earnings (dollars)	Number with earnings	Mean earnings (dollars)	Number with earnings	Mean earnings (dollars)	Number with earnings	Mean earnings (dollars)	Number with earnings	Mean earnings (dollars)	Number with earnings	Mean earnings (dollars)	Number with earnings
Female												
1975	4 968	40 584	3 438	9 303	4 802	18 480	5 019	7 066	6 963	3 804	9 818	1 931
1976	5 373	42 091	3 723	9 401	5 240	19 071	5 301	7 504	7 383	3 997	10 345	2 117
1977	5 804	43 678	4 032	9 485	5 624	19 850	5 856	8 057	7 923	4 016	10 848	2 271
1978	6 396	45 850	4 397	9 237	6 192	20 860	6 441	8 769	8 408	4 390	11 603	2 595
1979	7 099	48 362	4 840	9 072	6 741	22 179	7 190	9 393	9 474	4 862	12 717	2 856
1980	7 909	49 094	5 263	8 755	7 423	22 772	8 256	9 721	10 628	5 043	14 022	2 802
1981	8 619	49 754	5 673	8 595	8 063	22 897	8 811	9 975	11 384	5 186	15 647	3 101
1982	9 403	49 962	5 932	7 921	8 715	22 525	9 348	10 499	12 511	5 560	17 009	3 457
1983	10 111	51 279	6 292	7 644	9 147	23 111	9 981	10 947	13 808	5 919	18 593	3 658
1984	10 742	53 178	6 644	7 881	9 561	23 625	10 614	11 645	14 865	6 266	20 275	3 762
1985	11 493	54 212	6 874	7 555	10 115	24 178	11 504	12 017	16 114	6 579	21 202	3 883
1986	12 214	55 568	7 109	7 457	10 606	24 542	12 029	12 611	17 623	6 880	22 672	4 078
1987	13 049	56 923	7 504	7 631	11 309	24 834	13 158	12 971	18 217	7 211	24 004	4 277
1988	13 833	58 558	7 711	7 642	11 857	25 217	14 009	13 198	19 216	7 842	25 010	4 660
1989	14 809	59 296	8 268	7 363	12 468	25 377	14 688	13 694	21 089	8 030	26 977	4 831
1990	15 493	59 862	8 808	7 286	12 986	25 224	15 002	14 149	21 933	8 321	28 862	4 883
1991	16 320	60 226	8 818	6 875	13 523	22 398	15 643	17 657	22 802	9 348	32 929	3 948
1992	17 145	60 451	9 311	6 277	14 128	21 730	16 023	18 571	23 991	9 738	33 814	4 135
1993	17 900	61 937	9 462	6 425	14 446	21 391	16 555	19 897	25 232	10 005	37 212	4 218
1994	18 684	62 850	9 189	6 498	14 955	21 195	16 928	20 276	26 483	10 388	39 905	4 493
1995	19 414	63 587	9 790	6 678	15 970	21 073	17 962	20 224	26 841	11 034	37 813	4 578
1996	20 570	64 748	10 421	6 492	16 161	21 942	18 933	20 202	28 701	11 466	42 625	4 646
1997	21 528	65 771	10 725	6 614	16 906	21 824	19 856	20 442	30 119	12 027	42 744	4 863
1998	22 818	66 840	11 353	6 657	17 898	21 832	21 056	20 867	31 452	12 332	44 954	5 153
1999	23 551	68 409	12 145	6 819	18 092	21 847	21 644	22 687	32 546	12 533	46 307	5 523
2000[2]	25 228	69 647	12 739	6 890	19 162	21 538	22 779	22 348	35 328	13 113	49 368	5 757
2001	26 962	69 487	14 524	6 720	20 489	21 402	24 268	21 824	36 913	13 472	51 160	6 068
2002	27 271	69 735	13 459	6 404	21 141	21 233	23 905	22 176	37 909	13 589	50 756	6 330
2003[3]	28 367	69 790	14 214	6 108	21 659	20 772	24 848	22 514	38 447	13 823	53 579	6 572

Source: U.S. Census Bureau. 1947, and 1952 to 2002 March Current Population Survey; 2003 and 2004 Annual Social and Economic Supplement to the Current Population Survey (noninstitutionalized population, excluding members of the Armed Forces living in barracks); 1960 Census of Population, 1950 Census of Population, and 1940 Census of Population (resident population).

[1]For data prior to 1991, some college/associate degree equals 1 to 3 years of college completed; a bachelor's degree equals 4 years of college completed; and an advanced degree equals 5 or more years of college completed.
[2]Beginning in 2000, earnings data are from the expanded CPS sample and were calculated using population controls based on the 2000 census.
[3]Starting in 2003, respondents could choose more than one race. The race data in this table from 2003 onward represent those respondents who indicated only one racial identity.

Table A7-9. Mean Earnings of Workers 18 Years of Age and Over, by Educational Attainment, Race, Sex, and Hispanic Origin, 1975–2003—*Continued*

(Dollars, numbers in thousands.)

Sex and year	Total		Not a high school graduate		High school graduate		Some college/ associate degree		Bachelor's degree[1]		Advanced degree[1]	
	Mean earnings (dollars)	Number with earnings	Mean earnings (dollars)	Number with earnings	Mean earnings (dollars)	Number with earnings	Mean earnings (dollars)	Number with earnings	Mean earnings (dollars)	Number with earnings	Mean earnings (dollars)	Number with earnings
WHITE												
Both Sexes												
1975	8 815	86 894	6 438	20 696	8 005	35 799	8 525	15 423	12 597	8 955	16 920	6 021
1976	9 469	89 099	7 018	20 625	8 559	36 523	8 958	16 127	13 279	9 325	18 153	6 498
1977	10 191	91 254	7 415	20 492	9 173	37 521	9 771	16 968	14 462	9 534	19 337	6 739
1978	11 135	94 002	8 135	19 516	10 020	38 915	10 504	18 022	15 463	10 171	20 531	7 376
1979	12 155	97 544	8 827	19 504	10 431	40 458	11 574	18 835	16 758	10 807	22 085	7 940
1980	13 040	98 358	9 743	18 925	11 524	41 600	12 677	18 888	18 434	11 067	23 466	7 876
1981	14 027	99 510	9 737	18 298	12 355	42 080	13 424	19 102	19 389	11 450	25 564	8 582
1982	14 767	99 488	9 719	17 132	12 854	41 157	13 799	19 967	20 760	12 103	27 040	9 127
1983	15 556	101 035	10 239	16 568	13 357	42 007	14 486	20 452	21 914	12 577	28 532	9 430
1984	16 546	103 022	10 732	16 559	14 274	42 547	15 197	21 451	23 472	13 056	30 515	9 409
1985	17 709	104 818	11 115	16 149	14 815	43 347	16 701	22 131	25 376	13 670	33 401	9 522
1986	18 698	106 384	11 605	16 094	15 514	43 593	17 371	22 653	27 061	14 055	35 265	9 987
1987	19 599	108 407	12 502	16 165	16 339	44 235	18 265	23 083	27 741	14 624	36 175	10 300
1988	20 616	110 159	12 236	16 042	17 183	44 399	19 384	23 643	28 886	15 221	38 129	10 854
1989	22 035	111 243	12 654	15 628	18 011	44 726	20 678	24 212	31 266	15 723	41 610	10 952
1990	22 401	111 972	12 773	15 191	18 257	44 635	21 095	25 105	31 626	15 993	41 908	11 049
1991	22 998	111 830	12 914	14 041	18 766	39 764	21 013	30 973	31 837	18 033	46 498	9 019
1992	23 932	112 120	13 193	13 494	19 265	38 692	21 357	32 014	33 092	18 555	49 347	9 363
1993	25 440	113 342	13 171	13 480	19 918	37 826	21 924	33 728	35 846	18 922	56 964	9 386
1994	26 696	114 586	13 941	13 119	20 911	37 562	22 648	34 006	37 996	19 917	56 475	9 981
1995	27 556	115 636	14 234	13 869	22 154	37 802	24 349	33 850	37 711	20 203	57 054	9 914
1996	28 844	117 230	15 358	13 972	22 782	38 463	25 511	34 087	38 936	20 846	61 779	9 861
1997	30 515	117 985	16 596	13 780	23 618	38 409	26 906	34 274	41 439	21 528	65 058	9 994
1998	32 057	119 201	16 474	13 531	24 409	38 397	28 318	34 540	44 852	22 266	65 379	10 467
1999	33 326	120 916	16 623	13 585	25 270	38 428	29 105	35 634	46 894	22 322	68 910	10 949
2000[2]	35 527	123 039	18 285	14 172	26 444	38 133	30 638	36 334	50 969	23 110	71 983	11 288
2001	36 844	122 930	19 120	14 012	27 700	37 969	31 482	35 722	51 631	23 531	74 398	11 694
2002	37 376	122 699	19 264	13 740	28 145	37 380	31 878	36 023	52 479	23 638	73 870	11 916
2003[3]	38 053	122 599	19 110	13 094	28 708	36 951	32 346	36 318	52 259	24 010	75 638	12 226

Source: U.S. Census Bureau. 1947, and 1952 to 2002 March Current Population Survey; 2003 and 2004 Annual Social and Economic Supplement to the Current Population Survey (noninstitutionalized population, excluding members of the Armed Forces living in barracks); 1960 Census of Population, 1950 Census of Population, and 1940 Census of Population (resident population).

[1]For data prior to 1991, some college/associate degree equals 1 to 3 years of college completed; a bachelor's degree equals 4 years of college completed; and an advanced degree equals 5 or more years of college completed.
[2]Beginning in 2000, earnings data are from the expanded CPS sample and were calculated using population controls based on the 2000 census.
[3]Starting in 2003, respondents could choose more than one race. The race data in this table from 2003 onward represent those respondents who indicated only one racial identity.

Table A7-9. Mean Earnings of Workers 18 Years of Age and Over, by Educational Attainment, Race, Sex, and Hispanic Origin, 1975–2003—Continued

(Dollars, numbers in thousands.)

Sex and year	Total Mean earnings (dollars)	Total Number with earnings	Not a high school graduate Mean earnings (dollars)	Not a high school graduate Number with earnings	High school graduate Mean earnings (dollars)	High school graduate Number with earnings	Some college/associate degree Mean earnings (dollars)	Some college/associate degree Number with earnings	Bachelor's degree[1] Mean earnings (dollars)	Bachelor's degree[1] Number with earnings	Advanced degree[1] Mean earnings (dollars)	Advanced degree[1] Number with earnings
WHITE												
Male												
1975	11 448	51 510	8 110	13 191	10 726	19 361	11 028	9 096	16 079	5 587	19 858	4 275
1976	12 342	52 312	8 867	13 117	11 497	19 446	11 616	9 394	16 995	5 765	21 490	4 589
1977	13 329	53 174	9 366	12 903	12 377	19 773	12 657	9 853	18 521	5 941	23 093	4 704
1978	14 627	54 113	10 358	12 141	13 534	20 328	13 589	10 350	20 085	6 205	24 635	5 088
1979	15 971	55 556	11 127	12 291	13 916	20 834	15 043	10 572	21 785	6 464	26 645	5 395
1980	16 945	55 772	11 539	11 937	15 382	21 453	16 313	10 400	23 803	6 618	27 991	5 363
1981	18 141	56 397	12 094	11 523	16 352	21 809	17 303	10 448	24 943	6 824	30 396	5 794
1982	18 859	56 364	11 952	10 816	16 662	21 436	17 571	10 822	26 404	7 242	32 266	6 047
1983	19 812	56 641	12 573	10 387	17 281	21 733	18 388	10 974	27 726	7 379	33 981	6 168
1984	21 174	57 362	13 248	10 280	18 681	21 989	19 344	11 387	29 781	7 624	36 219	6 081
1985	22 604	58 385	13 579	10 163	19 203	22 357	21 240	11 831	32 165	7 970	40 358	6 064
1986	23 892	58 932	14 168	10 239	20 128	22 392	22 303	11 846	34 273	8 041	42 480	6 413
1987	24 898	59 468	15 303	10 132	21 012	22 682	23 310	11 771	34 865	8 384	43 440	6 499
1988	26 184	60 221	14 943	10 008	22 216	22 707	24 462	12 277	36 637	8 467	46 181	6 762
1989	28 013	60 877	15 217	9 805	23 291	23 029	26 260	12 582	39 654	8 750	51 031	6 710
1990	28 105	60 676	15 319	9 476	23 135	23 088	26 841	13 003	39 780	8 770	50 385	6 731
1991	28 516	60 770	15 499	8 720	23 475	20 765	26 090	15 873	39 547	9 893	55 257	5 519
1992	29 515	60 919	15 414	8 487	23 844	20 259	26 387	16 335	40 893	10 118	59 329	5 720
1993	31 719	61 356	15 295	8 430	24 781	19 835	27 297	16 959	44 505	10 452	70 000	5 680
1994	33 292	62 029	16 835	8 133	26 125	19 833	28 240	17 091	47 575	10 992	67 629	5 979
1995	34 276	62 520	17 032	8 660	27 467	19 982	30 529	17 136	47 016	10 851	70 155	5 891
1996	35 821	63 532	18 246	8 899	28 591	20 329	32 238	17 418	48 014	11 065	75 481	5 821
1997	37 933	63 738	20 071	8 670	29 298	20 426	33 691	17 423	51 678	11 340	80 322	5 879
1998	39 638	64 181	19 632	8 430	29 782	20 388	35 277	17 407	56 620	11 874	79 734	6 083
1999	41 598	64 856	19 320	8 286	31 279	20 526	36 518	17 928	59 606	11 851	85 345	6 265
2000[2]	44 181	66 222	21 561	8 859	32 528	20 553	38 476	18 179	64 831	12 271	89 812	6 359
2001	45 071	66 216	22 006	8 833	33 545	20 465	38 501	17 957	65 046	12 396	92 304	6 562
2002	45 793	66 202	22 539	8 841	33 920	20 156	39 605	18 068	65 439	12 512	92 733	6 623
2003[3]	46 114	66 199	21 791	8 500	34 224	20 238	39 594	18 060	65 264	12 665	94 017	6 734
Female												
1975	4 982	35 384	3 500	7 505	4 800	16 438	4 926	6 327	6 822	3 368	9 728	1 746
1976	5 383	36 787	3 788	7 508	5 214	17 077	5 250	6 733	7 262	3 560	10 131	1 909
1977	5 808	38 080	4 097	7 589	5 604	17 748	5 774	7 115	7 750	3 593	10 655	2 035
1978	6 398	39 889	4 476	7 375	6 176	18 587	6 342	7 672	8 231	3 966	11 404	2 288
1979	7 105	41 988	4 909	7 213	6 731	19 624	7 135	8 263	9 275	4 343	12 420	2 545
1980	7 926	42 586	6 675	6 988	7 415	20 147	8 221	8 488	10 447	4 449	13 809	2 513
1981	8 646	43 113	5 727	6 775	8 054	20 271	8 740	8 654	11 196	4 626	15 523	2 788
1982	9 419	43 124	5 896	6 316	8 714	19 721	9 336	9 145	12 352	4 861	16 779	3 080
1983	10 126	44 394	6 317	6 181	9 150	20 274	9 969	9 478	13 664	5 198	18 230	3 262
1984	10 732	45 660	6 614	6 279	9 561	20 558	10 504	10 064	14 617	5 432	20 092	3 328
1985	11 555	46 433	6 931	5 986	10 142	20 990	11 488	10 300	15 883	5 700	21 202	3 458
1986	12 247	47 452	7 123	5 855	10 641	21 201	11 964	10 807	17 418	6 014	22 320	3 574
1987	13 161	48 939	7 798	6 033	11 421	21 553	13 015	11 312	18 170	6 240	23 753	3 801
1988	13 902	49 938	7 747	6 034	11 915	21 692	13 898	11 366	19 169	6 754	24 824	4 092
1989	14 810	50 366	8 338	5 823	12 406	21 697	14 640	11 630	20 741	6 973	26 709	4 242
1990	15 559	50 905	8 725	5 715	13 031	21 547	14 922	12 102	21 725	7 223	28 694	4 318
1991	16 431	51 060	8 677	5 321	13 621	18 999	15 677	15 100	22 471	8 140	32 687	3 500
1992	17 289	51 200	9 428	5 007	14 233	18 434	16 116	15 679	23 738	8 437	33 675	3 643
1993	18 028	51 986	9 624	5 050	14 557	17 991	16 490	16 769	25 161	8 470	36 988	3 705
1994	18 912	52 557	9 220	4 987	15 078	17 729	16 998	16 915	26 198	8 925	39 816	4 002
1995	19 647	53 117	9 582	5 208	16 196	17 820	18 011	16 714	26 916	9 352	37 864	4 022
1996	20 590	53 697	10 290	5 073	16 270	18 134	18 482	16 669	28 667	9 781	42 049	4 041
1997	21 779	54 247	10 700	5 111	17 166	17 983	19 892	16 852	30 041	10 188	43 236	4 114
1998	23 213	55 020	11 255	5 102	18 327	18 009	21 246	17 132	31 406	10 393	45 462	4 384
1999	23 756	56 061	12 405	5 299	18 381	17 902	21 598	17 705	32 507	10 471	45 741	4 684
2000[2]	25 441	56 816	12 823	5 313	19 330	17 579	22 790	18 155	35 273	10 838	48 982	4 929
2001	27 240	56 714	14 197	5 178	20 866	17 503	24 387	17 764	36 698	11 135	51 499	5 131
2002	27 512	56 496	13 354	4 898	21 388	17 224	24 101	17 954	37 903	11 126	50 270	5 293
2003[3]	28 591	56 400	14 149	4 593	22 028	16 712	25 177	18 258	37 739	11 344	53 102	5 492

Source: U.S. Census Bureau. 1947, and 1952 to 2002 March Current Population Survey; 2003 and 2004 Annual Social and Economic Supplement to the Current Population Survey (noninstitutionalized population, excluding members of the Armed Forces living in barracks); 1960 Census of Population, 1950 Census of Population, and 1940 Census of Population (resident population).

[1]For data prior to 1991, some college/associate degree equals 1 to 3 years of college completed; a bachelor's degree equals 4 years of college completed; and an advanced degree equals 5 or more years of college completed.
[2]Beginning in 2000, earnings data are from the expanded CPS sample and were calculated using population controls based on the 2000 census.
[3]Starting in 2003, respondents could choose more than one race. The race data in this table from 2003 onward represent those respondents who indicated only one racial identity.

Table A7-9. Mean Earnings of Workers 18 Years of Age and Over, by Educational Attainment, Race, Sex, and Hispanic Origin, 1975–2003—*Continued*

(Dollars, numbers in thousands.)

Sex and year	Total Mean earnings (dollars)	Total Number with earnings	Not a high school graduate Mean earnings (dollars)	Not a high school graduate Number with earnings	High school graduate Mean earnings (dollars)	High school graduate Number with earnings	Some college/ associate degree Mean earnings (dollars)	Some college/ associate degree Number with earnings	Bachelor's degree[1] Mean earnings (dollars)	Bachelor's degree[1] Number with earnings	Advanced degree[1] Mean earnings (dollars)	Advanced degree[1] Number with earnings
BLACK												
Both Sexes												
1975	6 190	9 368	4 989	3 922	6 281	3 495	7 212	1 193	9 473	517	12 333	241
1976	6 716	9 744	5 304	4 008	6 805	3 515	7 331	1 370	10 331	547	15 013	305
1977	7 271	10 014	5 406	3 946	7 553	3 604	8 321	1 578	11 088	532	14 749	354
1978	7 981	10 420	5 918	3 841	8 152	3 944	9 026	1 689	12 870	557	15 076	389
1979	8 720	10 856	6 424	3 776	8 723	4 267	9 895	1 826	13 473	622	18 182	366
1980	11 085	5 576	8 421	2 054	11 563	2 119	12 393	964	15 616	283	19 960	353
1981	10 117	11 088	7 520	3 514	9 994	4 388	11 456	2 078	14 587	708	19 463	398
1982	10 612	11 081	7 799	3 188	10 287	4 591	11 119	2 067	15 152	747	22 959	488
1983	11 299	11 296	7 867	3 035	10 557	4 692	12 426	2 206	17 207	828	23 506	535
1984	12 002	11 948	8 725	3 127	10 882	4 927	12 890	2 396	19 330	937	24 072	561
1985	12 926	12 427	9 116	3 009	11 791	5 223	13 805	2 615	20 533	1 046	26 246	535
1986	13 494	12 729	9 365	3 028	12 276	5 470	14 743	2 662	21 403	1 004	27 503	564
1987	14 136	13 023	9 976	3 015	12 862	5 699	15 491	2 617	20 805	1 097	29 163	596
1988	15 318	13 356	10 202	2 970	13 835	5 760	16 760	2 802	23 689	1 204	30 802	621
1989	16 072	13 600	10 066	2 883	14 613	5 894	17 385	3 008	25 357	1 121	32 740	694
1990	16 627	13 731	11 184	2 853	14 794	6 049	18 209	3 004	26 448	1 217	32 962	607
1991	16 809	13 865	11 248	2 860	15 060	5 512	17 850	3 581	25 630	1 383	38 002	528
1992	17 416	13 836	11 077	2 451	15 260	5 379	18 719	4 054	27 457	1 429	41 439	523
1993	18 614	14 315	11 065	2 352	16 122	5 521	18 867	4 279	29 953	1 638	41 221	525
1994	19 772	14 754	12 705	2 290	16 446	5 596	19 631	4 610	30 938	1 679	48 653	579
1995	20 537	14 847	12 956	2 389	17 072	5 453	21 824	4 727	29 666	1 684	46 654	595
1996	21 978	15 255	13 110	2 383	18 722	5 844	23 628	4 783	31 955	1 655	48 731	590
1997	21 909	15 873	13 185	2 437	18 980	5 964	22 899	4 902	32 062	1 846	42 791	724
1998	22 829	16 201	13 672	2 402	19 236	6 053	23 927	4 559	36 373	1 897	44 760	764
1999	24 979	16 936	13 569	2 393	20 991	6 112	25 176	5 417	37 422	2 140	52 437	873
2000[2]	26 204	16 756	15 201	2 434	21 789	6 020	26 324	5 431	41 513	2 060	52 373	809
2001	27 031	16 683	17 248	2 382	21 743	5 729	26 907	5 481	40 165	2 212	55 771	877
2002	28 179	16 352	16 516	2 148	22 823	5 822	27 626	5 255	42 285	2 275	59 944	851
2003[3]	28 838	16 389	16 201	2 095	23 777	5 941	27 187	5 119	42 968	2 321	64 164	911
Male												
1975	7 541	4 864	6 364	2 247	7 847	1 684	8 505	599	11 318	213	13 720	121
1976	7 991	5 156	6 670	2 289	8 056	1 766	8 688	726	12 246	233	17 859	143
1977	8 710	5 220	6 648	2 230	9 332	1 770	10 023	799	12 978	234	16 385	188
1978	9 651	5 350	7 423	2 156	9 869	1 982	11 197	770	16 009	260	18 083	181
1979	10 403	5 581	7 938	2 138	10 662	2 087	11 971	931	16 161	259	21 092	166
1980	11 085	5 576	8 421	2 054	11 563	2 119	12 393	964	15 616	283	23 346	156
1981	11 937	5 651	9 266	1 925	11 905	2 191	13 740	1 002	16 624	327	21 082	205
1982	12 203	5 535	9 153	1 798	11 952	2 213	12 926	953	17 658	319	26 452	253
1983	12 789	5 707	9 094	1 768	11 956	2 312	15 113	996	20 370	363	25 466	268
1984	13 560	5 899	10 216	1 780	12 382	2 339	14 960	1 106	21 986	424	27 893	250
1985	14 932	6 237	10 802	1 716	13 721	2 572	16 415	1 230	23 818	477	31 947	243
1986	15 441	6 326	11 248	1 691	14 214	2 666	17 419	1 226	23 412	480	31 054	263
1987	16 171	6 505	11 899	1 711	14 800	2 769	18 081	1 250	23 345	482	34 073	294
1988	17 782	6 593	12 439	1 671	16 345	2 795	19 265	1 311	28 506	533	36 452	283
1989	18 108	6 654	11 827	1 614	16 658	2 848	20 253	1 352	27 493	515	38 166	326
1990	18 859	6 781	13 031	1 563	17 046	3 013	21 152	1 372	29 471	564	39 104	269
1991	18 607	6 830	15 714	1 624	17 352	2 731	20 548	1 570	26 075	650	43 927	255
1992	19 278	6 822	12 661	1 457	16 978	2 683	22 697	1 796	30 989	643	48 968	244
1993	21 108	6 833	13 074	1 305	18 668	2 775	21 734	1 804	35 147	721	47 372	228
1994	22 614	7 009	15 984	1 191	18 527	2 818	23 748	1 959	34 073	758	52 829	281
1995	23 876	7 090	14 877	1 280	19 514	2 812	26 846	2 047	36 026	659	57 186	293
1996	25 067	7 125	15 461	1 290	22 267	2 836	26 365	2 047	35 558	700	65 981	253
1997	25 080	7 370	15 423	1 304	22 440	2 862	27 215	2 108	35 792	818	49 940	278
1998	26 090	7 488	16 013	1 190	22 698	2 974	26 586	2 215	42 539	792	51 198	318
1999	28 821	7 806	16 391	1 199	25 849	2 934	28 442	2 338	42 530	971	59 587	365
2000[2]	30 109	7 700	17 992	1 235	25 219	2 942	30 966	2 291	49 270	880	60 207	349
2001	30 502	7 727	18 543	1 210	25 037	2 759	31 084	2 457	46 511	943	67 007	356
2002	31 790	7 483	19 294	1 072	25 582	2 832	32 764	2 283	47 018	974	75 050	321
2003[3]	32 545	7 469	17 915	1 039	28 102	2 910	31 556	2 156	45 635	966	76 871	397

Source: U.S. Census Bureau. 1947, and 1952 to 2002 March Current Population Survey; 2003 and 2004 Annual Social and Economic Supplement to the Current Population Survey (noninstitutionalized population, excluding members of the Armed Forces living in barracks); 1960 Census of Population, 1950 Census of Population, and 1940 Census of Population (resident population).

[1]For data prior to 1991, some college/associate degree equals 1 to 3 years of college completed; a bachelor's degree equals 4 years of college completed; and an advanced degree equals 5 or more years of college completed.
[2]Beginning in 2000, earnings data are from the expanded CPS sample and were calculated using population controls based on the 2000 census.
[3]Starting in 2003, respondents could choose more than one race. The race data in this table from 2003 onward represent those respondents who indicated only one racial identity.

Table A7-9. Mean Earnings of Workers 18 Years of Age and Over, by Educational Attainment, Race, Sex, and Hispanic Origin, 1975–2003—*Continued*

(Dollars, numbers in thousands.)

Sex and year	Total		Not a high school graduate		High school graduate		Some college/ associate degree		Bachelor's degree[1]		Advanced degree[1]	
	Mean earnings (dollars)	Number with earnings	Mean earnings (dollars)	Number with earnings	Mean earnings (dollars)	Number with earnings	Mean earnings (dollars)	Number with earnings	Mean earnings (dollars)	Number with earnings	Mean earnings (dollars)	Number with earnings
BLACK												
Female												
1979	6 940	5 275	4 448	1 638	6 866	2 180	7 735	895	11 555	363	15 766	200
1980	7 684	...	4 685	...	7 508	...	8 544	...	12 389	...	17 278	...
1981	8 225	5 437	5 404	1 589	8 088	2 197	9 329	1 076	12 839	381	17 743	193
1982	9 024	5 546	6 047	1 390	8 737	2 378	9 574	1 114	13 284	428	19 198	235
1983	9 778	5 589	6 154	1 267	9 197	2 380	10 215	1 210	14 738	465	21 539	267
1984	10 482	6 049	6 754	1 347	9 527	2 588	11 115	1 290	17 134	513	21 000	311
1985	10 904	6 190	6 879	1 293	9 918	2 651	11 488	1 385	17 779	569	21 502	292
1986	11 571	6 403	6 984	1 337	10 434	2 804	12 459	1 436	19 562	524	24 400	301
1987	12 106	6 518	7 452	1 304	11 030	2 930	13 123	1 367	18 815	615	24 383	302
1988	12 916	6 763	7 325	1 299	11 469	2 965	14 557	1 491	19 862	671	26 072	338
1989	14 122	6 946	7 827	1 269	12 701	3 046	15 044	1 656	23 541	606	27 933	368
1990	14 449	6 950	8 946	1 290	12 560	3 036	15 734	1 632	23 837	653	28 074	338
1991	15 065	7 034	9 151	1 237	12 810	2 781	15 743	2 010	25 235	733	32 467	273
1992	15 605	7 014	8 756	995	13 550	2 696	15 553	2 256	24 572	786	34 902	281
1993	16 336	7 481	8 562	1 048	13 550	2 746	16 778	2 475	25 865	917	36 485	296
1994	17 200	7 745	9 150	1 099	14 333	2 777	16 589	2 651	28 356	921	44 618	297
1995	17 485	7 757	10 739	1 108	14 473	2 641	17 985	2 679	25 577	1 025	36 585	304
1996	19 271	8 129	10 337	1 094	15 379	3 008	21 581	2 736	29 311	954	35 785	337
1997	19 161	8 503	10 607	1 132	15 789	3 102	19 643	2 794	29 091	1 027	38 392	448
1998	20 026	8 713	11 372	1 212	15 892	3 078	20 371	2 870	31 952	1 105	40 214	448
1999	21 694	9 130	10 734	1 194	16 506	3 178	22 699	3 080	33 184	1 170	47 358	509
2000[2]	22 884	9 056	12 321	1 198	18 510	3 078	22 937	3 140	35 719	1 179	46 416	459
2001	24 036	8 956	15 912	1 172	18 683	2 970	23 511	3 023	35 448	1 269	48 080	521
2002	25 131	8 868	13 748	1 075	20 209	2 989	23 679	2 972	38 741	1 301	50 766	529
2003[3]	25 735	8 919	14 513	1 056	19 623	3 030	24 007	2 963	41 066	1 355	54 346	514
NON-HISPANIC WHITE												
Both Sexes												
1998	33 336	105 523	16 837	8 488	24 801	34 344	23 897	31 459	45 342	21 175	65 461	10 059
1999	34 838	106 573	16 957	8 219	25 847	34 121	29 557	32 454	47 401	21 272	68 910	10 507
2000[2]	37 346	106 709	19 147	7 957	27 122	33 231	31 217	32 836	51 351	21 824	72 356	10 859
2001	38 711	106 384	19 659	7 812	28 426	33 050	31 905	32 118	52 300	22 204	74 932	11 198
2002	39 220	105 706	19 423	7 380	28 756	32 365	32 318	32 344	53 185	22 221	74 122	11 395
2003[3]	40 094	105 214	19 769	6 768	29 571	31 831	32 825	32 460	52 856	22 474	76 200	11 680
Male												
1998	41 612	56 246	20 781	5 152	30 429	18 048	29 555	15 849	57 346	11 335	79 524	5 862
1999	44 032	56 575	20 256	4 842	32 321	18 047	37 224	16 343	60 384	11 307	85 918	6 036
2000[2]	47 084	56 675	23 296	4 763	33 669	17 733	39 379	16 435	65 459	11 594	90 150	6 149
2001	47 973	56 528	23 096	4 749	34 627	17 672	39 133	16 114	66 196	11 692	92 954	6 299
2002	48 817	55 994	23 250	4 580	34 909	17 218	40 368	16 121	66 638	11 764	93 686	6 309
2003[3]	49 386	55 774	22 957	4 224	35 589	17 225	40 316	16 048	66 390	11 849	95 029	6 427
Female												
1998	23 891	49 277	10 746	3 336	18 568	16 295	18 198	15 610	31 516	9 840	45 805	4 196
1999	24 436	49 998	12 227	3 378	18 579	16 074	21 779	16 112	32 667	9 964	45 943	4 470
2000[2]	26 315	50 034	12 962	3 194	19 631	15 498	23 038	16 401	35 362	10 230	49 126	4 710
2001	28 210	49 856	14 328	3 062	21 301	15 378	24 628	16 004	36 844	10 512	51 756	4 898
2002	28 410	49 712	13 163	2 800	21 762	15 146	24 318	16 222	38 049	10 457	49 845	5 085
2003[3]	29 613	49 439	14 475	2 543	22 473	14 605	25 499	16 411	37 761	10 624	53 164	5 253
NON-HISPANIC BLACK												
Both Sexes												
1998	22 887	15 793	13 473	2 252	19 225	5 964	28 753	4 964	36 543	1 861	44 939	753
1999	25 066	16 423	13 441	2 241	20 979	5 942	25 190	5 290	37 531	2 100	52 746	849
2000[2]	26 165	16 227	15 041	2 304	21 734	5 854	26 450	5 285	41 072	1 991	51 859	792
2001	27 171	16 079	17 465	2 190	21 750	5 521	26 957	5 348	39 999	2 153	55 720	864

Source: U.S. Census Bureau. 1947, and 1952 to 2002 March Current Population Survey; 2003 and 2004 Annual Social and Economic Supplement to the Current Population Survey (noninstitutionalized population, excluding members of the Armed Forces living in barracks); 1960 Census of Population, 1950 Census of Population, and 1940 Census of Population (resident population).

[1]For data prior to 1991, some college/associate degree equals 1 to 3 years of college completed; a bachelor's degree equals 4 years of college completed; and an advanced degree equals 5 or more years of college completed.
[2]Beginning in 2000, earnings data are from the expanded CPS sample and were calculated using population controls based on the 2000 census.
[3]Starting in 2003, respondents could choose more than one race. The race data in this table from 2003 onward represent those respondents who indicated only one racial identity.
... = Not available.

Table A7-9. Mean Earnings of Workers 18 Years of Age and Over, by Educational Attainment, Race, Sex, and Hispanic Origin, 1975–2003—*Continued*

(Dollars, numbers in thousands.)

Sex and year	Total Mean earnings (dollars)	Total Number with earnings	Not a high school graduate Mean earnings (dollars)	Not a high school graduate Number with earnings	High school graduate Mean earnings (dollars)	High school graduate Number with earnings	Some college/ associate degree Mean earnings (dollars)	Some college/ associate degree Number with earnings	Bachelor's degree[1] Mean earnings (dollars)	Bachelor's degree[1] Number with earnings	Advanced degree[1] Mean earnings (dollars)	Advanced degree[1] Number with earnings
NON- HISPANIC BLACK												
Male												
1998	26 142	7 289	15 768	1 099	22 658	2 930	35 841	2 168	42 745	779	51 523	313
1999	28 959	7 542	16 288	1 111	25 853	2 850	28 404	2 277	42 572	954	61 078	350
2000[2]	29 979	7 427	17 835	1 151	25 131	2 859	31 120	2 219	47 746	853	59 504	343
2001	30 816	7 392	18 728	1 093	25 070	2 645	31 234	2 388	46 761	914	67 317	351
Female												
1998	20 097	8 504	11 283	1 153	15 910	3 034	33 330	2 795	32 076	1 082	40 275	440
1999	21 761	8 881	10 640	1 130	16 488	3 093	22 762	3 014	33 332	1 146	46 969	500
2000[2]	22 945	8 800	12 252	1 153	18 490	2 994	23 069	3 065	36 067	1 138	46 009	449
2001	24 068	8 686	16 206	1 096	18 697	2 875	23 507	2 960	35 014	1 239	47 769	513
HISPANIC OR LATINO[4]												
Both Sexes												
1975	6 567	4 078	5 462	2 028	6 759	1 293	7 154	474	10 573	173	15 756	111
1976	7 081	4 303	5 984	2 107	7 580	1 309	7 252	592	11 242	177	14 000	118
1977	7 761	4 752	6 547	2 306	8 079	1 461	8 172	656	12 572	210	16 660	118
1978	8 460	4 898	7 138	2 345	8 512	1 554	9 575	661	13 985	213	17 333	125
1979	9 248	5 545	7 683	2 533	9 338	1 812	10 181	768	14 940	240	18 273	190
1980	10 062	5 723	8 119	2 649	10 182	1 824	11 891	808	15 676	283	21 910	157
1981	10 872	5 930	8 645	2 648	11 046	1 966	12 971	834	16 114	320	24 082	161
1982	11 307	5 914	8 498	2 583	11 539	1 967	13 108	873	18 186	303	28 167	186
1983	11 901	6 222	9 473	2 674	12 077	2 030	13 371	976	17 972	320	24 352	222
1984	12 583	7 349	9 671	3 129	12 858	2 457	14 359	1 116	19 924	381	26 327	265
1985	13 120	7 840	9 956	3 223	13 044	2 661	15 318	1 226	20 878	458	28 357	273
1986	13 558	8 393	9 896	3 379	13 389	2 835	16 523	1 411	22 707	471	28 316	295
1987	14 695	8 817	10 961	3 457	13 958	2 982	16 899	1 400	23 105	644	34 413	335
1988	15 007	9 226	11 045	3 824	14 667	2 953	18 101	1 511	23 745	596	33 843	340
1989	15 714	9 570	11 500	3 985	14 901	3 188	18 707	1 513	28 157	535	39 273	349
1990	15 943	9 729	10 368	3 929	15 417	3 282	19 206	1 534	25 703	601	38 075	382
1991	16 300	10 006	11 335	3 906	16 142	3 045	19 123	2 080	26 623	665	40 154	311
1992	16 824	10 171	11 836	3 962	16 714	2 991	19 778	2 242	28 260	702	46 736	274
1993	17 102	11 644	11 852	4 425	16 591	3 367	19 043	2 728	30 359	799	45 034	325
1994	18 568	12 035	13 733	4 686	17 323	3 444	21 041	2 723	29 165	844	51 898	337
1995	18 262	12 434	13 068	4 784	18 333	3 594	19 923	2 856	30 602	866	45 612	334
1996	19 439	13 365	13 287	5 062	18 528	3 783	22 209	3 096	32 955	1 027	49 873	398
1997	20 766	13 972	15 069	5 238	19 558	4 082	22 001	3 075	33 465	1 140	58 571	437
1998	22 117	14 372	15 832	5 281	20 978	4 219	23 091	3 289	35 014	1 156	62 583	425
1999	22 096	15 122	16 106	5 601	20 704	4 539	24 577	3 392	36 212	1 117	55 352	472
2000[2]	23 855	17 161	17 156	6 428	22 009	5 145	25 276	3 737	44 661	1 395	63 908	455
2001	24 786	17 575	18 334	6 533	22 866	5 265	27 523	3 842	40 586	1 416	62 194	517
2002	25 824	18 409	18 981	6 748	24 163	5 499	27 757	4 024	40 949	1 568	67 679	569
2003[3]	25 810	18 786	18 349	6 767	23 472	5 517	28 494	4 235	43 676	1 663	62 794	603
Male												
1975	8 162	2 456	6 745	1 287	8 546	691	8 807	279	12 881	113	17 991	86
1976	8 787	2 571	7 440	1 321	9 640	712	8 843	342	13 650	114	16 184	81
1977	9 655	2 833	8 192	1 460	10 386	776	9 924	391	15 189	120	19 025	85
1978	10 473	2 915	8 836	1 498	10 940	815	11 545	393	16 898	127	20 702	82
1979	11 332	3 269	9 393	1 615	11 714	952	12 489	441	18 923	142	21 299	118
1980	12 310	3 401	9 825	1 707	13 108	961	14 331	451	19 224	167	24 642	114
1981	13 052	3 504	10 447	1 686	13 513	1 037	15 432	489	19 201	177	27 619	114
1982	13 484	3 480	10 108	1 622	13 883	1 083	15 560	495	22 565	153	34 474	125
1983	14 265	3 577	11 353	1 678	14 584	1 074	16 626	514	21 911	170	28 680	141
1984	14 957	4 344	11 441	2 022	15 763	1 319	17 261	611	23 835	223	30 727	168
1985	15 293	4 702	11 671	2 111	15 602	1 491	18 168	678	24 723	267	32 831	155
1986	15 624	5 037	11 262	2 262	15 948	1 546	19 675	778	27 427	274	32 538	176
1987	17 048	5 248	12 823	2 281	16 774	1 616	19 414	758	26 581	383	39 014	211
1988	17 357	5 477	12 836	2 517	17 446	1 621	21 631	811	26 935	333	40 916	194
1989	18 087	5 641	13 167	2 632	17 579	1 711	22 374	810	32 767	292	49 088	196
1990	18 320	5 745	13 182	2 562	18 100	1 812	22 376	852	31 485	314	47 479	205

Source: U.S. Census Bureau. 1947, and 1952 to 2002 March Current Population Survey; 2003 and 2004 Annual Social and Economic Supplement to the Current Population Survey (noninstitutionalized population, excluding members of the Armed Forces living in barracks); 1960 Census of Population, 1950 Census of Population, and 1940 Census of Population (resident population).

[1]For data prior to 1991, some college/associate degree equals 1 to 3 years of college completed; a bachelor's degree equals 4 years of college completed; and an advanced degree equals 5 or more years of college completed.
[2]Beginning in 2000, earnings data are from the expanded CPS sample and were calculated using population controls based on the 2000 census.
[3]Starting in 2003, respondents could choose more than one race. The race data in this table from 2003 onward represent those respondents who indicated only one racial identity.
[4]May be of any race.

Table A7-9. Mean Earnings of Workers 18 Years of Age and Over, by Educational Attainment, Race, Sex, and Hispanic Origin, 1975–2003—*Continued*

(Dollars, numbers in thousands.)

Sex and year	Total		Not a high school graduate		High school graduate		Some college/ associate degree		Bachelor's degree[1]		Advanced degree[1]	
	Mean earnings (dollars)	Number with earnings	Mean earnings (dollars)	Number with earnings	Mean earnings (dollars)	Number with earnings	Mean earnings (dollars)	Number with earnings	Mean earnings (dollars)	Number with earnings	Mean earnings (dollars)	Number with earnings
HISPANIC OR LATINO[4]												
Male												
1991	18 516	5 932	13 133	2 548	18 582	1 705	21 974	1 131	31 699	356	45 873	193
1992	18 842	6 034	13 313	2 633	19 357	1 665	23 033	1 193	33 430	380	53 645	164
1993	19 460	6 957	13 572	2 928	18 765	1 954	22 417	1 444	37 554	438	52 441	194
1994	21 288	7 117	16 355	3 111	19 667	1 937	24 517	1 410	33 797	450	60 858	210
1995	20 312	7 337	14 774	3 140	20 882	2 039	22 171	1 475	35 109	466	50 802	215
1996	21 870	7 975	14 986	3 382	21 593	2 116	26 682	1 687	38 130	531	49 307	259
1997	23 520	8 261	17 447	3 444	22 253	2 391	25 923	1 598	37 963	557	68 097	272
1998	25 534	8 288	17 756	3 428	24 739	2 413	26 483	1 652	40 889	569	83 754	226
1999	24 970	8 713	18 020	3 592	23 736	2 597	29 387	1 698	42 733	577	66 745	250
2000[2]	27 253	9 996	19 501	4 236	25 629	2 940	30 155	1 873	55 050	722	81 447	223
2001	27 964	10 258	20 614	4 289	26 745	2 985	32 595	1 962	45 445	748	75 746	272
2002	29 084	10 979	21 611	4 506	27 992	3 205	32 935	2 112	46 115	815	73 836	338
2003[3]	28 806	11 195	20 637	4 556	26 652	3 234	34 157	2 193	49 298	867	71 446	344
Female												
1975	4 152	1 622	3 233	741	4 708	602	4 790	195	6 226	60	8 067	25
1976	4 548	1 732	3 537	786	5 124	597	5 075	250	6 884	63	9 218	37
1977	4 964	1 919	3 707	846	5 466	685	5 588	265	9 082	90	10 569	33
1978	5 501	1 983	4 135	847	5 834	739	6 686	268	9 684	86	10 908	43
1979	6 255	2 276	4 675	918	6 708	860	7 069	327	9 168	98	13 313	72
1980	6 770	2 322	5 028	942	6 923	863	8 808	357	10 568	116	14 668	43
1981	7 723	2 426	5 486	962	8 292	929	9 483	345	12 292	143	15 503	47
1982	8 195	2 434	5 781	961	8 668	884	9 896	378	13 719	150	15 244	61
1983	8 704	2 645	6 305	996	9 261	956	9 750	462	13 507	150	16 817	81
1984	9 150	3 005	6 438	1 107	9 492	1 138	10 848	505	14 404	158	18 706	97
1985	9 865	3 138	6 699	1 112	9 784	1 170	11 791	548	15 503	191	22 480	118

Source: U.S. Census Bureau. 1947, and 1952 to 2002 March Current Population Survey; 2003 and 2004 Annual Social and Economic Supplement to the Current Population Survey (noninstitutionalized population, excluding members of the Armed Forces living in barracks); 1960 Census of Population, 1950 Census of Population, and 1940 Census of Population (resident population).

[1]For data prior to 1991, some college/associate degree equals 1 to 3 years of college completed; a bachelor's degree equals 4 years of college completed; and an advanced degree equals 5 or more years of college completed.
[2]Beginning in 2000, earnings data are from the expanded CPS sample and were calculated using population controls based on the 2000 census.
[3]Starting in 2003, respondents could choose more than one race. The race data in this table from 2003 onward represent those respondents who indicated only one racial identity.
[4]May be of any race.

Table A7-9. Mean Earnings of Workers 18 Years of Age and Over, by Educational Attainment, Race, Sex, and Hispanic Origin, 1975–2003—*Continued*

(Dollars, numbers in thousands.)

Sex and year	Total Mean earnings (dollars)	Total Number with earnings	Not a high school graduate Mean earnings (dollars)	Not a high school graduate Number with earnings	High school graduate Mean earnings (dollars)	High school graduate Number with earnings	Some college/ associate degree Mean earnings (dollars)	Some college/ associate degree Number with earnings	Bachelor's degree[1] Mean earnings (dollars)	Bachelor's degree[1] Number with earnings	Advanced degree[1] Mean earnings (dollars)	Advanced degree[1] Number with earnings
HISInterPANIC OR LATINO[4]												
Female												
1986	10 457	3 356	7 130	1 117	10 319	1 289	12 648	633	16 142	197	22 071	119
1987	11 234	3 569	7 350	1 176	10 627	1 366	13 929	642	18 003	261	26 584	124
1988	11 573	3 749	7 597	1 307	11 284	1 332	14 012	700	19 707	263	24 444	146
1989	12 307	3 929	8 256	1 353	11 799	1 477	14 482	703	22 617	243	26 700	153
1990	12 516	3 984	5 093	1 367	12 109	1 470	15 245	682	19 378	287	27 184	177
1991	13 069	4 072	4 809	1 358	13 043	1 339	15 721	948	20 791	309	30 721	117
1992	13 880	4 137	8 913	1 330	13 396	1 326	16 076	1 049	22 160	322	34 551	110
1993	13 602	4 687	8 489	1 498	13 584	1 413	15 250	1 284	21 627	361	34 001	131
1994	14 631	4 918	8 559	1 576	14 313	1 508	17 309	1 313	23 867	393	37 269	127
1995	15 310	5 096	9 809	1 644	14 989	1 555	17 521	1 380	25 338	399	36 255	118
1996	15 841	5 390	9 867	1 680	14 635	1 667	16 856	1 409	27 407	495	50 960	139
1997	16 781	5 711	10 503	1 794	15 747	1 691	17 759	1 477	29 173	584	43 051	165
1998	17 461	6 804	12 273	1 854	15 952	1 806	20 460	1 639	29 317	587	38 422	200
1999	18 187	6 409	12 684	2 010	16 653	1 943	19 754	1 694	29 249	540	42 503	222
2000[2]	19 115	7 164	12 622	2 191	17 180	2 204	20 372	1 864	33 489	672	47 057	232
2001	20 330	7 316	13 976	2 243	17 786	2 279	22 229	1 879	35 142	668	47 176	245
2002	21 008	7 430	13 694	2 241	18 810	2 293	22 035	1 911	35 357	753	58 623	230
2003[3]	21 391	7 591	13 632	2 210	18 967	2 283	22 411	2 042	37 550	795	51 294	258

Source: U.S. Census Bureau. 1947, and 1952 to 2002 March Current Population Survey; 2003 and 2004 Annual Social and Economic Supplement to the Current Population Survey (noninstitutionalized population, excluding members of the Armed Forces living in barracks); 1960 Census of Population, 1950 Census of Population, and 1940 Census of Population (resident population).

[1]For data prior to 1991, some college/associate degree equals 1 to 3 years of college completed; a bachelor's degree equals 4 years of college completed; and an advanced degree equals 5 or more years of college completed.
[2]Beginning in 2000, earnings data are from the expanded CPS sample and were calculated using population controls based on the 2000 census.
[3]Starting in 2003, respondents could choose more than one race. The race data in this table from 2003 onward represent those respondents who indicated only one racial identity.
[4]May be of any race.

Detailed Tables

Crime and Criminal Justice

Table A8-1. Estimated Number and Rate of Offenses Known to Police, 1960–2004

(Number, rate per 100,000 population.)

Year	Violent crime [1]	Property crime [1]	Murder and nonnegligent manslaughter	Forcible rape	Robbery	Aggravated assault	Burglary	Larceny-theft	Motor vehicle theft
Number of Offenses [2]									
1960	288 460	3 095 700	9 110	17 190	107 840	154 320	912 100	1 855 400	328 200
1961	289 390	3 198 600	8 740	17 220	106 670	156 760	949 600	1 913 000	336 000
1962	301 510	3 450 700	8 530	17 550	110 860	164 570	994 300	2 089 600	366 800
1963	316 970	3 792 500	8 640	17 650	116 470	174 210	1 086 400	2 297 800	408 300
1964	364 220	4 200 400	9 360	21 420	130 390	203 050	1 213 200	2 514 400	472 800
1965	387 390	4 352 000	9 960	23 410	138 690	215 330	1 282 500	2 572 600	496 900
1966	430 180	4 793 300	11 040	25 820	157 990	235 330	1 410 100	2 822 000	561 200
1967	499 930	5 403 500	12 240	27 620	202 910	257 160	1 632 100	3 111 600	659 800
1968	595 010	6 125 200	13 800	31 670	262 840	286 700	1 858 900	3 482 700	783 600
1969	661 870	6 749 000	14 760	37 170	298 850	311 090	1 981 900	3 888 600	878 500
1970	738 820	7 359 200	16 000	37 990	349 860	334 970	2 205 000	4 225 800	928 400
1971	816 500	7 771 700	17 780	42 260	387 700	368 760	2 399 300	4 424 200	948 200
1972	834 900	7 413 900	18 670	46 850	376 290	393 090	2 375 500	4 151 200	887 200
1973	875 910	7 842 200	19 640	51 400	384 220	420 650	2 565 500	4 347 900	928 800
1974	974 720	9 278 700	20 710	55 400	442 400	456 210	3 039 200	5 262 500	977 100
1975	1 039 710	10 252 700	20 510	56 090	470 500	492 620	3 265 300	5 977 700	1 009 600
1976	1 004 210	10 345 500	18 780	57 080	427 810	500 530	3 108 700	6 270 800	966 000
1977	1 029 580	9 955 000	19 120	63 500	412 610	534 350	3 071 500	5 905 700	977 700
1978	1 085 550	10 123 400	19 560	67 610	426 930	571 460	3 128 300	5 991 000	1 004 100
1979	1 208 030	11 041 500	21 460	76 390	480 700	629 480	3 327 700	6 601 000	1 112 800
1980	1 344 520	12 063 700	23 040	82 990	565 840	672 650	3 795 200	7 136 900	1 131 700
1981	1 361 820	12 061 900	22 520	82 500	592 910	663 900	3 779 700	7 194 400	1 087 800
1982	1 322 390	11 652 000	21 010	78 770	553 130	669 480	3 447 100	7 142 500	1 062 400
1983	1 258 087	10 850 543	19 308	78 918	506 567	653 294	3 129 851	6 712 759	1 007 933
1984	1 273 282	10 608 473	18 692	84 233	485 008	685 349	2 984 434	6 591 874	1 032 165
1985	1 327 767	11 102 590	18 976	87 671	497 874	723 246	3 073 348	6 926 380	1 102 862
1986	1 489 169	11 722 700	20 613	91 459	542 775	834 322	3 241 410	7 257 153	1 224 137
1987	1 483 999	12 024 709	20 096	91 111	517 704	855 088	3 236 184	7 499 851	1 288 674
1988	1 566 221	12 356 865	20 675	92 486	542 968	910 092	3 218 077	7 705 872	1 432 916
1989	1 646 037	12 605 412	21 500	94 504	578 326	951 707	3 168 170	7 872 442	1 564 800
1990	1 820 127	12 655 486	23 438	102 555	639 271	1 054 863	3 073 909	7 945 670	1 635 907
1991	1 911 767	12 961 116	24 703	106 593	687 732	1 092 739	3 157 150	8 142 228	1 661 738
1992	1 932 274	12 505 917	23 760	109 062	672 478	1 126 974	2 979 884	7 915 199	1 610 834
1993	1 926 017	12 218 777	24 526	106 014	659 870	1 135 607	2 834 808	7 820 909	1 563 060
1994	1 857 670	12 131 873	23 326	102 216	618 949	1 113 179	2 712 774	7 879 812	1 539 287
1995	1 798 792	12 063 935	21 606	97 470	580 509	1 099 207	2 593 784	7 997 710	1 472 441
1996	1 688 540	11 805 323	19 645	96 252	535 594	1 037 049	2 506 400	7 904 685	1 394 238
1997	1 636 096	11 558 475	18 208	96 153	498 534	1 023 201	2 460 526	7 743 760	1 354 189
1998	1 533 887	10 951 827	16 974	93 144	447 186	976 583	2 332 735	7 376 311	1 242 781
1999	1 426 044	10 208 334	15 522	89 411	409 371	911 740	2 100 739	6 955 520	1 152 075
2000	1 425 486	10 182 584	15 586	90 178	408 016	911 706	2 050 992	6 971 590	1 160 002
2001	1 439 480	10 437 189	16 037	90 863	423 557	909 023	2 116 531	7 092 267	1 228 391
2002	1 423 677	10 455 277	16 229	95 235	420 806	891 407	2 151 252	7 057 379	1 246 646
2003	1 383 676	10 442 862	16 528	93 883	414 235	859 030	2 154 834	7 026 802	1 261 226
2004	1 367 009	10 328 255	16 137	94 635	401 326	854 911	2 143 456	6 947 685	1 237 114

Source: Federal Bureau of Investigation. *Crime in the United States, 2004.*

[1]Violent crimes are offenses of murder and nonnegligent manslaughter, forcible rape, robbery, and aggravated assault. Property crimes are offenses of burglary, larceny-theft, and motor vehicle theft. Data are not included for the property crime of arson.
[2]All rates were calculated for the number of offenses before rounding.

Table A8-1. Estimated Number and Rate of Offenses Known to Police, 1960–2004
—Continued

(Number, rate per 100,000 population.)

Year	Violent crime [1]	Property crime [1]	Murder and nonnegligent manslaughter	Forcible rape	Robbery	Aggravated assault	Burglary	Larceny-theft	Motor vehicle theft
Rate of Offenses [2]									
1960	160.9	1 726.3	5.1	9.6	60.1	86.1	508.6	1 034.7	183.0
1961	158.1	1 747.9	4.8	9.4	58.3	85.7	518.9	1 045.4	183.6
1962	162.3	1 857.5	4.6	9.4	59.7	88.6	535.2	1 124.8	197.4
1963	168.2	2 012.1	4.6	9.4	61.8	92.4	576.4	1 219.1	216.6
1964	190.6	2 197.5	4.9	11.2	68.2	106.2	634.7	1 315.5	247.4
1965	200.2	2 248.8	5.1	12.1	71.7	111.3	662.7	1 329.3	256.8
1966	220.0	2 450.9	5.6	13.2	80.8	120.3	721.0	1 442.9	286.9
1967	253.2	2 736.5	6.2	14.0	102.8	130.2	826.6	1 575.8	334.1
1968	298.4	3 071.8	6.9	15.9	131.8	143.8	932.3	1 746.6	393.0
1969	328.7	3 351.3	7.3	18.5	148.4	154.5	984.1	1 930.9	436.2
1970	363.5	3 621.0	7.9	18.7	172.1	164.8	1 084.9	2 079.3	456.8
1971	396.0	3 768.8	8.6	20.5	188.0	178.8	1 163.5	2 145.5	459.8
1972	401.0	3 560.4	9.0	22.5	180.7	188.8	1 140.8	1 993.6	426.1
1973	417.4	3 737.0	9.4	24.5	183.1	200.5	1 222.5	2 071.9	442.6
1974	461.1	4 389.3	9.8	26.2	209.3	215.8	1 437.7	2 489.5	462.2
1975	487.8	4 810.7	9.6	26.3	220.8	231.1	1 532.1	2 804.8	473.7
1976	467.8	4 819.5	8.8	26.6	199.3	233.2	1 448.2	2 921.3	450.0
1977	475.9	4 601.7	8.8	29.4	190.7	240.0	1 419.8	2 729.9	451.9
1978	497.8	4 642.5	9.0	31.0	195.8	262.1	1 434.6	2 747.4	460.5
1979	548.9	5 016.6	9.7	34.7	218.4	286.0	1 511.9	2 999.1	505.6
1980	596.6	5 353.3	10.2	36.8	251.1	298.5	1 684.1	3 167.0	502.2
1981	593.5	5 256.5	9.8	36.0	258.4	289.3	1 647.2	3 135.3	474.1
1982	570.8	5 029.7	9.1	34.0	238.8	289.0	1 488.0	3 083.1	458.6
1983	538.1	4 641.1	8.3	33.8	216.7	279.4	1 338.7	2 871.3	431.1
1984	539.9	4 498.5	7.9	35.7	205.7	290.6	1 265.5	2 795.2	437.7
1985	558.1	4 666.4	8.0	36.8	209.3	304.0	1 291.7	2 911.2	463.5
1986	620.1	4 881.8	8.6	38.1	226.0	347.4	1 349.8	3 022.1	509.8
1987	612.5	4 963.0	8.3	37.6	213.7	352.9	1 335.7	3 095.4	531.9
1988	640.6	5 054.0	8.5	37.8	222.1	372.2	1 316.2	3 151.7	586.1
1989	666.9	5 107.1	8.7	38.3	234.3	385.6	1 283.6	3 189.6	634.0
1990	729.6	5 073.1	9.4	41.1	256.3	422.9	1 232.2	3 185.1	655.8
1991	758.2	5 140.2	9.8	42.3	272.7	433.4	1 252.1	3 229.1	659.0
1992	757.7	4 903.7	9.3	42.8	263.7	441.9	1 168.4	3 103.6	631.6
1993	747.1	4 740.0	9.5	41.1	256.0	440.5	1 099.7	3 033.9	606.3
1994	713.6	4 660.2	9.0	39.3	237.8	427.6	1 042.1	3 026.9	591.3
1995	684.5	4 590.5	8.2	37.1	220.9	418.3	987.0	3 043.2	560.3
1996	636.6	4 451.0	7.4	36.3	201.9	391.0	945.0	2 980.3	525.7
1997	611.0	4 316.3	6.8	35.9	186.2	382.1	918.8	2 891.8	505.7
1998	567.6	4 052.5	6.3	34.5	165.5	361.4	863.2	2 729.5	459.9
1999	523.0	3 743.6	5.7	32.8	150.1	334.3	770.4	2 550.7	422.5
2000	506.5	3 618.3	5.5	32.0	145.0	324.0	728.8	2 477.3	412.2
2001	504.5	3 658.1	5.6	31.8	148.5	318.6	741.8	2 485.7	430.5
2002	494.4	3 630.6	5.6	33.1	146.1	309.5	747.0	2 450.7	432.9
2003	475.8	3 591.2	5.7	32.3	142.5	295.4	741.0	2 416.5	433.7
2004	465.5	3 517.1	5.5	32.2	136.7	291.1	729.9	2 365.9	421.3

Source: Federal Bureau of Investigation. *Crime in the United States, 2004.*

[1]Violent crimes are offenses of murder and nonnegligent manslaughter, forcible rape, robbery, and aggravated assault. Property crimes are offenses of burglary, larceny-theft, and motor vehicle theft. Data are not included for the property crime of arson.
[2]All rates were calculated for the number of offenses before rounding.

Table A8-2. Arrest Rates, 1971–2004

(Rate per 100,000 population.)

Year	Total crime index [1]	Violent crime [2]	Property crime [3]
1971	897.1	175.8	721.4
1972	881.5	186.5	695.0
1973	883.4	187.3	696.1
1974	1 098.0	219.7	878.3
1975	1 059.6	206.7	852.9
1976	1 016.8	193.1	823.7
1977	1 039.4	202.7	836.7
1978	1 047.6	215.5	832.2
1979	1 057.2	212.5	844.7
1980	1 055.8	214.4	841.4
1981	1 070.0	216.8	853.2
1982	1 148.9	236.9	912.0
1983	1 071.9	221.1	850.8
1984	1 019.8	212.5	807.3
1985	1 046.5	212.4	834.0
1986	1 091.8	234.5	857.3
1987	1 120.1	233.8	886.4
1988	1 123.5	243.8	879.7
1989	1 173.1	268.6	904.4
1990	1 203.2	290.7	912.5
1991	1 198.8	293.0	905.8
1992	1 162.4	300.5	861.9
1993	1 131.6	302.9	828.8
1994	1 148.4	310.7	837.7
1995	1 140.3	315.2	825.0
1996	1 081.8	288.6	793.2
1997	1 042.9	273.6	769.3
1998	954.0	258.8	695.2
1999	880.0	244.5	635.5
2000	821.8	228.2	593.6
2001	807.3	225.6	581.8
2002	788.4	217.9	570.5
2003	. . .	205.3	558.4
2004	. . .	200.4	565.8

Source: Federal Bureau of Investigation. *Crime in the United States, 2004,* and previous years.

[1]Includes arson beginning in 1979. Discontinued beginning in 2003.
[2]Violent crimes are offenses of murder and nonnegligent manslaughter, forcible rape, robbery, and aggravated assault.
[3]Property crimes are offenses of burglary, larceny-theft, motor vehicle theft, and arson.
. . . = Not available.

Health

Table A9-1. Number of Deaths, Death Rates, and Age-Adjusted Death Rates, by Race and Sex, Selected Years, 1940–2002

(Number, rate per 100,000 population.)

Year	All races[1]			White			Black		
	Both sexes	Male	Female	Both sexes	Male	Female	Both sexes	Male	Female
Number of Deaths									
1940	1 417 269	791 003	626 266	1 231 223	690 901	540 322	178 743	95 517	83 226
1950	1 452 454	827 749	624 705	1 276 085	731 366	544 719	169 606	92 004	77 602
1960	1 711 982	975 648	736 334	1 505 335	860 857	644 478	196 010	107 701	88 309
1970	1 921 031	1 078 478	842 553	1 682 096	942 437	739 659	225 647	127 540	98 107
1980	1 989 841	1 075 078	914 763	1 738 607	933 878	804 729	233 135	130 138	102 997
1981	1 977 981	1 063 772	914 209	1 731 233	925 490	805 743	228 560	127 296	101 264
1982	1 974 797	1 056 440	918 357	1 729 085	919 239	809 846	226 513	125 610	100 903
1983	2 019 201	1 071 923	947 278	1 765 582	931 779	833 803	233 124	127 911	105 213
1984	2 039 369	1 076 514	962 855	1 781 897	934 529	847 368	235 884	129 147	106 737
1985	2 086 440	1 097 758	988 682	1 819 054	950 455	868 599	244 207	133 610	110 597
1986	2 105 361	1 104 005	1 001 356	1 831 083	952 554	878 529	250 326	137 214	113 112
1987	2 123 323	1 107 958	1 015 365	1 843 067	953 382	889 685	254 814	139 551	115 263
1988	2 167 999	1 125 540	1 042 459	1 876 906	965 419	911 487	264 019	144 228	119 791
1989	2 150 466	1 114 190	1 036 276	1 853 841	950 852	902 989	267 642	146 393	121 249
1990	2 148 463	1 113 417	1 035 046	1 853 254	950 812	902 442	265 498	145 359	120 139
1991	2 169 518	1 121 665	1 047 853	1 868 904	956 497	912 407	269 525	147 331	122 194
1992	2 175 613	1 122 336	1 053 277	1 873 781	956 957	916 824	269 219	146 630	122 589
1993	2 268 553	1 161 797	1 106 756	1 951 437	988 329	963 108	282 151	153 502	128 649
1994	2 278 994	1 162 747	1 116 247	1 959 875	988 823	971 052	282 379	153 019	129 360
1995	2 312 132	1 172 959	1 139 173	1 987 437	997 277	990 160	286 401	154 175	132 226
1996	2 314 690	1 163 569	1 151 121	1 992 966	991 984	1 000 982	282 089	149 472	132 617
1997	2 314 245	1 154 039	1 160 206	1 996 393	986 884	1 009 509	276 520	144 110	132 410
1998	2 337 256	1 157 260	1 179 996	2 015 984	990 190	1 025 794	278 440	143 417	135 023
1999	2 391 399	1 175 460	1 215 939	2 061 348	1 005 335	1 056 013	285 064	145 703	139 361
2000	2 403 351	1 177 578	1 225 773	2 071 287	1 007 191	1 064 096	285 826	145 184	140 642
2001	2 416 425	1 183 421	1 233 004	2 079 691	1 011 218	1 068 473	287 709	145 908	141 801
2002	2 443 387	1 199 264	1 244 123	2 102 589	1 025 196	1 077 393	290 051	146 835	143 216
Death Rate									
1940	1 076.4	1 197.4	954.6	1 041.5	1 162.2	. . .	. . .	. . .	. . .
1950	963.8	1 106.1	823.5	945.7	1 089.5	. . .	. . .	. . .	. . .
1960	954.7	1 104.5	809.2	947.8	1 098.5	800.9	1 038.6	1 181.7	. . .
1970	945.3	1 090.3	807.8	946.3	1 086.7	812.6	999.3	1 186.6	. . .
1980	878.3	976.9	785.3	892.5	983.3	806.1	875.4	1 034.1	733.3
1981	862.0	954.0	775.0	880.4	965.2	799.8	842.4	992.6	707.7
1982	852.4	938.4	771.2	873.1	951.8	798.2	823.4	966.2	695.5
1983	863.7	943.2	788.4	885.4	957.7	816.4	836.6	971.2	715.9
1984	864.8	938.8	794.7	887.8	954.1	824.6	836.1	968.5	717.4
1985	876.9	948.6	809.1	900.4	963.6	840.1	854.8	989.3	734.2
1986	876.7	944.7	812.3	900.1	958.6	844.3	864.9	1 002.6	741.5
1987	876.4	939.3	816.7	900.1	952.7	849.8	868.9	1 006.2	745.7
1988	886.7	945.1	831.2	910.5	957.9	865.3	888.3	1 026.1	764.6
1989	871.3	926.3	818.9	893.2	936.5	851.8	887.9	1 026.7	763.2
1990	863.8	918.4	812.0	888.0	930.9	846.9	871.0	1 008.0	747.9
1991	857.6	908.8	808.7	883.2	922.7	845.2	861.4	994.8	741.4
1992	848.1	896.1	802.4	875.8	912.2	840.8	841.8	967.6	728.6
1993	872.8	915.0	832.5	902.7	931.8	874.6	864.6	992.2	749.6
1994	866.1	904.2	829.7	897.8	922.6	873.8	849.0	970.2	739.7
1995	868.3	900.8	837.2	901.8	921.0	883.2	846.2	960.2	743.2
1996	859.2	882.8	836.7	896.0	907.1	885.3	819.7	915.3	733.3
1997	848.8	864.6	833.6	889.1	893.3	885.0	789.9	867.1	720.1
1998	847.3	856.4	838.5	889.5	887.3	891.6	782.3	848.2	722.6
1999	857.0	859.2	854.9	901.4	892.1	910.4	788.1	847.4	734.3
2000	854.0	853.0	855.0	900.2	887.8	912.3	781.1	834.1	733.0
2001	848.5	846.4	850.4	895.1	881.9	907.9	773.5	823.9	727.7
2002	847.3	846.6	848.0	895.7	884.0	907.0	768.4	816.7	724.4

Source: Centers for Disease Control and Prevention. National Center for Health Statistics. *National Vital Statistics Report* 53(15).

[1]For 1940–1991, includes deaths among races not shown separately; beginning in 1992, records coded as "other races" and records for which race was unknown, not stated, or not classifiable were assigned to the race of the previous record.
. . . = Not available.

Table A9-1. Number of Deaths, Death Rates, and Age-Adjusted Death Rates, by Race and Sex, Selected Years, 1940–2002—*Continued*

(Number, rate per 100,000 population.)

Year	American Indian and Alaska Native[2]			Asian or Pacific Islander[3]		
	Both sexes	Male	Female	Both sexes	Male	Female
Number of Deaths						
1940	4 791	2 527	. . .	. . .	. . .	. . .
1950	4 440	2 497	. . .	. . .	. . .	. . .
1960	4 528	2 658	. . .	. . .	. . .	. . .
1970	5 675	3 391	. . .	. . .	. . .	. . .
1980	6 923	4 193	2 730	11 071	6 809	4 262
1981	6 608	4 016	2 592	11 475	6 908	4 567
1982	6 679	3 974	2 705	12 430	7 564	4 866
1983	6 839	4 064	2 775	13 554	8 126	5 428
1984	6 949	4 117	2 832	14 483	8 627	5 856
1985	7 154	4 181	2 973	15 887	9 441	6 446
1986	7 301	4 365	2 936	16 514	9 795	6 719
1987	7 602	4 432	3 170	17 689	10 496	7 193
1988	7 917	4 617	3 300	18 963	11 155	7 808
1989	8 614	5 066	3 548	20 042	11 688	8 354
1990	8 316	4 877	3 439	21 127	12 211	8 916
1991	8 621	4 948	3 673	22 173	12 727	9 446
1992	8 953	5 181	3 772	23 660	13 568	10 092
1993	9 579	5 434	4 145	25 386	14 532	10 854
1994	9 637	5 497	4 140	27 103	15 408	11 695
1995	9 997	5 574	4 423	28 297	15 933	12 364
1996	10 127	5 563	4 564	29 508	16 550	12 958
1997	10 576	5 985	4 591	30 756	17 060	13 696
1998	10 845	5 994	4 851	31 987	17 659	14 328
1999	11 312	6 092	5 220	33 675	18 330	15 345
2000	11 363	6 185	5 178	34 875	19 018	15 857
2001	11 977	6 466	5 511	37 048	19 829	17 219
2002	12 415	6 750	5 665	38 332	20 483	17 849
Death Rate						
1940	. . .	. . .	. . .	. . .	. . .	. . .
1950	. . .	. . .	. . .	. . .	. . .	. . .
1960	. . .	. . .	. . .	. . .	. . .	. . .
1970	. . .	. . .	. . .	. . .	. . .	. . .
1980	487.4	597.1	380.1	296.9	375.3	222.5
1981	445.6	547.9	345.6	272.3	336.2	211.5
1982	434.5	522.9	348.1	271.3	338.3	207.4
1983	428.5	515.1	343.9	276.1	339.1	216.1
1984	419.6	502.7	338.4	275.9	336.5	218.1
1985	416.4	492.5	342.5	283.4	344.6	224.9
1986	409.5	494.9	325.9	276.2	335.1	219.9
1987	410.7	483.8	339.0	278.9	338.3	222.0
1988	411.7	485.0	339.9	282.0	339.0	227.4
1989	430.5	510.7	351.3	280.9	334.5	229.4
1990	402.8	476.4	330.4	283.3	334.3	234.3
1991	405.3	468.9	342.7	278.7	326.9	232.4
1992	406.6	474.1	340.0	282.1	331.1	235.3
1993	419.8	479.6	360.7	288.0	338.1	240.3
1994	408.2	468.8	348.3	294.6	344.0	247.7
1995	409.4	459.4	360.1	294.6	341.4	250.4
1996	399.5	441.5	358.0	294.4	340.2	251.1
1997	402.7	458.2	347.7	294.1	336.8	253.9
1998	397.8	441.9	354.2	293.8	335.4	254.9
1999	399.3	431.8	367.1	296.8	333.2	262.5
2000	380.8	415.6	346.1	296.6	332.9	262.3
2001	392.1	424.2	360.2	303.8	335.0	274.0
2002	403.6	439.6	367.7	299.5	331.4	269.7

Source: Centers for Disease Control and Prevention. National Center for Health Statistics. *National Vital Statistics Report* 53(15).

[2]Includes Aleuts and Eskimos.
[3]Includes Chinese, Filipino, Hawaiian, Japanese, and Other Asian or Pacific Islander.
. . . = Not available.

Table A9-1. Number of Deaths, Death Rates, and Age-Adjusted Death Rates, by Race and Sex, Selected Years, 1940–2002—*Continued*

(Number, rate per 100,000 population.)

Year	All races[1]			White			Black		
	Both sexes	Male	Female	Both sexes	Male	Female	Both sexes	Male	Female
Age-Adjusted Death Rate									
1940	1 785.0	1 976.0	1 599.4	1 735.3	1 925.2	1 550.4	. . .	. . .	. . .
1950	1 446.0	1 674.2	1 236.0	1 410.8	1 642.5	1 198.0	. . .	. . .	. . .
1960	1 339.2	1 609.0	1 105.3	1 311.3	1 586.0	1 074.4	1 577.5	1 811.1	1 369.7
1970	1 222.6	1 542.1	971.4	1 193.3	1 513.7	944.0	1 518.1	1 873.9	1 228.7
1980	1 039.1	1 348.1	817.9	1 012.7	1 317.6	796.1	1 314.8	1 697.8	1 033.3
1981	1 007.1	1 308.2	792.7	984.0	1 282.2	773.6	1 258.4	1 626.6	986.6
1982	985.0	1 279.9	776.6	963.6	1 255.9	758.7	1 221.3	1 580.4	960.1
1983	990.0	1 284.5	783.3	967.3	1 259.4	763.9	1 240.5	1 600.7	980.7
1984	982.5	1 271.4	779.8	959.7	1 245.9	760.7	1 236.7	1 600.8	976.9
1985	988.1	1 278.1	784.5	963.6	1 249.8	764.3	1 261.2	1 634.5	994.4
1986	978.6	1 261.7	778.7	952.8	1 230.5	758.1	1 266.7	1 650.1	994.4
1987	970.0	1 246.1	774.2	943.4	1 213.4	753.3	1 263.1	1 650.3	989.7
1988	975.7	1 250.7	781.0	947.6	1 215.9	759.1	1 284.3	1 677.6	1 006.8
1989	950.5	1 215.0	761.8	920.2	1 176.6	738.8	1 275.5	1 670.1	998.1
1990	938.7	1 202.8	750.9	909.8	1 165.9	728.8	1 250.3	1 644.5	975.1
1991	922.3	1 180.5	738.2	893.2	1 143.1	716.1	1 235.4	1 626.1	963.3
1992	905.6	1 158.3	725.5	877.7	1 122.4	704.1	1 206.7	1 587.8	942.5
1993	926.1	1 177.3	745.9	897.0	1 138.9	724.1	1 241.2	1 632.2	969.5
1994	913.5	1 155.5	738.6	885.6	1 118.7	717.5	1 216.9	1 592.8	954.6
1995	909.8	1 143.9	739.4	882.3	1 107.5	718.7	1 213.9	1 585.7	955.9
1996	894.1	1 115.7	733.0	869.0	1 082.9	713.6	1 178.4	1 524.2	940.3
1997	878.1	1 088.1	725.6	855.7	1 059.1	707.8	1 139.8	1 458.8	922.1
1998	870.6	1 069.4	724.7	849.3	1 042.0	707.3	1 127.8	1 430.5	921.6
1999	875.6	1 067.0	734.0	854.6	1 040.0	716.6	1 135.7	1 432.6	933.6
2000	869.0	1 053.8	731.4	849.8	1 029.4	715.3	1 121.4	1 403.5	927.6
2001	854.5	1 029.1	721.8	836.5	1 006.1	706.7	1 101.2	1 375.0	912.5
2002	845.3	1 013.7	715.2	829.0	992.9	701.3	1 083.3	1 341.4	901.8

Source: Centers for Disease Control and Prevention. National Center for Health Statistics. *National Vital Statistics Report* 53(15).

[1]For 1940–1991, includes deaths among races not shown separately; beginning in 1992, records coded as "other races" and records for which race was unknown, not stated, or not classifiable were assigned to the race of the previous record.
. . . = Not available.

Table A9-1. Number of Deaths, Death Rates, and Age-Adjusted Death Rates, by Race and Sex, Selected Years, 1940–2002—*Continued*

(Number, rate per 100,000 population.)

Year	American Indian and Alaska Native[2]			Asian or Pacific Islander[3]		
	Both sexes	Male	Female	Both sexes	Male	Female
Age-Adjusted Death Rate						
1940	. . .	. . .	. . .	. . .	. . .	. . .
1950	. . .	. . .	. . .	. . .	. . .	. . .
1960	. . .	. . .	. . .	. . .	. . .	. . .
1970	. . .	. . .	. . .	. . .	. . .	. . .
1980	867.0	1 111.5	662.4	589.9	786.5	425.9
1981	784.6	1 030.2	588.0	544.7	710.3	405.3
1982	757.0	940.1	604.4	550.4	738.2	410.3
1983	757.3	945.0	605.5	565.1	718.8	428.8
1984	761.7	946.0	567.9	574.4	724.7	443.1
1985	731.7	926.1	577.2	586.5	755.4	456.7
1986	720.8	926.7	549.3	576.4	730.5	445.4
1987	719.8	899.3	583.7	577.3	732.4	448.1
1988	718.6	917.4	563.6	584.2	732.0	451.0
1989	761.6	999.8	586.3	581.3	729.6	458.4
1990	716.3	916.2	561.8	582.0	716.4	469.3
1991	763.9	970.6	608.3	566.2	703.4	453.2
1992	759.0	970.4	599.4	558.5	697.3	445.8
1993	796.4	1 006.3	641.6	565.8	709.9	450.4
1994	764.8	953.3	618.8	562.7	702.5	452.1
1995	771.2	932.0	643.9	554.8	693.4	446.7
1996	763.6	924.8	641.7	543.2	676.1	439.6
1997	774.0	974.8	625.3	531.8	660.2	432.6
1998	770.4	943.9	640.5	522.4	646.9	426.7
1999	780.9	925.9	668.2	519.7	641.2	427.5
2000	709.3	841.5	604.5	506.4	624.2	416.8
2001	686.7	798.9	594.0	492.1	597.4	412.0
2002	677.4	794.2	581.1	474.4	578.4	395.9

Source: Centers for Disease Control and Prevention. National Center for Health Statistics. *National Vital Statistics Report* 53(15).

[2]Includes Aleuts and Eskimos.
[3]Includes Chinese, Filipino, Hawaiian, Japanese, and Other Asian or Pacific Islander.
. . . = Not available.

Table A9-2. Deaths and Death Rates for the 10 Leading Causes of Death in Specified Age Groups, 2003[1]

(Number, rate per 100,000 population.)

Age, rank, and cause of death	Number	Rate per 100,000 population
All Ages[2]		
All causes	2 443 930	840.4
1. Diseases of heart	684 462	235.4
2. Malignant neoplasms	554 643	190.7
3. Cerebrovascular diseases	157 803	54.3
4. Chronic lower respiratory diseases	126 128	43.4
5. Accidents (unintentional injuries)	105 695	36.3
Motor vehicle accidents	44 059	15.2
All other accidents	61 636	21.2
6. Diabetes mellitus	73 965	25.4
7. Influenza and pneumonia	64 847	22.3
8. Alzheimer's disease	63 343	21.8
9. Nephritis, nephrotic syndrome, and nephrosis	42 536	14.6
10. Septicemia	34 243	11.8
All other causes (residual)	536 265	184.4
1–4 Years		
All causes	4 911	31.1
1. Accidents (unintentional injuries)	1 679	10.6
Motor vehicle accidents	591	3.7
All other accidents	1 088	6.9
2. Congenital malformations, deformations, and chromosomal abnormalities	514	3.3
3. Malignant neoplasms	383	2.4
4. Assault (homicide)	342	2.2
5. Diseases of heart	186	1.2
6. Influenza and pneumonia	151	1.0
7. Septicemia	82	0.5
8. Certain conditions originating in the perinatal period	76	0.5
9. In situ neoplasms, benign neoplasms, and neoplasms of uncertain or unknown behavior	53	0.3
10. Chronic lower respiratory disease	47	0.3
All other causes (residual)	1 398	8.9
5–14 Years		
All causes	6 930	16.9
1. Accidents (unintentional injuries)	2 561	6.3
Motor vehicle accidents	1 592	3.9
All other accidents	970	2.4
2. Malignant neoplasms	1 060	2.6
3. Congenital malformations, deformations, and chromosomal abnormalities	370	0.9
4. Assault (homicide)	310	0.8
5. Intentional self-harm (suicide)	255	0.6
6. Diseases of heart	252	0.6
7. Influenza and pneumonia	134	0.3
8. Chronic lower respiratory disease	107	0.3
9. Septicemia	77	0.2
10. In situ neoplasms, benign neoplasms, and neoplasms of uncertain or unknown behavior	76	0.2
All other causes (residual)	1 728	4.2
15–24 Years		
All causes	33 022	80.1
1. Accidents (unintentional injuries)	14 966	36.3
Motor vehicle accidents	10 857	26.3
All other accidents	4 109	10.0
2. Assault (homicide)	5 148	12.5
3. Intentional self-harm (suicide)	3 921	9.5
4. Malignant neoplasms	1 628	4.0
5. Diseases of heart	1 083	2.6
6. Congenital malformations, deformations, and chromosomal abnormalities	425	1.0
7. Influenza and pneumonia	216	0.5
8. Cerebrovascular diseases	204	0.5
9. Chronic lower respiratory diseases	172	0.4
10. Human immunodeficiency virus (HIV) disease	171	0.4
All other causes (residual)	5 088	12.3

Source: Centers for Disease Control and Prevention. National Center for Health Statistics. *National Vital Statistics Report* 53(15).

[1]Preliminary data.
[2]Includes deaths under 1 year of age.

Table A9-2. Deaths and Death Rates for the 10 Leading Causes of Death in Specified Age Groups, 2003[1]—Continued

(Number, rate per 100,000 population.)

Age, rank, and cause of death	Number	Rate per 100,000 population
25–44 Years		
All causes	128 924	153.0
1. Accidents (unintentional injuries)	27 844	33.1
Motor vehicle accidents	13 582	16.1
All other accidents	14 261	16.9
2. Malignant neoplasms	19 041	22.6
3. Diseases of heart	16 283	19.3
4. Intentional self-harm (suicide)	11 251	13.4
5. Assault (homicide)	7 367	8.7
6. Human immunodeficiency virus (HIV) disease	6 879	8.2
7. Chronic liver disease and cirrhosis	3 288	3.9
8. Cerebrovascular diseases	3 004	3.6
9. Diabetes mellitus	2 662	3.2
10. Influenza and pneumonia	1 337	1.6
All other causes (residual)	29 968	35.6
45–64 Years		
All causes	437 058	636.1
1. Malignant neoplasms	144 936	211.0
2. Diseases of heart	101 713	148.0
3. Accidents (unintentional injuries)	23 669	34.5
Motor vehicle accidents	9 891	14.4
All other accidents	13 778	20.1
4. Diabetes mellitus	16 326	23.8
5. Cerebrovascular diseases	15 971	23.2
6. Chronic lower respiratory diseases	15 409	22.4
7. Chronic liver disease and cirrhosis	13 649	19.9
8. Intentional self-harm (suicide)	10 057	14.6
9. Human immunodeficiency virus (HIV) disease	5 917	8.6
10. Septicemia	5 827	8.5
All other causes (residual)	83 584	121.7
65 Years and Over		
All causes	1 804 131	5 022.8
1. Diseases of heart	564 204	1 570.8
2. Malignant neoplasms	387 475	1 078.7
3. Cerebrovascular diseases	138 397	385.3
4. Chronic lower respiratory diseases	109 199	304.0
5. Alzheimer's disease	62 707	174.6
6. Influenza and pneumonia	57 507	160.1
7. Diabetes mellitus	54 770	152.5
8. Nephritis, nephrotic syndrome, and nephrosis	35 392	98.5
9. Accidents (unintentional injuries)	33 976	94.6
Motor vehicle accidents	7 379	20.5
All other accidents	26 597	74.0
10. Septicemia	26 609	74.1
All other causes (residual)	333 895	929.6

Source: Centers for Disease Control and Prevention. National Center for Health Statistics. *National Vital Statistics Report* 53(15).

[1]Preliminary data.

Table A9-3. Serum Cholesterol Levels Among Persons 20 Years of Age and Over, According to Sex, Age, Race, and Hispanic Origin, Selected Years, 1960–2002

(Percent, except as noted.)

Sex, age, race, and Hispanic origin	1960–1962	1971–1974	1976–1980 [1]	1988–1994	1999–2002
PERCENT OF POPULATION WITH HIGH SERUM CHOLESTEROL					
20–74 Years, Age-Adjusted [2]					
Both sexes [3]	33.3	28.6	27.8	19.7	17.0
Male	30.6	27.9	26.4	18.8	16.9
Female	35.6	29.1	28.8	20.5	17.0
Not Hispanic or Latino					
White only, male	. . .	. . .	26.4	18.7	17.0
White only, female	. . .	. . .	29.6	20.7	17.4
Black or African American only, male	. . .	. . .	25.5	16.4	12.5
Black or African American only, female	. . .	. . .	26.3	19.9	16.6
Mexican male [4]	. . .	. . .	20.3	18.7	17.6
Mexican female [4]	. . .	. . .	20.5	17.7	12.7
20 Years and Over, Age-Adjusted [2]					
Both sexes [3]	. . .	. . .	. . .	20.8	17.3
Male	. . .	. . .	. . .	19.0	16.4
Female	. . .	. . .	. . .	22.0	17.8
Not Hispanic or Latino					
White only, male	. . .	. . .	. . .	18.8	16.5
White only, female	. . .	. . .	. . .	22.2	18.1
Black or African American only, male	. . .	. . .	. . .	16.9	12.4
Black or African American only, female	. . .	. . .	. . .	21.4	17.7
Mexican male [4]	. . .	. . .	. . .	18.5	17.4
Mexican female [4]	. . .	. . .	. . .	18.7	13.8
20 Years and Over, Crude					
Both sexes [3]	. . .	. . .	. . .	19.6	17.3
Male	. . .	. . .	. . .	17.7	16.6
Female	. . .	. . .	. . .	21.3	18.0
Not Hispanic or Latino					
White only, male	. . .	. . .	. . .	18.0	16.9
White only, female	. . .	. . .	. . .	22.5	19.1
Black or African American only, male	. . .	. . .	. . .	14.7	12.2
Black or African American only, female	. . .	. . .	. . .	18.2	16.1
Mexican male [4]	. . .	. . .	. . .	15.4	15.0
Mexican female [4]	. . .	. . .	. . .	14.3	10.7
Male					
20–34 years	15.1	12.4	11.9	8.2	9.8
35–44 years	33.9	31.8	27.9	19.4	19.8
45–54 years	39.2	37.5	36.9	26.6	23.6
55–64 years	41.6	36.2	36.8	28.0	19.9
65–74 years	38.0	34.7	31.7	21.9	13.7
75 years and over	. . .	. . .	. . .	20.4	10.2
Female					
20–34 years	12.4	10.9	9.8	7.3	8.9
35–44 years	23.1	19.3	20.7	12.3	12.4
45–54 years	46.9	38.7	40.5	26.7	21.4
55–64 years	70.1	53.1	52.9	40.9	25.6
65–74 years	68.5	57.7	51.6	41.3	32.3
75 years and over	. . .	. . .	. . .	38.2	26.5

Source: Centers for Disease Control and Prevention. National Center for Health Statistics. *Health, United States, 2005.*

[1] Data for Mexicans are for 1982–1984.

[2] Age adjusted to the 2000 standard population using five age groups. Age-adjusted estimates may differ from other age-adjusted estimates based on the same data and presented elsewhere if different age groups are used in the adjustment procedure.

[3] Includes persons of all races and Hispanic origin, not just those shown separately.

[4] Persons of Mexican origin may be of any race.

. . . = Not available.

Table A9-3. Serum Cholesterol Levels Among Persons 20 Years of Age and Over, According to Sex, Age, Race, and Hispanic Origin, Selected Years, 1960–2002 —*Continued*

(Percent, except as noted.)

Sex, age, race, and Hispanic origin	1960–1962	1971–1974	1976–1980 [1]	1988–1994	1999–2002
MEAN SERUM CHOLESTEROL LEVEL, MG/DL					
20–74 Years, Age-Adjusted [2]					
Both sexes [3]	222	216	215	205	203
Male	220	216	213	204	203
Female	224	217	216	205	202
Not Hispanic or Latino					
White only, male	. . .	. . .	213	204	202
White only, female	. . .	. . .	216	206	204
Black or African American only, male	. . .	. . .	211	201	195
Black or African American only, female	. . .	. . .	216	204	200
Mexican male [4]	. . .	. . .	209	206	205
Mexican female [4]	. . .	. . .	209	204	198
20 Years and Over, Age-Adjusted [2]					
Both sexes [3]	. . .	. . .	. . .	206	203
Male	. . .	. . .	. . .	204	202
Female	. . .	. . .	. . .	207	204
Not Hispanic or Latino					
White only, male	. . .	. . .	. . .	205	202
White only, female	. . .	. . .	. . .	208	205
Black or African American only, male	. . .	. . .	. . .	202	195
Black or African American only, female	. . .	. . .	. . .	207	202
Mexican male [4]	. . .	. . .	. . .	206	204
Mexican female [4]	. . .	. . .	. . .	206	199
20 Years and Over, Crude					
Both sexes [3]	. . .	. . .	. . .	204	203
Male	. . .	. . .	. . .	202	202
Female	. . .	. . .	. . .	206	204
Not Hispanic or Latino					
White only, male	. . .	. . .	. . .	203	203
White only, female	. . .	. . .	. . .	208	206
Black or African American only, male	. . .	. . .	. . .	198	194
Black or African American only, female	. . .	. . .	. . .	201	199
Mexican male [4]	. . .	. . .	. . .	199	200
Mexican female [4]	. . .	. . .	. . .	198	194
Male					
20–34 years	198	194	192	186	188
35–44 years	227	221	217	206	207
45–54 years	231	229	227	216	215
55–64 years	233	229	229	216	212
65–74 years	230	226	221	212	202
75 years and over	. . .	. . .	. . .	205	195
Female					
20–34 years	194	191	189	184	185
35–44 years	214	207	207	195	198
45–54 years	237	232	232	217	211
55–64 years	262	245	249	235	221
65–74 years	266	250	246	233	224
75 years and over	. . .	. . .	. . .	229	217

Source: Centers for Disease Control and Prevention. National Center for Health Statistics. *Health, United States, 2005.*

[1] Data for Mexicans are for 1982–1984.

[2] Age adjusted to the 2000 standard population using five age groups. Age-adjusted estimates may differ from other age-adjusted estimates based on the same data and presented elsewhere if different age groups are used in the adjustment procedure.

[3] Includes persons of all races and Hispanic origin, not just those shown separately.

[4] Persons of Mexican origin may be of any race.

. . . = Not available.

Table A9-4. Hypertension Among Persons 20 Years of Age and Over, According to Sex, Age, Race, and Hispanic Origin, 1988–1994 and 1999–2002

(Percent.)

Sex, age, race, and Hispanic origin	1988–1994	1999–2002
20–74 Years, Age-Adjusted [1]		
Both sexes [2,3]	21.7	25.5
Male	23.4	25.1
Female [2]	20.0	25.7
Not Hispanic or Latino		
White only, male	22.6	23.9
White only, female [2]	18.4	23.3
Black or African American only, male	34.3	36.8
Black or African American only, female [2]	34.9	39.4
Mexican male [4]	23.4	22.5
Mexican female [2,4]	20.9	23.4
20 Years and Over, Age-Adjusted [1]		
Both sexes [2,3]	25.5	29.9
Male	26.4	28.7
Female [2]	24.4	30.5
Not Hispanic or Latino		
White only, male	25.6	27.5
White only, female [2]	22.9	28.4
Black or African American only, male	37.5	40.4
Black or African American only, female [2]	38.2	43.4
Mexican male [4]	26.9	26.7
Mexican female [2,4]	25.0	27.8
20 Years and Over, Crude		
Both sexes [2,3]	24.1	30.1
Male	23.8	27.5
Female [2]	24.4	32.7
Not Hispanic or Latino		
White only, male	24.3	28.1
White only, female [2]	24.6	32.8
Black or African American only, male	31.1	35.8
Black or African American only, female [2]	32.3	42.0
Mexican male [4]	16.4	16.5
Mexican female [2,4]	15.9	18.8
Male		
20–34 years	*8.1	8.1
35–44 years	17.1	17.1
45–54 years	29.2	30.9
55–64 years	40.6	44.9
65–74 years	54.4	58.9
75 years and over	60.4	68.4
Female [2]		
20–34 years	*2.7	2.7
35–44 years	11.2	15.1
45–54 years	23.9	31.7
55–64 years	42.5	53.9
65–74 years	56.1	72.5
75 years and over	73.5	82.8

Source: Centers for Disease Control and Prevention. National Center for Health Statistics. *Health, United States, 2005.*

[1] Age adjusted to the 2000 standard population using five age groups, except for the 1999–2000 estimates, which are age adjusted using three age groups. However, the use of three rather than five age groups had virtually no effect on age-adjusted estimates.

[2] Excludes pregnant women.

[3] Includes persons of all races and Hispanic origins, not just those shown separately.

[4] Persons of Mexican origin may be of any race.

* = Figure does not meet standards of reliability or precision.

Table A9-5. Overweight, Obesity, and Healthy Weight Among Persons 20 Years and Over, According to Sex, Age, Race, and Hispanic Origin, Selected Years, 1960–2002

(Percent.)

Sex, age, race, and Hispanic origin	1960–1962	1971–1974	1976–1980[1]	1988–1994	1999–2002
PERCENT OF POPULATION OVERWEIGHT[2]					
20–74 Years, Age-Adjusted[3]					
Both sexes[4,5]	44.8	47.7	47.4	56.0	65.2
Male	49.5	54.7	52.9	61.0	68.8
Female[4]	40.2	41.1	42.0	51.2	61.7
Not Hispanic or Latino					
White only, male	. . .	. . .	53.8	61.6	69.5
White only, female[4]	. . .	. . .	38.7	47.2	57.0
Black or African American only, male	. . .	. . .	51.3	58.2	62.0
Black or African American only, female[4]	. . .	. . .	62.6	68.5	77.5
Mexican male[6]	. . .	. . .	61.6	69.4	74.1
Mexican female[4,6]	. . .	. . .	61.7	69.6	71.4
20 Years and Over, Age-Adjusted[3]					
Both sexes[4,5]	. . .	. . .	. . .	56.0	65.1
Male	. . .	. . .	. . .	60.9	68.8
Female[4]	. . .	. . .	. . .	51.4	61.6
Not Hispanic or Latino					
White only, male	. . .	. . .	. . .	61.6	69.4
White only, female[4]	. . .	. . .	. . .	47.5	57.2
Black or African American only, male	. . .	. . .	. . .	57.8	62.6
Black or African American only, female[4]	. . .	. . .	. . .	68.2	77.1
Mexican male[6]	. . .	. . .	. . .	68.9	73.2
Mexican female[4,6]	. . .	. . .	. . .	68.9	71.2
20 Years and Over, Crude					
Both sexes[4,5]	. . .	. . .	. . .	54.9	65.2
Male	. . .	. . .	. . .	59.4	68.6
Female[4]	. . .	. . .	. . .	50.7	62.0
Not Hispanic or Latino					
White only, male	. . .	. . .	. . .	60.6	69.9
White only, female[4]	. . .	. . .	. . .	47.4	58.2
Black or African American only, male	. . .	. . .	. . .	56.7	61.7
Black or African American only, female[4]	. . .	. . .	. . .	66.0	76.8
Mexican male[6]	. . .	. . .	. . .	63.9	70.1
Mexican female[4,6]	. . .	. . .	. . .	65.9	69.3
Male					
20–34 years	42.7	42.8	41.2	47.5	57.4
35–44 years	53.5	63.2	57.2	65.5	70.5
45–54 years	53.9	59.7	60.2	66.1	75.7
55–64 years	52.2	58.5	60.2	70.5	75.4
65–74 years	47.8	54.6	54.2	68.5	76.2
75 years and over	. . .	. . .	. . .	56.5	67.4
Female[4]					
20–34 years	21.2	25.8	27.9	37.0	52.8
35–44 years	37.2	40.5	40.7	49.6	60.6
45–54 years	49.3	49.0	48.7	60.3	65.1
55–64 years	59.9	54.5	53.7	66.3	72.2
65–74 years	60.9	55.9	59.5	60.3	70.9
75 years and over	. . .	. . .	. . .	52.3	59.9

Source: Centers for Disease Control and Prevention. National Center for Health Statistics. *Health, United States, 2005.*

[1] Data for Mexicans are for 1982–1984.

[2] Body mass index (BMI) greater than or equal to 25.

[3] Age adjusted to the 2000 standard population using five age groups, except for the 1999–2000 estimates, which are age adjusted using three age groups. However, use of three rather than five age groups had virtually no effect on age-adjusted estimates.

[4] Excludes pregnant women.

[5] Includes persons of all races and Hispanic origins, not just those shown separately.

[6] Persons of Mexican origin may be of any race.

Table A9-5. Overweight, Obesity, and Healthy Weight Among Persons 20 Years and Over, According to Sex, Age, Race, and Hispanic Origin, Selected Years, 1960–2002 —*Continued*

(Percent.)

Sex, age, race, and Hispanic origin	1960–1962	1971–1974	1976–1980[1]	1988–1994	1999–2002
PERCENT OF POPULATION OBESE[7]					
20–74 Years, Age-Adjusted[3]					
Both sexes[4,5]	13.3	14.6	15.1	23.3	31.1
Male	10.7	12.2	12.8	20.6	28.1
Female[4]	15.7	16.8	17.1	26.0	34.0
Not Hispanic or Latino					
White only, male	...	...	12.4	20.7	28.7
White only, female[4]	...	...	15.4	23.3	31.3
Black or African American only, male	...	...	16.5	21.3	27.9
Black or African American only, female[4]	...	...	31.0	39.1	49.6
Mexican male[6]	...	...	15.7	24.4	29.0
Mexican female[4,6]	...	...	26.6	36.1	38.9
20 Years and Over, Age-Adjusted[3]					
Both sexes[4,5]	...	...	...	22.9	30.4
Male	...	...	...	20.2	27.5
Female[4]	...	...	...	25.5	33.2
Not Hispanic or Latino					
White only, male	...	...	...	20.3	28.0
White only, female[4]	...	...	...	22.9	30.7
Black or African American only, male	...	...	...	20.9	27.8
Black or African American only, female[4]	...	...	...	38.3	48.8
Mexican male[6]	...	...	...	23.8	27.8
Mexican female[4,6]	...	...	...	35.2	38.0
20 Years and Over, Crude					
Both sexes[4,5]	...	...	...	22.3	30.5
Male	...	...	...	19.5	27.5
Female[4]	...	...	...	25.0	33.4
Not Hispanic or Latino					
White only, male	...	...	...	19.9	28.4
White only, female[4]	...	...	...	22.7	31.3
Black or African American only, male	...	...	...	20.7	27.5
Black or African American only, female[4]	...	...	...	36.7	48.8
Mexican male[6]	...	...	...	20.6	26.0
Mexican female[4,6]	...	...	...	33.3	37.0
Male					
20–34 years	9.2	9.7	8.9	14.1	21.7
35–44 years	12.1	13.5	13.5	21.5	28.5
45–54 years	12.5	13.7	16.7	23.2	30.6
55–64 years	9.2	14.1	14.1	27.2	35.5
65–74 years	10.4	10.9	13.2	24.1	31.9
75 years and over	...	...	...	13.2	18.0
Female[4]					
20–34 years	7.2	9.7	11.0	18.5	28.4
35–44 years	14.7	17.7	17.8	25.5	32.1
45–54 years	20.3	18.9	19.6	32.4	36.9
55–64 years	24.4	24.1	22.9	33.7	42.1
65–74 years	23.2	22.0	21.5	26.9	39.3
75 years and over	...	...	...	19.2	23.6

Source: Centers for Disease Control and Prevention. National Center for Health Statistics. *Health, United States, 2005.*

[1]Data for Mexicans are for 1982–1984.
[3]Age adjusted to the 2000 standard population using five age groups, except for the 1999–2000 estimates, which are age adjusted using three age groups. However, use of three rather than five age groups had virtually no effect on age-adjusted estimates.
[4]Excludes pregnant women.
[5]Includes persons of all races and Hispanic origins, not just those shown separately.
[6]Persons of Mexican origin may be of any race.
[7]Body mass index (BMI) greater than or equal to 30.

Table A9-5. Overweight, Obesity, and Healthy Weight Among Persons 20 Years and Over, According to Sex, Age, Race, and Hispanic Origin, Selected Years, 1960–2002 —Continued

(Percent.)

Sex, age, race, and Hispanic origin	1960–1962	1971–1974	1976–1980[1]	1988–1994	1999–2002
PERCENT OF POPULATION WITH A HEALTHY WEIGHT[8]					
20–74 Years, Age-Adjusted[3]					
Both sexes[4,5]	51.2	48.8	49.6	41.7	32.9
Male	48.3	43.0	45.4	37.9	30.2
Female[4]	54.1	54.3	53.7	45.3	35.6
Not Hispanic or Latino					
White only, male	. . .	. . .	45.3	37.4	29.5
White only, female[4]	. . .	. . .	56.7	49.2	39.7
Black or African American only, male	. . .	. . .	46.6	40.0	35.5
Black or African American only, female[4]	. . .	. . .	35.0	28.9	21.3
Mexican male[6]	. . .	. . .	37.1	29.8	25.6
Mexican female[4,6]	. . .	. . .	36.4	29.0	27.5
20 Years and Over, Age-Adjusted[3]					
Both sexes[4,5]	. . .	. . .	. . .	41.6	33.0
Male	. . .	. . .	. . .	37.9	30.2
Female[4]	. . .	. . .	. . .	45.0	35.7
Not Hispanic or Latino					
White only, male	. . .	. . .	. . .	37.3	29.6
White only, female[4]	. . .	. . .	. . .	48.7	39.5
Black or African American only, male	. . .	. . .	. . .	40.1	34.7
Black or African American only, female[4]	. . .	. . .	. . .	29.2	21.7
Mexican male[6]	. . .	. . .	. . .	30.2	26.5
Mexican female[4,6]	. . .	. . .	. . .	29.7	27.5
20 Years and Over, Crude					
Both sexes[4,5]	. . .	. . .	. . .	42.6	32.9
Male	. . .	. . .	. . .	39.4	30.4
Female[4]	. . .	. . .	. . .	45.7	35.4
Not Hispanic or Latino					
White only, male	. . .	. . .	. . .	38.2	29.2
White only, female[4]	. . .	. . .	. . .	48.8	38.7
Black or African American only, male	. . .	. . .	. . .	41.5	35.9
Black or African American only, female[4]	. . .	. . .	. . .	31.2	21.9
Mexican male[6]	. . .	. . .	. . .	35.2	29.4
Mexican female[4,6]	. . .	. . .	. . .	32.4	29.4
Male					
20–34 years	55.3	54.7	57.1	51.1	40.3
35–44 years	45.2	35.2	41.3	33.4	29.0
45–54 years	44.8	38.5	38.7	33.6	24.0
55–64 years	44.9	38.3	38.7	28.6	23.8
65–74 years	46.2	42.1	42.3	30.1	22.8
75 years and over	. . .	. . .	. . .	40.9	32.0
Female[4]					
20–34 years	67.6	65.8	65.0	57.9	42.6
35–44 years	58.4	56.7	55.6	47.1	37.1
45–54 years	47.6	49.3	48.7	37.2	33.1
55–64 years	38.1	41.1	43.5	31.5	27.6
65–74 years	36.4	40.6	37.8	37.0	26.4
75 years and over	. . .	. . .	. . .	43.0	36.9

Source: Centers for Disease Control and Prevention. National Center for Health Statistics. *Health, United States, 2005.*

[1] Data for Mexicans are for 1982–1984.

[3] Age adjusted to the 2000 standard population using five age groups, except for the 1999–2000 estimates, which are age adjusted using three age groups. However, use of three rather than five age groups had virtually no effect on age-adjusted estimates.

[4] Excludes pregnant women.

[5] Includes persons of all races and Hispanic origins, not just those shown separately.

[6] Persons of Mexican origin may be of any race.

[8] Body mass index (BMI) from 18.5 to less than 25.

Table A9-6. Age-Adjusted [1] Prevalence of Current Smoking by Persons [2] 25 Years of Age and Over, According to Sex, Race, and Education, Selected Years, 1974–2003

(Percent.)

Sex, race, and education	1974 [3]	1979 [3]	1985 [3]	1990 [3]	1995 [3]	1998	1999	2000	2001	2002	2003
All Persons [4]	36.9	33.1	30.0	25.4	24.5	23.4	22.7	22.6	22.0	21.4	21.1
No high school diploma or GED	43.7	40.7	40.8	36.7	35.6	34.4	32.2	31.6	30.5	30.5	29.7
High school diploma or GED	36.2	33.6	32.0	29.1	29.1	28.9	28.0	29.2	28.1	27.9	27.8
Some college, no bachelor's degree	35.9	33.2	29.5	23.4	22.6	23.5	23.3	21.7	22.2	21.5	21.1
Bachelor's degree or higher	27.2	22.6	18.5	13.9	13.6	10.9	11.1	10.9	10.8	10.0	10.2
All Males [4]	42.9	37.3	32.8	28.2	26.4	25.1	24.5	24.7	23.8	23.5	23.3
No high school diploma or GED	52.3	47.6	45.7	42.0	39.7	37.5	36.2	36.0	34.2	34.0	34.4
High school diploma or GED	42.4	38.9	35.5	33.1	32.7	32.0	30.4	32.1	30.2	31.0	29.9
Some college, no bachelor's degree	41.8	36.5	32.9	25.9	23.7	25.4	24.8	23.3	24.3	23.2	22.7
Bachelor's degree or higher	28.3	22.7	19.6	14.5	13.8	11.0	11.8	11.6	11.2	11.0	11.2
White Males [4, 5]	41.9	36.7	31.7	27.6	25.9	24.8	24.2	24.7	23.7	23.5	23.2
No high school diploma or GED	51.5	47.6	45.0	41.8	38.7	37.4	36.3	38.2	34.8	35.6	33.6
High school diploma or GED	42.0	38.5	34.8	32.9	32.9	32.2	30.5	32.4	30.3	31.0	29.6
Some college, no bachelor's degree	41.6	36.4	32.2	25.4	23.3	25.2	24.7	23.5	24.5	23.2	23.3
Bachelor's degree or higher	27.8	22.5	19.1	14.4	13.4	10.9	11.8	11.3	11.2	11.1	11.2
Black or African American Males [4, 5]	53.4	44.4	42.1	34.5	31.6	30.4	29.1	26.4	28.4	27.2	26.3
No high school diploma or GED	58.1	49.7	50.5	41.6	41.9	42.9	43.8	38.2	37.9	37.2	37.4
High school diploma or GED	*50.7	48.6	41.8	37.4	36.6	32.8	32.5	29.0	33.4	31.3	33.4
Some college, no bachelor's degree	*45.3	39.2	41.8	28.1	26.4	28.4	23.4	19.9	24.1	25.6	19.5
Bachelor's degree or higher	*41.4	*36.8	*32.0	*20.8	*17.3	*15.3	11.3	14.6	11.3	*10.8	*10.3
All Females [4]	32.0	29.5	27.5	22.9	22.9	21.7	20.9	20.5	20.4	19.3	19.1
No high school diploma or GED	36.6	34.8	36.5	31.8	31.7	31.3	28.2	27.1	26.9	26.9	24.9
High school diploma or GED	32.2	29.8	29.5	26.1	26.4	26.2	25.9	26.6	26.4	25.2	25.8
Some college, no bachelor's degree	30.1	30.0	26.3	21.0	21.6	21.8	21.9	20.4	20.4	20.0	19.7
Bachelor's degree or higher	25.9	22.5	17.1	13.3	13.3	10.7	10.4	10.1	10.5	9.0	9.3
White Females [4, 5]	31.7	29.7	27.3	23.3	23.1	22.3	21.4	21.0	21.3	20.2	19.6
No high school diploma or GED	36.8	35.8	36.7	33.4	32.4	33.0	29.5	28.4	29.2	29.0	25.0
High school diploma or GED	31.9	29.9	29.4	26.5	26.8	27.1	27.2	27.8	28.3	26.8	26.8
Some college, no bachelor's degree	30.4	30.7	26.7	21.2	22.2	22.2	22.3	21.1	21.3	20.5	20.6
Bachelor's degree or higher	25.5	21.9	16.5	13.4	13.5	11.5	10.5	10.2	10.9	9.6	9.4
Black or African American Females [4, 5]	35.6	30.3	32.0	22.4	25.7	23.0	21.4	21.6	19.1	18.4	18.9
No high school diploma or GED	36.1	31.6	39.4	26.3	32.3	32.8	30.1	31.1	26.3	27.1	26.9
High school diploma or GED	40.9	32.6	32.1	24.1	27.8	24.3	22.4	25.4	21.3	19.5	23.3
Some college, no bachelor's degree	32.3	*28.9	23.9	22.7	20.8	21.7	22.3	20.4	17.4	20.7	17.0
Bachelor's degree or higher	*36.3	*43.3	26.6	17.0	17.3	9.0	13.4	10.8	11.6	*7.7	11.4

Source: Centers for Disease Control and Prevention. National Center for Health Statistics. *Health, United States, 2005.*

[1] Estimates are age adjusted to the year 2000 standard population using four age groups: 25–34 years, 35–44 years, 45–64 years, and 65 years and over.

[2] Beginning in 1993, current cigarette smokers reported ever smoking 100 cigarettes in their lifetime and smoking now on every day or some days.

[3] Data prior to 1997 are not strictly comparable with data for earlier years, due to the 1997 questionnaire redesign.

[4] Includes unknown education. Education quantities shown apply to 1997 and subsequent years. GED stands for General Educational Development high school equivalency diploma. In 1974–1995, the following categories based on the number of years of school completed were used: less than 12 years, 12 years, 13–15 years, 16 years or more.

[5] The race groups, White and Black, include persons of Hispanic and non-Hispanic origin. Starting with data year 1999, race-specific estimates are tabulated according to the 1997 Standards for Federal Data on Race and Ethnicity and are not strictly comparable with estimates for earlier years. The single race categories shown in the table conform to 1997 Standards. Starting with data year 1999, race-specific estimates are for persons who reported only one racial group. Prior to data year 1999, data were tabulated according to the 1977 Standards. Estimates for single race categories prior to 1999 included persons who reported one race or, if they reported more than one race, identified one race as best representing their race.

* = Figure does not meet standards of reliability or precision.

Table A9-7. Use of Selected Substances in the Past Month by Persons 12 Years of Age and Over, According to Age, Sex, Race, and Hispanic Origin, 2002–2003

(Percent.)

Age, sex, race, and Hispanic origin	Any illicit drug[1]		Marijuana		Nonmedical use of any psychotherapeutic drug[2]	
	2002	2003	2002	2003	2002	2003
12 years and over	8.3	8.2	6.2	6.2	2.6	2.7
Age						
12–13 years	4.2	3.8	1.4	1.0	1.7	1.8
14–15 years	11.2	10.9	7.6	7.2	4.0	4.1
16–17 years	19.8	19.2	15.7	15.6	6.2	6.1
18–25 years	20.2	20.3	17.3	17.0	5.4	6.0
26–34 years	10.5	10.7	7.7	8.4	3.6	3.4
35 years and over	4.6	4.4	3.1	3.0	1.6	1.5
Sex						
Male	10.3	10.0	8.1	8.1	2.7	2.7
Female	6.4	6.5	4.4	4.4	2.6	2.6
Age and Sex						
12–17 years	11.6	11.2	8.2	7.9	4.0	4.0
Male	12.3	11.4	9.1	8.6	3.6	3.7
Female	10.9	11.1	7.2	7.2	4.3	4.2
Hispanic Origin and Race						
Non-Hispanic						
White only	8.5	8.3	6.5	6.4	2.8	2.8
Black or African American only	9.7	8.7	7.4	6.7	2.0	1.8
American Indian and Alaska Native only	10.1	12.1	6.7	10.3	3.2	4.8
Native Hawaiian and Other Pacific Islander only	7.9	11.1	4.4	7.3	3.8	3.2
Asian only	3.5	3.8	1.8	1.9	0.7	1.7
Two or more races	11.4	12.0	9.0	9.3	3.5	2.4
Hispanic (of any race)	7.2	8.0	4.3	4.9	2.9	3.0

Age, sex, race, and Hispanic origin	Alcohol use		Binge alcohol use[3]		Heavy alcohol use[4]	
	2002	2003	2002	2003	2002	2003
12 years and over	51.0	50.1	22.9	22.6	6.7	6.8
Age						
12–13 years	4.3	4.5	1.8	1.6	0.3	0.1
14–15 years	16.6	17.0	9.2	9.4	1.9	2.2
16–17 years	32.6	31.8	21.4	21.2	5.6	5.5
18–25 years	60.5	61.4	40.9	41.6	14.9	15.1
26–34 years	61.4	60.2	33.1	32.9	9.0	9.4
35 years and over	52.1	50.7	18.6	18.1	5.2	5.1
Sex						
Male	57.4	57.3	31.2	30.9	10.8	10.4
Female	44.9	43.2	15.1	14.8	3.0	3.4
Age and Sex						
12–17 years	17.6	17.7	10.7	10.6	2.5	2.6
Male	17.4	17.1	11.4	11.1	3.1	2.9
Female	17.9	18.3	9.9	10.1	1.9	2.3
Hispanic Origin and Race						
Non-Hispanic						
White only	55.0	54.4	23.4	23.6	7.5	7.7
Black or African American only	39.9	37.9	21.0	19.0	4.4	4.5
American Indian and Alaska Native only	44.7	42.0	27.9	29.6	8.7	10.0
Native Hawaiian and Other Pacific Islander only	*	43.3	25.2	29.8	8.3	10.4
Asian only	37.1	39.8	12.4	11.0	2.6	2.3
Two or more races	49.9	44.4	19.8	21.8	7.5	6.1
Hispanic (of any race)	42.8	41.5	24.8	24.2	5.9	5.2

Source: Centers for Disease Control and Prevention. National Center for Health Statistics. *Health, United States, 2005.*

Note: Due to methodological differences among the National Survey on Drug Use & Health (formerly called NHSDA), Monitoring the Future Study (MTF), and Youth Risk Behavior Survey (YRBS), rates of substance use measured by these surveys are not directly comparable.

[1] Any illicit drug includes marijuana/hashish, cocaine (including crack), heroin, hallucinogens (including LSD and PCP), inhalants, and any prescription-type psychotherapeutic drug used nonmedically.

[2] Psychotherapeutic drugs include prescription-type pain relievers, tranquilizers, stimulants, and sedatives; does not include over-the-counter drugs.

[3] Binge alcohol use is defined as drinking 5 or more drinks on the same occasion on at least 1 day in the past 30 days. Occasion is defined as at the same time or within a couple of hours of each other.

[4] Heavy alcohol use is defined as drinking 5 or more drinks on the same occasion on each of 5 or more days in the past 30 days; all heavy alcohol users are also "binge" alcohol users.

* = Figure does not meet standards of reliability or precision.

Table A9-7. Use of Selected Substances in the Past Month by Persons 12 Years of Age and Over, According to Age, Sex, Race, and Hispanic Origin, 2002–2003
—Continued

(Percent.)

Age, sex, race, and Hispanic origin	Any tobacco[5]		Cigarettes		Cigars	
	2002	2003	2002	2003	2002	2003
12 years and over	30.4	29.8	26.0	25.4	5.4	5.4
Age						
12–13 years	3.8	3.2	3.2	2.5	0.7	0.8
14–15 years	13.4	13.3	11.2	11.0	3.8	3.9
16–17 years	29.0	27.0	24.9	23.2	9.3	8.8
18–25 years	45.3	44.8	40.8	40.2	11.0	11.4
26–34 years	38.2	38.8	32.7	33.4	6.6	6.9
35 years and over	27.9	27.0	23.4	22.6	4.1	3.9
Sex						
Male	37.0	35.9	28.7	28.1	9.4	9.0
Female	24.3	24.0	23.4	23.0	1.7	2.0
Age and Sex						
12–17 years	15.2	14.4	13.0	12.2	4.5	4.5
Male	16.0	15.6	12.3	11.9	6.2	6.2
Female	14.4	13.3	13.6	12.5	2.7	2.7
Hispanic Origin and Race						
Non-Hispanic						
White only	32.0	31.6	26.9	26.6	5.5	5.4
Black or African American only	28.8	30.0	25.3	25.9	6.8	7.2
American Indian and Alaska Native only	44.3	41.8	37.1	36.1	5.2	8.3
Native Hawaiian and Other Pacific Islander only	28.8	37.0	*	33.1	4.1	8.0
Asian only	18.6	13.8	17.7	12.6	1.1	1.8
Two or more races	38.1	34.4	35.0	30.7	5.5	6.2
Hispanic (of any race)	25.2	23.7	23.0	21.4	5.0	4.9

Source: Centers for Disease Control and Prevention. National Center for Health Statistics. *Health, United States, 2005.*
Note: Due to methodological differences among the National Survey on Drug Use & Health (formerly called NHSDA), Monitoring the Future Study (MTF), and Youth Risk Behavior Survey (YRBS), rates of substance use measured by these surveys are not directly comparable.

[5]Any tobacco product includes cigarettes, smokeless tobacco (i.e., chewing tobacco or snuff), cigars, and pipe tobacco.
 * = Figure does not meet standards of reliability or precision.

Table A9-8. Health Insurance Coverage Status and Type of Coverage, 1987–2004

(Number in thousands, percent.)

Year	Total population	Covered by private or government health insurance								Not covered
		Total	Private health insurance		Government health insurance					
			Total	Employ-ment based	Total	Medicaid	Medicare	Military health care[1]		

ALL RACES

Number

Year	Total population	Total	Total	Employ-ment based	Total	Medicaid	Medicare	Military health care[1]	Not covered
1987[2]	241 187	210 161	182 160	149 739	56 282	20 211	30 458	10 542	31 026
1988	243 685	211 005	182 019	150 940	56 850	20 728	30 925	10 105	32 680
1989	246 191	212 807	183 610	151 644	57 382	21 185	31 495	9 870	33 385
1990	248 886	214 167	182 135	150 215	60 965	24 261	32 260	9 922	34 719
1991	251 447	216 003	181 375	150 077	63 882	26 880	32 907	9 820	35 445
1992[3]	256 830	218 189	181 466	148 796	66 244	29 416	33 230	9 510	38 641
1993[4]	259 753	220 040	182 351	148 318	68 554	31 749	33 097	9 560	39 713
1994[5]	262 105	222 387	184 318	159 634	70 163	31 645	33 901	11 165	39 718
1995	264 314	223 733	185 881	161 453	69 776	31 877	34 655	9 375	40 582
1996	266 792	225 077	187 395	163 221	69 000	31 451	35 227	8 712	41 716
1997[6]	269 094	225 646	188 532	165 091	66 685	28 956	35 590	8 527	43 448
1998	271 743	227 462	190 861	168 576	66 087	27 854	35 887	8 747	44 281
1999[7]	276 804	236 576	198 841	175 101	67 683	28 506	36 923	8 648	40 228
1999	274 087	231 533	194 599	172 023	66 176	27 890	36 066	8 530	42 554
2000[8]	279 517	239 714	201 060	177 848	69 037	29 533	37 740	9 099	39 804
2001	282 082	240 875	199 860	176 551	71 295	31 601	38 043	9 552	41 207
2002	285 933	242 360	198 973	175 296	73 624	33 246	38 448	10 063	43 574
2003	288 280	243 320	197 869	174 020	76 755	35 647	39 456	9 979	44 961
2004	291 155	245 335	198 262	174 174	79 086	37 514	39 745	10 680	45 820

Percent

Year	Total population	Total	Total	Employ-ment based	Total	Medicaid	Medicare	Military health care[1]	Not covered
1987[2]	100.0	87.1	75.5	62.1	23.3	8.4	12.6	4.4	12.9
1988	100.0	86.6	74.7	61.9	23.3	8.5	12.7	4.1	13.4
1989	100.0	86.4	74.6	61.6	23.3	8.6	12.8	4.0	13.6
1990	100.0	86.1	73.2	60.4	24.5	9.7	13.0	4.0	13.9
1991	100.0	85.9	72.1	59.7	25.4	10.7	13.1	3.9	14.1
1992[3]	100.0	85.0	70.7	57.9	25.8	11.5	12.9	3.7	15.0
1993[4]	100.0	84.7	70.2	57.1	26.4	12.2	12.7	3.7	15.3
1994[5]	100.0	84.8	70.3	60.9	26.8	12.1	12.9	4.3	15.2
1995	100.0	84.6	70.3	61.1	26.4	12.1	13.1	3.5	15.4
1996	100.0	84.4	70.2	61.2	25.9	11.8	13.2	3.3	15.6
1997[6]	100.0	83.9	70.1	61.4	24.8	10.8	13.2	3.2	16.1
1998	100.0	83.7	70.2	62.0	24.3	10.3	13.2	3.2	16.3
1999[7]	100.0	85.5	71.8	63.3	24.5	10.3	13.3	3.1	14.5
1999	100.0	84.5	71.0	62.8	24.1	10.2	13.2	3.1	15.5
2000[8]	100.0	85.8	71.9	63.6	24.7	10.6	13.5	3.3	14.2
2001	100.0	85.4	70.9	62.6	25.3	11.2	13.5	3.4	14.6
2002	100.0	84.8	69.6	61.3	25.7	11.6	13.4	3.5	15.2
2003	100.0	84.4	68.6	60.4	26.6	12.4	13.7	3.5	15.6
2004	100.0	84.3	68.1	59.8	27.2	12.9	13.7	3.7	15.7

Source: U.S. Census Bureau. Current Population Reports. *Health Insurance Coverage: 2004.*

[1] Includes CHAMPUS (Comprehensive Health and Medical Plan for Uniformed Services)/Tricare, veterans', and military health care.
[2] Implementation of a new CPS ASEC processing system.
[3] Implementation of 1990 census population controls.
[4] Data collection method changed from paper and pencil to computer-assisted interviewing.
[5] Health insurance questions were redesigned. Increases in estimates of employment-based and military health care coverage may be partially due to questionnaire changes. Overall coverage estimates were not affected.
[6] Beginning with the 1998 CPS ASEC, people with no coverage other than access to Indian Health Service are no longer considered covered health insurance; instead, they are considered to be uninsured. The effect of this change on the overall estimates of health insurance coverage is negligible; however, the decrease in the number of people covered by Medicaid may be partially due to this change.
[7] Estimates reflect the results of follow-up verification questions and implementation of Census 2000-based population controls.
[8] Implementation of a 28,000 household sample expansion.

Table A9-8. Health Insurance Coverage Status and Type of Coverage, 1987–2004
—Continued

(Number in thousands, percent.)

Year	Total population	Covered by private or government health insurance								Not covered
		Total	Private health insurance		Government health insurance					
			Total	Employ-ment based	Total	Medicaid	Medicare	Military health care[1]		

WHITE ALONE[9]

Number
2002	230 809	198 103	167 151	146 210	57 072	22 171	33 135	8 065		32 706
2003	232 254	198 270	165 852	144 780	59 495	23 959	33 765	8 105		33 983
2004	234 077	199 289	165 327	144 246	61 311	25 586	34 084	8 567		34 788

Percent
2002	100.0	85.8	72.4	63.3	24.7	9.6	14.4	3.5		14.2
2003	100.0	85.4	71.4	62.3	25.6	10.3	14.5	3.5		14.6
2004	100.0	85.1	70.6	61.6	26.2	10.9	14.6	3.7		14.9

WHITE[10]

Number
1987[2]	203 745	179 845	161 338	132 264	44 028	12 163	27 044	8 482		23 900
1988	205 333	180 122	160 753	133 050	44 477	12 504	27 293	8 305		25 211
1989	206 983	181 126	161 363	132 882	44 868	12 779	27 859	8 116		25 857
1990	208 754	181 795	160 146	131 836	47 589	15 078	28 530	8 022		26 959
1991	210 257	183 130	159 628	131 646	49 699	17 058	28 940	7 867		27 127
1992[3]	213 198	183 479	158 612	129 685	51 195	18 659	29 341	7 556		29 719
1993[4]	215 221	184 732	158 586	128 855	53 222	20 642	29 297	7 689		30 489
1994[5]	216 751	186 447	160 414	137 966	54 288	20 464	29 978	8 845		30 305
1995	218 442	187 337	161 303	139 151	54 141	20 528	30 580	7 656		31 105
1996	220 070	188 341	161 806	139 913	54 004	20 856	30 919	6 981		31 729
1997[6]	221 650	188 409	161 682	140 601	52 975	19 652	31 108	6 994		33 241
1998	223 294	189 706	163 690	143 705	51 690	18 247	31 174	7 140		33 588
1999[7]	225 794	195 929	168 730	147 583	53 175	18 977	32 144	6 902		29 865
1999	224 806	192 943	166 191	145 878	52 139	18 676	31 416	6 848		31 863
2000[8]	228 208	198 133	170 071	149 364	54 287	19 889	32 695	7 158		30 075
2001	230 071	198 878	169 180	148 371	56 200	21 535	33 006	7 788		31 193

Percent
1987[2]	100.0	88.3	79.2	64.9	21.6	6.0	13.3	4.2		11.7
1988	100.0	87.7	78.3	64.8	21.7	6.1	13.3	4.0		12.3
1989	100.0	87.5	78.0	64.2	21.7	6.2	13.5	3.9		12.5
1990	100.0	87.1	76.7	63.2	22.8	7.2	13.7	3.8		12.9
1991	100.0	87.1	75.9	62.6	23.6	8.1	13.8	3.7		12.9
1992[3]	100.0	86.1	74.4	60.8	24.0	8.8	13.8	3.5		13.9
1993[4]	100.0	85.8	73.7	59.9	24.7	9.6	13.6	3.6		14.2
1994[5]	100.0	86.0	74.0	63.7	25.0	9.4	13.8	4.1		14.0
1995	100.0	85.8	73.8	63.7	24.8	9.4	14.0	3.5		14.2
1996	100.0	85.6	73.5	63.6	24.5	9.5	14.0	3.2		14.4
1997[6]	100.0	85.0	72.9	63.4	23.9	8.9	14.0	3.2		15.0
1998	100.0	85.0	73.3	64.4	23.1	8.2	14.0	3.2		15.0
1999[7]	100.0	86.8	74.7	65.4	23.6	8.4	14.2	3.1		13.2
1999	100.0	85.8	73.9	64.9	23.2	8.3	14.0	3.0		14.2
2000[8]	100.0	86.8	74.5	65.5	23.8	8.7	14.3	3.1		13.2
2001	100.0	86.4	73.5	64.5	24.4	9.4	14.3	3.4		13.6

Source: U.S. Census Bureau. Current Population Reports. *Health Insurance Coverage: 2004.*

[1]Includes CHAMPUS (Comprehensive Health and Medical Plan for Uniformed Services)/Tricare, veterans', and military health care.
[2]Implementation of a new CPS ASEC processing system.
[3]Implementation of 1990 census population controls.
[4]Data collection method changed from paper and pencil to computer-assisted interviewing.
[5]Health insurance questions were redesigned. Increases in estimates of employment-based and military health care coverage may be partially due to questionnaire changes. Overall coverage estimates were not affected.
[6]Beginning with the 1998 CPS ASEC, people with no coverage other than access to Indian Health Service are no longer considered covered health insurance; instead, they are considered to be uninsured. The effect of this change on the overall estimates of health insurance coverage is negligible; however, the decrease in the number of people covered by Medicaid may be partially due to this change.
[7]Estimates reflect the results of follow-up verification questions and implementation of Census 2000-based population controls.
[8]Implementation of a 28,000 household sample expansion.
[9]The 2003 CPS asked respondents to choose one or more races. White alone refers to people who reported White and did not report any other race category. The use of this single-race population does not imply that it is the preferred method of presenting or analyzing data. The Census Bureau uses a variety of approaches. Information on people who reported more than one race, such as White and American Indian and Alaska Native or Asian and Black or African American, is available from Census 2000 through American FactFinder. About 2.6 percent of people reported more than one race in Census 2000.
[10]The 2001 CPS and earlier years asked respondents to report only one race. The reference groups for these years are: White, White not Hispanic, Black, and Asian and Pacific Islander.

Table A9-8. Health Insurance Coverage Status and Type of Coverage, 1987–2004
—Continued

(Number in thousands, percent.)

Year	Total population	Covered by private or government health insurance	Private health insurance		Government health insurance				Not covered
		Total	Total	Employ-ment based	Total	Medicaid	Medicare	Military health care[1]	
WHITE ALONE, NOT HISPANIC[9]									
Number									
2002	194 421	173 639	150 422	130 801	47 736	14 984	30 718	7 465	20 782
2003	194 877	173 295	149 084	129 261	49 743	16 247	31 458	7 563	21 582
2004	195 301	173 319	148 069	128 368	50 806	17 241	31 640	7 952	21 983
Percent									
2002	100.0	89.3	77.4	67.3	24.6	7.7	15.8	3.8	10.7
2003	100.0	88.9	76.5	66.3	25.5	8.3	16.1	3.9	11.1
2004	100.0	88.7	75.8	65.7	26.0	8.8	16.2	4.1	11.3
WHITE, NOT HISPANIC[10]									
Number									
1987[2]	185 044	166 922	151 817	124 068	39 792	9 143	26 054	7 883	18 122
1988	186 047	167 048	151 009	124 622	40 259	9 522	26 224	7 743	19 000
1989	187 078	167 889	151 424	124 311	40 624	9 759	26 738	7 567	19 188
1990	188 240	168 015	150 306	123 261	42 732	11 423	27 313	7 528	20 224
1991	189 216	168 810	149 798	123 109	44 228	12 750	27 695	7 402	20 406
1992[3]	189 113	167 394	147 967	120 482	44 649	13 390	27 853	7 104	21 719
1993[4]	191 087	168 306	147 729	119 861	46 158	14 980	27 795	7 243	22 781
1994[5]	192 771	170 541	150 181	128 633	47 475	15 052	28 467	8 318	22 230
1995	191 271	169 272	149 686	128 378	46 501	14 381	28 918	7 163	21 999
1996	191 791	169 699	149 262	128 355	46 772	15 082	29 211	6 537	22 092
1997[6]	192 178	169 043	148 426	128 280	45 691	14 046	29 213	6 504	23 135
1998	193 074	170 184	149 910	130 956	44 699	12 985	29 222	6 675	22 890
1999[7]	192 858	173 958	152 984	133 123	45 540	13 157	30 256	6 326	18 901
1999	193 633	172 271	151 539	132 381	44 749	13 120	29 457	6 306	21 363
2000[8]	193 931	175 247	153 816	134 253	46 297	13 788	30 642	6 564	18 683
2001	194 822	175 412	152 821	133 295	47 661	15 035	30 811	7 144	19 409
Percent									
1987[2]	100.0	90.2	82.0	67.0	21.5	4.9	14.1	4.3	9.8
1988	100.0	89.8	81.2	67.0	21.6	5.1	14.1	4.2	10.2
1989	100.0	89.7	80.9	66.4	21.7	5.2	14.3	4.0	10.3
1990	100.0	89.3	79.8	65.5	22.7	6.1	14.5	4.0	10.7
1991	100.0	89.2	79.2	65.1	23.4	6.7	14.6	3.9	10.8
1992[2]	100.0	88.5	78.2	63.7	23.6	7.1	14.7	3.8	11.5
1993[4]	100.0	88.1	77.3	62.7	24.2	7.8	14.5	3.8	11.9
1994[5]	100.0	88.5	77.9	66.7	24.6	7.8	14.8	4.3	11.5
1995	100.0	88.5	78.3	67.1	24.3	7.5	15.1	3.7	11.5
1996	100.0	88.5	77.8	66.9	24.4	7.9	15.2	3.4	11.5
1997[6]	100.0	88.0	77.2	66.8	23.8	7.3	15.2	3.4	12.0
1998	100.0	88.1	77.6	67.8	23.2	6.7	15.1	3.5	11.9
1999[7]	100.0	90.2	79.3	69.0	23.6	6.8	15.7	3.3	9.8
1999	100.0	89.0	78.3	68.4	23.1	6.8	15.2	3.3	11.0
2000[8]	100.0	90.4	79.3	69.2	23.9	7.1	15.8	3.4	9.6
2001	100.0	90.0	78.4	68.4	24.5	7.7	15.8	3.7	10.0

Source: U.S. Census Bureau. Current Population Reports. *Health Insurance Coverage: 2004.*

[1]Includes CHAMPUS (Comprehensive Health and Medical Plan for Uniformed Services)/Tricare, veterans', and military health care.
[2]Implementation of a new CPS ASEC processing system.
[3]Implementation of 1990 census population controls.
[4]Data collection method changed from paper and pencil to computer-assisted interviewing.
[5]Health insurance questions were redesigned. Increases in estimates of employment-based and military health care coverage may be partially due to questionnaire changes. Overall coverage estimates were not affected.
[6]Beginning with the 1998 CPS ASEC, people with no coverage other than access to Indian Health Service are no longer considered covered health insurance; instead, they are considered to be uninsured. The effect of this change on the overall estimates of health insurance coverage is negligible; however, the decrease in the number of people covered by Medicaid may be partially due to this change.
[7]Estimates reflect the results of follow-up verification questions and implementation of Census 2000-based population controls.
[8]Implementation of a 28,000 household sample expansion.
[9]The 2003 CPS asked respondents to choose one or more races. White alone refers to people who reported White and did not report any other race category. The use of this single-race population does not imply that it is the preferred method of presenting or analyzing data. The Census Bureau uses a variety of approaches. Information on people who reported more than one race, such as White and American Indian and Alaska Native or Asian and Black or African American, is available from Census 2000 through American FactFinder. About 2.6 percent of people reported more than one race in Census 2000.
[10]The 2001 CPS and earlier years asked respondents to report only one race. The reference groups for these years are: White, White not Hispanic, Black, and Asian and Pacific Islander.

Table A9-8. Health Insurance Coverage Status and Type of Coverage, 1987–2004 —Continued

(Number in thousands, percent.)

Year	Total population	Covered by private or government health insurance								Not covered
		Total	Private health insurance		Government health insurance					
			Total	Employ-ment based	Total	Medicaid	Medicare	Military health care[1]		

BLACK ALONE[11]

Number

2002	35 806	28 578	19 347	18 002	12 058	8 289	3 776	1 268	7 228
2003	36 121	29 041	19 320	17 924	12 585	8 797	3 989	1 225	7 080
2004	36 546	29 360	19 596	18 122	12 878	8 943	3 925	1 369	7 186

Percent

2002	100.0	79.8	54.0	50.3	33.7	23.1	10.5	3.5	20.2
2003	100.0	80.4	53.5	49.6	34.8	24.4	11.0	3.4	19.6
2004	100.0	80.3	53.6	49.6	35.2	24.5	10.7	3.7	19.7

BLACK[10]

Number

1987[2]	29 417	23 555	15 358	13 055	10 380	7 046	2 918	1 497	5 862
1988	29 904	24 029	15 818	13 418	10 415	7 049	3 064	1 385	5 875
1989	30 392	24 550	16 520	14 187	10 443	7 123	3 043	1 340	5 843
1990	30 895	24 802	15 957	13 560	11 150	7 809	3 106	1 402	6 093
1991	31 439	24 932	15 466	13 297	11 776	8 352	3 248	1 482	6 507
1992[3]	32 535	25 967	15 994	13 545	12 464	9 122	3 154	1 459	6 567
1993[4]	33 040	26 279	16 590	13 693	12 588	9 283	3 072	1 331	6 761
1994[5]	33 531	26 928	17 147	15 607	12 693	9 007	3 167	1 683	6 603
1995	33 889	26 781	17 106	15 683	12 465	9 184	3 316	1 171	7 108
1996	34 218	26 799	17 718	16 358	12 074	8 572	3 393	1 357	7 419
1997[6]	34 598	27 166	18 544	17 077	11 157	7 750	3 573	1 100	7 432
1998	35 070	27 274	18 663	17 132	11 524	7 903	3 703	1 111	7 797
1999[7]	35 893	28 775	20 442	18 854	11 361	7 652	3 615	1 216	7 119
1999	35 509	27 973	19 805	18 363	11 165	7 495	3 588	1 198	7 536
2000[8]	35 597	28 915	20 485	18 922	11 579	7 735	3 871	1 372	6 683
2001	36 023	29 190	20 363	18 975	11 616	7 994	3 783	1 192	6 833

Percent

1987[2]	100.0	80.1	52.2	44.4	35.3	24.0	9.9	5.1	19.9
1988	100.0	80.4	52.9	44.9	34.8	23.6	10.2	4.6	19.6
1989	100.0	80.8	54.4	46.7	34.4	23.4	10.0	4.4	19.2
1990	100.0	80.3	51.6	43.9	36.1	25.3	10.1	4.5	19.7
1991	100.0	79.3	49.2	42.3	37.5	26.6	10.3	4.7	20.7
1992[3]	100.0	79.8	49.2	41.6	38.3	28.0	9.7	4.5	20.2
1993[4]	100.0	79.5	50.2	41.4	38.1	28.1	9.3	4.0	20.5
1994[5]	100.0	80.3	51.1	46.5	37.9	26.9	9.4	5.0	19.7
1995	100.0	79.0	50.5	46.3	36.8	27.1	9.8	3.5	21.0
1996	100.0	78.3	51.8	47.8	35.3	25.1	9.9	4.0	21.7
1997[6]	100.0	78.5	53.6	49.4	32.2	22.4	10.3	3.2	21.5
1998	100.0	77.8	53.2	48.9	32.9	22.5	10.6	3.2	22.2
1999[7]	100.0	80.2	57.0	52.5	31.7	21.3	10.1	3.4	19.8
1999	100.0	78.8	55.8	51.7	31.4	21.1	10.1	3.4	21.2
2000[8]	100.0	81.2	57.5	53.2	32.5	21.7	10.9	3.9	18.8
2001	100.0	81.0	56.5	52.7	32.2	22.2	10.5	3.3	19.0

Source: U.S. Census Bureau. Current Population Reports. *Health Insurance Coverage: 2004.*

[1]Includes CHAMPUS (Comprehensive Health and Medical Plan for Uniformed Services)/Tricare, veterans', and military health care.
[2]Implementation of a new CPS ASEC processing system.
[3]Implementation of 1990 census population controls.
[4]Data collection method changed from paper and pencil to computer-assisted interviewing.
[5]Health insurance questions were redesigned. Increases in estimates of employment-based and military health care coverage may be partially due to questionnaire changes. Overall coverage estimates were not affected.
[6]Beginning with the 1998 CPS ASEC, people with no coverage other than access to Indian Health Service are no longer considered covered health insurance; instead, they are considered to be uninsured. The effect of this change on the overall estimates of health insurance coverage is negligible; however, the decrease in the number of people covered by Medicaid may be partially due to this change.
[7]Estimates reflect the results of follow-up verification questions and implementation of Census 2000-based population controls.
[8]Implementation of a 28,000 household sample expansion.
[10]The 2001 CPS and earlier years asked respondents to report only one race. The reference groups for these years are: White, White not Hispanic, Black, and Asian and Pacific Islander.
[11]Black alone refers to people who reported Black or African American and did not report any other race category.

Table A9-8. Health Insurance Coverage Status and Type of Coverage, 1987–2004
—Continued

(Number in thousands, percent.)

Year	Total population	Covered by private or government health insurance								Not covered
		Total	Private health insurance		Government health insurance					
			Total	Employ-ment based	Total	Medicaid	Medicare	Military health care[1]		

ASIAN ALONE[12]

Number

2002	11 558	9 426	7 939	6 932	2 132	1 202	988	270		2 132
2003	11 869	9 641	8 143	7 210	2 244	1 229	1 067	295		2 228
2004	12 311	10 241	8 704	7 612	2 396	1 267	1 098	360		2 070

Percent

2002	100.0	81.6	68.7	60.0	18.4	10.4	8.5	2.3		18.4
2003	100.0	81.2	68.6	60.7	18.9	10.4	9.0	2.5		18.8
2004	100.0	83.2	70.7	61.8	19.5	10.3	8.9	2.9		16.8

ASIAN AND PACIFIC ISLANDER[10]

Number

1987[2]	6 326	5 440	4 468	3 691	1 394	702	357	475		886
1988	6 447	5 329	4 392	3 599	1 353	763	401	322		1 118
1989	6 679	5 532	4 615	3 661	1 414	792	444	322		1 147
1990	7 023	5 832	4 887	3 883	1 410	771	463	364		1 191
1991	7 193	5 886	4 917	3 995	1 451	727	560	347		1 307
1992[3]	7 782	6 230	5 202	4 207	1 460	823	507	314		1 552
1993[4]	7 444	5 927	5 026	3 970	1 408	802	474	345		1 517
1994[5]	6 656	5 312	4 267	3 774	1 551	883	501	426		1 344
1995	9 653	7 671	6 347	5 576	2 075	1 272	586	424		1 982
1996	10 071	7 946	6 718	5 888	1 768	1 071	667	275		2 125
1997[6]	10 492	8 320	7 100	6 290	1 877	1 093	700	334		2 173
1998	10 897	8 596	7 202	6 511	2 113	1 201	819	351		2 301
1999[7]	11 964	9 673	8 189	7 331	2 204	1 179	897	450		2 292
1999	10 925	8 653	7 285	6 588	2 023	1 087	825	412		2 272
2000[8]	12 693	10 405	8 916	8 104	2 249	1 288	886	443		2 287
2001	12 500	10 222	8 643	7 684	2 312	1 257	949	414		2 278

Percent

1987[2]	100.0	86.0	70.6	58.3	22.0	11.1	5.6	7.5		14.0
1988	100.0	82.7	68.1	55.8	21.0	11.8	6.2	5.0		17.3
1989	100.0	82.8	69.1	54.8	21.2	11.9	6.6	4.8		17.2
1990	100.0	83.0	69.6	55.3	20.1	11.0	6.6	5.2		17.0
1991	100.0	81.8	68.4	55.5	20.2	10.1	7.8	4.8		18.2
1992[3]	100.0	80.1	66.8	54.1	18.8	10.6	6.5	4.0		19.9
1993[4]	100.0	79.6	67.5	53.3	18.9	10.8	6.4	4.6		20.4
1994[5]	100.0	79.8	64.1	56.7	23.3	13.3	7.5	6.4		20.2
1995	100.0	79.5	65.8	57.8	21.5	13.2	6.1	4.4		20.5
1996	100.0	78.9	66.7	58.5	17.6	10.6	6.6	2.7		21.1
1997[6]	100.0	79.3	67.7	60.0	17.9	10.4	6.7	3.2		20.7
1998	100.0	78.9	66.1	59.8	19.4	11.0	7.5	3.2		21.1
1999[7]	100.0	80.8	68.4	61.3	18.4	9.9	7.5	3.8		19.2
1999	100.0	79.2	66.7	60.3	18.5	9.9	7.5	3.8		20.8
2000[8]	100.0	82.0	70.2	63.8	17.7	10.1	7.0	3.5		18.0
2001	100.0	81.8	69.1	61.5	18.5	10.1	7.6	3.3		18.2

Source: U.S. Census Bureau. Current Population Reports. *Health Insurance Coverage: 2004.*

[1]Includes CHAMPUS (Comprehensive Health and Medical Plan for Uniformed Services)/Tricare, veterans', and military health care.
[2]Implementation of a new CPS ASEC processing system.
[3]Implementation of 1990 census population controls.
[4]Data collection method changed from paper and pencil to computer-assisted interviewing.
[5]Health insurance questions were redesigned. Increases in estimates of employment-based and military health care coverage may be partially due to questionnaire changes. Overall coverage estimates were not affected.
[6]Beginning with the 1998 CPS ASEC, people with no coverage other than access to Indian Health Service are no longer considered covered health insurance; instead, they are considered to be uninsured. The effect of this change on the overall estimates of health insurance coverage is negligible; however, the decrease in the number of people covered by Medicaid may be partially due to this change.
[7]Estimates reflect the results of follow-up verification questions and implementation of Census 2000-based population controls.
[8]Implementation of a 28,000 household sample expansion.
[10]The 2001 CPS and earlier years asked respondents to report only one race. The reference groups for these years are: White, White not Hispanic, Black, and Asian and Pacific Islander.
[12]Asian alone refers to people who reported Asian and did not report any other race category.

Table A9-8. Health Insurance Coverage Status and Type of Coverage, 1987–2004
—Continued

(Number in thousands, percent.)

Year	Total population	Covered by private or government health insurance							Not covered
		Total	Private health insurance		Government health insurance				
			Total	Employ-ment based	Total	Medicaid	Medicare	Military health care[1]	
HISPANIC (OF ANY RACE)									
Number									
1987[2]	19 428	13 456	9 845	8 490	4 482	3 214	1 029	631	5 972
1988	20 076	13 684	10 188	8 831	4 414	3 125	1 114	594	6 391
1989	20 779	13 846	10 348	8 914	4 526	3 221	1 180	595	6 932
1990	21 437	14 479	10 281	8 948	5 169	3 912	1 269	519	6 958
1991	22 096	15 128	10 336	8 972	5 845	4 597	1 309	522	6 968
1992[3]	25 682	17 242	11 330	9 786	7 099	5 703	1 578	523	8 441
1993[4]	26 646	18 235	12 021	9 981	7 873	6 328	1 613	530	8 411
1994[5]	27 521	18 244	11 743	10 729	7 829	6 226	1 677	630	9 277
1995	28 438	18 964	12 187	11 309	8 027	6 478	1 732	516	9 474
1996	29 703	19 730	13 151	12 140	7 784	6 255	1 806	474	9 974
1997[6]	30 773	20 239	13 751	12 790	7 718	5 970	1 974	526	10 534
1998	31 689	20 493	14 377	13 310	7 401	5 585	2 026	503	11 196
1997[7]	34 773	23 311	16 634	15 275	8 168	6 253	1 979	626	11 462
1999	32 804	21 853	15 424	14 214	7 875	5 946	2 047	589	10 951
2000[8]	36 093	24 210	17 114	15 893	8 566	6 552	2 141	682	11 883
2001	37 438	25 021	17 322	15 965	9 227	7 074	2 295	704	12 417
2002	39 384	26 627	18 108	16 714	10 280	7 946	2 535	724	12 756
2003	40 425	27 188	18 183	16 788	10 716	8 505	2 462	639	13 237
2004	41 839	28 160	18 714	17 208	11 462	9 123	2 618	694	13 678
Percent									
1987[2]	100.0	69.3	50.7	43.7	23.1	16.5	5.3	3.2	30.7
1988	100.0	68.2	50.7	44.0	22.0	15.6	5.5	3.0	31.8
1989	100.0	66.6	49.8	42.9	21.8	15.5	5.7	2.9	33.4
1990	100.0	67.5	48.0	41.7	24.1	18.2	5.9	2.4	32.5
1991	100.0	68.5	46.8	40.6	26.5	20.8	5.9	2.4	31.5
1992[3]	100.0	67.1	44.1	38.1	27.6	22.2	6.1	2.0	32.9
1993[4]	100.0	68.4	45.1	37.5	29.5	23.7	6.1	2.0	31.6
1994[5]	100.0	66.3	42.7	39.0	28.4	22.6	6.1	2.3	33.7
1995	100.0	66.7	42.9	39.8	28.2	22.8	6.1	1.8	33.3
1996	100.0	66.4	44.3	40.9	26.2	21.1	6.1	1.6	33.6
1997[6]	100.0	65.8	44.7	41.6	25.1	19.4	6.4	1.7	34.2
1998	100.0	64.7	45.4	42.0	23.4	17.6	6.4	1.6	35.3
1997[7]	100.0	67.0	47.8	43.9	23.5	18.0	5.7	1.8	33.0
1999	100.0	66.6	47.0	43.3	24.0	18.1	6.2	1.8	33.4
2000[8]	100.0	66.8	46.3	42.6	24.6	18.9	6.1	1.9	33.2
2001	100.0	67.6	46.0	42.4	26.1	20.2	6.4	1.8	32.4
2002	100.0	67.1	47.4	44.0	23.7	18.2	5.9	1.9	32.9
2003	100.0	67.3	45.0	41.5	26.5	21.0	6.1	1.6	32.7
2004	100.0	67.3	44.7	41.1	27.4	21.8	6.3	1.7	32.7

Source: U.S. Census Bureau. Current Population Reports. *Health Insurance Coverage: 2004.*

[1]Includes CHAMPUS (Comprehensive Health and Medical Plan for Uniformed Services)/Tricare, veterans', and military health care.
[2]Implementation of a new CPS ASEC processing system.
[3]Implementation of 1990 census population controls.
[4]Data collection method changed from paper and pencil to computer-assisted interviewing.
[5]Health insurance questions were redesigned. Increases in estimates of employment-based and military health care coverage may be partially due to questionnaire changes. Overall coverage estimates were not affected.
[6]Beginning with the 1998 CPS ASEC, people with no coverage other than access to Indian Health Service are no longer considered covered health insurance; instead, they are considered to be uninsured. The effect of this change on the overall estimates of health insurance coverage is negligible; however, the decrease in the number of people covered by Medicaid may be partially due to this change.
[7]Estimates reflect the results of follow-up verification questions and implementation of Census 2000-based population controls.
[8]Implementation of a 28,000 household sample expansion.

Leisure, Volunteerism, and Religiosity

Table A10-1. Average Hours Per Day Spent by Persons 18 Years of Age and Over Caring for Household Children Under 18 Years of Age, 2004

(Hours.)

Child care activities	Total	Men	Women
Persons in Households with Children Under 18, Total			
Caring for household children as a primary activity	1.34	0.84	1.76
Physical care	0.47	0.22	0.67
Education-related activities	0.10	0.06	0.13
Reading to/with children	0.04	0.02	0.05
Talking to/with children	0.05	0.02	0.07
Playing/doing hobbies with children	0.26	0.23	0.29
Looking after children	0.08	0.06	0.11
Attending children's events	0.06	0.05	0.06
Travel related to care of household children	0.17	0.10	0.23
Other child care activities	0.12	0.06	0.17
Persons in Households with Youngest Child 6 to 17 Years			
Caring for household children as a primary activity	0.79	0.52	1.00
Physical care	0.15	0.06	0.23
Education-related activities	0.12	0.07	0.16
Reading to/with children	0.02	. . .	0.03
Talking to/with children	0.06	0.03	0.09
Playing/doing hobbies with children	0.06	0.08	0.04
Looking after children	0.05	. . .	0.06
Attending children's events	0.08	0.07	0.08
Travel related to care of household children	0.15	0.11	0.19
Other child care activities	0.10	0.06	0.12
Persons in Households with Youngest Child Under 6 Years			
Caring for household children as a primary activity	2.02	1.21	2.73
Physical care	0.85	0.41	1.22
Education-related activities	0.07	. . .	0.10
Reading to/with children	0.06	0.04	0.08
Talking to/with children	0.03	. . .	0.04
Playing/doing hobbies with children	0.51	0.41	0.60
Looking after children	0.13	0.09	0.16
Attending children's events	0.04	. . .	0.04
Travel related to care of household children	0.19	0.09	0.27
Other child care activities	0.15	0.07	0.22

Source: U.S. Bureau of Labor Statistics. American Time Use Survey 2004.

. . . = Not available.

Table A10-2. Average Hours Per Day Spent in Leisure and Sports Activities, 2004

(Hours.)

Characteristic	Total, all days	Total, all leisure and sports activities		Participating in sports, exercise, and recreation		Socializing and communicating		Watching TV	
		Weekdays	Weekends and holidays	Weekdays	Weekends and holidays	Weekdays	Weekends and holidays	Weekdays	Weekends and holidays
Sex									
Men	5.56	5.00	6.86	0.35	0.52	0.56	1.04	2.61	3.43
Women	4.82	4.45	5.71	0.20	0.19	0.61	1.21	2.36	2.62
Age									
Total, 15 years and over	5.18	4.71	6.28	0.27	0.35	0.59	1.13	2.48	3.02
15–24 years	5.68	5.26	6.62	0.50	0.57	0.81	1.27	2.36	2.77
25–34 years	4.40	3.63	5.93	0.18	0.46	0.55	1.27	2.02	2.78
35–44 years	4.15	3.59	5.55	0.25	0.28	0.46	1.14	1.94	2.67
45–54 years	4.51	3.99	5.77	0.21	0.28	0.48	1.00	2.18	2.89
55–64 years	5.45	5.04	6.56	0.21	0.28	0.59	0.99	2.79	3.32
65 years and over	7.31	7.17	7.68	0.27	0.17	0.65	1.00	3.82	4.04
Race/Ethnicity									
White	5.14	4.67	6.30	0.28	0.37	0.59	1.15	2.40	2.94
Black or African American	5.65	5.35	6.23	0.23	0.16	0.58	0.95	3.15	3.62
Hispanic or Latino (of any race)	4.81	4.24	5.85	0.25	0.41	0.57	1.24	2.41	2.95
Employment Status									
Employed	4.24	3.61	5.73	0.23	0.37	0.50	1.09	1.87	2.71
Full-time workers	4.07	3.33	5.74	0.22	0.37	0.43	1.07	1.79	2.78
Part-time workers	4.83	4.52	5.67	0.27	0.38	0.72	1.17	2.16	2.42
Not employed	6.82	6.64	7.29	0.34	0.32	0.74	1.19	3.53	3.59
Earnings of Full-Time Wage and Salary Workers									
$450 and lower	4.21	3.56	5.64	0.21	0.32	0.45	1.09	2.04	2.80
$451–$675	4.21	3.42	5.96	0.11	0.37	0.44	1.00	1.95	3.13
$676–$1,050	4.17	3.45	5.82	0.23	0.31	0.47	1.14	1.80	2.98
$1,051 and higher	3.84	3.05	5.70	0.32	0.45	0.40	1.15	1.40	2.30
Presence and Age of Children									
No household children under 18 years	5.74	5.32	6.75	0.27	0.33	0.59	1.13	2.84	3.27
Household children under 18 years	4.35	3.79	5.62	0.28	0.38	0.59	1.12	1.93	2.67
Children 13–17 years, none younger	4.62	4.03	6.24	0.32	0.41	0.60	1.10	1.91	2.78
Children 6–12 years, none younger	4.50	3.91	5.81	0.34	0.40	0.58	1.15	1.97	2.77
Youngest child under 6 years	4.06	3.54	5.17	0.21	0.36	0.59	1.11	1.91	2.54
Marital Status and Sex									
Married, spouse present	4.77	4.30	5.92	0.24	0.31	0.55	1.12	2.28	2.88
Men	5.09	4.50	6.47	0.29	0.43	0.50	1.08	2.46	3.32
Women	4.45	4.11	5.33	0.19	0.18	0.60	1.16	2.12	2.40
Other marital statuses	5.68	5.24	6.70	0.31	0.40	0.64	1.14	2.72	3.18
Men	6.19	5.68	7.37	0.43	0.64	0.65	0.99	2.80	3.56
Women	5.24	4.86	6.12	0.21	0.20	0.62	1.27	2.66	2.86
Educational Attainment, 25 Years and Over									
Less than a high school diploma	6.13	5.91	6.57	0.15	0.21	0.59	1.11	3.72	3.85
High school graduates, no college	5.45	5.07	6.38	0.18	0.29	0.56	1.09	2.95	3.37
Some college or associate degree	4.89	4.37	6.16	0.20	0.30	0.52	1.03	2.32	3.03
Bachelor's degree and higher	4.33	3.73	5.85	0.32	0.37	0.51	1.16	1.67	2.39

Source: U.S. Bureau of Labor Statistics. American Time Use Survey 2004.

Table A10-2. Average Hours Per Day Spent in Leisure and Sports Activities, 2004 —Continued

(Hours.)

Characteristic	Reading		Relaxing/thinking		Playing games and computer use for leisure, including travel		Other leisure and sports activities	
	Weekdays	Weekends and holidays	Weekdays	Weekends and holidays	Weekdays	Weekends and holidays	Weekdays	Weekends and holidays
Sex								
Men	0.30	0.37	0.31	0.29	0.43	0.46	0.44	0.75
Women	0.42	0.49	0.28	0.26	0.25	0.29	0.34	0.65
Age								
Total, 15 years and over	0.36	0.43	0.29	0.28	0.34	0.37	0.38	0.70
15–24 years	0.12	0.13	0.20	0.21	0.71	0.70	0.56	0.97
25–34 years	0.16	0.17	0.17	0.20	0.23	0.38	0.32	0.67
35–44 years	0.22	0.30	0.23	0.23	0.22	0.28	0.27	0.63
45–54 years	0.30	0.47	0.24	0.27	0.24	0.22	0.34	0.63
55–64 years	0.53	0.66	0.31	0.29	0.23	0.32	0.37	0.70
65 years and over	0.95	1.11	0.64	0.53	0.38	0.27	0.46	0.56
Race/Ethnicity								
White	0.39	0.47	0.27	0.26	0.35	0.38	0.40	0.73
Black or African American	0.26	0.24	0.52	0.39	0.27	0.30	0.35	0.56
Hispanic or Latino (of any race)	0.21	0.15	0.27	0.19	0.22	0.22	0.32	0.67
Employment Status								
Employed	0.23	0.33	0.20	0.22	0.23	0.32	0.34	0.69
Full-time workers	0.21	0.32	0.20	0.23	0.18	0.31	0.31	0.66
Part-time workers	0.30	0.35	0.21	0.19	0.39	0.35	0.46	0.80
Not employed	0.59	0.62	0.45	0.38	0.52	0.47	0.46	0.71
Earnings of Full-Time Wage and Salary Workers								
$450 and lower	0.13	0.21	0.26	0.28	0.22	0.25	0.25	0.69
$451–$675	0.19	0.25	0.21	0.20	0.18	0.41	0.35	0.61
$676–$1,050	0.28	0.32	0.21	0.23	0.17	0.23	0.29	0.61
$1,051 and higher	0.26	0.49	0.14	0.23	0.18	0.30	0.35	0.79
Presence and Age of Children								
No household children under 18 years	0.47	0.57	0.36	0.32	0.39	0.39	0.41	0.74
Household children under 18 years	0.20	0.23	0.20	0.22	0.25	0.35	0.35	0.65
Children 13–17 years, none younger	0.21	0.32	0.21	0.30	0.38	0.54	0.41	0.78
Children 6–12 years, none younger	0.23	0.25	0.21	0.21	0.22	0.37	0.37	0.67
Youngest child under 6 years	0.16	0.16	0.18	0.19	0.21	0.24	0.29	0.57
Marital Status and Sex								
Married, spouse present	0.38	0.48	0.29	0.27	0.24	0.26	0.32	0.60
Men	0.34	0.43	0.31	0.30	0.26	0.28	0.34	0.63
Women	0.43	0.53	0.27	0.24	0.22	0.24	0.29	0.58
Other marital statuses	0.34	0.38	0.30	0.28	0.46	0.50	0.47	0.81
Men	0.25	0.29	0.30	0.29	0.67	0.69	0.57	0.91
Women	0.41	0.45	0.29	0.28	0.28	0.34	0.39	0.73
Educational Attainment, 25 Years and Over								
Less than a high school diploma	0.34	0.32	0.63	0.51	0.19	0.10	0.30	0.47
High school graduates, no college	0.39	0.39	0.38	0.35	0.29	0.31	0.33	0.59
Some college or associate degree	0.42	0.51	0.24	0.22	0.30	0.37	0.37	0.69
Bachelor's degree and higher	0.46	0.70	0.17	0.18	0.22	0.32	0.37	0.72

Source: U.S. Bureau of Labor Statistics. American Time Use Survey 2004.

Detailed Tables
Voting

Table A11-1. Reported Voting and Registration by Race, November 1964 to November 2004

(Number in thousands, percent.)

Year	Total voting-age population (thousands)	Percent registered	Percent voted
All Groups			
1964	110 604	. . .	69.3
1966	112 800	70.3	55.4
1968	116 535	74.3	67.8
1970	120 701	68.1	54.6
1972	136 203	72.3	63.0
1974	141 299	62.2	44.7
1976	146 548	66.7	59.2
1978	151 646	62.6	45.9
1980	157 085	66.9	59.3
1982	165 483	64.1	48.5
1984	169 963	68.3	59.9
1986	173 890	64.3	46.0
1988	178 098	66.6	57.4
1990	182 118	62.2	45.0
1992	185 684	68.2	61.3
1994	190 267	62.5	45.0
1996	193 651	65.9	54.2
1998	198 228	62.1	41.9
2000	202 609	63.9	54.7
2002	210 421	60.9	42.3
2004	215 694	65.9	58.3
White			
1964	110 604	. . .	70.7
1966	112 800	71.7	57.0
1968	116 535	75.4	69.1
1970	120 701	70.8	56.0
1972	136 203	73.4	64.5
1974	141 299	64.6	46.3
1976	146 548	68.3	60.9
1978	151 646	63.8	47.3
1980	157 085	68.4	60.9
1982	165 483	65.6	49.9
1984	169 963	69.6	61.4
1986	173 890	65.3	47.0
1988	178 098	67.9	59.1
1990	182 118	63.8	46.7
1992	185 684	70.1	63.6
1994	190 267	64.6	47.3
1996	193 651	67.7	56.0
1998	198 228	63.9	43.3
2000	202 609	65.7	56.4
2002	210 421	63.1	44.1
2004	215 694	67.9	60.3
White, Non-Hispanic			
1978	151 646	65.4	48.6
1980	157 085	70.3	62.8
1982	165 483	67.5	51.5
1984	169 963	71.6	63.3
1986	173 890	67.7	48.9
1988	178 098	70.8	61.8
1990	182 118	66.7	49.0
1992	185 684	73.5	66.9
1994	190 267	68.1	50.1
1996	193 651	71.6	59.6
1998	198 228	67.9	46.5
2000	202 609	70.0	60.4
2002	210 421	67.9	48.0
2004	215 694	73.5	65.8
Black			
1964	110 604	. . .	58.5
1966	112 800	60.2	41.7
1968	116 535	66.2	57.6
1970	120 701	64.5	43.5
1972	136 203	65.5	52.1
1974	141 299	54.2	33.8
1976	146 548	58.5	48.7
1978	151 646	57.1	37.2
1980	157 085	60.0	50.5
1982	165 483	59.1	43.0
1984	169 963	66.3	55.8
1986	173 890	64.0	43.2
1988	178 098	64.5	51.5
1990	182 118	58.8	39.2
1992	185 684	63.9	54.1
1994	190 267	58.5	37.1
1996	193 651	63.5	50.6
1998	198 228	60.2	39.6
2000	202 609	63.6	53.5
2002	210 421	58.5	39.7
2004	215 694	64.4	56.3

Source: U.S. Census Bureau.
Note: Percentages would be slightly higher if non-citizens were excluded from voting-age population.

. . . = Not available.

Table A11-1. Reported Voting and Registration by Race, November 1964 to November 2004—*Continued*

(Number in thousands, percent.)

Year	Total voting-age population (thousands)	Percent registered	Percent voted
Asian/Pacific Islander			
1990	182 118	28.4	20.3
1992	185 684	31.2	27.3
1994	190 267	28.7	21.8
1996	193 651	32.6	25.7
1998	198 228	29.1	19.3
2000	202 609	30.7	25.4
2002	210 421	30.7	19.4
2004	215 694	34.9	29.8
Hispanic (of any race)			
1972	136 203	44.4	37.5
1974	141 299	34.9	22.9
1976	146 548	37.8	31.8
1978	151 646	32.9	23.5
1980	157 085	36.4	29.9
1982	165 483	35.3	25.3
1984	169 963	40.1	32.7
1986	173 890	35.9	24.2
1988	178 098	35.5	28.8
1990	182 118	32.3	21.0
1992	185 684	35.0	28.9
1994	190 267	31.3	20.2
1996	193 651	35.7	26.8
1998	198 228	33.7	20.0
2000	202 609	34.9	27.5
2002	210 421	32.6	18.9
2004	215 694	34.3	28.0
Men			
1964	110 604	. . .	71.9
1966	112 800	72.2	58.2
1968	116 535	76.0	69.8
1970	120 701	69.6	56.8
1972	136 203	73.1	64.1
1974	141 299	62.8	46.2
1976	146 548	67.1	59.6
1978	151 646	62.6	46.6
1980	157 085	66.6	59.1
1982	165 483	63.7	48.7
1984	169 963	67.3	59.0
1986	173 890	63.4	45.8
1988	178 098	65.2	56.4
1990	182 118	61.2	44.6
1992	185 684	66.9	60.2
1994	190 267	61.2	44.7
1996	193 651	64.4	52.8
1998	198 228	60.6	41.4
2000	202 609	62.2	53.1
2002	210 421	58.9	41.4
2004	215 694	64.0	56.3
Women			
1964	110 604	. . .	67.0
1966	112 800	68.6	53.0
1968	116 535	72.8	66.0
1970	120 701	66.8	52.7
1972	136 203	71.6	62.0
1974	141 299	61.7	43.4
1976	146 548	66.4	58.8
1978	151 646	62.5	45.3
1980	157 085	67.1	59.4
1982	165 483	64.4	48.4
1984	169 963	69.3	60.8
1986	173 890	65.0	46.1
1988	178 098	67.8	58.3
1990	182 118	63.1	45.4
1992	185 684	69.3	62.3
1994	190 267	63.7	45.3
1996	193 651	67.3	55.5
1998	198 228	63.5	42.4
2000	202 609	65.6	56.2
2002	210 421	62.8	43.0
2004	215 694	67.6	60.1

Source: U.S. Census Bureau.
Note: Percentages would be slightly higher if non-citizens were excluded from voting-age population.

. . . = Not available.

Table A11-2. Reported Voting and Registration by Age and Region, November 1964 to November 2004

(Percent.)

Year	Age				Region			
	18 to 24 years	25 to 44 years	45 to 64 years	65 years and over	Northeast	Midwest	South	West
Voted								
1964	50.9	69.0	75.9	66.3	74.4	76.2	56.7	71.9
1966	31.1	53.1	64.5	56.1	...	...	...	...
1968	50.4	66.6	74.9	65.8	...	...	...	...
1970	30.4	51.9	64.2	57.0	...	...	...	...
1972	49.6	62.7	70.8	63.5	...	...	...	...
1974	23.8	42.2	56.9	51.4	48.7	49.3	36.0	48.1
1976	42.2	58.7	68.7	62.2	59.5	65.1	54.9	57.5
1978	23.5	43.1	58.5	55.9	48.1	50.5	39.6	47.5
1980	39.9	58.7	69.3	65.1	58.5	65.8	55.6	57.2
1982	24.8	45.4	62.2	59.9	49.8	54.7	41.8	50.7
1984	40.8	58.4	69.8	67.7	59.7	65.7	56.8	58.5
1986	21.9	41.4	58.7	60.9	44.4	49.5	43.0	48.4
1988	36.2	54.0	67.9	68.8	57.4	62.9	54.5	55.6
1990	20.4	40.7	55.8	60.3	45.2	48.6	42.4	45.0
1992	42.8	58.3	70.0	70.1	61.2	67.2	59.0	58.5
1994	20.1	39.4	56.7	61.3	45.6	48.9	40.9	47.1
1996	32.4	49.2	64.4	67.0	54.5	59.3	52.2	51.8
1998	16.6	34.8	53.6	59.5	41.2	47.3	38.6	42.3
2000	32.3	49.8	64.1	67.6	55.2	60.9	49.9	53.5
2002	17.2	34.1	53.1	61.0	41.4	47.1	41.6	39.0
2004	41.9	52.2	66.6	68.9	58.6	65.0	56.4	54.4
Registered								
1964	...	...	...	...	...	...	...	...
1966	44.1	67.6	78.9	73.5	...	...	...	...
1968	56.0	72.4	81.1	75.6	...	...	...	...
1970	40.9	65.0	77.5	73.7	...	...	...	...
1972	58.9	71.3	79.7	75.6	...	...	...	...
1974	41.3	59.9	73.6	70.2	62.2	66.6	59.8	59.8
1976	51.3	65.5	75.5	71.4	65.9	72.3	64.6	63.2
1978	40.5	60.2	74.3	72.8	62.3	68.2	60.1	59.1
1980	49.2	65.6	75.8	74.6	64.8	73.8	64.8	63.3
1982	42.4	61.5	75.6	75.2	62.5	71.1	61.7	60.6
1984	51.3	66.6	76.6	76.9	66.6	74.6	66.9	64.7
1986	42.0	61.1	74.8	76.9	62.0	70.7	63.0	60.8
1988	48.2	63.0	75.5	78.4	64.8	72.5	65.6	63.0
1990	39.9	58.4	71.4	76.5	61.0	68.2	61.3	57.7
1992	52.5	64.8	75.3	78.0	67.0	74.6	67.2	63.6
1994	42.3	57.9	71.7	76.3	61.5	68.9	61.1	58.9
1996	48.8	61.9	73.5	77.0	64.7	71.6	65.9	60.8
1998	39.2	57.7	71.1	75.4	60.8	68.2	62.7	56.0
2000	45.4	59.6	71.2	76.1	63.7	70.2	56.9	64.5
2002	38.2	55.4	69.4	75.8	60.8	66.5	61.6	54.0
2004	51.5	60.1	72.7	76.9	65.3	72.8	65.5	60.1

Source: U.S. Census Bureau.
Note: Prior to 1972, data are for people 21 years of age and over with the exception of those age 18 years and over in Georgia and Kentucky, 19 years and over in Alaska, and 20 years and over in Hawaii. Registration data were not collected in the 1964 Current Population Survey.

... = Not available.

Table A11-3. Reported Voting and Registration by Age, Race, and Sex, November 1964 to November 2004

(Number in thousands, percent.)

| Year | Total voting-age population | Percent | | | | | | | |
		Total	White	White, non-Hispanic	Black	Asian/Pacific Islander	Hispanic [1]	Male	Female
18 TO 24 YEARS									
Voted									
1964	9 919	50.9	52.1	. . .	44.2	. . .	. . .	51.5	50.5
1966	10 751	31.1	32.6	. . .	21.9	. . .	. . .	32.3	30.3
1968	11 602	50.4	52.8	. . .	38.9	. . .	. . .	50.3	50.6
1970	13 027	30.4	31.5	. . .	22.4	. . .	. . .	30.6	30.0
1972	24 612	49.6	51.9	. . .	34.7	. . .	30.9	48.8	50.4
1974	25 719	23.8	25.2	. . .	16.1	. . .	13.3	24.6	23.1
1976	26 953	42.2	44.7	. . .	27.9	. . .	21.8	40.9	43.4
1978	27 678	23.5	24.2	. . .	20.1	. . .	11.5	23.2	23.9
1980	28 138	39.9	41.8	. . .	30.1	. . .	15.9	38.5	41.2
1982	28 823	24.8	25.0	. . .	25.5	. . .	14.2	25.1	25.7
1984	27 976	40.8	41.6	. . .	40.6	. . .	21.9	38.7	42.8
1986	26 425	21.9	21.6	. . .	25.1	. . .	11.6	21.2	22.5
1988	25 569	36.2	37.0	. . .	35.0	. . .	16.8	34.1	38.2
1990	24 831	20.4	20.8	. . .	20.2	. . .	8.7	19.8	21.0
1992	24 371	42.8	45.4	. . .	36.6	. . .	17.6	40.5	45.1
1994	25 182	20.1	21.1	23.1	17.4	10.6	10.1	18.6	21.5
1996	24 650	32.4	33.3	36.9	32.4	19.2	15.1	29.8	35.0
1998	25 537	16.6	17.2	19.2	15.6	9.7	9.0	15.7	17.6
2000	26 712	32.3	33.0	37.2	33.9	15.9	15.4	30.0	34.6
2002	27 377	17.2	17.4	19.9	19.3	8.1	10.0	15.7	18.6
2004	27 808	41.9	42.6	48.5	44.1	23.5	20.4	38.8	44.9
Registered									
1964	9 919	. . .	. . .	. . .	. . .	. . .	. . .	. . .	. . .
1966	10 751	44.1	43.6	. . .	34.5	. . .	. . .	44.4	43.8
1968	11 602	56.0	57.9	. . .	46.4	. . .	. . .	56.1	55.9
1970	13 027	40.9	40.6	. . .	33.0	. . .	. . .	41.2	40.6
1972	24 612	58.9	60.6	. . .	47.7	. . .	38.9	58.3	59.4
1974	25 719	41.3	42.8	. . .	33.6	. . .	23.1	41.8	40.8
1976	26 953	51.3	53.7	. . .	38.8	. . .	29.0	50.8	51.9
1978	27 678	40.5	37.2	. . .	37.2	. . .	20.5	39.5	41.5
1980	28 138	49.2	51.0	. . .	41.3	. . .	22.5	48.0	50.4
1982	28 823	42.4	43.2	. . .	41.8	. . .	24.3	42.4	42.5
1984	27 976	51.3	52.0	. . .	53.7	. . .	29.8	49.6	53.0
1986	26 425	42.0	42.0	. . .	46.1	. . .	22.0	41.0	43.0
1988	25 569	48.2	48.7	. . .	49.8	. . .	25.3	45.5	50.8
1990	24 831	39.9	40.5	. . .	40.2	. . .	19.3	39.5	40.2
1992	24 371	52.5	54.6	. . .	49.2	. . .	24.9	50.5	54.4
1994	25 182	42.3	43.9	48.1	42.0	18.3	20.0	40.9	43.7
1996	24 650	48.8	49.8	54.3	49.4	29.5	27.6	46.5	51.0
1998	25 537	39.2	36.4	45.0	37.6	17.7	22.2	36.4	42.0
2000	26 712	45.4	46.3	51.7	48.0	22.2	23.2	42.3	48.5
2002	27 377	38.2	39.2	44.2	39.6	20.8	21.7	34.9	41.6
2004	27 808	51.5	52.5	59.1	53.1	29.1	27.6	48.2	54.9

Source: U.S. Census Bureau.
Note: Prior to 1972, data are for people 21 years of age and over with the exception of those age 18 years and over in Georgia and Kentucky, 19 years and over in Alaska, and 20 years and over in Hawaii. Registration data were not collected in the 1964 Current Population Survey.

[1]May be of any race.
. . . = Not available.

Table A11-3. Reported Voting and Registration by Age, Race, and Sex, November 1964 to November 2004—*Continued*

(Number in thousands, percent.)

Year	Total voting-age population	Percent							
		Total	White	White, non-Hispanic	Black	Asian/Pacific Islander	Hispanic [1]	Male	Female
25 TO 44 YEARS									
Voted									
1964	45 296	69.0	70.1	. . .	61.5	. . .	. . .	70.0	68.0
1966	45 061	53.1	54.4	. . .	43.9	. . .	. . .	54.1	52.1
1968	46 103	66.6	67.7	. . .	60.3	. . .	. . .	67.2	66.1
1970	47 056	51.9	53.0	. . .	44.1	. . .	. . .	52.3	51.5
1972	49 173	62.7	64.0	. . .	61.4	. . .	39.5	62.5	62.9
1974	51 663	42.2	47.6	. . .	36.4	. . .	24.2	42.0	42.4
1976	54 302	58.7	60.6	. . .	49.6	. . .	33.2	57.9	59.5
1978	57 536	43.1	44.4	. . .	36.7	. . .	22.4	42.5	43.6
1980	61 285	58.7	60.3	. . .	51.9	. . .	30.4	57.1	60.1
1982	66 881	45.4	46.5	. . .	43.5	. . .	22.2	44.5	46.2
1984	71 023	58.4	60.0	. . .	40.6	. . .	31.1	56.3	60.5
1986	74 927	41.4	42.2	. . .	41.2	. . .	21.7	40.3	42.4
1988	77 863	54.0	55.9	. . .	48.0	. . .	27.1	51.8	56.1
1990	80 541	40.7	42.1	. . .	37.8	. . .	19.7	39.1	42.2
1992	81 319	58.3	60.6	. . .	52.1	. . .	26.4	55.8	60.6
1994	83 006	39.4	41.5	44.6	33.3	17.4	17.5	38.6	40.2
1996	83 393	49.2	50.8	55.1	47.8	22.8	22.9	46.8	51.5
1998	82 993	34.8	35.8	39.1	36.4	12.9	16.1	33.5	36.1
2000	81 780	49.8	51.2	56.3	52.1	22.2	23.2	47.3	52.3
2002	82 228	34.1	35.3	39.7	36.1	15.3	14.0	32.7	35.4
2004	82 133	52.2	54.0	61.6	54.0	23.9	23.0	49.0	55.2
Registered									
1964	45 296	. . .	. . .	. . .	. . .	. . .	. . .	. . .	. . .
1966	45 061	67.6	68.7	. . .	61.9	. . .	. . .	68.1	67.3
1968	46 103	72.4	73.3	. . .	68.7	. . .	. . .	73.0	71.9
1970	47 056	65.0	65.9	. . .	60.9	. . .	. . .	65.3	64.8
1972	49 173	71.3	72.1	. . .	68.7	. . .	46.0	71.2	71.4
1974	51 663	59.9	65.0	. . .	58.3	. . .	37.2	42.4	60.8
1976	54 302	65.5	67.0	. . .	59.5	. . .	38.4	64.8	66.1
1978	57 536	60.2	61.5	. . .	56.9	. . .	32.7	59.5	60.9
1980	61 285	65.6	67.0	. . .	59.5	. . .	36.0	64.3	66.8
1982	66 881	61.5	62.9	. . .	59.4	. . .	30.8	60.3	62.6
1984	71 023	66.6	68.0	. . .	53.7	. . .	38.4	64.5	68.6
1986	74 927	61.1	61.9	. . .	64.0	. . .	34.5	59.4	62.8
1988	77 863	63.0	64.4	. . .	62.1	. . .	33.2	60.6	65.4
1990	80 541	58.4	59.9	. . .	57.2	. . .	30.4	56.4	60.3
1992	81 319	64.8	66.8	. . .	62.0	. . .	32.0	62.6	67.0
1994	83 006	57.9	59.9	64.0	55.4	24.4	28.4	55.9	59.7
1996	83 393	61.9	63.6	68.5	61.4	28.5	31.8	59.6	64.1
1998	82 993	57.7	59.4	64.3	59.5	23.2	29.8	55.5	59.9
2000	81 780	59.6	61.2	66.8	62.0	26.7	31.1	57.3	61.8
2002	82 228	55.4	57.4	63.8	55.8	28.9	25.6	52.8	57.9
2004	82 133	60.1	62.0	70.2	62.2	28.9	28.8	57.6	62.5

Source: U.S. Census Bureau.
Note: Prior to 1972, data are for people 21 years of age and over with the exception of those age 18 years and over in Georgia and Kentucky, 19 years and over in Alaska, and 20 years and over in Hawaii. Registration data were not collected in the 1964 Current Population Survey.

[1] May be of any race.
. . . = Not available.

Table A11-3. Reported Voting and Registration by Age, Race, and Sex, November 1964 to November 2004—*Continued*

(Number in thousands, percent.)

Year	Total voting-age population	Percent							
		Total	White	White, non-Hispanic	Black	Asian/Pacific Islander	Hispanic [1]	Male	Female
45 TO 64 YEARS									
Voted									
1964	38 121	75.9	77.2	. . .	64.1	. . .	. . .	78.5	73.5
1966	39 171	64.5	66.2	. . .	48.4	. . .	. . .	66.9	62.2
1968	40 362	74.9	76.1	. . .	64.5	. . .	. . .	76.6	73.3
1970	41 477	64.2	65.4	. . .	53.3	. . .	. . .	66.3	62.3
1972	42 344	70.8	71.9	. . .	61.9	. . .	43.5	72.2	69.6
1974	42 961	56.9	58.3	. . .	45.9	. . .	34.2	59.1	55.0
1976	43 293	68.7	69.9	. . .	62.3	. . .	40.3	69.7	67.9
1978	43 431	58.5	59.9	. . .	48.4	. . .	38.5	59.8	57.4
1980	43 569	69.3	70.7	. . .	61.2	. . .	42.7	69.8	68.9
1982	44 180	62.2	63.8	. . .	54.3	. . .	39.9	62.9	61.6
1984	44 307	69.8	69.8	. . .	66.2	. . .	44.2	69.8	69.8
1986	44 825	58.7	59.7	. . .	56.6	. . .	38.3	58.9	58.5
1988	45 862	67.9	69.2	. . .	64.8	. . .	39.2	68.1	67.7
1990	46 871	55.8	57.4	. . .	49.4	. . .	28.7	55.9	55.7
1992	49 147	70.0	71.8	. . .	64.9	. . .	40.4	69.8	70.2
1994	50 934	56.7	58.4	60.6	51.6	31.5	29.9	56.8	56.6
1996	53 721	64.4	61.7	68.6	66.1	32.1	38.3	63.7	65.1
1998	57 436	53.6	54.7	57.0	52.7	29.8	30.7	53.5	53.6
2000	61 352	64.1	65.6	68.4	62.9	32.0	38.3	62.7	65.3
2002	66 924	53.1	54.8	57.5	50.0	28.7	29.7	52.6	53.5
2004	71 014	66.6	68.6	72.0	62.6	38.3	38.5	65.3	67.9
Registered									
1964	38 121	. . .	. . .	. . .	. . .	. . .	. . .	. . .	. . .
1966	39 171	78.9	80.2	. . .	67.8	. . .	. . .	80.9	77.1
1968	40 362	81.1	82.1	. . .	72.1	. . .	. . .	82.4	79.8
1970	41 477	77.5	78.3	. . .	71.2	. . .	. . .	78.9	76.3
1972	42 344	79.7	80.5	. . .	74.2	. . .	50.3	80.4	79.1
1974	42 961	73.6	74.6	. . .	67.2	. . .	46.3	74.7	72.7
1976	43 293	75.5	76.4	. . .	70.6	. . .	46.4	76.1	74.9
1978	43 431	74.3	75.2	. . .	69.3	. . .	46.6	75.0	73.7
1980	43 569	75.8	77.0	. . .	69.4	. . .	50.6	76.3	75.3
1982	44 180	75.6	77.1	. . .	69.8	. . .	50.5	75.8	75.5
1984	44 307	76.6	76.6	. . .	73.7	. . .	51.8	76.6	76.6
1986	44 825	74.8	75.8	. . .	74.5	. . .	49.3	74.5	75.1
1988	45 862	75.5	76.7	. . .	74.6	. . .	45.6	75.7	75.3
1990	46 871	71.4	72.9	. . .	68.9	. . .	41.3	71.2	71.6
1992	49 147	75.3	76.9	. . .	72.4	. . .	45.9	74.9	75.7
1994	50 934	71.7	73.3	75.8	69.8	37.9	42.4	70.9	72.5
1996	53 721	73.5	71.1	77.8	75.1	40.0	45.2	72.6	74.4
1998	57 436	71.1	72.6	75.3	69.5	40.4	44.3	70.4	71.8
2000	61 352	71.2	72.7	75.5	70.9	38.1	45.1	69.8	72.6
2002	66 924	69.4	71.3	74.2	66.9	43.6	41.1	68.4	70.3
2004	71 014	72.7	74.6	78.1	69.6	43.4	44.4	71.6	73.8

Source: U.S. Census Bureau.
Note: Prior to 1972, data are for people 21 years of age and over with the exception of those age 18 years and over in Georgia and Kentucky, 19 years and over in Alaska, and 20 years and over in Hawaii. Registration data were not collected in the 1964 Current Population Survey.

[1] May be of any race.
. . . = Not available.

Table A11-3. Reported Voting and Registration by Age, Race, and Sex, November 1964 to November 2004—*Continued*

(Number in thousands, percent.)

Year	Total voting-age population	Percent							
		Total	White	White, non-Hispanic	Black	Asian/Pacific Islander	Hispanic [1]	Male	Female
65 YEARS AND OVER									
Voted									
1964	17 269	66.3	68.1	. . .	45.3	. . .	. . .	73.7	60.4
1966	17 817	56.1	57.9	. . .	35.3	. . .	. . .	64.2	49.8
1968	18 468	65.8	67.4	. . .	49.9	. . .	. . .	73.1	73.3
1970	19 141	57.0	58.6	. . .	39.3	. . .	. . .	65.4	50.8
1972	20 074	63.5	64.8	. . .	50.6	. . .	26.7	70.7	58.4
1974	20 955	51.4	52.8	. . .	38.5	. . .	28.1	58.7	46.2
1976	22 001	62.2	63.2	. . .	54.3	. . .	29.9	68.3	58.0
1978	23 001	55.9	57.2	. . .	45.6	. . .	24.9	62.6	51.3
1980	24 094	65.1	66.0	. . .	59.4	. . .	36.8	70.4	61.3
1982	25 598	59.9	61.1	. . .	50.8	. . .	29.5	65.3	56.2
1984	26 658	67.7	68.7	. . .	61.5	. . .	40.5	71.9	64.8
1986	27 712	60.9	61.9	. . .	53.3	. . .	36.5	66.8	56.7
1988	28 804	68.8	69.8	. . .	63.5	. . .	45.6	73.3	65.6
1990	29 874	60.3	61.7	. . .	51.3	. . .	40.5	66.0	56.3
1992	30 846	70.1	71.5	. . .	64.1	. . .	39.7	74.5	67.0
1994	31 144	61.3	62.8	63.9	51.6	33.8	37.6	66.5	57.6
1996	31 888	67.0	68.1	69.2	63.7	34.3	47.6	70.9	64.1
1998	32 263	59.5	60.5	61.7	56.2	35.4	41.9	64.6	55.8
2000	32 764	67.6	68.8	70.0	64.7	37.9	50.0	71.4	64.8
2002	33 892	61.0	62.7	64.0	54.8	41.5	29.0	65.4	57.7
2004	34 738	68.9	70.5	72.2	64.1	38.2	45.9	71.9	66.7
Registered									
1964	17 269	. . .	. . .	. . .	. . .	. . .	. . .	. . .	. . .
1966	17 817	73.5	75.5	. . .	56.2	. . .	. . .	79.9	69.2
1968	18 468	75.6	77.1	. . .	62.7	. . .	. . .	81.7	71.1
1970	19 141	73.7	75.0	. . .	61.5	. . .	. . .	79.8	69.2
1972	20 074	75.6	76.5	. . .	67.9	. . .	34.7	81.9	71.1
1974	20 955	70.2	71.2	. . .	62.9	. . .	37.8	75.8	66.2
1976	22 001	71.4	72.5	. . .	64.5	. . .	36.5	76.6	67.8
1978	23 001	72.8	73.7	. . .	67.6	. . .	33.5	77.6	69.5
1980	24 094	74.6	75.4	. . .	70.1	. . .	44.1	78.8	71.6
1982	25 598	75.2	76.3	. . .	68.4	. . .	40.6	78.9	72.6
1984	26 658	76.9	77.7	. . .	73.0	. . .	46.7	80.2	74.7
1986	27 712	76.9	77.9	. . .	71.4	. . .	47.0	80.6	74.3
1988	28 804	78.4	75.9	. . .	79.2	. . .	51.0	81.6	76.1
1990	29 874	76.5	77.7	. . .	71.2	. . .	53.2	79.7	74.2
1992	30 846	78.0	79.1	. . .	74.2	. . .	47.9	81.1	75.7
1994	31 144	76.3	77.5	78.7	72.4	40.7	50.2	79.2	74.3
1996	31 888	77.0	78.1	79.3	75.2	39.2	54.2	79.7	75.0
1998	32 263	75.4	76.4	77.6	73.6	44.1	56.5	78.5	73.2
2000	32 764	76.1	77.3	78.6	74.3	42.8	56.7	78.8	74.2
2002	33 892	75.8	77.3	78.7	73.5	54.8	37.2	77.3	74.7
2004	34 738	76.9	78.4	80.0	73.7	43.5	55.0	78.5	75.6

Source: U.S. Census Bureau.
Note: Prior to 1972, data are for people 21 years of age and over with the exception of those age 18 years and over in Georgia and Kentucky, 19 years and over in Alaska, and 20 years and over in Hawaii. Registration data were not collected in the 1964 Current Population Survey.

[1] May be of any race.
. . . = Not available.

Table A11-4. Selected Characteristics of Persons Reporting Voting and Registration, November 2004

(Number in thousands, percent.)

Characteristic	Total voting-age population	Registered		Voted	
		Number	Percent	Number	Percent
AGE					
Both Sexes					
Total, 18 years and over	215 694	142 070	65.9	125 736	58.3
18 to 24 years	27 808	14 334	51.5	11 639	41.9
25 to 44 years	82 133	49 371	60.1	42 845	52.2
45 to 64 years	71 014	51 659	72.7	47 327	66.6
65 to 74 years	18 363	14 125	76.9	13 010	70.8
75 years and over	16 375	12 581	76.8	10 915	66.7
Male					
Total, 18 years and over	103 812	66 406	64.0	58 455	56.3
18 to 24 years	13 960	6 731	48.2	5 415	38.8
25 to 44 years	40 618	23 403	57.6	19 913	49.0
45 to 64 years	34 471	24 676	71.6	22 520	65.3
65 to 74 years	8 438	6 534	77.4	6 119	72.5
75 years and over	6 325	5 062	80.0	4 489	71.0
Female					
Total, 18 years and over	111 882	75 663	67.6	67 281	60.1
18 to 24 years	13 848	7 603	54.9	6 224	44.9
25 to 44 years	41 515	25 967	62.5	22 932	55.2
45 to 64 years	36 544	26 984	73.8	24 807	67.9
65 to 74 years	9 926	7 591	76.5	6 891	69.4
75 years and over	10 049	7 519	74.8	6 426	63.9
RACE/ETHNICITY					
White, non-Hispanic	151 410	111 318	73.5	99 567	65.8
Asian/Pacific Islander	9 291	3 247	35.0	2 768	29.8
Hispanic [1]	27 129	9 308	34.3	7 587	28.0
Black	24 910	16 035	64.4	14 016	56.3
REGION					
Northeast	41 006	26 785	65.3	24 040	58.6
Midwest	48 419	35 242	72.8	31 495	65.0
South	77 188	50 556	65.5	43 512	56.4
West	49 080	29 486	60.1	26 689	54.4
EDUCATION					
Less than 9th grade	12 574	4 090	32.5	2 971	23.6
9th to 12th grade, no diploma	20 719	9 479	45.7	7 161	34.6
High school graduate	68 545	42 180	61.5	35 894	52.4
Some college or associate degree	58 913	43 434	73.7	38 922	66.1
Bachelor's degree	36 591	28 158	77.0	26 579	72.6
Advanced degree	18 352	14 730	80.3	14 210	77.4
LABOR FORCE					
Not in labor force	69 612	44 859	64.4	39 124	56.2
Civilian labor force	146 082	97 211	66.5	86 612	59.3
Government workers	20 469	16 471	80.5	15 389	75.2
Private industry	107 642	69 089	64.2	60 979	56.7
Self-employed	10 720	7 570	70.6	6 881	64.2
Unemployed	7 251	4 081	56.3	3 362	46.4

Source: U.S. Census Bureau.

[1] May be of any race.

Detailed Tables
Government

Table A12-1. Total Tax Revenue as Percentage of GDP, Selected Years, 1975–2004

(Percent; ranked by 2003 figures.)

Country	1975	1985	1990	1995	2000	2001	2002	2003	2004, provisional
Sweden	42.0	48.2	53.2	48.5	53.8	51.9	50.1	50.6	50.7
Denmark	40.0	47.4	47.1	49.4	49.6	49.9	48.7	48.3	49.6
Belgium	40.6	45.6	43.2	44.8	45.7	45.9	46.2	45.4	45.6
Finland	36.8	40.2	44.3	46.0	48.0	46.0	45.8	44.8	44.3
France	35.9	43.8	43.0	43.9	45.2	44.9	43.4	43.4	43.7
Norway	39.3	43.1	41.5	41.1	43.2	43.4	43.8	43.4	44.9
Austria	37.4	41.9	40.4	41.6	43.4	45.2	43.6	43.1	42.9
Italy	26.1	34.4	38.9	41.2	43.2	43.0	42.5	43.1	42.2
Luxembourg	37.5	45.1	40.8	42.3	40.2	40.7	41.3	41.3	40.6
Iceland	29.7	28.5	31.5	31.8	39.4	38.1	38.5	39.8	41.9
Netherlands	41.3	42.8	42.9	41.9	41.2	39.8	39.2	38.8	39.3
Hungary	. . .	. . .	. . .	42.4	39.0	39.0	38.8	38.5	37.7
Czech Republic	. . .	. . .	. . .	39.8	39.0	38.5	37.0	37.7	37.6
Portugal	20.8	26.6	29.2	33.6	36.4	35.6	36.5	37.1	. . .
Greece	21.8	28.6	29.3	32.4	38.2	36.6	37.1	35.7	. . .
United Kingdom	35.3	37.7	36.5	35.0	37.4	37.2	35.6	35.6	36.1
Germany	35.3	37.2	35.7	38.2	37.8	36.8	35.4	35.5	34.6
New Zealand	28.5	31.3	37.7	37.0	33.4	33.3	35.0	34.9	35.4
Spain	18.8	27.8	33.2	32.8	35.2	35.0	34.8	34.9	35.1
Poland	. . .	. . .	. . .	37.0	32.5	31.9	34.7	34.2	. . .
Canada	31.9	32.5	35.9	35.6	35.6	35.0	34.0	33.8	33.0
Turkey	16.0	15.4	20.0	22.6	32.3	35.1	31.1	32.8	31.1
Australia	26.5	29.1	29.3	29.6	31.8	30.4	31.4	31.6	. . .
Slovak Republic	. . .	. . .	. . .	. . .	34.0	31.6	33.0	31.1	30.8
Ireland	29.1	35.0	33.5	32.8	32.2	30.1	28.7	29.7	30.2
Switzerland	27.0	25.8	26.0	27.8	30.5	30.0	30.1	29.5	29.4
United States	25.6	25.6	27.3	27.9	29.9	28.9	26.3	25.6	25.4
Japan	20.8	27.4	30.2	27.8	27.1	27.4	25.8	25.3	. . .
Korea	14.5	16.0	18.1	19.4	23.6	24.1	24.4	25.3	24.6
Mexico	. . .	17.0	17.3	16.7	18.5	18.8	18.1	19.0	18.5

Source: Organisation for Economic Co-operation and Development (OECD).

. . . = Not available.

Table A12-2. Real Gross State Product (Total and for Government), 1993 and 2003

(Millions of chained [2000] dollars, percent; ranked according to government as a percent of total real gross state product for 2003.)

State	Total GSP		Government portion of GSP		Government portion as percent of GSP		Rank	Difference from 1993 to 2003
	1993	2003	1993	2003	1993	2003		
United States	7 240 810	10 289 220	1 052 950	1 175 255	14.5	11.4		-3.1
District of Columbia	55 199	64 137	23 723	22 118	43.0	34.5	1	-8.5
Hawaii	41 936	42 964	9 780	9 192	23.3	21.4	2	-1.9
Alaska	28 572	28 103	6 061	5 494	21.2	19.5	3	-1.7
New Mexico	36 819	54 183	8 372	10 091	22.7	18.6	4	-4.1
Mississippi	51 790	66 646	9 123	11 066	17.6	16.6	5	-1.0
West Virginia	35 649	43 158	5 846	7 131	16.4	16.5	6	0.1
Oklahoma	73 322	93 750	14 072	15 280	19.2	16.3	7	-2.9
Maryland	144 433	198 334	28 719	32 263	19.9	16.3	8	-3.6
Virginia	194 750	283 922	43 697	45 912	22.4	16.2	9	-6.3
Montana	18 047	23 493	3 480	3 790	19.3	16.1	10	-3.2
Alabama	93 722	122 675	17 372	18 961	18.5	15.5	11	-3.1
North Dakota	14 263	19 909	2 857	3 014	20.0	15.1	12	-4.9
South Carolina	83 909	119 973	16 116	17 606	19.2	14.7	13	-4.5
Wyoming	15 929	19 940	2 512	2 818	15.8	14.1	14	-1.6
Nebraska	43 397	60 672	7 667	8 489	17.7	14.0	15	-3.7
Kentucky	88 926	120 508	14 611	16 762	16.4	13.9	16	-2.5
Utah	43 741	71 605	8 509	9 896	19.5	13.8	17	-5.6
Maine	28 648	38 097	4 779	5 175	16.7	13.6	18	-3.1
Washington	159 045	229 680	27 173	31 185	17.1	13.6	19	-3.5
Kansas	64 936	86 814	10 815	11 523	16.7	13.3	20	-3.4
Idaho	23 130	38 849	4 088	5 028	17.7	12.9	21	-4.7
Louisiana	115 024	130 733	15 116	16 639	13.1	12.7	22	-0.4
Vermont	14 189	19 562	1 979	2 420	13.9	12.4	23	-1.6
Arkansas	51 140	69 734	7 422	8 624	14.5	12.4	24	-2.1
Georgia	191 094	302 966	29 141	37 223	15.2	12.3	25	-3.0
South Dakota	17 286	25 609	3 089	3 095	17.9	12.1	26	-5.8
North Carolina	187 725	295 897	29 221	35 427	15.6	12.0	27	-3.6
Oregon	69 619	116 113	11 558	13 841	16.6	11.9	28	-4.7
Arizona	91 709	175 536	16 190	20 346	17.7	11.6	29	-6.1
Tennessee	133 056	191 186	18 328	22 100	13.8	11.6	30	-2.2
Rhode Island	27 111	36 547	3 678	4 194	13.6	11.5	31	-2.1
Colorado	104 714	178 327	17 269	20 370	16.5	11.4	32	-5.1
Florida	343 546	517 855	52 180	59 023	15.2	11.4	33	-3.8
Iowa	67 594	95 569	9 757	10 716	14.4	11.2	34	-3.2
Texas	505 783	769 410	70 896	86 102	14.0	11.2	35	-2.8
Missouri	132 946	181 638	17 272	20 094	13.0	11.1	36	-1.9
Ohio	285 610	375 740	36 533	39 416	12.8	10.5	37	-2.3
Wisconsin	131 738	186 350	17 129	19 488	13.0	10.5	38	-2.5
California	927 133	1 369 235	127 179	142 909	13.7	10.4	39	-3.3
Michigan	247 453	340 972	32 547	33 496	13.2	9.8	40	-3.3
New York	616 896	801 038	75 922	78 467	12.3	9.8	41	-2.5
Minnesota	128 346	198 526	16 730	19 342	13.0	9.7	42	-3.3
Nevada	47 072	83 603	5 720	8 051	12.2	9.6	43	-2.5
New Jersey	276 229	371 806	32 634	35 389	11.8	9.5	44	-2.3
Illinois	353 296	470 101	40 161	43 868	11.4	9.3	45	-2.0
Indiana	143 295	201 263	17 588	18 599	12.3	9.2	46	-3.0
Pennsylvania	320 424	415 281	38 882	38 360	12.1	9.2	47	-2.9
New Hampshire	29 605	45 874	3 379	3 972	11.4	8.7	48	-2.8
Connecticut	121 635	164 137	12 451	13 840	10.2	8.4	49	-1.8
Massachusetts	194 471	284 286	20 767	23 261	10.7	8.2	50	-2.5
Delaware	29 133	46 952	2 846	3 765	9.8	8.0	51	-1.8

Source: Bureau of Economic Analysis.

Table A12-3. Local Governments and Public School Systems, 2002

(Number.)

State	Total	General purpose					Special purpose				
		Total	County [1]	Subcounty			Total	Special districts	Public school systems		
				Total	Municipal	Town or township			Total	School districts	Dependent public school systems [2]
United States	87 525	38 967	3 034	35 933	19 429	16 504	48 558	35 052	15 014	13 506	1 508
Alabama	1 171	518	67	451	451	0	653	525	128	128	0
Alaska	175	161	12	149	149	0	14	14	54	0	54
Arizona	638	102	15	87	87	0	536	305	245	231	14
Arkansas	1 588	574	75	499	499	0	1 014	704	310	310	0
California	4 409	532	57	475	475	0	3 877	2 830	1 107	1 047	60
Colorado	1 928	332	62	270	270	0	1 596	1 414	182	182	0
Connecticut	580	179	0	179	30	149	401	384	166	17	149
Delaware	339	60	3	57	57	0	279	260	19	19	0
District of Columbia	2	1	0	1	1	0	1	1	2	0	2
Florida	1 191	470	66	404	404	0	721	626	95	95	0
Georgia	1 448	687	156	531	531	0	761	581	180	180	0
Hawaii	19	4	3	1	1	0	15	15	1	0	1
Idaho	1 158	244	44	200	200	0	914	798	116	116	0
Illinois	6 903	2 824	102	2 722	1 291	1 431	4 079	3 145	934	934	0
Indiana	3 085	1 666	91	1 575	567	1 008	1 419	1 125	294	294	0
Iowa	1 975	1 047	99	948	948	0	928	542	386	386	0
Kansas	3 887	2 030	104	1 926	627	1 299	1 857	1 533	324	324	0
Kentucky	1 439	543	119	424	424	0	896	720	176	176	0
Louisiana	473	362	60	302	302	0	111	45	66	66	0
Maine	826	505	16	489	22	467	321	222	295	99	196
Maryland	265	180	23	157	157	0	85	85	39	0	39
Massachusetts	841	356	5	351	45	306	485	403	330	82	248
Michigan	2 804	1 858	83	1 775	533	1 242	946	366	739	580	159
Minnesota	3 482	2 734	87	2 647	854	1 793	748	403	345	345	0
Mississippi	1 000	378	82	296	296	0	622	458	167	164	3
Missouri	3 422	1 372	114	1 258	946	312	2 050	1 514	536	536	0
Montana	1 127	183	54	129	129	0	944	592	352	352	0
Nebraska	2 791	1 070	93	977	531	446	1 721	1 146	575	575	0
Nevada	210	35	16	19	19	0	175	158	17	17	0
New Hampshire	559	244	10	234	13	221	315	148	177	167	10
New Jersey	1 412	587	21	566	324	242	825	276	624	549	75
New Mexico	858	134	33	101	101	0	724	628	96	96	0
New York	3 420	1 602	57	1 545	616	929	1 818	1 135	715	683	32
North Carolina	960	641	100	541	541	0	319	319	175	0	175
North Dakota	2 735	1 745	53	1 692	360	1 332	990	764	226	226	0
Ohio	3 636	2 338	88	2 250	942	1 308	1 298	631	667	667	0
Oklahoma	1 798	667	77	590	590	0	1 131	560	571	571	0
Oregon	1 439	276	36	240	240	0	1 163	927	236	236	0
Pennsylvania	5 031	2 630	66	2 564	1 018	1 546	2 401	1 885	516	516	0
Rhode Island	118	39	0	39	8	31	79	75	36	4	32
South Carolina	701	315	46	269	269	0	386	301	85	85	0
South Dakota	1 866	1 314	66	1 248	308	940	552	376	176	176	0
Tennessee	930	441	92	349	349	0	489	475	138	14	124
Texas	4 784	1 450	254	1 196	1 196	0	3 334	2 245	1 090	1 089	1
Utah	605	265	29	236	236	0	340	300	40	40	0
Vermont	733	298	14	284	47	237	435	152	283	283	0
Virginia	521	324	95	229	229	0	197	196	133	1	132
Washington	1 787	318	39	279	279	0	1 469	1 173	296	296	0
West Virginia	686	289	55	234	234	0	397	342	55	55	0
Wisconsin	3 048	1 922	72	1 850	585	1 265	1 126	684	444	442	2
Wyoming	722	121	23	98	98	0	601	546	55	55	0

Source: U.S. Census Bureau. *Government Organization, 2002.*

[1] Excludes areas that correspond to counties but have no organized governments.
[2] Systems operated by a state, county, municipal, or township government. These are not included in total of local governments.

Table A12-4. State Rankings for Per Capita Amounts of Federal Expenditures, Fiscal Year 2003

(Rank.)

State	Total	Retirement and disability	Other direct payments	Grants	Procurement	Salaries and wages
Alaska	1	50	49	1	4	1
Virginia	2	4	40	48	1	3
Maryland	3	12	14	17	3	4
New Mexico	4	20	41	5	2	6
North Dakota	5	23	1	4	31	5
Hawaii	6	14	43	20	6	2
Wyoming	7	22	42	2	26	7
Connecticut	8	33	18	19	5	45
Alabama	9	2	9	23	7	19
South Dakota	10	17	2	6	38	13
Massachusetts	11	36	4	10	11	36
West Virginia	12	1	11	12	45	20
Montana	13	8	17	8	36	12
Missouri	14	16	8	21	9	25
Maine	15	5	32	11	19	24
Kentucky	16	10	25	16	13	18
Mississippi	17	13	10	13	21	23
Rhode Island	18	18	13	9	32	17
Pennsylvania	19	6	3	22	27	38
Tennessee	20	19	24	18	12	33
Oklahoma	21	9	22	24	25	8
New York	22	40	7	3	42	43
Vermont	23	31	33	7	20	31
Washington	24	29	31	26	17	10
Louisiana	25	38	5	14	24	30
Arizona	26	35	44	40	8	28
South Carolina	27	11	35	30	22	21
Arkansas	28	7	12	15	49	40
Kansas	29	24	16	43	23	16
Florida	30	3	6	49	29	34
Texas	31	47	37	42	10	26
Colorado	32	46	46	38	15	9
Idaho	33	42	45	36	16	27
Nebraska	34	25	21	28	47	22
New Jersey	35	37	15	37	30	41
California	36	48	30	27	18	32
Delaware	37	15	28	29	50	29
North Carolina	38	27	38	32	41	15
Ohio	39	28	26	34	35	42
Georgia	40	44	36	45	33	11
Oregon	41	26	29	31	48	39
Iowa	42	21	20	39	44	47
Illinois	43	43	19	44	40	37
Michigan	44	32	23	41	43	49
Utah	45	49	50	46	14	14
Indiana	46	34	27	47	37	48
New Hampshire	47	30	47	25	34	44
Wisconsin	48	39	34	33	46	50
Minnesota	49	45	39	35	39	46
Nevada	50	41	48	50	28	35

Source: U.S. Census Bureau. *Consolidated Federal Funds Report: Fiscal Year 2003.*

Table A12-5. State and Local Government Finances, 2002–2003

(Dollars in millions, except where noted.)

Item	Total	State and local		Per capita [1] (dollars)		
		State	Local	State and local	State	Local
REVENUE [2]	2 047 337	1 295 659	1 140 633	7 040	4 455	3 922
Intergovernmental Revenue	389 264	361 617	416 601	1 339	1 243	1 433
Total Revenue from Own Sources	1 658 073	934 042	724 032	5 702	3 212	2 490
General revenue from own sources	1 373 948	750 732	623 216	4 725	2 582	2 143
Taxes [3]	938 972	548 991	389 981	3 229	1 888	1 341
Property	296 683	10 471	286 213	1 020	36	984
Individual income	199 407	181 933	17 475	686	626	60
Corporation income	31 369	28 384	2 985	108	98	10
Sales and gross receipts	337 787	273 811	63 975	1 162	942	220
General	229 222	184 597	44 626	788	635	153
Selective [3]	108 564	89 215	19 350	373	307	67
Motor fuel	33 379	32 269	1 110	115	111	4
Alcoholic beverages	4 757	4 399	358	16	15	1
Tobacco products	11 807	11 482	325	41	39	1
Public utilities	21 015	10 557	10 458	72	36	36
Motor vehicle and operators' licenses	17 379	16 009	1 370	60	55	5
Charges and miscellaneous [3]	434 976	201 741	233 235	1 496	694	802
Current charges [3]	269 560	106 357	163 204	927	366	561
Education [3]	78 522	60 215	18 307	270	207	63
School lunch sales	6 074	19	6 055	21	0	21
Higher education	66 831	59 392	7 440	230	204	26
Natural resources	3 018	2 160	857	10	7	3
Hospitals	68 927	24 131	44 796	237	83	154
Sewerage	28 237	27	28 210	97	0	97
Solid waste management	11 559	416	11 143	40	1	38
Parks and recreation	7 342	1 202	6 140	25	4	21
Housing and community development	4 589	565	4 024	16	2	14
Airports	12 759	871	11 888	44	3	41
Sea and inland port facilities	2 930	809	2 121	10	3	7
Highways	8 503	5 351	3 152	29	18	11
Interest earnings	58 317	29 730	28 587	201	102	98
Special assessments	5 808	306	5 502	20	1	19
Sale of property	1 773	608	1 165	6	2	4
Utility and liquor store revenue	108 388	17 036	91 352	373	59	314
Insurance trust revenue	175 737	166 274	9 463	604	572	33
EXPENDITURE	2 164 176	1 359 048	1 194 932	7 442	4 673	4 109
Intergovernmental Expenditure	4 404	382 197	12 011	15	1 314	41
Direct Expenditure	2 159 772	976 852	1 182 920	7 427	3 359	4 068
General expenditure [3]	1 817 513	781 772	1 035 741	6 250	2 688	3 562
Education [3]	621 335	170 685	450 650	2 137	587	1 550
Elementary and secondary education	428 503	4 691	423 812	1 473	16	1 457
Higher education	164 187	137 349	26 838	565	472	92
Public welfare	306 463	265 105	41 358	1 054	912	142
Hospitals	93 175	38 023	55 152	320	131	190
Health	61 703	30 351	31 353	212	104	108
Highways	117 696	72 455	45 241	405	249	156
Police protection	67 361	9 860	57 501	232	34	198
Fire protection	27 854	0	27 854	96	0	96
Corrections	55 471	36 938	18 533	191	127	64
Natural resources	22 808	17 110	5 699	78	59	20
Sewerage	32 540	1 003	31 537	112	3	108
Solid waste management	19 183	2 693	16 491	66	9	57
Housing and community development	35 275	4 608	30 668	121	16	105
Governmental administration	98 658	42 846	55 813	339	147	192
Parks and recreation	31 765	4 636	27 129	109	16	93
Interest on general debt	77 277	31 295	45 982	266	108	158
Utility	144 594	22 405	122 189	497	77	420
Liquor store expenditure	4 402	3 697	706	15	13	2
Insurance trust expenditure	193 263	168 979	24 285	665	581	84
By character and object:						
Current operation	1 579 290	656 989	922 301	5 431	2 259	3 171
Capital outlay	263 198	91 943	171 255	905	316	589
Construction	203 035	72 374	130 661	698	249	449
Equipment, land, and existing structures	60 162	19 568	40 594	207	67	140
Assistance and subsidies	35 080	25 901	9 179	121	89	32
Interest on debt (general and utility)	88 940	33 040	55 900	306	114	192
Insurance benefits and repayments	193 263	168 979	24 285	665	581	84
Expenditure for salaries and wages [4]	647 211	183 386	463 826	2 226	631	1 595

Source: U.S. Census Bureau. Governments Division.

[1] Based on estimated resident population as of July 1.
[2] Aggregates exclude duplicative transactions between levels of government.
[3] Includes amounts not shown separately.
[4] Included in items shown above.

Index